UNIVERSITY OF NORTH CAROLINA AT CHAPEL HILL
DEPARTMENT OF ROMANCE LANGUAGES

NORTH CAROLINA STUDIES
IN THE ROMANCE LANGUAGES AND LITERATURES

*Founder:* URBAN TIGNER HOLMES
*Editor:* MARÍA A. SALGADO

*Distributed by:*

UNIVERSITY OF NORTH CAROLINA PRESS

CHAPEL HILL
North Carolina 27515-2288
U.S.A.

NORTH CAROLINA STUDIES IN THE
ROMANCE LANGUAGES AND LITERATURES
Number 248

TEXT AS TOPOS IN RELIGIOUS LITERATURE
OF THE SPANISH GOLDEN AGE

# TEXT AS TOPOS
IN
# RELIGIOUS LITERATURE
OF THE
# SPANISH GOLDEN AGE

BY
M. LOUISE SALSTAD

CHAPEL HILL

NORTH CAROLINA STUDIES IN THE ROMANCE
LANGUAGES AND LITERATURES
U.N.C. DEPARTMENT OF ROMANCE LANGUAGES

1995

**Library of Congress Cataloging-in-Publication Data**

Salstad, M. Louise.
　　Text as topos in the religious literature of Spanish Golden age / by M. Louise Salstad.
　　466 p. – cm. – (North Carolina Studies in the Romance Languages and Literatures: no. 248)
　　Includes bibliographical references.
　　ISBN 0-8078-9252-1 (alk. paper)
　　1. Spanish literature – Classical period, 1500-1700 – Themes, motives – Indexes.
2. Christian literature, Spanish – Themes, motives – Indexes.　I. Title.　II. Series.
PQ6066.S18　1995　　　　　　　　　　　　　　　　　　　　　　　　　　95-16972
860.9'003 – dc20　　　　　　　　　　　　　　　　　　　　　　　　　　　　　CIP

© 1995. Department of Romance Languages. The University of North Carolina at Chapel Hill.

ISBN 0-8078-9252-1

DEPÓSITO LEGAL: V. 4.141 - 1995　　　I.S.B.N. 84-401-2148-2

ARTES GRÁFICAS SOLER, S. A. - LA OLIVERETA, 28 - 46018 VALENCIA - 1995

## TABLE OF CONTENTS

|  | *Page* |
|---|---|
| Acknowledgments | 11 |
| Explanation of Terms | 13 |
| General Introduction | 15 |
| Introduction to Motif Index | 63 |
| Motif Index | 72 |
| Writers and Works | 308 |
| Chronology | 324 |
| Anthology | 332 |
| Works Consulted | 419 |
| Alphabetical Key Word Index of English Motifs | 437 |
| Alphabetical Key Word Index of Spanish Motifemes | 462 |

*To the Sisters of St. Scholastica Priory*
*Duluth, Minnesota*

## ACKNOWLEDGMENTS

This book is the outcome of an idea first suggested to me by Professor Royston Jones, whose interest in my work I shall always remember with gratitude. I have also benefited from the breadth and depth of scholarship of the late Professor Mack Singleton of the University of Wisconsin, Madison. A research grant from North Carolina State University allowed me to obtain microfilms of manuscripts from the Biblioteca Nacional de Madrid. As I talked through my ideas, I found constant encouragement from my friend Elizabeth Evasdaughter. Finally, the unfailing patience and expertise of Debora Godfrey ensured that this book materialized in the correct format.

Excerpts from *El libro español antiguo: Análisis de su estructura* by José Simón Díaz (Bibliografías y catálogos 1). Copyright © 1983 by Edition Reichenberger. Reprinted by permission of the publisher.

Excerpts from *Obras de Santo Tomás de Villanueva. Sermones de la Virgen y obras castellanas*, edited by Santos Santamarta (Biblioteca de Autores Cristianos 96). Copyright © 1952 by La Editorial Católica, S. A. Reprinted by permission.

Excerpts from *Primera parte de las diferencias de libros q̃ ay en el universo*. Prologue by Daniel Eisenberg. Facsimile of 1546 Toledo edition of Juan de Ayala. Copyright © 1983 by Libros Puvill, S.A. Reprinted by permission of the publisher.

Excerpt from *Rimas* of Juan de Jáurequi. Vol. 1 of *Obras*, edited by Inmaculada Ferrer de Alba. Copyright © 1973 by Espasa-Calpe, S.A. Reprinted by permission.

Excerpts from *Romancero espiritual* of José de Valdivielso, edited by J. M. Aguirre. Copyright © 1984 by Espasa-Calpe, S.A. Reprinted by permission.

Excerpts from *Vida y poesía de Alonso de Ledesma: Contribución al estudio del conceptismo español*, by Miguel D'Ors. Copyright © 1974 by E.U.N.S.A. (Universidad de Navarra). Reprinted by permission.

# EXPLANATION OF TERMS AS USED IN THIS STUDY

Motif: A specific repeated articulation of a topos. It may be a motifeme or an expansion of a motifeme.

Motifeme: An irreducible signifying unit in the form of a noun or verb.

Referent: The subject that vehicle and tenor help to illuminate.

Tenor: The most specific or immediate physical, metaphysical, or spiritual reality (entity or action) to which a motif is linked.

Topos: A symbolic image-idea construct (e.g., the book of nature), which has been codified by the cultural tradition and which, developed and modified by the individual, can be employed in rhetoric in the service of a thesis.

Vehicle: The metaphorical image (entity or action) by which a tenor is signified.

## GENERAL INTRODUCTION

The immediate purpose of this work is to contribute to a more systematic study of topoi than has been undertaken, to my knowledge, until now. I have chosen as a paradigm the cluster of metaphors whose nucleus is the written text. Ernst Robert Curtius, in *European Literature and the Latin Middle Ages*, states that "The use of writing and the book in figurative language occurs in all periods of world literature, but with characteristic differences which are determined by the course of the culture in general" (303). The period I have selected by way of example encompasses the sixteenth and seventeenth centuries of Spanish literature, a period more or less equivalent to the Golden Age, of which Curtius says, "In the history of the modern literatures, the Spanish *siglo de oro* stands alone by the abundance and the preciosity of its imagery, including that derived from writing and the book" (343).

I have focused on works of a religious or moral nature, primarily poetry, sermons, and *autos sacramentales*. This selection produces a body of texts large enough to yield a more or less complete repertory of motifs and also allows for potential comparison among genres in terms of the functioning of the topos. At the same time the corpus is coherent enough to serve as a basis of comparison with other groupings of topical texts.

In his discussion of Curtius' work, Francisco López Estrada lays out a program for the student of literary history who would write on topoi:

> En su estudio el crítico tiene que recoger su aparición [de los topicos] en los escritores y establecer el desarrollo que tuvieron como tales piezas de expresión, y qué significación se les confió y cómo la mantuvieron. . . . El estudio de su variación ofrece un elemento de juicio para el historiador de la cultura; y en el dominio literario, para valorar el sentido de originalidad de un escritor. (119)

I see the present work as a contribution to the realization of this program. Besides the literary historian, the cultural historian interested in theology and spirituality or in the history of the book, and the art historian as well, will find here, I hope, useful information. For Golden Age scholars this study complements other sources on imagery of the period, such as Daniel Heiple's *Mechanical Imagery in Spanish Golden Age Poetry*, Manuel Morales Borrero's *La geometría mística del alma en la literatura española del Siglo de Oro*, and Francisco Rico's *El pequeño mundo del hombre*.

I envision this study as serving several kinds of comparison, such as between Spanish and French religious literature of the sixteenth and seventeenth centuries, Spanish religious literature of the medieval period and that of the Golden Age, or religious and secular literature of the Spanish Golden Age. For example, many religious poetic texts are based on already existing secular texts. One would thus expect to find many of the same vehicles in the secular poems, linked to different tenors. On the other hand, I venture the hypothesis that the elaboration of the topos is more varied and often more extensive in religious than in secular literature, in part because religious writers used the topos primarily, though by no means exclusively, for didactic ends, whereas in secular writing it served mainly as ornamentation. Ultimately I hope this study will be one small building block in the ongoing construction of a solid comparison among national literatures and cultures. What follows in this general introduction is an overview of the topos as it is used in my corpus of texts.

Of the ninety writers identified in this study, at least fifty-five are clerics or members of male religious orders, although several were ordained or professed late in life; four of the six women are nuns. At least eight are said to be of Jewish descent; three of them eventually returned to Judaism. Many of the writers were preachers, with thorough knowledge of Sacred Scripture and theological tradition. Many, too, taught in the universities. Several were *censores de libros*. In various ways, then, written texts were an important part of their lives.

The birthplaces of the seventy-four writers for whom I was able to establish one spread over most of the map of Spain. Of the various regions, Castilla la Nueva has the largest number, followed by Andalucía and Castilla la Vieja-León. Together these three regions represent about three-fourths of the writers. The other fourth are mostly from Navarra, Aragón, Cataluña, Valencia, Extremadura, and La Gran Canaria. Two writers were born in Portugal, one in Naples. Many of them lived in various parts of the country during the course of their lives. I have also included one writer, Hernando Domínguez Camargo, who was from the New World (Santa Fe de Bogotá), because his poetry was notably influenced by Góngora and was sent to Spain for publication, since its editor believed he would be more appreciated there.

We seldom have such explicit information about the influence of one writer on another as in the case of Domínguez Camargo. Certainly many of them knew one another, personally or through their works. Marco Antonio Camós indicates in the first dialogue of his *Microcosmia* that he was very familiar with Luis de León's *Nombres de Cristo* (qtd. in Santiago Vela 554). According to Luis G. Alonso-Getino, Luis de Granada was for Alonso de Cabrera "maestro de predicación, . . . al que estudiaba religiosamente. . . . Tan discípulo suyo se muestra, que muchas veces le copia textualmente sin citarle, y se ve que lo sabía de coro" (Cabrera, *Navidad* lxxii). Alarcos García remarks on Luis de Góngora's friendship with Hortensio Félix Paravicino and what he sees as a mutual influence in their writing (229-35). In the case of Domínguez Camargo, the influence was unidirectional. Antonio Navarro Navarrete, in his dedication to the *S. Ignacio de Loyola*, speaks of "el supremo Numen de Gongora, cuyo espiritu parece que le heredó, o bebió en sus versos. . . . De algunos versos enteros se valió de Gongora (como primogenito de su espiritu) . . . para ilustrar su Poema. . . ." Perhaps the images in lines 32-35 of the excerpt in the Anthology (Ant. Do) are an imitation of the following cluster in the *Soledades*: "En brazos dividido caudalosos / De islas, que paréntesis frondosos / Al periodo son de su corriente" (Castro1:464). Valdivielso was a friend of most of the writers of his time, including Lope de Vega, Pérez de Montalban, and Salas Barbadillo (Valdivielso. *Romancero* xvi). Pérez de Montalban was a close enough friend of Lope's to write his biography. In a later period, Pedro Calderón de la Barca and Manuel Guerra y Ribera were friends. Valdivielso, Lope, Calderón, and Guerra y Ribera are four of the writers in this corpus who use the topos most often.

Who else provided an audience or readership for these works in which we find the symbol of the written text? Cultural historians like Manuel Fernández Alvarez state that at least eighty percent of the population of Golden Age Spain was in effect illiterate (11). Potential readers would have been found in the following groups: clerics; nobles; those whom we would today call technologists and intellectuals; higher-ranking bureaucrats; professors; members of the liberal professions, such as lawyers, notaries, doctors, architects, and painters; merchants; a small number of tradesmen and artisans; middle-level bureaucrats and servants (Chevalier 20). In spite of the relatively small number of readers, however, it is not quite accurate to say, as Chevalier does, that the others are excluded from the "práctica del libro" (19), because we know that reading aloud to a group was still a common practice.

Whether listeners-spectators or readers, we are likely to categorize them as *culto*, although by the seventeenth century the distinction between this term and *popular* is ambiguous. In the baroque period "los cultos," those who "conocen y les son habituales los motivos bíblicos, mitológicos, históricos," according to José Antonio Maravall in "La literatura de emblemas," constitute "una verdadera masa" (182). With regard to the works in this corpus, the following at least were probably intended for or enjoyed by a popular or mixed group: most of the *autos sacramentales*; the pieces composed for the *justas poéticas* celebrated on popular occasions like the beatification or canonization of a saint; many of the other poems, especially the shorter ones (J. M. Aguirre affirms as an incontrovertible fact that "la mayor parte de la poesía religiosa española del siglo XVII se crea cara al pueblo, para el pueblo, y desde el punto de vista del pueblo" [145]); and some of the sermons. Tomás de Villanueva's biographer, Bishop Muñatones, marvels that "hombres de todo orden, estado y condición . . . acudían porfiadamente a sus sermones." They included "el gentío inmenso de confusa muchedumbre," as well as

> los próceres, . . . los grandes y . . . magistrados, varones distinguidos de entre los caballeros . . . hombres eruditos e ilustres predicadores, y miembros de casi todas las corporaciones; finalmente, todos los hombres famosos en las letras. (Qtd. in Villanueva 33)

In the words of Miguel Mir, Cabrera used in his sermons "una plática familiar y al alcance del vulgo" (xix). When one reads that Ignacio de Vitoria's sermon on the occasion of Lope's obsequies was heard by "el mayor concurso que se ha visto" (Vega Carpio, *Colección* 499), one assumes a mixed audience.

On the other hand, the *auto* titled *Actio quae inscribitur examen sacrum* was performed in the Jesuit Colegio of Salamanca (González Pedroso 133). Most of the longer narrative poems were doubtless written for well-educated readers. Domínguez Camargo's editor declares in the dedication that he was anxious that the *S. Ignacio* "gozasse el aplauso de los Doctos, bien entendidos, y mejor intencionados." Many of the sermons, too, were mainly directed to a cultured audience. Juan Bautista Ballester's *Aclamacion festiva* was preached primarily to university faculty. His is an example of a *suelto*, which Hilary Dansey Smith explains as a sermon originally published individually, usually very shortly after the occasion on which it was preached, and intended as a record of what the preacher actually said. In contrast, *sermonarios* or sermon collections, individual sermons of which were often called *discursos predicables, consideraciones, oraciones evangélicas,* etc. rather than *sermones,* usually represent a preacher's personal selection of his sermons, often spanning the whole of his preaching career, and seem to be intended as models for apprentice preachers, or as compendia of *materia predicable,* rather than a verbatim record (29-30). Both internal evidence and preliminary sections of numerous *sermonarios* support the view that they were primarily directed to preachers. However, Smith points out that arguments presented by preachers themselves for publishing their sermons in the vernacular indicate they are going to be read by the laity. Indeed, by the 1630's it is taken for granted that sermons will be quite widely used as books of private devotion (38-40).

The earliest date that can be definitely assigned within this corpus is 1508, year of publication of Ambrosio Montesino's *Cancionero*; the latest is 1694, which saw the publication of Juan Francisco de Enciso's *Christiada*. Roughly one-fourth of the works were written or published before 1600. Poetry, prose, and drama are more or less equally represented. The Anthology contains some one hundred sixty-five single poems or poetic excerpts, thirteen of them from long narrative poems. In many cases, several poems are taken from the same collection, and some are quite short. Of the seventy-six prose works, fifty-nine are sermons. The dramatic genre includes eighty-two *autos*, fifty-nine by Calderón, and eleven *loas* or *entremeses*.

The criteria according to which I selected illustrative texts call for brief comment. First, they are texts in which the topos occurs as part of the surface structure. Since in the Golden Age people were still accustomed to experiencing the world the way one would read a text, had I taken into account deep structure, I should probably never have finished this study. I have excluded texts in which the topical motifs seemed to me to be "frozen," in which the writer gives little or no evidence of consciously using a metaphor. Such, for instance, are many passages which employ a simple *imprimir* or *borrar* with respect to the heart. Certain terms that we today connect with a written text, such as *autor*, did not always have the same meaning in the Golden Age. When I could not be sure of the denotation, I rejected the passage. Nor have I included texts that play on the letters in a person's name.

When I began my study, as I intended to include only examples in which the tenor was a human being or the natural world, as a whole or in any of their parts, I did not gather passages that referred exclusively to Christ's divine nature. Only later, in accord with the vision of the essential unity of nature, a nature which, as Camós states in *Microcosmia*, constitutes together with God a single book (Ant. Cam: 51-54), did I decide to include whatever symbolic writing images I found in the texts to which I had access. For that reason, images for which the tenor is other than a human person or the natural world are proportionately fewer in this study than in the literature itself.

Another, closely related, pair of issues with which I wrestled was the ambiguity of the spoken and the written word and that of writing vis-a-vis painting. Here Mary J. Carruthers' *The Book of Memory: A*

*Study of Memory in Medieval Culture* came to my aid. Carruthers shows how a memorial culture regarded the spoken and the written or the pictorial and the verbal as aspects of the same basic phenomenon (Whitaker 96). One sees vestiges of this attitude in my corpus of texts. The mixing or even identification of the oral with the written is probably due in part to the continuation of such traditional reading habits and customs as reading aloud to oneself – the *voce tenui* of memory work and meditation (Carruthers 6), that is, subvocalization or murmuring, as well as reading aloud to others in *viva voce* (170). It would have been reinforced by the coexistence in the Golden Age of a healthy body of oral literature with handwritten and printed texts.

Two examples will suffice to show the continuation into the Golden Age of the medieval concept of reading as a " 'hermeneutical dialogue' between two memories," expressed in the phrase " 'voces paginarum,' 'the voices of the pages' " (Carruthers 169-70). Alejo Venegas says in the prologue to *Primera parte de las diferencias de libros que ay en el universo*, published in 1540, "Los libros son como vnos preceptores: que avn que no por palabras vocales: a lo menos por señas hablan con los ausentes" (1). Seventy-eight years later Lope asks rhetorically in *Triunfo de la fe en los reinos del Japón*:

> Pues ¿qué diré de aquellos apostólicos varones que . . . tienen la propagación de la fe desde la ardiente lumbre de Domingo, de la sangre del mártir de Verona, y de tanta *como nos muestran a los oidos los libros*, y a los ojos las teñidas efigies de sus mártires. . . ?
> (*Colección escogida* 161, emphasis added)

Venegas' and Lope's statements illuminate the initially surprising or puzzling alternation between images of orality and literacy that one finds in many metaphorical passages in this corpus. One example is from Gálvez de Montalvo's "El llanto de San Pedro":

> Y lo que puede asconderse
> Dentro de un alma amorosa,
> Sin escribirse o leerse,
> Con la vista es fácil cosa
> Escucharse y entenderse. (Ant. Gal)

In *Consideraciones del Martes después del Domingo cuarto de Cuaresma*, Cabrera speaks of the blessed in heaven as reading in the book of life, that is, enjoying direct or unmediated communication with the Godhead, in contrast with the mediated knowledge of God granted to humans on earth in the humanity of Christ. However, when Cabrera asks, "¿qué me aprovechara a mí, Señor, que tú leyeras esa doctrina tan alta, y por modo tan alto allá en el templo de tu gloria, si no tuvieras por bien de bajar al templo de tu iglesia a enseñar a estos pequeñuelos hombres. . . ?" (Ant. Cab8: 8-14), he reveals that for him reading the book of life in heaven is identical to hearing it read aloud. Valdivielso's *exposición parafrástica* of Psalm 18 converts what was originally a metaphor based on the spoken word into one that alternates between the oral and the written. When the "sonoras / vozes" of the first verses become "vozes mudas" in verse 15, one is inclined to interpret the latter image as writing (Ant.Va 4).

Similarly, Carruthers tells us that in medieval culture looking at pictures, or picturing, was an act equivalent to reading (222), or from a different point of view, writing and making pictures were identical. This link also holds true in the Golden Age. Lope's *Laurel de Apolo* observes, "Dos cosas son al hombre naturales, / O pintar o escribir en tiernos años, / Que plumas y pinceles son iguales" (*Colección escogida* 219). And Pedro de Navarra's *Rústico* states, "los santos que tú vees en los templos pintados son como escrituras que leemos de las santas obras y vidas que han hecho . . ." (163). Just as the medieval scribe who wrote out the letters was often identified as the "painter" of the manuscript (Carruthers 225), so in a metaphorical passage in "Coplas en gloria de nuestra Señora," Montesino refers to "el sol escribano, / Que el verano pinta" (Ant. Mon5:3-4). Venegas' use of the motif "to delight in the beautiful letters without understanding their meaning" also equates *pintura* with *escriptura*: "no hagamos como los niños o como los locos: que viendo en el libro las letras muy galanas i muy luminadas[,] deleytanse en la pintura sin curar de lo que interiormente en la tal escriptura se representa" (Ant. Ven:224-29). Lope de Vega links calligraphy and painting to the art of embroidery in a 'Silva moral' from "El siglo de Oro," *Vega del Parnaso*:

> No de otra suerte que la alfombra pinta
> El tracio con la seda de colores,
> En cada rueda de labor distinta,
> Arábicos carácteres y flores. . . . (Ant. VgC23: 3-6)

Here the "Arábicos carácteres" are the tendrils among the blossoms, blending with the painted / embroidered flowers in such a way that it is difficult to discern where one ends and the other begins.

The ambiguity of some texts does not derive solely from the mingling of words referring to writing with those alluding to painting. Certain terms, such as *borrador*, *cifra*, *ejemplar*, *copia*, and *estampar* are identical in the contexts of both writing and painting, so that it can be difficult to tell if one or the other is meant, or perhaps both. A passage from Montesino's "Itinerario de la Cruz" is a case in point: "Te pido, oh Reina sin par, / Que tu claro original / Resplandezca en mi traslado" (Ant. Mon8:1-3). Besides being ambivalent in this way, a term like *rasgo* is also a cross between writing and drawing. Other terms, such as *pinzel* and *retrato*, identify objects primarily related to painting but which can be associated with written texts. A fine brush might be used to make illuminated letters in a manuscript, and a book might include a portrait. The passage from Guerra y Ribera's *Oracion en la beatificacion de onze Martyres, y San Francisco Solano* included in the Anthology illustrates two of these types of ambiguity (Ant. Gue10). In addition, entities like the emblem or map usually incorporate both writing and drawing. I have included examples that seemed to me to refer either exclusively or inclusively to written texts.

Sometimes a writer uses the same image with first one denotation and then the other in closely placed passages. In Felipe Godínez' *Auto del nacimiento de Christo* the motif of the *borrón* occurs first in the context of writing: "es gran ventura / ser borron en la Escritura / de los Salmos de Dauid" (Ant. Go1:3-6). Shortly afterwards it appears in the context of painting: "Pinto Dios el mundo, / y fueron / estos negros venturosos / borrones de su pinzel" (J. Fernández 110). At other times the denotation or connotation of a word may shift between painting and writing within the same passage, as in the case of *borrador* in Cabrera's *Consideraciones del Viernes después del Domingo primero de Cuaresma* (Ant. Cab7).

The topos is long-lived, and many of its motifs have become frozen. We tend to use expressions like "to read someone like a book," "you can't judge a book by its cover," and "it's written all over your face" in fixed form and with little or no attention to the presence of metaphor. Some writers, however, manage to infuse new life into these topical motifs. Perhaps one reason for the revitalizing of the topos in our times has to do with such factors as the environmental movement, which among other things has renewed our appreciation of paper; the literacy issue; and computerization, which has made us conscious of books in a different way.

Examples I have gathered through random reading indicate that all three basic tenors – God, the human being, and the natural world – are alive and well in users of the topos today. I have found motifs in many different media and genres, from books, through newspapers and magazines to television; from a park guide to an advertisement for the Infinity ("It reads the road as if it had written the book"), from a poem to an article on a presidential candidate, from baby books to memoirs, from historical novels to science fiction, from detective novels to essays on spirituality.

One advantage I have already experienced as a result of having assembled the present motif index is that when I come across examples of the topos, the motifs sort themselves into those which are virtually unchanged, those which have been updated, those whose articulation is especially creative, etc. When one of the interlocutors on the *NOVA* program "Decoding the Book of Life" observes, "Then there was the problem of interpreting the text. What did all those A's, C's, G's and T's mean?" (6), I immediately discern the old motif "to recognize the characters without understanding their meaning." Upon reflection, I can also see quite readily both change and similarity in the relationship between two of the referents of the topos, from the Golden Age to now. Whereas in the earlier period the book of the universe and the book of the person were related as macrocosm to microcosm, or vast tome to compendium, in the script for the aforementioned program the book of the human being is one variant of an original it had in common with, for example, the book of the mouse or the book of cotton. The book of the person and the various other books that constitute the universe are related through their common alphabet, DNA.

Twentieth-century writers and the Spanish writers presented in this study work within and help extend a tradition whose foundation is, it would seem, primarily Biblical and classical. Several more or less synonymous motifs, such as the tablet of the heart / soul / memory appear in both the Bible and classical writers. The Church Fathers, early Christian poets, and medieval poets, mystics, and philosopher-theologians carry on the tradition, adding elements from their own cultural milieu in their formulations of the topoi. Not only their own, however; Arabic literature also plays a role in the formation of the topos. As Maria Rosa Menocal observes in *The Arabic Role in Medieval Literary History: A Forgotten Heritage*:

> There was no doubt that access to the works of many of those who wrote in Arabic was more than abundant [in 12th century Europe and after], because it was provided, not only surreptitiously but also through the most respectable of Christian channels, by the translations of the venerable abbot of Cluny himself, for example. (55)

Curtius remarks that many of the metaphors based on textual images were transmitted to the Spanish writers of the Golden Age via medieval Latin mannerist literature (316), that is, literature of basically the same period to which Menocal refers. Al-Andalus "was very much at the heart of the renaissance of the twelfth [century]" (Menocal 66), and "El amor por la lectura y por los libros han sido dos pasiones de los andaluces" (Peres 450). While Curtius points out that Arabic and Persian poetry and poetics, transmitted to Andalucía, where they flourished between the tenth and thirteenth centuries, were themselves doubtless influenced by Hellenistic models (340-41), María Rosa Lida de Malkiel, in *La tradición clásica en España*, counters that in fact, Hellenistic literature was greatly influenced by Oriental, and especially Hebrew, literature (294-95). In whichever direction we view the current as flowing, the fact remains that "Oriental and Spanish sensibility unite in it [Andalusian poetry]. . . . This delicate poetry . . . is one of the channels through which the spirit of Islamic art could find its way into the Spanish poetry of the *siglo de oro*" (Curtius 341). Curtius summarizes what he sees as the principal reasons for the extraordinary "abundance and preciosity" of metaphors in Spanish literature, including those based on writing and the book:

> [T]wo reasons, I think, suggest themselves: first, the influence of medieval Latin poetry (far stronger in Spain than elsewhere); second, the community of culture which existed for centuries between Christian and Moorish Spain. The medieval Latin and the Eastern ornamental styles could meet and mingle only in Spain. (343)

Dietrich Briesemeister observes in "Die Buchmetaphorik in den Autos sacramentales" that Calderón's "bibliofilia" is linguistically expressed in the *comedias* through some forty different phrases, that is, similes and metaphors related to writing, and that there are still others in the *autos* (98). This fact is a less astonishing, while no less admirable, manifestation of *inventio* when one is aware of the wealth of forms assumed by the topos in the Spanish Golden Age.[1] Virtually all the comparisons mentioned by Curtius, not only in connection with Spanish writers but throughout the entire chapter "The Book as Symbol," are present in my corpus, as are others that he does not treat. In fact, it is difficult to think of potential motifs that do not appear in some guise. The only ones that have occurred to me are the pirating of books (though lines 9-10 of the excerpt from Gerónimo de la Fuente's *décimas* may allude to it), the borrowing or loaning of books, the recycling of books that have not sold, and the laudatory poems often found preceding the main text. With regard to this last, some of the Spanish writers may have viewed as such their own poems in praise of the metaphorical text.

Within this corpus can be found writers from each of the two groups alluded to by María Rosa Lida de Malkiel in the following passage: "Tradición literaria es en los verdaderos poetas recreación y reactualización de los temas, por más que en todos los tiempos haya versifi-

---

[1] Among the motifs missing in the texts from Calderón, although they occur in several other writers, are papyrus and parchment, products of a technology much earlier than his own, as well as motifs connected with the printing or censoring of a book, processes well established by his time.

cadores que los usen como repetición de tópicos retóricos" ("La tradición clásica" 38). I will treat "reactualización" a bit later in this introduction, in relation to influences from the cultural milieu. Nearly all of these writers defamiliarize the topical motifs, using such techniques as repeating, elaborating or dramatizing the central image, transforming, punning, and joking. For instance, Calderón alludes in humorous vein to the frequency of one motif when *Judaísmo* remarks in *La vacante general*, "Mucho lo temo / oír metáforas de pluma, / cuando de David me acuerdo" (Ant. Ca62:24-26). Some writers, Calderón among them, recreate old motifs in superior ways, arresting with the beauty of their imagery or entrancing with a motif raised, as it were, to the second power. By means of the topos they also defamiliarize or thaw frozen doctrine or ideas. For example, we may forget that the expression "original sin," a frequent tenor of various topical vehicles, is itself a metaphor, but Calderón makes us aware of this fact in passage after passage. He uses new metaphors to illuminate the old one, such as when he alludes to the mysterious way in which all people throughout human history are jointly responsible for and inevitably enmeshed in the alienating behavior many call sin, or to the fact that so-called original sin and actual sin are not separable entities but different perspectives on the same reality, through his unique articulation of the motif of writing on a tree.

I am not concerned in this section with determining the source of particular motifs, but rather with suggesting a few ways in which the Spanish Golden Age writers transmitted and at the same time changed the topos as they received it from whatever source. Whether from earlier writers or contemporaries, as Menocal observes, "Influence is clearly more diffuse in some cases than in others, sometimes explicit and marked, and other times not, sometimes manifest in absorption, adaptation, and rewriting, and other times in a denial, a countertext, or a void" (61). She does not explain precisely what she means by these terms, so I have assigned them descriptions of my own in aid of a coherent comparison of examples. I consider absorption to have occurred when a writer uses an earlier motif with both the same vehicle and the same tenor, or when s/he alludes to it only partially, assuming the reader's familiarity with it. Adaptation means that a writer uses virtually the same wording in the vehicle but with a different tenor, or substitutes in the vehicle an image that is substantially the same but accidentally different, such as a more contemporary type of writing material. Rewriting signifies that a motif has undergone more radical change, in semantics or structure. Denial involves the explicit negative formulation of an existing motif normally expressed positively, whereas a countertext is the positively expressed contradiction or contrary of another motif. A void exists if a motif shines by its absence. It seems to me that adaptation and rewriting are the most commonly occurring forms of influence, whether marked or diffuse, in this corpus of texts.

Seemingly the easiest way to identify direct or marked influence would be by citation or quotation on the part of the writer, most likely to be found in the sermons or other prose works.[2] In neither case, however, can one take for granted that the topos occurs in the original as articulated by the Golden Age writer. One reason is that in the case of a simple citation, the writer or source named may be an indirect or secondary influence. Speaking in reference to Golden Age sermons, Smith observes that every preacher's library contained "voluminous collections of commonplaces and 'potted' erudition" (26). Andrés Soria Ortega mentions, for example, the presence of a 1624 edition of the *Glosa Ordinaria* in the library of Guerra y Ribera (283). Smith finds that many preachers freely borrow similes from Pedro Mexía's "anthology" *Silva de varia lección* (Seville 1540), acknowledging only the name of the person who first conceived them (87). It should be said, however, that writers do sometimes refer explicitly to such a collection, as in Ángel Manrique's sermon *Del glorioso san Pedro de Castilnuouo* (Ant. ManA3:27).

Another reason is the tradition Carruthers discusses in relation to medieval culture and which continues into the Golden Age. The highly valued art of memory was actually the art of recollection (*memoria ad res*), tracking down through association, distinct from the ability to reproduce something exactly (*memoria ad verbum*) (20). In many cases, then, writers would have drawn on a vast repertory of ideas and images that had become part of their mental furnishings, among which they could move, and which they could move about, with ease. Habits of reading and reflecting upon what was read, formed through meditation upon Scripture, created networks of texts in the mind of the writer, texts that intermingle, play off of and set up resonances among one another. Thus, for example, although Luis de Granada declares that God taught Job to philosophize "en este gran libro de las criaturas" (Ant. Grn:15), one would search in vain for the explicit image of the "libro de

---

[2] One example in the dramatic genre is from Calderón's *La nave del mercader.* I see in the following excerpt a pointed allusion to the influence of the Italian poet Marino, who was apparently one of the channels for the transmission of the classical motif of writing as plowing. Calderón raises the conceit to the second power:

> Que si en sacras lecciones
> las vagas ondas son tribulaciones,
> no (para algún concepto) sin disculpa
> marino monstruo, a tribular la Culpa
> hoy sulca de la vida los pasajes. (Ant. Ca36:2-6)

las criaturas" in the Book of Job. Rather, Fray Luis seems to be referring to the last four chapters of the Biblical book, which express in other terms the idea of nature as manifesting God's power and wisdom. Juan Suárez de Godoy's supposedly direct quotation from Mercurius Trismegistus seems to be another example (Ant. Sua: 26-31), although the problem may lie in the translation of the *Poemandres* that I consulted.

Many times, of course, the citation or quotation does in fact indicate an apparently direct source of the specific motif. For example, in his sermon *En la fiesta de las llagas* Murillo cites Canticles and paraphrases 8.6, translating the original "signaculum" as "señal de recuerdo" and "señal de memoria" (Ant. Mu3: 49-51). Both vehicle and tenor are virtually the same, so the passage is very likely an example of absorbed direct influence.

In comparison, Ángel Manrique deals more freely with the cited and quoted Biblical sources in his sermon on Mary's nativity. His point of departure is the *liber generationis Iesu Christi* of Matthew 1.1, an image whose meaning in Scripture is literal but which Manrique converts to a metaphorical one, applying it to Mary. Of course, this procedure is not really different from the traditional method of Biblical exegesis, with its literal and spiritual interpretations, or from the practice of accommodation, that is, modifying the usual interpretation given to a text in order to achieve one's particular purpose on a specific occasion. In the same sermon Manrique follows the Scripture in applying the image of the "virens folium" of Proverbs 11.28 to the saints, but he changes the literal denotation of the leaves from those on a tree to ones in a book (Ant. ManA2: 82-86). The foregoing passages are thus adaptations of a direct influence, unless, of course, we think that these same transformations could be found in some other earlier text or texts.

A second approach to detecting possible direct influence might be to ascertain that the vehicle, tenor, and referent are all identical in both writers.[3] Compare, for example the following excerpts from Cairasco de Figueroa's "Apariencia santa" and Calderón's *Sueños hay que verdad son*. The former contains two of his many definitions:

> Es la bella Apariencia un sobrescrito
> Que declara cuál es y lo que vale
> La interna calidad que esta encubierta.
> . . . .
> Aquesta es una carta encarecida
> Que escribe de favor naturaleza
> A los humanos ojos. . . . (Ant. Cai2)

---

[3] See Introduction to Motif Index pp. 64-65 for an explanation of these terms.

Calderón's *Copero* affirms of Joseph, temporarily imprisoned by Pharaoh:

> La buena presencia es
> el sobrescrito primero
> de las cartas de favor,
> que escribe piadoso el cielo. (Ant. Ca60)

I am inclined to call this a case of marked influence in the form of adaptation, although as Peter M. Daly observes with respect to emblems and other poetic images, a similarity or even an exact correspondence does not necessarily indicate direct influence, since it is always possible that both texts have been inspired by the same common source (55).

Another example is a pair of texts based on the primary motif of the book of nature and the secondary one of delighting in the beautiful letters without understanding their meaning. Here the likelihood of direct influence is even greater, since the vehicles, tenors, and referents are all the same, and the wording itself is strikingly similar. Venegas declares:

> En este libro leya sant Anton el gran poder de dios en la creación: la sabiduria de dios en la gouernación: la bondad de dios en la comunicación. A cuyo exemplo en la lición deste libro nosotros podemos ser induzidos a temer a dios por razon de su immenso poder: a creerle por razon de su infinito saber[,] a amarle por su infinita bondad: porque no hagamos como los niños o como los locos: que viendo en el libro las letras muy galanas i muy luminadas[,] deleytanse en la pintura sin curar de lo que interiormente en la tal escriptura se representa. (Ant. Ven:216-29)

The Benedictine Pierre Bersuire, or Petrus Berchorius (ca. 1290-1362), declares in his *Repertorium morale*:

> Primo ergo dico, quod liber naturae, qui est liber inductivus, & iste nihil aliud est, quam universitas creaturarum, quae nihil aliud quam quaedam scripturae, vel lecturae, ubi, & in quibus homo potest legere.
>
>                 Potestatem in creatione,
> Dei         Sagacitatem in gubernatione,
>                 Bonitatem in communicatione.
>
> Et ideo in isto possumus induci ad Deum timendum ratione potentiae: ad Deum credendum ratione sapientiae: ad Deum amandum ra-

> tione bonitatis & influentiae. Peccatores tamen sunt sicut pueri & fatui, vel laici, qui videntes in libro literas pulchras & pictas, ibi taliter delectantur, quod de sensu literali non curant. (3-4:462)

Of course, rather than direct influence in the form of absorption, this might be another case of "potted erudition," Venegas having drawn upon Berchorius via an intermediary, or it might be that both Berchorius and Venegas utilized some other common source.

On the other hand, when a less remarkable similarity involves a somewhat unique motif, the possibility of direct influence should not be disregarded either. Antonio Coello's *auto El reyno en cortes, y rey en campaña* and Calderón's *El lirio y la azucena* use the motif of the *libro verde* in strikingly similar ways (Ant. Co1, Ca30). Given the added considerations that the topical vehicle derives at least in part from a phenomenon peculiar to Spanish culture, that these two writers are the only ones in this corpus in whom I have found it, and that they collaborated on several plays, direct influence in the form of rewriting and adaptation seems quite possible.

However, one could also view this as an instance of diffuse influence, given that, according to Otis H. Green, Hugh of Folieto wrote of four books of life, the first of which was written in Paradise by God on the human heart (2: 179). If this is the case, the book of life has been only slightly modified to a green book, green being the symbol of life. The tenor has remained the same in Coello, i.e., Paradise or the Garden of Eden, while Calderón gives it the three levels of meaning traditional to Biblical exegesis, the literal – Garden of Eden, the allegorical – Mt. Sinai, and the tropological – Mt. Calvary, in conjunction with their three respective "laws," the natural, the Mosaic, and that of grace.

A third clue to direct influence on the topical motifs is the fact of a work's being a *contrafactum* of a known secular text. Sebastián de Córdoba's "Soneto V" is an *a lo divino* version of Garcilaso. Córdoba retains the vehicles and tenors and simply changes the referent from the lady to Christ.

Examples of diffuse influence are obviously much more plentiful. Here I offer only a few, to illustrate the various forms in which it is manifested. The motif of rubrication with reference to the shedding of blood, used by Peter the Venerable in apostrophizing the martyr St. Cyprian of Carthage (Curtius 316), occurs several times in my writers without change, that is, in the verb form *rubricar* or the noun form *rúbrica*. For this reason I consider it a fully absorbed motif. Another absorbed motif is that of the book that was consumed. Lope (Ant. VgC5: 6) and Enciso (Ant. Enc:7-8) assume it is familiar to their readers, as indicated by "el que" and the demonstrative, and thus identify it only partially (Enciso is a bit more complete). The image occurs in Scripture, in both Ezekiel 3.1-3 and Apocalypse 10.10, but Enciso especially is closer to the former text.[4]

In some cases the absorbed motifs are implicit. Paravicino's "A la santa Cruz" contains the following lines: "Que aquesos papeles rotos / La escritura son contraria / Que clava el fiador famoso" (Ant. Par1:9-11). The topical motifs are embedded in the image of a fortress under siege, reminiscent of the Biblical passage on the kingdom of heaven suffering violence and the violent bearing it away (Matt. 11.12). The "papeles rotos" refer on the one hand to the "Desmantelado ... globo / Impíreo" of eight lines back; here Paravicino counts on the reader's familiarity with the much used motif of the paper of the heavens. On the other hand they are "La escritura ... contraria / Que clava el fiador famoso." What they are contrary to is first, the idea that Dimas' action is a theft, since Christ's redemption has opened the fortress of heaven to all, including a repentant thief, converting slaves into heirs of the kingdom. Thus they are a *carta de horro*, in contradistinction to the underlying motif of the *carta de venta*, or to the *S y clavos* of the branded slave. In addition they are contrary to the *escritura de obligación*, whose familiarity to the reader Paravicino also assumes; that is, they are a *carta de pago*. The poet's playing off these implicit motifs is expressed paradoxically; a document appears to be constructed by its own deconstruction, reflecting the supreme paradox of the Cross, in which death is but the other face of resurrection. Paravicino emphasizes this idea by converting the negative image of the original source, "chirographum decreti, quod erat *contrarium* nobis ... affigens illud cruci" (Col. 2.14) to the positive one of the "escritura ... *contraria* / Que clava el fiador famoso" (emphasis added). The tearing up of the *escritura de obligación is* the new document; grace is freedom from the Law. The final motif concretizes this paradoxical act of redemption in the "papeles rotos" of the body of Christ, torn by the nails that fix him to the Cross.

Probably the simplest type of adapted diffuse motif involves the same wording but a different tenor or referent. The image of the *digitus Dei*, signifying the power or Spirit of God, as writing the text appears in such Biblical passages as Exodus 8.19 and 31.18, in the respective contexts of the plagues wrought as punishment for Pharaoh's hardness of heart and the tablets of the Law given Moses on Mt. Sinai. Hugh of St. Victor, twelfth-century head of the Augustinian monastery

---

[4] Enciso might have been indirectly influenced also by St. Bernard's famous image for the name of Jesus: "Jesus, mel in ore, in aure melos, in corde jubilus" (qtd. in Cabrera, *Navidad* 143, 179). Perhaps Bernard's final phrase is a countertext to the last part of Apoc. 10.10.

of that name in Paris, is among the medieval writers who use the motif as a metaphor, specifically for God's work in creation. In this corpus the referents of the motif are quite varied. Another motif that appears in several writers is the *cartilla*. Curtius explains that at least from the twelfth century it was common to teach the alphabet in schools by writing it on a large leaf of parchment stretched over a wooden board and sometimes nailed to the wall. From this custom arose a metaphor that the thirteenth-century Cistercian Odo of Cheriton articulates as follows: "Sicut enim carta, in qua scribitur doctrina parvulorum, quatuor clavis affigitur in postem, sic caro Christi extensa est in cruce" (qtd. in Curtius 319). While this motif appears substantially unchanged in Lope de Vega's "Sentimientos a los agravios de Cristo" (Ant. VgC24: 26-31), many Golden Age writers adapt it by applying it to other tenors than the crucified Christ.

An adapted motif with a somewhat modified vehicle is the *lámina*, which occurs in Job 19.23-24: "Quis mihi tribuat ut scribantur sermones mei? Quis mihi det ut exarentur in libro, stylo ferreo et plumbi lámina, vel celte sculpantur in cilice?" Curtius asserts that this passage was the source of the metaphor of the "lead tablet," so popular in the Middle Ages (311). However, in the Golden Age writers in this study the *lámina* is never of lead; on the contrary, the text often implies or states that it is of some precious material. In Calderón's *El árbol del mejor fruto*, it is a "verde lámina" (Ant. Ca8: 27), perhaps a fusion of the Biblical image with the Emerald Tablet of Mercurius or Hermes Trismegistus (Goodrich-Dunn 17).

Curtius informs us that the metaphor of the *album* first appears in the late Latin period and that the word originally signified "the white tablet for official notices, then a register of officeholders" (309). Carruthers speaks of the "shining white substance" on which, according to Jewish tradition, the sins of all men were preserved (9). The motif appears in Calderón's *La inmunidad del sagrado* as

> ... blanco volumen,
> en que cuantos nazcan consten,
> hasta que su cargo ajusten,
> y de la cárcel del mundo
> salgan.... (Ant. Ca26: 16-20)

In this slightly more complex form of adaptation, Calderón appears to have combined the secular vehicle, which undergoes a solely linguistic change, and its literal meaning with the metaphoric tenor of the sacred tradition.

Juan de Avila's sermon on St. Francis of Assisi (Ant. Av7) contains what appears to be a rewriting of the motif "to prepare a parchment for writing" as it is found in a medieval sermon attributed to Hildebert of Lavardin. In his development of Deut. 4.1, "Audi, Israel, praecepta vitae, et scribe ea in corde tuo," Hildebert describes the process of bookmaking:

> First the scribe cleanses the parchment of fat and coarse dirt with a knife. Then he removes the hairs and fibers with a pumice stone. If he did not do this, the written letters [would] be worthless and impermanent. Then he rules the parchment, so that the writing will be regular. All this you too must do with your hearts . . . (Qtd. in Curtius 318-19)

Avila omits the motif of tracing lines on the parchment and repeats terms related to its purity. Perhaps the title of the Spanish writer's celebrated treatise *Audi, Filia* and the thematic verse of the medieval sermon are more than coincidentally alike, but I am hesitant to call this a case of direct influence.

A somewhat more transformed rewriting, this time of a passage originating in St. Augustine, occurs in Alonso de Ledesma's verses "A S. Ivan Evangelista recostado al pecho de Cristo" (Ant. Led12). In a paraphrase of a passage from *De Genesi ad litteram*, Villanueva says that Augustine "llama matutino al conocimiento que los ángeles tienen en el Verbo, y vespertino al que tienen según su propia naturaleza, porque es mucho más clara, perfecta y distinta la primera noticia que la segunda" (173). I think Ledesma's "liciones de prima," witnessed by St. John in his mystical experience at the Last Supper, can be traced back to Augustine's *conocimiento matutino* enjoyed by the angels.

The idea of God and the world together constituting one book, which occurs in Camós' *Microcosmia* (Ant. Cam:51-54), is found also, in different terms, in St. Bonaventure's *Breviloquium*: "Duplex est liber, unos scilicet scriptus intus, qui est Dei aeterna ars et sapientia, et alius scriptus foris, scilicet mundus sensibilis" (qtd. in Curtius 321). In his sermon on Christ's wounds (Ant. Mu3), Murillo develops the image of the "anillo de memoria" in a manner strikingly reminiscent of Cabrera's "sortija" and "libro de memoria" in *Consideraciones del Domingo en la octava de la Pascua de Resurrección* (Ant. Cab11), with echoes of the "cinco anillos" in Montesino's "Del glorioso san Francisco" (Ant. Mon7). Murillo's text could be a rewriting of Cabrera, or more likely, both could have drawn on a common source. One of the most thoroughgoing rewritings, which I have discussed at some length elsewhere (Salstad, "Illuminating"), is Juan Bautista Aguilar's sonnet "A Christo Señor nuestro," in which he transforms a passage from Berchorius.

St. Teresa speaks in *Libro de la vida* of certain aids to spiritual recollection, a simultaneous quieting and awakening of the mind, aids which include the beauties of nature: "campo o agua, flores; en estas cosas hallaba yo memoria del Criador, digo que me despertaban y recogían y servían de libro" (Ant. Ter:4-7). I see this passage as an example of both adaptation and rewriting. It is an articulation of the motif of the *libro de memoria*, which had a long and complex development. In it I perceive an echo from a hymn of Proclus, fifth-century Greek Neoplatonist, in which he refers to " 'spirit-awakening books,' " which as gifts of the Muses purify spirits imprisoned in the earthly (qtd. in Curtius 308).

Another combination of adaptation and rewriting is Jaime Torres' development of the motif of the book with seven seals, in "Desafío moral del hombre." He equates the seals with "varios accidentes" (Ant. To:5), as does Berchorius in the following gloss on Apocalypse 5.1 in *Repertorium morale*:

> Iste liber fuit nobis clausus, signatus, velatus in Sacramento altaris, quia pro certo ibi sunt sigilla septem, id est, septem accidentia, quibus substantia corporis occultatus. Ista sunt sapor, color, odor, figura, quantitas, actio, passio; . . . . & sub istis accidentibus, & sigillis celatur & absconditur corpus Christi. (1: 228)

Whereas the Benedictine applies the image to the Eucharistic body of Christ, Torres speaks of his human figure. In comparison, the tenor of José de Valdivielso's book with seven seals in "Romance al Santíssimo Sacramento" is the Eucharistic Christ (Ant. Val3:5-8). His rewriting incorporates a motif expressed in different terms in *The Lauds* of the thirteenth-century poet Jacopone da Todi, that of Christ's wounds as five illuminated or rubricated seals: "I am the book of life, sealed with the seven seals; / When I am opened you will find five signs, / The color of red, red blood. Ponder them" (141).

An Oriental text proffers an image that could have been a diffuse influence on a passage in Luis de Granada's *Introducción del Símbolo de la Fe* (Ant. Grn:76-88). In *The Thousand and One Nights* "a trained ape," reminiscence of the Egyptian god of writing, Thoth, "writes successive quatrains in cursive hand, slim hand, steep hand, round monumental hand, large document hand, and large decorated hand" (qtd. in Curtius 341-42). Granada's writer, a metaphor for the Creator, is a "grande escribano, que quiere asentar en una ciudad escuela de escribir." The "muchas diferencias de letras" he composes are also of six types, several of them more or less synonymous with certain ones in the previous passage: "unas de tirado, otras de redondo, otras de letra escolástica, otras de hacienda, otras quebradas, otras iluminadas." Granada's apologizing for the lowliness of his comparison is somewhat curious in that this last does not seem any more "common" than certain other analogies for which he does not feel compelled to apologize. One explanation might be that he had in mind the trained ape of *The Thousand and One Nights*. Or the apology might reflect a social prejudice toward the *escribano*.

Another example involves a less problematic adaptation of tenors. Curtius mentions the appearance of the 'Book of Fate' in the *Dionysiaca* of the poet Nonnus: "The primordial spirit . . . inscribed the future history of the world on tablets in vermilion letters" (308). Certain lines in Calderón's *La inmunidad del sagrado* look much like a rewriting of this motif, Calderón's "primordial spirit" being Christ, the "vermilion letters," his blood, with which he creates anew the future of humankind (Ant. Ca26:55-64, 88-94).

The motif of the tools as inadequate to the subject occurs in two of my texts, Ambrosio Montesino's "Coplas en gloria de nuestra Señora" (Ant. Mon5) and Pedro de Padilla's "Cancion al sanctissimo nombre de Iesus" (Ant. Pad2). Of the earlier sources of this motif which I have found, the one that seems closest to Montesino in terms of discrete images, though not its tenor, is an elegy of Henry of Settimello, two of whose verses read as follows: "Pagina sit caelum, sint frondes scriba, sit unda / Incaustrum: mala non nostra referre queant" (qtd. Curtius 316). Padilla's text, on the other hand, is similar, but not identical, in both vehicle and tenor to one translated by Ilse Lichtenstadtler in *Introduction to Classical Arabic Literature*. Certain Jewish rabbis visiting the apostle at Medina are told concerning the Torah, " 'If all the trees in the world were pens and the ocean were ink, though the seven seas reinforced it, the words of God would not be exhausted' " (198).

Calderón's *La vacante general* contains a most interesting passage in which several intimately related motifs are juxtaposed (Ant. Ca62: 45-65). The ultimate source of this reworking is doubtless Apocalypse 20.12: "et libri aperti sunt, et alius liber apertus est qui est vitae, et judicati sunt mortui ex his quae scripta erant in libris, secundum opera ipsorum." Jesse M. Gellrich quotes the Dominican Hugh of St. Cher's interpretation of the first of the pair of images as " 'libri conscientiarum, vel cordium.' " Hugh then follows other exegetes in contrasting these books with the book of presence. The *Allegoria in sacram scripturam* identifies the *liber praesentia* with the book of life (Gellrich 163). It seems to me that the *praesentia* might be a mutation of *presciencia*, as it appears, for example, in St. Augustine's *City of God*. Glossing Apocalypse 20.15, he comments:

> No sirve este libro de memoria a Dios para que no se engañe por olvido, sino que significa la predestinación de aquellos a quienes ha de darse la vida eterna. Porque no los ignora Dios, y para saberlos lee en este libro, sino que antes la misma presciencia que tiene de

ellos, que es la que no se puede engañar, es el libro de la vida, donde están los escritos, esto es, los conocidos para la vida eterna. (Villanueva 172)

Instead of contrasting the books of conscience and the book of life, Calderón emphasizes the idea that the human conscience always lies open to God by fusing all four of the above motifs, three of which appear on the surface: the *libro de memoria*, the *libro de la consciencia*, and the *libro de presencia* or *libro de la [pre]Ciencia*, the underlying image being the *libro de la vida*. The book of each person's conscience is part of the eternal knowledge of the Book of Life.

Examples of diffuse influence in the forms of denial, contradiction, or a void are less frequent but not totally lacking in this group of texts. An epitaph from the High Middle Ages which Curtius believes to have been written possibly by Peter Riga includes the following thought: "Nature made a splendid man and painted him with moral excellences – but Death dyes him with his ink" (Curtius 316-17). Gerónimo de la Fuente, in his *dézimas* in praise of Mary's immaculate conception and the stigmata of St. Francis, denies the idea expressed by the final motif in this cluster when he declares that "ni aun tinta se consiente" in the forming of the excellent book of Mary, "Porque no manche el papel" (Ant. Fue: 38-39). A poem by Alonso de Bonilla in praise of Mary, published less than a decade later, does not go so far as to deny but qualifies:

> Porque quando en la impressión
> naturaleza dio tinta,
> la gracia os hizo distinta
> del mundo en la perfección. (Ant. Bo15: 41-44)

*Critilo* in Baltasar Gracián's *El Criticón* asserts in reference to the book of the heavens: "Fáciles son de entender esos brillantes caracteres, por más que algunos los llamen dificultosos enigmas. La dificultad la hallo yo en leer y entender lo que está de las tejas abajo . . ." (Ant. Grc: 30-32). He may be referring through a countertext to a tradition that emphasized the mystery of the natural world, such as it is iterated in Berchorius in a gloss on Isaiah 29.11:

> Visio enim omnium creaturarum est sicut liber unus clausus & signatus, quia scil. sub exteriori apparentia signata sunt, & latent in creaturis divina mysteria. . . . In isto enim libro studuerunt Philosophi, sed quia signatus erat, in pluribus erraverunt, unde de caelo dicitur Apo. 6. *Caelum rescessit sicut liber involutus.* (4: 462)

Gracián transfers the idea expressed in the phrase "sub exteriori apparentia signata sunt" to the human heart, of which he declares: "porque como todo ande en cifra y los humanos corazones estén tan sellados y inescrutables, asegúroos que el mejor letor se pierde" (Ant. Grc:32-35).

Calderón assigns to the figure *Luna* in *El verdadero Dios Pan* the following observation in reference to both the

> ... manchada oveja,
> que sobre el blanco vellón
> negros lunares la hacían
> más bella.... (Calderón 1251)

and herself:

> que no desluce el borrón
> los primores, que antes llenos
> de mil aciertos verás,
> pues donde se borra más,
> es donde se yerra menos. (Ant. Ca65: 17-22)

It is certainly tempting to see this as a counter to texts like Paravicino's denunciation in *Iesv Cristo desagraviado*, of those who claim to find spots in sun and moon (Ant. Par3).

I earlier described the form of diffuse influence Menocal designates a void, as a motif that shines by its absence. In the following excerpt from Aguilar's *romances* in praise of Mary, a shining is caused by absence in more than one sense:

> En vuestra Concepcion pura,
> blancas hojas miro, y veo
> en abismos de candores,
> sin Letras, muchos conceptos.
>     Negras lineas, que me dizen
> sacros discursos diversos,
> son del Espiritu Santo
> luzes, que sombra os hizieron. (Ant. Ag2:25-32)

The blank / white leaves of Mary's soul shine in the fullness of grace or complete absence of sin. Letters are lacking because Mary's life has not yet been written out in time, but from God's eternal perspective, all is present; her immaculate conception is the first of many mysteries of her life, including her virginal conception of the divine Word, which is its raison d'etre. The occurrence of the "Negras lineas" in the verse following "sin Letras" is paradoxical. One possible explanation for the seeming contradiction is that "sin Letras, muchos conceptos" is a clue that the next motif cluster contains a void. That void, I think, is the agricultural analogy deriving from classical literature and passing by way of St. Isidore of Seville to the Middle Ages, in which among other comparisons, the tablet or parchment written upon was likened to a plowed field. "Negras lineas" could be a transformation of an image of the seed, such as in the following "formulilla de copista" discovered in a Mozarabic missal of the eighth or ninth century and translated by Curtius: " 'Aguijoneaba a los bueyes, araba campos blancos y sostenía un arado blanco y sembraba una semilla negra' " (440). In the case of the virginal conception of Christ in Mary's womb by the power of the overshadowing Spirit, the black lines are actually "luzes."

What María Rosa Lida de Malkiel calls "reactualización" also plays a role in the topical transformations that occur in the Spanish Golden Age. Perhaps the most *actualizado* of all examples is the application of the topos to Lope himself in Ignacio de Vitoria's *Oracion funeral panegyrica*. In the next few pages I consider the texts in the light of certain cultural factors that helped shape specific formulations of the topos and determine its applications. I have limited the discussion to aspects of culture that either were specific to the Golden Age or, if they existed earlier, were prominent in that period. Here, too, one can speak in terms of both direct or marked influence and more diffuse influence. In this context I mean by marked influence that either vehicle or tenor has been shaped primarily by what can be considered a single specific event that can be tied to a particular point in time, or by a unique entity. Anything else is considered diffuse influence. In most cases the cultural phenomenon converges with an already existing topical motif, corroborating Lida de Malkiel's observation that "Lo más corriente y lo más fecundo es la acomodación espontánea de la realidad a la convención artística vigente" (323). In some cases, though, specific new motifs result from a new cultural situation, as with printing. At times two separate cultural factors meld in the formation or use of a motif; an example is the *privilegio*.

The Protestant Reformation obviously had a diffuse influence on this corpus of texts, even on the level of individual motifs, not only in terms of the tenor but also, in some cases, of the vehicle. As Hilary Dansey Smith observes, "The boundaries of Spanish Catholicism are defined and fortified by the ... refutation ... of the Protestant heresies of Northern Europe" (140). She is speaking of preachers, but we could equally well add poets and dramatists. Although the Reformation dates from about 1520, it is especially after the Council of Trent (1545-63) that the impact of the Counter-Reformation is felt. The great majority of texts in this study were published during or after Trent. One of the means by which the Roman Catholic Church reaffirmed the teachings of Trent on the tenets of the faith was the catechism published in 1566 under the title *Catechismus ex decreto Concilii Tridentini ad Parochos, Pii V Pon. Max. jussu editus*. It was intended to provide parish priests with an official book of instruction for the faithful, to be used in their preaching (*Catechism* xxiii, xxv).[5]

One area of controversy, as is well known, was the doctrine of justification, or the relative importance between faith and works with respect to salvation. For the most part Spanish preachers took the middle way, "stressing the cooperative effort required from the human being as an adjunct, not cause, of salvation" (Smith 140). It seems to me that Calderón's fusing of the images of the book of conscience and the book of life in *La vacante general*, discussed above, reflects this point of view. Juan de Pineda offers a much more explicit example in his *Diálogos familiares* (Ant. Pin:1-125). The attention given to the doctrine of justification doubtless contributed in a general way to the popularity of the motif of the book of life and others related to it.

An emphasis on *obras* in a few texts may be another echo of the controversy. For instance, although in *El Criticón* Gracián evidently contrasts a person's deeds with the lines on the palm as deciding his or her fate, one could see an allusion to works
in opposition to a fatalistic understanding of predestination in the Calvinist sense (Ant. Grc:17-20).

The sacraments were another area of theological contention, particularly the Eucharist. The *Catechism* of the Council of Trent, speaking of the mystery of the Real Presence in the Eucharist and citing 1 Corinthians 9.28-29, alludes to the Reformers' objections to this dogma: "If, as heretics continually repeat, the Sacrament presents nothing to our veneration but a memorial and sign of the Passion of Christ, why was there need to exhort the faithful, in language so energetic, to prove themselves?" (229). The doctrine of the Real Presence, or of Transubstantiation, is a referent for such vehicles as the book with seven seals, an emblem book (Ant. Va13: 5-7,10), a white page (Ant. Ca10: 17-18), and paper written in invisible ink (Ant. Brn); the Eucharist as reenactment of Christ's Passion and resurrection, for vehicles like the *libro de memoria* (Ant. Va13: 1), the *memorial* presented by a soldier (Ant. Ca49: 6 passim), and the final copy (Ant. Gue17). The

---

[5] This work was in part a response to the numerous catechisms disseminated by the Reformers, aided by the recent invention of the printing press. About forty different catechisms were produced by Luther's disciples between 1522-29, followed by Luther's own larger *Deutsch Catechismus* in 1530. Among the numerous other catechisms published were Calvin's *Formulary of Instruction* of 1536, that of the Anglicans contained in the *Book of Common Prayer* in 1549, and the Heidelberg catechism of the Dutch Reformed Church in 1563 (*Catechism* xxii).

*memorial* is particularly interesting from the point of view that the term for the vehicle chosen to express the Catholic dogma is precisely that used in a different sense by the Reformers.

A sacramental reality that serves simultaneously as vehicle and tenor in many texts of Calderón is the "character," the term St. Augustine had given the Church to express the belief that the three sacraments of Baptism, Confirmation, and Orders were not to be repeated. The nature of the character was the subject of much theological debate in the thirteenth and fourteenth centuries. The Council of Trent defined it as a "sign," a "certain indelible mark," that is "imprinted on the soul" (*New Catholic*). This definition is echoed in Joan Timoneda's *Aucto de la fuente de los siete sacramentos* (Ant. Ti: 4-5). The Council's *Catechism* declares: "This caracter is, as it were, a distinctive impression stamped on the soul which perpetually inheres and cannot be blotted out" (159). Apart from Juan Dávila, who uses it once (Ant. Da: 22), Calderón is the only writer is this group who explicitly uses *carácter* in reference to the sacraments, although he also employs *sello*, a term that occurs often in the Fathers of the Church before Augustine.

Reformers differed with the Church also over the relative role of the Bible in divine revelation. "For the post-Tridentine Church revelation embraces both the written canon of Scripture and the whole legacy of apostolic tradition" (Smith 154), rather than Scripture alone, as the Lutherans claimed. In *La vacante general* Calderón dramatizes this doctrine clearly in the passage that begins with the appearance of *Iglesia* "en un trono con un libro en la mano, corona y cetro" (Ant. Ca62: 37-38). We have already seen that one designation of the book is "El que ser / mereció por su presencia / de memoria" (62: 50-52). *Iglesia* states that

> . . . porque malicia
> no se arguya al elegir,
> la Inocencia le ha de abrir
> y yo he de guardar justicia. (62: 57-60)

I perceive in Calderón's *El árbol del mejor fruto* a very similar, if less direct, allusion to the important role of apostolic tradition as safeguarded and interpreted by the Church, most particularly in the passage in which *Saba* addresses Solomon as

> . . . de la presencia
> oráculo . . . vivo,
> libro con voz y archivo
> en quien la Providencia
> supo depositar Poder y Ciencia. (Ant. Ca8: 62-66).

This passage contrasts with the earlier one in which *Idolatría* and others attempt unsuccessfully to interpret, first individually and then together, the fragments of the prophecy contained on the "hojas descuadernadas" which had been scattered by the wind.

In the case of the Eucharist, popular devotion goes hand in hand with theology. Mercedes Dexeus de Moll speaks of the climate of "exaltación eucarística" in post-Tridentine Spain (122), and Ludwig Pfandl affirms that together with the Immaculate Conception, the mystery of the Eucharist and concomitant celebration of Corpus Christi were the "centros condensadores de toda la piedad y del dogma católico" (156). One manifestation of this exaltation and piety was the founding in Madrid of the "Hermandad de los esclavos del Santísimo Sacramento" in 1608, by the friar Alonso de la Purificación and don Antonio Robles y Guzmán (Barrera 118). Several writers in this corpus were admitted, including Paravicino, Quevedo, Salas Barbadillo, Valdivielso, Lope de Vega, Calderón, Solís, and apparently Prado. Texts by four of them (Ant. Va10, VgC20, PrA, Ca66) employ the image of the slave brand voluntarily borne, in reference to the Eucharist. I see these as examples of marked or direct cultural influence.[6]

Devotion to the other central mystery mentioned by Pfandl, the Immaculate Conception, or rather to the person at its center, is both a direct and diffuse influence. Debate over this dogma existed since the thirteenth century. Mary's exemption from original sin was mentioned in the fifth session of the Council of Trent (Smith 149), but it was in the early seventeenth century that the controversy reached a climax. Attacks by Protestant Reformers were certainly a factor. A *pliego de cordel* published in Seville in 1615 contained a piece by Pedro de Monsalve that includes these lines:

> Y pues con sabios hablo,
> Razón es defenderla:
> Que los sectarios, y el infiel Caluino
> Nos salen al camino
> Contra la Virgen pura. (Qtd. in Aguirre 152)

Seville was in fact the center of a movement to define and proclaim the Immaculate Conception as dogma, in which Philip III himself became involved. Bonilla's prologue to certain poems to Mary included in his *Nuevo jardín* refers to "el vniversal y nueuo alarido que se oyó en España el año de 1614 (y hasta oy perseuera)" (qtd. in Aguirre 151-52).

---

[6] Although Valdivielso's "Ensaladilla buelta al Santíssimo Sacramento" is a *contrafactum*, "Brasildo, Tyrsi y Damón, / Froniso" might allude to the first four writers named, all of whom became members of the confraternity in 1609.

In 1622 Gregory V imposed absolute silence on adversaries of this doctrine (Valdivielso, *Romancero* 322), and in 1662 Alexander VII pronounced, though not ex cathedra, in favor of the *inmaculistas* (Smith 116).

With regard to the texts in this study, one begins to see the topos applied to the Immaculate Conception at roughly the same time, i.e., the first part of the seventeenth century. Angel Manrique's first sermon from Book 1 of his *Sanctoral*, published in 1610 and again in 1613, is a salient example (Ant. ManA: 1). The next instances, those most directly linked to a specific event related to this mystery, are the compositions by Gerónimo de la Fuente and Gaspar de Ovando for the *justa poética* in honor of the Immaculate Conception held in Granada in 1615 (Ant. Fue, Ov). Alonso de Bonilla's *Nombres y atribvtos de la impecable siempre virgen María Señora Nuestra*, published in 1624, two years after Gregory V's decree, contains two poems in which he applies the topos to the Immaculate Conception, one through the motif of the binding, whose imagery corresponds to the iconology of the mystery (Ant. Bo1:9-14), the other much more explicitly (Bo6). Of the several examples in texts published after that date, the last is Juan Bautista Aguilar's "A la Virgen Santissima," one of whose image clusters for the Immaculate Conception is the printed text copied without *erratas* from the original (Ant. Ag2: 45-48), a synthetic version of Manrique's treatment in the sermon mentioned above.

Devotion to the saints was yet another area of Roman Catholic practice attacked by Luther and Calvin. Many texts under consideration here are devoted to saints who were beatified or canonized in the Golden Age, including Ignatius of Loyola (b. 1610, c. 1622), Teresa of Avila (b. 1614, c. 1622), Isidore of Madrid (b. 1620/21?, c. 1622), John of Mata (b. 1666), Peter of Alcantara (b. 1622, c. 1669), Francis Borgia (b. 1624, c. 1671), and Francis Solano (b. 1675). In many cases they were composed for that specific occasion. The saints themselves usually serve as new tenors for old topical motifs. Of the saints long established in the liturgical calendar, the one to whom the topos is applied most frequently is Francis of Assisi, the stigmata being the source of inspiration for many topical conceits. St. John of Mata was co-founder, with St. Felix of Valois, of the Order of the Most Holy Trinity in the late twelfth century. Their names are the basis of a pun that introduces the vehicle of a topical motif in Calderón's *La redención de cautivos* (Ant. Ca53: 2-9). Lope's *Triunfo de la Fe en los reinos del Japón, por los años de 1614 y 1615* was published just three years after the events related in it had taken place. Lope converts a literal reality into a metaphorical and spiritual one when he equates the branding of the missionaries on the forehead by their tormenters with the corresponding Biblical motif from Ezekiel 9.4 and Apocalypse 7.2-3 (Ant. VgC22:7-25).

According to Smith, a popular subject in Counter-Reformation art was conversion, and a subject of meditation for popular devotion, the tears of repentance shed by St. Peter and by Mary Magdalene (142). While the literature of tears may derive from the Petrarchan lover, Spanish poets of the seventeenth century were also influenced by Tansillo and Erasmo de Valvasone, whose respective works *Le lagrime di San Pietro* and *Le lagrime della Magdalena* were published in 1560 and 1592, the Spanish translation of both appearing in 1613 (Aguirre 159-60). The theme of tears in general was, in Maravall's view, "one of the various aspects in which the baroque prefigured romantic sensibility." Weeping was in fact a sign of masculinity (*Cultura* 170n99). Luis Gálvez de Montalvo's "El llanto de San Pedro" applies the topos to the moment when Christ looks upon Peter, a prelude to his bitter weeping. Mary's tears and those of the poet-observer are the focus of an extended topical development in Dávila's *Passion del Hombre-Dios* (Ant. Da:41-62). In Guerra y Ribera's *Sermón de la Conversion*, the *borrones* of Mary Magdalene's tears erase the *borrones* of her sins (Ant. Gue1).

Among philosophical influences on the shaping of the topos in these texts, Neoplatonism was one of the most diffuse and many-leveled. Most importantly, perhaps, it was integral to the very foundation of the topos in a religious context, since Christian Neoplatonists saw in the platonic archetypes or exemplary ideas a foreshadowing of the eternal Logos of the prologue to John's Gospel. Venegas, for example, identifies the "libro Archetypo" and "exemplar" with the "verbo eterno: en el qual y por el qual cría [Dios] todas las cosas" (Ant. Ven: 22-23; 36-38). Valdivielso uses like terminology in his exposition of Psalm 138, when he changes the original "& in libro tuo omnes scribentur" of verse 15 to "porque teneys escriptos exemplares / en las ideas vuestras libro eterno" (Ant. Va9). The allusion in Villanueva's sermon on Mary's nativity is a bit less evident. Here the incarnate Word is the "libro ejemplar, manifiesto e ideal," in which God "transcribió prácticamente ... cuanto nos había enseñado teóricamente en el libro de la naturaleza y en el libro de la Escritura" (Ant. Vi3:212-16). Christ is the ideal book that is at the same time and for that very reason the most real of books, taking priority over not only the natural world but even the Bible. This link with Neoplatonism may be one reason, among several, why the motif of the *concepto* is so often used for the divine Word.

The relationship between nature and Scripture as a source of knowledge of God is the referential context for topical motifs in many texts. The *Catechism* of the Council of Trent, in its exposition on the first article of the Apostles' Creed, states:

> These great and sublime truths regarding the nature of God, which are in full accord with Scripture, the philosophers were able to learn from an investigation of God's works. But even here we see the necessity of divine revelation if we reflect that not only does faith, as we have already observed, make known clearly and at once to the rude and unlettered, those truths which only the learned could discover, and that by long study; but also that the knowledge obtained through faith is much more certain and more secure against error than if it were the result of philosophical inquiry.... But how much more exalted must not that knowledge of the Deity be considered, which cannot be acquired in common by all from the contemplation of nature, but is peculiar to those who are illumined by the light of faith? (18)

Venegas, Villanueva, and others, in their exploitation of such topical motifs as the original and its translations, the contents of the book and its covers, express substantially the same convictions (Ant. Ven: 167-94, 392-408, Vi3: 176-89). However, they tend to modify the idea that the divine truths manifest in nature could be discovered only by the learned. A number of motifs, such as the primer, the common book, the text that is easy to understand, and the writing of a book for everyone, make a rather different point.

The discovery of the New World does not have as much of an apparent effect upon the formation of the topos in these texts as one might expect. One of the few exceptions is Granada's passage on the *escribano* discussed above. Applying the metaphor of the various types of letter to the abundant animal species, Granada indicates in the conclusion to the passage that he has been inspired in part by that new world: "mayormente que cada dia en nuevas tierras se descubren nuevos animales y nuevas habilidades y propriedades dellos, que nunca en estas nuestras tierras han sido conoscidas" (214). In *El lirio y la azucena* Calderón incorporates a reference to the New World within the vehicle. [*Brazo*] *Seglar* refers to the baptismal character and new life of grace as follows:

> pues por agua imprimo el sello,
> carácter de nuevo mundo,
> como chanciller supremo
> de las Indias de su Ophir. (Ant. Ca30: 25-28)

Scientific discoveries, too, play a part in formulations of the topos. One of the most marked is the discovery of sun-spots by Fabricius in 1611 and independently by Scheiner and Galileo in 1612 (Bayley 156), made possible by the invention of the telescope. This particular cultural influence is reflected in Paravicino's *Iesv Cristo desagraviado* and

Calderón's *El verdadero Dios Pan*, discussed above in relation to countertexts.

Still closely related to astronomy in that period, but a much more diffuse influence in these texts, is astrology, as well as the practice of magic. Although Pfandl relates that the magic arts were less important in Spain than in any other part of Europe in that period (166), belief in them was still very strong among a certain group. In a paradigmatic sermon for the Tuesday after the second Sunday of Lent, Villanueva gives us an idea of how the Church looked upon astrology and magic, as well as some of the specific forms assumed by the latter:

> Contra esta Deidad hacen los adivinos (que usurpan el oficio de Dios, queriendo adivinar lo que ha de venir). . . . Aun el astrólogo, que trata según su ciencia, que es lícita, si afirmase determinadamente lo que ha de venir (lo que ve en las causas materiales) sin tener respeto a que Dios lo puede ordenar de otra manera, . . . es pecado gravísimo. Aquí entran los que adivinan por las manos, o fisonomías del rostro, o por agüeros, como son graznidos de aves, aullidos de perros, etcétera, dicen esto sucederá o el otro; los que dan crédito a los sueños. A lo menos sabe te aprovechar, si son buenos. (622)

The year after Villanueva's death, in 1556, Pedro Ciruelo published *Reprobación de las supersticiones y hechicerías*, which saw many editions. The practice of palm reading affects the vehicle of a motif in Gracián's *El Criticón* (Ant. Grc: 17-19). Valdivielso's "libro de vn nigromante" in the *auto El hombre encantado* may contain an allusion to Doctor Eugenio Torralba, "el único nigromante que produjeron los siglos XVI y XVII" in Spain, tried by the Inquisition of Cuenca in 1531 (Pfandl 169, *Diccionario U.T.E.H.A.*). Calderón normally makes a distinction between astrology and the more earthly arts of divination. In *Los encantos de la Culpa*, for example, *Culpa* practices "Quiromancía," reading the occult messages in flames and flowers (Ant. Ca18: 10-19). Similarly *Sombra* in *La vida es sueño* is an "agricultora," who "en ella apura, / y en los demás elementos, / las cualidades ocultas," whereas *Sabiduría* is a student of the stars (Ant. Ca68).

Physiognomy was another science or pseudoscience that functions as a diffuse influence on several texts. Maravall states that the baroque century saw a great development of studies in this area, which he views as one aspect of the emphasis on empirical knowledge of the human being, based on observation and directed toward a practical end (*Cultura* 149). Such emphasis would have converged with the topical tradition through motifs like "to write on the face" and "the outside corresponds to the inside." Perhaps the most obvious example is the following *décima* from Dávila:

> Corre por los circunstantes
> Sin oirse la Sentencia,
> Pues quien, no oyó su violencia,
> La leía en los semblantes:
>
> Eran tan desemejantes,
> Como sus facciones son,
> Y en cada qual su affeccion
> Tantas letras escribía,
> Que en su rostro se leía
> A todos el corazon. (Ant. Da: 30-39)

The seventeenth century was ravaged by plagues (Maravall, *Teatro* 298). One of them appears as a direct influence in Juan Valero Pradas' sermon on Our Lady of Montserrat, in which he cites another preacher who had named her "libro celestial de Medicina contra la peste," in both a literal and spiritual sense (Ant. PrJ).

Golden Age technology produces a group of marked influences on the topos. One is *papel de corazón*, also called *papel de Génova*. It was used in very special books and was "llamado seguramente así por su filigrana, papel que ha de ser, además, limpio, sano, sin costeras y sin entremeterse en la edición otro papel de la tierra" (Amezua 349). This motif, applied to the heart or soul, was thus simultaneously a vehicle and a combination of vehicle and tenor. It is one variant of the old motif "to write on the heart."

By far the most important technological influence was printing. For a good part of the period covered by these texts, printing was still a relatively new phenomenon in many parts of Spain. Seville, Segovia, Barcelona, Valencia, Saragossa, and Guadalajara, among other cities, had a printing press by the 1470's; Salamanca, Valladolid, Huete, Toledo, and Burgos, in the 1480's; Granada, in 1496; Alcalá de Henares, in 1502; Madrid, not until 1566 (Salstad, *Illustration* 5-7). Numerous writers in this study employ motifs tied explicitly to a printed text, such as the press, type, typecase, printer, printer's mark, and misprints, in addition to the *texto impreso* itself. In many passages, too, the printed text is implied by motifs like those related to the anatomical structure of a printed book, as well as to the process of having it approved.[7]

---

[7] As is well known, Golden Age literature often criticizes the printing press. One instance is Antonio Enríquez Gómez' "Elegía III":

> ¿Causa menos gustoso desvarío
> La imprenta, mi señora, con su alarde?
> Tanto libro, ¿es pequeño señorío?
> Tanta redonda letra ¿no es tesoro?
> La mayor parte buena para un río.

The first example occurs at the very beginning of the period, in Ambrosio Montesino's "Coplas [del sudor de sangre en Getsemaní]" (Ant. Mon6). The last example is Guerra y Ribera's "Aprobación" for Rodríguez Monforte's *Sueños misteriosos de la Escritura*, in which the motif of the *aprobación* or *censura* implies a printed book (Ant. Gue12:13-16). In the course of the Golden Age many convents had their own printing press, a fact to which Antonio Balvás Barona perhaps alludes in "Romance a San Francisco" (Ant. BaB:1-4).

Guerra y Ribera's articulation of the motif in the paragraph of *Sermón de la Conversión* in which Christ affirms, "Eran sus caracteres malditos porque se imprimían sus voces en el mundo, pero ahora son hermosos porque se imprimen en mis plantas" (Ant. Gue1: 105-08) is surely an oblique reference to Christopher Plantin. Besides the aptness of his name, other factors that lead me to perceive such wordplay are the fame he enjoyed for the beauty of his printing and his having been appointed in 1570 printer to King Philip II, obtaining from the Holy See through Philip's influence a monopoly for printing the liturgical books used in all the countries under the monarch's rule (McMurtrie 361-62).

At the same time, as Curtius notes, the art of calligraphy continued to flourish in Spain long after the invention of the printing press (483). Pedro de Madariaga wrote his *Honra de escribanos* in 1565. The calligrapher José de Casanova's *Arte de escrivir todas formas de letras* appeared in Madrid in 1650, containing a sonnet on the subject written by Calderón (Cotarelo, *Ensayo* 59, Briesemeister 98). The passages from his *autos* included in this corpus reveal that Calderón in fact preferred images of handwriting and illuminated manuscripts to those of the printed text.

---

¿Causó más daño idolatrando el oro?
¿Hay más vano y gustoso desatino?
Aquí del juicio, que me vuelvo moro.
No ha emborrachado tanto el señor vino
Como locos ha vuelto esta señora;
Dígalo su carácter peregrino. (Castro 2:378)

Like many such criticisms, this one is ambivalent, a left-handed compliment, as it were. Other texts display uninhibited enthusiasm for the press. Francisco Terrones del Caño says in *Instrucción de predicadores*, "Gran cosa es la emprenta, pues en tan breve tiempo como un día hacen mil y quinientos pliegos; como era cosa cansada y enfadosa hacer libros manuscritos" (122). One of the three examples of the marvellous inventions of human *ingenio* proffered by Antonio de Orozco is "la agudeza y arte de la impression de los libros: adonde poniendo las letras al reues, salen tan ordenadas y tan concertadas, quan gran señal y insignia son, del alto ingenio del hombre" (Prologo, *Historia de la reyna*). The fact that in this corpus Christ and Mary are among the tenors of the printing press suggests a generally positive attitude toward the invention.

Gonzalo Díaz-Migoyo advances the idea that the introduction and spread of printing introduces an important change in the relation between the text as conceived in the mind of its author and its material realization: "a partir de entonces [la existencia del texto impreso] los textos no pueden diferenciarse más que por sus características ideales. De ahí a entender que el texto ideal no sólo coincide con su manifestación material sino que ésta misma adquiere un caracter ideal, no hay más que un paso" (6). The passage from Villanueva treated above in relation to Neoplatonism, in which the Word as manifest in his humanity is the ideal book, suggests that the preacher has made this last connection. However, the book described by Villanueva is written by hand.

Closely related to the technological phenomenon of the printed book is the more specifically cultural one of getting it published, which in the Golden Age necessarily included submitting the manuscript for censoring or approval. A number of texts, as a glance at sections A.3.16 and B.2.3.2. of the Motif Index evinces, incorporate as topical vehicles any number of the various procedures involved. I will point out examples that correspond to the discrete steps, as they are explained by Agustín Amezúa y Mayo and José Simón Díaz.

Beginning in 1502 the *licencia*, with its concomitant *aprobación* or *censura*, had to be obtained from the local bishop; after 1554, from the Consejo Real. When the work was an important one, the original manuscript had to be presented to the Council to ensure that once printed, no alteration had been introduced into the text. In 1558 another *pragmática* obliged an *escribano de la Cámara* to rubricate each leaf (Amezúa 333-35). One text that clearly reflects these realities is Ángel Manrique's sermon for Mary's nativity; among the contrasts he uses to emphasize her superiority to all the other saints is that between the *libro* and the *cartapacio*. One difference is the fact that

> en los cartapacios no todo lo que se escribe esta aprouado, . . . pero en los libros no puede auer nada, que no lleue su aprouacion, y su censura. . . . Que ellos, como no son libros, si no cartapacios, por mas enquadernados que traygan todas las hojas de su vida, y de sus obras, . . . y aunque en algunas tengan aprobacion, y en otras aprouacion y Priuilegio, en muchas es muy cierto que no llegaron a tener lo vno, ni lo otro. . . . Solo la Reyna de los Angeles es libro, . . . y assi es fuerza, que no tenga hoja perdida, ni que carezca de aprobacion, y priuilegio. . . . Todas en particular aprouacion del Cielo. . . . (Ant. ManA2: 139-91)

The possibility of illicit textual alteration appears in Guerra y Ribera's sermon on Mary Magdalene's conversion. Christ, she says, "bajó a encuadernarme los libros y borrar las hojas prohibidas que introdujo Adán en nuestros mortales cuerpos" (Ant. Gue1:79-82).

Both Bonilla and Aguilar refer to Mary, as printed book, having been approved by all three divine Persons (Ant. Bo15:33-36, Ag2:17-20). This motif probably derives from the necessity for members of religious orders to obtain, from at least 1626 on, three *aprobaciones* and *licencias*, one from the civil authority, a second from the ecclesiastical hierarchy, and a third from a superior of the Order to which they belonged (Simón Díaz, *El libro español* 25, 27, 33). Moreover, in the case of subjects considered especially delicate, e.g. the Immaculate Conception, "se solicitaba el juicio de una corporación en vez de un individuo, por lo general de una Facultad universitaria o de un convento" (Simón Díaz 106). Thus the two poets specify the divine Censor as the God who is One in Three.

The censors were not supposed to praise the work they approved or to write laudatory poems for it, although sometimes "la personalidad del autor transformaba por sí sola la Aprobación en Elogio" (Simón Díaz 101). Such is the case in Aguilar's poem on the book of Mary; God is her Author, and the Trinity not only approve her but do so "en docto aplauso escriviendo / azia vuestra Gracia glorias" (Ant. Ag2:18-19).

After obtaining the *licencia*, the second step was getting past the Holy Office of the Inquisition, which became increasingly more inclined to forbid titles permitted by the bishops. A work might end up, from 1551, on the Index of forbidden books, and the copies already printed might be burned or parts of them deleted with black ink (Amezúa 339-40, Simón Díaz 23, Pfandl 82). The motif of burning a forbidden book occurs in Suárez de Godoy (Ant. Sua:24-44), that of deleting condemned segments from a printed text, in several writers. Some of them, such as Damián de Vegas (Ant. Vgs4), may have been exclusively inspired by the motif, already important in Scripture, of removing a name from the book of life, but for others, like Valdivielso (Ant. Va7), who was himself a *censor de libros*, the contemporary reality of censorship was surely a secondary influence. For still others, including Guerra and Aguilar, the latter influence seems by far the stronger (Ant. Gue1:55-61,87-94,etc., Ag2:70-73).

The third step was obtaining the *privilegio*, the counterpart of a copyright, granted by the Council in the name of the king (Amezúa 341). At first, as the term implies, it was not widely granted, but with the passage of time it became more common (Simón Díaz 89). In spite of this change, the motif is usually applied to Mary's immaculate conception, as a singular divine privilege. However, Bonilla's use of the term in "Redondillas de la Virgen" (Ant. Bo15:5-8) may illustrate

Simón Díaz's observation that a so-called *privilegio* was often in fact a royal license for a single *impresión* (89).

An author also had to obtain money to pay for the printing of a book. The most common means was to sell the *privilegio* to the printer or bookseller (Amezúa 345), a fact reflected in Fuente (Ant. Fue: 31-35). Another was to secure the support of a noble patron, to whom the book would be dedicated (Amezúa 343). God and the king were also common dedicatees of actual books of the period (Simón Díaz 93). The metaphorical books in this corpus are, of course, dedicated to God (BaB: 14, Ag2: 21), who is both King and noble Patron. The name of this last, his titles, and his coat of arms would be on the title page (Amezúa 343), a separate plate, or at the beginning of the dedication (Simón Díaz 97). The "escudo" in Antonio Balvás Barona's "Romance a San Francisco" displays "un árbol del parayso," i.e., the Cross, coat of arms of Francis' Patron. According to Amezúa, the proofs of a book were usually not corrected by the author, since he would have sold his *privilegio* to the printer (354), but sometimes they were the object of a double correction, by the author and the person responsible for that task at the press (Simón Díaz 114). Guerra y Ribera's Mary Magdalene observes that as author of the book, it is her responsibility to correct the errors (Ant. Gue1: 74-76). This may be an allusion to the double correction, or, in light of Guerra's being a Trinitarian, it may reflect the fact that many convents had their own press.

Besides their own proofreader, all presses had a *Corrector general*, appointed by the Consejo de la Cámara. This official was responsible for ascertaining that the censored manuscript and printed edition were identical. His certification, included among the preliminaries, was indicated by the formula, "Este libro corresponde con su original, y para testimonio de ello doy fe." On a separate sheet he had to note all the *faltas y erratas* (Amezúa 355). Angel Manrique, in his sermon on the Immaculate Conception, develops the first idea at some length, concluding with a reference to the complete absence of *erratas* (Ant. ManA1: 7-54).

Another preliminary was the *tasa*, which stated the maximum fixed price at which the book could be sold. An invariable accompaniment of all printed books, its purpose was to keep the price down (Amezúa 358). Thus Mary's being without a *tasa* (Ant. Bo15: 64, Ag2: 41) underscores her preciousness and uniqueness.

*Pliegos sueltos* or broadsides were also an important product of the printing press in the Golden Age. With rare exceptions, they were anonymous and represent the cultural level and literary tastes of the commonfolk (Pfandl 201). In addition to the motif of the *cartapacio*, treated above, Manrique applies that of *hojas sueltas* to the saints, to suggest their spiritual inferiority in comparison to the book of Mary (Ant. ManA2: 81-105).

The printing press played a key role in the diffusion of a different cultural phenomenon, the emblem. Beginning with Andrea Alciati's *Emblematum liber* in 1531, over six hundred writers produced over two thousand emblem-books during the sixteenth and seventeenth centuries (Daly 185). Both Valdivielso and Gracián use the emblem book as an explicit vehicle, the former for the Eucharist, the latter for the created universe. But such books were only one indication of the immense popularity of emblems:

> En las grandes fiestas que en las ciudades se organizan por cualquier fausto motivo, así como en las solemnidades necrológicas, que tienen también mucho carácter de festejo público, en calles y plazas se levantan representaciones con figuras que llevan al pie un oscuro y sutil epigrama y que, por tanto, son emblemas. . . . Hubo incluso fiestas públicas de epigramas . . . . (Maravall, "Literatura" 183)

Miguel de Dicastillo's *Avla de Dios* contains among its *silvas* a description of a "comun Sepulcro" upon which flowers grow in such a way as to form "funebres Geroglificos" and an "Epitafio lugubre" (Ant. Di). Nature is an emblem of a spiritual truth, that life arises out of death. Fernando Cardoso's imagery in his *Oracion funebre* in honor of Lope de Vega is also emblematic, the pictorial element constituted by the various natural entities, which are accompanied by "Epigramas y Epitaphios" (Ant. Car).

Dicastillo's use of *jeroglífico*, which together with *cifra* and *enigma* could be synonymous with *emblema*, points to the influence initially exercised on emblem literature by the ancient Egyptian hieroglyphs. Renaissance humanists regarded these as an ideographical form of writing used by Egyptian priests, as Peter Daly puts it, "to shadow forth enigmatically divine wisdom" (Maravall, "Literatura" 155, Daly 11). The element of obscurity, which Maravall claims was dear to the baroque (*Cultura* 442), is emphasized especially in some of Calderón's formulations of the emblem motif (Ant. Ca20: 18, 35:2-3).

The relationship between emblems and topical motifs in this body of texts is evident not only in the occurrence of terms denoting emblems, but also in images that formed the basis of many emblems. The *letra de cambio* is one example (Valdivielso *Romancero* 29). Alonso de Ledesma's "Hieroglifico XVI" describes such an emblem, applied to St. Ignatius Loyola. Another topical motif, the name written on the heart, received visual treatment in emblem books (Daly 62-63). Determining the direction of the influence can be difficult, however, with respect to particular images.

The literary style known as *conceptismo* in one sense underlies this whole corpus. Among the texts in which it is most evident are those of Alonso de Ledesma and Alonso de Bonilla, considered its originators in poetry. The topical vehicle that perhaps best epitomizes the influence of *conceptismo* is the term *concepto* itself, mentioned earlier in relation to Neoplatonism. As Hilary Dansey Smith remarks, the conceit "requires a forging of conceptual links between apparent contraries, or an 'acto del entendimiento' which at times looks like a leap of faith" (78). The term *concepto* is very aptly, then, applied to the incarnate Word, its most usual tenor, emphasizing the mystery of the divine and the human brought together in Christ, as well as that of Mary, his virgin mother.

A diffuse influence from the realm of painting is the technique of chiaroscuro, a feature of works by renaissance and, even more, baroque masters. One of the texts most obviously affected by this development is that in which Antonio Hurtado de Mendoza alludes to Dionysius the Areopagite, convert of St. Paul, who for some time was confused with the sixth-century Neoplatonist author of works like *Mystic Theology*:

> El Atheniense más sabio,
> Por el borrado contexto
> De obscuridades, las dudas
> Leyó claras en el Cielo. (Ant. Hu: 6-9)

Another is the following excerpt from Dávila's description of Mary's grief over the Passion of her Son:

> Todos caracteres son
> De Cruz, y nos los declara
> Vna beldad, que está clara,
> Entre vn llanto, que es borron. (Ant. Da: 59-62)

I spoke earlier of the "Hermandad de los esclavos del Santísimo Sacramento" as a direct influence on certain motifs, such as the slave brand. A more diffuse influence, one lying behind the religious ideal of total spiritual surrender to God, is the social reality of slavery, which according to Defourneaux reached a peak at the beginning of the seventeenth century (84). "Lo normal era que el pudiente, incluso al norte del Sistema Central, se sirviera de esclavos domésticos" (Fernández Álvarez 1: 143), but slaves were most abundant in the Court, western Andalucía, and Valencia. The granting of liberty to domestic slaves, a fairly frequent occurrence (Fernández Álvarez 1: 145), was probably a factor in the use of the motif of the letter of manumission.

Analogous to this last motif is the certificate of ransom, indication of the existence in that period of the Christian captive fallen into the hands of the Moslem Turks. The captive and galley slave were figures in the society who, in the words of Fernández Álvarez "la marcaban a fuego" (1:218). In Calderón's *La hidalga del valle* the "esclavo" and "cautivo" are synonymous (Ant. Ca22: 9-10). Calderón thus fuses two types who according to Fernández Alvarez were in reality quite distinct: the Muslim captive whose situation in Spain was equivalent to that of an *esclavo*, and the *cautivo*, a word that for the Spaniard had a very specific meaning, one who was or had been in the hands of the Turks (1:208).

On the other end of the social scale were the privileged upper nobility, who were exempt from the *pecho* paid to the Crown. Fernández Alvarez records an incident illustrative of the degree to which the nobles held this privilege sacrosanct. When in 1538 Charles V, in dire financial straits, tried to get the Cortes to impose a temporary *sisa* that would have included the nobility, their response was as follows:

> Toda la fama y honra de nuestros pasados se convertiría en infamia y mengua y deshonra de nuestras personas, si perdiésemos esta libertad ganada y conservada por tantos años y perpetuamente quedaría en nuestro linaje, para todos nuestros descendientes, la *mancilla de habernos hecho pecheros*. (Qtd. in 1:152, emphasis added)

Calderón plays on this idea in *Las órdenes militares*, in which he applies the motifs of the blot and the *padrón de pecheros* to the descendants of Adam in bondage to sin, with the exception of Christ and Mary (Ant. Ca43: 1-21,63-92). Antonio Domínguez Ortiz observes that nobles tried to obtain posts in municipal councils because of the advantage of being able to manipulate these *padrones* (23). Calderón alludes to this fact also through the figure of *Culpa*, not only in this *auto* but also in *La hidalga del valle*.

Nevertheless, in the seventeenth century

> no pocos señores quedaron arruinados por donativos que no tenían de tales sino el nombre, pero lo esencial era que su nombre no figurase en aquellos *padrones de pecheros*.... Los antiguos privilegios apenas subsisten más que en nombre. (Domínguez Ortiz 100-102)

This is the situation that gives literal sense to the following lines from Balvás Barona, whose intelligibility would be lacking were *privilegio* to be read only in relation to the meaning of copyright:

> El priuilegio Real,
> en honra de tantos hijos,

> seruirá de executoria
> en la Yglesia, y sus archiuos.
> La tassa, no si se aduierte,
> es del priuilegio antiguo,
> que en manos, y cuerpo impresso,
> muestra valor excessiuo. (Ant. BaB: 37-44)

Closely related to the issue of class distinctions and privilege was that of purity of blood, i.e., descent from Old Christians with no taint of Jewish or Muslim ancestry. Proof of pedigree became especially important after 1530, when the Inquisition ordered its tribunals "to record for future reference the names of all those who had had dealings with the Holy Office over questions relating to their faith" (Defourneaux 38). According to Domínguez Ortis, "El siglo XVII recibió esta herencia, concretada para los miembros de las Ordenes Militares, Inquisición y muchos cabildos eclesiásticos y civiles en minuciosos reglamentos, los *estatutos de limpieza de sangre*, y para la alta burocracia en una tradición no escrita pero eficaz..." (26). In Calderón's *Las órdenes militares*, *Naturaleza*, on behalf of *Segundo Adán*, presents *Judaísmo* with a *memorial* that constitutes "los actos positivos / de su limpieza y nobleza" (Ant. Ca43: 57-58). The *memorial* is a frequent topical motif in Calderón, sometimes functioning importantly in the structure of an *auto* or *loa*. Its presence corresponds to the situation in the Spanish Court. Since no regulated procedures existed for obtaining higher level posts, the king had to depend on the *memoriales* submitted by innumerable *pretendientes* (Domínguez Ortiz 17-18).

Marcelin Defourneaux asserts that it was the malign disposition of the public, "always disposed to attack the *poderosos*," which led to the appearance of the "green books." These contained family trees, only some of which were authentic, that attributed ancient Muslim or Jewish roots to the great Spanish families (Defourneaux 38-39). The motif of the *libro verde* in Coello and Calderón, discussed above as an example of possible direct influence, is also affected by this social reality. In *El lirio y la azucena* the motif, with its attendant social connotations, is linked to that of *privilegio*. The reality of the "green books" and the concomitant blot on a family's honor are, I think, also overtones in Calderón's repeated use of the tree on which original sin has left its apparently ineradicable characters (Ant. Ca7: 1-13; 17: 10-27; 28: 29-35, etc.).

In the economic sphere the early Golden Age was the period when, in Fernández Alvarez' opinion, "Empieza... la lucha de la burguesía por hacerse con el poder" (1:9). It seems to me that the increasing influence of this group, and the concomitant growth of mercantilism, might be one reason for the frequency in this body of texts, of poems to St. Francis of Assisi, a well-to-do merchant's son who had exchanged a life of extravagance for one of evangelical poverty. Doubtless it is also an important diffuse influence in the popularity of motifs like the *letra de cambio*, which arose in the heart of Medina del Campo (Fernández Álvarez 1: 101), the promissory note, and several others related to the financial account.

The account book was already an important image in the Old Testament and throughout the medieval period, but in the Golden Age a specific new development made its influence felt on the topos, double-entry bookkeeping. The Italian friar Luca Pacioli included the first published treatise on *contabilidad por partida doble* as a section of his *Suma de arithmetica*, which appeared in 1494 (Yamey 19). The first book in Spanish to give instruction on the system applied to a merchant's affairs was written by Bartolomé Salvador de Solórzano and published in Madrid in 1590 (15). Poems by Ledesma, Valdivielso, and Balvás Barona published well after that date use paired motifs that suggest the double-entry system (Ant. Led14: 17-21, Va18: 3, BaB: 5-6). The title of one chapter in Solórzano's exposition instructs "que todas las cuentas se escrivan en estos dos libros [the *libro de caja* or ledger and the journal], y no en papelejos, ni en libretes de memoria" (qtd. in Yamey 15). The *libro de caja*, *libro de los días*, and *libro de memoria* all appear in texts in this study; they are usually bisemous in their literal significance.

Another innovation in the economic realm that left its mark on the topos was the introduction in 1637 of *papel sellado*, attributed to both Hurtado de Mendoza (Davies 37-38) and the Jesuit Hernando de Salazar, friend of Count Duke Olivares (Domínguez Ortiz 19). It was "señalado con las armas del Rey, y sirve para autorizar los instrumentos legales y jurídicos. Hácese todos los años, y tiene diferente precio cada pliego, segun el instrumento para que se toma, y su producto es para el Rey" (*Diccionario de autoridades*). It appears seven years later in Calderón's *La humildad coronada de las plantas*, as a vehicle for the baptized soul (Ant. Ca23: 32-39).

It is difficult to discern a "decorum of motifs" in this corpus, i.e., a set of implicit "rules" or virtually inviolable conventions, for the relationships between vehicles and tenors or referents. Certainly there seems to be little or no rigidity in terms of what motifeme is applied to what tenor or referent. Even "original" has several tenors. Nearly every motifeme with both a single tenor and single referent occurs in only one, or at most two, writers, providing little basis for drawing conclusions. In the case of other one-tenor motifemes, like "autobiography," "approbation," "errata sheet," "virgin copy," "cross," and "to dedicate," the tenor is usually inherent, and the motifeme has two or more referents.

One would expect to find more examples of exclusivity in a more delimited or specified vehicle, and this is in fact the case. In the group of expanded motifs that in this corpus have only one tenor and one referent, the most significant examples are probably those which occur in a relatively large number of writers, since the likelihood of finding the identical vehicle, tenor, and referent in all writers involved decreases as the number of writers increases. Even a single writer often applies the same vehicle to different tenors. If we subtract all examples that involve only two writers, we are left with seven cases, and only two involve more than three writers. One of the two, "God writes his Word / Concept in Mary," which occurs in six writers, is a mixed motif, i.e., it incorporates in its articulation one or more tenors or referents. It is always used in reference to the incarnation of the Second Person of the Trinity. The other, "Saint Anthony read the book," which occurs in four writers, can be considered an unmixed motif, one which by the Golden Age was firmly ensconced in the topical tradition. It invariably refers to St. Anthony's meditation on nature as evidence of God's perfections.

In comparison, among the motifs with virtually a single tenor but more than one referent, approximately twelve occur in more than two writers, eight of them in more than three, two in more than four. Those two are unmixed motifs. "Red ink" and its equivalents, which occur in seven writers, was in the Golden Age a very old vehicle for the tenor "blood," while "without misprint," found in five writers, was probably an updated version of or variation on an old vehicle like "without error." It always signifies sinlessness or absence of any imperfection; although it usually refers to Mary or her immaculate conception, one writer also applies it to Christ.

In spite of the greater frequency of one-to-one linkage among expanded motifs, here, too, flexibility predominates. Although one begins to expect certain motifs to be attached to particular realities, such as "a book with broken binding" to the crucified Christ or "to sign a promissory note" to the circumcision and naming of Jesus, this is not to say that these same vehicles are never associated with other subjects, or that numerous other vehicles are not linked to the same subject. Indeed, "the book with seven seals" has more than one tenor. This adaptability is not unlike the diverse interpretations given to Biblical texts in Church tradition. In some cases the Spanish writer himself sets forth the different tenors or referents found in earlier glosses.[8]

Also related to a potential decorum is the question of what types of tenor are involved when a single vehicle is applied to several. For ex-

---

[8] Manrique, for example, in the sermon *Del glorioso san Pedro de Castilnuouo* presents three traditional interpretations of Col. 2. 14.

ample, can the same vehicle signify both God and a human person or the natural world, in harmony with the notion of the planes of correspondence?[9] It can. "A closed book," to name just one motif, metaphorizes the Godhead, the Second Person of the Trinity, Mary, and the natural world, among other entities. Even a motif formulated in the superlative can be applied to tenors on different planes; "the best book" signifies the eternal Word, the incarnate Word, Mary, the natural world, and the remembrance of benefits received. In writers like Paravicino and Calderón a single occurrence of an image often alludes to two or three planes of correspondence. Examples are the "papeles rotos" of "A la santa Cruz" (Ant. Par1:9) and the "rasgos de carmín" of *La protestación de la Fe* (Ant. Ca48:15).

One might wonder, however, how disparate the various tenors of a single vehicle can be. Can the same vehicle be used to signify both a very positive and a very negative reality? It would seem so, for two of the tenors of the vehicle "original" are God and original sin; of "illuminated letters," the heavenly bodies and the punishment attendant on God's wrath. As Daly observes in connection with medieval nature symbolism, a single object could be seen from many different points of view, connoting as many meanings, which could be good or bad depending on the qualities involved (32). Not only can a conventionally positive vehicle be attached to a negative reality; the converse is also true. The earlier-mentioned "slave brand" is one example; another is the *borrón* used as metaphor for one of the three Wise Men in Godínez' *Auto del nacimiento de Christo* (Ant. Go1:3-5). A somewhat ambivalent passage in Paravicino's *Iesv Cristo desagraviado* suggests that the positive or negative character of the image-reality depends not so much on quality as perspective: "Aviasele de caer a Dios al escrevir essos cielos, como David dijo, alguna gota de tinta en lo batido de essas ojas azules, papel de sus maravillas entre letras de plata i oro, que cuando allá passasse por rasgo, pudiesse acá parecer borron?" (Ant. Par3:6-12).

A closely related aspect of a hypothetical decorum of motifs involves the ways in which a single vehicle is adapted when applied to different tenors or referents. One approach for the student of the topos is to examine a vehicle with various tenors, each of which occurs in different writers, to see if the adaptations for a particular tenor are always the same. One such vehicle is "character." All but one text in which the tenor is the Word refer to the Incarnation; that one, to the Eucharist. The relatively few descriptors are mostly abstract. Without exception, the *letra* or *carácter* is identified or conjoined with the *palabra* or *Verbo* (Ant. Vi3:23, Leo2:12-13, Bo5:5-6, 13-14, Go2:4-5, Brn:1-6).

---

[9] E. M. Tillyard explains this concept in *The Elizabethan World Picture* (77-95).

When the tenor is nature or creatures in general, the Spanish *letra* or *carácter* is always qualified by nouns and adjectives that emphasize aliveness, beauty, and variety. They are, for example, *letras vivas* (Ant. Grn: 53, Pin: 154), "letras muy galanas i muy luminadas" (Ant. Ven: 226), "hermosos caracteres" (Ant. Vi3: 119), "letras iluminadas y doradas" (Ant. Grn: 46), "caracteres de varios colores" (Ant. Gar: 2), "las letras que tenía el prolijo ABC" (Ant. Bo16: 6-7). Furthermore, the passages involved state explicitly that the characters teach of God and his perfections, while several incorporate the motif "to delight in the beautiful letters without understanding their meaning."

In reference to stars or other heavenly bodies, the vehicle "character" is sometimes described by words denoting or connoting brilliance (Ant. Grc: 29, Gue2: 4-5). The *letras* or *caracteres* are always read against the explicit backdrop of the heavens, presented as simply *cielo* (Ant. Ca8: 31) or, more often, metaphorized as "libro" (Ant. Va4: 3-4), "pergamino" (Ant. Grc: 25-26), "cuaderno" (Ant. Ca8: 33-34), "azul campo de yelo" (Ant. Ca65: 2-4), "lámina bella" (Ant. Ca31: 31-36), or "láminas de zafiros" (Ant. Ca4: 6-7). Calderón describes the characters as composed of irregular strokes (Ant. Ca65: 4-5). *Letras* or *caracteres* also frequently signify the wounds of Christ, the former term always used when the wounds are those of the Crucified. They are either explicitly red (Ant. Mu2: 4,12-13,33, Da: 20-22) or gold (Ant. Va18: 2) or described as borne on the hands, feet, or side (Ant. Mu3: 36-38,42-44). When the wounds are the stigmata imprinted on St. Francis, both Spanish terms are employed; the nature of the description varies in each case (Ant. Fue: 25-26,28, BaB: 71, Gue10: 4-5).

Another tenor, which occurs in Fuente and often in Calderón, is sin. With this negative signification, the *letra* or *carácter* is sometimes qualified with an explicitly negative term, as in "letra de afrenta" (Ant. Fue: 36) or "el confuso enigma / de este carácter" (Ant. Ca20: 18-19). However, when Lucifer or his equivalent is speaking, the description is positive or at least neutral; the vehicle becomes, for example, a "carácter inmortal" (Ant. Ca64: 9) or a "letra gótica y clara" (Ant. Ca64: 14;17:22).

As indicated above, the two Spanish terms *letra* and *carácter* are interchangeable for all these tenors. The five discussed suffice to justify the assertion that certain types of qualification seem to be linked only to, or never linked with, specific tenors; for instance, "letras vivas" metaphorizes only natural creatures in general. Other types, however, can designate various tenors; "illuminated letters" or "letters of gold" can signify creatures in general, the stars specifically, or the glorified wounds of Christ.

Another approach to possible rules for the adaptation of vehicles to different tenors is to look at motifs one might have expected to be applied exclusively to one tenor, to see if their articulation is noticeably different when the tenor changes. One vehicle that offers this opportunity is "the book with seven seals," derived from Apocalypse 5.1. Tenors include not only Christ as incarnate Word or as present in the Eucharist (Ant. To: 1+4, Va13:5-7;3:24, Ca44:13;10:12), but also Mary (Ant. Va15:1-2, Ag2:68-69) and the just person (Ant. Sua:44-45). I discern no special distinctions in the application of the vehicle. All the above texts reinforce the allusion to the Biblical book in one way or another, such as naming it explicitly, referring to St. John, or juxtaposing the motif of "the book with seven seals" with others from the same Scriptural passage. These techniques appear to be used without regard to tenor. For example, the motif "to be written on the inside and the outside" occurs in texts whose tenor is the Eucharist, the person of Christ, and the just human being.

A third approach is to pay attention to the application of different Spanish counterparts of the English formulation of a motifeme. Here one finds a bit more evidence of implicit rules in adapting a vehicle to different tenors. For example, *dicción, palabra, verbo,* and *voz* are all counterparts of the English "word." Not surprisingly, the Latinate *verbo* is reserved for the incarnation and birth of the divine Word. *Voz* and *dicción* are never linked with this tenor, and *palabra,* while usually signifying the Word, can have different meanings. Similarly, whenever the tenor of "character" is the distinctive and enduring quality or potency conveyed by the sacraments of Baptism, Confirmation, or Holy Orders, only the term *carácter,* never *letra,* is used, and only by Calderón. *Rubricar,* one of the three Spanish terms for "to sign," always signifies wounding or the shedding of blood, whereas *firmar* can have this or other meanings.

Space constraints preclude more than a few general observations on structural aspects of topical passages in this corpus. With respect to its function within a work as a whole, the topos may be simply ornamental or an integral element in the structure. By ornament I mean a topical motif or cluster of motifs that embellishes a work and does not contribute in an essential way to the line of argument or theme. It could be removed or replaced without impairing the work's coherence or fundamental design. Examples are the motif of Arabic characters in Lope de Vega's 'Silva moral' from "El siglo de Oro," *Vega del Parnaso,* the motif of reading superficially in Avila's sermon for the fourth Wednesday of Lent, and the motif cluster based on the name written in the book of life in the *Aucto de los desposorios de Josef.*

A structuring element, on the other hand, is a motif or cluster that does contribute in some substantial way to argument or theme, so that its removal would leave the work less unified or comprehensible, or at least less richly significant. Its contribution may take a number of forms. For instance, it may occur solely at the beginning of the composition but in such a way as to orient or frame one's interpretation, as in Córdoba's "Soneto V" and Guerra y Ribera's sermon on the Blessed Sacrament. It may occur only at the end of the work, in such a way as to recapitulate or refocus the whole, as in Ledesma's gloss "Al juicio final y particular del hombre." Guerra y Ribera's "Aprobación" for Rodríguez Monforte's *Sueños misteriosos* ends, appropriately enough, with the topical motif of the *aprobación*; although the function of the topos in other passages is simply ornamental, in the conclusion it is, I think, structurally significant. The motif or motif cluster may organize a relatively sizeable section of a work, such as the *exordio* or *salutación* in a sermon, i.e. the introductory section leading up to the "Ave María" that precedes the sermon proper, or one of the *consideraciones* in the body of the sermon, a scene in an auto, a stanza or two in a short poem, or a series of stanzas in a longer one. The exordium of Guerra y Ribera's *Sermón de la Conversión* and the "Consideración sexta" of Cabrera's sermon for the Sunday in the Octave of Easter are structured by a fusion of topical motifs. The penultimate scene in Calderón's *¿Quién hallará mujer fuerte?* constitutes an emblem based on the motif of the slave brand. The topical motifs that occur at the end of Cairasco's "Causa pia" are integral to his whole cluster of images. Among the various topical passages in Domínguez Camargo's *S. Ignacio de Loyola*, the motif cluster from the second canto of Book 2 structures an important moment in the saint's conversion of life. The motif/s may also appear at several significant moments in the work, creating an added dimension of meaning. Such is one function of the topical motifs in Calderón's *La cena del rey Baltasar* and *No hay más fortuna que Dios*.

When the motifs are major building blocks of the argument or of a unifying theme, appearing at strategic intervals throughout the piece, I consider them to constitute its structuring framework, or at least one level of this framework. For example, Aguilar's sonnet "A Christo Señor nuestro" is structured by motifs related to the making of a printed book. Angel Manrique builds his sermon on Mary's nativity on topical motifs whose center is the *libro de generación*. In the *auto Las órdenes militares*, as well as the *loa* for *Psiquis y Cupido* (Madrid), Calderón uses the *memorial* as a primary structuring element of both the action and the theme.

Statements about the relative proportions of passages in which the topos serves each of the above three functions must be approximate because inevitably, some passages straddle two categories, i.e., ornament and structuring element or structuring element and framework; my classification of one or the other text might differ from someone else's. Also, if a work contains several passages and these have different functions, I subsume the more discrete function/s under the more global one, which I consider the topos as performing in the work as a whole. Counting individual works regardless of length, I find that in about two thirds of the pieces in my corpus the topos has an ornamental function, in one-fourth it is a structuring element, and in one tenth it constitutes the framework. In terms of the three basic genres, the three functions represent 66 %, 21 %, and 13 %, respectively, for poetry; 68 %, 27 %, and 5 % for prose; and 70 %, 25 %, and 5 % for drama.

When one attempts to determine if the proportions change over the course of the Golden Age, conclusions become even more approximate, because the date of composition of many works is uncertain. I have grouped the texts by quarter centuries, omitting those which cannot be thus dated with at least relative certainty. The following table shows percentages of the three functions in each period, without respect to genre:

| PERIOD | FUNCTION | | |
| --- | --- | --- | --- |
| | *Ornament* | *Structuring Element* | *Framework* |
| 1500-24 | 100 % | – | – |
| 1525-49 | 70 % | 18 % | 12 % |
| 1550-74 | 86 % | 14 % | – |
| 1575-99 | 57 % | 39 % | 4 % |
| 1600-24 | 59 % | 24 % | 17 % |
| 1625-49 | 77 % | 18 % | 5 % |
| 1650-74 | 70 % | 23 % | 7 % |
| 1675-99 | 71 % | 23 % | 6 % |

Although it must be borne in mind that in some instances the absolute numbers are very small, the table suggests that for this group of writers as a whole the period of greatest exploitation or development of the topos was 1575-1624, before Calderón.

When genre is taken into account, when one looks, for example, at the percentage of all the examples from poetry for a particular period in which the topos has an ornamental function, the figures look like this:

## POETRY

| PERIOD | FUNCTION | | |
| --- | --- | --- | --- |
| | Ornament | Structuring Element | Framework |
| 1500-24 | 100 % | 0 % | 0 % |
| 1525-49 | 100 % | 0 % | 0 % |
| 1550-74 | 50 % | 50 % | 0 % |
| 1575-99 | 57 % | 36 % | 7 % |
| 1600-24 | 62 % | 21 % | 17 % |
| 1625-49 | 81 % | 13 % | 6 % |
| 1650-74 | 50 % | 50 % | 0 % |
| 1675-99 | 60 % | 0 % | 40 % |

## PROSE

| PERIOD | FUNCTION | | |
| --- | --- | --- | --- |
| | Ornament | Structuring Element | Framework |
| 1500-24 | – | – | – |
| 1525-49 | 70 % | 15 % | 15 % |
| 1550-74 | 100 % | 0 % | 0 % |
| 1575-99 | 57 % | 43 % | 0 % |
| 1600-24 | 33 % | 45 % | 22 % |
| 1625-49 | 100 % | 0 % | 0 % |
| 1650-74 | 100 % | 0 % | 0 % |
| 1675-99 | 69 % | 31 % | 0 % |

## DRAMA

| PERIOD | FUNCTION | | |
| --- | --- | --- | --- |
| | Ornament | Structuring Element | Framework |
| 1500-24 | 100 % | 0 % | 0 % |
| 1525-49 | 0 % | 100 % | 0 % |
| 1550-74 | 100 % | 0 % | 0 % |
| 1575-99 | 67 % | 33 % | 0 % |
| 1600-24 | 60 % | 40 % | 0 % |
| 1625-49 | 71 % | 25 % | 4 % |
| 1650-74 | 67 % | 23 % | 10 % |
| 1675-99 | 79 % | 21 % | 0 % |

In general, the structural possibilities of the topos seem to have been explored first in prose and poetry. The first work in this corpus in which the topos serves as framework is Venegas' prose treatise, written between 1538 and 1539; in poetry, the first example is Ledesma's *Conceptos espirituales*, published in 1600. When Calderón appears on the scene, its potential is realized also in drama. Of the dramatists in this corpus, he is the only one to use the topos as framework, the first time in *Lo que va del hombre a Dios*, written around 1640. Thus whichever aspect of topical development one considers, *recreación*, *reactualización*, or structural exploitation, Calderón is confirmed in his reputation as one of the most creative writers of the Golden Age. Still, he was not the first, nor was he the last in this period, to stretch the limits of the metaphor of the written text.

Although one might find an occasional exception, perhaps more apparent than actual, the examples in this corpus suggest certain underlying assumptions about texts and reading. Among them is that the primary function of a written text is to communicate with the reader or listener; in this sense the text cannot be separated from its author. The original is the "true" text; copies are valued according to their degree of fidelity to the original. Another assumption is that meaning is found in the text, as Scholz observes of the way a seventeenth-century emblematist perceived his activity: "Reading the book of nature, uncovering what he believed was the God-given meaning of the inventory of this world for him amounted to an act of hermeneutic piety rather than an imposition of meaning" (67). Making the book one's own through subjective interpretation is viewed negatively, as Fernando de la Torre's translation of one of Martial's epigrams indicates:

> El libro que lees por tuyo
> Mio es. Cierto Fidentino;
> Mas desde que lo lees mal,
> Comienza a ser tuyo el libro. (Castro 2:568)

There are correct and incorrect ways to read if one wishes to discern the true meaning. Being content with the surface meaning means not really reading at all. A text may be more or less difficult to understand, but misreadings are not inevitable; they are often due to the reader's inattention or even bad faith. In addition, we belong to a community of readers; the testimony of previous readers of long-standing reputation can and should be taken into account in our interpretation of the text, although we can also offer humbly our own insights. Furthermore, texts are to be learned from not only intellectually or theoretically; the learning should result in right acts. Therefore what one reads does matter.

# INTRODUCTION TO MOTIF INDEX

## Ways in Which the Index Might Be Used

The motif index is the core of the present volume. My primary reason for giving the study this particular shape was to provide a comprehensive, precise, and flexible infrastructure for future studies of the topos, as it appears not only in Spanish Golden Age literature of a religious nature, but also in different genres, periods, or countries. I thought, too, that such an index might be a useful tentative model to researchers of comparable, non-narrative topics.

The index synthesizes a good deal of information in a relatively short space. For example, a glance at the topical divisions and English terms readily reveals not only the wealth of motifs through which the topos was articulated, but also the specific aspects of written texts represented by the motifs and which of them were more fully exploited, which less so, and which possibilities inherent in the comparison tended to be ignored. Perusal of the Spanish terms and the citations that follow them discloses the linguistic variety in which a single motif could be clothed, which motifs were used most often, and which writers used a particular motif. An additional brief look at the tenors and referents of a motif indicates the variety of ideas expressed by it in general, and invites a comparison among the applications of a term by different writers, or by a single writer who uses it many times.

A more extensive examination discloses the several motifs for which the same Spanish term was used and the diversity of motifs used for the same reality or idea, as well as the variety of motifs used by a particular writer and those which seem to be his or her favorites. To cite just a few examples, the term *cifra* means, on different occasions, an abbreviation, emblem, character, or code; *cuaderno*, a book, census book, account book, or quire; *escritura*, a document, receipt, promissory note, text, script, or an act of writing. Among the motifs used to express the reality of the Holy Spirit are the pen, binder, printer, writer, law book, leaf, and writing. The idea of redemption through Christ's death on the Cross is conveyed through the interplay between the account book in which large sums are credited to one's account and type being separated in the typecase, through the motifs of the guarantor of a contract, transferring of a debt from one account to another, document of closure of an account, receipt of discharge of a debt, promissory note, bill of exchange, certificate of ransom, and letter of manumission, among others. One writer who employs a great variety of motifs is, not surprisingly, Calderón. Within the group "writing equipment" alone, he uses at least ten distinct motifs, the most frequent being pen and paper, which appear in ten *autos*.

I have cited in brackets after each term the writers and texts in which I have found it, in the order in which they appear in the chronological table. Used in conjunction with the table, the motif index thus offers an incipient chronology for the emergence, rise, and decline of individual motifs. For instance, in this group of texts the motif of the printing press first appears in Damián de Vegas' *Comedia llamada jacobina*, published in 1590, although the motif of the printed text occurs already in Ambrosio Montesino. While one finds the motif of the account book in a sermon by Juan de Avila for the First Sunday of Advent, printed sometime between 1529-69, that of the double entry does not appear until Alonso de Ledesma'a "A la certidumbre de la muerte," published in a collection of 1611. The term *letra* is used for the motif of the character throughout the period, whereas *carácter*, although it does occur in an early writer, Tomás de Villanueva, is much more frequent in the seventeenth century. The chronology can be helpful in the study of the intersecting of individual creativity with the topical tradition and is suggestive of changing cultural realities in the course of the Golden Age. Concomitantly, the chronology suggests approximately when a particular Spanish word came into use for a specific motif and who helped popularize it. In all the above ways the index provides a helpful context for the exploration of any particular text.

Together, the motif index and the anthology provide a more detailed comparison between or among writers who use the same motif. In some cases the comparison strongly suggests direct imitation, but more often it interests because of the differences it reveals. For example, one meaning of the *letras quebradas* in Luis de Granada's *Introducción del símbolo de la Fe* is that of creatures, as manifesting the beauty and wisdom of the Creator. In comparison, Pedro Calderón de la Barca's *El Año Santo en Madrid* uses the image as a metaphor on two levels of signification, the physical one of wrinkles or cracks in the bark of a tree and the metaphysical one of sin as affecting the entire human race. Manuel de Guerra y Ribera's *Oracion a la Vncion de la Madalena* applies it to Mary Magdalene's unbound hair. The associations for vehicle, tenor, and referent are all positive in Granada and in Guerra y Ribera, while in Calderón tenors and referent are predominantly negative. Whereas Granada is more abstract and philosophical in his use of the image, Guerra y Ribera is quite sensorial, and Calderón is both.

In addition, the index and anthology used jointly throw light on the ways in which a particular writer rings changes on certain motifs, even when he applies them to the same reality. In Calderón these variations disclose an ongoing refinement in understanding and expression of certain theological issues. For instance, to trace his use of the motif of the character in reference to original sin, selecting only those texts in which he employs the above-mentioned tenor of wrinkles on tree bark, one will look at four plays: *El veneno y la triaca*, *El gran mercado del mundo*, *El Año Santo en Madrid*, and *El divino Orfeo* (first version), written around 1634, 1634-35, 1651-52, and 1663, respectively. The pertinent passages in the first and last of these plays are identical in many lines, but the changes seem to me significant. The "algún tronco" of *El veneno y la triaca* (Ant. Ca64:8) becomes "estos troncos" in *El divino Orfeo* (Ant. Ca17:16). The wording of lines 16-19 identifies "estos troncos" with the "tronco herido" and thereby reinforces the link between individual sinners and the original sinner, Adam, the reality of the actual sin of each human being as one more concrete manifestation of original sin. In addition, lines 20-24 of *Orfeo* express more clearly than lines 12-16 of *Veneno* the inevitable and ever-growing manifestation of sin as part and parcel of the multiplication of the human race. Calderón introduces the image of multiple trees in *El gran mercado* (Ant. Ca20:13-14) but does not yet identify them so unmistakably with the one tree. In *Orfeo* he also refines the articulation of his theology by correctly omitting the adversative "a pesar de" of *Año Santo* (Ant. Ca7:8).

Furthermore, perusal of the multiple occurrences of a term within a single passage occasionally uncovers a sometimes subtle shift in that term's meaning or connotations. Such is the case of the vehicle *privilegio* in Antonio Balvás Barona's "Romance a San Francisco," which shifts from the royal copyright (Ant. BaB:37) to the nobleman's exemption from the *pechero* (Ant. BaB:42). Another example, this time in relation to the tenor, is the motif of the *libro* in Calderón's *La vacante general*. In the course of vv. 37-63 (Ant. Ca62) Calderón further articulates the image, identifying it as *libro de memoria*, *libro de casos de conciencia*, and *libro de Ciencia*, subtly weaving together the realities of divine omniscience and human conscience. In a third instance, from his "Loa" to *Psiquis y Cupido*, Calderón consistently links the vehicle of the *memorial* to the tenor of the Eucharist while shifting the referent, to bring out the many dimensions of the mystery.

Expansion on the meaning of "motif" and related terms

In this study a motif is a recurring specific articulation of the topos. A motif may consist of what I have chosen to call a motifeme, that is, an irreducible signifying unit in the form of a noun or verb. It may also be an expansion of a motifeme. I have articulated each of these expansions as a noun phrase, verb phrase, or complete sentence.

I consider an actual motif to be a specific articulation of the topos that occurs at least three times in the corpus and in more than one writer. Where both possible and appropriate, I have subsumed motifemes and expansions that occur only once or twice under more encompassing motifs. However, I have listed independently several cases of what I believe are motifs, articulations for which I would expect to find other examples, were more texts included in the corpus. The criteria I have used are both extrinsic and intrinsic. If it is mentioned in Curtius, occurs in the Bible, is a motif in secular literature of the period, or appears in at least two writers in my corpus, or if a writer refers explicitly to an earlier source of the image, I consider a topical articulation a probable motif. I do likewise if it is a motifeme that denotes an entity directly related to a written text; if it is a variant of an established motif (e.g. the "verde lámina" in Calderón 8:27, an apparent variant of Hermes Trismegistus' Emerald Tablet); or if it can be described as concise, graphic, and allowing of several metaphorical applications (e.g. "to apply the press" and "Parchment shrivels near fire"). Other articulations I have, for the time being, judged to be a writer's unique expression of the topos. I have not included dramatized forms of a motif unless accompanied by textual references, in either dialogue or stage directions.

In this study I have borrowed or adapted terms used by I. A. Richards in his definition of metaphor in *The Philosophy of Rhetoric*. While I use "vehicle" in basically the same way he does, "tenor" has a somewhat different meaning from his. I apply it to the most specific or immediate physical, metaphysical, or spiritual reality (entity or action) to which the motif is linked. It may be more or less global; for example, flower petals, a meadow, and the universe are all tenors, as are the finger of Christ, Christ's human nature, and God. The tenor may also be concrete (the face, starlight, the imprinting of the stigmata), abstract (the soul, love, sin, time's relentlessness), or both (the heavens / mystical body of Christ). I realize that in many cases, most particularly, though not always and not exclusively, in Calderón, identifying a tenor is difficult and may even seem opposed to the poet's technique of creating for an image multiple associations from various sources which together evoke a mental and emotional response but which cannot be reduced to a single analogue. My intention is not so much to isolate a single tenor as to convey an idea of the various kinds of reality to which a topical image is linked in these Spanish writers.

For the subject that vehicle and tenor help to illuminate I use the term "referent." Like the tenor, the referent may be more or less global (birth of Christ, God's action in the world) and either concrete (Christ's scourging) or abstract (devotion to Jesus). The same reality may serve as either tenor or referent, depending on the particular text. I have distinguished between tenor and referent in order to make clearer the differences among writers in the use of a motif. Those motifs I have designated "unmixed expansions" consist of vehicle alone; those designated "mixed expansions," of vehicle and some aspect of the tenor or referent.

Organization of the Index

Throughout the index motifemes are followed, where relevant, by the related expansions, first the unmixed, then the mixed. In both groups noun phrases precede verb phrases, which in turn precede complete sentences. I have given tenors and referents for motifemes only, in part to conserve space but also because the meaning of an expanded motif can normally be easily deduced by consulting the referent for the pertinent instance of the corresponding motifeme. I have listed tenors and referents in the order in which their vehicles occur in the text under consideration but have avoided repetitions of identical tenor-referent combinations.

Rather than establish a priori semantic categories, I let them grow out of the topical material. I do not imagine that the index is exhaustive; on the contrary, I would expect to find other motifs, given texts enough and time. However, I doubt that new motifs would necessitate radical change in the present organization of the index. At any rate, in setting it up, I have endeavored to allow for future expansion in the various divisions and subdivisions.

I have assigned the motifs to two main categories, taking into account both grammar and meaning. The category "Entities" consists principally of nouns and noun phrases but also includes verb phrases or sentences in which the noun is the focus of interest. The category "Actions or States" includes, in addition to verbs and verb phrases, a few noun phrases in which an embedded verb is the focus of interest or the noun has verbal import, as well as sentences in which the verb is of primary interest.

I have ordered the subdivisions within each of these two main categories, and the motifemes within each subdivision, according to a logic based on the interplay of various factors. These include:

1. degree of abstractness (generic terms precede specific terms);

2. English word grouping (e.g., since in English one says "pen and ink," the subdivision *Writing Instruments*, which includes "pen," precedes *Other Writing Equipment*, which includes "ink"; because the English interrogatives "who," "what," "how," and "how much" are usually listed in that order, the equivalent unmixed expansions of TO READ THE TEXT follow the same order; "inside" precedes "outside");

3. prevalence of use, i.e., prototypes, or centrality (e.g., the subdivisions that include equipment for writing by hand precede *Printing Equipment*; under the subdivision TO PRINT THE TEXT, equivalents of "to print" precede the motifs related to preparing the type, which is more peripheral to the act of printing);

4. temporal sequence of existence (e.g., the division EQUIPMENT FOR THE PRODUCTION OF THE TEXT precedes the other divisions in the category of entities; TO PREPARE THE EQUIPMENT FOR PRODUCING THE TEXT, in the category of actions and states; "to trim the binding" precedes "to adorn the binding"; the motifeme "original" precedes "copy");

5. temporal sequence of awareness on the part of a reader (e.g., the subdivision TEXT FORMAT precedes GENRES, FORMS OR TYPES OF TEXT; *Binding* precedes *Leaves / Pages*);

6. comprehensiveness or globality (e.g., the subdivision CONTENT precedes PORTION; OVERALL STRUCTURE precedes INTERNAL STRUCTURE; *Layout* precedes *Characters and Parts of Characters*; however, in the subdivision PORTION OR EXTENT, entities are arranged in approximate order of length from shortest to longest);

7. hierarchy of value (e.g., "New Testament" is the first motifeme in the subdivision *Books* under GENRES, FORMS OR TYPES OF TEXT);

8. association or commonality (e.g., LANGUAGE leads naturally to STYLE; motifemes for *Writing Instruments* are ordered by form and function: pen – reed – artist's brush – engraving tool – seal / signet ring / stamp – branding iron).

Where other bases seemed nonexistent or not helpful, I have followed alphabetical order. When various factors conflict, I have relied upon internal logic in deciding which should take precedence.

Subdivisions and motifemes that had negative connotations in the period generally appear at the end of a list. Thus within the division THE TEXT ITSELF, the last major subdivision is DEFECTS AND CORRECTIONS; within the subdivision *Books*, of GENRES, FORMS OR TYPES, the last entry is "book of magic." An exception is the strictly alphabetical ordering of subdivisions in the section TO NOT PRESERVE THE TEXT, which is already basically negative. The negative formulation of a verbal motif (e.g. to not do X) follows its positive formulation in both subdivisions and motifemes.

I have arranged the expansions, whether mixed or unmixed, on the following basis. Among noun phrases, I respect whatever natural semantic groupings appear, i.e., groupings based on commonality or association; otherwise I observe alphabetical order. Qualifiers with strongly negative meaning appear at the end of each list, since there are relatively few of them. In general, expanded motifs are ordered according to the following sequence of elements: (1) numbers, (2) particularization, (3) possessor, (4) constituting entities or composing material, (5) size, (6) colors, (7) other concrete descriptors, (8) other abstract descriptors.

Verb phrases are alphabetized on a grammatical basis: first by the verb, second by the direct complement, third by the preposition, fourth by the object of the preposition, fifth by the adverb. True passives follow the entire group of active phrases. This order is superseded by strong pairs or series, such as contraries or contradictories, synonyms, and traditional groups like the elements.

Sentences are alphabetized first by the subject in the noun clause, second by the adjective that modifies identical subjects, third by the main verb, fourth by the direct complement or the predicate adjective. Passive sentences follow the entire group of active sentences. This order is superseded by strong pairs, such as contradictory statements.

LANGUAGE

In view of the possible use of this index by researchers in various national literatures, I have used English terms for the subdivisions and motifs because it is the currently predominant international language. However, a few Spanish terms for which I could find no satisfactory English equivalent appear in the original language. Explanatory endnotes accompany such terms. For each English motifeme I list all the Spanish equivalents I have found in the texts. The numbers in brackets after each Spanish term refer to the anthology entries in which the term occurs. The numbers are in chronological order; those following a colon indicate lines. Citations in brackets immediately after the English term refer to paraphrases or circumlocutions.

I have counted past participles as verbs and subsumed them under the appropriate infinitive. Similarly, passive articulations of a verbal motifeme are subsumed under the active form. I have also included with the Spanish verbs a few nouns that in context signify an action. In general, I have assigned all Spanish terms to their respective subdivisions according to their specific meaning in the texts from which they were taken. In several cases, therefore, the same Spanish word appears in more than one category. Terms that appear with the same citation in more than one subdivision do so because they are the basis of puns. The strictly alphabetical Spanish index at the end of this volume will bring together all uses of a particular term.

CROSS REFERENCES

I have assigned the expanded motifs to the English motifeme that predominates in each. SEE and SEE ALSO references point the reader to synonymous and subsumed motifs. By the latter I mean a motif that occurs both independently and also as part of a more encompassing motif. The interested reader can identify additional variations of a motif by perusing the Tenor column under likely motifemes. For example, to identify variants of "to write with blood," s/he can check under "ink." I do not cross-reference motifs that simply cluster with others, for example, all motifs in which the motifeme "pen" occurs, or all motifs that include the descriptor "blue." The alphabetical English index provides for the reader who wants to trace such clusters.

A WORD ON METAPHOR

I do not include in this index text-related images that are purely and simply literal. However, I do include images that are both literal and metaphorical and are an integral part of a more overarching comparison. Several images in this category derive from Scripture. An example is the image of the tablets of the Old Law given by God to Moses on Mt. Sinai. This image is already in Scripture an example of what Northrop Frye calls the "metaphorical literal" (69). In my texts it is also often accompanied by images whose metaphorical nature is more immediately apparent, such as the *buril* for the finger of God. It may, in addition, be contrasted with the metaphorical New Law of grace.

I also include images that have no identifiable tenor but that contribute to the extended metaphor as a whole, such as by making it more vivid, and that acquire a quasi metaphorical character by interaction with the other images. Images from this group have a – in the Tenor column. An example is "pluma con pelo" from Cabrera's *Con-*

*sideraciones del Viernes después del Domingo Primero de Cuaresma*; it is an image with an empty tenor slot, but as an integral part of the extended metaphor of the letter written to a subordinate in rank, identified with God's work in the Creation, it needs to be included in the index. Normally metaphors for Scripture do not appear in this index, but in some cases these metaphors are so interwoven into the texture of the more encompassing metaphor or allegory that it would be artificial to omit them. An example is the "recado de escribir" used by Moses and Joshua in *Las órdenes militares*. It is one in a cluster of images and figures that allude to the Old Testament books named for Moses and Joshua. While metaphorical in itself, its tenor involves a literal text, Scripture, not a person, a supernatural being, or the natural world. Nevertheless, because it is an integral part of the topical allegory used by Calderón in reference to Christ, I have included it.

# MOTIF INDEX

## A. ENTITIES

### A.1. *EQUIPMENT FOR THE PRODUCTION OF THE TEXT*

#### A.1.1. WRITING EQUIPMENT – GENERIC

**writing equipment**
  escribanía [Bo7:8]
  instrumentos (para escribir) [Cab6:8,4; Gue8:4,7]
  recado de escribir [Ca43:102-103]

| *Tenor* | *Referent* | *No.* |
|---|---|---|
| human beings | God's transformation of weak human beings into instruments of his power | Cab3 |
| arguments of scribes and Pharisees | superiority of Christ's authority to that of scribes and Pharisees | Bo7 |
| composition of scriptural books of Moses and Joshua | Moses and Joshua, Old Testament leaders of Hebrews to promised land, as prophets of Christ's divine and human lineage | Ca43 |
| scholars | scholars' lives as inevitably filled with self-sacrifice | Gue8 |

#### A.1.2. WRITING EQUIPMENT – SPECIFIC

##### A.1.2.1. *Writing Instruments*

**pen**
  cálamo [Cai20:12]
  estilo [Va16:2; Do:3,87]
  péndola [Cai20:5,14]
  pluma [Mon5:6; Vi3:232,247,249; Pad2:6; Led3:4; Cab3:3,11; 7:6;11:31,48, 49; ManA2:43,62,63; Gon:3; Led1:1; Va13:11;17:4; Bo8:11; Mu4:20;

Tel:16; Va3:11; Bo3:10;5:9; Ca64:6; VgC24:20;23:11; Ca14:2;62:17,80; 37:30; Do:20,21,43,83,98; Ca8:52;43:16;17:14;26:91; 68:35;36:31; Cas:11; Gue8:5,9; Ca5:8]

| Tenor | Referent | No. |
|---|---|---|
| sun ray | Mary's greatness and beauty | Mon5 |
| Holy Spirit | Incarnation | Vi3 |
| grain of sand | immensity of name of Jesus | Pad2 |
| feathered arrows | martyrdom of St. Sebastian | Led3 |
| human beings | God's transformation of weak human beings into instruments of his power | Cab3 |
| — | work of Creation as inferior to work of Redemption | Cab7 |
| nails | Crucifixion | Cab11 |
| love | devotion to Jesus | Cab11 |
| prong on whip | Christ's scourging | ManA2 |
| Holy Spirit | Incarnation | ManA2 |
| two Negresses | participation in Corpus Christi procession | Gon |
| Holy Spirit | Mary's exaltation of God | Cai20 |
| noble eloquence | sacred poetry as divine in origin | Cai20 |
| Cross | Crucifixion | Led1 |
| love | Eucharist | Va13 |
| reed or thorns | Christ's being wounded on head and crowned with thorns | Va16 |
| nails | Crucifixion | Va17 |
| composition of prophetic books of Bible | long history of human sin as recounted by prophets | Bo8 |
| the finger of God | stigmata of St. Francis | Mu4 |
| theoretical knowledge | necessity of supplementing theoretical understanding of virtue with practical experience | Tel |
| human appetite | pursuit of worldly illusions | Va3 |
| love | Incarnation | Bo3 |
| Holy Spirit | Incarnation | Bo5 |
| knife | redemption through Christ's death on Cross | Ca64 |
| angels' wings | angels faithful to God who follow Michael as their leader in battle against Lucifer | VgC24 |
| weapons | history of human violence | VgC23 |
| feathered arrows | Pascual Vivas' supposed heroism in battle | Ca14 |
| oar | John the Evangelist's renown as beloved disciple of Christ, and Apostles as successors to patriarchs of Old Dispensation | Ca62 |

| Tenor | Referent | No. |
|---|---|---|
| waves of sea | nature's turbulence at Second Coming of Christ | Ca62 |
| knife | Fall: eating from tree of knowledge of good and evil | Ca37 |
| — | fruitfulness of St. Ignatius of Loyola's life and teaching | Do |
| fame | wounding of St. Ignatius | Do |
| sun ray | St. Ignatius' recognition of God's greatness in natural world | Do |
| starlight | creation of heavens | Do |
| God's power | God's giving Law to Moses | Do |
| time's relentlessness | aged and wise hermit | Do |
| making known | fame of Saba | Ca8 |
| devices of evil | link between Immaculate Conception Incarnation and Redemption | Ca43 |
| knife | redemption through Christ's death on Cross | Ca17 |
| lance | Crucifixion and piercing of Christ's side | Ca26 |
| bird feathers | sin's domination of world | Ca68 |
| time as dimension in which human life is lived and human acts must be accounted for | obligation to use wisely one's gifts | Ca36 |
| angels' wings | birth of Christ | Cas |
| scholars; St. Catherine of Alexandria | scholar as chief vehicle for transmission of learning and needing to sacrifice self to produce works of wisdom, as exemplified in St. Catherine | Gue8 |
| fame | enduring honor of a city and its governor | Ca5 |

**pen:** unmixed expansions
   the pen of a notary [SEE ALSO: A.1.2.1. pen:ue. the pen of a skillful scribe]
      [Gon:3]
   the pen of a skillful scribe [Mon5:6; Vi3:247-48]
   a diamond pen [Do:83]
   an iron pen [SEE ALSO: A.1.2.1. pen: *estilo*]
      [Cab11:31,48; Va17:4; Do:98]
   a golden pen [Cai20:12,14]
   a well-cut pen [Cab3:3; Gue8:13]
   an ill-cut pen [Cab7:6; Ca26:89-91; Gue8:12]
   to cut the pen [SEE ALSO: A.1.2.1. pen:ue. a well-cut pen;
      an ill-cut pen]
      [Gue8:9-11,15-16]
   to dip the pen in ink [Do:20]

## MOTIF INDEX

**reed**
  caña [Cab3:1,11; Ca26:91]

| Tenor | Referent | No. |
|---|---|---|
| weak human beings | God's transformation of weak human beings into instruments of his power | Cab3 |
| lance | Crucifixion and piercing of Christ's side | Ca26 |

**artist's brush** (for illuminating)
  pinzel [BaB:64; Ca20:8; Gue10:9]

| Tenor | Referent | No. |
|---|---|---|
| Christ's action in imprinting stigmata | stigmata of St. Francis | BaB |
| moonlight | reading horoscope in night sky | Ca20 |
| Christ's action in imprinting stigmata | stigmata of St. Francis | Gue10 |

**engraving tool** [SEE ALSO: A.1.2.1. pen: *estilo*; A.1.2.1. pen:ue. an iron pen]
  buril [Mu3:28; Ca22:26;20:9;45:36;50:11; GarE:7]
  cincel [Ca40:8]
  punzón [Vi2:7-8,9-10]

| Tenor | Referent | No. |
|---|---|---|
| sexual intercourse | Incarnation | Vi2 |
| lance or spear | wounding of Christ's side | Mu3 |
| the finger of God | God's giving Law to Moses | Ca40 |
| the finger of God | God's giving Law to Moses | Ca22 |
| shadow | reading horoscope in night sky | Ca20 |
| Christ's finger | Christ's writing on ground "Let him who is without sin. . . ." | Ca45 |
| the finger of God | God's giving Law to Moses | Ca50 |
| intelligent wit | spiritual power of St. Peter of Alcantara's eloquent preaching | GarE |

**seal / signet ring / stamp** [Rod2:2]
  anillo [Mon7:11]
  sello [Mon7:6; VgC20:2;18:13; Jau:19,25; VgC22:20; Ca32:6]

| Tenor | Referent | No. |
|---|---|---|
| wounds on hands, feet and side of Christ | stigmata of St. Francis as work of divine love | Mon7 |

| Tenor | Referent | No. |
|---|---|---|
| Mary Magdalene's mouth | kissing feet of Christ | Rod2 |
| Eucharistic host | Eucharist as God | VgC20 |
| Christ | stigmata of St. Francis | VgC18 |
| Christ | Christ as God and man | Jau |
| act of identifying or distinguishing | identification of God's faithful servants | VgC22 |
| baptismal character or grace | John's baptism of Christ as inauguration of sacrament of Baptism | Ca32 |

**seal / signet ring / stamp:** unmixed expansions
  five signet rings [Mon7:11]
  a royal seal [Ca32:6]
  to forge a stamp [Mon7:20; Jau:19-20]

**branding iron**
  hierro [VgC22:11-12; Ca22:5]

| Tenor | Referent | No. |
|---|---|---|
| — | branding of certain Franciscan martyrs in Japan as ironically confirming their witness to Christ | VgC22 |
| sin | enslavement of human race through sin | Ca22 |

A.1.2.1.ue. *Writing Instruments: Unmixed Expansions*

  an inept writing instrument [SEE ALSO: A.1.2.1. pen:ue. an ill-cut pen] [Cab3:6]

A.1.2.2. *Other Writing Equipment*

**ink** [Gue14:3]
  tinta [Mon5:2; Vi3:233,295; Av5:21; Grn:64; Pad2:4; Cab7:8;11:32; ManA2:61,63; Gon:2; Led7:7; Cai4:5; Bo8:8; Mu4:19; Fue:38; Ov:2,10; Bo15:42;3:8;5:23; Ca14:6;47:4; Do:21,27,83,97; Ca43:76;26:94; Lud:12; Gue7:4]

| Tenor | Referent | No. |
|---|---|---|
| sea | Mary's greatness and beauty | Mon5 |
| Mary's blood | Incarnation | Vi3 |
| inner effects of human acts | conscience as informed by one's acts, revealed at Last Judgment | Vi3 |
| — | Holy Spirit's inspiring people to follow the Gospel | Av5 |

## MOTIF INDEX 77

| Tenor | Referent | No. |
|---|---|---|
| effect of chance | creation of world | Grn |
| sea | immensity of name of Jesus | Pad2 |
| —— | work of Creation as inferior to work of Redemption | Cab7 |
| Christ's blood | Crucifixion and Redemption | Cab11 |
| Mary's blood | Incarnation | MaA2 |
| sweat | copious sweating of two Negresses participating in Corpus Christi procession | Gon |
| intentions of the heart | outward manifestation of St. Ignatius of Loyola's love | Led7 |
| tears | contrition | Cai4 |
| Christ's blood | flowing of blood and water from Christ's side, pierced in Crucifixion | Bo8 |
| Christ's blood | stigmata of St. Francis | Mu4 |
| tendency to sin | Immaculate Conception | Fue |
| blood of all the redeemed, including Mary | link between Immaculate Conception Incarnation and Redemption | Ov |
| Christ's blood | link between Immaculate Conception Incarnation and Redemption | Ov |
| human nature | Immaculate Conception | Bo15 |
| Mary's blood | Incarnation | Bo3 |
| God's action | Incarnation | Bo5 |
| human blood | performance of heroic deeds | Ca14 |
| sin | Pontius Pilate's moral responsibility in Christ's death | Ca47 |
| St. Ignatius' blood | wounding of St. Ignatius | Do |
| light of heavenly bodies | creation of heavens | Do |
| blood | aged hermit | Do |
| sin | Immaculate Conception | Ca43 |
| Christ's blood | Crucifixion | Ca26 |
| sin | St. Peter of Alcantara's holiness | Lud |
| human merits | St. Ann's election as mother of Mary | Gue7 |
| inner effects of human acts (?) | conscience as informed by one's acts, revealed at Last Judgment (?) | Gue14 |

**ink:** unmixed expansions
    invisible ink [SEE: A.1.2.2. ink:ue. Letters written in invisible ink appear when held before the fire / to the light.]
    black ink [SEE ALSO: A.3.9. line of writing:ue. black lines]
        [Ca47:4; Lud:12]
    gold ink [Do:83]
    red ink [SEE ALSO: A.3.7.2. note / gloss:ue. a note in red ink]
        [Bo8:8;3:8; Do:20-21,97]
    pale ink [SEE ALSO: A.1.2.2. ink:ue. to water the ink]
        [Cab7:8]

to water the ink [Bo8:12]
The ink stains one's fingers. [Ca47:4-5]
Letters written in invisible ink appear when held before the fire / to the light.
 [Vi3:285-89; Gue14:3-4; Brn:2-4]

**inkwell**
 tintero [Bo8:7]

| Tenor | Referent | No. |
|---|---|---|
| Christ's side | Christ's side as drained of blood in Crucifixion | Bo8 |

**inkwell:** unmixed expansions
 The inkwell runs dry. [Bo8:7]

**ruler**
 regla [Led21:17]

| Tenor | Referent | No. |
|---|---|---|
| rules of virtue | study and practice of virtue | Led21 |

A.1.2.3. *Material Written On*

A.1.2.3.1. *Generic Terms*

**writing material**
 materia [ManA2:252]

| Tenor | Referent | No. |
|---|---|---|
| Mary's flesh | Incarnation | ManA2 |

A.1.2.3.2. *Vegetable Matter*

**paper**
 papel [Av5:6; Pin:50; ASF:1,4; Pad2:2; Snt1:2,3,4; Sua:67; Rod1:9; Cab1:5;7:7; Led10:2,10,18; Mu3,10,14,16; ManA2:42,61,64,246,248,249,252,254,257; Led7:3,4,6; Cai14:2; Led21:18;15:2; Va11:5; Bo14:2;7:7; VgC3:9;18:16; Mu4:14; Fue:39; Ov:2; Es:8; Bo3:11;5:3,5,18,23,24; 6:1,6,10,12,31,37; Per:8; Par3:9; Ca64:11;40:4; VgC23:13; Ca18:8,13;62:18,34; Do:11; Ca8:21; 34:5;17:19; 41:5;26:92;36:31; Gue1:6,31,123;2:3; Brn:2]

| Tenor | Referent | No. |
|---|---|---|
| — | coming of Holy Spirit at Pentecost | Av5 |
| — | the divine essence | Pin |

## MOTIF INDEX

| Tenor | Referent | No. |
|---|---|---|
| St. Francis | stigmata of St. Francis | ASF |
| Mary | Incarnation | ASF |
| heavens | immensity of name of Jesus | Pad2 |
| ordinary Christians ? | God's transformation of human nature through grace | Snt1 |
| Mary's flesh | Incarnation | Sua |
| Mary's flesh | Incarnation | Rod1 |
| — | power of name of Jesus | Cab1 |
| — | work of Creation as inferior to work of Redemption | Cab7 |
| Mary | link between Incarnation and Immaculate Conception | Led10 |
| human nature | original sin | Led10 |
| purified heart or soul | God's transformation of weak human beings into instruments of his power | Mu1 |
| Christ's back | Christ's Passion | ManA2 |
| Mary's womb | Incarnation | ManA2 |
| face | St. Ignatius of Loyola's face as manifesting love of his heart | Led7 |
| soul | practice of virtue | Cai14 |
| soul | study and practice of virtue | Led21 |
| memory | sinner's review of sinful life | Led15 |
| heaven | praise of the Eucharist | Va11 |
| heart | conscience | Bo14 |
| sand | superiority of Christ's authority to that of scribes and Pharisees | Bo7 |
| heart | learning the "Our Father" | VgC3 |
| body and soul of St. Francis | stigmata of St. Francis | VgC18 |
| body of St. Francis | stigmata of St. Francis | Mu4 |
| soul | Immaculate Conception | Fue |
| flesh of Mary and of all the redeemed | link between Immaculate Conception, Incarnation and Redemption | Ov |
| the infant Mary | Mary's beauty | Es |
| Mary's flesh | Incarnation | Bo3 |
| Mary's soul | Mary's fullness of grace | Bo5 |
| Mary | Mary's role in Incarnation as planned by God from eternity | Bo5 |
| human flesh | Incarnation of Word | Bo5 |
| Mary | Mary's preservation from original sin, or fullness of divine grace, from first moment of conception, in view of her role as mother of God | Bo6 |
| earth | creation of human race | Per |

| Tenor | Referent | No. |
|---|---|---|
| heavens | creation of heavens | Par3 |
| tree trunk; human nature | original sin | Ca64 |
| rock | God's giving Law to Moses | Ca40 |
| history of human violence | long history of human violence | VgC23 |
| heavens | God's promise of peace to human race | Ca18 |
| smoke | illusion of sin's allurements | Ca18 |
| waves | John the Evangelist's renown as beloved disciple of Christ, and Apostles as successors to patriarchs of Old Dispensation | Ca62 |
| air | preaching of John the Baptist | Ca62 |
| soul | effect on souls of St. Ignatius of Loyola's teaching | Do |
| wind; various doctrines among which Gentiles vacillated before finding true Wisdom | Queen Saba's vision of Redemption through God's Word | Ca8 |
| lily petals | Mount Horeb, sacred mountain | Ca34 |
| tree trunk; human nature | original sin | Ca17 |
| air | preaching of John the Baptist | Ca41 |
| tree bark; Cross | Christ's death as instituting New Dispensation | Ca26 |
| time as dimension in which human life is lived and human acts must be accounted for | obligation to use one's gifts wisely | Ca36 |
| heavens | heavens as God's handiwork | Gue1 |
| Mary Magdalene's soul | effects of sin on Mary Magdalene | Gue1 |
| heavens | Mary Magdalene's sorrow for her sins | Gue1 |
| heavens | correspondence between star called "Aguila" and new rector of Salamanca | Gue2 |
| Eucharistic host | Real Presence in Eucharist | Brn |

**paper:** unmixed expansions
*papel de corazón*[1] [Led10:5;14:20; Co2:8] / *hoja de corazón* [Bo9:12]

| Tenor | Referent | No. |
|---|---|---|
| Mary's soul | link between Incarnation and Immaculate Conception | Led10 |
| human heart | God's knowledge of the secrets of conscience | Led14 |

---

[1] See explanation in General Introduction p. 43.

| human heart | divine mission of John the Baptist | Bo9 |
| soul | devotion to mysteries of the rosary | Co2 |

*papel de culebrilla*[2] [Led10:7]

| Tenor | Referent | No. |
|---|---|---|
| unredeemed human nature | original sin | Led1 |

*papel de estraza*[3] [Bo5:24-25; Vel:3]

| Tenor | Referent | No. |
|---|---|---|
| sinful human nature | all human beings but Mary as affected by original sin | Bo5 |
| Cain | Judas' betrayal of Christ as much worse than Cain's betrayal of Abel | Vel |

*papel sellado*[4] [Ca23:32,38]

| Tenor | Referent | No. |
|---|---|---|
| baptized soul | God's desire that all people be saved | Ca23 |

blue paper [Gue1:6,7;2:3]
    white paper [Pad2:2; Led10:3; Mu1:3; ManA2:257; Led15:2; Bo5:23;6:6-7; Gue1:31; Brn:2]
    burnished paper [ASF:1; Pad2:2; ManA2:42; Bo6:35]
    clean paper [ASF:3-4; Pad2:2; Led10:2,6; ManA2:257; VgC18:16; Bo6:36-37]
    smooth paper [Led10:18; Mu1:3-4]
    fine paper [SEE ALSO: A.1.2.3.2. paper:ue. *papel de corazón*; to make fine paper]
    [Ov:1-2; Bo6:1]
    inferior paper [SEE: A.1.2.3.2. paper:ue. *papel de culebrilla; papel de estraza;* The paper bleeds.]
    to make fine paper [SEE ALSO: A.1.2.3.2. paper:ue. to make fine paper from old rags]
    [Bo6:31-35; Par3:8-9]
    to make fine paper from old rags [Snt1:1-2; Mu1:1-4,8-14]
    The paper bleeds. [Cab7:7; Led7:4-7]

---

[2] "Cierto papel para escribir, que parece se hacia en lo antiguo, y tenia por marca una figura de culebra" (*Diccionario de autoridades*).

[3] "El tosco y grossero, fabricado de trapo gruesso de lana, cañamo y lienzo basto, que sirve para envolver mercaderías y otros usos" (*Diccionario de autoridades*).

[4] See explanation in General Introduction p. 52.

**palm leaf**
hoja de palma [Bo5:5]

| Tenor | Referent | No. |
|---|---|---|
| Mary | Mary's being chosen by God from eternity to be mother of the Word | Bo5 |

**palm leaf:** unmixed expansions
Palm leaf was the first paper. [Bo5:5]

**papyrus** [Do:4]
papiro [Vi3:260]

| Tenor | Referent | No. |
|---|---|---|
| Mary | Incarnation | Vi3 |
| — | fruitfulness of St. Ignatius of Loyola's life and teaching | Do |

**tree bark** [Do:8-9]
corteza [Ca64:7;20:14;7:7;37:3,42;17:15;26:103;28:5]

| Tenor | Referent | No. |
|---|---|---|
| human soul | original sin | Ca64 |
| human soul | original sin | Ca20 |
| human soul | original sin | Ca7 |
| human soul | original sin | Ca37 |
| Cross | Redemption | Ca37 |
| — | fruitfulness of St. Ignatius of Loyola's life and teaching | Do |
| human soul | original sin | Ca17 |
| Cross | Christ's death as instituting New Dispensation | Ca26 |
| Cross | eternal life through Christ's death | Ca28 |

**wax**
cera [Pin:49; VgC5:41;20:19; Es:20; Do:2]
nema [VgC18:21]

| Tenor | Referent | No. |
|---|---|---|
| — | the divine essence | Pin |
| St. Isidore of Madrid | St. Isidore's virtue | VgC5 |
| body and soul of St. Francis | stigmata of St. Francis | VgC18 |
| flesh wound from circumcision | link between Christ's circumcision and Redemption | Es |
| — | fruitfulness of St. Ignatius of Loyola's life and teaching | Do |

**wax:** unmixed expansions
red wax [Es:20]

A.1.2.3.3. *Animal Matter*

**parchment** [SEE ALSO: A.1.2.3.3. skin]
membrana [Vi3:294]
pergamino [Ven:239,248; Vi3:233,262,272; Av7:3; Pin:50; Va13:2; VgC1:5; Grc:25]

| Tenor | Referent | No. |
| --- | --- | --- |
| heavens | heavens as revelation of God | Ven |
| Mary's womb | Incarnation | Vi3 |
| conscience | conscience as informed by and ultimate judge of one's acts | Vi3 |
| soul | soul purified by self-denial in preparation for grace | Av7 |
| — | the divine essence | Pin |
| Eucharistic host | Eucharist as mystery of faith | Va13 |
| soul | death to self in union with God | VgC1 |
| heavens | heavens as revelation | Grc |

**parchment:** unmixed expansions
a white parchment [Av7:2-3; Va13:2]
a clean parchment [Vi3:261-62,272; Av7:2-4]
a parchment saturated with ink [Vi3:294-95]
a smooth parchment [Av7:2-3]
to prepare a parchment for writing [Av7:2-4]
Parchment shrivels near fire. [VgC1:5-7]

**skin** [SEE ALSO: A.3.18.1. binding / boards: *piel*]
pellejo [Ven:237,248; Grc:8]
piel [Grc:24; Do:6-7,30]

| Tenor | Referent | No. |
| --- | --- | --- |
| heavens | heavens as revelation of God | Ven |
| appearance | people empty of substance | Grc |
| heavens | heavens as revelation of God | Grc |
| — | fruitfulness of St. Ignatius of Loyola's life and teaching | Do |
| heavens | St. Ignatius' recognition of God's greatness in natural world | Do |

**skin:** unmixed expansions
a blue skin [Do:30]

an unrolled skin [SEE ALSO: B.3.3.1. to unroll:ue. to unroll a skin] [Grc:24-25]

### A.1.2.3.4. *Mineral Matter*

**bronze**
bronce [Ca48:20; GarE:7; Ca38:5;24:22,26]

| Tenor | Referent | No. |
|---|---|---|
| heart | Queen Christina of Sweden's response to letter from Philip II of Spain | Ca48 |
| aptitude of St. Peter of Alcantara's preaching | spiritual power of St. Peter of Alcantara's eloquent preaching | GarE |
| heart | devotion to Mary | Ca38 |
| lastingness | immortal fame of the union of divine and human in Christ | Ca24 |

**clay** [LoU1:2]

| Tenor | Referent | No. |
|---|---|---|
| weak human nature | human being as created in God's image | LoU1 |

**marble**
mármol [Ca22:25;6:5;50:10;69:38]

| Tenor | Referent | No. |
|---|---|---|
| tablets of Law | God's giving Law to Moses | Ca22 |
| tablets of Law | lastingness of Decalog | Ca6 |
| tablets of Law | God's giving Law to Moses | Ca50 |
| heart | New Law of grace | Ca69 |

**precious stone**
piedra preciosa [Cab4:10]
carbunclo [Cab4:11]
diamante [Cab4:10-11; VgC24:24]
perla [Cab4:6,8]
zafiro [Ca4:6]

| Tenor | Referent | No. |
|---|---|---|
| Christ | following of Christ | Cab4 |
| heart and soul | strong faith of Spanish Christians | VgC24 |

MOTIF INDEX 85

| Tenor | Referent | No. |
|---|---|---|
| color and limpidity of heavens | heavens, from which Christ descends | Ca4 |

**stone**
  piedra [Av5:7; Cab4:15; Mu3:8; VgC1:10]
  piedrecita [Cab4:5]

| Tenor | Referent | No. |
|---|---|---|
| — | coming of Holy Spirit at Pentecost, contrasted with Mosaic Law | Av5 |
| Christ | Christ as reward of his faithful followers | Cab4 |
| hands, feet, side, heart | Christ's wounds as motivated by and manifestation of his eternal love for humankind | Mu3 |
| heart | contrition for hardness of heart in face of God's love | VgC1 |

A.1.2.4. *Printing Equipment*

**form**
  molde [Ven:117]

| Tenor | Referent | No. |
|---|---|---|
| free will | importance of free will in forming virtue | Ven |

**printing press**
  imprenta [Vgs4:3; Va14:1; Fue:32,57; Ov:9; BaB:3]

| Tenor | Referent | No. |
|---|---|---|
| group of fallen angels | fall of angels through pride | Vgs4 |
| death | preservation of Christ's image on his burial shroud | Va14 |
| conception in the womb | Immaculate Conception | Fue |
| Christ or Christ's action | stigmata of St. Francis | Fue |
| Christ | link between Immaculate Conception, Incarnation and Redemption | Ov |
| Christ | stigmata of St. Francis | BaB |

**printing press:** unmixed expansions
  to apply the press [Fue:57]

**type** [Ti:1+4-5]

| Tenor | Referent | No. |
|---|---|---|
| strength of the sacramental character | sacraments of Baptism, Confirmation Holy Orders | Ti |

**typecase**
  caja [Bo7:13;10:1;15:31]

| Tenor | Referent | No. |
|---|---|---|
| Godhead | superiority of Christ's authority to that of scribes and Pharisees | Bo7 |
| Cross | redemption through Christ's death | Bo10 |
| Godhead | Incarnation | Bo15 |

A.1.ue. *Equipment for the production of the text: unmixed expansions*

The tools are inadequate to the subject. [Mon5:1-7; Pad2:1-10]
The writing materials are consumed. [SEE: A.1.2.1. pen:ue. to cut the pen; A.1.2.2. inkwell:ue. The inkwell runs dry; A.3.3.3. tablet:ue. a worn tablet]

A.2. PERSONS INVOLVED IN THE PRODUCTION, TRANSMISSION AND RECEPTION OF THE TEXT

A.2.1. PERSONS INVOLVED IN THE PRODUCTION OF THE TEXT

**binder**
  artifice [Bo1:11]

| Tenor | Referent | No. |
|---|---|---|
| Holy Spirit | link between Immaculate Conception and Incarnation | Bo1 |

**censor**
  fiscal [ManA1:40; Fue:5]
  oidor de Consejo [ManA1:31,36-37]

| Tenor | Referent | No. |
|---|---|---|
| patriarchs and prophets | Immaculate Conception | ManA1 |
| sinners who were Mary's ancestors | Immaculate Conception | ManA1 |
| Satan | Immaculate Conception; holiness of St. Francis | Fue |

## MOTIF INDEX

**chancellor**
    canciller [Ca32:3,8]
    chanciller supremo [Ca30:27]

| Tenor | Referent | No. |
|---|---|---|
| John the Baptist | John's baptism of Christ as inauguration of sacrament of Baptism | Ca32 |
| Baptism | sacrament of Baptism | Ca30 |

**guarantor of a contract** [ManA3:68-69,91-92]
    fiador [Av3:10; Led2:1,4; Bo10:2; Par1:11; Ca22:32]

| Tenor | Referent | No. |
|---|---|---|
| infant Christ | link between Christ's circumcision and Redemption | Av3 |
| Christ | redemption through Christ's death | ManA3 |
| Christ | redemption of Adam and his descendants through Christ | Led2 |
| crucified Christ | redemption through Christ's death | Bo10 |
| crucified Christ | redemption through Christ's death | Par1 |
| grace | Mary's exemption from original sin | Ca22 |

**printer**
    impresor [Ra:2; PrJ:5; Ag2:46]

| Tenor | Referent | No. |
|---|---|---|
| Holy Spirit | Incarnation | Ra |
| Trinity | Mary as co-Redemptrix | PrJ |
| God | Immaculate Conception | Ag2 |

**printer:** unmixed expansions
    a skillful printer [Ra:2; Ag2:46]

**printer's assistant** (i.e. *batidor*)[5] [Bo15:41-42]

| Tenor | Referent | No. |
|---|---|---|
| nature | Mary's conception in womb of St. Ann | Bo15 |

---

[5] The *batidor* "reparte la tinta, compuesta de aceite de linaza, trementina y humo de pez, en las formas ya listas" (Amezúa 348).

**witness to a contract**
    testigo [Cab5:3; Ca9:22]

| Tenor | Referent | No. |
|---|---|---|
| St. Stephen | St. Stephen's martyrdom as witness to truth of Gospel | Cab5 |
| Adam, David, Job | inevitability of death for every person | Ca9 |

**writer**
    author [VgC15:3]
        autor [Grn:43; Cam:73; Mu2:26; ManA2:214,221; Va4:13; VgC4:5; BaB:1,19; Ca21:2; Gue1:74; Ag1:3,9;2:9]

| Tenor | Referent | No. |
|---|---|---|
| God | natural world as manifestation of its Creator | Grn |
| God | natural world as manifestation of its Creator | Cam |
| God the Father | Christ as fulfillment of Scripture | Mu2 |
| God | glory due God because of Word's taking flesh of Virgin Mary as infinitely greater than that of famous writers of past | ManA2 |
| God | effects of God's presence in holy priest as manifest on his face even in death | VgC15 |
| God | heavens as manifestation of their Creator | Va4 |
| God | natural world as manifestation of its Creator | VgC4 |
| God | stigmata of St. Francis | BaB |
| God | world as God's creation | Ca21 |
| Mary Magdalene | sinner's responsibility for amendment of life in preparation for God's saving grace | Gue1 |
| God | mysteries of life of Christ, God and man | Ag1 |
| God | Mary as special creation of God | Ag2 |

**author:** unmixed expansions
    a wise author [Grn:43; Ag1:3]
    The text immortalizes its author. [ManA2:213-14,220-21; Jau:9-12,37-40,49-52]

**calligrapher**
    escribano [Mon5:3; Grn:77; Cab3:4]

# MOTIF INDEX 89

| Tenor | Referent | No. |
|---|---|---|
| sun | Mary's greatness and beauty | Mon5 |
| God | manifestation of God's providence in the various species | Grn |
| God | God's transformation of weak human beings into instruments of his power | Cab3 |

**calligrapher**: unmixed expansions
  a skillful calligrapher [SEE ALSO: A.1.2.1. pen:ue. the pen of a skillful scribe]
  [Grn:77-83; Cab3:1-4]

**chronicler**
  coronista [Ca8:70]

| Tenor | Referent | No. |
|---|---|---|
| fame | fame of King Solomon's wisdom | Ca8 |

**copyist / adaptor / translator**
  amanuense [Vi3:231,247]
  traslador / trasladador [Ven:144,188]

| Tenor | Referent | No. |
|---|---|---|
| God | natural world and human reason as imperfect manifestations of God | Ven |
| God | Incarnation | Vi3 |

**notary / clerk**
  escribano [Gon:3; Cai4:3; Led19:11; Bo8:11; Mu4:8]

| Tenor | Referent | No. |
|---|---|---|
| — | copious sweating of two Negresses participating in Corpus Christi procession | Gon |
| truth | zeal for a pious cause | Cai4 |
| time | gratitude for favors received and readiness to repay them | Led19 |
| biblical prophets | long history of human sin | Bo8 |
| God | stigmata of St. Francis | Mu4 |

**notary / clerk**: unmixed expansions
  the king as notary / clerk [Mu4:6-8]

**notary / clerk**: mixed expansions
  time as notary / clerk [Cai10:1; Led19:11; Ca36:30-31,70-75]

**secretary**
  secretario [Ca32:18]

| Tenor | Referent | No. |
|---|---|---|
| John the Baptist | John's baptism of Christ in witness to Christ as Redeemer | Ca32 |

**writer**
  escritor [ASF:5; Roc:4; Ca44:9; Gue1:8]

| Tenor | Referent | No. |
|---|---|---|
| God | Incarnation | ASF |
| Holy Spirit | desire for constancy in dedication to God's law | Roc |
| John the Baptist | John the Baptist as precursor of Christ | Ca44 |
| God | heavens as God's handiwork | Gue1 |

**writer:** unmixed expansions
  The writer is present in his / her writing. [Ven:182-83; Leo1:1-6; VgC15:3-5]

## A.2.2. PERSONS INVOLVED IN THE TRANSMISSION AND RECEPTION OF THE TEXT

**dictator**
  dictador [Cai20:8]

| Tenor | Referent | No. |
|---|---|---|
| God | Mary's outpouring of praise of God as divinely inspired | Cai20 |

**mail carrier**
  correo [Cai5:6;16:1]

| Tenor | Referent | No. |
|---|---|---|
| resolved will | promptness in doing good | Cai5 |
| good and holy thoughts | life of holy solitude | Cai16 |

**reader**
  lector [Ven:373; Led18:5; Va16:4; BaB:82; VgC24:31; Grc:35,46,49]

| Tenor | Referent | No. |
|---|---|---|
| each person | understanding the moral and metaphysical implications to be | Ven |

MOTIF INDEX 91

| Tenor | Referent | No. |
|---|---|---|
| | derived from the marvellous composition and functioning of one's body | |
| person desirous of imitating the saints in virtue | the putting out of St. Lucy's eyes in her martyrdom as example for Christians to relinquish all that deflects from love of God | Led18 |
| person contemplating Christ's Passion | Christ's being wounded on head and crowned with thorns | Va16 |
| person contemplating St. Francis' stigmata | stigmata of St. Francis | BaB |
| Prince Baltasar Carlos, son of Philip IV | Christ as model for the prince and future king | VgC24 |
| person who tries to understand another | difficulty of understanding human intentions | Grc |

**reader:** unmixed expansions
  a good reader [Grc:35,46]
  a poor reader [SEE ALSO: B.3.4.ue. to read poorly] [Grc:49]

**student**
  discípulo [Bo5:27]
  estudiante [Vi3:48; VgC5:15]
  la enseñada [Va4:11]
  oyente [Cab8:15]

| Tenor | Referent | No. |
|---|---|---|
| angels and saints | beatific vision | Vi3 |
| St. Isidore of Madrid | imitation of Christ | VgC5 |
| human beings | incarnate Christ as manifestion of God accessible to human beings | Cab8 |
| successive nights | heavens as manifestation of their Creator | Va4 |
| nature | Immaculate Conception | Bo5 |

**student:** unmixed expansions
  the outstanding student of a single book [Vi3:47-49; VgC5:15-16]

**teacher**
  ayo [Bo16:4]
  maestro [Ven:204; Vi3:48; Cab8:3; Led16:8; Bo7:1; Va4:9; Bo15:27;5:28;6:21]
  teólogo [Bo15:72]

| Tenor | Referent | No. |
|---|---|---|
| — | natural world as clear manifestation of God | Ven |
| God | beatific vision | Vi3 |
| God | God's becoming man so that we could know him | Cab8 |
| Christ | Christ as model of all virtues | Led16 |
| scribes and Pharisees | superiority of Christ's authority to that of scribes and Pharisees | Bo7 |
| God | natural world as source of knowledge of God | Bo16 |
| successive nights | heavens as manifestation of their Creator | Va4 |
| God | Mary's perfect holiness linked to her being mother of God | Bo15 |
| God | Mary's simultaneous virginity and divine maternity as unique act of God | Bo15 |
| grace | Immaculate Conception | Bo5 |
| God | original sin | Bo6 |

## A.3. THE TEXT ITSELF

### A.3.1. GENERIC TERMS FOR THE TEXT

**copy**
 copia [Gue10:6]

| Tenor | Referent | No. |
|---|---|---|
| Christ and St. Francis | stigmata of St. Francis | Gue10 |

**document / piece of writing**
 documento [Cai1:1; Gue12:4,8-9]
 escritura [Leo1:6; Snt2:6; ManA3:10-11; LoA:7,16; Jau:51]
 impreso [ManA1:26; Ca37:41]

| Tenor | Referent | No. |
|---|---|---|
| — | faithful following of St. Teresa's teachings by her spiritual daughters | Leo1 |
| learning | value of memory | Snt2 |
| Mary | Immaculate Conception | ManA1 |
| Old Law; eternal condemnation; recompense for sin | redemption and freedom through Christ's death | ManA3 |

| Tenor | Referent | No. |
|---|---|---|
| good words, thoughts and deeds | effects of Christian love in a soul | Cai1 |
| Moses' deeds | Moses as example of the Law he was to receive from God | LoA |
| merits of the saints | merits of saints as hidden through humility in this life | LoA |
| life of Christ | Eucharist as culmination of Christ's redemptive acts | Jau |
| crucified Christ | Redemption | Ca37 |
| deeds, specifically, practice of Christian detachment | exemplification of virtue in one's life as more convincing than preaching alone | Gue12 |

**document / piece of writing:** unmixed expansions

    a royal document [SEE ALSO: A.3.4.2.4. letters patent:ue. royal letters patent; A.3.16. copyright:ue. a royal copyright] [Led11:2]

    a blank document [SEE ALSO: A.3.2.1.ue. a blank book; A.3.4.2.6.2. petition:ue. a blank petition] [Va2:29-30; VgC9:3]

    a closed document [SEE: A.3.2.1.ue. a closed book; A.3.4.2.5. will:ue. a closed will; A.3.3.2. envelope / folded sheet]

    an open document [SEE: A.3.2.1.ue. an open book; A.3.4.2.5. will:ue. an open will]

    a signed and sealed document [SEE: A.3.4.2.3.1. promissory note:ue. a signed and sealed promissory note]

    an important document [SEE ALSO: A.3.4.2.6.3.ue. an important letter] [Snt2:6; Gue12:8-9]

**document / piece of writing:** mixed expansions
    a living document [LoA:7]

**work**
    obra [Vi3:163; Lem:4; ManA2:201; Bo9:3,21; Va4:23-24; BaB:20,45; Ca68:20]

| Tenor | Referent | No. |
|---|---|---|
| heavens | heavens as God's handiwork | Vi3 |
| a person's life | conversion of life | Lem |
| Mary's life | link between Mary's fullness of grace and Incarnation | ManA2 |
| John the Baptist | sanctification of John the Baptist in his mother's womb | Bo9 |
| heavens | heavens as manifestation of God | Va4 |
| St. Francis | life of St. Francis as imitation of that of crucified Christ | BaB |

| Tenor | Referent | No. |
|---|---|---|
| terrestrial creatures; acts of sin | sin's domination of the world | Ca68 |

**work:** unmixed expansions
   a polished work [SEE ALSO: A.3.1. work:ue. to polish a work] [Bo9:21]
   to polish a work [Ca68:20]


## A.3.2. TEXT FORMATS – GENERIC

### A.3.2.1. Book[6]

**book**
   cuaderno [Vgs5:1; Va7:6; Bo1:3; Ca18:17;37:6;2:13,14;8:32]

| Tenor | Referent | No. |
|---|---|---|
| code of the worldly | vices of worldly persons | Vgs5 |
| communion of saints in heaven | exclusion of unrepentant sinners from communion of saints | Va7 |
| the incarnate Word | Hypostatic Union and Incarnation | Bo1 |
| flowers | allurements of sin | Ca18 |
| tree trunk; unredeemed human nature | original sin as affecting whole human race | Ca37 |
| St. John the Evangelist | divine mysteries revealed to St. John the Evangelist in a vision | Ca2 |
| Christ | divine mysteries of Christ revealed to St. John the Evangelist | Ca2 |
| heavens; God's eternal Wisdom | Queen Saba's vision of Redemption through God's Word | Ca8 |

**libro / librito / librete**
   [Mon2:1,6,12;6:2;4:5;3:12;1:13; Ven:10,16,24,27,32,35,40,51,56,58,61,64,66,69-
   70,76,77,79,89,96,102,122,139,143,144,153,168,172,178,182,184,196,198,204,
   209,213,216,220,226,231,238,239,244,250,264,267,311,370,374,384; Cstj2:6;1:3;
   Vi3:1,3,4,5,8,15,18,22,25,27,32,35,37,40,44,49,51,52,54,59,63,65,76,78,81,

---

[6] Nepaulsingh throws light on the relationships between certain terms for "book" and their elaboration in various texts in this corpus. The basic unit of the medieval book was the quaternion, formed by folding a large sheet of paper or parchment twice to make a gathering of four folios. In order to meet the great demand for books brought about by the rise of universities, the official university stationer and scribes employed by him copied the original text and then divided the copy into *quaterni*. This separation of a book into parts and their circulation among students who each rented one quaternion at a time and copied it, added flexibility to the concept "book," as something that could be added to or subtracted from by a person collecting it in parts (203, 207).

## MOTIF INDEX 95

84,87,94,96,108,110,111,114,116,155,160,166,170,182,214,217,220,224, 231,235,240,260,276,277,279,281,300; 1:1;2:5-6,19; Av2: 2,3,5,6,8,10,11; Ter:7,9,20,29,30; Si:3; Lem:3; ADJ:2,9; To:1; Pin:2,6,9,12,17,18,19,22, 26,28,32,35,36,40,43,48,62,65,68,74,78,83,84,97,101,103,113,128,141; Grn:7,15,16,18,19,20,33,45,51,92,98,101,104; Pad1:4; Mat:4,14; Leo1:2,6; Vgs8:4;4:4; Cam:13,25,33,37,50,54,57,58,61,70,75; Os:1; Var: 1,7,9,12,17; VgC5:6,12,16,23,38; Sua:2,11,16,21,22,35,36,38,40,42,44,49,52,53,57,59,61; Led1:11; Cab6:3;8:5;10:3,6,9; Led12:5;22:7; Sal:1; Mu2:3,6,19,26,29; ManA1:2,6,19,23,28,33,51; 2:6,12,16,22,27,37,38,72,82,87,97,107,110,131, 134,143,147,149,155,181,192,195,202,206,209,211,213,215,218,222,226,238, 244,245,248,251,253,260,262,265,267,271,278,280,293,295,298,333,335,344, 351,352,353,358;3:54; Cai12:5; Led21:8;16:11; 19:6;20:1; Va13:4,5,14,19; 16:1;19:1; VgC8:4,6; Bo9:1,6,14,18,28;14:5; VgC13:4;17:1,10; Fue:3,6,11, 16,30,33,37,53; Bo13:3;12:1; Tel:5,12; Jau:4,13; Va4:3;6:2;7:3;8:4;9:2; VgC4:2; Va3:13,18,23,24,27;1:3; VgC8.1:5,7,13; Bo15:8,9,21,26,40,53,55,56,57,63;5: 37,39,41;6:17;1:1,10; BaB:4,29,35,62,70,75,87,89,93; VgC1:1; Hu:17; Ra:1,5; VgC10:2; Ca9:4,7;22:53;33:2;62:38,45,46,48;12:5; Grc:4,23; Ca67:3;2:5;54:10; Do:54,81; Ca8:11,64;43:5,15,65,72,92;41:24,27;26:8,11,56,66,67,98; GarE:8; Ca55:2,8,15,25,34,44,51,61;68:13,30;3:5;36:24; Gar:1; Ca57:6;44:13; Gue1: 1,12,16,20,28,32,36,41,44,50,52,56,63,66,69,80,83,96,101,103,113,115; PrJ:2; Gue5:4,8;3:4;15:1,2,6;16:2; Ag1:1;2:2,5,7,49,53,66,69,70,71,73; Ca24:6; 10:12; Gue12:2,6,12,15; Enc:3,8]

| Tenor | Referent | No. |
|---|---|---|
| soul of John the Baptist | John the Baptist's ascetic and contemplative life | Mon2 |
| mirrors | vanity of certain widows | Mon2 |
| Jesus and John the Baptist in the womb | communication between unborn Jesus and John on occasion of Mary's visit to Elizabeth | Mon2 |
| heart | contemplation of Christ's Passion | Mon6 |
| Mary | Virgin Birth | Mon4 |
| St. John the Evangelist | imitation of virtues of St. John | Mon3 |
| eternal life | eternal life won by early Christian martyrs | Mon1 |
| God's self-knowledge | God's eternal self-knowledge, in which he knows all things | Ven |
| the Word | God's self-knowledge in the Word as source of creation | Ven |
| rational soul | reason as a God-given source of knowledge of himself | Ven |
| God; created beings | distinction between direct and indirect knowledge of God | Ven |
| God | understanding of Godhead as not intended for the ordinary person or for this life | Ven |
| God | God's infinite self-knowledge | Ven |
| God | beatific vision | Ven |

| Tenor | Referent | No. |
|---|---|---|
| created beings | making good use of sources of knowledge of God intended for our use in this life | Ven |
| God; creatures | creatures as manifestation of God, though purposely incomplete and inferior | Ven |
| natural world | natural world as source of knowledge of God accessible to reason | Ven |
| human reason | human reason as manifestation of God superior to natural world but still needing to be supplemented by Scripture | Ven |
| natural world | natural world as very clear manifestation of God and more trustworthy than books written by human beings | Ven |
| natural world | natural world as manifestation to St. Anthony and to all who know how to interpret it correctly, of God's power, wisdom and goodness | Ven |
| heavens; natural world | heavens as manifestation of God as First Cause or Creator | Ven |
| natural world | natural world as God's self-communication intended for all people | Ven |
| natural world | natural world as based on matter | Ven |
| natural world | knowledge of God through natural world as needing to be supplemented by faith | Ven |
| one's body | harmony of one's body as source of metaphysical and moral understanding, and of one's place in society | Ven |
| flattery | danger of believing flattery | Cstj2 |
| memory | ingratitude and forgetfulness of service rendered on part of unjust and inhumane king | Cstj1 |
| God in his divinity, nature, Scripture, example and thought (later Christ), conscience | importance for the Christian of the various sources of spiritual understanding mentioned in Scripture | Vi3 |
| God's mind | God's foreknowledge of the elect | Vi3 |
| the Word | the Word, in whom all things live and have their being | Vi3 |

| Tenor | Referent | No. |
|---|---|---|
| the Word or divine Wisdom | infinite riches of God's Wisdom enoyed by the angels and saints | Vi3 |
| God's foreknowledge of the elect | predestination as an unchangeable gift of God | Vi3 |
| God | direct knowledge of God as granted to very few mortals in this life | Vi3 |
| natural world | natural world as indirect manifestation of God intended for all people | Vi3 |
| God | beatific vision or direct knowledge of God, destiny of the elect at end of time | Vi3 |
| heavens | end of the world | Vi3 |
| natural world | natural world as a worthy manifestation of God, though inferior to direct knowledge of him | Vi3 |
| natural world | paucity of writers who have taught us to understand the natural world as a manifestation of God | Vi3 |
| God | God's direct self-communication to angels | Vi3 |
| natural world | God's indirect self-communication to humankind through natural world | Vi3 |
| natural world | knowledge of God through natural world as needing to be supplemented by Scriptures | Vi3 |
| natural world | natural world as a theoretical source of knowledge of God | Vi3 |
| Christ | Christ as the clear epitome and practical model for humankind of all God's teachings, imitated by faithful Christians | Vi3 |
| Christ | Incarnation as God's self-communication | Vi3 |
| Mary | Incarnation | Vi3 |
| God's foreknowledge of the elect | Last Judgment | Vi3 |
| conscience | Last Judgment | Vi3 |
| God | Second Coming | Vi3 |
| Mary | Mary's virtue and modesty | Vi1 |
| Mary | Incarnation | Vi2 |
| conscience | Last Judgment | Av2 |
| God's foreknowledge of the elect | Last Judgment | Av2 |
| natural world (fields, water, flowers) | natural world as source of spiritual recollection for St. Teresa | Ter |
| converted life | St. Teresa's life as completely given over to God | Ter |

| Tenor | Referent | No. |
|---|---|---|
| God | St. Teresa's visions | Ter |
| humility | practice of humility as preparation for a holy death, and meditation on death as source of humility | Si |
| converted life | grace-inspired life of a converted sinner | Lem |
| God's mind | eternal existence of all creatures in God's mind | ADJ |
| Christ | Christ as one divine Person with both human and divine natures | To |
| God's knowledge or essence | God's foreknowledge of or graces to the elect | Pin |
| conscience | conscience of each of the elect | Pin |
| second Person of Trinity | divine Son as mirroring and conserving exemplary ideas emanating from Father | Pin |
| God's knowledge of the elect | God's knowledge of the elect as eternal and dependent on grace | Pin |
| newly created soul | newly created soul as devoid of all knowledge, potency without act | Pin |
| soul or understanding | understanding of wise persons | Pin |
| creatures | creatures as source of knowledge of God for many philosophers and saints | Grn |
| universe | universe as manifestation of Creator, intended for all people but whose deeper significance is too often missed | Grn |
| world | world and all creatures in it as created for service of humankind | Grn |
| Mary | Mary as epitome of the beauties of creation | Pad1 |
| crucified Christ | crucified Christ as source of all St. Bonaventure's wisdom | Mat |
| — | faithful following of St. Teresa's teachings by her spiritual daughters | Leo1 |
| God's foreknowledge of the elect | soul's ignorance of its final destiny | Vgs8 |
| eternal life | Fall of angels | Vgs4 |
| universe of creatures | order and harmony of natural universe as manifesting God's universal kingship, recognized by philosophers and saints | Cam |
| creatures and God together | creatures as emanating from, united to and manifesting God | Cam |
| divine essence | understanding of God in this life by means of created universe | Cam |
| Christ | Christ's Ascension | Os |

# MOTIF INDEX

| Tenor | Referent | No. |
|---|---|---|
| meditation | meditation as essential and readily available means to progress in the spiritual life | Var |
| divine mysteries | St. Isidore of Madrid's infused understanding of Christ and his mysteries | VgC5 |
| Christ | St. Isidore of Madrid's faithful following of Christ | VgC5 |
| natural world (fields, water, flowers) | natural world as source of spiritual understanding for St. Isidore of Madrid | VgC5 |
| natural world | natural world and its beauty as manifestation of God's greatness accessible to all and recognized by philosophers and saints | Sua |
| human being | human being as synthesis of natural world and manifestation of God | Sua |
| human being | contrast between the just and sinners and their destinies | Sua |
| Mary | link between Mary's perfection and Incarnation | Sua |
| Christ | Crucifixion | Led1 |
| — | person transformed by grace as incarnating principles of virtue | Cab6 |
| God's essence | beatific vision | Cab8 |
| divine mysteries | Christ's life as fulfillment and revelation of the Old Testament prophecies | Cab10 |
| Christ | St. John the Evangelist's vision at the Last Supper | Led12 |
| God's mind | God's eternal knowledge of all sins of humankind | Led22 |
| Christ | John the Baptist as precursor of Christ | Sal |
| Christ's life and person | mystery of Christ's life and person as synthesized in his name Jesus | Mu2 |
| Mary | link between Immaculate Conception and Incarnation | ManA1 |
| Mary | Mary's nativity, in which her role in Redemption was not yet apparent | ManA1 |
| Mary | Mary as God's instrument in conquering sin | ManA2 |
| Mary | Incarnation | ManA2 |
| Mary | Mary as more graced by God than all the other saints together | ManA2 |

| Tenor | Referent | No. |
|---|---|---|
| Mary | Mary's integral and unfailing virtue | ManA2 |
| Mary | Mary's perfect holiness and perpetual virginity | ManA2 |
| Mary | Mary's fullness of grace or sinlessness from first moment of conception | ManA2 |
| Mary | Mary's glorious Assumption | ManA2 |
| Mary | glory accruing to God in creating Mary mother of the Word | ManA2 |
| — | glory accruing to God through Incarnation as infinitely greater than that of any author of wordly fictions | ManA2 |
| Mary together with the incarnate Word in her womb | Mary together with the incarnate Word in her womb as equal to the Father | ManA2 |
| Mary | Mary as giver of life to Life or the Word | ManA2 |
| Mary's memory | Mary as help of Christians | ManA2 |
| human accountability for sin | redemption through Christ's death | ManA3 |
| eternal life | prayer as anticipation of eternal union with God | Cai12 |
| virtue | study and practice of virtue | Led21 |
| Christ | Christ as embodiment and model of all virtues | Led16 |
| memory of favors received | gratitude for favors received and readiness to repay them | Led19 |
| conscience | last particular judgment of each person | Led20 |
| Eucharist | Eucharist as mystery of faith | Va13 |
| Eucharist | Eucharist as Christ in both his humanity and divinity | Va13 |
| Eucharist | Eucharist as triune God, who is eternal life | Va13 |
| Christ | Christ's crowning with thorns | Va16 |
| Mary | Assumption of virgin Mary | Va19 |
| infant Christ | birth of Christ, God and man | VgC8 |
| infant Christ | infant Christ's hidden divinity, later mysteriously revealed in his Passion and death on Cross | VgC8 |
| John the Baptist | John the Baptist's singular holiness | Bo9 |
| John the Baptist | esteem in which John the Baptist was held for his holiness | Bo9 |
| John the Baptist | conversions effected by John the Baptist's preaching and example | Bo9 |

# MOTIF INDEX 101

| Tenor | Referent | No. |
|---|---|---|
| John the Baptist | sanctification of John the Baptist in his mother's womb | Bo9 |
| heart | conscience as guide and judge in observance of natural law | Bo14 |
| Christ | God's becoming man in Christ and dying unrecognized as God by those to whom he could not reveal himself because of their lack of faith | VgC13 |
| effects of original sin | principle of vengeance in contrast to forgiveness taught by Christ | VgC17 |
| Christ's face | Christ's meekness in his Passion, specifically, when struck by high priest's servant | VgC17 |
| Mary | Mary's Immaculate Conception and complete sinlessness | Fue |
| St. Francis | St. Francis' likeness to Christ, even to bearing his wounds | Fue |
| Christ | crucified Christ, who bestows his own wounds on St. Francis | Fue |
| person who does not mortify the flesh | importance of fasting for spiritual integrity | Bo13 |
| God | the wonder of the one and triune God | Bo12 |
| fear of God | experience as worthy teacher of fear of God | Tel |
| redeemed world | Christ's redemption of humankind | Jau |
| St. Peter the Apostle | institution of sacraments of Eucharist and Holy Orders | Jau |
| heavens | heavens as manifestation of God | Va4 |
| God | predestination of the elect and redemption by the Word | Va6 |
| sinners | eternal condemnation of unrepentant sinners | Va7 |
| converted life | conversion of the sinner | Va8 |
| God's mind | God's providence or foreknowledge of all creatures | Va9 |
| flowers with open petals | creatures as manifestation of God | VgC4 |
| worldly delights | pursuit of worldly illusions | Va3 |
| Christ | Christ as source of power to reject worldly illusions | Va3 |
| truth | incompatibility of worldly delights and truth | Va1 |
| Christ | Christ as source of all wisdom and as all that one needs to know | VgC8.1 |
| all human sources of wisdom | Christ as only source of true wisdom | VgC8.1 |

| Tenor | Referent | No. |
|---|---|---|
| Mary | Mary's unique holiness | Bo15 |
| Mary | Mary as recipient of God's special grace and as mother of God or the Word | Bo15 |
| Mary | Immaculate Conception | Bo15 |
| Mary | link between Mary's perfection and her divine motherhood | Bo15 |
| Mary | Mary's Immaculate Conception as embodying the new creation, redeemed humanity | Bo15 |
| human being | whole human race, except Mary, affected by original sin | Bo15 |
| Mary | Immaculate Conception | Bo15 |
| Mary | Mary as manifestation of divine Wisdom | Bo15 |
| Mary | Mary's perpetual virginity and simultaneous divine motherhood | Bo15 |
| Mary | Mary as help of Christians in conquering sin | Bo15 |
| Mary | Mary's embodiment of both the Old Law and, through Incarnation, of New Law | Bo5 |
| human race | original sin | Bo6 |
| Mary together with the incarnate Word | link between Immaculate Conception and Incarnation | Bo1 |
| St. Francis | stigmata as impression of Christ's own wounds | BaB |
| St. Francis | St. Francis' profound or boundless faith | BaB |
| St. Francis | stigmata as divine testimony to Francis' holiness or sanctity | BaB |
| St. Francis | Francis as replica of crucified Christ | BaB |
| Christ | Christ as infinite Wisdom | VgC1 |
| Holy Spirit | coming of Holy Spirit to Apostles at Pentecost | Hu |
| Mary | link between Immaculate Conception and Incarnation | Ra |
| infant Christ | Christ's nativity | VgC10 |
| end of human life | humankind as forgetful of its end rather than mindful of death as motivation for upright life | Ca9 |
| subjection to sin on part of human race | original sin and Immaculate Conception | Ca22 |
| divine Wisdom | God's foreknowledge of the elect | Ca33 |
| divine Word | Church as guardian and interpreter of the Word | Ca62 |

## MOTIF INDEX

| Tenor | Referent | No. |
|---|---|---|
| divine Word or Wisdom | God's foreknowledge of the elect | Ca62 |
| conscience | conscience as revealing divine election | Ca62 |
| sacred history | accessibility to all peoples of salvation through faith in Christ | Ca12 |
| universe | universe as manifestation of God, as understood by the truly wise | Grc |
| natural world | natural world as teaching a wisdom superior to all human teaching | Grc |
| God's eternal Idea, Word or Wisdom | God's foreknowledge of the whole history of sin and redemption | Ca67 |
| the divine Word | St. John the Evangelist's ecstatic vision of the mystery of the Word | Ca2 |
| St. Augustine's reasoning mind | St. Augustine's conversion, surrender to faith | Ca54 |
| natural world | St. Ignatius' response to God, whose perfections he recognizes in natural world | Do |
| heavens | heavens as God's handiwork | Do |
| Queen Saba; Gentiles | Queen Saba's or Gentiles' spiritual confusion or lack of wholeness before finding true wisdom in Christ | Ca8 |
| King Solomon | Solomon as symbol of God's power and wisdom | Ca8 |
| subjection to sin on part of human race | original sin | Ca43 |
| subjection to sin on part of human race | Christ's and Mary's freedom from original sin | Ca43 |
| salvation in the Word | salvation in and through faith in the Word as available to all people | Ca41 |
| the Word | divine foreknowledge of the saved and damned as including their free acceptance or rejection of faith in the Word | Ca41 |
| human life | unredeemed human life as subject to suffering and death | Ca26 |
| time or human history | future time as redeemed by Christ | Ca26 |
| time or human history | time or history from the perspective of grace | Ca26 |
| time or human history | time or history from the perspective of sin | Ca26 |
| time or human history | time under the dispensation of grace | Ca26 |

| Tenor | Referent | No. |
|---|---|---|
| St. Peter of Alcantara's preaching | spiritual power of St. Peter of Alcantara's eloquent preaching | GarE |
| Cross | beginnings of conversion to Christianity on the part of a Jew; emergence of New Law of Christ from Old Law | Ca55 |
| external laws | King Ferdinand as not needing external laws to guide him because his soul is informed by divine truth, in contrast to Jews, who need such external laws | Ca55 |
| God's Wisdom | King Ferdinand's longing to better understand mysteries of divine Providence | Ca55 |
| Cross | conversion of a Jew to Christianity through understanding of crucified Christ as fulfillment of Old Law; Spain's role in defense of Christianity | Ca55 |
| universe in both its temporal and spatial dimensions | God's foreknowledge of human history | Ca68 |
| waves of sea | sin's dominion over world | Ca68 |
| the divine Word | St. John the Evangelist's ecstatic vision of the mystery of the Word | Ca3 |
| Christ | revelation of mystery of Christ | Ca36 |
| natural world | natural world as manifestation of God's wisdom | Gar |
| remembrance of benefits received | importance of remembering God's benefits and so remaining grateful to him | Ca57 |
| Christ | Christ's self-revelation through his death | Ca44 |
| person who leads life of penance and mortification | world's rejection of, and God's delight in, person who leads life of penance and mortification | Gue1 |
| converted sinner | converted sinner's longing for God and everlasting union with God | Gue1 |
| people | people's lives as alternating between sin and repentance | Gue1 |
| Mary Magdalene: her entire personhood and her soul | Mary Magdalene's consideration of her past sinful life | Gue1 |

| Tenor | Referent | No. |
|---|---|---|
| Mary Magdalene | the repentant Mary Magdalene's earnest haste to seek Christ's forgiveness | Gue1 |
| Mary Magdalene | Mary Magdalene's life as having much to teach | Gue1 |
| Mary Magdalene | Mary Magdalene's beauty as occasion of her many sins and her disgust with same | Gue1 |
| Mary Magdalene | integrity of the whole person that Christ's coming was meant to effect | Gue1 |
| Mary Magdalene | Mary Magdalene's fear of not obtaining Christ's forgiveness because of her many sins | Gue1 |
| Mary Magdalene | harsh judgments of Mary Magdalene by those with Christ | Gue1 |
| Mary Magdalene | Christ's forgiveness and gracing of converted Mary Magdalene | Gue1 |
| Mary | Our Lady of Montserrat as protector from plague and sin | PrJ |
| Christ's wounds | Christ's Passion and death as glorious and joyous event | Gue5 |
| Mary Magdalene's unbound hair | Mary Magdalene's loving haste to seek Christ's forgiveness | Gue3 |
| human life | death as a transformation of human life | Gue15 |
| Cardinal Cisnero's death | Cardinal Cisnero's death as illuminated by his life | Gue15 |
| St. Teresa | St. Teresa's humility | Gue16 |
| Christ | mysteries of life of Christ | Ag1 |
| Mary | Mary as model of wisdom and virtue | Ag2 |
| Mary | Mary's unique holiness, including freedom from original sin, as part of God's eternal plan | Ag2 |
| Mary | foreknowledge of Mary's role in Redemption granted to certain patriarchs | Ag2 |
| Mary | Mary as a source of John the Evangelist's understanding of Christ | Ag2 |
| Mary | Marian mysteries | Ag2 |
| Aguilar and every Christian | participation in communion of saints in heaven through Mary's intercession | Ag2 |
| history of sin | judgment of sins of humankind | Ca24 |

| Tenor | Referent | No. |
|---|---|---|
| Christ | understanding of divine mysteries of Christ given through faith | Ca10 |
| natural world | nature as teaching *desengaño* | Gue12 |
| Christian detachment | actual practice of Christian detachment | Gue12 |
| Rodríguez Monforte | regret at thought of eventual loss to world of wisdom of Rodríguez Monforte | Gue12 |
| God | God as the only judge of each soul | Gue12 |
| Mary | Mary's perpetual virginity | Enc |
| name of Jesus | spiritual joy in devotion to Jesus | Enc |

registro [Mat:14; Ca53:15]

| Tenor | Referent | No. |
|---|---|---|
| crucified Christ | crucified Christ as source of all St. Bonaventure's wisdom | Mat |
| clerics' mindfulness of sinners in their charge | spiritual preparation for coming of Redeemer | Ca53 |

**tome**

cuerpo [Bo13:3; Jau:8; BaB:4; Hu:18; Do:76,94; Gue1:82]

| Tenor | Referent | No. |
|---|---|---|
| body of person who does not mortify the flesh | importance of fasting for spiritual integrity | Bo13 |
| people | spread of Christian faith | Jau |
| body of St. Francis | stigmata of St. Francis | BaB |
| Apostles | coming of Holy Spirit to Apostles at Pentecost | Hu |
| bones of the dead | meditation on death as motivation to conversion of life | Do |
| hermit's unkempt body | aged and wise hermit | Do |
| body | transmission of original sin to all people | Gue1 |

volumen[7] [Ven:211; Jau:30; BaB:29; Ca12:7;13:8; Do:22,68,72,94; Ca8:57; Ba:3; Ca26:16,60; Mrn:2; RodC:4; Ca68:7;46:10;61:17;11:6,15]

| Tenor | Referent | No. |
|---|---|---|
| creatures of natural world | natural world as manifestation of God | Ven |

---

[7] Some Golden Age texts may retain the association of the Latin *volumen* with the image of a scroll.

| Tenor | Referent | No. |
|---|---|---|
| — | Eucharist as inexhaustible source of truth, surpassing most learned human books | Jau |
| faith of St. Francis | immense and profound faith of St. Francis | BaB |
| sacred history | sacred history from beginning of human race to present of speaker | Ca12 |
| heavens; Mystical Body of Christ | rising of sun; Christ's resurrection | Ca13 |
| life of St. Ignatius | heroic life of St. Ignatius | Do |
| the adult Christ | Christ's perfect humanity and divinity, both present in the infant Christ | Do |
| grave | meditation on death as motivation to conversion of life | Do |
| hermit's body | aged and wise hermit | Do |
| night sky | astrological knowledge | Ca8 |
| heavens | end of the world | Ba |
| mortal life | human life as under the sway of death before redemption by Christ | Ca26 |
| time or human history | all time, including future time, as redeemed by Christ | Ca26 |
| heavens | power of St. Peter of Alcantara's intercession with God | Mrn |
| natural world | human being as synthesis of perfections of all creation | RodC |
| heavens | order of heavens as manifestation of God's wisdom | Ca68 |
| time | rapid passage of time | Ca46 |
| Scripture and Christ | Christ as the Word of God revealed in Scripture | Ca61 |
| heavens; Christ | sunrise; Redemption | Ca11 |
| knowledge of good and evil | sin's dominion over unredeemed world | Ca11 |

A.3.2.1.ue. *Book: Unmixed Expansions*

five books [Vi3:1]
a single book [SEE ALSO: A.2.2. student:ue. the outstanding student of a single book; B.3.2.ue. to have / need only one book] [Cam:54]
a common book [SEE ALSO: B.2.1.ue. to write a book for everyone; A.3.2.1.ue. The book is open to all.] [Ven:231,264,374; Vi3:96]
a little book [Vi3:116; Sua:38]

a large / vast book [Pin:141; Grn:15,33,92; Sua:2; ManA2:87-89; Bo16:7; Jau:30; BaB:29-30; RodC:4; Gue1:41,50-51;12:1-2]
a blue book [Mrn:2]
a golden book [Ca68:13]
the green book [SEE: A.3.4.1. genealogy]
a white book [BaB:56; Ca26:16]
a blank book [Pin:128]
a bound book [SEE ALSO: B.2.6. to bind] [Fue:52-53; Bo5:37; Ca13: 8; 68:7]
a book with broken binding [SEE ALSO: B.4.2.5. to (cause to) come unbound:ue. for a book to come unbound] [Led1:11-12; Fue:29-30; Bo13:3-4; Ca8:11-12; Gue3:4]
an illuminated book [SEE ALSO: B.2.2.ue. to illuminate a book] [Lem:3-4; Sua:11; BaB:75-76]
a printed book [SEE ALSO: B.2.4. to print] [Bo10:1;15:29; BaB:89]
a closed book [SEE ALSO: B.3.3.2.ue. to close a book] [Mon4:5-6; To:1; Cam:65; ManA1:6-7;2:106; Va13:5+7; 15:1-2;19:1; VgC8:6-7; Fue:55; Va1:3; VgC8.1:7; Grc:23-24; Ca2:5;3:5;36:24;44:12-13; Ag2:60]
an open book [SEE ALSO: A.3.2.1.ue. The book is open to all; B.3.3.1.ue. to open a book] [Ven:231-34; Os:1; VgC8:6-7;17:10-12; Fue:56; VgC4:2; BaB:5; Ca12:5-6; Grc:24; Ag2:61; Ca10:16]
a beautiful book [Vi3:117-19; Pad1:4-5; Sua:2; Fue:24; Do:68; Gue1:103-114,114-15; 3:4]
a complete book [ManA2:87; Ag2]
a new book [SEE ALSO: A.3.2.1.ue. to begin a new book; A.3.4.1. primer:ue. a new primer; B.2.1.1. to correct:ue. to be so emended as to seem a new book] [Ter:9; Jau:4; Bo15:40]
a more advanced book [Vi3:114]
a learned book [Ag2:5]
an inexhaustible book [Ven:61-62; Vi3:51-52]
a marvelous book / book of marvels [ADJ:9; Grn:33,51]
a rare book [Bo9:1;12:1;15:7-8; Ra:1; Ag2:5]
a true / trustworthy book [Ter:29-30; ManA2:226-27; VgC13:4]
a highly esteemed book [SEE ALSO: B.3.5.ue. to value a book highly] [ManA2:295; Bo9:6,18;15:39]
a famous book [SEE ALSO: B.3.5.ue. The text is well received.] [Sal:1]
a fruitful book [Var:9; Bo9:13-14;15:48]
a good / excellent book [SEE ALSO: A.3.2.1.ue. the best book; a great book][Ven:369-70; ManA2:211; Fue:37; Gue5:4]
the best book [Sua:57; Bo1:3; Grc:22-23; Ca67:3;57:5]
a great book [SEE ALSO: A.3.2.1.ue. a supreme book] [Grn:15,33,92; Sua:2; Bo10:1;15:21; Ca30:32; Gue1:41,50-51;15:6;12:1-2]
a perfect book [SEE ALSO: A.3.20.1.1. flaw:ue. without flaw] [Ag1:1]
a supreme book [Bo1:1; Ca33:2;61:17]
a crude book [Ca37:6; Do:94]
a false book [Sua:40-41; ManA2:222]

MOTIF INDEX 109

a forbidden book [Sua:42-43; Va7:3]
a scandalous book [Gue1:83,95-96]
the book as weapon [ManA2:6-22; Bo15:75-76]
to begin a new book [Lem:3-4; Va8:4]
to complete a book [Jau:51; Ca26:59-60]
The book is open to all. [SEE ALSO: A.3.2.1.ue. a common book; B.3.4.1.ue. The text is easy to understand.]
   [Ven:247-50; Ca41:24-25]
The book does not suffice by itself. [Ven:185-87; Vi3:181-82]


A.3.2.1.me. *Book: Mixed Expansions*

the book that flies to heaven [Va19:1-3; Gue1:3-4,12-14,19-20,36-39]
the book that was consumed [VgC5:6; Enc:8]
the book with seven seals [To:1+4; Sua:44-45; Va13:5-7; 15:1-2;3:23; Ca44:13; Ag2:68-69; Ca10:12]
God's book [Vi3:27,281; Bo15:21,29; BaB:75; Ca33:3-4]
the book of heaven [VgC8:4,6]
the book of the just [Vi3:71,224-25; Va7:4-5]
the book of justice [Os:1; Led16:11]
the book of life / glory [SEE ALSO: B.2.1.me. to write a name in the book of life / glory; B.4.2.2. to erase / blot out:me. to erase from the book of life / glory] [Vi3:3,8-9,15,18-19,25,27,32-33,35-36,40,94,277,300; Av2:3, 8-9; Pin:18,32,35,36,40,43-44,68,84,113; Cab8:5-6; ManA2:278,293-94,298-99; Cai12:6; Va13:19; Va7:6; Ca26:8]
the book of truth [SEE ALSO: A.3.2.1.ue. a true / trustworthy book] [Os:1-2; Sal:1-2]
a living book [SEE ALSO: A.3.4.1. New Testament:ue. a living New Testament] [Ter:20; Gue1:28;12:6]


A.3.2.2. *Notebook*

**notebook**
   cartapacio [ManA2:130,132,140,145,155,179]

| *Tenor* | *Referent* | *No.* |
| saints | Mary as superior to all the saints | ManA2 |


A.3.2.3. *[a] Paper*

**paper**
   papel [Vi3:285; Led7:3; Es:18; Par1:9; Ca9:30,39,51,57; 31:3,10;43:26;49:2]

| Tenor | Referent | No. |
|---|---|---|
| heart | revelation of secrets of conscience in Last Judgment | Vi3 |
| St. Ignatius of Loyola | intentions of St. Ignatius' heart as revealed on his face | Led7 |
| Christ's flesh | Christ's circumcision | Es |
| heavens; punishment due because of sin; Christ's flesh | rending of the heavens; redemption through Christ's death | Par1 |
| remembrance of death | remembrance of ineluctability of death as motive for upright life, but ignored or rejected by sinner | Ca9 |
| divine judgment | intimation of divine judgment experienced through conscience of sinner | Ca9 |
| Christ's promise of a hundredfold reward | almsgiving and its heavenly reward | Ca31 |
| Christ's deeds | redemptive acts of Christ's life and death | Ca43 |
| Eucharistic host | Eucharist as representation and reminder of Christ's Passion | Ca49 |

A.3.2.3.ue. *[a] Paper: Unmixed Expansions*

a torn paper [SEE: B.4.2.2. to tear up:ue. to tear up a document]

A.3.3. TEXT FORMATS – SPECIFIC

A.3.3.1. *Book*

**compendium** [BaB:74]
   compendio [BaB:5; RodC:1; Ag2:50]
   epítome [RodC:2]
   libro universal [Bo16:14; Gue1:21;13:1]
   suma [Ven:356; Or:3; Pad2:7; Led3:1; Mu4:16;Tel:14; Va3:10; VgC24:19; 23:12; Ca62:84]

| Tenor | Referent | No. |
|---|---|---|
| human being | human being as epitome of creation | Ven |
| Golden Rule | Golden Rule as epitome of natural law | Or |
| totality of creation | impossibility of explaining all the spritual riches in Jesus | Pad2 |
| group of martyred saints | St. Sebastian's inclusion among number of the saints | Led3 |

## MOTIF INDEX

| Tenor | Referent | No. |
|---|---|---|
| God | God as the One in whom all creatures have their being | Bo16 |
| stigmata of St. Francis | stigmata of St. Francis as reminder of and sharing in Christ's redemptive death, supreme act of compassionate love | Mu4 |
| long experience | necessity to supplement theory with practice in learning virtue | Tel |
| worldly delights as epitome of human desires | pursuit of worldly illusions | Va3 |
| St. Francis | stigmata of St. Francis as marks that epitomize Christ's redemptive acts | BaB |
| ranks of angels | St. Michael as leader of angels faithful to God and opposing Lucifer | VgC24 |
| long history of human violence | Same as tenor | VgC23 |
| waves of sea | subsiding of sea at death of Christ | Ca62 |
| human being | human being as synthesis of perfections of creation | RodC |
| world or mortal life | mortal life in itself as basically tragic | Gue1 |
| intellect | intellect as matrix of all branches of learning | Gue13 |
| Mary | Mary as epitome of all that is good | Ag2 |

**compendium:** unmixed expansions
    a compendium of the Law [Or:3; VgC23:11-12]

**compendium:** mixed expansions
    the human being as compendium of nature [Ven:356-57; Pad1:4-6; Es:8-9; RodC:1-4]

**scroll** [SEE ALSO: A.3.2.1. tome: *volumen*]
    [Vi3:107-11; LoA:15-16]
    libro arrollado [Ven:239-40]
    libro envuelto [Gue14:2]

| Tenor | Referent | No. |
|---|---|---|
| heavens | heavens as revelation of God | Ven |
| heavens | end of the world | Vi3 |
| merits of saints | merits of saints as hidden through humility | LoA |
| heavens | end of the world | Gue14 |

### A.3.3.2. [a] Paper

**sheet**
  carta [Av5:18,20; Do:4]
  pliego [Led10:13; ManA2:149]

| Tenor | Referent | No. |
|---|---|---|
| (soul of) Christians | Holy Spirit's inspiration of Christians to live the Gospel | Av5 |
| Mary | Incarnation | Led10 |
| period of life | Mary's fullness of grace or freedom from sin from beginning of her existence | ManA2 |
| — | fruitfulness of St. Ignatius of Loyola's life and teaching | Do |

**broadsheet / broadside** [SEE: A.3.18.2.ue. a loose leaf]

**half-sheet**
  medio pliego [Cab1:5]

| Tenor | Referent | No. |
|---|---|---|
| — | power of name of Jesus | Cab1 |

**envelope / folded sheet**
  pliego cerrado [Rod2:3-4]
  pliego [Re:6; Ca43:132]

| Tenor | Referent | No. |
|---|---|---|
| Christ as God and man | Mary Magdalene's kissing feet of Christ | Rod2 |
| God's mind | God's sure knowledge of all a person's sins | Re |
| mystery of Christ's identity | union of human and divine natures in Christ | Ca43 |

### A.3.3.3. Other

**coin**
  moneda [Led9:1,7]

| Tenor | Referent | No. |
|---|---|---|
| St. Ignatius of Loyola | St. Ignatius' total dedication to Christ | Led9 |

# MOTIF INDEX

**column**
columna [Gue6:8,12,15-16]

| Tenor | Referent | No. |
|---|---|---|
| St. John of Matha and St. Felix of Valois | sanctity of Sts. John of Matha and Felix of Valois as long unrecognized | Gue6 |

**jewel**[8]
anillo de memoria [Mu3:4-5,19-20]
joyel [Cab11:3,13,18]
sortija [Cab11:3,13,16]

| Tenor | Referent | No. |
|---|---|---|
| wounds on Christ's hands, feet, side | Christ's wounds glorified in Resurrection and borne by him on his Ascension as manifestation of his eternal love for humankind | Cab11 |
| hands, feet, side, heart | Christ's wounds as motivated by and manifestation of his eternal love for humankind | Mu3 |

**metal plate**
lámina [Va5:2; Ca9:79;64:10;40:8;31:31; Mrl:2; Ca8:27;45:35;17:18;50:5;38:5;4:6]

| Tenor | Referent | No. |
|---|---|---|
| heart | just person's faithful observance of God's law | Va5 |
| time | superseding of the Old Law by the New Law of grace | Ca9 |
| tree trunk; human nature | original sin | Ca64 |
| rock | God's giving Law to Moses | Ca40 |
| heavens | heavens as revealing human destinies | Ca31 |
| ice | martyrdom of St. Peter of Verona | Mrl |
| sky at time of Christ's death; Cross | Queen Saba's vision of redemption through God's Word | Ca8 |

---

[8] Carruthers observes that jewels were used in the Middle Ages not only in the covers of precious books but also as a motif of illumination: "jewels – often pearls, rubies, and other stones mentioned in the Bible – were commonly painted into the margins of Books of Hours at the end of the Middle Ages, an allusion to their nature as memorial shrines and *thesauri*" (41). Christ's wounds are explicitly associated in my corpus with the motif of illumination, as well as that of jewels.

114       TEXT AS TOPOS IN RELIGIOUS LITERATURE

| | | |
|---|---|---|
| earth | Christ's writing on ground "Let him who is without sin. . . ." | Ca45 |
| tree trunk; human nature | original sin | Ca17 |
| heart | natural law | Ca50 |
| breast (heart) | devotion to Mary | Ca38 |
| heavens | heavens, from which Christ descends | Ca4 |

**metal plate:** unmixed expansions
  a green metal plate [Ca8:27]

**tablet**
  tabla [Vi2:8; Av5:2; Pin:139; Roc:4; Cab9:7; ManA2:41,52; 3:56,136; LoA:5; Bo5:37; Do:25; Da:26; Ca1:4;26:71]

| Tenor | Referent | No. |
|---|---|---|
| Mary's womb | Incarnation | Vi2 |
| — | coming of Holy Spirit at Pentecost as promulgation of New Law, one that informs heart, in contrast to Mosaic Law | Av5 |
| human understanding | beginning learner as having nothing in his or her understanding | Pin |
| heart | desire for constancy in dedication to God's law | Roc |
| Christ's will | love of God and people that inspired Christ's life | Cab9 |
| Cross | Crucifixion | ManA2 |
| manger | Christ's nativity | ManA2 |
| Cross | redemption through Christ's death | ManA3 |
| — | Moses as embodying the Law he was to receive from God | LoA |
| Mary's embodiment of Old Law | Mary's embodiment of both the Old Law and the New Law | Bo5 |
| memory | immortal memory of St. Ignatius' deeds | Do |
| — | Christ's meekness when struck by high priest's servant, contrasted with law of talion | Da |
| Cross | inauguration of New Law of grace with Christ's death | Ca1 |
| humankind's history of sin | humankinds's history of sin against both natural law and Mosaic law | Ca26 |

**tablet:** unmixed expansions
  the tablets of the Law [Vi2:8; Av5:2; Roc:2-4; Cab9:7-8; LoA:1-5; Bo5:36-45; Da:25-26; Ca1:4-6;26:71-73]
  a blank tablet[Pin:139]
  a worn tablet [ManA2:52]

# MOTIF INDEX

**wall**
pared [Led15:1; Grc:13]

| Tenor | Referent | No. |
|---|---|---|
| memory | sinner's review of sinful life | Led15 |
| minds of the wise | importance of true self-knowledge | Grc |

## A.3.4. GENRES, FORMS OR TYPES OF TEXT

### A.3.4.1. *Books*

**New Testament**
Testamento Nuevo [Hu:4]

| Tenor | Referent | No. |
|---|---|---|
| Christ | Incarnation | Hu |

**New Testament:** mixed expansions
a living New Testament [Hu:4]

**wisdom book** [Vi3:153-55,116-18; Sua:58-60; ManA1:8-9;2:215-16; Gar:1-4]
libro de sabiduría [Bo15:2]

| Tenor | Referent | No. |
|---|---|---|
| the Word | the Word as inexhaustible divine Wisdom enjoyed by blessed in heaven | Vi3 |
| natural world | natural world as manifestation of God's wisdom | Vi3 |
| Mary | Incarnation | Sua |
| Mary | birth of Christ | ManA1 |
| Mary | Incarnation | ManA2 |
| Mary | Incarnation | Bo15 |
| natural world | natural world as manifestation of God's wisdom | Gar |

**chant book**
libro de canto [Par2:4]

| Tenor | Referent | No. |
|---|---|---|
| St. Stephen | St. Stephen's martyrdom by stoning and his prayer | Par2 |

**Holy Rule**
regla [Mon7:4]

| Tenor | Referent | No. |
|---|---|---|
| St. Francis | stigmata as Christ's confirmation of holiness of St. Francis | Mon7 |

**Mariology**
  marial [Bo15:4]

| Tenor | Referent | No. |
|---|---|---|
| Mary | Mary's special graces | Bo15 |

**saint's life** [SEE ALSO: A.3.4.1. autobiography]
  libro de santo [BaB:13]

| Tenor | Referent | No. |
|---|---|---|
| St. Francis | sanctity of St. Francis | BaB |

**book of theology** [SEE ALSO: A.3.4.1. book of moral theology / canon law] [Ven:110; Bo15:69-72]

| Tenor | Referent | No. |
|---|---|---|
| natural world | natural world as manifestation of God's wisdom, power and goodness | Ven |
| Mary | unique mystery of Mary's simultaneous divine maternity and virginity | Bo15 |

**book of moral theology / canon law** [Ca62:55]
  libro de la Ciencia [Ca62:63]]

| Tenor | Referent | No. |
|---|---|---|
| conscience | conscience as manifesting judgments of divine wisdom | Ca62 |
| God's Word or law of grace | Church as interpreter of the Word | Ca62 |

**penitential**
  libro de mortificación [Gue1:10]
  libro de penitencia [Gue1:48-49,117]

| Tenor | Referent | No. |
|---|---|---|
| person who leads life of mortification | the repugnance felt by the worldly for mortification | Gue1 |
| Mary Magdalene's life | Mary Magdalene's conversion of life as model for sinners | Gue1 |

**manual**
 guía [Bo7:3]
 manual [Vi3:225-26; Grc:47]

| Tenor | Referent | No. |
|---|---|---|
| Christ | Christ as model of spiritual life | Vi3 |
| Christ | Christ as teaching in his own person who God is | Bo7 |
| knowledge that is very present to awareness | constant need for discernment in interpreting human appearances | Grc |

**book of philosophy** [SEE ALSO: B.3.4.ue. Philosophers and wise men have read the book.] [Vi3:147-59; Grn:14-15,17-20]

| Tenor | Referent | No. |
|---|---|---|
| natural world | divine philosophy revealed by natural world as largely ignored by famous philosophers of past | Vi3 |
| natural world | natural world as manifestatiton of God's wisdom and power | Grn |

**law book** [Vgs5:1; Mu2:6-8; Bo14:1-2+5;5:36-40; Hu:17; Ca26:67-74]

| Tenor | Referent | No. |
|---|---|---|
| code of the worldly | vices of worldly persons | Vgs5 |
| Christ's life and person | Christ as fulfillment of Scripture | Mu2 |
| heart | conscience as guide amd judge in observance of natural law | Bo14 |
| Mary | Mary's embodiment of both the Old Law and the New Law; Mary's perfect observance of Old Law, and Incarnation | Bo5 |
| Holy Spirit | coming of Holy Spirit to Apostles at Pentecost | Hu |
| humankind's history of sin | humankind's history of sin against both natural law and Mosaic law | Ca26 |

**book of medicine**
 libro de medicina [PrJ:2-3]

| Tenor | Referent | No. |
|---|---|---|
| Mary (Our Lady of Montserrat) | Our Lady of Montserrat as protector from plague and from sin | PrJ |

**music book**
libro de solfa [Ca27:6-7]

| Tenor | Referent | No. |
|---|---|---|
| world | physical and metaphysical harmony of the universe | Ca27 |

**chronicle / annals**
anales [Ca14:7]
crónica [BaB:9; Ca8:35]
historia de corona [Car:14]
historia de los días [Do:71]
partidas [BaB:8]
registro de los años [Gue5:9]

| Tenor | Referent | No. |
|---|---|---|
| St. Francis | holy life of St. Francis | BaB |
| account of human history | immortal fame of St. Francis' sanctity | BaB |
| flower *corona de rey* | *corona de rey* reminder of Lope's writings on kings | Car |
| time | fame accruing to noble deeds | Ca14 |
| human life of an individual and in general | meditation on death as motivation to conversion of life | Do |
| heavens; God's eternal Wisdom | Queen Saba's vision of redemption through God's Word | Ca8 |
| Christ's wounds | Christ's Passion and death as glorious and joyous | Gue5 |

**book of heroic exploits** [Jau:2-4; Do:22]
libro de hazañas [VgC14:6-7]

| Tenor | Referent | No. |
|---|---|---|
| acts of Christ | Christ's love for each soul | VgC14 |
| Christ's redemptive acts | Christ's redemption of humankind | Jau |
| life of St. Ignatius | immortal fame of St. Ignatius | Do |

**genealogy** [ManA2:38-39]
libro de (la) generación [Cam:57; ManA2:67,267,300,333-34,341-42; Bo15:28]
libro verde [Co1:12; Ca30:20,32,44]

| Tenor | Referent | No. |
|---|---|---|
| God and his creation | unity of all being | Cam |
| Mary | Mary as mother of, giver of life to, the Word and Redeemer | ManA2 |

| Tenor | Referent | No. |
|---|---|---|
| Mary | Mary as giver of life to all Christians through her motherhood of the Savior | ManA2 |
| Mary | Mary as mother of Christ | Bo15 |
| Garden of Eden | free will bestowed on humankind at creation | Co1 |
| Mt. Sinai and Mosaic Law; Garden of Eden and natural law; Calvary and law of grace | discord fomented by perverse minds between natural law or free will, and law of grace; conflict alleged by Jewish leaders between Mosaic Law and Christ's teachings | Ca30 |
| Mt. Calvary, law of grace | acceptance of the New Law of grace, which subsumes natural law and fulfills Old Law | Ca30 |

**encyclopedia / miscellany**
varia lección [Ca37:17-18]

| Tenor | Referent | No. |
|---|---|---|
| moral lessons | moral lessons taught through good and bad examples in human history and learned by the prudent | Ca37 |

**emblem book** [Grc:4-5]
libro de cifras [Va13:10]

| Tenor | Referent | No. |
|---|---|---|
| Eucharist | Eucharist as sacrament and embodiment of divine love | Va13 |
| universe | creatures as manifestations or signs of divine perfections | Grc |

**art of memory**[9] [SEE ALSO: A.3.4.1. memorandum book]
arte de memoria [Ca57:5]

| Tenor | Referent | No. |
|---|---|---|
| remembrance of benefits received | importance of remembering God's benefits and so remaining grateful to him | Ca57 |

---

[9] According to Carruthers, after the twelfth century all treatises on the study of *memoria* are called *artes memorativae*, though the term was rarely used before that time (154).

**autobiography**
vida [Led18:1,8,11,14,18]
libro de la vida [Gue1:86]

| Tenor | Referent | No. |
|---|---|---|
| life of St. Lucy | St. Lucy's life, and particularly her martyrdom and blinding, as example for Christians to relinquish all that deflects from love of God | Led18 |
| life of Mary Magdalene | Mary Magdalene's self-surrender to Christ | Gue1 |

**novel of chivalry**
libro de caballería [Ca28:25-26]

| Tenor | Referent | No. |
|---|---|---|
| history of human struggle between good and evil | enticement of the senses by sin | Ca28 |

**primer** [Vi3:84-86,116; Sua:1-10; Ca55:51-54]
A.B.C. / abecé [Ven:258,324; VgC5:9; Bo16:4,7,12;2:3]
abecedario [Do:78]
cartilla [Pin:151-52; Led21:9;16:23; BaB:15; VgC24:26; Grc:64; Ca42:28]

| Tenor | Referent | No. |
|---|---|---|
| natural world | natural world as evident manifestation of God as Creator | Ven |
| natural world | creatures as manifestation of power, wisdom and goodness of Creator | Ven |
| natural world | natural world as a first, indirect, source of knowledge of God | Vi3 |
| natural world | natural world as indirect source of knowledge of God | Pin |
| — | St. Isidore of Madrid's imitation of Christ | VgC5 |
| natural world | natural world as source of knowledge of God | Sua |
| virtue | study and practice of virtue as foundation for Christian life | Led21 |
| God's will | union of Christ's human will with the divine will | Led16 |

MOTIF INDEX 121

| Tenor | Referent | No. |
|---|---|---|
| natural world | immense variety of natural word as a first source of knowledge of God | Bo16 |
| childhood | martyrdom of Sts. Justus and Pastor as children | Bo2 |
| St. Francis | St. Francis' imitation of Christ, even to his wounds | BaB |
| Christ as suffering Servant | Christ as model for Prince Baltasar Carlos | VgC24 |
| bones of the dead | meditation on death as motivation to conversion of life | Do |
| knowledge possessed by everyone | knowledge of certain kinds of discrepancy between human appearances and human reality as possessed by everyone | Grc |
| childhood | dedication to Christ of Sts. Justus and Pastor as children | Ca42 |
| Cross | conversion of a Jew to Christianity | Ca55 |

**primer:** unmixed expansions
   a new primer [Led21:9]

**census book** (of *pecheros*) [Ca22:51-53;43:5-8,11-12]
   cuaderno [Ca43:21]
   padrón de registros [Ca43:69]

| Tenor | Referent | No. |
|---|---|---|
| subjection to sin on part of human race | original sin and Immaculate Conception | Ca22 |
| subjection to sin on part of human race | original sin | Ca43 |
| subjection to sin on part of human race | Christ's and Mary's freedom from original sin | Ca43 |

**register** [SEE ALSO: A.3.4.1. census book; customs book]
   catálogo [Cai12:2; Va7:5]
   registro [ADJ:8; Ca39:12;28:39]

| Tenor | Referent | No. |
|---|---|---|
| God's mind | eternal existence of all creatures in God's mind | ADJ |
| eternal life | prayer as prelude to beatific vision | Cai12 |
| communion of saints | exclusion of unrepentant sinners from communion of saints | Va7 |
| Christ | hiddenness of Christ's divinity in Eucharist | Ca39 |

| Tenor | Referent | No. |
|---|---|---|
| sinners | Christ's and Mary's freedom from sin | Ca28 |

**register:** unmixed expansions
a sacred register [Va7:5; Ca39:12]

**roster** [Pin:70-71]
libro de ejércitos [Ca59:4-5]
matrícula [Pin:115]

| Tenor | Referent | No. |
|---|---|---|
| God's knowledge or providence | God's foreknowledge of the elect | Pin |
| ranks of Christians | Baptism as initiation of Christians | Ca59 |

**account book / ledger** [SEE ALSO: A.3.4.1. memorandum book]
[Av2:3-7; Led22:5-7; ManA2:344-46;3:54-56; Led19:6-7;20:1-2]
cuaderno [Ca22:33]
libro de caja [Bo10:1;15:29; BaB:5-6]
libro de cuentas [Vi3:279-80]
registro [Ca22:42]

| Tenor | Referent | No. |
|---|---|---|
| conscience | conscience as final judge of a person's life | Vi3 |
| conscience | Last Judgment | Av2 |
| God's knowledge | Last Judgment | Av2 |
| God's knowledge of all human acts | God's redemption of humankind from sin through Christ's death | Led22 |
| memory of favors received | gratitude for favors received and readiness to repay them | Led19 |
| Mary | Mary as mother of Redeemer | ManA2 |
| human accountability for sin | redemption through Christ's death | ManA3 |
| conscience | last judgment of the individual at death | Led20 |
| Cross | redemption through Christ's death | Bo10 |
| Mary | incarnation of Redeemer | Bo15 |
| St. Francis | St. Francis' life as participation in Christ's redemption of sinners | BaB |
| sins of humankind | punishment accruing to humankind for sin | Ca22 |
| sins of humankind | Christ's freedom from sin | Ca22 |

# MOTIF INDEX

**customs book**
registro [Led14:14]

| Tenor | Referent | No. |
|---|---|---|
| God's knowledge of even most secret thoughts | last judgment of the individual at death | Led14 |

**memorandum book**[10] [Ter:5-7; ManA2:358-59; Ca9:4-5;54:10;24:5-6]
libro de los días [Ca6:9-10;24:9-10,12-13]
libro de memoria [Cab11:6; Led14:18; Va13:1; BaB:51; Ca9:12,13-14;33:3; 62:48-52;54:3-4,6,13-14,20]
registro [Ca24:30]

| Tenor | Referent | No. |
|---|---|---|
| natural world | natural world as reminder of God | Ter |
| wounds on Christ's hands, feet and side | Christ's glorious wounds as reminder of his love for sinners | Cab11 |
| Mary's mind | Mary's intercession with God on behalf of sinners | ManA2 |
| God's mind | judgment of the soul at death | Led14 |
| Eucharist | Eucharist as commemoration of Christ's Passion | Va13 |
| St. Francis | stigmata of St. Francis as reminder of Christ's Passion | BaB |
| God's mind | divine judgment on sinners, manifested through conscience | Ca9 |
| conscience | remembrance of death and judgment | Ca9 |
| God's mind | God's foreknowledge of the eternal destiny of all people | Ca33 |
| God's mind | God's foreknowledge of the eternal destiny of all people | Ca62 |

---

[10] Terms such as *libro de los días*, *libro de memoria*, and *memorial* are sometimes ambivalent even in their literal signification in this corpus. Yamey helps clarify the mercantile context. The merchant or an assistant made an abridged entry in the journal (day book) or memorial book, with a reference to the page of the invoice book on which the transaction was written out at length (31). The *libro de los días* was also a diary; Albrecht Dürer's diary of his journey to the Netherlands in November 1520 is a combination of diary and account-book in narrative form (126). The very term "account-book" is, of course, ambivalent. The aptness of Cabrera's development of the image of the *libro de memoria* depends more on the concept as presented in the *Diccionario de autoridades*:

> El librito que se suele traher en la faltriquera, cuyas hojas están embetunadas y en blanco, y en él se incluye una pluma de metal, en cuya punta se inxiere un pedazo agudo de piedra lápiz, con la qual se annota en el librito todo aquello que no se quiere fiar a la fragilidad de la memoria: y se borra despues para que vuelvan a servir las hojas, que tambien se suelen hacer de marfil.

| Tenor | Referent | No. |
|---|---|---|
| God's mind | humanity's desire for divine forgiveness | Ca6 |
| St. Augustine's reasoning mind | St. Augustine's reasoning about mysteries of faith | Ca54 |
| St. Augustine's reasoning mind | St. Augustine's conversion, surrender to faith | Ca54 |
| history of sin | judgment on humankind for sin | Ca24 |
| God's mind | desire of sinners, represented by King David, for divine forgiveness | Ca24 |
| history of sin | meticulous recalling of sins of humankind | Ca24 |

**book of magic**
libro de nigromante [Va3:19-20]

| Tenor | Referent | No. |
|---|---|---|
| illusion of worldly delights | pursuit of worldly illusions | Va3 |

A.3.4.2. *Papers*

A.3.4.2.1. *Official Documentation – General*

**dispatch**
despacho [Vgs2:8; Ca32:3]

| Tenor | Referent | No. |
|---|---|---|
| St. Francis | stigmata of St. Francis | Vgs2 |
| the baptized and specifically, Christ | John's baptism of Christ as inauguration of sacrament of Baptism | Ca32 |

A.3.4.2.2. *Ecclesiastical*

**episcopal letter**
carta [Av5:18,20; Mu1:17]
epístola [Av5:19]

| Tenor | Referent | No. |
|---|---|---|
| (soul of) Christians | Holy Spirit's inspiration of Christians to live the Gospel | Av5 |

# MOTIF INDEX

| Tenor | Referent | No. |
|---|---|---|
| Gospel as lived by Christians | Christians transformed by grace as manifestations of God to the world | Mu1 |

**papal brief**
  buleto [Vgs2:7]

| Tenor | Referent | No. |
|---|---|---|
| St. Francis | stigmata of St. Francis | Vgs2 |

**papal bull of canonization**
  bula [de canonización] [GarE:3]

| Tenor | Referent | No. |
|---|---|---|
| miracle | St. Peter of Alcantara's walking on water | GarE |

A.3.4.2.3. *Financial*

A.3.4.2.3.1. *pertaining to debts*

**document of closing of an account**
  finiquito [Ca36:92]

| Tenor | Referent | No. |
|---|---|---|
| redemption of humankind | redemption through Christ's death | Ca36 |

**receipt given to one who has paid on behalf of another** (= *carta de pago y lasto*)
  escritura [Led11:1-2,15]

| Tenor | Referent | No. |
|---|---|---|
| crucified Christ | redemption through Christ's death, of which St. Francis' stigmata are reminder | Led11 |

**receipt of discharge of a debt**
  carta de pago [Ca36:92-93]
  escritura [VgC21:1; Par1:10]
  recados [Vgs2:13; ManA3:141-42]

| Tenor | Referent | No. |
|---|---|---|
| stigmata of St. Francis | stigmata of St. Francis as sign of God's mercy to sinners | Vgs2 |

| Tenor | Referent | No. |
|---|---|---|
| Christ's death on Cross | redemption through Christ's death | ManA3 |
| redemption of humankind | redemption through Christ's death | VgC21 |
| redemption of humankind | redemption through Christ's death | Par1 |
| redemption of humankind | redemption through Christ's death | Ca36 |

**memorandum**
memorial [Led11:18; Ca9:29,43]

| Tenor | Referent | No. |
|---|---|---|
| St. Francis of Assisi | stigmata of St. Francis as reminder of redemption through Christ's death | Led11 |
| remembrance of death | ineluctability of death | Ca9 |
| remembrance of death | sinner's forgetfulness of death | Ca9 |

**promissory note** (= *escritura de obligación*)
escrito [Cai8:1-2]
escritura [Av3:16; Led19:10;2:3; Es:15,17; Va2:1,9,22,29; Per:27; Ca9:21; 31:65,69;36:49,65,72,84,101]
escritura de obligación [ManA3:132]
obligación [Av3:11; Led19:7; Bo8:1,6,13; Ca9:11]

| Tenor | Referent | No. |
|---|---|---|
| Christ's promise of redemption | Christ's circumcision as promise of redemption | Av3 |
| subjection to punishment for sin | redemption through Christ's death | Av3 |
| Christ's death on Cross | redemption through Christ's death | ManA3 |
| grace | grace as assurance of God's gift of eternal glory | Cai8 |
| memory of favors received | gratitude for favors received and acknowledgment of obligation to repay them | Led19 |
| debt of sin owed by humankind | redemption through Christ's death | Led2 |
| Christ's promise of redemption | Christ's circumcision as promise of redemption; his death as fulfillment of that promise | Bo8 |
| subjection to punishment for sin | redemption through Christ's death | Bo8 |
| infant Christ | Jesus' naming and circumcision as promise of redemption | Es |
| soul as subject to punishment for sin | redemption through Christ's death, mediated through Church | Va2 |
| subjection to punishment for sin | condemnation accruing to sinner and redemption by Christ | Per |

| Tenor | Referent | No. |
|---|---|---|
| subjection to death | remembrance of ineluctability of death | Ca9 |
| subjection to death | acknowledgment of ineluctability of death | Ca9 |
| subjection to death and punishment for sin, as contained in Sacred Scripture | condemnation to death and punishment on part of whole human race because of original sin | Ca31 |
| subjection to death and accountability for one's acts | acknowledgment of ineluctability of death and of one's responsibility towards God | Ca36 |
| subjection to death and accountability for one's acts | promise of redemption through Christ's death | Ca36 |
| Sacred Scripture | Sacred Scripture as history of sins of humankind and promise of redemption through Christ's death | Ca36 |

**promissory note:** unmixed expansions
   a signed and sealed promissory note [Cai8:1-2; Es:4-20]


A.3.4.2.3.2. *other*

**bill of exchange** [Ca31:10-12]
   letra (de cambio) [Led1:18-19; Brv:5; Led10:15;8:1; 19:2-3;5:4; Va12:5; Ca31:25]

| Tenor | Referent | No. |
|---|---|---|
| debt of sin owed by humankind | Christ's paying debt of sin in humankind's stead through his death on Cross | Led1 |
| intentions of heart | God's knowledge of thoughts and desires of the heart | Brv |
| incarnate Word | Incarnation as beginning of Redemption | Led10 |
| Society of Jesus | official papal confirmation of Society of Jesus | Led8 |
| memory of favors received | gratitude for favors received | Led19 |
| money | money as motive for Judas' betrayal of Christ | Led5 |
| name of Jesus | name of Jesus given at his circumcision as signifying salvation or redemption for those who believe in him | Va12 |

| Tenor | Referent | No. |
|---|---|---|
| Christ's promise of a hundredfold reward | almsgiving and its heavenly reward, interpreted literally by the worldly minded | Ca31 |

**carte blanche**
firma en blanco [Cab1:4,10-11,13; Va12:9]

| Tenor | Referent | No. |
|---|---|---|
| name of Jesus | power of name of Jesus | Cab1 |
| name of Jesus | salvation through faith in Jesus | Va12 |

A.3.4.2.4. *Governmental*

**census list**
padrón [Ca43:2,11]

| Tenor | Referent | No. |
|---|---|---|
| human race | human race in bondage to sin as result of Fall | Ca43 |
| human race in bondage to sin | Christ's freedom from sin | Ca43 |

**letter**
carta [VgC22:9]

| Tenor | Referent | No. |
|---|---|---|
| certain Franciscan martyrs | torture of certain Franciscan martyrs in Japan as ironically confirming their witness to Christ | VgC22 |

**letter of credential**
carta de crédito [Vaz:2]

| Tenor | Referent | No. |
|---|---|---|
| God's testifying to Christ's divine sonship | God's testifying to Christ's divine sonship at his baptism by John | Vaz |

**letters patent**
cédula [Cab1:8; Que1:4]

# MOTIF INDEX

| Tenor | Referent | No. |
|---|---|---|
| name of Jesus | power of name of Jesus | Cab1 |
| constancy in fortune | downfall of Alvaro de Luna | Que1 |

**letters patent:** unmixed expansions
   royal letters patent [Cab1:8-9]

**peace treaty**
   concordia [Ri4:4]

| Tenor | Referent | No. |
|---|---|---|
| peace between God and human race | peace between God and human race won through Christ's death | Ri4 |

## A.3.4.2.5. Legal

**certificate of ransom** [Led10:2-4; Va15:9]
   ejecutoria de rescate [ManA3:124]

| Tenor | Referent | No. |
|---|---|---|
| Mary | Incarnation of Redeemer | Led10 |
| redemption | redemption through Christ's death on Cross | ManA3 |
| Christ | presence of Redeemer in Mary's womb perceived by John the Baptist in his mother's womb | Va15 |

**contract** [SEE ALSO: A.3.4.2.3.1. promissory note]
   contrato [Ca41:16;69:16]

| Tenor | Referent | No. |
|---|---|---|
| God's covenant with Israel | justice of God's establishing New Covenant with Church because of Israel's lack of faith | Ca41 |
| God's covenant with Israel | Israel's bad faith | Ca69 |

**judicial report**
   memorial ajustado [Ca26:25,31]
   proceso [Led6:6; Ca32:16]

| Tenor | Referent | No. |
|---|---|---|
| last particular judgment | judgment of soul as saved or condemned | Led6 |
| guilt of original sin | Baptism as conteracting original sin | Ca32 |

| Tenor | Referent | No. |
|---|---|---|
| history of human race as sinful | condemnation deserved by humankind because of sin | Ca26 |

**letter of manumission**
    acto de libertad [ManA3:122]
    carta de horro [Led1:3]

| Tenor | Referent | No. |
|---|---|---|
| redemption | redemption through Christ's death on Cross | Led1 |
| redemption | redemption through Christ's death on Cross | ManA3 |

**will**
    testamento [VgC5:31; Ca69:8]

| Tenor | Referent | No. |
|---|---|---|
| effects of original sin | human life, specifically life of St. Isidore of Madrid, as one of unceasing toil and suffering as result of original sin | VgC5 |
| New Covenant established by God | Israel's being given first opportunity to accept Christ and New Covenant | Ca69 |

**will: unmixed expansions**
    a closed will [VgC5:31-32]
    an open will [VgC5:31+33]


A.3.4.2.6. *Personal*

A.3.4.2.6.1. *documentation – generic*

**documentation**
    información [Ca43:151]
    prueba [Cai10:1; Ca43:131,141]
    testimonio [Ca45:8,9,17,19]

| Tenor | Referent | No. |
|---|---|---|
| long-suffering | nature and effects of virtue of long-suffering | Cai10 |
| evidence of Christ's person and life | Christ's person and life as testifying to his being the Messiah but rejected as such by the Jews | Ca45 |

MOTIF INDEX                          131

| Tenor | Referent | No. |
|---|---|---|
| Christ's divinity and humanity | union of human and divine natures in Christ, to which Old Testament bears testimony | Ca43 |
| Christ's divinity and humanity | Israel's rejection of Christ | Ca43 |
| evidence of Christ's lineage or identity | Christ's fulfillment of Old Law and inauguration of New Law | Ca43 |

A.3.4.2.6.2. *documentation – specific*

**baptismal certificate**
    fe de bautismo [Ca43:152]

| Tenor | Referent | No. |
|---|---|---|
| Christ's baptism | John's baptism of Christ as inauguration of sacrament of Baptism and occasion of God's witnessing to Christ's divine sonship | Ca43 |

**certificate of having received the Eucharist**
    cédula de Comunión [Ca43:155]

| Tenor | Referent | No. |
|---|---|---|
| institution of Eucharist | Christ's institution of, and sharing with disciples in, sacrament of Eucharist at Last Supper | Ca43 |

**certificate of military service** [SEE: A.3.4.2.6.2.petition]

**certificate of purity of blood**
    acto de limpieza [Ca43:57-58]

| Tenor | Referent | No. |
|---|---|---|
| Christ as son of Mary in his human nature | Christ's nobility and holiness as son of Mary, who was immaculately conceived and descended from David's line | Ca43 |

**letters patent of nobility** [Ov:2+4]
    acto de nobleza [Ca43:57-58]
    carta ejecutoria [Cai18]
    cédula [VgC7:3]
    ejecutoria [Led11:8; Cai15:2; BaB:39; GarE:8]

origen [Ca43:47]
título [Snt2:6-7; VgC7:2; Ca49:46,53; GarE:10]

| Tenor | Referent | No. |
|---|---|---|
| noble acts | memory as preserving noble acts of humankind | Snt2 |
| divine sonship and daughtership of human race | loss of divine sonship and daughtership of human race through original sin and its recovery through Christ's death | Led11 |
| eternal life | eternal life as inheritance of true sons and daughters of God, those who are obedient to him | Cai15 |
| moral and spiritual victory | moral and spiritual victory as both proof and reward of virtue | Cai18 |
| justice of homage due Mary and infant Christ | affirmation in faith of new-born Christ as God and Mary as mother of God | VgC7 |
| Mary | affirmation in faith of newborn Christ as God and Mary as mother of God | VgC7 |
| divine sonship and daughtership of Christians | divine sonship and daughtership of Christians in Christ through Incarnation and Redemption | Ov |
| stigmata of St. Francis | stigmata of St. Francis as proof of God's favor and as honor for his Order | BaB |
| Christ's Sonship | Christ's divine Sonship as second Person of Trinity | Ca43 |
| Christ's noble descent | Christ's noble descent, in his human nature, from King David's line | Ca43 |
| Christ's divine kingship | crucified Christ as divine King | Ca49 |
| sublimity and immortal fame of St. Peter of Alcantara's preaching | spiritual power of St. Peter of Alcantara's eloquent preaching | GarE |

**passport**
pasaporte [Ca45:3]

| Tenor | Referent | No. |
|---|---|---|
| authentication | authentication of Christ's being Messiah | Ca45 |

**petition**
fe de oficio [Ca43:27]
memorial [Led11:18; Ca39:5;23:14,17,19,21,25,26,35,49,55;42:2,7,16,19,34;
  43:29,44,49,54,59,95,103,117,118,124,133;49:3,6,8,13,17,19,24,26,34,38,
  44,61]
petición [Cai4:6]

| Tenor | Referent | No. |
| --- | --- | --- |
| St. Francis | stigmata of St. Francis as reminder of redemption through Christ's death | Led11 |
| prayers | zeal for a pious cause | Cai4 |
| Christ | Eucharist as commemoration of Christ's Passion and proof of his love | Ca39 |
| justification presented by various religions or virtues for supremacy over the others | Eucharist as sacrament of God's substantial presence under lowly forms of bread and wine, example of his exaltation of the humble | Ca23 |
| cases of various figures from Old and New Testaments, and of other saints, who appeal to divine love | response of divine love to suffering of various sinners and holy persons | Ca42 |
| acts of Christ's life | acts of Christ's life as manifestations of his divine mission and identity | Ca43 |
| evidence of Christ's divine and human lineage | human and divine natures in Christ | Ca43 |
| evidence of Christ's divinity and of his nobility as man | Christ as Son of God and son of Mary, descendant of King David | Ca43 |
| evidence of Christ's lowly human origin | Christ as son of Adam and of Joseph the carpenter | Ca43 |
| evidence of Christ's divine and human lineage | apparently conflicting evidence as to whether Christ was human or divine | Ca43 |
| Eucharistic host | Eucharist as commemoration of Christ's Passion | Ca49 |
| Eucharistic host | Eucharist as mystery of faith | Ca49 |
| Eucharist | Eucharist as commemoration of Christ's Passion and glorification | Ca49 |

**petition:** unmixed expansions
a blank petition [Ca49:8-9,19-20]


A.3.4.2.6.3. *letters*

**letter**
carta [Ven:86; AD:5; Cab7:5; ManA2:316,320,329; Cai5:7;14:1; 16:2;17:1]

| Tenor | Referent | No. |
|---|---|---|
| mystery of God in his divinity | creatures as legitimate source of study in order to know God in this world | Ven |
| Mary's suffering in Christ's Passion | original sin as cause of Christ's Passion and death | AD |
| natural world | God's creation of natural world as inferior to work of redemption | Cab7 |
| one of King David's prayers or psalms | King David's mode of addressing awe-inspiring God of Old Testament | ManA2 |
| good intentions | prompt execution of good | Cai5 |
| virtuous soul | perseverance in virtue | Cai14 |
| holy inspirations and desires | prayer in solitude | Cai16 |
| serenity of spirit | serenity as God's gift to soul detached from world | Cai17 |

**letter of recommendation**
carta de favor [Cai2:5-6;13; Ca60:4]

| Tenor | Referent | No. |
|---|---|---|
| beautiful appearance | beautiful and virtuous appearance of the good as gift of nature that favorably disposes others | Cai2 |
| prayer | power of prayer in obtaining God's mercy for others | Cai13 |
| person's natural gifts | Joseph's beautiful and virtuous appearance as having won sympathy of Pharaoh's cup-bearer | Ca60 |


A.3.4.2.6.3.ue. *letters: unmixed expansions*

an important letter [Cai5:7]

### A.3.4.2.7. *Pertaining to Arts and Letters*

**map** [SEE ALSO: A.3.4.2.7. navigational map]
  mapa [VgC2:6]

| Tenor | Referent | No. |
|---|---|---|
| incarnate Word | Christ as human and divine | VgC2 |

**navigational map**
  carta de marear [Ven:240-41]

| Tenor | Referent | No. |
|---|---|---|
| heavens | heavens as revelation of God | Ven |

**sheet of music** [Va11:4-5]

| Tenor | Referent | No. |
|---|---|---|
| Eucharist | desire to praise God for mystery of Eucharist | Va11 |

### A.3.4.2.8. *Publicity*

**poster**
  cartel [Ca25:2;5:3]

| Tenor | Referent | No. |
|---|---|---|
| wind | consideration of grace as remedy for sin | Ca25 |
| announcement | announcement of a contest | Ca5 |

### A.3.4.3. *Other*

**memorial**
  padrón [Ca64:18;20:17;31:39;7:6;37:4,29,41; Da:2; Ca28:32]

| Tenor | Referent | No. |
|---|---|---|
| sin | original sin as manifest in sins of whole human race | Ca64 Ca20 |
| starry sky | stars as manifesting human fortune for good or ill | Ca31 |
| human nature as affected by original sin | condemnation of human race because of original sin, and redemption through Christ's death on Cross | Ca7 Ca37 |

| Tenor | Referent | No. |
|---|---|---|
| permanent mark from blow to Christ's cheek | blow given Christ by high priest's servant | Da |
| fallen human nature | entire human race as affected by original sin | Ca28 |

## A.3.5. CONTENT OF THE TEXT – GENERIC TERMS

**context**
  contexto [Hu:7]

| Tenor | Referent | No. |
|---|---|---|
| darkened sky | darkening of sky at Christ's death and conversion of St. Dionysius (seems to be fused with centurion of Luke 23:47, Mt. 27:54) | Hu |

**text / contents** [SEE ALSO: A.3.14. inside]
  [ManA2:247,254,294]
  escrito [BaB:36]
  lo escrito [Vi3:289; Bo6:15; Gue12:10]
  escritura [Ven:213; Av8:1; ManA2:249,250]
  lectura [Vi3:257; Bo15:60]
  letra [Mu4:23; Do:49,77; Ca42:29;17:26; Gue6:21]
  texto [Ca26:52]

| Tenor | Referent | No. |
|---|---|---|
| natural world | natural world as God's creation a more perfect manifestation of truth than books written by people | Ven |
| incarnate Word | incarnate Word as manifestation of God for all people | Vi3 |
| secrets of conscience | revelation of secrets of the individual conscience at Last Judgment | Vi3 |
| predestination | predestination as God's loving foreknowledge of, and gift of glory to, the elect | Av8 |
| incarnate Word | Mary together with the incarnate Word in her womb as equal to the Father | ManA2 |
| incarnate Word | Mary as giver of life to Life | ManA2 |
| stigmata of St. Francis | stigmata of St. Francis, identical to Christ's wounds, | Mu4 |

| Tenor | Referent | No. |
|---|---|---|
| | as sign of New Law of grace and redemption | |
| incarnate Word | Mary as mother of the Word | Bo15 |
| incarnate Word | link between Immaculate Conception and Incarnation | Bo6 |
| St. Francis | extraordinary holiness of St. Francis | BaB |
| natural world | manifestation of God in natural world as moving St. Ignatius spiritually | Do |
| lesson taught by bones of the dead | meditation on death as motivation to conversion of life | Do |
| Christ | dedication to Christ of Sts. Justus and Pastor as children | Ca42 |
| original sin | original sin as manifested in sins of whole human race | Ca17 |
| Christ | redemption through Christ | Ca26 |
| significance of acts | lack of recognition of sanctity of Sts. John of Matha and Felix of Valois | Gue6 |
| deeds | actual practice of Christian detachment | Gue12 |

**text / contents:** unmixed expansions
   a counter text [SEE ALSO: A.3.19.5.1. code breaker] [Va3:27-30; Par1:10; Ca56:9-10;37:41]
   The text is both clear and unclear. [Hu:7-9; Da:50-52]
   The text is illegible. [SEE ALSO: A.1.2.2. ink:ue. Letters written in invisible ink appear when held before the fire / to the light; A.3.7.1. word:ue. A formerly unreadable word becomes readable.]
   [Ca43:76-84; Gue6:14,20-21]


## A.3.6. CONTENT OF THE TEXT – ABSTRACT TERMS

**accuracies**
   aciertos [Ca65:20; Ag2:48]

| Tenor | Referent | No. |
|---|---|---|
| virtues | love and virtue of the sinner who has been forgiven | Ca65 |
| grace | Mary's fullness of grace at conception | Ag2 |

**doctrine**
doctrina [Cab8:10,14; Mu1:16,17; Jau:8; Bo15:47,71]
teórica [Led16:4]

| Tenor | Referent | No. |
|---|---|---|
| mysteries of the Godhead | communication of mysteries of Godhead directly, in beatific vision, and on earth, in Christ | Cab8 |
| Gospel | Christians transformed by grace as manifestations of God to the world | Mu1 |
| long-suffering and forgiveness of injuries | imitation of virtues Christ taught by his life | Led16 |
| Christ's teachings | transmission of Christ's teachings | Jau |
| lessons of Mary's virtuous life | Mary's fullness of virtue; power of what she taught more by deed than words | Bo15 |
| the Word | Incarnation | Bo15 |

**doctrine:** unmixed expansions
lofty doctrine [Cab8:10; Led16:4]

**idea**
concepto [Vi3:242; Pin:171,173-74; Sua:51,54,65; Rod1:1,7; Bo9:33,35; VgC15:4; Bo15:32;5:19,43;6:5;1:2,10; Ra:3,4; Go2:5,8,14; Ca67:2; So:6; Ca44:25; Ag2:28]
razón [Cab7:9; ManA2:296]

| Tenor | Referent | No. |
|---|---|---|
| the Word | Incarnation | Vi3 |
| understanding of the deeper significance | understanding through reason divine significance of creatures and world | Pin |
| intentions | sinner as hypocrite, appearing good but with wicked intentions | Sua |
| the Word | Incarnation | Sua |
| the Word | incarnation of the Word as God's self-communication to humankind | Rod1 |
| — | work of Creation as inferior to work of Redemption | Cab7 |
| the Word | Mary as mother of the Word | ManA2 |
| teachings of John the Baptist | John the Baptist's preaching as heralding a new age; mystery of John's sanctification in womb | Bo9 |
| spiritual joy | joyful death of the saintly priest Gregorio de Valmaseda | VgC15 |

| Tenor | Referent | No. |
|---|---|---|
| the Word | Incarnation | Bo15 |
| the Word | Incarnation | Bo5 |
| the Word | Incarnation | Bo6 |
| the Word | Incarnation | Bo1 |
| the Word | Incarnation | Ra |
| the Word | birth of Christ, manifestation of divine Word | Go2 |
| the Word | God's omniscience through his Word, in whom all things have their eternal being | Ca67 |
| significance of death, *desengaño* | conversion of St. Francis Borgia upon contemplating the cadaver of the Empress | So |
| a thought | essential inalterability of angelic thought, specifically, rebellion of Lucifer | Ca44 |
| mysteries and graces of Mary's life | mysteries and special graces of Mary's life inherent in her immaculate conception | Ag2 |

**science / branch of learning / letters**
ciencia [Vi3:86-87,230; VgC5:23; Led1:9;16:19; Bo7:3; 15:15,18,58; VgC1:1; ManL:3; Ca17:36;55:45;68:3; Gue13:3]
letras [VgC5:36; ManA2:356,360; Led21:4;5:4; Tel:8; Ca45:27]

| Tenor | Referent | No. |
|---|---|---|
| revelation through natural world | manifestation of God through natural world as insufficient without Scripture | Vi3 |
| wisdom | Christ as model of spiritual life | Vi3 |
| — | natural world rather than book learning as source of St. Isidore of Madrid's spiritual understanding | VgC5 |
| natural world (fields, water, flowers) | natural world as source of spiritual understanding for St. Isidore of Madrid | VgC5 |
| wisdom | divine wisdom taught by Christ's last words on Cross | Led1 |
| wisdom | Mary as the finest of God's instruments in the victory over evil, and as help of Christians | ManA2 |
| humility | humility taught by Christ's entire life | Led16 |
| wisdom | humility as foundation of true wisdom | Led21 |

| Tenor | Referent | No. |
|---|---|---|
| money | money as motive for Judas' betrayal of Christ | Led5 |
| God, eternal wisdom | Christ as teaching in his own person who God is | Bo7 |
| theoretical learning | necessity of supplementing theoretical understanding of virtue with practical experience | Tel |
| virtues and perfections | Mary as graced with all perfection | Bo15 |
| mystery of Mary's life and person | God alone as capable of explaining mystery of Mary | Bo15 |
| divine Wisdom | Incarnation | Bo15 |
| Christ | Christ as infinite Wisdom | VgC1 |
| understanding | understanding of who one is in relation to God | ManL |
| Jews' misinterpretation of Scripture as among instruments of Christ's death | mutual responsibility of Jews and Romans for Christ's death | Ca45 |
| knowledge of good and evil | temptation of Eve | Ca17 |
| God's mind | mysteries of God's providence | Ca55 |
| wisdom and knowledge | order of heavens as manifestation of God's wisdom | Ca68 |
| disciplines | intellect as matrix of all branches of learning | Gue13 |

**science / branch of learning / letters:** unmixed expansions
  arms and letters [ManA2:356-57; Ca45:27]
  a lofty / profound science [Led16:19; ManL:3; Ca17:36]

**subject matter / discourse**
  asunto [BaB:70; Ca8:46]
  discurso [Bo9:34; BaB:10,90; VgC6:3; Ag2:30; Ca10:6]
  estudios [Mon2:2]
  materia [Ven:318; Cam:23; Led21:13;16:7;4:4; Bo15:45,49,52; 6:22; BaB:25; Ca21:6; Grc:52]
  material [Ca49:64]

| Tenor | Referent | No. |
|---|---|---|
| conscience | John the Baptist's ascetic and contemplative life | Mon2 |
| natural world | natural world as source of knowledge of God | Ven |
| order, variety and beauty of the world | natural world as manifestation of God | Cam |

| Tenor | Referent | No. |
|---|---|---|
| virtue | study of virtue | Led21 |
| observance of religious laws and rites | Christ as model of all virtues | Led16 |
| preaching | St. John the Baptist's preaching | Bo9 |
| sin, flesh as sinful | Christ's person and life as teaching victory over sin | Led4 |
| mysteries of Mary's life | spiritual power of Mary's life | Bo15 |
| incarnate Word | Mary as mother of Word and Redeemer | Bo15 |
| God's law | original sin | Bo6 |
| life of St. Francis in its interior aspect | evangelical poverty and humility manifested in life of St. Francis | BaB |
| holy zeal and acts of penance | ascetic life of St. Francis | BaB |
| imitation of crucified Christ | stigmata of St. Francis | BaB |
| reasonings | examples of love, including divine love | VgC6 |
| prime matter | God's informing matter in creation | Ca21 |
| human intentions | difficulty of interpreting human intentions | Grc |
| various prophecies pertaining to redemption and salvation | fruitlessness of search for true wisdom without faith and divine grace | Ca8 |
| Eucharist | adoration of the Eucharist | Ca49 |
| mysteries | sacred mysteries of Mary's life | Ag2 |
| mortal life | life on earth as interruption of one's true life with God, and death as transformation of life | Ca10 |

**subject matter / discourse:** unmixed expansions
difficult subject matter [Grc:52-53]


## A.3.7. CONTENT OF THE TEXT – TYPE

### A.3.7.1. *Generic Type*

**superscription**
   sobrescrito [Ven:86; AD:17; Pad3:5; Cab4:13-14; ManA2:320,324,328; Cai2:1; 9:1; Jau:28; Vit:5; Mad:6; Ca60:3; Gue5:6]

| Tenor | Referent | No. |
|---|---|---|
| creatures | creatures as manifestation of God | Ven |
| name of Mary | Mary's suffering in Christ's Passion | AD |
| name of Jesus | name of Jesus, which means saviour, as source of hope for Christians | Pad3 |
| name of Jesus | naming of Jesus at his circumcision | Cab4 |
| name of God: *Terribili* | the awe-inspiring God of the Old Testament | ManA2 |
| beautiful appearance | beautiful appearance of the virtuous as outward sign of character | Cai2 |
| modesty | modesty as an outward sign of a virtuous heart | Cai9 |
| bread and wine of Eucharist | Eucharist as mystery of faith | Jau |
| quality of excellence | quality of excellence in one of God's creatures as enhancing its manifestation of God's greatness; Lope de Vega as specific example | Vit |
| zeal | St. Peter of Alcantara's zeal as sign of his imitation of Christ | Mad |
| beautiful appearance | Joseph's beautiful and virtuous appearance as having won sympathy of Pharaoh's cup-bearer | Ca60 |
| pain and sorrow | Christ's wounds, though apparently a cause for sorrow, as in fact a sign of glory and cause for joy | Gue5 |

**superscription:** unmixed expansions
    a name as superscription [SEE ALSO: B.2.1.1. to superscribe:ue. to superscribe a name] [Pad3:1+5; Cab4:13-16; ManA2:327-29]
    the superscription on a letter [Ven:86; AD:2+17; ManA2:319-20,327-29; Ca60:3-4]
    The superscription corresponds to the content. [Brv:9-10; Cai2:1-3;9:1-2]
    The superscription does not correspond to the content. [Gue5:6-7]

**word**
    palabra [Vi2:8; Leo2:12; Vgs2:11; Mu1:5; ManA2:239,263,273,282; Va4:14; Bo5:14;6:4; Go2:4,6,15]
    verbo [Vi2:11; Sua:62; ManA2:66,335; Go2:2; Brn:5]
    voz [Vi3:146,165,173; Cam:41; Par2:5; Va4:15; Do:46; Gue1:58,106]

| Tenor | Referent | No. |
|---|---|---|
| significance of creatures | creatures as not only meant for human utility but as manifestations of God to all people | Vi3 |

| Tenor | Referent | No. |
|---|---|---|
| evidence of God's action | heavens as manifestation of God | Vi3 |
| the Word | Incarnation | Vi2 |
| the Word | incarnation of the divine Word | Leo2 |
| the Word | Christ's wounds as God's authentication of his Word | Vgs2 |
| creatures | creatures as manifestations of God | Cam |
| the Word | Incarnation | Sua |
| St. Stephen's words | St. Stephen's prayer for God's forgiveness of those who stoned him | Par2 |
| Christ | Christians transformed by grace as manifestations of Christ to world | Mu1 |
| the Word | Incarnation | ManA2 |
| evidence of God's action | heavens as manifestation of God | Va4 |
| the Word | Incarnation | Bo5 |
| the Word | Incarnation | Bo6 |
| the Word | birth of Christ as manifestation of divine Word to world | Go2 |
| heavenly spheres | heavens as manifestation of God to St. Ignatius | Do |
| inclination of heart | Mary Magdalene's previously sinful life and her conversion | Gue1 |
| the Word | Incarnation | Brn |

**word:** unmixed expansions
A formerly unreadable word becomes readable. [Leo2:12-13; Go2:2-12]


A.3.7.2. *Specific Type*

**account / account entry**
   cuenta [Ven:355; Av2:6; Led22:6; ManA3:56,72,91,98,101-02,111; Led14:22; 20:2; Ca31:42,70; Enr:3; Ca69:26]
   cuenta de suma [Ven:181]
   partida [ManA2:345-46;3:71,91-92,96,131; Led19:6; Bo10:3; BaB:8; Ca31:58]
   cargo [ManA3:97; Led14:21; Ca26:18]
   descargo [Led14:21]
   cuento [BaB:6]
   gasto [Led14:19]
   recibo [Led14:19; BaB:6; Enr:3]
   debe [Va18:3]
   ha de haber [Va18:3; VgC21:4]

| Tenor | Referent | No. |
|---|---|---|
| human being | human being as epitome of creation | Ven |
| obligation | humankind's obligation to praise God on behalf of all creation | Ven |
| totality of one's acts | God's knowledge of one's every act | Av2 |
| totality of one's acts | God's knowledge of all one's sins | Led22 |
| the incarnate Word | Mary as mother of the Word and Saviour | ManA2 |
| responsibility for sin and concomitant punishment or recompense | Christ's making recompense for sin in place of humankind by his death on Cross | ManA3 |
| responsibility for sin and concomitant punishment | God's forgiveness of King David's sin in view of Christ's sacrificial death | ManA3 |
| one's gifts and one's use of them | God's total knowledge of each person | Led14 |
| punishment and reward due for bad and good acts | conscience as judge of one's life | Led14 |
| accountability | irrevocable accountability for all one's acts | Led14 |
| specific favors received | gratitude for favors received and readiness to repay them | Led19 |
| judgment | strict judgment facing each person at death | Led20 |
| condemnation and pardon | Christ's wounds as indication of both punishment due humankind for sin, and eternal life won for humankind through Christ's redemptive death | Va18 |
| grace won by Christ on behalf of human race | Crucifixion | Bo10 |
| eternal life | redemption through Christ's death | VgC21 |
| graces given to St. Francis and his use of them; stigmata | stigmata as manifestation of God's grace; as replica of Christ's wounds, sign of punishment due humankind for sin and grace of redemption won through Christ's death | BaB |
| ages | stigmata as extraordinary grace given St. Francis by Christ in person and celebrated throughout ages | BaB |

| Tenor | Referent | No. |
|---|---|---|
| total use one has made of the five senses in one's lifetime | use of the five senses in pursuit of worldly delights | Ca31 |
| totality of humankind's or individual's sins | Christ's death as redeeming humankind from infinite offense of sin | Ca31 |
| judgment before one has paid one's spiritual debts | unpreparedness for death and judgment | Enr |
| burden of guilt | examination of conscience and making amends in preparation for death and judgment | Ca26 |
| totality of good and bad acts | postponement of examination and reformation of life | Ca69 |

**account / account entry:** unmixed expansions
  to add an account [Ven:181-82; Ca31:49-50]
  to settle an account [Led20:1; Ca26:18;69:26]
  The account shows debits and credits. [Led14:19-21; Va18:1-3; BaB:5-6]
  The account shows an excessive debt. [Led22:7-8; ManA3:61-63; Ca31:78-79]

**copy material**
  materia [Led21:13; Bo6:22]

| Tenor | Referent | No. |
|---|---|---|
| virtue | practice of virtue | Led21 |
| God's law | original sin | Bo6 |

**decree**
  decreto [ManA3:47; Ca9:3;39:5;45:28;49:65; Gue7:4]
  edicto [Ca62:33;41:4,19]
  orden [Ca53:8]
  pregón [Ca41:3]

| Tenor | Referent | No. |
|---|---|---|
| condemnation to spiritual and eternal death | redemption through Christ's death | ManA3 |
| death | God's mercy in giving a person an opportunity to repent before dying | Ca9 |
| Eucharist | Eucharist, which Christ ordained be celebrated by his followers in remembrance of his Passion | Ca39 |
| proclamation | John the Baptist's proclamation of Christ as Messiah, and process of Paul's conversion | Ca62 |

| Tenor | Referent | No. |
|---|---|---|
| determination that Christ must die | mutual responsibility of Jews and Romans for Christ's death | Ca45 |
| proclamation of New Law of grace through faith in Christ | grace through faith in Christ offered to both Jews and Gentiles | Ca41 |
| adoration | adoration of God in Eucharist under signs of bread and wine | Ca49 |
| Mercedarian and Trinitarian Orders; incarnate Word | institution of religious orders dedicated to redemption of captives; Annunciation and incarnation of Redeemer | Ca53 |
| predestination of individual | St. Ann's election as mother of Mary | Gue7 |

**dirge**
endecha [Gue1:26]

| Tenor | Referent | No. |
|---|---|---|
| birth and death | mortal life in itself as basically tragic | Gue1 |

**entry on a census list**
partida [Ca43:14]

| Tenor | Referent | No. |
|---|---|---|
| subjection to sin on part of an individual | Christ's and Mary's freedom from sin | Ca43 |

**entry on a roster of prisoners**
partida [Ca26:9]

| Tenor | Referent | No. |
|---|---|---|
| human birth | human life as subjugated to death before redemption by Christ | Ca26 |

**epigram**
epigrama [Car:7-8]

| Tenor | Referent | No. |
|---|---|---|
| flora of riverbank | plants and flowers on banks of Manzanares as reminders of Lope and his writings | Car |

MOTIF INDEX                                                        147

**epitaph** [Ca7:11-13;37:11-12,36-37;28:34-35]
  epitafio [Car:8; Di:16]

| Tenor | Referent | No. |
|---|---|---|
| flora of riverbank | plants and flowers on banks of Manzanares as reminders of Lope and his writings | Car |
| spiritual signficance conveyed by flowers growing on a common grave | death of certain holy monks as leading to their eternal life | Di |
| spiritual death and eternal condemnation | spiritual death and eternal condemnation to which human race is subject because of sin | Ca7 |
| spiritual death and eternal condemnation | spiritual death and eternal condemnation to which human race is subject because of sin | Ca37 |
| spiritual death and eternal condemnation | spiritual death and eternal condemnation to which human race is subject because of sin | Ca28 |

**fable**
  apólogo [VgC13:3]
  fábula [ManA2:222]

| Tenor | Referent | No. |
|---|---|---|
| — | glory accruing to God through Incarnation as infinitely greater than that of any author of wordly fictions | ManA2 |
| — | incarnation of infinite God as vulnerable human being as a true transformation, in contrast to secular fables | VgC13 |

**law**
  ley [Ven:331,335,396; Vi2:3,6,8; Av5,6,8,12,18,23; Or:3; Grn:74; Vgs5:1,3; Roc:2; Cab6:2,13; Bo14:1,11,14; LoA:3; Mu4:22; Va5:3;6:8; Sar:3; Bo6:22; Hu:17; Ca9:76;40:2; VgC23:11; Ca62:2;30:2,9,18,37; Da:25,27; GoT:2; Ca1:4,6;26:41,50,73,78,85,89,99;50:2; Lud:6,9,11; Ca53:17;46:16]
  precepto [Bo14:7; Ca6:2;69:41]

| Tenor | Referent | No. |
|---|---|---|
| principles of higher reason | rational soul as source of knowledge of God | Ven |
| principles of higher reason | rational soul as source of knowledge of God superior to natural world and inferior to Scripture | Ven |
| principles of higher reason | rational soul as source of realization that human being desires beatitude | Ven |
| Mary | Incarnation of the Word of God through virgin Mary | Vi2 |
| Gospel or Spirit of Christ | law of grace, with which Holy Spirit informs soul, contrasted with Mosaic Law | Av5 |
| Gospel | law of grace or indwelling of Holy Spirit as Gospel in primary sense | Av5 |
| principles of higher reason | Golden Rule as epitome of rational behavior | Or |
| order of nature | ocean tides as following an established order | Grn |
| principles of behavior | vengeance for injuries and other worldly principles | Vgs5 |
| divine principles | divine judgment on those who live by worldly principles | Vgs5 |
| principles taught by Christ | desire to live life inspired by Holy Spirit | Roc |
| principles of virtue | spiritually perfected Christians as manifestations of principles of virtue | Cab6 |
| spiritually perfected Christians | will of perfected Christian as in complete harmony with will of God, as exemplified in whole person | Cab6 |
| principles of higher reason | conscience as judge and justification of life according to principles of higher reason | Bo14 |
| Moses | Moses as manifesting in his own person Law he was to receive from God and transmit to Israelites | LoA |
| — | stigmata of St. Francis as replica of Christ's wounds, sign of rule of grace in contrast to fear-inspiring Mosaic Law | Mu4 |

# MOTIF INDEX

| Tenor | Referent | No. |
|---|---|---|
| divinely inspired principles of living | just person as continually meditating on God's will | Va5 |
| divine will | Christ's willing obedience unto death | Va6 |
| order of nature | order of natural world as manifestation of God to St. Ignatius | Sar |
| principles of higher reason, natural justice | original sin | Bo6 |
| principles taught by Christ | Holy Spirit as source of understanding and loving fulfillment of Christ's teaching by disciples | Hu |
| principles taught by Christ | Eucharist as sacrament of New Dispensation | Ca9 |
| principles of higher reason | Ten Commandments as embodying principles of higher reason | Ca40 |
| principles of higher reason | history of human violence | VgC23 |
| principles of higher reason and grace | God-given principles of human living in period before Moses | Ca62 |
| principles of Decalog as principles of higher reason | principles of Decalog as eternal principles, and so not annulled with rest of Mosaic Law with inauguration of New Dispensation | Ca6 |
| principles of higher reason and principles taught by Christ | Mosaic Law as historically appearing between natural law and law of grace | Ca30 |
| — | Mosaic Law seen by certain Jewish leaders as threatened, but in reality fulfilled, by Christ's teaching | Ca30 |
| principle of forgiveness of injuries | forgiveness of injuries taught by Christ in his own person, contrasted with principle of strict retribution of Mosaic Law | Da |
| principles taught by Christ | Christ's death on Cross as inauguration of dispensation of grace and salvation | GoT |
| Christ | crucified Christ as embodiment of principles he taught | Ca1 |
| principles taught by Christ | inauguration of New Dispensation by Christ's death | Ca1 |
| moral principles | humankind's disregard of all principles of higer reason and of Mosaic Law | Ca26 |

| Tenor | Referent | No. |
|---|---|---|
| principles taught by Christ | inauguration of New Dispensation by Christ's death | Ca26 |
| principles of higher reason | human history to time of Christ seen in terms of two ages, that of natural law and that of written or Mosaic Law | Ca50 |
| order of nature | ocean tides as following an established order | Lud |
| principles taught by Christ | St. Peter of Alcantara's holiness | Lud |
| principles of higher reason | confession of sins against natural and written laws | Ca53 |
| principles taught by Christ | superseding of Mosaic Law by New Dispensation of grace or faith | Ca69 |
| principle that "the last shall be first," the humble will be exalted; New Dispensation | Rebecca as biblical type of Mary | Ca46 |

**statute-law rights and privileges**
fueros / privilegios [Co1:5,11; Ca30:17,21,31,43]

| Tenor | Referent | No. |
|---|---|---|
| free will, reason, immortality, etc., of human soul | powers and qualities with which God endowed human soul in creation, engaged in struggle between good and evil | Co1 |
| Israel's status and privileges | status and privileges conferred on Israel as God's chosen people through Law given to Moses | Ca30 |
| Isreael's status and privileges | Israel's refusal to accept New Dispensation | Ca30 |
| status and privileges | superseding and fulfillment of Old Dispensation by New Dispensation of grace, which bestows status and privileges of divine sonship and daughtership through union with Christ | Ca30 |

**law: unmixed expansions**
a new law [SEE: B.2.1.ue. to write a new law]

MOTIF INDEX                                               151

the Old Law vis-a-vis the New Law [Av5:1-7; Cab7:1-4;9:7-10; Mu4:22-23; Ca9:76-79; Da:24-28]

**law:** mixed expansions
  the law written on the heart / soul [Ven:331-32,335-37; Av5:3-7,12-13,23; Or:3-5; Roc:2-4; Cab6:2-4; Bo14:1-2; Va5:1+3;6:8+10; Ca62:2-6;50:2-5]
  a living law [Cab6:13; LoA:3-4]

**lesson**
  lección [Ven:50,55,66,73,80,124,145,158,161,187,191,220,234,244,286,288, 291,297,299,302,313,319,363,396,406-07; Led1:8;12:4; Bo7:1; Led4:2; Bo15:49; VgC24:30; ManL:6; SF2:3]

| Tenor | Referent | No. |
|---|---|---|
| mysteries of Godhead | beatific vision as reward promised to the just | Ven |
| mysteries of Godhead | understanding of mysteries of Godhead as not intended for ordinary person | Ven |
| mysteries of Godhead | understanding of mysteries of Godhead as not intended for this life | Ven |
| knowledge of God derived from created beings | importance of using one's time in this life to learn to know God through created beings | Ven |
| knowledge of God derived from created beings | God's self-communication through created beings as intended to stir human desire to know him more perfectly in heaven, although people too often content with less | Ven |
| direct knowledge of mystery of Godhead | perfect understanding of Godhead as not spiritually desirable for mortals | Ven |
| mysteries of Godhead | human being as insufficient in itself as means of knowing God | Ven |
| mysteries of Godhead | mysteries of Godhead enjoyed in beatific vision as revealed in Scripture | Ven |
| power, wisdom and goodness of God | power, wisdom and goodness of God as manifested in natural world and leading human beings to fear, believe and love him | Ven |
| knowledge of God | natural world as clear source of knowledge of God accessible to all people | Ven |

| Tenor | Referent | No. |
|---|---|---|
| spiritual principles | spiritual principles analogous to functioning of nature | Ven |
| enlightenment | spiritual enlightenment provided by faith as superior to that derived through reason | Ven |
| power, wisdom and goodness of God | importance of natural world as source of knowledge of God | Ven |
| spiritual and moral understanding | rational soul as source of spiritual and moral understanding, more efficacious when aided by faith | Ven |
| divine enlightenment | divine enlightenment as necessary for understanding true destiny of humankind | Ven |
| knowledge of God and of self | natural world and rational soul as sources of knowledge of God and of moral and spiritual truths about human person, but insufficient without supernatural enlightenment | Ven |
| utterance | last utterances of crucified Christ | Led1 |
| mysteries of Godhead | St. John the Evangelist's vision at Last Supper | Led12 |
| hypocrisy | hypocrisy of scribes and Pharisees, teachers of Mosaic Law | Bo7 |
| example | entire life and person of Christ as example of victory over sin | Led4 |
| Christ; Christ's teachings | Mary as mother of Word and Redeemer; Mary as embodiment of Christ's teachings | Bo15 |
| Christ as suffering Servant | Christ as model for Prince Baltasar Carlos | VgC24 |
| understanding of self in relation to God | distractions from contemplative prayer | ManL |
| spiritual detachment | importance of detachment from world and self-will for contemplatives | SF2 |

**lesson:** unmixed expansions
seven lessons [Led1:8]
a morning ("prime time") lesson [Led12:4]
a clear lesson [Ven:161,234]
an important lesson [ManL:6]
to derive a lesson [Mon3:12; Ven:286,288,291,296-97,299,363,406-07]

**lyrics**
  letra [Cai11:1; Va11:4; Ca17:2]

| Tenor | Referent | No. |
|---|---|---|
| human being | praise of God by angels and saints in heaven | Cai11 |
| saints? | poet's desire to join in praise of Eucharist by angels and saints | Va11 |
| heavens and earth | harmony of created universe | Ca17 |

**maxim**
  dicho [Be:4]
  máxima [Vi3:127]
  sentencia [Do:31]

| Tenor | Referent | No. |
|---|---|---|
| creatures of natural world | human ignorance of deeper spiritual significance of natural world in entrancement with its physical beauty and wonder | Vi3 |
| mortality of every human life | rivers as reminder of death | Be |
| each star | natural world as manifestation of God | Do |

**name** [SEE ALSO: A.3.7.2. entry on a census list; entry on a roster of prisoners]
  nombre [Mon1:12; Vi3:12,24,56; ADJ:3,6; LoU1:1,4,9,12,17,20; Cab5:4; 4:6,15-16;11:4,13,25,30,36,43,50; Mu3:11,30-31,32,35; ManA2: 328,331; Ri1; Bo14:6; VgC19:3;22:14;8.1:6; Bo3:4,6,13;5:12;6:24; VgC1:9; Ca9:85;20:15; 62:19;48:2; 43:78,79,84;1:18,26,30; Gue6:9-10,16,25-26; Ca57:16]

| Tenor | Referent | No. |
|---|---|---|
| person | eternal life won by early Christian martyrs | Mon1 |
| person | predestination of the elect | Vi3 |
| person | election of Asenet, biblical type of Mary and of soul | ADJ |
| (angelic) being | eternal beatitude of angel | ADJ |
| image of God | human soul as created in the image of God, i.e., eternal and incorruptible | LoU1 |
| divine sonship or daughtership | Christian's sharing in Jesus' divine sonship or daughtership | LoU1 |
| testimony | St. Stephen's martyrdom as testimony to truth of Gospel | Cab5 |

| Tenor | Referent | No. |
|---|---|---|
| Jesus, Savior | naming of Jesus at his circumcision as indication of his being Savior | Cab4 |
| Jesus | Jesus as Lord of Christians, their leader and Savior in struggle against sin and their reward in victory | Cab4 |
| presence in love | Christ's eternal love for Church and each soul, manifested in glorified wounds, sign of his victory | Cab11 |
| presence in love | Christian's love for and continual remembrance of Christ | Cab11 |
| presence in love | Christ's eternal love for humankind, manifested in his wounds | Mu3 |
| fear or awe inspired by the divine | God of the Old Testament as inspiring awe | ManA2 |
| presence in love | Mary's, and the soul's, continual remembrance and contemplation of God | Ri1 |
| presence | God's presence in human conscience | Bo14 |
| knowledge and love of Jesus | St. Ignatius' desire to spread Christianity in foreign lands | VgC19 |
| Jesus Christ | torture of certain Franciscan martyrs in Japan as ironically confirming their witness to Christ | VgC22 |
| Christ | Christ as God's wisdom and salvation | VgC8.1 |
| Jesus | Jesus as God and man, God's self-communication to humankind | Bo3 |
| divine Word | Incarnation | Bo5 |
| human nature | original sin | Bo6 |
| remembrance | compunction for sin | VgC1 |
| identity | conversion from idolatry to adoration of true God, in Eucharist | Ca9 |
| presence | presence of sin in all humankind | Ca20 |
| remembrance | John the Evangelist's renown as beloved disciple of Christ, and Apostles as successors to patriarchs of Old Dispensation | Ca62 |
| identity or character | Queen Christina of Sweden's conversion to Roman Catholicism, seen as most complete form of Christianity | Ca48 |

| Tenor | Referent | No. |
|---|---|---|
| person | Immaculate Conception | Ca43 |
| presence in love | devotion to Mary | Ca1 |
| divine grace or glory | sanctity of Sts. John of Matha and Felix of Valois, long unrecognized | Gue6 |
| remembrance | celebration of a sacred festival | Ca57 |

**name:** unmixed expansions
   the name Jesus [SEE ALSO: A.3.8. Jesus] [LoU1:9-10,17; Cab4:15-16; VgC8.1:6; Bo3:13]
   the name of the beloved [Cab11:4-5]
   a name as (part of) a coat of arms [Cab4:14-16;11:43-45; Led9:1+8; VgC22:14]
   a new name [Cab4:6-7,16-17]

**note / gloss**
   cota [ManA2:139]
   nota [Va16:3; BaB:22]

| Tenor | Referent | No. |
|---|---|---|
| fullness of virtue | Mary's fullness of virtue | ManA2 |
| wounds | wounds on Christ's head in his Passion | Va16 |
| notable humility | extraordinary humility of St. Francis | BaB |

**note / gloss:** unmixed expansions
   a marginal note [ManA2:138-39; Va16:1-3; BaB:22]
   a note in red ink [Va16:3]

**poetry**
   gozos [Mon2:8; Gue1:33,105]
   poema [Ca17:6,8]
   poesía [Ca17:5]
   poética [Cai20:8]
   verso [Ca17:6,8; Gue1:25,33,38]

| Tenor | Referent | No. |
|---|---|---|
| divine graces and mercies | communication between unborn Jesus and John on occasion of Mary's visit to Elizabeth | Mon2 |
| Mary's exaltation of God | Holy Spirit as inspirer of Mary's outpouring of praise | Cai20 |
| heavens and earth | harmony of created universe | Ca17 |
| joy | mortal life in itself as basically tragic, though relieved by an occasional joy | Gue1 |

| Tenor | Referent | No. |
|---|---|---|
| worldly delights | Mary Magdalene's repentance for and conversion from her sinful life | Gue1 |

**point of discussion**
punto [BaB:24; Ca62:41,65; Ag2:40]

| Tenor | Referent | No. |
|---|---|---|
| touchiness regarding one's honor | humility of St. Francis | BaB |
| aspects of New Dispensation | aspects of New Dispensation as taught by Church, e.g. sacraments, faith, preaching | Ca62 |
| mysteries of Mary's life | mysteries of Mary's life, beginning with Immaculate Conception and Virgin Birth | Ag2 |

**prophecy**
oráculo [Di:9; Ca8:63;68:28]
vaticinio [Ca8:39]

| Tenor | Referent | No. |
|---|---|---|
| interlaced flowers, jointly and distinctly | flowers on common grave of holy monks, which teach that death, and death to self, is a transformation that leads to eternal life | Di |
| prophecy of Redemption | fruitless search for wisdom by worshippers of false Gods | Ca8 |
| King Solomon | King Solomon as biblical type of God's power and wisdom | Ca8 |
| stars | sin's dominion over world | Ca68 |

**prophecy: mixed expansions**
a living prophecy [Ca8:63]

**signature** [SEE ALSO: A.3.8. Jesus]
firma [AD:13; Act:6; Cab1:9; Led10:14; Cai8:1; Led19:9; VgC7:3; Bo8:4; VgC21:7; Ca43:122]

| Tenor | Referent | No. |
|---|---|---|
| Cross | Crucifixion as culmination of Mary's sorrows in Christ's Passion, result of original sin | AD |

| Tenor | Referent | No. |
|---|---|---|
| physical appearance | luxury of worldly members of religious order | Act |
| divine promise | power of name of Jesus | Cab1 |
| the Word | Incarnation | Led10 |
| promise | grace as a promise of God's freely given gift of eternal life | Cai8 |
| moral obligation | gratitude for favors received and readiness to repay them | Led19 |
| infant Christ | affirmation in faith of newborn Christ as God and Mary as mother of God | VgC7 |
| wound | Christ's circumcision as promise of redemption; his death as fulfillment of that promise | Bo8 |
| wounds | wounds on Christ's hands, feet and side in Crucifixion as sign of redemption | VgC21 |
| power | Christ's and Mary's freedom from power of sin | Ca43 |

**signature:** unmixed expansions
  five signatures [VgC21:7]
  a cross as signature [AD:12-13; Cai19]
  the signature on a promissory note [SEE ALSO: A.3.4.2.3.1. promissory note:ue: a signed and sealed promissory note; B.2.1.1. to sign:ue. to sign a promissory note] [Led19:7-9; Bo8:1-4]
  the king's signature [SEE ALSO: B.2.1.1. to sign:ue. to be signed by the king] [Cab1:5-6+9]
  to lack a signature [Ca43:122]

**signature:** mixed expansions
  God's signature [SEE ALSO: B.2.1.1. to sign:me. God signs a promissory note]
  [Led10:14; VgC7:3]

**story**
  historia [Fue:27,61; Jau:9; VgC6:3; Gue1:64]

| Tenor | Referent | No. |
|---|---|---|
| life of St. Francis | stigmata as sign of God's grace and reminder of Crucifixion | Fue |
| God's giving stigmata to St. Francis | stigmata as God's special gift and reminder of Crucifixion | Fue |

| Tenor | Referent | No. |
|---|---|---|
| life of Christ | Christ's saving acts, epitomized in Eucharist | Jau |
| true examples | examples of love, including divine love | VgC6 |
| sinful life | Mary Magdalene's sinful life | Gue1 |

**story:** unmixed expansions
a love story [VgC6:1-3]

**title / emblematic motto**
mote [Ca47:3]
nombre [BaB:87; Ag2:11]
rótulo [Gue4:5]
rúbrica [Mu2:7,12]
título [Mon1:4; Mu2:2,4,27,32,37,40; BaB:17; PrJ:11; Ag1:14; 2:13,15]

| Tenor | Referent | No. |
|---|---|---|
| Christ's kingship | divine kingship of the crucified Christ | Mon1 |
| name of Jesus together with his circumcision | name of Jesus as epitomizing his life and person | Mu2 |
| name of Jesus together with his circumcision | Christ as fulfillment of Scripture | Mu2 |
| "Lady Poverty" (title of St. Francis' "bride")? "Il poverello"? | St. Francis' imitation of crucified Christ | BaB |
| "saint" | St. Francis' sanctity as confirmed by God's gift of stigmata | BaB |
| "king" | Pilate's having affixed to Cross inscription INRI, i.e., "Jesus the Nazarene, King of the Jews" | Ca47 |
| "Our Lady of Montserrat" | Our Lady of Montserrat as protector from plague and from sin | PrJ |
| manifestation | more plainly evident manifestation of the divine in burning bush on Mt. Horeb than in crucified Christ | Gue4 |
| "Jesus the Nazarene, King of the Jews" | Pilate's having inscription affixed to Cross | Ag1 |
| honorary title | Mary's being graced by God as virgin, mother, queen, bride, etc. | Ag2 |
| "Mother" and "Queen" | Mary's being mother of God and queen of heaven, an example of God's exaltation of the humble | Ag2 |

| Tenor | Referent | No. |
|---|---|---|
| "slave" | Mary's calling herself slave of the Lord at the Annunciation | Ag2 |

**tragedy**
  tragedia [Car:16; Gue1:23]

| Tenor | Referent | No. |
|---|---|---|
| cypress | cypress as reminder of Lope's tragedies | Car |
| mortal life | mortal life in itself as basically tragic | Gue1 |

**verdict / sentence**
  sentencia [ManA3:28-29; Led6:7; Ca9:71;37:31,33; Da:31; Ca50:18]
  sentencia de muerte [ManA3:47-48]

| Tenor | Referent | No. |
|---|---|---|
| condemnation to spiritual and eternal death | redemption through Christ's death | ManA3 |
| eternal destiny | each soul as destined to eternal life or damnation | Led6 |
| condemnation | conquest of King Balshazzar's kingdom by Persians and Medes as punishment for his profanation of sacred vessels; condemnation of soul who profanes Eucharist | Ca9 |
| condemnation to spiritual and eternal death | condemnation of human race because of original sin | Ca37 |
| condemnation to death | diverse responses of crowd to Christ's sentencing | Da |
| condemnation to death; declaration of nonbelief | Pilate's handing Jesus over to death; rejection of Christ by Jews and Gentiles; unbelief in Real Presence in Eucharist | Ca50 |

**versicle**
  verso [Va3:30]

| Tenor | Referent | No. |
|---|---|---|
| Christ's words | Christ as source of power to reject worldly illusions | Va3 |

## A.3.8. CONTENT OF THE TEXT – SPECIFIC ENTITY

Christus [VgC5:10; Led21:6;16:23; Va13:13;15:3; Bo2:3; BaB:16; VgC24:28; Ca42:30;55:53,54]

| Tenor | Referent | No. |
|---|---|---|
| Christ's life and teachings | St. Isidore of Madrid's imitation of Christ | VgC5 |
| Christ's life and teachings | imitation of Christ as basis of true honor | Led21 |
| obedience unto death | union of Christ's human will with the divine will | Led16 |
| Christ | Christ as present whole and entire, body and blood, soul and divinity, in Eucharist | Va13 |
| Christ | unborn John the Baptist's recognition of Christ in Mary's womb | Va15 |
| death in witness to Christ | martyrdom of Sts. Justus and Pastor as children | Bo2 |
| Christ's life and teachings | St. Francis' imitation of Christ as basis of his life | BaB |
| Christ | Christ, the suffering Servant, as model for Prince Baltasar Carlos | VgC24 |
| Christ's life and teachings | martyrdom of Sts. Justus and Pastor as children | Ca42 |
| crucified Christ | conversion of a Jew to Christianity through contemplation of crucified Christ | Ca55 |

**Christus:** unmixed expansions
 the Christus as the first lesson of the primer [Bo2:3-4; BaB:15-16; VgC24:26-30]
 The Christus is the only lesson one needs to learn. [VgC24:26-31]

**Creed**
 credo [Mon9:8; VgC22:5]

| Tenor | Referent | No. |
|---|---|---|
| faith | John the Evangelist's sublime faith and love | Mon9 |
| faith | martyrdom of St. Peter of Verona | VgC22 |

**Jesus** [SEE ALSO: A.3.7.2. name:ue. the name Jesus]
  Jesús [Cab2:7; Led8:2;9:8]

| Tenor | Referent | No. |
|---|---|---|
| person of Jesus | St. Ignatius of Antioch's reverence and love for Christ, who dwelt within | Cab2 |
| person of Jesus | dedication to Jesus of order founded by St. Ignatius of Loyola, and his authorizing it | Led8 |
| person of Jesus | St. Ignatius of Loyola's dedication to Jesus | Led9 |

A.3.9. PORTION OF THE TEXT

**jot**
  añadidura [Grc:57]
  ápice [ManA2:9; Grc:42; Ca61:10]
  puntillo [Grc:57]
  punto [Ca7:18; Mrt:8]
  tilde [Ven:58; Grc:40,58]

| Tenor | Referent | No. |
|---|---|---|
| aspect of infinity or perfection | God's infinitely perfect self-knowledge | Ven |
| least act | Mary's life and person in every aspect as God's instrument for salvation of humankind | ManA2 |
| sin committed in a single moment | loss of grace and meriting of condemnation through even consenting in thought to mortal sin | Ca7 |
| smallest action of a person | difficulty of understanding human intentions | Grc |
| petty human beings | petty human beings who pretend to be more than they are | Grc |
| any attempt to imagine horrors of hell | St. Margaret of Hungary's vision of hell | Mrt8 |
| smallest detail | Christ's entire life and person as manifesting the divine | Ca61 |

**stroke**
  rasgo [Ca9:66; Grc:39; Ca35:9,13;17:34; Mrt:8; Gue9:5; SF1:3]

| Tenor | Referent | No. |
|---|---|---|
| — | the divine judgment on King Balshazzar for profanation of sacred vessels | Ca9 |
| least aspect | difficulty of understanding anything of a person's true intentions | Grc |
| angel Gabriel | angel who saves three young men from fiery furnace as prefiguration of Word, who redeems human nature | Ca35 |
| bread and wine of Eucharist | Eucharist as presence of Christ whole and entire, and epitome of his saving acts | Ca35 |
| tree of knowledge of good and evil | tree of knowledge of good and evil as containing lofty divine mysteries | Ca17 |
| any attempt to imagine horrors of hell | St. Margaret of Hungary's vision of hell | Mrt |
| rose | fleeting beauty of rose | Gue9 |
| sum of all earthly joys | earthly joys compared to joys of heaven | SF1 |

**stroke:** unmixed expansions
a brief stroke [Ca9:66;35:9,13;17:34; Gue9:5]

**letter**
letra [Ven:58; Vi3:89; Pin:158,165; Sua:5; ManA2:9; Led17:1; Grc:39]

| Tenor | Referent | No. |
|---|---|---|
| aspect of infinity or perfection | God's infinitely perfect self-knowledge | Ven |
| — | natural world as source of knowledge of God | Vi3 |
| each creature | individual creatures apprehended by exterior senses | Pin |
| four elements | natural world as manifestation of God | Sua |
| least act | Mary's life and person in every aspect as God's instrument for salvation of humankind | ManA2 |
| Christ ? | existence of all things in God | Led17 |
| smallest action of a person | difficulty of understanding human intentions | Grc |

# MOTIF INDEX 163

**letter:** unmixed expansions
a single letter [Pin:158; Led17:1]

**syllable**
sílaba [Ven:58; Sua:6-7]

| Tenor | Referent | No. |
|---|---|---|
| aspect of infinity or perfection | God's infinitely perfect self-knowledge | Ven |
| imperfect mixtures of the four elements | natural world as manifestation of God | Sua |

**abbreviation**
abreviatura [Led10:20; Grc:58-59]
cifra [Grc:59]
síncopa [Ca10:9]

| Tenor | Referent | No. |
|---|---|---|
| Christ in Mary's womb | conception of Christ | Led10 |
| petty human beings | petty human beings who pretend to be more than they are | Grc |
| human being as mortal | mortal life as interruption in one's eternal life in or with God | Ca10 |

**word / phrase**
dicción [Ven:57; Sua:7-8]
palabra [Vi3:89; Pin:166-67; Led10:16; ManA2:65; Jau:11; VgC11:2; Grc:39]
verbo [ManA2:256; Ag2:12]

| Tenor | Referent | No. |
|---|---|---|
| aspect of infinity or perfection | God's infinitely perfect self-knowledge | Ven |
| — | natural world as source of knowledge of God | Vi3 |
| signification | divine signification of creatures | Pin |
| compounds in which the four elements are perfectly mixed | natural world as manifestation of God | Sua |
| the Word | Incarnation | Led10 |
| the Word | Incarnation | ManA2 |
| words of consecration: "Este es mi cuerpo." | Eucharist as epitome of Christ's saving acts | Jau |
| the Word | child Jesus as infinite Wisdom | VgC11 |
| single action of a person | difficulty of understanding human intentions | Grc |
| the Word | Incarnation | Ag2 |

**word:** unmixed expansions
four words [Jau:11]
a single word [SEE ALSO: B.2.1.1. to synthesize:ue. to synthesize in a single word] [ManA2:256]

**line of writing**
línea [Ag2:29; Ca29:16]
renglón [Ven:57; Pin:148; Cab7:8-9; ManA2:8; Bo15:73; VgC24:4; Ca18:7; Do:51; Ca49:60;11:32; Gue12:7]
surco [Tel:15]

| *Tenor* | *Referent* | *No.* |
|---|---|---|
| aspect of infinity or perfection | God's infinitely perfect self-knowledge | Ven |
| — | human being's virtually infinite capacity for wisdom, since it is spiritual | Pin |
| — | work of creation as inferior to work of redemption | Cab7 |
| least act | Mary's life and person in every aspect as God's instrument for salvation of humankind | ManA2 |
| practical experience and theoretical knowledge | necessity of supplementing theoretical understanding of virtue with practical experience | Tel |
| Mary's virtue | Mary as model of virtue | Bo15 |
| sacrileges already committed | sacrilegious treatment by Jews, of Christian figures, specifically St. Peter | VgC24 |
| rainbow | God's promise of peace to human race | Ca18 |
| order of nature | St. Ignatius' recognition of God in natural world | Do |
| Christ's resurrection | Resurrection as culmination of Christ's redemptive acts | Ca49 |
| Mary's suffering and joy | sacred mysteries of Mary's life, in which joy of Incarnation and glory of Resurrection inseparably linked to sorrow of Crucifixion | Ag2 |
| glorified wounds of crucified Christ | Constantine's vision, symbolic of redemption through Christ's death | Ca29 |
| degree of intensity | devil's despair over Christ's victory | Ca11 |
| degree | death to self or loss of self as highest degree of Christian detachment | Gue12 |

# MOTIF INDEX 165

**line of writing:** unmixed expansions
  the last line [Ca49:60;11:32]
  black lines [Ag2:29]
  illuminated lines [Ca18:7;29:16]
  crooked lines [Cab7:8-9]

**sentence**
  cláusula [Do:33; Ca26:2]
  oración [Sua:8-9]
  sentencia [Pin:159]

| Tenor | Referent | No. |
|---|---|---|
| signification | apprehension of creatures through the exterior senses as distinct from understanding their divine meaning | Pin |
| animals | natural world as manifestation of God | Sua |
| waves of sea | St. Ignatius' recognition of God in natural world | Do |
| four elements | nature as subservient to God | Ca26 |

**paragraph**
  párrafo [VgC23:15; Ca13:7]

| Tenor | Referent | No. |
|---|---|---|
| period | early period in history of human violence | Vg23 |
| sun; Christ | rising of sun; resurrected Christ as head of Mystical Body | Ca13 |

**paragraph:** unmixed expansions
  the first paragraphs [VgC23:15]

**passage**
  pasaje [Ca36:9]

| Tenor | Referent | No. |
|---|---|---|
| events or periods in life | human life as under dominion of sin and suffering | Ca36 |


A.3.10. STAGE IN THE PROCESS OF COMPOSITION OF THE TEXT

**rough draft** [SEE ALSO: B.2.1.1. to sketch]
  borrador [Pad1:7; Cab7:11,17,22,26]
  en borrón [Gue8:2]

| Tenor | Referent | No. |
|---|---|---|
| creatures | Mary as epitome and culmination of the beauties of all God's creatures | Pad1 |
| prefigurations | mysteries of New Dispensation as prefigured in and superseding Old Testament | Cab7 |
| wisdom | human wisdom as manifesting divine Wisdom, even if imperfectly | Gue8 |

**final copy** [Pad1:4-7; Cab7:24-25; Gue8:2-3]
  en limpio [Ven:190-91; Cab7:12; Gue17]

| Tenor | Referent | No. |
|---|---|---|
| teachings found in Scripture | Scripture as teaching more clearly or explicitly what is also taught by nature and the rational soul | Ven |
| Mary | Mary as epitome and culmination of the beauties of all God's creatures | Pad1 |
| New Dispensation of grace in Christ | New Dispensation as prefigured in and superseding Old Dispensation | Cab7 |
| Godhead, divine Wisdom | human wisdom as manifesting divine Wisdom, even if imperfectly | Gue8 |
| Eucharist | Eucharist as reenactment of Christ's Passion | Gue17 |

## A.3.11. VERSION OF THE TEXT

**original**
  dechado [Ven:38]
  ejemplar [Ven:38,165,187; Va9:1]
  libro arquetipo [Ven:36-37,125,140]
  libro ejemplar [Ven:162-63,167; Vi3:212-13]
  libro original [Ven:395,400]
  original [Mon8:2;9:8; Ven:342; ASF:7; Mat:8; Led11:3,11,15; ManA1:20,25,
    30-31,34,48,49; Fue:42; Bo15:72; Ca64:18;17:26; Gue10:7,8; Ag2:47]
  primer ejemplar [Mad:1-2]

| Tenor | Referent | No. |
|---|---|---|
| Christ | poet's desire to portray Christ worthily in his poetry | Mon8 |

| Tenor | Referent | No. |
|---|---|---|
| St. John the Evangelist | St. John the Evangelist's sublime faith and love | Mon9 |
| God | beatific vision | Ven |
| God | understanding of mysteries of Godhead as not intended for this life | Ven |
| God | creatures as intentionally incomplete and inferior manifestation of God, meant to awaken one's longing for him | Ven |
| God | natural world and human soul as manifestations of God needing to be supplemented by that of Scriptures | Ven |
| Christ | Christ as the clear epitome and model for humankind, of all God's teachings | Vi3 |
| God | Christ as manifestation of God | ASF |
| crucified Christ | crucified Christ as source of all St. Bonaventure's wisdom | Mat |
| Christ | stigmata of St. Francis as replica and reminder of Christ's wounds, which are the ones that won human salvation | Led11 |
| Christ | Mary as perfect likeness of Christ from first instant of her conception | ManA1 |
| Christ | link between Mary's immaculate conception and her being mother of God | ManA1 |
| Mary | Mary's immaculate conception as unique gift of God | Fue |
| the Word | the Word, in and through whom all things have their being | Va9 |
| God | Mary's immaculate conception as unique gift of God | Bo15 |
| original sin | original sin as manifested in sins of entire human race | Ca64 |
| original sin | original sin as manifested in sins of entire human race | Ca17 |
| Christ | St. Peter of Alcantara's imitation of Christ | Mad |
| Christ | stigmata of St. Francis as replica of Christ's wounds | Gue10 |
| God | Immaculate Conception | Ag2 |

**copy / adaptation / translation**
libro metagrapho [Ven:37,132-33,134-35]
libro trasladado [Ven:163]
traslado [Mon9:7; Ven:39,134,139,149,153,161-62,167,188,295,342,343; ASF:6; Led3:3;11:4,12,13,17; Cai5:1; Fue:43; Gue10:7; Ca61:8]
trasunto [Ven:39,133; Vgs2:3; Va14:2]

| Tenor | Referent | No. |
|---|---|---|
| St. John the Evangelist | St. John the Evangelist's sublime faith and love | Mon9 |
| indirect sources of knowledge of God | knowledge of God in this life as indirect | Ven |
| indirect sources of knowledge of God | manifestations of God in this life as intentionally incomplete and imperfect | Ven |
| indirect sources of knowledge of God | even indirect sources of knowledge of God as difficult to understand fully | Ven |
| indirect sources of knowledge of God | manifestations of God in this life: natural world, rational soul, Scripture | Ven |
| rational soul | rational soul as superior to natural world as source of knowledge of God but inferior to Scripture | Ven |
| contemplative life | contemplative life on earth as similar to beatific vision | Ven |
| natural world | natural world as manifestation of divine perfections | Ven |
| Christ | Christ as manifestation of God | ASF |
| St. Francis | stigmata of St. Francis as exact replica of Christ's wounds | Vgs2 |
| St. Sebastian | St. Sebastian's meriting to be included among the saints through his martyrdom or imitation of Christ | Led3 |
| St. Francis | stigmata of St. Francis as replica and reminder of Christ's wounds, which are the ones that won human salvation | Led11 |
| constancy in virginity | constancy in virginity as state similar to angels | Cai5 |
| likeness | preservation of Christ's image on his burial shroud | Va14 |
| St. Francis | stigmata of St. Francis as exact replica of Christ's wounds | Fue |

| Tenor | Referent | No. |
|---|---|---|
| St. Francis | stigmata of St. Francis as exact replica of Christ's wounds | Gue10 |
| Christ | Christ as divine Son of God | Ca61 |

**first impression**
primera impresión [ManA1:5,15]

| Tenor | Referent | No. |
|---|---|---|
| conception in the womb | Mary's immaculate conception | ManA1 |

A.3.11.ue. VERSION OF THE TEXT: UNMIXED EXPANSIONS

three versions [Ven:167-72]
twelve copies [Hu:18]
a faithful copy [SEE ALSO: A.3.11.ue. The copy is indistinguishable from the original; The first impression corresponds to the original.] [Ven:295; ASF:6-7; Leo1:6]
to compare the first impression with the original [ManA1:18-21]
The copy is indistinguishable from the original. [Fue:43-45; Gue10:6-8]
The copy serves as a reminder of the original. [Led11:17-18]
The first impression corresponds to the original. [ManA1:47-48]
The copy / adaptation / translation is not as complete as the original. [Ven:139-43]
The copy / adaptation / translation is not as valuable as the original. [Ven:139-41; Led11:13-16]

A.3.11.me. VERSION OF THE TEXT: MIXED EXPANSIONS

a living copy [Leo1:6]

A.3.12. LANGUAGE OF THE TEXT

**language**
idioma [Vi3:172; To:8; Ca7:10]
lengua [Ca55:11;28:14]
lenguaje [Vi3:172; Pad1:2; Jau:31; Va4:14,19; So:2]

| Tenor | Referent | No. |
|---|---|---|
| aspect of universality | natural world as clear manifestation of God able to be understood by everyone | Vi3 |

| Tenor | Referent | No. |
|---|---|---|
| Scriptures | Christ as fulfillment of Old Testament prefigurations and prophecies | To |
| harmonious order and beauty of the stars | birth of Mary | Pad1 |
| mystery | Eucharist as *magnum mysterium* | Jau |
| harmonious order and beauty of the heavens | heavens as clear manifestation of God able to be understood by everyone | Va4 |
| fissures on tree bark; rupture between God and humanity and among people, signified and caused by sin | original sin as manifested in sins of entire human race | Ca7 |
| three languages of inscription on Cross | beginning of a Jew's conversion to Christianity through contemplation of crucified Christ | Ca55 |
| grace | conversion of St. Francis Borgia upon contemplating cadaver of the Empress | So |
| three languages of inscription on Cross, mysteriously signifying Trinity | redemption through death of Christ, who is one with Trinity | Ca28 |

A.3.12.ue. LANGUAGE OF THE TEXT: UNMIXED EXPANSIONS

three languages [SEE: A.3.12.ue. to be written in three languages]
mute language [Pad1:2; Va4:15]
to be written in three languages [Ca55:10-11;28:14]
The book is written in every language. [Vi3:171-73; Va4:19]

A.3.12.me. LANGUAGE OF THE TEXT: MIXED EXPANSIONS

the language of God / heaven [Jau:31; So:2]

A.3.13. STYLE OF THE TEXT

**style**
estilo [Jau:32; BaB:10]

| Tenor | Referent | No. |
|---|---|---|
| way of communicating or understanding | profound mystery of God's presence in Eucharist under signs of bread and wine, which cannot be understood by a literal-minded person | Jau |
| manner of life | evangelical poverty and humility practiced by St. Francis as signs of holiness and divine grace | BaB |

**rhetorical figures**
  retóricos colores [VgC5:25]
  cultas flores [Do:38]
  tropo [Do:31]

| Tenor | Referent | No. |
|---|---|---|
| beauty of natural world | natural world as source of spiritual understanding for St. Isidore of Madrid | VgC5 |
| beauty of natural world | St. Ignatius' recognition of God in harmony, order and beauty of natural world | Do |
| each star | St. Ignatius' recognition of God in harmony, order and beauty of natural world | Do |

**in good taste**
  de buen gusto [Gue1:70-71]

| Tenor | Referent | No. |
|---|---|---|
| physical beauty | Mary Magdalene's physical attraction as occasion of her sinful life | Gue1 |

A.3.13.ue. STYLE OF THE TEXT: UNMIXED EXPANSIONS

  a polished style [BaB:10-12; Do:29-48; Ag2:9-12]
  an unpolished / low style [Jau:32; BaB:10-11]

A.3.14. OVERALL STRUCTURE OF THE TEXT

**inside** [Jau:25; Bo5:39-40]
  lo escrito [Bo5:45]
  dentro / de dentro / lo de dentro / por dentro / por de dentro [Ven:44,45,85; Vi1:2-3,7; Cam:60,64; Sua:46-47,50; Gue1:66]
  el / lo interior [Gue1:67,102]

| Tenor | Referent | No. |
|---|---|---|
| Godhead | ineffability of mystery of Godhead | Ven |
| mysteries of Godhead | beauty of natural world as indication of divine Beauty | Ven |
| virtue | Mary's fullness of virtue | Vi1 |
| mysteries of Godhead | direct knowledge of God as inaccessible to humans in this life | Cam |
| heart | the just as praising God both in their hearts and by their deeds | Sua |
| heart | the wicked as hypocrites, appearing good but filled with evil intentions | Sua |
| Christ's divinity, present in Eucharist | Eucharist as mystery of faith | Jau |
| the Word, who is God | Incarnation | Bo5 |
| heart, soul | Mary Magdalene's recognition that her physical beauty belies her sinfulness | Gue1 |
| heart, soul | condemnation of Mary Magdalene by those aware of her reputation as a sinner but not of her conversion of heart | Gue1 |

**outside** [SEE ALSO: A.3.7.1. superscription; A.3.18.1. binding]
la exterioridad [Gue1:101-02]
de fuera / por fuera/ por defuera [Ven:44,47,78,82,129; Vi1:3,7-8; Cam:60; Sua:47,50; Bo1:12]

| Tenor | Referent | No. |
|---|---|---|
| humanity assumed by God in Christ | mystery of Christ's divinity, revealed but also concealed by his humanity | Ven |
| creatures as manifestation | beauty, excellence and truth of creatures as manifestation of God | Ven |
| modesty | Mary's fullness of virtue | Vi1 |
| manifestation | creatures as manifestation of Good | Cam |
| deeds | the just as praising God both in their hearts and by their deeds | Sua |
| outward impression | the wicked as hypocrites, appearing good but filled with evil intentions | Sua |

| Tenor | Referent | No. |
|---|---|---|
| Mary's beauty | Mary's unique spiritual beauty, her immaculate conception | Bo1 |
| reputation | condemnation of Mary Magdalene by those aware of her reputation as a sinner but not of her conversion of heart | Gue1 |

## A.3.14.ue. OVERALL STRUCTURE OF THE TEXT: UNMIXED EXPANSIONS

The outside corresponds to the inside. [SEE ALSO: A.3.7.1. superscription:ue. The superscription corresponds to the content; A.3.18.1.ue. The binding corresponds to the content.]
[Sua:45-49; Da:38-39]
The outside does not correspond to the inside. [SEE ALSO: A.3.7.1. superscription:ue. The superscription does not correspond to the content; A.3.19.5.1.ue. to need a code breaker in order to read the text]
[Sua:49-51; Gue1:65-67,101-02]

## A.3.15. INTERNAL STRUCTURE OF THE TEXT

**beginning** [SEE ALSO: A.3.15.ue. the first part of a text]
 entrada [Mu2:19]
 principio [Vi3:50; Mu2:3,13,28; Va13:20;6:1,2; VgC4:8; Bo2:4; VgC24:37; Ca12:10; Ag2:52]

| Tenor | Referent | No. |
|---|---|---|
| creation of angels, beginning of a saint's life of glory | beatific vision enjoyed by angels and saints in eternal glory | Vi3 |
| beginning of Christ's life | Christ's naming and circumcision as key to his mission | Mu2 |
| from eternity | Incarnation and Redemption as God's eternal plan | Mu2 |
| beginning in time | eternity of Christ's divinity, present in Eucharist | Va13 |
| primacy of place | God's eternal begetting of the Word | Va6 |
| beginning in time | eternity of God and his Word | Va6 |
| First Cause, God as Creator | natural world as manifestation of its eternal and infinite Creator | VgC4 |

| Tenor | Referent | No. |
|---|---|---|
| childhood; entry into life of glory | martyrdom of Sts. Justus and Pastor as children | Bo2 |
| God | God as source of all ruler's actions | VgC24 |
| material cause | Christ's inauguration of New Dispensation, rejected by Jews and accepted by Gentiles, as occasion of enmity among religions of world | Ca12 |
| birth | Mary's birth | Ag2 |

**beginning:** unmixed expansions
    the beginning of a book [Vi3:50-51; Mu3,19,28-29; Va6:1-2; Ca12:4+10; Ag2: 49+52]
    from beginning to end [SEE: A.3.18.2.ue. from the first to the last page; B.3.4.ue. to read from beginning to end]
    without a beginning [Va13:20;6:2]

**body**
    cuerpo [BaB:70]

| Tenor | Referent | No. |
|---|---|---|
| body of St. Francis | stigmata of St. Francis | BaB |

**ending** [SEE ALSO: A.3.15.ue. the last part of a text] [ManA2:200-01]
    fin [Vi3:51; Mu2:25; ManA1:23,51; Va13:20; VgC4:8; Ca48:14; Ag2:51; Gue12:12]

| Tenor | Referent | No. |
|---|---|---|
| end of time | eternity of beatific vision | Vi3 |
| Christ | Christ as fulfillment of Scripture | Mu2 |
| completed act of Mary's conception | Mary's sinlessness or fullness of grace even in her conception | ManA1 |
| death | Mary's death and glorious assumption into heaven | ManA2 |
| end in time | eternity of Christ's divinity, present in Eucharist | Va13 |
| end in time | natural world as manifestation of its eternal and infinite Creator | VgC4 |
| disappearance of cloud, as at sunrise or sunset; Christ's death and resurrection | dream or vision of Queen Christina of Sweden, pertaining to sacrifice of Cross and of altar | Ca48 |

# MOTIF INDEX

| Tenor | Referent | No. |
|---|---|---|
| Coronation | mystery of Mary's coronation as Queen of Heaven | Ag2 |
| death | regret at thought of eventual death of Rodriguez Monforte | Gue12 |

**ending:** unmixed expansions [SEE ALSO: A.3.15. beginning:ue. from beginning to end]
the ending of a book [Vi3:51; ManA1:23,51; Ag2:49+51; Gue12:12]
without an ending [Va13:20; VgC4:8]

**chapter**
capítulo [Var:17-18; Mu2:7-8,9-10,12; Gue1:52-53,64;15:7; Ag2:73; Ca10:16]

| Tenor | Referent | No. |
|---|---|---|
| topics of meditation | importance of meditation in order to progress in spiritual life | Var |
| mysteries of Christ's life | mysteries of Christ's life as epitomized in his name and circumcision | Mu2 |
| periods of life or acts thereof | consideration of Mary Magdalene's life before and after conversion | Gue1 |
| periods and acts | consideration of life of Cardinal Cisneros | Gue15 |
| periods of life or acts thereof | intercession for Mary's aid in amendment of life, divine forgiveness and eternal salvation | Ag2 |
| mysteries | divine mysteries revealed by Christ and accessible through faith | Ca10 |

**chapter:** mixed expansions
the chapters of a life [Gue1:52-53;15:7-8]

**treatise**
tratado [PrJ:6]

| Tenor | Referent | No. |
|---|---|---|
| stage in the spiritual life | Mary as embodying the three stages in the spiritual life, virtues of the first two infused by special grace from conception, so that she was always in perfect union with God | PrJ |

**treatise:** unmixed expansions
three treatises [SEE: A.3.15. treatise:ue. a book of three treatises]
a book of three treatises [PrJ:6]

**clause**
cláusula [Ca69:7]
estancia [Ca24:3]

| Tenor | Referent | No. |
|---|---|---|
| place in New Dispensation | Jews as first people to whom God offered participation in New Dispensation | Ca69 |
| ages of human history | history of sins of humankind | Ca24 |

**clause:** unmixed expansions
the first clause in a will [Ca69:7-8]


A.3.15.ue. INTERNAL STRUCTURE OF THE TEXT: UNMIXED EXPANSIONS

the first part of a text [SEE: A.3.8. Christus:ue. the Christus as the first lesson of the primer; A.3.9. paragraph:ue. the first paragraphs; A.3.15. clause:ue. the first clause in a will; A.3.16. title page; A.3.18.2. quire:ue. the first quire; A.3.18.2.ue. the first page]
the last part of a text [SEE: A.3.9. line of writing:ue. the last line; A.3.18.2.ue. the last page]


A.3.16. ANATOMICAL STRUCTURE OF A BOOK

**approbation**
aprobación [ManA2:144,159,160,175-76,183,190; Fue:2; Bo15:36; BaB:72; Gue1:77,114]
censura [ManA2:145; Gue1:83]

| Tenor | Referent | No. |
|---|---|---|
| special divine grace or favor | Mary's fullness of grace from first moment of conception and in every act | ManA2 |
| special divine grace or favor | saints as subject to sin or as having committed some sins or faults, in contrast to Mary | ManA2 |
| divine grace, favor or approval | God's special favor or grace to Mary in her immaculate conception and to St. | Fue |

MOTIF INDEX                                        177

| Tenor | Referent | No. |
|---|---|---|
|  | Francis in stigmata; divine approval expressed through Church's celebration of same |  |
| special divine grace or favor | Mary's unique graces as work of Trinity | Bo15 |
| special divine grace or favor | stigmata of St. Francis as special divine favor and sign of divine approval or sanctity | BaB |
| special divine grace or favor | Christ's forgiveness and gracing of repentant Mary Magdalene | Gue1 |

**approbation:** unmixed expansions

three approbations [Bo15:36; Ag2:17]
without an approbation [ManA2:159-62,175-76,183]

**certification of fidelity to the original** [Va13:4]
    certificación [ManA1:24]
    fe [BaB:29]

| Tenor | Referent | No. |
|---|---|---|
| Church's affirmation of Mary's fullness of grace from first moment of conception | Immaculate Conception and divine maternity of Mary | ManA1 |
| Eucharist as truly Christ whole and entire | Eucharist as mystery of faith, and as truly what it is claimed to be | Va13 |
| St. Francis' faith and fidelity | St. Francis' profound faith in and fidelity to Christ | BaB |

**copyright**
    privilegio [ManA2:146,148,150,160,173,184,197; Bo15:5; BaB:37,42; Ag2:20]

| Tenor | Referent | No. |
|---|---|---|
| freedom from subjection to sin | Mary's complete freedom from sin, from first moment of conception, as unique gift of God | ManA2 |
| freedom from subjection to sin | saints as subject to original and actual sin, with occasional exception | ManA2 |

| Tenor | Referent | No. |
|---|---|---|
| | owing to special divine grace at certain times | |
| freedom from subjection to sin | Mary's complete freedom from sin, from first moment of conception, as unique gift of God | Bo15 |
| stigmata | stigmata of St. Francis as unique gift of God | BaB |
| freedom from subjection to sin and its effects | Mary's complete freedom from sin, from first moment of conception, as unique gift of God | Ag2 |

**copyright:** unmixed expansions
a royal copyright [11] [ManA2:150-51; BaB:37]
an old copyright [BaB:42]
a unique copyright [ManA2:97-98]
without a copyright [ManA2:160-62,170-73,183-84]

**dedication**
carta dedicatoria [BaB:21]

| Tenor | Referent | No. |
|---|---|---|
| dedication to God | St. Francis' dedication to the crucified Christ, as manifested by his humility | BaB |

**errata sheet** [ManA1:21-23]
fe de erratas [BaB:31]

| Tenor | Referent | No. |
|---|---|---|
| sins or faults | Mary's complete freedom from sin, from first moment of conception | ManA1 |
| sins | St. Francis' faith as reproof to sinners | BaB |

**index** [Var:16-18]
índice [Sal:1; Do:69]

---

[11] In fact, every *privilegio* "es una concesión real. Al no existir un rey de España, no puede haber un privilegio para España. El rey concede privilegios para los reinos de Castilla y, en su nombre, los virreyes para los demás reinos" (Moll 55).

| Tenor | Referent | No. |
|---|---|---|
| topics of meditation | importance of meditation in order to progress in spiritual life | Var |
| John the Baptist | John the Baptist as precursor of Christ | Sal |
| Christ Child | Christ in his childhood as both indication and epitome of beauty and spiritual riches of the mature Christ, God and man | Do |

**license**
licencia [Gue1:77]

| Tenor | Referent | No. |
|---|---|---|
| Christ's authoritative affirmation | Christ's affirmation of Mary Magdalene's divine forgiveness and absolution from past sin | Gue1 |

**list of signatures** [*registrum chartarum*]
registro [BaB:72]

| Tenor | Referent | No. |
|---|---|---|
| stigmata | stigmata of St. Francis | BaB |

**price limit**
tasa [Bo15:64; BaB:41; Ag2:41]

| Tenor | Referent | No. |
|---|---|---|
| virtue, holiness | Mary's immeasurable virtue or holiness | Bo15 |
| grace | stigmata of St. Francis as exceedingly great grace | BaB |
| esteem | exceedingly great esteem in which Mary is held by those devoted to her | Ag2 |

**price limit:** unmixed expansions
an extremely high price limit [BaB:41-44]
without a price limit [Bo15:64; Ag2:41]

**prologue**
prólogo [Cai12:5; BaB:22; Ca61:28]

| Tenor | Referent | No. |
|---|---|---|
| prayer | prayer as anticipation of eternal union with God | Cai12 |
| St. Francis' humility | St. Francis' humility as basis of his sanctity and special divine graces | BaB |
| mountains on which sun rises; Wise Men from East | mountains on which sun rises as indicating that day is breaking; Wise Men from East who recognized infant Christ as God | Ca61 |

**prologue:** unmixed expansions
a clear prologue [Ca61:28]
an elegant prologue [Cai12:5]

**table of contents**
registro [Ca67:5]
tabla [Ca26:71; Ag2:50]

| Tenor | Referent | No. |
|---|---|---|
| existence of all things in the Word | God's foreknowledge of the whole history of sin and redemption | Ca67 |
| humankind's history of sin | humankind's history of sin against both natural law and Mosaic Law | Ca26 |
| epitome of all good | Mary's fullness of all grace | Ag2 |

**title page**
hoja del principio [BaB:18]
primer hoja [Jau:14]
título [Gue1:65]

| Tenor | Referent | No. |
|---|---|---|
| St. Peter as "first among equals," Bishop of Rome | institution of sacraments of Eucharist and Holy Orders | Jau |
| outward manifestations | poverty, humility, stigmata of St. Francis as indications of God's working in him | BaB |
| physical appearance | Mary Magdalene's physical beauty, as contrasted with her sinfulness | Gue1 |

**title page:** unmixed expansions
a beautiful title page [Gue1:65]

## A.3.17. CONDITION OF THE TEXT [SEE ALSO: B.4. *TO PRESERVE / NOT PRESERVE THE TEXT*]

**virgin copy**
 virginal libro / libro virginal [Va15:1; Bo15:69]

| Tenor | Referent | No. |
|---|---|---|
| Mary | unborn John the Baptist's recognition of Christ in Mary's virginal womb | Va15 |
| Mary | Mary as virgin-mother | Bo15 |

## A.3.18. PHYSICAL COMPONENTS OF THE TEXT [SEE ALSO: A.1.2.3. *Material Written On*]

### A.3.18.1. *Binding*

**adornments**
 argentería [Bo1:13]
 doraduras y lindezas [Cam:68-69]
 florones [Bo1:12]
 rayos [Gue3:5]

| Tenor | Referent | No. |
|---|---|---|
| beauty of creation | beauty of creation as indication of perfection of Creator | Cam |
| spiritual or heavenly beauty | Mary's exceptional spiritual graces, particularly her immaculate conception | Bo1 |
| strands of hair | Mary Magdalene's beautiful hair, flying in wind | Gue3 |

**binding / boards**
 cubiertas [Cam:62,68,75]
 encuadernación [Ven:75-76,77-78,82,96,102,121-22,128,394-95,399; Cam:62-63,69; Ov:6; Bo5:38,45; BaB:81; Gue15:2]
 pergamino [Va19:4]
 piel [Do:93]
 tablas [To:2; Bo5:37;1:7,11; Ca55:2,7]

| Tenor | Referent | No. |
|---|---|---|
| creatures | beauty and perfection of natural world as marvelous manifestation of God | Ven |
| creatures | truth manifest in creatures as leading to understanding of God as supreme truth, power, wisdom and goodness | Ven |
| truth | metaphysical truth manifested in creatures as revelation of God | Ven |
| truth | metaphysical truth manifested in creatures as only source of knowledge of Godhead possible in this life, apart from Scripture | Ven |
| truth | metaphysical truth manifested in creatures as source of knowledge of free will | Ven |
| body and soul | Christ's uniting both human and divine natures in one divine Person | To |
| creatures | natural world as manifesting God in its beauty, order and perfection | Cam |
| body | Mary's Assumption | Va19 |
| Incarnation | Mary's divine maternity as final cause, and Redemption as efficient cause, of her fullness of grace, including immaculate conception | Ov |
| Old Law | Mary's perfect fulfillment of Old Law as prelude to her being mother of Christ, embodiment of New Law | Bo5 |
| Mary as virgin-mother | Mary as immaculately conceived virgin-mother of God | Bo1 |
| appearance | St. Francis' imitation of crucified Christ | BaB |
| human flesh | aged hermit | Do |
| Cross | beginning of conversion of a Jew to Christianity through contemplation of crucified Christ | Ca55 |
| mode of being | death as a transformation from mortality to immortality | Gue15 |

# MOTIF INDEX 183

**binding / boards:** unmixed expansions
two boards [To:2; Bo1:7]

**fastenings / ligatures**
ataduras [To:9]
cerraduras [ManA2:110]
correas [To:9]
manecillas / manillas [Cab10:5; ManA2:112]

| Tenor | Referent | No. |
|---|---|---|
| Hypostatic Union | union in Christ of human and divine natures in one divine Person | To |
| mysteries of Old Testament Scriptures concerning Messiah | enlightenment of Christ's followers after his resurrection, regarding himself as fulfillment of Old Testament prophecies | Cab10 |
| virtue | Mary's impregnable virtue and fullness of grace | ManA2 |

A.3.18.1.ue. *Binding: Unmixed Expansions*

a precious binding [Ven:82-83; To:2; Cam:68-69; Bo1:9-14]
a faded binding [Do:93; Gue15:3]
a loose binding [Do:93]
The binding corresponds to the content. [Ven:75-78,82-85; Cam:67-70; Bo5:38-40;1:9-10]

A.3.18.2. *Leaves / Pages*

**leaf**
hoja [Ven:57,245,264; To:6; ManA2:4,13,83,86,88,95,98,100,103,117,132,136, 157,170,174,182,192,239;3:71,97,99 Cai6:1; Led6:1,5; Va13:12,21;14:3;18:1; VgC18:4; Jau:5; VgC4:2; Va3:14; Bo15:48,75;6:18;1:3; BaB:49; Par3:9; Ca9:50; Car:8; Di:8; Ca12:2,9;48:16; Do:95; Ca8:4,11,20,38;34:5;43:4,17;26:36,55; GarE:3; Ca65:14;55:10;53:7; 68:14; Gue1:17,20,22,30,44,59,66,80,90,111;3:4; Ag2:26; Ca29:15;10:18;11:7]

| Tenor | Referent | No. |
|---|---|---|
| aspect | God's infinitely perfect self-knowledge | Ven |
| constituent parts | natural world, and particularly the heavens, as clear manifestation of God | Ven |

| Tenor | Referent | No. |
|---|---|---|
| manner of understanding, aspect | three manners of understanding nature: particular substances or beings, order or laws of nature, power inherent in each thing by which it functions | Ven |
| each of Christ's natures, human and divine | Hypostatic Union | To |
| holy persons | holy persons as God's instruments in victory over evil | ManA2 |
| individual saints | the saints, united to God, who is Life | ManA2 |
| grace, virtue | grace given Mary as surpassing that of all the saints together | ManA2 |
| virtue | different saints as exemplifying different virtues, in contrast to Mary, who exemplifies them all | ManA2 |
| virtue | virtue of saints as subject to being lost or diminished through sins or faults | ManA2 |
| virtue | Mary's fullness of and constancy in virtue through special divine grace | ManA2 |
| period of life | Mary's superiority to all the saints in that every period of her life, from conception to death, was filled with God's special grace, manifested in her virtuous acts and freedom from all sin or fault | ManA2 |
| womb | gestation of incarnate Word | ManA2 |
| human soul | redemption through Christ's death | ManA3 |
| Cross | redemption through Christ's death | ManA3 |
| acts or periods of a person's life | prudence as informing all one's acts | Cai6 |
| possible judgments | salvation or damnation as destiny of each soul | Led6 |
| Eucharistic host | Christ as present whole and entire, body and blood, soul and divinity, in Eucharistic host | Va13 |

MOTIF INDEX 185

| Tenor | Referent | No. |
|---|---|---|
| divine Person | triune God as substantially present in Eucharist | Va13 |
| burial shroud | preservation of Christ's image on his burial shroud | Va14 |
| Christ in his Ascension | redemption through Christ's death on Cross | Va18 |
| petals of hyacinth | dew formed on flowers at dawn | VgC18 |
| each of the twelve Apostles | twelve Apostles as first to follow Christ | Jau |
| open flower petals | creatures as manifestation of God | VgC4 |
| allurement of worldly delights | pursuit of worldly illusions | Va3 |
| years or other temporal measure | Mary's fullness of virtue and grace; Incarnation | Bo15 |
| virtue | Mary's virtue as powerful aid in victory over evil | Bo15 |
| Mary | Mary as only human being preserved from original sin, because of her election as mother of God | Bo6 |
| nature | union of divine and human natures in one divine Person in Christ | Bo1 |
| immortal glory | St. Francis's immortal glory on earth and in heaven, for his spiritual victory | BaB |
| heavens | God's creation of heavens | Par3 |
| mindfulness of death | heedlessness of death through human vanity | Ca9 |
| leaves or petals of flowering plants | plants and flowers on banks of Manzanares as reminders of Lope and his writings | Car |
| flower petals | flowers growing on grave as signifying that death of certain holy monks leads to their eternal life | Di |
| subject; period in history | change of subject, from spread of Christian faith throughout world, battle against Church, and enmity of world's religions, to unhappy fate of Jews; return to subject | Ca12 |
| portions of sky as at sunrise or sunset; | dream or vision of Queen Christina of Sweden, | Ca48 |

| Tenor | Referent | No. |
|---|---|---|
| flesh of crucified and risen Christ | pertaining to sacrifice of Cross and altar | |
| skin | wrinkled, translucent skin of hermit, in whom physical and spiritual effects of time are manifest | Do |
| heavens; angels | dream or vision of King Solomon | Ca8 |
| soul | distraught state of Queen Saba as she seeks true wisdom; Gentiles in unredeemed state, before finding true Wisdom | Ca8 |
| prophecies | mysterious prophecies pertaining to Redemption, with which Queen Saba has been inspired | Ca8 |
| lily petals | natural world as glorifying the Creator | Ca34 |
| members of human race | human race in state of grace before original sin | Ca43 |
| category "sinner" | sin's powerlessness over Christ and Mary | Ca43 |
| heavens; flesh of Christ | prayer for God's mercy and coming of Christ | Ca26 |
| period of time | time after period of Old Law, seen as not yet redeemed or graced through Christ's death | Ca26 |
| water | St. Peter of Alcantara's walking on water | GarE |
| heavens | invocation of Diana, goddess of moon, figure of Mary | Ca65 |
| Persons of Trinity | redemption as work of triune God | Ca55 |
| heart | Mary's dedication to God and role in Redemption | Ca53 |
| heavenly sphere | eleven spheres of the heavens, in Christianized Ptolemaic universe | Ca68 |
| acts | penance and mortification as necessary for salvation | Gue1 |
| heart, soul | repentant sinner as loving greatly | Gue1 |
| human lives, taken together | mortal life in itself as basically tragic | Gue1 |
| human lives, taken individually | people's lives as alternating between sin and repentance | Gue1 |
| acts | Mary Magdalene's repentance for her sins | Gue1 |

| Tenor | Referent | No. |
|---|---|---|
| acts | Mary Magdalene's abandonment of her former sins | Gue1 |
| sin and its effects | human race as afflicted by original and actual sin | Gue1 |
| hair | Mary Magdalene's beautiful and carefully arranged hair, which was occasion of sin for many | Gue3 |
| Mary's body and soul | Immaculate Conception as first of Mary's many sublime graces | Ag2 |
| Mary's future | the many graces and mysteries of Mary's life, present potentially in her immaculate conception but not yet lived | Ag2 |
| grace; flesh of crucified Christ | Constantine's vision, symbolic of redemption through Christ's death | Ca29 |
| Mary | link between Immaculate Conception and Incarnation | Ca10 |
| Eucharistic host | Eucharist as sacrament of incarnate Word | Ca10 |
| heavens at sunrise; flesh of crucified and risen Christ | redemption through Christ's death | Ca11 |

**page**

página [Ca2:8; Do:55-82; Ca3:8;36:27; Gar:1]
plana [ManA2:137,149,196,199;3:130; Led18:3; Ca43:74]

| Tenor | Referent | No. |
|---|---|---|
| period of one's life life | each period of Mary's life as filled with God's special graces | ManA2 |
| accumulated sin of human race | redemption through Christ's death | ManA3 |
| life event | St. Lucy's martyrdom | Led18 |
| sacred mysteries | St. John the Evangelist's sublime understanding of divine mysteries of which he wrote | Ca2 |
| natural world | beauty of natural world as effective instrument of God to capture St. Ignatius' love | Do |
| heavens | God's creation of heavens | Do |
| category "sinner" | sin's powerlessness over Mary | Ca43 |

| Tenor | Referent | No. |
|---|---|---|
| sacred mysteries (or raptures, depending on version) | St. John the Evangelist's ecstatic vision of divine mysteries of which he wrote | Ca3 |
| raptures | St. John the Evangelist's ecstatic vision of divine mysteries of which he wrote | Ca36 |
| expanses of natural world (heavens, earth, seas) | natural world as source of knowledge of God | Gar |

**quire**
  cuaderno [Jau:6; Bo15:13; Ca46:9]

| Tenor | Referent | No. |
|---|---|---|
| group of Christians | twelve Apostles as first to follow Christ | Jau |
| categories of divine virtue and perfection | Mary's fullness of virtue and wisdom | Bo15 |
| ages or periods of time | immortal memory of Abraham's offering of Isaac, biblical type of God's sacrificing his only Son | Ca46 |

**quire:** unmixed expansions
  the first quire [Jau:6]
  a quire of twelve leaves [Jau:5-6]


A.3.18.2.ue. *Leaves / Pages: Unmixed Expansions*

  two leaves [Led6:5; Va14:3; Bo1:3]
  three leaves [Va13:21; Ca55:10]
  five leaves [Ca34:5]
  eleven leaves [Ca68:14]
  twelve leaves [SEE: A.3.18.2. quire:ue. a quire of twelve leaves]
  a single page [SEE ALSO: A.3.18.2.ue. One page alone is free of blots.] [Ca10:17-18]
  the first page [SEE ALSO: A.3.16. title page; A.3.18.2.ue. from the first to the last page] [ManA2:149,170,195-96]
  the last page [SEE ALSO: A.3.18.2.ue. from the first to the last page] [ManA2:199]
  from the first to the last page [ManA2:136-37]
  the chief pages [Ven:245]
  pages of gold [ManA2:98]

a spacious page [Gar:1-2]
a blue page [Par3:9; Do:82; GarE:3]
a green page [ManA2:86; Ca43:4]
a purple page [Ca29:15]
a white page [Va13:12; Ag2:26; Ca10:17-18]
a marbled page [SEE ALSO: B.3.3.1. to display:ue. to display marbled pages] [Ca8:4-5]
a blank page [ManA2:132-33,185-88,192; Ca26:55,97-98]
illuminated pages [Ca8:4]
a loose leaf [SEE ALSO: A.3.18.2.ue. Loose leaves are easily lost or torn.] [ManA2:88,117]
a beautiful page [SEE ALSO: A.3.16. title page:ue. a beautiful title page] [Va18:1; Do:82]
well-ordered pages [ManA2:96-98,103-05; Gue3:7-8]
a wrinkled page [Do:95]
a forbidden page [SEE: A.3.18.2.ue. to insert a forbidden page into a book]
a worthless page [Ca9:50]
to fill a page with writing [ManA2:137-39,190-94; Cai6:1-2; Ca26:59]
to insert a forbidden page into a book [Gue1:80-82]
to turn the page [Ca12:2; Do:95]
to turn back to a preceding page [Ca12:4,9]
One page alone is free of blots. [Bo6:16-18]
Loose leaves are easily lost or torn. [ManA2:95-96,100-02; Ca8:11-13]
Blank leaves and written leaves are juxtaposed. [ManA2:132-33; VgC9:3]

## A.3.19. GRAPHIC ELEMENTS OF THE TEXT

### A.3.19.1. *Generic Terms*

**impress / impression**
  estampa [BaB:82]
  impresión [Fue:30,34; Bo15:11,41; BaB:69]

| *Tenor* | *Referent* | *No.* |
|---|---|---|
| stigmata | stigmata of St. Francis | Fue |
| conception | Mary's immaculate conception | Fue |
| God | Incarnation of the Word | Bo15 |
| conception | Mary's immaculate conception | Bo15 |
| stigmata | stigmata of St. Francis | BaB |

### A.3.19.2. *Layout*

**column**
  columna [Ag1:13]

| Tenor | Referent | No. |
|---|---|---|
| pillar | Christ's scourging | Ag1 |

**margin**
  margen [ManA2:138,193; Led21:18;18:1; Va16:1; Bo14:5]

| Tenor | Referent | No. |
|---|---|---|
| smallest act | every act of Mary's, no matter how small, as sanctified and salvific | ManA2 |
| exception to a rule | humble obedience in practice of virtue | Led21 |
| end of one's life | martyrdom of St. Lucy | Led18 |
| Christ's head and forehead | Christ's being wounded on head and crowned with thorns | Va16 |
| conscience | conscience as guide and judge in observance of natural law | Bo14 |

**ruled lines** [SEE ALSO: B.1. to rule the page] [Bo15:73-74]
  guías [Bo7:4]
  pauta [Ca8:60]

| Tenor | Referent | No. |
|---|---|---|
| Christ's ribs or back | Christ's scourging | Bo7 |
| Mary's virtue | Mary as model of virtue | Bo15 |
| orbits of stars in zodiac | great astrological knowledge of Saba | Ca8 |

A.3.19.3. *Full-page Illustrations*

**plate**
  tabla [BaB:93]

| Tenor | Referent | No. |
|---|---|---|
| St. Francis' body | stigmata of St. Francis as exact replica of Christ's wounds | BaB |

**portrait**
  retrato [BaB:94]

| Tenor | Referent | No. |
|---|---|---|
| stigmata | stigmata of St. Francis as exact replica of Christ's wounds | BaB |

## A.3.19.4. *Illuminated Figures and Symbolic Designs*

### A.3.19.4.1. *Illuminated Figures*

**illuminated figure**
figura [Sua:9]

| Tenor | Referent | No. |
|---|---|---|
| entities of natural world | natural world as manifesting God and his greatness | Sua |

### A.3.19.4.2. *Symbolic Designs*

**coat of arms**
armas [Cab4:14; Led9:1; Jau:19; VgC22:10,14; BaB:60; Da:67]
blasón [VgC18:20; BaB:46; Ca42:42;38:4]
empresa [Cab11:44; BaB:46]
escudo [BaB:45]

| Tenor | Referent | No. |
|---|---|---|
| name of Jesus | naming of Jesus at his circumcision | Cab4 |
| Christ's wounds | Christ's glorified wounds as sign of his love for Church and each soul | Cab11 |
| cause | Christ as leader to whose cause St. Ignatius of Loyola was dedicated | Led9 |
| the crucified Christ | stigmata of St. Francis and his total devotion to the crucified Christ | VgC18 |
| Christ | Christ as God's instrument in Redemption, present in Eucharistic host | Jau |
| Cross | torture of certain Franciscan martyrs in Japan by branding with cross on forehead as ironically confirming their witness to Christ the King | VgC22 |
| Cross or crucified Christ | crucified Christ as eternal life, whose protection, love and honoring of St. Francis are signified in the stigmata | BaB |
| Cross and wounds | St. Francis, imagined with outstretched arms and stigmata, as replica of crucified Christ | BaB |

| Tenor | Referent | No. |
|---|---|---|
| Christ's wounds | wounds on hands, feet, and side of crucified Christ | Da |
| charity | charity of St. Francis of Paola (?), specifically, his Order's work of burying those executed for crimes | Ca42 |
| devotion to Mary | devotion to Mary as source of spiritual fortitude | Ca38 |

**design**
designio [BaB:60; Do:90; Ca29:26]

| Tenor | Referent | No. |
|---|---|---|
| Cross and wounds | St. Francis, imagined with outstretched arms, and stigmata, as replica of crucified Christ and reminder of Redemption | BaB |
| idea | God's inspiring St. Ignatius with idea of Company of Jesus | Do |
| Cross, in its form and purpose | Constantine's wondering as to meaning of his vision of Cross | Ca29 |

**emblem**
cifra [Ca20:16;62:77; Grc:4; Ca35:3]
emblema [Ca63:4]
enigma [Ca20:18; Grc:30]
jeroglífico [Di:13; Ca23:5;58:6;63:12;52:13]

| Tenor | Referent | No. |
|---|---|---|
| actual sin | mysterious interrelationship between original sin and actual sins of entire human race | Ca20 |
| flowers on a common grave | death as transformation that leads to eternal life | Di |
| crown suspended in air | appearance of angels with crown, intended for victor in spiritual competition | Ca23 |
| strange appearance of sun, confusing sun- rise and sunset; crucified Christ | Christ's death as ending era of Old Law and beginning new era of grace | Ca62 |
| creatures | creatures as manifestations of God's perfections | Grc |
| "O" antiphons, recited | integrity of Mary in her per- | Ca58 |

| Tenor | Referent | No. |
|---|---|---|
| in Divine Office December 17-23; virginal integrity and eternal life | petual virginity, and of other virgin saints; immortality won by martyrs | |
| sin | sin's illusory and fatal attraction | Ca63 |
| stars and other heavenly bodies | difficulty of astrological determinations | Grc |
| human heart | impossibility for anyone but God, of understanding intentions or desires of the heart | Ca35 |
| Sisara with nail in his forehead; victory over Satan | Jael's triumph over Sisara; Mary's triumph over Satan through giving birth to Redeemer | Ca52 |

**emblem:** unmixed expansions
an obscure emblem [Ca20:18; Grc:30; Ca35:2-3]
printers mark [Jau:15-16; BaB:17-20]

| Tenor | Referent | No. |
|---|---|---|
| Eucharistic host | Christ's institution of sacraments of Eucharist and Holy Orders at Last Supper | Jau |
| Cross, inscription and wounds | St. Francis' imitation of crucified Christ, including stigmata | BaB |

**seal**
figura [Sua:45]
sello [To:4; Vgs2:1,9,12; Cab10:3-4,13; Cai8:1;9:1; Va13:7; 15:2; VgC13:6; Mu4:4,9; Bo11:3; Es:19; Va3:23; Ca23:33,43;30:25; Ag2:68; Ca10:12]
señal [Mon7:16; VgC22:24]
signo [Ca2:15;36:26]

| Tenor | Referent | No. |
|---|---|---|
| stigmata | stigmata of St. Francis as God's work | Mon7 |
| "accidents" or secondary characteristics of Christ's humanity | Christ as one divine Person with both human and divine natures | To |
| stigmata | stigmata of St. Francis as exact replica of Christ's wounds | Vgs2 |
| gifts of the Holy Spirit | the just person, graced by the Holy Spirit | Sua |

| Tenor | Referent | No. |
|---|---|---|
| mysteries | Christ's enlightening of his disciples regarding himself as fulfillment of mysteries of the Scriptures | Cab10 |
| guarantee | grace as a promise of God's freely given gift of eternal life | Cai8 |
| modesty | modesty as affirmation and safeguard of a virtuous heart | Cai9 |
| "accidents" or secondary characteristics of Christ's humanity and of Eucharist | Eucharist as mystery of faith, in which Christ's humanity and divinity are hidden beneath accidents of bread and wine | Va13 |
| Christ's glorious wounds | Eucharist as commemoration and reenactment of Christ's Passion and resurrection | Va13 |
| virginity | Mary as simultaneously virgin and pregnant with the Word | Va15 |
| incomprehensibility of mysteries of Christ | hiddenness of Christ's divinity in his Passion | VgC13 |
| stigmata | stigmata of St. Francis as testimony to fullness of God's grace | Mu4 |
| identity | Saul's persecution of Christians | Bo11 |
| distinguishing characteristic | distinguishing characteristic of faithful servants of God | VgC22 |
| Jesus | Jesus as God's guarantee of redemption | Es |
| mysteries of Christ | Christ as source of power to reject worldly illusions | Va3 |
| baptismal character or grace | God's desire that all people be saved | Ca23 |
| incomprehensibility of mysteries of Christ | divine mysteries of Christ as revealed to St. John the Evangelist | Ca2 |
| baptismal character or grace | sacrament of Baptism | Ca30 |
| mysteries of Christ | revelation of mysteries of Christ after his death | Ca36 |
| mystery | Marian mysteries | Ag2 |
| incomprehensibility of mysteries of Christ | understanding of divine mysteries of Christ given through faith | Ca10 |

MOTIF INDEX                195

**seal:** unmixed expansions
  five seals [Va13:8]
  seven seals [See: A.3.2.1:me. the book with seven seals]
  a royal seal [Es:19]
  a mysterious seal [Ca23:33]
  to bear an identical seal [Vgs2:9-12]
  to lack a seal [Ca23:43]

**stamp**
  estampa [VgC18:15; BaB:59; Per:4; Ca32:7,15]

| Tenor | Referent | No. |
|---|---|---|
| the crucified Christ | stigmata of St. Francis and his total devotion to the crucified Christ | VgC18 |
| stigmata | stigmata of St. Francis as replica of the crucified Christ | BaB |
| human being | human being as created in the image and likeness of God | Per |
| baptismal character or grace | John's baptism of Christ as inauguration of sacrament of Baptism | Ca32 |
| baptismal character or grace | Baptism as annulling original sin | Ca32 |

**watermark**
  marca [Led10:10]
  figura [Led10:12]

| Tenor | Referent | No. |
|---|---|---|
| original sin | God's preservation of Mary from original sin | Led10 |

A.3.19.5. *Characters and Parts of Characters* [SEE ALSO: A.3.9. jot; stroke; letter]

**character / lettering**
  carácter [Vi3:120,124-25,237,242-43,287; Luc:2; VgC6:6; Ca16:4;64:9; Go2: 5; Ca20:19; VgC23:6; Di:7; Ca19:14;51:7,14;31:36;23:34;18:14;56:9,10,16; 62:7; Grc:14; Ca7:9; Grc:29; Ca13:15;32:7,11; Do:84; Ca30:26; Da:22,59; Ca8: 33,59; 17:20;1:12; Gue6:14; Lud:12; GarE:5-6; Ca65:4;55:19;68:24; Gar:2; Gue10:4; Ca44:25; Gue1:105;2:6;8:3,10;4:3;3:6; Ca29:5,24,50;11:26;4:7]
  cifra [Grc:51]
  letra [Ven:226; Vi3:287; Av5:14; Pin:51,154; Grn:41,45,79; Leo2:13; Grn:94, 99; Cab2:7; Mu2:4,13,33;3:37-42 ManA2:49; Led7:3;17:4;5:4; Ri2:6; Va18: 2;

Bo16:6; VgC15:4;18:3; Fue:22,26,28,36; Ov:7; Bo12:2; Va4:3;5:2; Es:4; Bo15:33;5:6,32,33; BaB:71; Par3:10; Ca9:58;64:14; 31:25; Grc:12; Ca58: 9;48:5,26,28; Grc:28,54,57; Do:25,58,73; Da:37,55;Ca8:31,57;17:22; 49:48; Gue6:20,22; So:1,3; Ca28:13;15:7; Gue8:14; Ag2:28; Brn:2]

señal [Ti:4]

| Tenor | Referent | No. |
|---|---|---|
| entities of natural world | beauty of natural world as intended to lead us beyond itself to knowledge of its Creator | Ven |
| creatures | beauty of natural world as intended to lead us beyond itself to knowledge of its Creator | Vi3 |
| the incarnate Word | Incarnation as God's self-revelation | Vi3 |
| thoughts or intentions motivating one's acts | manifestation of secrets of conscience at Last Judgment | Vi3 |
| —— | Holy Spirit, dwelling in heart, as making knowledge of God's will possible even without written Law | Av5 |
| sign of the Cross; distinctive and enduring quality or potency | sacraments of Baptism, Confirmation and Holy Orders | Ti |
| —— | the divine essence | Pin |
| creatures | natural world as source of knowledge of God | Pin |
| animal species | manifestation of God's providence in many animal species | Grn |
| creatures | beauty of natural world as intended to lead us beyond itself to knowledge of Creator's beauty and wisdom | Grn |
| creatures | each creature as manifesting glory of God in special way | Grn |
| Christ's human soul and human body | union of divine nature with human nature in Jesus so that people might know God better | Leo2 |
| reverence and love | St. Ignatius of Antioch's reverence and love for Christ, who dwelt within | Cab2 |
| love | profoundly moving effect of a vision of Christ | Luc |
| wound | Christ's circumcision and naming | Mu2 |

MOTIF INDEX 197

| Tenor | Referent | No. |
|---|---|---|
| wounds | wounds of crucified Christ | Mu3 |
| — | wounds of crucified Christ | ManA2 |
| thoughts and intentions of heart | manifestation of intentions of St. Ignatius of Loyola's heart on his face | Led7 |
| — | all things as having their being in God | Led17 |
| money | money as motive for Judas' betrayal of Christ | Led5 |
| sands of Guadalquivir | immortal fame of Christ's Ascension | Ri2 |
| Christ's glorified wounds | Christ in his Ascension as bearing the wounds that are reminder of Redemption | Va18 |
| entities of natural world | natural world as manifestation of God | Bo16 |
| expression on face | the joy experienced in God's presence in both life and death as informing the expression on the face of a dead priest | VgC15 |
| dew | dew formed on flowers at dawn | VgC18 |
| extraordinary grace | Immaculate Conception | Fue |
| stigmata | stigmata of St. Francis as sign of grace and as exact replica of Christ's wounds | Fue |
| sin | Mary's sinlessness from first moment of conception | Fue |
| blood of Christ and of Mary | link between Incarnation, Immaculate Conception and Redemption | Ov |
| worlds | world or universe as source of knowledge of God | Bo12 |
| stars | heavens as manifestation of God | Va4 |
| grace | just person's faithful observance of God's law | Va5 |
| marks on melon rind | fruitfulness of season when Mary was born | Es |
| graces | Mary's extraordinary graces | Bo15 |
| the Word | Mary as mother of the Word | Bo5 |
| Mary | Mary as most perfect of human beings, naturally and supernaturally | Bo5 |
| stigmata | stigmata of St. Francis | BaB |
| thoughts, emotions, acts | examples of love, including divine love | VgC6 |
| Satan's acts | Satan's dominion over world before Redemption | Ca16 |

| Tenor | Referent | No. |
|---|---|---|
| heavenly bodies | God's creation of heavens | Par3 |
| warning | divine warning given to King Balshazzar and to sinner who profanes Eucharist | Ca9 |
| sin | original sin as affecting whole human race | Ca64 |
| the Word | divine Personhood of Christ | Go2 |
| actual sin | original sin as manifested in sins of entire human race | Ca20 |
| interlaced flowers and tendrils of vines | nature in golden age of history | VgC23 |
| interlaced flowers | flowers on common grave of certain holy monks, which teach that death is a transformation of life | Di |
| Cross | redemption, and restoration of peace between God and humankind through Christ's death on Cross | Ca19 |
| essential quality | heretic as essentially attracted to Faith even in the act of heresy | Ca51 |
| distinctive and enduring quality or potency | heretic as retaining baptismal character | Ca51 |
| — | almsgiving in hope of literal hundredfold return | Ca31 |
| stars | stars as indicating human fortune | Ca31 |
| distinctive and enduring quality or potency | baptized soul | Ca23 |
| flames | illusion of sin's allurements | Ca18 |
| distinctive and enduring quality or potency | Baptism as annulling original sin | Ca56 |
| sin | Baptism as annulling original sin | Ca56 |
| distinctive and enduring quality or potency | Baptism as irreversible | Ca56 |
| grace and nature | natural and supernatural reason as guiding principles of humankind in period from Adam to Moses | Ca62 |
| high regard | high regard in which the wise hold true self-knowledge | Grc |
| wrinkles on tree bark; sin | whole human race as affected by original sin | Ca7 |

# MOTIF INDEX

| | | |
|---|---|---|
| integrity | Mary's integrity as virgin mother | Ca58 |
| God | Queen Christina of Sweden's conversion to Roman Catholicism, seen as most complete form of Christianity, in which God is truly found | Ca48 |
| stars and other heavenly bodies | heavens as clear revelation of God | Grc |
| human actions or appearances | lack of correspondence between human actions and intentions, and failure of most people to interpret former correctly | Grc |
| human persons | human beings who are less than persons | Grc |
| flight of birds | flight and song of birds as presaging a divine mystery | Ca13 |
| distinctive and enduring quality or potency | John's baptism of Christ as inauguration of sacrament of Baptism | Ca32 |
| deeds | immortal memory of St. Ignatius' deeds | Do |
| entities of natural world | love of God evoked in St. Ignatius by manifestation of divine beauty in natural world | Do |
| reminder of death in ashes from bones of dead | meditation on death as motivation to conversion of life | Do |
| stars | God's creation of heavens | Do |
| distinctive and enduring quality or potency | Baptism as gift of new life of grace | Ca30 |
| wound | wound caused by blow on Christ's cheek during Passion as manifesting spiritual fortitude, also signified in blow administered in sacrament of Confirmation | Da |
| expression on face | diverse responses of crowd to Christ's sentencing manifested on their faces | Da |
| tears | Mary's grief in Christ's Passion | Da |
| stars | Queen Saba's vision of redemption through God's Word | Ca8 |

| Tenor | Referent | No. |
|---|---|---|
| grace | Queen Saba's vision of redemption through God's Word | Ca8 |
| stars | great astrological knowledge of Saba | Ca8 |
| sin | original sin as manifested in sins of whole human race | Ca17 |
| distinctive and enduring quality or potency | baptized person, sharing in Christ's priesthood, as obligated to holiness | Ca1 |
| — | divine kingship of Christ, signified by inscription on Cross | Ca49 |
| grace-filled acts | sanctity of Sts. John of Matha and Felix of Valois, long unrecognized | Gue6 |
| grace | St. Peter of Alcantara's holiness | Lud |
| sun | God's creation of world | GarE |
| stars | stars as influencing human fortune | Ca65 |
| — | letters affixed to Cross in Greek, Latin and Hebrew, proclaiming Christ King of the Jews | Ca55 |
| reminder of death | contemplation of ashes of the dead as God-given reminder of human mortality | So |
| plants | sin's dominion over world | Ca68 |
| entities of natural world | natural world as manifestation of God's wisdom | Gar |
| Christ's death; paradoxical manifestation of Jesus' kingship | Christ's victory and humankind's eternal glory won through Christ's death on Cross | Ca28 |
| stigmata | stigmata of St. Francis as exact replica of Christ's wounds | Gue10 |
| realized act | angels as pure intelligences, such that in them thought is act | Ca44 |
| God's wrath | idolatry as enemy of the true Faith | Ca15 |
| acts | Mary Magdalene's previously sinful life; her acts of love and penitence, represented by her kissing | Gue1 |

| Tenor | Referent | No. |
|---|---|---|
| | Christ's feet, washing them with her tears and drying them with her hair | |
| stars | correspondence between star known as "Aguila" and new head of University of Salamanca | Gue2 |
| wisdom | human wisdom as manifesting divine wisdom, even if imperfectly | Gue8 |
| wisdom | necessity of great self-sacrifice and self-detachment on part of scholar devoted to true wisdom | Gue8 |
| glory | obligation of noblemen to defend a noble cause with their lives | Gue4 |
| disordered strands of hair | Mary Magdalene's loving haste to seek Christ's forgiveness | Gue3 |
| realized acts | mysteries and special graces of Mary's life inherent in her immaculate conception | Ag2 |
| distinctive and enduring quality or potency | baptism of St. Helen, mother of Constantine | Ca29 |
| Cross | vision of Constantine and his conversion to Christianity | Ca29 |
| Cross | sin in conflict with faith | Ca29 |
| distinctive and enduring quality or potency | sacrament of Baptism | Ca11 |
| stars | the divine Word's becoming flesh | Ca4 |
| Christ's humanity and divinity | Eucharist as hiding both Christ's humanity and divinity, whereas his humanity conceals but also reveals his divinity | Brn |

**character / lettering:** unmixed expansions
  two letters [Leo2:13]
  four letters [Ca49:48]
  five letters [Fue:26]
  Arabic characters [VgC23:6]
  Gothic lettering (black letter) [SEE: A.3.19.5. character / lettering:ue. clear Gothic lettering]

a character from (a language of) the New World [Ca30:26]
letras quebradas [12] [Grn:41-42,81-82; Ca7:10;8:26;65:4-5; Gue3:6]
a character composed of two strokes [Ca19:14]
a character composed of five strokes [Da:20-22]
illuminated letters [SEE ALSO: A.3.19.5. character / lettering:ue. gold lettering; silver lettering; A.3.19.5. initial; stroke / flourish or adornment on initial]
  [Ven:226-27; Grn:41-42,45-46,82; Di:7+12; Grc:26-28; Gar:2; Ca15:7]
gold lettering [Grn:45-46; Cab2:7; Led5:4; Ri2:5-6; Va18:2;5:2; Es:4;Par3:10; Grc:12]
silver lettering [Led5:4; Fue:22; Par3:10]
purple lettering [Gue4:2-3]
red lettering [Mu2:4,13,33; BaB:71; Ca48:15; Da:20]
ancient lettering [Gue6:14-15,20]
an indelible character [Ca56:16-17;29:4-5;11:26-27]
letters written on a mantle [VgC2:2+9]
beautiful letters [SEE ALSO: A.3.19.5. character / lettering:ue. to delight in the beautiful letters without understanding their meaning]
  [Vi3:119-20; Di:7; Gue6:13-14;10:4;1:105-107;8:14;Brn:2-3]
clear lettering [SEE: A.3.19.5. character / lettering: ue. clear Gothic lettering]
clear Gothic lettering [Ca64:14;17:22]
immortal characters [SEE ALSO: A.3.19.5. character / lettering: ue. an indelible character; B.4.1:ue. to not (ever) erase]
  [Ri2:6; Ca64:9;17:22+25; So:3; Gue4:2-3]
a rare character [Bo15:33-34; Ca29:23-24]
ill-formed characters [Ca28:13; Gue1:105-106]
an obscure character [SEE ALSO: A.3.19.4.2. emblem:ue. an obscure emblem; A.3.19.5.1. Code; B.3.4.1:ue. to not understand a character; B.3.4:ue. The text is illegible.]
  [Ca16:4;29:50]
without letters [Av5:14; Ag2:28]
to add a letter [Leo2:12-13; Ca48:5+10]
to remove a letter [Ca66:3]
to be missing a letter [Ca48:5-6,25-26]
to delight in the beautiful letters without understanding their meaning
  [Ven:225-29; Vi3:124-25; Grn:44-49]
to make different styles of letter [Grn:78-79]
The spirit gives life to the letter. [ManA2:292-99; VgC15:3-4]

**character / lettering:** mixed expansions
the baptismal character [Ca51:14;23:34;32:10-11;29:5]

---

[12] A sample of *letras quebradas* appears in Oxford University Press' 1960 facsimile of the 1550 edition of The *Arte Subtilissima, por la qual se enseña a escreuir perfectamente* (fol. H6r). The latter was a product of the joint efforts of Juan de Yciar, calligrapher and teacher, and Juan de Vingles, engraver.

a sacramental character [SEE ALSO: A.3.19.5. character / lettering:me. the baptismal character]
 [Da:19-22; Ca1:11-12]
God's characters [Gue10:4-5;8:3]
living letters [Grn:53; Pin:154]

**initial**
letra mayúscula [Bo15:10]
letras y figuras [Bo16:10]
rasgo [Grc:27; Ca29:10]
rasgos + letras [Led1:14]

| Tenor | Referent | No. |
|---|---|---|
| wounds from whip | scourged and crucified Christ | Led1 |
| entities of natural world | natural world as source of knowledge of God | Bo16 |
| Mary's extraordinary graces | link between all of Mary's extraordinary graces and her being mother of God | Bo15 |
| sun and moon | heavens as revelation | Grc |
| rainbow bearing angel with Cross | Constantine's vision, symbolic of redemption through Christ's death | Ca29 |

**alphabet**[13]
A.B.C. [SEE: A.3.4.1. primer]
abecedario [SEE: A.3.4.1. primer]
alfabeto [Pin:152]

| Tenor | Referent | No. |
|---|---|---|
| creatures | creatures as manifestation of God | Pin |

"A"
A [Ca48:6]
alfa [Led17:3; Ca48:7,9,28]

---

[13] Carruthers points out that the alphabet was in medieval culture one of the most basic mnemonic devices, used to lay out one's memory grid. In order to further mark the material stored in that grid for immediate, secure recollection, one used various sorts of vivid images to clothe the alphabet, such as the type of pictures found in bestiaries and lapidaries (127). The idea found in topical passages, of each creature being a living letter is doubtless owing at least in part to this practice.

| Tenor | Referent | No. |
|---|---|---|
| God | God as source of all that is | Led17 |
| God | God as source of all that is | Ca48 |

"E"
  E [VgC2:9]

| Tenor | Referent | No. |
|---|---|---|
| "Esposa", soul | love of soul as motive for Incarnation and Redemption | VgC2 |

"O"
  O [Ca58:5,9]
  omega [Led17:3; Ca48:9]

| Tenor | Referent | No. |
|---|---|---|
| God | God as destiny of all that is | Led17 |
| integrity | integrity of Mary in her perpetual virginity, and of other virgin saints | Ca58 |
| immortality | immortality won by martyrs | Ca58 |
| God | God as destiny of all that is | Ca48 |

"S"
  S [Va10:3; Ca66:3,6]

| Tenor | Referent | No. |
|---|---|---|
| *sclavus* | total devotion to God, expressed in devotion to Eucharist | Va10 |
| jealousy; *sclavus* | abandonment of jealousy and conversion of one's energy into zeal for God's honor | Ca66 |

taw (Hebrew character)
Thao / Tau / Tao [VgC5:48;22:18; Mrt:3]

| Tenor | Referent | No. |
|---|---|---|
| Cross | St. Isidore of Madrid's honoring of the Cross | VgC5 |
| Cross | torture of certain Franciscan martyrs in Japan as ironically confirming their witness to Christ | VgC22 |

MOTIF INDEX 205

| Tenor | Referent | No. |
|---|---|---|
| Cross | St. Ladislaus of Hungary's devotion to Christ and the Faith | Mrt |

**taw: mixed expansions**
  the taw written on the forehead [VgC5:48-49;22:18+23-24; Mrt:3]

**alphabet: mixed expansions**
  God as Alpha and Omega [Led17:3; Ca48:9]

**Tetragrammaton**
  Tetragrammatón [Fe:5; ActE:4]

| Tenor | Referent | No. |
|---|---|---|
| crucified Christ | crucified Christ as sovereign God | Fe |
| Christ | high priest's complaint that Christ's demands are excessive | ActE |

**stroke** / flourish or adornment on initial [SEE ALSO: A.3.9. stroke]
  azote [Bo7:4; VgC24:28]
  línea [Ca19:14; Da:20; Ca8:26;65:4;29:30,36;11:16]
  paje [Bo16:3,10]
  rasgo [ManA2:44; Par3:11; Ca21:5;23:9; Mi2:5;1:5; Ca18:2; 48:15; Gue6:7;8:2]
  rasguño [Do:88]
  rayo [Ca4:5]

| Tenor | Referent | No. |
|---|---|---|
| wounds from whip strokes | Christ's scourging | ManA2 |
| wounds from whip strokes | Christ's scourging | Bo7 |
| entities of natural world | natural world as source of knowledge of God | Bo16 |
| sunspot as seen from celestial perspective | objection to idea of sunspots, as imperfection in creation | Par3 |
| form of world | world as God's creation | Ca21 |
| lashes of whip | Christ's scourging | VgC24 |
| bars of Cross | redemption and restoration of peace between God and | Ca19 |

| Tenor | Referent | No. |
|---|---|---|
| | humankind through Christ's death on Cross | |
| Lucifer | Lucifer's pride as cause of his rebellion against idea of Incarnation and thus of his fall | Mi2 |
| every person | humility based on position of every person in relation to God | Mi1 |
| crown suspended in air | appearance of angels with crown, intended for victor in spiritual competition | Ca23 |
| rainbow | God's promise of peace to human race | Ca18 |
| red streaks in sky as at sunrise or sunset; wounds of crucified and risen Christ | dream or vision of Queen Christina of Sweden, pertaining to sacrifice of Cross and altar | Ca48 |
| divine inspiration | God's inspiring St. Ignatius with idea of Company of Jesus | Do |
| marks of wound caused by impact of hand | wound caused by blow on Christ's cheek during Passion | Da |
| lines of constellations, divided by stars that compose them; lines of Cross, divided by Christ's body | Queen Saba's vision of redemption through God's Word | Ca8 |
| heavenly bodies | heavenly bodies as manifesting distance between the material and spiritual | Gue6 |
| lines of constellations; favorable and unfavorable influence | stars as influencing human fortune | Ca65 |
| stars of constellations | God's creation of heavens | Gue1 |
| human wisdom | human wisdom as manifesting divine Wisdom, even if imperfectly | Gue8 |
| glorified wounds of crucified Christ | Constantine's vision, symbolic of redemption through Christ's death | Ca29 |
| bars of Cross | vision of Cross, which inspires Constantine and his followers | Ca29 |

MOTIF INDEX 207

| Tenor | Referent | No. |
|---|---|---|
| | in battle; Cross as source of victory over sin | |
| sky with its stars and earth with its flowers | sin's dominion over world | Ca11 |
| sun rays; divinity of the Word | impression of ship formed by sun rays as symbol of divinity of the Word who becomes flesh | Ca4 |

**stroke / flourish:** unmixed expansions
    two strokes [SEE: A.3.19.5. character / lettering:ue. a character composed of two strokes]
    three strokes [Ca9:66]
    five strokes [SEE: A.3.19.5. character / lettering:ue. a character composed of five strokes]
    illuminated strokes [Ca23:8;11:16-18]

**stroke / flourish:** mixed expansions
    strokes of light [Ca23:9;18:2; Gue6:7;1:9]

A.3.19.5.1. *Code*

**code**
    cifra [Grc:33,41]

| Tenor | Referent | No. |
|---|---|---|
| enigmatic relationship between outward actions and intentions of heart | difficulty of understanding human intentions | Grc |

**code breaker**
    contracifra [Grc:37,48]

| Tenor | Referent | No. |
|---|---|---|
| insight into relationship between outward actions and intentions of heart | difficulty of understanding human intentions | Grc |

A.3.19.5.1.ue. *Code: Unmixed Expansions*

    to need a code breaker in order to read the text [Grc:36-40]
    to be written in code [Grc:32-33,41]

A.3.19.6. *Script / Writing*

**script / writing**
escritura [Ven:228; Vi3:243,254,256,259,261,297,298; Av5:14; Cab11:42]
lo escrito [Cam:67]

| Tenor | Referent | No. |
|---|---|---|
| entities of natural world | beauty of natural world as intended to lead beyond itself to knowledge of God | Ven |
| the incarnate Word | Incarnation as God's self-revelation | Vi3 |
| work of Holy Spirit in conception of Christ | divine mystery of Christ's conception | Vi3 |
| the incarnate Word | Christ's becoming incarnate of the virgin Mary | Vi3 |
| acts of conscience | revelation of secrets of conscience at Last Judgment | Vi3 |
| — | Holy Spirit, dwelling in heart, as making knowledge of God's will possible even without written Law | Av5 |
| structure and functioning of entities of natural world | natural world as manifestation of God's perfection | Cam |
| marks of Christ's wounds | Christ's bearing his glorified wounds even in heaven, as reminder of his love for Church and each soul | Cab11 |

**handwriting**
letra [Led1:4; Cab3:2; Brv:5; Led10:15;7:8;21:15; Bo7:2,11; VgC21:2; Mu4:10; Per:6; Da:50; Gue6:26;1:43]

| Tenor | Referent | No. |
|---|---|---|
| Christ | redemption through Christ's death on Cross | Led1 |
| acts, works | God's using flawed human beings to accomplish his purposes | Cab3 |

| Tenor | Referent | No. |
|---|---|---|
| thoughts and desires of heart | God's knowledge of thoughts and desires of the heart | Brv |
| Christ in his divinity | Incarnation | Led10 |
| thoughts and intentions of heart | manifestation of intentions of St. Ignatius of Loyola's heart on his face | Led7 |
| acts | study and practice of virtue | Led21 |
| words and deeds | hypocritical role of scribes and Pharisees in Christ's Passion and death | Bo7 |
| words and deeds | superiority of Christ's authority to that of scribes and Pharisees | Bo7 |
| wounds of crucified Christ | Christ's death as voluntary act for sake of redemption of humankind | VgC21 |
| Christ's imprinting of his own wounds | stigmata of St. Francis as replica of Christ's own wounds | Mu4 |
| image and likeness of God | creation of human beings in image and likeness of God | Per |
| Mary's weeping | Mary's weeping as manifest indication of her grief during Christ's Passion | Da |
| sanctity | sanctity of Sts. John of Matha and Felix of Valois, long unrecognized | Gue6 |
| acts | Mary Magdalene's acts of repentance and amendment, compared to her sinful acts | Gue1 |

**handwriting:** unmixed expansions
 clear handwriting [Da:50]
 better handwriting [Cab3:2; Gue1:43]
 to not recognize the handwriting [Gue6:26]

A.3.19.6.1. *Style of Handwriting*

**slanted writing**
 bastardillo [Bo7:9]

| Tenor | Referent | No. |
|---|---|---|
| corruption of scribes and Pharisees and their distortion of teachings of Law | superiority of Christ's authority to that of scribes and Pharisees | Bo7 |

**straight writing / printed letters**
de caja [Bo7:12]

| Tenor | Referent | No. |
|---|---|---|
| divine truth and authority of Christ and his teaching | superiority of Christ's authority to that of scribes and Pharisees | Bo7 |

A.3.19.6.ue. *Script / Writing: Unmixed Expansions*

Hebrew script [ManA2:48-50]
   a beautiful script [SEE ALSO: A.3.19.5. character / lettering:ue. beautiful letters]
      [Vi3:258-59; Gue6:26]
   a clear script [SEE: A.3.19.5. character / lettering:ue. clear lettering; handwriting:ue. clear handwriting]

A.3.19.7. *Punctuation* [SEE ALSO: A.3.9. jot]

**comma**
coma [ManA2:10; SF1:3]

| Tenor | Referent | No. |
|---|---|---|
| least act | Mary's life and person in every aspect as God's instrument for salvation of humankind | ManA2 |
| sum of all earthly joys | earthly joys compared to joys of heaven | SF1 |

**exclamation mark**
admiración [Ag2:33]

| Tenor | Referent | No. |
|---|---|---|
| response of wonder | marvelling of angels at Mary's fullness of grace | Ag2 |

**period**
punto [ManA2:49; Do:34; Ag2:37]

| Tenor | Referent | No. |
|---|---|---|
| puncture wounds from nails | Crucifixion | ManA2 |
| sands that bound sea | St. Ignatius' recognition of God in natural world | Do |

# MOTIF INDEX

| Tenor | Referent | No. |
|---|---|---|
| sorrows | Mary's sorrows in connection with Christ, beginning with his birth in a stable | Ag2 |

**parenthesis**
paréntesis [Do:35; Ca30:4;61:20;10:4,8]

| Tenor | Referent | No. |
|---|---|---|
| islands that curb sea | St. Ignatius' recognition of God in natural world | Do |
| discord, linked to Mosaic Law | discord fomented by perverse minds between natural law or free will, and law of grace; Mosaic Law as incorporating natural law through Decalog but in other respects in conflict with natural law and law of grace | Ca30 |
| dream | revelation through Christ as transition for Gentiles from paganism to Christian faith | Ca61 |
| mortal life | mortal life as interruption in one's eternal life in or with God, and death as return to that life | Ca10 |

**parenthesis:** unmixed expansions
to close a parenthesis [Ca10:4-5]

**parenthesis:** mixed expansions
a parenthesis in life [Ca61:20;10:2-4]


A.3.19.8. *Marginal Symbols and Superscripts*

A.3.19.8.1. *Generic Terms*

**superscript**
sobrescrito [Bo5:2]

| Tenor | Referent | No. |
|---|---|---|
| divine grace | Mary's fullness of grace | Bo5 |

A.3.19.8.2. *Specific Terms*

**asterisk**
   astro [Bo5:2; Ca29:45]
   estrella [Ag1:9]

| Tenor | Referent | No. |
|---|---|---|
| divine grace | Mary's fullness of grace | Bo5 |
| star of Bethlehem | God's leading Wise Men to Christ by a star | Ag1 |
| Cross, seen in sky | Cross as source of victory over sin | Ca29 |

**eyes**
   ojos [Led18:2,8,11,14,18]

| Tenor | Referent | No. |
|---|---|---|
| St. Lucy's eyes, put out in her martyrdom | St. Lucy's life, and particularly her martyrdom, as example for Christians to relinquish all that deflects from love of God | Led18 |

**pointing finger**
   índice [Ca44:5]

| Tenor | Referent | No. |
|---|---|---|
| John the Baptist's index finger, his role as precursor of Christ | John the Baptist's pointing out Christ as the long-awaited Messiah | Ca44 |

A.3.19.9. *Marks / Signs*

A.3.19.9.1. *Generic Terms*

**mark / sign**
   marca [Vi3:255; Fue:46; Ca29:4]
   seña [Do:58]
   señal [Brv:10; Mu3:1,14,35,42,46,49,50; Fue:46; Ca29:29,35]
   symbolo [Mu3:5]

| Tenor | Referent | No. |
|---|---|---|
| work of Holy Spirit in conception of Christ | divine mystery of Christ's conception | Vi3 |

## MOTIF INDEX

| Tenor | Referent | No. |
|---|---|---|
| lines on forehead | St. Benedict's compassion as shown on his countenance | Brv |
| wounds | Christ's wounds as sign of his eternal love for souls | Mu3 |
| Christ | love of Christ as motive of Christian's every act | Mu3 |
| stigmata | stigmata of St. Francis as exact replica of Christ's wounds | Fue |
| manifestation of divine beauty in natural world | love of God evoked in St. Ignatius by manifestation of divine beauty in natural world | Do |
| distinctive and enduring effect | baptism of St. Helen, mother of Constantine | Ca29 |
| Cross | vision of Cross, which inspires Constantine and his followers in battle; Cross as source of victory over sin | Ca29 |

A.3.19.9.2. *Type of Mark*

**brand** [SEE ALSO: A.3.19.5. alphabet: "S"]
 cruz [VgC22:12]
 hierro [Ca22:12,17;56:3,7,25,30;36:16; Ag2:16]
 letras [VgC20:5]
 sello [Ca19:6,9]
 seña [Ca22:21;52:7]
 señal [PrA:6]
 signo [Ca22:13]

| Tenor | Referent | No. |
|---|---|---|
| IHS (letters on Eucharistic host); grace | grace of sacrament of Eucharist; strengthening of bond between soul and Christ | VgC20 |
| Cross | torture of certain Franciscan martyrs in Japan as ironically confirming their witness to Christ | VgC22 |
| divine mercies and graces | total devotion to God, expressed in devotion to Eucharist | PrA |

| Tenor | Referent | No. |
|---|---|---|
| sin or effects of sin | human nature as vitiated by original sin, manifested in actual sins of human race | Ca22 |
| sin | original sin as subjugating human race to power of Satan | Ca19 |
| sin or effects of sin | original sin and its annulment through Baptism | Ca56 |
| sin or effects of sin | habit of sin as enslaving human being | Ca56 |
| original sin | original sin and its annulment through Baptism | Ca36 |
| subjection | death of Sisara; Satan's defeat through Mary and Christ | Ca52 |
| sin | Mary's sinlessness | Ag2 |

**brand:** unmixed expansions
   slave brand [SEE ALSO: B.2.1.2. to brand:ue. to brand a slave]
     [Va10:2-3; PrA:1+6; Ca22:3-5,9-12;66:3-5;36:16-17; 52:7; Ag2:16]
   without a brand [Ag2:16]

**brand:** mixed expansions
   to bear God's brand [Va10:3-4; VgC20:1-5; PrA:1-7]

A.3.19.9.3. *Specific Mark*

**cross**
   cruz [AD:5,12; BaB:17,58; Da:60; Ca43:145;36:75,80;29:29, 35,50]

| Tenor | Referent | No. |
|---|---|---|
| Cross | Christ's death as culmination of Mary's sorrows, caused by original sin | AD |
| Cross | St. Francis' imitation of crucified Christ | BaB |
| Cross | contemplation of Mary's grief during Christ's Passion | Da |
| Cross | religious leaders of Jews as responsible for Christ's death | Ca43 |
| Cross | redemption through Christ's Passion and death | Ca36 |
| Cross | Constantine's vision of the Cross; Cross as sign of redemption | Ca29 |

**cross:** unmixed expansions
  a cross as part of a coat of arms [VgC22:9-12; BaB:58-60]
  to mark with a cross [AD:5; Cai19; VgC22:11-12; Ca43:144-45; 36:75,78-80]

A.3.19.9.ue. *Marks / Signs: Unmixed Expansions*

  a mysterious mark [SEE: A.3.19.4.2. emblem:ue. an obscure emblem; A.3.19.4.2. seal:ue. a mysterious seal; A.3.19.5. character:ue. an obscure character]
  to bear an identical mark [SEE ALSO: A.3.19.4.2. seal:ue. to bear an identical seal]
    [Fue:46-48]

A.3.19.9.me. *Marks / Signs: Mixed Expansions*

  the sign of the cross [Ca29:29,35]

A.3.20. DEFECTS AND CORRECTIONS IN THE TEXT

A.3.20.1. *Defects in Content*

A.3.20.1.1. *General Terms*

**flaw**
  falta [Cai7:4; Bo9:26]
  imperfección [Bo15:25,61]

| *Tenor* | *Referent* | *No.* |
|---|---|---|
| sins | God's mercy to repentant sinners who amend their life | Cai7 |
| original sin and its effects | sanctification of John the Baptist in his mother's womb | Bo9 |
| spiritual imperfection | Mary's fullness of grace or complete freedom from sin and fault | Bo15 |

**flaw:** unmixed expansions
  without flaw [Bo15:25-26,61]

A.3.20.1.2. *Types of Defect*

**error**
  error [BaB:31; Gue1:30,53,60,88,90,109]

| Tenor | Referent | No. |
|---|---|---|
| sins | St. Francis' faith as reproof to sinners | BaB |
| sins | people's lives as alternating between sin and repentance | Gue1 |
| sins | Mary Magdalene's sins and conversion | Gue1 |

**error:** unmixed expansions
to be full of errors [Gue1:88-89]

**excess**
demasía [Bo9:15,26]

| Tenor | Referent | No. |
|---|---|---|
| effects of original sin | sanctification of John the Baptist in his mother's womb | Bo9 |

**lack** [SEE ALSO: A.3.19.5. character:ue. to be missing a letter]
falta [Bo9:26]

| Tenor | Referent | No. |
|---|---|---|
| lack of sanctifying grace | sanctification of John the Baptist in his mother's womb | Bo9 |

A.3.20.2. *Defects in Appearance or Graphics*

**blot / drop of ink**
borrón [ManA2:175; Ov:10; Bo15:54;6:25,39; Par3:12; Go1:5; Mi2:7; Roj:3; Ca43:83,91,92; Mrt:8; Ca65:17; Gue1:31; 8:13;16:3]
gota de tinta [Par3:8]
mancha [Bo6:8,28,40]

| Tenor | Referent | No. |
|---|---|---|
| sins | saints as having been guilty of occasional sin, and some of many sins | ManA2 |
| sin | Christ as incapable of sin; Mary as preserved by God from all sin | Ov |
| sin | Mary as only human person free from original sin | Bo15 |

| Tenor | Referent | No. |
|---|---|---|
| sin | Mary's preservation from original sin and its effects | Bo6 |
| sin | original sin | Bo6 |
| spots on sun or moon | God's creation of heavens | Par3 |
| Balthazar | visit of Wise Men to newborn Christ, as prefigured in Scripture | Go1 |
| defect | Lucifer's pride as cause of his rebellion against idea of Incarnation and thus of his fall | Mi2 |
| work | work as painful but necessary for salvation | Roj |
| annulment | total annulment of sin's power in case of Mary, through retroactive grace won by Christ's death | Ca43 |
| sin | Mary's preservation from original sin | Ca43 |
| any attempt to imagine horrors of hell | St. Margaret of Hungary's vision of hell | Mrt |
| black spot on sheep; sin | God's mercy and grace to sinners, and the love of the forgiven sinner | Ca65 |
| sin | Mary Magdalene's sinful life and conversion | Gue1 |
| errors | necessity of self-sacrifice on part of scholar devoted to true wisdom | Gue8 |
| sins | St. Teresa of Avila's humility | Gue16 |

**blot:** unmixed expansions
   to be full of blots [SEE ALSO: A.3.18.2:ue. One page alone is free of blots.]
     [ManA2:175]
   without blot [SEE ALSO: B.4.1:ue. to not (ever) blot]
     [Bo15:53-55; Mi2:7]

**blot:** mixed expansions
   the blot of Adam [Bo15:54]

**blurring / overlapping** (as of letters)
   borrón [Pin:143; Da:62; Gue1:68]

| Tenor | Referent | No. |
|---|---|---|
| confusion | supposed confusion among vast number of ideas in minds of the wise | Pin |
| weeping | Mary's beauty as evident even amidst her weeping during Christ's Passion | Da |
| tears | Mary Magdalene's penitence | Gue1 |

**misprint**
errata [ManA1:54; Fue:23; Ov:9; Bo15:68; Ra:6; Ag2:45,48]
falta [ManA1:21]

| Tenor | Referent | No. |
|---|---|---|
| sin, particularly original sin | Mary's freedom from sin from first moment of conception | ManA1 |
| original sin | Immaculate Conception | Fue |
| sin | Christ as incapable of sin; Mary as preserved by God from all sin | Ov |
| sin | Mary's sinlessness | Bo15 |
| sin | Immaculate Conception | Ra |
| sin | Mary's freedom from all sin | Ag2 |

**misprint:** unmixed expansions
without misprint [ManA1:53-54; Fue:23; Bo15:65-68; Ra:6; Ag2:45,48]

**strike-out**
rayo [BaB:52]

| Tenor | Referent | No. |
|---|---|---|
| being forgotten | lasting memory of St. Francis | BaB |

A.3.20.3. *Corrections*

**correction**
corrección [Bo15:64]
enmienda [Fue:23]

| Tenor | Referent | No. |
|---|---|---|
| need to annul effects of original sin | Immaculate Conception | Fue |
| amendment for sin | Mary's sinlessness | Bo15 |

A.3.20.3.ue. *Corrections: Unmixed Expansions*

without correction [Fue:23; Bo15:64]


A.3.20.ue. DEFECTS AND CORRECTIONS IN THE TEXT: UNMIXED EXPANSIONS

without defect [SEE: A.3.20.1.1. flaw:ue. without flaw; A.3.20.2. blot:ue. without blot; misprint:ue. without misprint; A.3.20.3:ue. without correction; B.2.3.2. to expurgate: ue. without expurgation]


A.4. CIRCUMSTANCES OF THE TEXT (ACCOMPANYING OR SURROUNDING DETAIL)

A.4.1. PLACES WHERE THE TEXT IS PRESERVED OR TRANSMITTED

**bookstore**
librería [Var:8,10]

| *Tenor* | *Referent* | *No.* |
|---|---|---|
| heart | importance of meditation in order to progress in the spiritual life | Var |

**library**
biblioteca [Vi3:6; Do:99; Gue11:4]
librería [Ven:210; Mat:1; Led12:2; Va19:3; Bo15:66; Do:17,75; Gue11:2; Ca61:2; Ag2:74]

| *Tenor* | *Referent* | *No.* |
|---|---|---|
| natural world | natural world as rich source of knowledge of God | Ven |
| heart and mind | importance for the Christian of the various sources of spiritual understanding mentioned in Scripture | Vi3 |
| crucified Christ | crucified Christ as source of all St. Bonaventure's wisdom | Mat |
| Christ | St. John the Evangelist's vision of divine mysteries while leaning on Christ's breast at Last Supper | Led12 |
| heaven | Mary's Assumption to heaven, and communion of angels and saints in God | Va19 |

| Tenor | Referent | No. |
|---|---|---|
| human race | Mary's unique preservation from sin | Bo15 |
| Jesuit communities | St. Ignatius of Loyola's life and teaching as inspiring many to join the order he founded | Do |
| disintegrated corpses or graves of the dead | meditation on death as motivation to conversion of life | Do |
| hermit | aged and wise hermit as source of wisdom for future generations | Do |
| wise people | number of wise persons in a city as the true measure of its greatness | Gue11 |
| sources of knowledge | Gentiles' seeking wisdom, specifically, understanding of astrological signs | Ca61 |
| heaven | desire for eternal life or participation in communion of saints | Ag2 |

**library:** unmixed expansions
  a great library [Bo15:66; Gue11:1-2]

**library:** mixed expansions
  Adam's library [Bo15:66-67]
  a living library [Gue11:4]

**professorial chair**
  cátedra [Led16:9;5:1; Bo15:70; Hu:15; Ca62:70; Mrl:7]

| Tenor | Referent | No. |
|---|---|---|
| Temple | Christ's example of obedience to the Law | Led16 |
| principles, teaching | Judas as example of Jews' putting money before wisdom | Led5 |
| Mary | Mary as "Seat of Wisdom" or mother of the Word | Bo15 |
| Mary | Mary as "Seat of Wisdom" or mother of the Word | Hu |
| Cross | Crucifixion | Ca62 |
| site of St. Peter Martyr's death | St. Peter Martyr's death as teaching mysteries of the Faith | Mrl |

**professorial chair:** unmixed expansions
  *cátedra de prima* [SEE ALSO: A.3.7.2. lesson:ue. a morning ("prime time") lesson]
  [Led1:6]

| Tenor | Referent | No. |
|---|---|---|
| Cross | divine mysteries taught by dying Christ | Led1 |

**school**
  escuela [Vi3:47,106,167,170,175,301; Grn:78; Cab8:2; Led16:2; Bo7:5,14; Tel:7]

| Tenor | Referent | No. |
|---|---|---|
| beatific vision | beatific vision enjoyed by angels and saints in heaven | Vi3 |
| world or mortal life | indirect knowledge of God through natural world, especially heavens | Vi3 |
| natural world | manifestation of God's providence in diverse animal species | Grn |
| God's direct self-communication | beatific vision enjoyed by blessed in heaven, compared to God's self-communication in human form in Christ | Cab8 |
| Christ's life in world | Christ as model of all virtues | Led16 |
| scribes and Pharisees as a group | plot of scribes and Pharisees to have Jesus put to death | Bo7 |
| God the Father | Christ as Father's eternal Wisdom | Bo7 |
| learning moral lessons through experience | necessity of supplementing theoretical understanding of virtue with practical experience | Tel |

**school:** unmixed expansions
  a school of calligraphy [Grn:78]
  a school of advanced students [SEE ALSO: A.4.1. school:me. the school of the angels]
    [Vi3:47-48; Cab8:2+6-8]
  a children's school [Vi3:106,301; Cab8:3-4+13-15]

**school:** mixed expansions
  the school of the angels [Vi3:166-67,301-02]

A.4.2. ACCOUTREMENTS (Items that Facilitate the Preparation, Preservation or Handling of the Text)

**archive**
archivo [Snt2:6; Led18:15; BaB:40; Ca2:21;8:64;55:43;36:61; 57:17;29:56]

| Tenor | Referent | No. |
| --- | --- | --- |
| faculty of memory | memory as preserving important and noble acts, and learning, of humankind | Snt2 |
| guardian, conserver | wife as guardian of husband's honor | Led18 |
| history of Church | stigmata of St. Francis as enduring honor for Franciscan Order | BaB |
| gifts or treasures of grace | divine grace as source of spiritual healing administered by Church | Ca2 |
| Solomon | Solomon's God-given wisdom, biblical type of divine Wisdom | Ca8 |
| mysteries of Godhead | God's merciful providence | Ca55 |
| heaven | divine grace as soul's riches | Ca36 |
| memory of humankind | commemoration of a sacred festival | Ca57 |
| mysteries of Godhead | divine Providence | Ca29 |

**archive:** unmixed expansions
open archives [Ca55:42-43]

**bookmark**[14]
registro [Ca2:9;68:8;3:9;36:28;29:20]

| Tenor | Referent | No. |
| --- | --- | --- |
| spiritual ecstasy | St. John the Evangelist's ecstatic vision of the divine mysteries of which he wrote | Ca2 |
| sun | order of heavens as manifestation of God's wisdom | Ca68 |
| spiritual ecstasy | St. John the Evangelist's ecstatic vision of the divine mysteries of which he wrote | Ca3 C36 |

---

[14] Carruthers mentions a medieval bookmark that explains the key to the pagination scheme of the volume in which it is found (100). The term *registro* in the examples cited is in accord with this description.

MOTIF INDEX                 223

| Tenor | Referent | No. |
|---|---|---|
| Cross | Constantine's vision of the Cross in heavens | Ca29 |

**chain**
  cadena [Vi3:97; Do:51]
  eslabones [Do:53]

| Tenor | Referent | No. |
|---|---|---|
| "great chain of being"; constant accessibility | natural world as source of knowledge of God intended for all people | Vi3 |
| "great chain of being"; being captivated | manifestation of God in order of natural world as capturing St. Ignatius' love | Do |

**desk**
  bufete [Ca43:101,119;61:2]
  escritorio [Va15:6]

| Tenor | Referent | No. |
|---|---|---|
| Mary | unborn John the Baptist's recognition of Redeemer in Mary's womb | Va15 |
| — | Moses and Joshua, Old Testament leaders of Hebrews to promised land, as prophets of Christ's divine and human lineage | Ca43 |
| — | Christ in his human nature as free from sin | Ca43 |
| — | Gentiles' seeking wisdom, specifically, understanding of astrological signs | Ca61 |

**lectern / shelf**[15]
  atril [Led1:11]
  retril [Led13:1]

---

[15] The *Diccionario de autoridades* depicts the *atril* as "tabla pequeña fundada sobre cuatro pies, levantada por una parte, y con un listoncito de madera en la parte interior, que sirve para poner y asegurar el Misal, u otro qualquier libro." A passage from Umberto Eco's *The Name of the Rose* translated by Díez Borque describes a medieval scriptorium: "Junto a cada escribiente, o bien en la parte más alta de las mesas, que tenían una inclinación, había un atril sobre el que estaba apoyado el códice que se estaba copiando" (53). I think Ledesma's poem mingles elements found in both these descriptions. It identifies Christ with a liturgical book displayed in a church and at the same time links him with a worn-out book that is being copied in order to preserve it.

| Tenor | Referent | No. |
|---|---|---|
| Cross | Cross upon which Christ hung | Led1<br>Led13 |

**scrinium**[16]
  custodia [LoA:14-15]
  escritorio [Snt2:2; Led14:10]
  vasija [Vi3:245]

| Tenor | Referent | No. |
|---|---|---|
| Christ | Incarnation | Vi3 |
| faculty of memory | memory as preserving important and noble acts, and learning, of humankind | Snt2 |
| heart | revelation at death and judgment of secrets of heart | Led14 |
| humility | merits of saints as hidden through humility | LoA |

**portfolio**
  cartera [Ca45:9;36:30]

| Tenor | Referent | No. |
|---|---|---|
| Christ's life | witness provided by Christ's life to his being Messiah | Ca45 |
| — | temporal dimension of human life and obligation to use one's gifts prudently | Ca36 |

---

[16] In classical Latin, the word *scrinium* denotes "a letter-case or book-box, or any chest in which papers are kept" (Carruthers 39). DeVinne provides a drawing of a Roman *scrinium* containing manuscript scrolls (43). "In the late Empire the word came to mean the state archives.... In Christian usage it seems to have been associated with the keeping of all valuable ecclesiastical items, including records, books, and relics – things for remembering. These meanings are still present in the English word 'shrine'.... A *scrinium*, at least in the earlier Middle Ages, was also a *secretorium*; the words suggest a repository for (written) things that are hidden and closed away as well as precious, as treasure is laid or hidden away.... *Scrinium* maintained its association with books as well as saints through the Carolingian period at least" (Carruthers 39-40).

MOTIF INDEX 225

## B. ACTIONS AND STATES

### B.1. TO PREPARE THE EQUIPMENT FOR PRODUCING THE TEXT

[SEE ALSO: A.1.2.1. pen:ue. to cut the pen; A.1.2.1. seal / signet ring / stamp:ue. to forge a stamp; A.1.2.2. ink:ue. to water the ink; A.1.2.3.2. paper:ue. to make fine paper; A.1.2.3.3. parchment:ue. to prepare a parchment for writing; B.2.4.1. *To Prepare the Type*]

**to rule the page**
arar pauta [Do:85]
correr las líneas [Gue1:8]
pautar [Ca27:6]

| Tenor | Referent | No. |
|---|---|---|
| to fix the orbit | God's fixing the orbits of stars | Do |
| to fix the order and relationships | physical and metaphysical harmony of the universe | Ca27 |
| to fix the orbit | God's fixing the orbits of stars | Gue1 |

### B.2. TO PRODUCE THE TEXT

### B.2.1. TO WRITE THE TEXT

B.2.1.1. *To Write*

**to abbreviate**
abreviar [Ca62:83]

| Tenor | Referent | No. |
|---|---|---|
| to calm, to diminish | diminishment of waves of sea at death of Christ, submission of nature in face of divine mystery | Ca62 |

**to abbreviate:** unmixed expansions
to abbreviate a word so it will fit on the paper [Led10:17-20]

**to address**
sobrescribir [ManA2:326; Cai14:3]

| Tenor | Referent | No. |
|---|---|---|
| to address, use a certain title | the awe-inspiring God of the Old Testament | ManA2 |
| to complete and eternalize | perseverance in virtue | Cai14 |

**to address:** unmixed expansions
  to address a letter [ManA2:319-20; Cai14:1-3]

**to compose**
  componer [Vi3:250; Cab1:6; ManA2:209-10; Bo9:2; Di:16; Ca17:2; Ag2:10]
  dar forma [Vi3:249; Ca21:6]

| Tenor | Referent | No. |
|---|---|---|
| to engender, to give human form | Mary's conceiving Christ by the Holy Spirit | Vi3 |
| to ask for | power of prayer in Jesus' name | Cab1 |
| to be the origin of | God the Father's election of Mary as mother of his eternal Word, with all the special graces implied | ManA2 |
| to beget | Zachary's begetting John the Baptist | Bo9 |
| to create | God as Creator of world | Ca21 |
| to convey symbolically | interlaced flowers growing on common grave of holy monks as symbolizing a spiritual truth | Di |
| to create | God's creation of heavens and earth in and through his Word | Ca17 |
| to be the origin of | God's election of Mary as mother of the Word, with all the special graces implied | Ag2 |

**to compose:** unmixed expansions [SEE ALSO: A.3.2.1:ue. to begin a new book; to complete a book]
  to compose with great care [Cab7:10-12; Ag2:9-10]

**to copy / adapt / translate**
  copiar [Va4:11; Mad:2-3]
  traducir [Jau:7]
  transcribir [Vi3:212]
  trasladar [Ven:143; Fue:20; Va3:12]

## MOTIF INDEX

| Tenor | Referent | No. |
|---|---|---|
| to manifest in a different way | indirect manifestations of God in this life | Ven |
| to communicate in a different way | Christ as clear and concrete manifestation of God | Vi3 |
| to imitate | St. Francis' imitation of crucified Christ, even to his wounds | Fue |
| to transmit | spread of Christianity by the Apostles | Jau |
| to recur | orderly succession of days and nights as manifestation of Creator | Va4 |
| to conceive a desire for, incline towards | pursuit of worldly delights | Va3 |
| to imitate | St. Peter of Alcantara's imitation of Christ | Mad |

**to copy / adapt / translate:** unmixed expansions
  to adapt a text according to the intended reader / listener [Ven:143-46; Cab8:14-15]
  to copy from the original [SEE ALSO: B.2.4:ue. to print from the original] [Ven:138-40,162-64,185-88; Mad:1-4]
  to make many copies [Jau:7-8]

**to correct**
  apurar [Bo9:28,40]
  cercenar [Bo9:15,16]
  corregir [Bo15:68; Gue1:35,57,74-75,92]
  emendar / enmienda [Gue1:74,76,85,93,112]

| Tenor | Referent | No. |
|---|---|---|
| to remove all effects of original sin | sanctification of John the Baptist in his mother's womb | Bo9 |
| to annul sin | Mary's sinlessness | Bo15 |
| to absolve | Mary Magdalene's seeking Christ's forgiveness and absolution of her sin | Gue1 |
| to amend (amending) one's life | Mary Magdalene's conversion | Gue1 |

**to correct:** unmixed expansions
  to be so emended as to seem a new book [Gue1:112-13]
  Correcting the text is the author's responsibility. [Gue1:74-75]

**to dedicate**
dedicar [Ca53:9; Ag2:21]
dirigir [BaB:14]

| Tenor | Referent | No. |
|---|---|---|
| to dedicate one's self | St. Francis' dedication to God in imitation of crucified Christ | BaB |
| to dedicate one's self | Mary's complete dedication to God, as manifested in Annunciation; Mercedarian and Trinitarian Orders' dedication to God and to work of rescuing Christian captives | Ca53 |
| to dedicate one's self | Mary's complete dedication to God | Ag2 |

**to dedicate:** unmixed expansions
to dedicate a book [SEE ALSO: B.2.1.1. to dedicate:ue. to dedicate a book to the king]
[BaB:13-14]
to dedicate a book to the king [Ag2:21]

**to entitle** [Ag1:14;2:13]
intitular [Mon1:9]
dar nombre [BaB:85]

| Tenor | Referent | No. |
|---|---|---|
| to proclaim someone's power | manifestation of Christ's divine power in the Crucifixion | Mon1 |
| to declare a particular dignity of someone | God's sanctifying St. Francis and manifesting his sanctity | BaB |
| to declare a particular dignity of someone | God's mysterious manifestation of Christ's divine kingship in the Crucifixion | Ag1 |
| to give someone a particular role or relationship | God's electing Mary as mother of God and queen of heaven | Ag2 |
| to assume a particular role or relationship | Mary's proclaiming herself God's slave | Ag2 |

## to gloss
acotar [ManA2:194; Bo14:7,14]

| Tenor | Referent | No. |
|---|---|---|
| to attest | God's attesting to perfect holiness of Mary's every act through his special grace | ManA2 |
| to attest and interpret | God's working through conscience to interpret natural law, to affirm its rightness, and to judge one's adherence to it | Bo14 |

## to inscribe
inscribir / inscripción [Vi3:17; Ag1:14]

| Tenor | Referent | No. |
|---|---|---|
| knowing | God's foreknowledge of the elect | Vi3 |
| to declare | God's using Pilate's inscription on Cross to declare Christ's divine kingship | Ag1 |

## to mark
señalar [ManA2:43; Fue:28; VgC22:18; Ca32:2]

| Tenor | Referent | No. |
|---|---|---|
| to wound | Christ's scourging | ManA2 |
| to wound | stigmata of St. Francis | Fue |
| to identify | torture of certain Franciscan martyrs in Japan as ironically confirming their identity as Christians | VgC22 |
| to baptize | John the Baptist's baptizing Christ | Ca32 |

## to note down [Tel:4]
anotar [Ca43:18]
apuntar [BaB:53,55; Ca26:9]
asentar [Mon1:12; Ven:354-55; ADJ:3; Pin:115; Led22:7; ManA2:345;3:56,72, 73,97,101,113; Led14:17; Ca33:5;62:52; 67:5;43:65]
consignar [Vi3:282]
hacer apuntamientos [Ca54:3-4]

notar / notación [Vi3:59; Ca2:13]
registrar [Ca42:12]

| Tenor | Referent | No. |
|---|---|---|
| to merit inclusion | eternal life won by early Christian martyrs | Mon1 |
| to hold someone responsible for | humankind's responsibility to praise God on behalf of all creation | Ven |
| divine election | divine election as gift of God not dependent on a person's merits | Vi3 |
| to inform | revelation of secrets of conscience at Last Judgment | Vi3 |
| to include | to include among the elect | ADJ |
| to include | God's foreknowledge of the elect | Pin |
| to know | God's knowledge of all human acts | Led22 |
| to engender | incarnation of the Redeemer | ManA2 |
| to hold someone responsible for | redemption from sin through Christ's death | ManA3 |
| to know | God's knowledge of even the most secret human acts | Led14 |
| to serve purposes of, to be an aspect of | learning fear of God through experience as serving purposes of, or as an aspect of, understanding or rational intellect | Tel |
| to point out; to mark with stigmata | stigmata of St. Francis as signal grace of God | BaB |
| to know | God's foreknowledge of the elect | Ca33 |
| to know | God's foreknowledge of the elect | Ca62 |
| to know or to be the source of existtence of | God's eternal knowledge of, or eternal existence of, all things in the Word | Ca67 |
| to know | revelation of divine mysteries to St. John the Evangelist in a vision | Ca2 |
| to reason | St. Augustine's application of human reason to divine mysteries | Ca54 |
| to attend to | loving attention to human needs and sufferings | Ca42 |

# MOTIF INDEX 231

| Tenor | Referent | No. |
|---|---|---|
| to include | Christ as not included among group of sinners | Ca43 |
| to include | every human being as sinful | Ca43 |
| to include | every person when born into this life as under the sway of death | Ca26 |

**to portray**
retratar [BaB:61,63]

| Tenor | Referent | No. |
|---|---|---|
| to manifest | St. Francis' imitation of the crucified Christ, even to his wounds | BaB |

**to punctuate** [SEE ALSO: A.3.19.7. parenthesis:ue. to close a parenthesis] [Ag2:33-35]

| Tenor | Referent | No. |
|---|---|---|
| to marvel | marveling of angels at Mary's spiritual splendor | Ag2 |

**to register** [ADJ:6-8; Cai12:2-3; Ca43:63-69]
alistar [Ca59:6]
escribir por huésped [VgC16:3]
registrar [Led14:2,7,12]

| Tenor | Referent | No. |
|---|---|---|
| to know | mystery of the angels as known only to God, not to humankind | ADJ |
| to grant eternal life to | prayer as prelude to beatific vision | Cai12 |
| to know or make known | secrets of conscience of the dying known only to God and to conscience itself | Led14 |
| to give mortal life to | detachment from this brief temporary life | VgC16 |
| to incorporate | incorporation of the baptized into ranks of Christ's followers | Ca59 |
| to make subject to sin and its effects | Christ's absolute freedom from sin | Ca43 |

**to revise** [SEE ALSO: A.3.19.5. character / lettering:ue. to add a letter; to remove a letter]
[VgC24:3-4]

| Tenor | Referent | No. |
|---|---|---|
| to devise new and more terrible sacrileges | sacrilegious treatment of Christian figures, specifically St. Peter, by certain Jews of Lope's time | VgC24 |

**to rubricate**
rubricar [Mon8:11;7:17; Mu2:40-41; Ag1:13]

| Tenor | Referent | No. |
|---|---|---|
| to shed blood upon | Golgotha or Mt. Calvary | Mon8 |
| to mark with blood; to attest | stigmata of St. Francis as God's attestation to his sanctity | Mon7 |
| to wound | Jesus' circumcision and naming | Mu2 |
| to mark with blood | Christ's scourging | Ag1 |

**to sign**
afirmar [Ca36:45]
firmar [Mon8:15; Av3:12; Cab5:3; Led11:13; Cai19;10:1; Ri4:4; Es:2,17; Per:27; Ca22:39;31:57,58,60; Que1:3; Ca32:4;43:108,109,112;41:10; 50:18; Gue6:25; Ca36:86,87; 69:16,32,33]
rubricar [Led11:20; Va12:8; Da:21]

| Tenor | Referent | No. |
|---|---|---|
| to be wounded | piercing of Christ's side, rather than breaking of his bones, as symbol of unity among Christians desired by Christ | Mon8 |
| to wound; to attest | naming and circumcision of Jesus as sign and promise of redemption | Av3 |
| to shed blood; to attest | martyrdom of St. Stephen as witness to Gospel of Christ | Cab5 |
| to wound; to attest | stigmata of St. Francis as direct imprinting by Christ of his own wounds | Led11 |
| to attest | Cross as instrument of salvation or eternal glory | Cai19 |

| Tenor | Referent | No. |
|---|---|---|
| to attest | long-suffering as proof of love and constancy | Cai10 |
| to confirm | Christ's death as confirma- of peace between God and humankind | Ri4 |
| to confirm with one's blood | naming and circumcision of Jesus as sign and promise of redemption | Va12 |
| to give evidence | appearance of melon as evidence of its ripeness | Es |
| to wound; to attest | naming and circumcision of Jesus as sign and promise of redemption | Es |
| to die; to redeem | redemption through Christ's death | Per |
| to guarantee | Christ's absolute freedom from sin and therefore from any punishment due because of sin | Ca22 |
| to put oneself in a compromising situation | pursuit of pleasure and its spiritual or eternal price | Ca31 |
| to guarantee | inconstancy of human fortune | Que1 |
| to authorize | Baptism as conferring sancti- fying grace, which justi- fies the soul and makes it God's own | Ca32 |
| to cause to bleed; to confirm | bleeding caused by blow to Christ's cheek as confirmation of his patience in suffering | Da |
| to certify | Scriptural testimony to Christ's human and di- vine lineage | Ca43 |
| to attest | Scriptural attestation to Israel as God's bride | Ca41 |
| to ratify | Gentiles' role in handing Jesus over to death; Gentiles' rejection of Christ and his teach- ings, specifically, Real Presence in Eucharist | Ca50 |
| to attest | sanctity of Sts. John of Matha and Felix of Valois, as God's pres- ence or grace | Gue6 |

| Tenor | Referent | No. |
|---|---|---|
| to acknowledge | acknowledgment of one's mortality and obligation to use one's gifts wisely in this world | Ca36 |
| to promise | promise of redemption through Christ's death | Ca36 |
| to promise | Israel's promise to keep covenant with God | Ca69 |
| to promise | Herod's promise to Salome, resulting in beheading of John the Baptist; Israel's breach of promise and rejection of prophets sent to her | Ca69 |

**to sign:** unmixed expansions
    to sign and seal [SEE ALSO: A.3.1. document:ue. a signed and sealed document]
        [Cai19;10:1; Ca32:4-6]
    to sign a death sentence [Ca50:18]
    to sign a peace treaty [Ri4:4]
    to sign a promissory note [SEE ALSO: A.3.7.2. signature:ue. the signature on a promissory note; A.3.7.2.m.e. God signs a promissory note]
        [Per:27; Ca31:58-65;36:35-37+44-45;69:16]
    to sign as guarantor [Av3:10-12; Per:23-27; Ca22:32-34,39,41-42;36:82-86]
    to sign as witness [Cab5:3-4]
    to sign without reading [Ca69:32-33]
    to be signed by the king [SEE ALSO: A.3.7.2. signature:ue. the king's signature]
        [Mon8:13-15; Led11:13-14,19-20]

**to sign:** mixed expansions
    to sign with blood [Av3:12; Cab5:3; Led11:12-13; Va12:78; Bo8:3-4; VgC21:7; Es:17]
    God signs a promissory note. [Av3:7-12; Cai8:1-2; Bo8:1-4; Es:13-16]

**to sketch** [SEE ALSO: A.3.10. rough draft]
    bosquejar [Led15:3]
    rasgar [Ca46:15]

| Tenor | Referent | No. |
|---|---|---|
| to be the occasion of imagining | idleness as occasion of sin | Led15 |
| to symbolize | Rebecca as symbolizing principle that "the last shall be first" | Ca46 |

MOTIF INDEX 235

**to spell out** [SEE ALSO: A.3.19.5. character / lettering:ue. to add a letter]
deletrear [Ven:148-49,257,273; Bo12:4,5]

| Tenor | Referent | No. |
|---|---|---|
| to manifest plainly | knowledge of God in this world as intentionally less clear and complete than in heaven | Ven |
| to manifest plainly | natural world as very evident manifestation of God | Ven |
| to manifest plainly | matter as very evident manifestation of stability or constancy of God | Ven |
| to manifest plainly | natural world as evident manifestation of God | Bo12 |

**to superscribe** [SEE ALSO: B.2.1.1. to address]
señalar [Ag1:9]
sobrescribir [Cab4:6; Brv:10; Gue6:9,10]

| Tenor | Referent | No. |
|---|---|---|
| to give a name | redemptive power of name of Jesus, reward of faithful Christian | Cab4 |
| to manifest | St. Benedict's compassion, manifested on face or forehead | Brv |
| to manifest | sanctity of Sts. John of Matha and Felix of Valois as manifesting God's grace | Gue6 |
| to identify | God's identifying Christ as divine King by the star that guided the Wise Men | Ag1 |

**to superscribe:** unmixed expansions
  to superscribe a name [SEE ALSO: A.3.7.1. superscription:ue. a name as superscription]
    [Cab4:6; Gue6:9-10]

**to synthesize**
  cifrar [Sua:66; VgC2:6; Led10:17; Mu2:42; Va13:13; Jau:12; BaB:59; VgC11:3]
  epilogar [Es:8]
  hacer una suma [Mu2:8-9]
  reducir [Ca35:13]

| Tenor | Referent | No. |
|---|---|---|
| to assume finite form | Incarnation | Sua |
| to assume finite form | Incarnation | VgC2 |
| to assume finite form | Incarnation | Led10 |
| to express succinctly | name of Jesus as expression of his being | Mu2 |
| to embody succinctly | Christ as fulfillment of Scripture | Mu2 |
| to assume finite form | Incarnation and Eucharist | Va13 |
| to recapitulate | Eucharist as recapitulation of Christ's redemptive acts | Jau |
| to embody succinctly | Mary as embodying all the beauties of creation | Es |
| to manifest succinctly | stigmata of St. Francis as reminder of Christ's redemptive death | BaB |
| to be in succinct form | infant Christ as infinite Wisdom | VgC11 |
| to recapitulate | Eucharist as presence of Christ whole and entire, and epitome of his saving acts | Ca35 |

**to synthesize:** unmixed expansions
  to synthesize in a single word [Led10:16-17; Mu2:2+40-42; ManA2:64-65; VgC11:2-4]
  to synthesize on a small amount of paper [Sua:65-67; VgC2:6; Led10:17-18; Va13:12-13; Es:8-9]

**to write** [Ri2:6; VgC14:6]
  configurar [Vi3:236]
  conscribir [Do:82]
  dibujar [Pin:50]
  escribir / escritura [Ven:43,71,146,148,183,189,197,213-14,264,319,332,336; Cstj3:3; Vi3:24-25,36,42-43,58,62,127,229,234,238,246,248,251-52,279,286, 296;1:2;2:2; Av2:6,9,12;5:6,13,18,21,23,24-25,26;6:2;3:4;7:4-5;1:3-4; Or:4; ADJ:6; Cor:1,3,4; Pin:20-21,23,29,34,41,44,68,70,73,77,80,86,92,121,129,152; Grn:34,73,78; LoU2:1; Mal:4; Grn:92; Pad2:4; Gal:3; Vgs7:1;3:5;1:2;8:3; Cam:33,60,61-62; VgC5:56,59; Sua:2,53,62,64; Be:3-4; Rod1:4,10; Cab2:4,7; 4:17-18;6:4;7:4,10-11;9:8;11:13,21,34,37,39,49; Brv:3; Led10:3,11,14;22: 5; Mu1:4,15;2:3,13,19,29,33;3:38,43,49; ManA1:8;2:38,40,59,64,65,73,107, 133,136,140,218,221,227,247,254,256,264,273,279,294,304,305,310,314-15,324,330,335,352,354,358;3:55,135; Led7:4;8:2; Cai20:5,12;2:6;3:4;4:6;6: 2;7:4;9:2;14:1;17:2; Led21:12,17;14:21;6:1,3; Ri3:4; Va13:6,13;16:2;17:2;18:2; Bo7:6,9,12; VgC3:8; 15:3,7; 21:2; 18:4; LoA:5; Mu4:14,21,30; Fue:22,26; Ov:4; Bo12:12; VgC22:5; Va5:1; 6:10; 9:1; Es:13; Va3:8,29; Sar:4; VgC8.1:6;

Bo15:32;3:4-5,6,14;5:6,12,14,19-20,27,43;6:3,13,14,20,23;1:2; VgC1:10; Per:17; VgC9:3;12:1; Par3:7; Ca9:57,64,72;22:32,52; VgC24:3,15; Di:9; Ca14:5; 19:3;33:5;31:45; Enr:1; Que2:2; Roj:4; Ca18:17,19;62:4,35,77; Grc:18; Co1:12; Ca7: 10;47:3; Mrl:2; Grc:25; Ca54:8; Do:30,43,74,96; Ca30:21; Da:28, 37, 71; GoT:3; Ca8:19,33;42:43;43:15,80,81;41:6,29;1:6;26:79,82,89,102; 49: 7,18,47; Gue6:6,19,23; GarE:2-3; Ca60:5;55:10; So:4; Ca53:7;36:39,40, 81; Cas:6,12; Ca28:6; Gue1:42,63,122;7:3-4;2:4;8:13-14;4:2;9:1;14:3; Ag2: 7,18; Ca5:9; Brn:2,6; Enc:9]
esculpir [Ca46:8]
pintar [Mon5:4]

| Tenor | Referent | No. |
|---|---|---|
| to produce | sun as agent of beauty and fruitfulness of summer | Mon5 |
| to be in a certain mode | God in divine and human modes | Ven |
| to create | God's created works as sources of knowledge of himself intended for humankind's instruction | Ven |
| to create | God's created works as intentionally incomplete sources of knowledge of himself | Ven |
| to create | rational human soul as created in likeness of God | Ven |
| to communicate | God's self-communication through Scripture | Ven |
| to create | God's creation as truer source of wisdom than books written by human beings | Ven |
| to create | natural world, created as source of knowledge of God for all people | Ven |
| to create | excellence of natural world as source of knowledge of God | Ven |
| to inform | rational soul as source of knowledge of God | Ven |
| to have a lasting effect | meditation on Christ's Passion as having lasting effect on mind and heart | Cstj3 |
| to know | God's eternal knowledge of the elect | Vi3 |
| to know as not saved | God's eternal knowledge of the damned | Vi3 |

| Tenor | Referent | No. |
|---|---|---|
| — | beauty of the natural world as manifesting God but whose meaning is often ignored | Vi3 |
| to exemplify | Christ as embodiment of his teachings | Vi3 |
| to conceive | conception of Christ in Mary | Vi3 |
| to give human form to | incarnation of the Word as God's self-communication to humankind | Vi3 |
| to engender | engendering of Christ through work of Holy Spirit in Mary | Vi3 |
| to inform | revelation of secrets of conscience at Last Judgment | Vi3 |
| to produce | Mary's fullness of virtue | Vi1 |
| to engender | incarnation of God's Word in Mary | Vi2 |
| to know | God's knowledge of all a person's acts | Av2 |
| to know as saved | God's foreknowledge of the elect | Av2 |
| to inform | Holy Spirit's informing hearts of faithful | Av5 |
| to be lovingfully mindful of | God's saving love | Av6 |
| to inform | St. Ignatius' devotion to Jesus | Av3 |
| to give | mortification of the flesh as preparation for God's gifts of grace | Av7 |
| to be lovingly mindful of | God's love for sinners | Av1 |
| to inform | Golden Rule as epitome of natural law | Or |
| to know | angel's being known by or existing in God | ADJ |
| to be lovingfully mindful of | soul's devotion to Christ | Cor |
| to effect | God's grace as causing the soul's devotion, God's presence as causing the very desire for his presence | Cor |
| to know | God's eternal knowledge of the elect and of their merits | Pin |

| Tenor | Referent | No. |
|---|---|---|
| to inform | conscience of the just as informed by just acts | Pin |
| — | eternal emanation of ideal forms in God, resulting in second Person of Trinity | Pin |
| to know as saved | being in state of grace as necessary for salvation | Pin |
| to inform | the soul as informed by its acts | Pin |
| to create | natural world as source of knowledge of God | Pin |
| to create | natural world as source of knowledge of God intended for all people | Grn |
| to create as part of the nature of | ocean tides as following natural order | Grn |
| to create | marvelous variety of animals as all manifesting God's providence | Grn |
| to act | futility of acting according to one's own rather than God's will | LoU2 |
| to know | God's eternal knowledge of all that exists | Mal |
| to create | natural world as God's creation | Grn |
| — | the inexpressible greatness of the name of Jesus | Pad2 |
| — | wordless communication between loving souls | Gal |
| to be ever mindful of | mindfulness of soul's immortality | Vgs7 |
| to be ever mindful of | sin as essentially committed by faculty of the will, but awareness of having sinned as burden of memory | Vgs3 |
| to be lovingfully mindful of | devotion to the angels | Vgs1 |
| to include | ignorance as to one's eternal destiny | Vgs8 |
| to create | creation as manifestation of God | Cam |
| to manifest | direct and indirect manifestation of God, in himself and through his creatures | Cam |

| Tenor | Referent | No. |
|---|---|---|
| to spot | a spotted horse | VgC5 |
| to mark | a melon with its markings | VgC5 |
| to fill with divine meaning; to manifest this meaning | natural world as manifestation of God | Sua |
| to engender | Incarnation as work of God | Sua |
| to manifest | river as reminder of death | Be |
| to give human form to | Incarnation | Rod1 |
| to indwell | St. Ignatius of Antioch's reverence and love for Christ, who dwelt within | Cab2 |
| to manifest | blood shed by Jesus in his circumcision as manifestation of his role as Savior, signified by his name | Cab4 |
| to inform | spiritually perfected Christians as manifestations of principles of virtue | Cab6 |
| — | the works of Redemption as superior to the work of Creation | Cab7 |
| to inform | love of God and neighbor as informing Christ's will | Cab9 |
| to wound; to be the motive of; to be lovingly mindful of | Christ's glorious wounds as motivated by his eternal love for Church and each soul | Cab11 |
| to be constantly and lovingly mindful of | love of soul for Christ | Cab11 |
| to devote one's thoughts and desires | God's knowledge of the thoughts and desires of the heart | Brv |
| to effect; to engender | incarnation of the Redeemer | Led10 |
| to know | God's knowledge of all a person's sins | Led22 |
| to inform | Christians transformed by grace as manifestations of Gospel | Mu1 |
| to wound; to name; to manifest | Jesus' circumcision and naming as manifestation of himself as fulfillment of Scripture | Mu2 |
| to wound; to be lovingly mindful of | Christ's wounds as motivated by his eternal love for souls | Mu3 |

## MOTIF INDEX

| Tenor | Referent | No. |
|---|---|---|
| to be constantly and lovingly mindful of | love of soul for Christ | Mu3 |
| to give human form to | Incarnation | ManA1 |
| to engender | Incarnation | ManA2 |
| to effect | Incarnation, Crucifixion and other mysteries of Christ's life | ManA2 |
| to have an effect on | God as sole agent of Mary's every act | ManA2 |
| to actualize | Mary's actualizing all the virtues | ManA2 |
| to act, to do | Mary's every act as one of virtue and grace, in contrast to saints, who could or did sin | ManA2 |
| to be present | God's presence through grace | ManA2 |
| to be present | God's substantial presence in faithful through Eucharist | ManA2 |
| to direct oneself to | David's praying to God | ManA2 |
| to be mindful of | prayer for Mary's spiritual help | ManA2 |
| to hold someone responsible for | redemption from sin through Christ's death | ManA3 |
| to assume responsibility for | redemption from sin through Christ's death | ManA3 |
| to inform | intentions that inform the heart as manifested in the face | Led7 |
| to inform | Society of Jesus as informed by dedication to Jesus | Led8 |
| to inspire, imbue | Mary's outpouring of praise of God | Cai20 |
| to inspire | divine inspiration as source of noble poetry | Cai20 |
| to give | beautiful and virtuous appearance of the good as gift of nature that favorably disposes others | Cai2 |
| to be present | God's presence in soul filled with charity | Cai3 |
| to form or express | zeal for a pious cause | Cai4 |
| to conceive in the intellect and will | prudence | Cai6 |
| to commit | God's mercy to repentant sinner who amends his / her life | Cai7 |

| Tenor | Referent | No. |
|---|---|---|
| to effect or produce | modesty as outward manifestation and safeguard of a virtuous heart | Cai9 |
| to give form to; to dispose towards | virtue's informing the soul and disposing it to receive God's grace | Cai14 |
| to give | spiritual peace as gift of God to soul who seeks him in solitude | Cai17 |
| to practice | study and practice of virtue | Led21 |
| to affect spiritually | secrets of conscience | Led14 |
| to predestine | predestination of each person | Led6 |
| to manifest | Annunciation | Ri3 |
| to immortalize | immortal memory of Christ's glorious ascension or victory over sin, among the Spanish people | Ri2 |
| to be in a certain mode | Christ as human and divine; Eucharist as Christ in both his humanity and divinity | Va13 |
| to engender; to give a certain form to | Incarnation; Christ's substantial presence in Eucharist under form of host | Va13 |
| to wound | Christ's being wounded on head and crowned with thorns | Va16 |
| to wound; to be mindful of | Christ's glorious wounds as motivated by his eternal love for Church and each soul | Va17 |
| to manifest and bear witness to | Christ's glorious wounds as manifestation and witness to his redemption of humankind | Va18 |
| to teach | superiority of Christ's authority to that of scribes and Pharisees | Bo7 |
| to inform | "Our Father" as prayer taught to humankind by Christ, which is meant to inform their lives | VgC3 |
| to praise and celebrate | to celebrate Christ's redemptive acts of love | VgC14 |
| to inform | lasting spiritual effects of | VgC15 |

| Tenor | Referent | No. |
|---|---|---|
|  | love of God and work of Holy Spirit which informed soul of now deceased priest |  |
| to imprint wounds; to attest | stigmata of St. Francis as attesting to redemption through Christ's death | VgC21 |
| to form drops of dew | dew formed on flowers at dawn | VgC18 |
| to effect | Moses as embodiment of God's Law | LoA |
| to wound | stigmata of St. Francis as imprinted by Christ in person | Mu4 |
| to manifest | stigmata of St. Francis, replica of Christ's wounds and thus manifestation of New Dispensation of grace | Mu4 |
| to conceive | Immaculate Conception | Fue |
| to manifest | stigmata of St. Francis as manifestation of God's grace | Fue |
| to effect | ennobling or transformation of humankind through Christ's incarnation and redemption | Ov |
| to exist | eternal existence in God of all that is | Bo12 |
| to witness to | martyrdom of St. Peter of Verona | VgC22 |
| to inform | soul as informed by God's will | Va5 |
| to inform | Christ's will as one with the Father's | Va6 |
| to exist | eternal existence in God of all that is or will be | Va9 |
| to mark | a melon with its markings | Es |
| to turn the will toward | pursuit of worldly delights | Va3 |
| to be in a certain mode | Christ, the God-Man, as source of victory over sin | Va3 |
| to inform; to inspire | laws or order with which God informed nature; grace with which he inspired St. Ignatius | Sar |

| Tenor | Referent | No. |
|---|---|---|
| to identify as | Christ as the only true wisdom | VgC8.1 |
| to engender | Incarnation | Bo15 |
| to give a certain mode of being to | God's assuming human nature in order that humankind might share in the divine nature | Bo3 |
| to manifest | manifestation of God in Christ | Bo5 |
| to engender, to give human form to | Incarnation | Bo5 |
| to form | nature as governed by grace in Mary's creation | Bo5 |
| to engender, to give human form to | Incarnation | Bo6 |
| to act | original sin | Bo6 |
| to give a certain mode of being to | Hypostatic Union | Bo1 |
| to create a deep spiritual effect | compunction for one's spiritual hardness of heart | VgC1 |
| to remember | punishment due humankind for sin | Per |
| to spot | spotted lambs and kids | VgC9 |
| to spot | spotted lambs | VgC12 |
| to create | God's creation of the heavens | Par3 |
| to manifest | God's manifestation of punishment of King Balshazzar for profanation of sacred vessels, figure of soul who profanes Eucharist; manifestation of guilty conscience | Ca9 |
| to obligate | humankind's obligation to make recompense for sin | Ca22 |
| to include | Mary's exemption from sin from first moment of conception | Ca22 |
| to do, commit | to add new sacrileges to those already committed | VgC24 |
| to manifest | fidelity to God manifested by Michael and other angels | VgC24 |
| to manifest | intertwined flowers on common grave of holy monks as manifesting that death, | Di |

| Tenor | Referent | No. |
|---|---|---|
| | including death to self, leads to eternal life | |
| to immortalize | honor won for noble deeds | Ca14 |
| to manifest | original sin as manifested in humankind's suffering | Ca19 |
| to be eternally mindful of | God's eternal knowledge of the elect | Ca33 |
| to desire, to pursue | pursuit of worldly delights | Ca31 |
| to intend | to intend to do good and to do ill instead | Enr |
| to manifest | lightning as symbol of God's swift justice and punishment for sin | Que2 |
| to make | work as painful but necessary for salvation | Roj |
| to mark | flower petals with their markings | Ca18 |
| to manifest | flowers as manifestation of nature's mysteries | Ca18 |
| to communicate | principles of higher reason and grace by which humankind lived in beginning of history | Ca62 |
| to proclaim | John the Baptist's proclamation of the Messiah | Ca62 |
| to bring forth | sun's bringing forth the day; Christ's inauguration of new era of grace | Ca62 |
| to manifest | destiny of each person as determined through their acts rather than revealed through lines of the palm | Grc |
| to endow inalienably | God's endowing human soul in creation with free will, reason, immortality, etc. | Col |
| to affect; to manifest | unredeemed human nature as manifesting the effects of original sin | Ca7 |
| to proclaim | Pilate's having affixed to Cross inscription "Jesus the Nazarene, King of the Jews" | Ca47 |
| to bear witness | martyrdom of St. Peter of Verona | Mrl |
| to create | heavens with stars and other luminous bodies | Grc |

| Tenor | Referent | No. |
|---|---|---|
| to reason | St. Augustine's application of human reason to divine mysteries | Ca54 |
| to create | God's creation of stars | Do |
| to form | sun as creative agent under God's direction | Do |
| to form; to manifest | bones of the dead, which form ashes or dust, as manifesting transitory or illusory nature of mortal life | Do |
| to create | God's creation of heavens | Do |
| to leave an effect on | physical and spiritual effects of time on old and holy hermit | Do |
| to give | powers with which God endowed human soul in its creation, and special relationship between himself and Israel created in Mosaic Law | Ca30 |
| to manifest | Christ's patient acceptance of insult and injury in his Passion as manifestation of God's new law or ethic | Da |
| to manifest | wounds on face and head of crucified Christ as manifestations of his divine kingship | Da |
| to manifest | diverse responses of crowd to Christ's sentencing, revealed on their faces | Da |
| to inaugurate, to bring into being | Christ's death on Cross as inauguration of New Dispensation of grace and salvation | GoT |
| to manifest | Queen Saba's, i.e., Gentiles', manifesting truth of salvation revealed by God | Ca8 |
| to manifest | wounds of crucified Christ as manifesting salvation | Ca8 |
| to manifest | manifest charity of St. Francis of Paola (?), specifically, his Order's | Ca42 |

| Tenor | Referent | No. |
|---|---|---|
| | work of burying those executed for crimes | |
| to include | Christ as not included among group of sinners | Ca43 |
| to include | Mary's preservation from original sin | Ca43 |
| to proclaim | John the Baptist's proclamation of the Messiah | Ca41 |
| to know | God's foreknowledge of the elect | Ca41 |
| to inaugurate or bring into being | Christ's death on Cross as inauguration of New Dispensation of grace | Ca1 |
| to inaugurate, to bring into being | Christ's death on Cross as inauguration of New Dispensation of grace | Ca26 |
| to embody | Eucharist as embodying the mysteries of Redemption | Ca49 |
| to proclaim | divine kingship of crucified Christ | Ca49 |
| to manifest | heavenly bodies as manifesting immense difference between material and spiritual reality | Gue6 |
| to manifest | sanctity of Sts. John of Matha and Felix of Valois as clearly manifesting God's glory | Gue6 |
| to cause or effect | sanctity of Sts. John of Matha and Felix of Valois as work of Trinity | Gue6 |
| to walk; to attest, to manifest | St. Peter of Alcantara's walking on water as testimony to and manifestation of his sanctity | GarE |
| to give | God-given natural gifts with which a person, specifically Joseph, is endowed | Ca60 |
| — | inscription on Cross pertaining to Christ's kingship | Ca55 |
| to manifest | dust of mortal remains as manifesting illusory character of all worldly good | So |

| Tenor | Referent | No. |
|---|---|---|
| to create; to make known | creation of Trinitarian and Mercedarian Orders, dedicated to redemption of captives; Annunciation | Ca53 |
| to indicate; to be the essential dimension of | time as the essential dimension of human mortality and as indicator of same | Ca36 |
| to indicate the fullness of time; to be the dimension in which redemption is accomplished | redemption of humankind through Christ's death | Ca36 |
| to form | transformation of world through Christ's birth | Cas |
| to manifest | presence of multitude of angels as manifesting birth of God | Cas |
| to affect; to manifest | unredeemed human nature as manifesting the sinfulness or spiritual death that affects the whole human race | Ca28 |
| to be the dimension of; to transmit | immortal memory of Abraham's offering of Isaac, biblical type of God's sacrificing his only Son, the most awe inspiring event in history of world | Ca46 |
| to manifest | Mary Magdalene as model of converted sinner | Gue1 |
| to cause, to be the occasion of | Mary Magdalene's beauty as occasion of her sins | Gue1 |
| to manifest | colors of rainbow manifested by sun in droplets of water; God's grace manifested in repentant and weeping Mary Magdalene | Gue1 |
| to determine | predestination of an individual as taking into account his / her own freely willed acts | Gue7 |
| to manifest | star called "Aguila" as manifestation of character of new head of University of Salamanca | Gue2 |

| Tenor | Referent | No. |
|---|---|---|
| to discover and reveal | scholar honed by self-abnegation as channel of true wisdom | Gue8 |
| to spill blood; to manifest; to win | defense of a noble cause with one's life as manifesting true nobility and winning immortal glory | Gue4 |
| to manifest | lightning around mountain peaks, corresponding to severe judgment of those in high and powerful position | Gue9 |
| to inform | secrets of conscience | Gue14 |
| to give human form to | Mary's creation in time | Ag2 |
| to bestow | grace and glory bestowed on Mary by triune God | Ag2 |
| to make known | enduring fame of a city and its governor | Ca5 |
| to be, to be present | presence of God in Christ and, totally hidden, in Eucharist | Brn |
| to be inherent in | spiritual delight inherent in name and person of Jesus | Enc |

### B.2.1.2. *To Imprint*

**to brand**
escribir [Cab11:25,30; PrA:1; Ca22:18]
esculpir [Ca19:7]
herrar [Cab11:27; Ca22:4]
imprimir [VgC22:11; Ca22:5;56:3,33]
marcar [Ca22:13]
sellar [VgC20:5]
señalar [Ca22:12]

| Tenor | Referent | No. |
|---|---|---|
| to wound; to be present to | Christ's glorious wounds as motivated by his eternal love for Church and each soul | Cab11 |
| to radically affect the soul | prayer for grace to be constant in surrender to God's will, expressed in devotion to Eucharist | VgC20 |

| Tenor | Referent | No. |
|---|---|---|
| — | torture of certain Franciscan martyrs in Japan as ironically confirming their identity as Christians | VgC22 |
| to commit, to surrender | to commit oneself completely to God, as expressed in devotion to Eucharist | PrA |
| to be inherent in, to subject | human nature as subject to sin | Ca22 |
| to manifest | human beings as manifesting their inherent sinfulness | Ca22 |
| to subject | subjection of all human beings to sin and condemnation | Ca19 |
| to be inherent in | original sin as inherent in every member of human race but annulled through Baptism | Ca56 |
| to radically affect the soul | human subjection to sin | Ca56 |

**to brand:** unmixed expansions
    to brand a slave [SEE ALSO: A.3.19.9.2. brand:ue. slave brand]
        [Cab11:25-27; VgC20:5-7; PrA:1; Ca22:3-5,9-13;19:6-7,9; 56:3-4,30-33;66:3-5]

**to cut / engrave**
    bosquejar [Ca4:5]
    escribir [Av5:6; Cab11:4,18,47; Mu3:11,24,26,27,30,31-32; VgC1:9; Ca64:7; 22: 27; 20:14; VgC24:24; Ca37:9,10,29; 45:37;17:15; 69:37;28:33; 24:22,26]
    esculpir [Vi2:7,11; Cab4:14; VgC15:5;19:2; Ca64:12;31:32; 8:27;17:20;44:22]
    grabar [Vi3:13,242; Roc:6; Ca1:17; Gue6:18; Ca55:31;38:4]
    imprimir / impresión [Ca6:4;48:21;50:3,8]

| Tenor | Referent | No. |
|---|---|---|
| to know eternally | God's eternal knowledge of the elect | Vi3 |
| to give human form to | incarnation of the Word | Vi3 |
| to engender | conception of Christ by Holy Spirit | Vi2 |
| — | coming of Holy Spirit at Pentecost, contrasted with Mosaic Law | Av5 |

| Tenor | Referent | No. |
|---|---|---|
| to inform | desire for constancy in dedication to God's law | Roc |
| to christen, to name | naming and circumcision of Christ | Cab4 |
| to be eternally mindful of | Christ's wounds as motivated by and manifestation of his love for Church and souls | Cab11 |
| to wound; to be lovingly and eternally mindful of | Christ's wounds as motivated by and manifestation of his love for humankind | Mu3 |
| to inform | lasting spiritual effects of love of God and work of Holy Spirit in now deceased priest | VgC15 |
| to leave a profound effect | St. Ignatius' desire to spread Christianity in foreign lands | VgC19 |
| to attempt to make an impression on | compunction for spiritual hardness of heart | VgC1 |
| to radically affect | sin as radically affecting whole human race | Ca64 |
| — | God's giving Decalog to Moses | Ca22 |
| to radically affect | sin as radically affecting whole human race | Ca20 |
| to be forever lovingly mindful of | strong faith of Spanish Christians | VgC24 |
| to produce | human fortune as manifested by stars produced in heavens | Ca31 |
| to inform | principles of the Decalog, which embody natural law, as informing human conscience | Ca6 |
| to radically affect | sin as radically affecting whole human race | Ca37 |
| to remember forever | Queen Christina of Sweden's response to letter from Philip II of Spain | Ca48 |
| to manifest | stars as mysterious manifestation of God; crucified Christ as manifesting salvation | Ca8 |
| to leave a lasting reminder | Christ's writing on ground "Let him who is without sin . . . ." | Ca45 |

| Tenor | Referent | No. |
|---|---|---|
| to radically affect | sin as radically affecting whole human race | Ca17 |
| to be forever lovingly mindful of | devotion to Mary | Ca1 |
| informing | humankind's being guided by natural law | Ca50 |
| — | God's giving Decalog to Moses | Ca50 |
| to inform; to manifest | informing of Sts. John of Matha and Felix of Valois by God's grace; their sanctity as glorifying God | Gue6 |
| to inform | profound faith of St. Ferdinand, King | Ca55 |
| to inform | Mosaic Law as superseded by New Dispensation of grace, which informs the soul through faith | Ca69 |
| to be forever lovingly mindful of or devoted to | devotion to Mary as source of fortitude and salvation | Ca38 |
| to manifest | eternal life through Christ's death, mysteriously manifested by a tree (Cross) | Ca28 |
| to will inalterably | fall of Lucifer | Ca44 |
| to immortalize | immortal fame of the incarnation of the divine Word | Ca24 |
| to be the essence of | impression of ship formed by sun rays; divinity of the Word made flesh | Ca4 |

**to cut / engrave:** unmixed expansions

    to cut in stone / marble [SEE ALSO: B.2.1:ue. to write a name on rock / stone]
        [Av5:6-7; Ca22:25-27;6:4-5;50:8-10; Gue6:15-18; Ca69:38]
    to cut on a tree [Ca64:6-8;20:13-14;37:8-10,27-30;17:14-16, 18-20;28:32-33]
    to engrave on bronze [Ca48:19-21; GarE:6-8; Ca38:4-5; 24:22,26]
    to engrave on a jewel / precious stone [SEE ALSO: B.2.1.2. to cut / engrave:ue. to engrave a name on a jewel / precious stone]
        [VgC24:24; Ca4:5-6]
    to engrave a name on a jewel / precious stone [Cab4:5-16; 11:3-5,12-18]
    to engrave on a metal plate [Ca31:31-32;8:27;45:35-37; 50:3-5;38:4-5]
    to engrave with a burin [Mu3:27-28; Ca22:26-27;45:36-37; 50:8-11; GarE:6-7]

MOTIF INDEX                                              253

**to impress / imprint**
   esculpir [VgC18:22]
   estampar [Vi3:243; ASF:4; LoU1:17; Vgs6:4; VgC5:42; Cab11:49-50; VgC24:8;
      Car:11; Da:3,25; Ca55:28]
   grabar [Vi3:261]
   imprimir / impresión [Cstj3:5; Vi3:88; Ter:31; Vgs2:1,12; Cab11:50-51; Luc:1;
      Ri1; VgC15:2;18:15,25; Bo11:6; Es:20; Ca9:66;51:15;18:6;62:6,19; Co2:7;
      Ca32:6,14; Do:58; Ca30:25; Da:11; Ca1:12,25; Lud:7,8,10; Ca38:3; Gue10:1;
      Ca29:46;11:28]

| *Tenor* | *Referent* | *No.* |
|---|---|---|
| to leave lasting effect on mind and heart | meditation on Christ's Passion | Cstj3 |
| to manifest | natural world as source of knowledge of its Creator | Vi3 |
| to give bodily form to | Incarnation of the Word | Vi3 |
| to manifest unforgettably | St. Teresa's visions of Christ | Ter |
| to give human form to | Incarnation | ASF |
| to inform | creation of humankind in God's image, i.e., with reason, free will, immortality; redemption in Christ | LoU1 |
| to remind symbolically | ashes applied to forehead on Ash Wednesday as reminder of mortality | Vgs6 |
| to wound | stigmata of St. Francis | Vgs2 |
| to inform | St. Isidore of Madrid's virtue | VgC5 |
| to be forever lovingly mindful of | Christian's love for Christ, in response to his saving love | Cab11 |
| to affect profoundly | profoundly moving effect of a vision of Christ | Luc |
| to be constantly mindful of | Mary's, and the Christian's, devotion to God | Ri1 |
| to inform; to manifest | love of God or presence of Holy Spirit manifested on face of deceased priest | VgC15 |
| to wound; to transform | imprinting of stigmata on St. Francis and his inward transformation into resemblance with crucified Christ | VgC18 |

| Tenor | Referent | No. |
|---|---|---|
| to be present | Christ's presence through grace in Christians | Bo11 |
| to circumcise; to confirm | Christ's circumcision as confirmation of promise of salvation signified in naming of Jesus | Es |
| ——— | the divine judgment on King Balshazzar for profanation of sacred vessels | Ca9 |
| to inflict with a whip | sacrilegious treatment by Jews, of Christian figures, specifically, St. Peter | VgC24 |
| to remind of | particular types of flower as reminiscent of certain genres of Lope's work | Car |
| to inform | sacrament of Baptism | Ca51 |
| to manifest | rainbow as manifestation of peace between God and humankind | Ca18 |
| to inform | natural and supernatural reason as guiding principles of humankind in period from Adam to Moses | Ca62 |
| to immortalize | immortal name won by John the beloved disciple and Evangelist | Ca62 |
| to be devoted to | devotion to mysteries of rosary | Co2 |
| to produce | sacrament of Baptism as producing a distinctive and enduring quality or potency | Ca32 |
| to produce a visual impression, to affect profoundly | love of God evoked in St. Ignatius by manifestation of divine beauty in natural world | Do |
| to produce | sacrament of Baptism as producing a distinctive and enduring quality or potency | Ca30 |
| to produce in lasting form | blow given Christ by high priest's servant | Da |
| to manifest | blow given Christ by high priest's servant as both insult and injury | Da |

| Tenor | Referent | No. |
|---|---|---|
| — | law of talion contrasted with bearing of injuries taught by Christ | Da |
| to produce | Baptism, which is a sharing in Christ's priesthood, as producing a distinctive quality in soul | Ca1 |
| to be forever lovingly mindful of | devotion to Mary | Ca1 |
| to cause to inhere in | ocean tides as following an established natural order | Lud |
| to inform | St. Peter of Alcantara's constant following of principles taught by Christ | Lud |
| to inform | profound faith of St. Ferdinand, King | Ca55 |
| to be forever lovingly mindful of or devoted to | devotion to Mary as source of fortitude and salvation | Ca38 |
| to wound | stigmata of St. Francis | Gue10 |
| to manifest | Cross, manifested in sky, as source of victory over sin | Ca29 |
| to produce | sacrament of Baptism as producing a distinctive and enduring quality or potency that annuls original sin | Ca11 |

**to impress / imprint:** unmixed expansions
   to impress in clay [LoU1:1-3+17]
   to impress in wax [VgC5:41-42;18:19-22; Es:20]
   to imprint a character [SEE ALSO: B.2.1.2. to impress / imprint:me. to imprint a character on the soul]
      [Luc:1-2; Ca62:6-7;32:6-7;30:25-26]
   to imprint a seal [Led9:8; VgC18:13-15; Es:19-20; Ca30:25]
   to stamp on a coin [Led9:7-8]

**to impress / imprint:** mixed expansions
   to imprint a character on the soul [Ti:4-5; Ca51:14-16; 1:12-13;11:25-28]

**to seal** [SEE ALSO: B.2.1.2. to impress / imprint:ue. to imprint a seal; B.3.3.2. to seal]
   echar el sello [Jau:18,36,54; Ag2:69]
   marcar [Ca32:5]

sellar [Ven:336; AD:5; Vgs2:11; Sua:45; Cai19; Led9:8; Cai10:1;14:3; Mu4:5; Bo11:6; VgC22:8,23; Es:18; VgC11:3; Da:16]

| Tenor | Referent | No. |
|---|---|---|
| to inform | rational soul as source of knowledge of God | Ven |
| to culminate | Christ's crucifixion as culmination of Mary's sorrows, the result of original sin | AD |
| to wound; to confirm | wounds of crucified Christ as confirmation of redemption | Vgs2 |
| to give; to confirm or authenticate | the just person as confirmed in grace with the gifts of the Holy Spirit | Sua |
| to confirm | Cross as instrument of salvation or eternal glory | Cai19 |
| to inform | St. Ignatius of Loyola as informed by Christ | Led9 |
| to confirm | long-suffering as confirmation of love and constancy | Cai10 |
| to confirm | perseverance in virtue as confirmation of that virtue | Cai14 |
| to authenticate | sanctity of St. Francis authenticated by stigmata, replica of Christ's own wounds | Mu4 |
| to attest | lives of early Christians as attesting to Christ's presence | Bo11 |
| to imprint with letters IHS; to be present substantially | imprinting of Eucharistic host with letters that represent Jesus' name; Christ's substantial presence in Eucharist | Jau |
| to torture; to authenticate | torture of certain Franciscan martyrs in Japan as ironically confirming their witness to Christ | VgC22 |
| to identify | identifying of God's faithful servants | VgC22 |
| to confirm | Christ's circumcision as confirmation of promise of salvation signified in naming of Jesus | Es |

# MOTIF INDEX 257

| Tenor | Referent | No. |
|---|---|---|
| to embody; to attest | infant Christ as embodying and attesting to infinite Wisdom | VgC11 |
| to confer | Baptism as conferring a distinctive and enduring divine quality or potency | Ca32 |
| to confirm | bleeding caused by blow to Christ's cheek as confirmation of his patience in suffering | Da |
| to attest | John's attesting in Apocalypse to Mary as mother of Messiah and thus source of wisdom and salvation | Ag2 |

**to seal:** unmixed expansions [SEE ALSO: B.2.1.1. to seal:ue. to sign and seal]
to seal a letter [AD:2-5; Cai14:1+3; VgC22:8-9]


## B.2.1.ue. TO WRITE THE TEXT: UNMIXED EXPANSIONS

to learn to write [SEE ALSO: B.2.1.ue. The pupil writes skillfully because the teacher guides his hand.]
[Led21:12-14; Bo7:12;6:21-23]
to teach to write [SEE: B.2.1.ue. to learn to write]
to put an idea in writing [SEE ALSO: B.2.1. me. God writes his Word / Concept in Mary]
[Vi3:241-43; Go2:12-15; Ca44:24-25]
to write all one knows [ManA2:64-65; Bo6:20; VgC11:3-4]
to write a book for everyone [SEE ALSO: A.3.2.1.ue: a common book]
[Ven:264-65; Vi3:256-58; Grn:33-38]
to write a letter to a king [Cab7:10-11; Mu1:4-7; Cai14:1-2]
to write a name on rock / stone [SEE ALSO: B.2.1.2. to cut / engrave:ue. to engrave a name on a jewel / precious stone]
[Mu3:8-11; VgC1:9-10]
to write by hand [SEE ALSO: B.2.1.ue. to write in one's own hand]
[Cai4:6; Bo3:14;5:9; Ca9:70-72;21:3-5; Vit:5; Do:80-82]
to write in one's own hand [SEE ALSO: B.2.1.ue. to write by hand; to write with the right hand]
[Ven:188-90,264-65; Led1:4;11:19-20; Bo14:6-7; VgC21:2; Mu4:10,29-30; Per:5-6]
to write with the right hand [Ca39:8-9; Do:88-90]
to write in an account book [Vi3:279-80; Led22:5-7; ManA2:344-46;3:55-56; Led14:17-19; Ca26:8-10+16-18]
to write in a memorandum book [ManA2:358-59; BaB:51-53; Ca33:3-5;62:48-53;54:3-4]

to write in dust / ashes [Ov:2-4; Do:73-74; So:4]
to write on a tree [SEE ALSO: B.2.1.2. to cut / engrave:ue. to cut on a tree]
[Ca7:7-10;26:102-103;28:5-7]
to write on a wall [Led15:1-4; Grc:12-13]
to write in the margin [SEE ALSO: B.2.1.1. to gloss]
[Led18:1-2; Va16:1-2]
to write well [SEE ALSO: A.1.2.1. pen:ue. the pen of a skillful scribe; B.2.1.ue. to write well with a poor instrument; The pupil writes skillfully because the teacher guides his hand.]
[Ven:319; Vi3:251-55; ManA2:135-36; Led21:15; Gue6:18-19]
to write well with a poor instrument [Cab3:1-3,10-11]
to write poorly [SEE ALSO: A.3.19.5. character / lettering:ue. ill-formed characters]
[Bo7:2;6:23]
to be written on the inside and the outside [Ven:43-44; Vi1:2-3; Cam:59-60; Sua:2-3,44-47; Mu3:49-51; Va13:6; 3:28-29]
to be written indelibly [SEE ALSO: A.3.19.5. character / lettering:ue. immortal characters]
[Vi3:12-13; Av3:4-6; Ter:30-32; LoU1:1-4; Roc:6-7; Ca51:15;6:4-6; Do:23-27; Ca55:31-33;44:25-28]
The pupil writes skillfully because the teacher guides his hand. [Bo5:27-28]

B.2.1.me. TO WRITE THE TEXT: MIXED EXPANSIONS

plowing as writing / writing as plowing [Tel:16; Do:3,10-11,85; Ca36:8-9]
a written animal [VgC5:55-56;9:2-3;12:1]
a written melon [VgC5:59; Es:3]
to write a law in the sand [Grn:71-74; Lud:5-7,8-9]
to write (a name) in the book of life / glory [Mon1:12-13; Vi3:24-25,56-57,62-63; Av2:8-12; ADJ:2-3; Pin:19-21,68,83-86; Vgs8:3-4; Va6:1-4; Ca41:27-30]
to write a name on the hands / feet [Cab11:12-14,21-22,36-39,47; Mu3:22, 26,29-32,37-38,42-43; Va17:1-2]
to write a name on the heart / breast [Cab2:4-7;11:12-15,36-37,47-48,50-51; Mu3:9-11,27-28,42-44,48-50; Va17:1-2; VgC19:2-3;1:9-11; Ca1:17-19,24-26]
to write a name on the soul [LoU1:7-10; Ca1:24-26]
to write what God dictates [Do:43-44; Ca8:19-22]
to write on air [Ca62:34-35;29:46]
to write on water [LoU2:1; Be:3-4; Ca62:18-19; GarE:2-3]
to write on wind [LoU2:1]
to write on the arm [Mu3:49-51]
to write on the body / in the flesh [SEE ALSO: B.2.1.2. to brand:ue. to brand a slave; B.2.1.me. to write on the arm; to write on the breast; to write on the face; to write on the forehead; to write on the hands / feet; to write on the side; God writes his Word / Concept in Mary]
[Cab11:25-26,29-30; ManA2:43-44; VgC18:15-17; Mu4:14-15; Bo3:4-5;6:1-6; BaB:43; Hu:18]

MOTIF INDEX 259

to write on the breast [SEE ALSO: B.2.1.me. to write a name on the heart / breast]
[Av6:1-2;8:1-2]
to write on the face [ManA2:43+46; Led7:1-4; VgC15:2,7-8; Ca22:5,18;19:7; Da:10-11,28,37-38,71; Ca66:3-4]
to write on the forehead [SEE ALSO: A.3.19.5. alphabet: taw:ue. the taw written on the forehead]
[Vgs6:4-5;1:1-2; Brv:10; ManA2:43-45; Ri1; VgC22:11-12,23-24; Ca19:9]
to write on the hands / feet [SEE ALSO: B.2.1.me. to write a name on the hands / feet]
[ManA2:47-49; VgC21:2-3; BaB:43; Gue1:105-08]
to write on the side [Cab11:36-37; Mu3:37-38; ManA2:43-46; VgC21:2-3]
to write on the soul [SEE ALSO: B.2.1.2. to impress / imprint:me. to imprint a character on the soul; B.2.1.me. to write a name on the soul; to write on the conscience; to write on the heart; to write on the memory; to write on the will][17]
[Av7:5-6; Or:4-5; Cor:1; Vgs1:2; Cai20:5;3:1-4;14:1-2; VgC18:15+18; Bo6:12-14; Ca56:16-17;62:6; Grc:14-15; Co2:7; Do:58-59,88-89; Lud:10; Ca38:3]
to write on the conscience [Cai9:2; Bo14:5-7,13-14]
to write on the heart [SEE ALSO: A.3.7.2. law:me. the law written on the heart; B.2.1.me. to write a name on the heart / breast]
[Cstj3:3,5; Av3:4;1:3-4; Brv:2-3; Mu1:15; Luc:1; Led7:1-4; Va10:3-4; VgC3:8-11; Va3:8,12; Ca48:19-21; 55:28;53:6-7]
to write on the memory [SEE ALSO: A.3.4.1. memorandum book]
[Vi3:17-19; Mal:4-5; Vgs7:1;3:1+5; Led15:1-4; Ca26:28-31]
to write on the will [Cab9:8-10]
to write with blood [SEE ALSO: A.1.2.1. pen:ue. to dip the pen in ink; A.3.19.5. character / lettering:ue. red lettering; B.2.1.1. to rubricate; to sign:ue. to sign with blood]
[Mon8:10-11; Cstj3:4-5; Vi3:235-37; Led1:1-3; Cab4:17-18; Mu2:33-34,40-41; ManA3:135-36; Mu4:5; Fue:25-26; VgC22:4-5; Bo3:6-8; VgC23:11-12; Ca19:3; Mrl:2-3; Da:10-11; GoT:3; Ca26:102; Gue4:2]
to write with fire [Ri3:4; VgC6:6; Gue9:1+6; Ca29:29-30, 35-36]
to write with tears [VgC18:1-4; Da:54-55; Gue1:105-10,120-23]
to write with the voice [Ca62:34-35;41:5-6]
to be written with the finger of God [Vi1:2;2:10-11; Av5:20-22; ADJ:6-7; Grn:92-93; Roc:5-6; Cab3:9-11;9:8-10; Sar:4; Bo3:14-15; Ca9:64,71-72;45:36-37;1:5-6]
to write without the usual equipment [SEE ALSO: B.2.4:me. to print without the usual equipment]
[Vi2:9-11; Av5:6-7,20-22]
Appetite writes. [Va3:11-12; Ca31:44-46]

---

[17] To write on the soul or to write on the heart was in medieval culture understood as a synonym for writing in one's memory, i.e. for reading in the true sense of the word: "Merely running one's eyes over the written pages is not reading at all, for the writing must be transferred into memory, from graphemes on parchment or papyrus or paper to images written in one's brain by emotion and sense." One had not truly read a work unless one had made it part of oneself (Carruthers 44, 10).

Fame writes. [Ca14:4-5;8:51-52]
God writes his Word / Concept in Mary. [Vi2:10-12; Sua:52-54,61-62; Rod1:1-4; ManA2:64-66,254-58,309-10,333-36; Bo15:29-32;5:13-14,17-23,41-43;6:1-5;1:1-2+9-10; Ra:1-4]
Time writes. [SEE ALSO: A.2.1. writer: notary / clerk:me. time as notary / clerk]
[Ca7:7-10; Do:95-96; Ca5:9;24:22,26]

## B.2.2. TO ILLUMINATE THE TEXT [ManA1:7; Ca11:17]

**to illuminate**
adornar [Sua:11]
iluminar [Ven:226-27; Lem:4; Grn:42,46,82; ManA1:12; Va13:8; BaB:76; Ca23:9; Grc:26-27; Ca8:4;15:7; Ag1:15; Ca29:16; 11:2]
ilustrar [Ca43:36]
rasgar [Ca8:3]

| Tenor | Referent | No. |
|---|---|---|
| to create as beautiful | beauty of natural world as intended to lead beyond itself to understanding of God | Ven |
| to inspire with grace | conversion to a life inspired by grace | Lem |
| to create as beautiful | beauty of natural world as manifestation of God's beauty | Grn |
| — | God's providence manifested in diverse animal species | Grn |
| to create as beautiful | beauty of natural world created by God | Sua |
| to glorify | Mary's Assumption and Coronation | ManA1 |
| to glorify | glorious wounds of the risen Christ | Va13 |
| to illumine understanding; to transform through grace | interior illumination, and transformation of St. Francis on occasion of his receiving stigmata | BaB |
| to cause to shine | shining crown suspended in air, brought by angels; spiritual victory and glory | Ca23 |
| to make beautiful and bright | God's creation of sun, moon and stars | Grc |
| to make bright; to make gloriously manifest | brightness of heavens or angels seen by King | Ca8 |

| Tenor | Referent | No. |
|---|---|---|
| | Solomon in dream or vision; manifestation in glory of Messiah | |
| to glorify | to transform the tree or Cross from symbol of shame to one of glory | Ca43 |
| to manifest clearly | God's wrath manifested in apocalyptic manner | Ca15 |
| to transfigure | Christ's transfiguration on Mt. Tabor | Ag1 |
| to make bright; to glorify | Constantine's vision of angel in rainbow, with crucifix in hand, as symbol of Christ's glorification and human redemption | Ca29 |
| to make bright; to glorify | glorious appearance of heavens at sunrise; glorification of Christ, and redemption of all creation, through his death | Ca11 |
| to manifest | stars as manifesting existaence of mysteries | Ca11 |

## B.2.2.ue. TO ILLUMINATE THE TEXT: UNMIXED EXPANSIONS

to illuminate a book [SEE ALSO: A.3.2.1:ue. an illuminated book] [ManA1:2+12; Ag1:1+15]

## B.2.3. TO PERFORM AN OFFICIAL ACT REGARDING THE TEXT
[SEE ALSO: B.2.1.1. to rubricate; to sign; B.2.1.2. to seal]

### B.2.3.1. *To Authorize the Text*

**to authorize**
autorizar [Mon7:3; Cab1:9; Mu4:9; Da:14]

| Tenor | Referent | No. |
|---|---|---|
| to manifest approval of | stigmata of St. Francis as manifestation of his sanctity | Mon7 |
| to empower | name of Jesus as spiritually empowering the Christian | Cab1 |

| Tenor | Referent | No. |
|---|---|---|
| to validate | stigmata of St. Francis as imprinted by Christ himself | Mu4 |
| to bear witness to | violence of blow given Christ by high priest's servant as demonstrating his spiritual strength | Da |

**to dispatch / issue**
despachar [ManA3:121; Ca39:8;43:148]

| Tenor | Referent | No. |
|---|---|---|
| to effect | redemption through Christ's death | ManA3 |
| to send | Christ, second person of Trinity, sent in human form by the Father to redeem world | Ca39 |
| to execute | Christ's Passion and death | Ca43 |

B.2.3.2. *To Censor / Submit to the Censors*

**to approve**
aplaudir [Ag1:12]
aprobar [Sua:40; ManA2:141; Bo15:34; BaB:33,35; Gue1:61,84; PrJ:4; Ag2:17; Gue12:13,14]

| Tenor | Referent | No. |
|---|---|---|
| to grace or show favor, to save | God's gracing and salvation of the just | . Sua |
| to approve, to grace | certain acts of the saints as not approved by God, not informed by his grace | ManA2 |
| to grace | Mary's perfect holiness as grace of triune God | Bo15 |
| to grace | God's gracing of St. Francis as manifested in stigmata | BaB |
| to grace | Christ's gracing of the repentant Mary Magdalene | Gue1 |
| to grace | Mary as graced by God | PrJ |
| to recognize Jesus' wisdom and understanding | doctors of Law as astounded at Jesus' wisdom and understanding of the Law at age twelve | Ag1 |

| Tenor | Referent | No. |
|---|---|---|
| to grace | Mary as graced by triune God | Ag2 |
| to judge | God as the only judge of his creations | Gue12 |

**to censor**
censurar / censura [Bo9:8,10,20,22,32,44; Gue1:83,84,92,94,97,99,100;12:15]

| Tenor | Referent | No. |
|---|---|---|
| to sanctify | sanctification of John the Baptist in his mother's womb | Bo9 |
| to judge | Mary Magdalene's seeking Christ's forgiveness and grace | Gue1 |
| to condemn or find fault | criticism and condemnation of Mary Magdalene by Christ's disciples and Pharisee | Gue1 |
| judgment | desire that in final judgment Rodriguez Monforte will be found worthy of reward | Gue12 |

**to expurgate** [SEE ALSO: B.4.2.2. to erase / blot out:ue. to erase a section of the text; to erase an error; to erase from the book; B.4.2.2. to tear out:ue. to tear out pages]
expurgar / expurgatorio [Bo15:22; Gue1:60]

| Tenor | Referent | No. |
|---|---|---|
| absolution, expiation | Mary's sinlessness | Bo15 |
| to amend and expiate | amendment of life and expiation for sin as necessary for absolution | Gue1 |

**to expurgate:** unmixed expansions
without expurgation [Bo15:22]

**to forbid / condemn**
condenar [Gue1:97]
prohibir [Sua:43; Va7:3; Gue1:81]
reprobar [Sua:40]
vedar [Va7:3]

| Tenor | Referent | No. |
|---|---|---|
| to reject, to condemn | eternal condemnation of unrepentant sinners | Sua |

| Tenor | Referent | No. |
|---|---|---|
| to reject, to condemn | eternal condemnation of unrepentant sinners | Va7 |
| to condemn as sinful | redemption through Christ from effects of sinful acts | Gue1 |
| to condemn | condemnation of Mary Magdalene by Pharisee | Gue1 |

B.2.3.2.ue. *To Censor / Submit to the Censors: Unmixed Expansions*

**to censor a book / submit a book to the censors** [SEE ALSO: A.3.11:ue. to compare the first impression with the original]
[ManA1:11-21,28-32; Ag1:11-12]
to judge a book by the outside [Gue1:101-02]


B.2.4. TO PRINT THE TEXT

**to print**
dar a la estampa [Ag1:1-2]
estampar [ManA2:172; Va14:3; Fue:17]
imprimir / impresión [Mon6:2; Ti:5; ManA1:19,22,28,32;2:150; Va14:2; Bo9:7,11,19,31,43;14:1; Fue:9,47,48,54; Jau:2; Bo15:7,38,40; BaB:33,43; Hu:18; Ra:3; Gue1:56,61,106,108; Ag1:4;2:23,24]
sacar impreso [BaB:2-3]

| Tenor | Referent | No. |
|---|---|---|
| to affect profoundly | contemplation of Christ's Passion as leaving profound and lasting effect on heart or soul | Mon6 |
| to cause or produce | God's producing a distinctive and enduring quality in soul through sacraments of Baptism, Confirmation and Holy Orders | Ti |
| to be conceived | Immaculate Conception | ManA1 |
| to be conceived | all saints as conceived in original sin, while Mary was immaculately conceived | ManA2 |
| to imprint | impression of Christ left on his burial shroud | Va14 |

| Tenor | Referent | No. |
|---|---|---|
| to cause to be given birth, to be born | sanctification of John the Baptist in his mother's womb | Bo9 |
| to affect profoundly | effects of John the Baptist's life and preaching | Bo9 |
| to inform | natural and supernatural reason as guiding principles of humankind | Bo14 |
| to be conceived | Mary's immaculate conception | Fue |
| to be present | God's presence through grace in Mary from first moment of conception | Fue |
| to imprint | Christ's imprinting his own wounds on St. Francis | Fue |
| to manifest | redemptive acts manifested by Christ during his life on earth | Jau |
| to produce | Mary's unique holiness and freedom from original sin and its effects | Bo15 |
| conception | Immaculate Conception | Bo15 |
| to imprint | imprinting of stigmata on St. Francis | BaB |
| to inform | Holy Spirit's informing Apostles | Hu |
| to engender | Mary's conception of the divine Word | Ra |
| to act | Mary Magdalene's sinful acts | Gue1 |
| to make anew | Mary Magdalene's new life of grace | Gue1 |
| to be oriented to | Mary Magdalene's actions and spiritual energies as formerly sinful or self-oriented, later oriented to Christ | Gue1 |
| to become incarnate | Incarnation | Ag1 |
| to be conceived | conception of Christ in Mary's womb | Ag1 |
| to be conceived | Immaculate Conception, and other extraordinary graces linked with this mystery, by which Mary perfectly images God | Ag2 |

**to proofread** [SEE: B.2.1.1. to punctuate]

B.2.4.1. *To Prepare the Type*

**to cast type** [Ti:4]
  imprimir [Ven:118]

| Tenor | Referent | No. |
|---|---|---|
| to be formative principle of | free will as formative principle of virtue | Ven |
| to make the sacramental signs | sacraments as effecting what they signify | Ti |

**to separate type**
  desencajar [Bo10:4]

| Tenor | Referent | No. |
|---|---|---|
| to disarticulate or disjoint | Crucifixion | Bo10 |


B.2.4.ue. TO PRINT THE TEXT: UNMIXED EXPANSIONS [SEE ALSO: A.1.2.4. printing press:ue. to apply the press]

to print from the original [ManA1:32-35; Ag2:47]


B.2.4.me. TO PRINT THE TEXT: MIXED EXPANSIONS

to print without the usual equipment [Fue:38]


B.2.5. TO PUBLISH THE TEXT

**to publish**
  sacar a luz [ManA2:30; Bo9:4; Ag1:5]
  salir a luz [ManA1:6; BaB:73; Gue1:76;13:4]
  salir a volar [Bo9:41]

| Tenor | Referent | No. |
|---|---|---|
| to be born | Mary's birth | ManA1 |
| to preach | preaching of the Gospel text Matt.1 on all Marian feasts | ManA2 |
| to cause to be given birth | Zachany's role in birth of John the Baptist | Bo9 |

| Tenor | Referent | No. |
|---|---|---|
| to make known; to be sent out | sanctification of John the Baptist in his mother's womb in preparation for his special mission | Bo9 |
| to be imprinted with stigmata | stigmata of St. Francis | BaB |
| to be transformed through grace | Mary Magdalene's conversion to a new life of grace | Gue1 |
| to be actualized | intellect as matrix of all branches of learning | Gue13 |
| to be born | Christ's birth | Ag1 |

**to assume costs**
correr por la cuenta de uno [Fue:35]

| Tenor | Referent | No. |
|---|---|---|
| to be the unique source or cause of | God as cause of Mary's immaculate conception, through retroactive effect of grace won by Christ's death, part of his eternal plan | Fue |

## B.2.6. TO BIND THE TEXT

**to accommodate for binding**
acomodar[18] [Vi3:235]

| Tenor | Referent | No. |
|---|---|---|
| to adjust | accommodation of divine Word to Mary's womb | Vi3 |

**to bind**
cubrir [Ag1:10]
dar a la encuadernación [Bo1:8]

---

[18] Because of the sequence "escrito, acomodado, y encuadernado," I have assigned the second verb the meaning "to accomodate for binding." However, it might also at least connote, if not denote, "to accomodate a text" in the sense of altering it slightly to better fit a speaker's or writer's context and purpose on a specific occasion. As Carruthers observes, even Scripture was often altered in this way (91). Here, the divine text would be altered to fit the context of Mary's womb, that is, assume human nature, the ultimate purpose for such accommodation being the redemption of the world.

**encuadernar** [Vi3:235; ManA2:96,103,120,121,126-27,128,156; Led16:14; Va13:14; Fue: 52; Bo15:16;5:37; Ca13:8;43:5;68:7; Gue1:79-80;15:3,5; Ag2:8]

| Tenor | Referent | No. |
|---|---|---|
| to assume human flesh | Incarnation | Vi3 |
| to make whole and complete, to protect | completeness and fullness of virtue in Mary, and this integrity as protection against sin | ManA2 |
| to make whole | spiritual and moral integrity of saints as less complete or actualized than that of Mary | ManA2 |
| to integrate | Christ's integration of justice and mercy in his own person | Led16 |
| to incorporate and integrate | Eucharist as Christ himself in his humanity and divinity | Va13 |
| to protect; to integrate | Mary's fullness of grace or absence of original sin at conception | Fue |
| to incorporate | God's incorporating all virtues and perfections in Mary | Bo15 |
| to be faithful to | Mary's fidelity to Old Law, as preparation for her motherhood of Christ, embodiment of the New Law | Bo5 |
| to cause to be simultaneously | Mary's simultaneous divine maternity and perpetual virginity | Bo1 |
| to constitute as orderly and harmonious system; to reintegrate | rising of sun as part of orderly and harmonious system; resurrected Christ as head of reintegrated human race or Mystical Body | Ca13 |
| to make subject to | subjection of human race to effects of original sin | Ca43 |
| to create as an ordered structure and system | heavens as ordered structure and system | Ca68 |
| to make whole | redemption or reintegration of humankind as purpose of Incarnation | Gue1 |

# MOTIF INDEX

| Tenor | Referent | No. |
|---|---|---|
| to give a form or mode of being | human life in this world as mortal, death as transition to immortal life | Gue15 |
| to hide or protect | Holy Family's flight into Egypt to escape Herod | Ag1 |
| to make whole and complete | God's eternal election of Mary as mother of the Word, with all the extraordinary graces implied, including freedom from original sin | Ag2 |

**to trim the binding**
cortar [Ag1:6]

| Tenor | Referent | No. |
|---|---|---|
| to circumcise | Christ's circumcision | Ag1 |

**to adorn the binding** [Bo1:13-14]
argentar [Bo1:11]
guarnecer [Ven:97]
rayar [ManA1:10]

| Tenor | Referent | No. |
|---|---|---|
| to be clearly manifest | presence of God, or truth, in his creation as clearly manifest | Ven |
| to inflict great pain | Mary's suffering at Christ's crucifixion | ManA1 |
| to grace in an extraordinary way | Immaculate Conception | Bo1 |

**to remove the binding**
descuadernar [Gue15:4]

| Tenor | Referent | No. |
|---|---|---|
| to transform | death as transformation from mortality to immortality | Gue15 |

**to gild the edges of pages**
lucir [BaB:76]

| Tenor | Referent | No. |
|---|---|---|
| to manifest God's presence | manifestation of God's grace or presence in St. Francis on occasion of his receiving stigmata | BaB |

B.2.6.ue. TO BIND THE TEXT: UNMIXED EXPANSIONS

to bind together in a book [ManA2:96-97; Led16:11-14; Va13:14-16; Bo15:13-16; Ca43:4-6; Gue1:79-80]
to bind skillfully [Va13:14-15; Bo1:8]
to change the binding [Gue15:4-5]


B.3. *TO OBTAIN AND USE THE TEXT*

B.3.1.ue. TO OBTAIN THE TEXT: UNMIXED EXPANSIONS

to buy a book [Var:12-14; Gue1:12-14]
to find a (replacement for a) lost text [Cab6:2-4; Ca54:19-21]
A text falls into one's hands. [Ven:86-87; Ca55:61-63]


B.3.2.ue. TO POSSESS THE TEXT: UNMIXED EXPANSIONS

to have a book in one's library [Vi3:6]
to have many books [Ven:69-70]
to have / need only one text [SEE: A.3.8. Christus:ue. The Christus is the only lesson one needs to learn; B.3.2.ue. to have / need only one book]
to have / need only one book [SEE ALSO: A.2.2. student:ue. the outstanding student of a single book]
    [Ven:209-10; Ter:27-29; Mat:14-15; VgC8.1:5-13;1:1-3]


B.3.3. TO OPEN OR CLOSE THE TEXT

B.3.3.1. *To Open the Text*

**to cut the pages**
rasgar [Fue:56; Ca8:3;65:13]

| Tenor | Referent | No. |
|---|---|---|
| to wound | stigmata of St. Francis | Fue |
| to manifest | King Solomon's vision | Ca8 |
| to appear in the midst of | appearance of moon in midst of a cloud, which appears in midst of sky, symbolic of Incarnation | Ca65 |

**to display / unfold**
desplegar [Ca48:14;26:35;65:14;11:5]

MOTIF INDEX                     271

| Tenor | Referent | No. |
|---|---|---|
| to manifest | manifestation of colors of sunrise or sunset; redemption through crucified and risen Christ | Ca48 |
| to manifest | manifestation of colors of sunrise; Incarnation and Redemption | Ca26 |
| to manifest | manifestation of moon in midst of cloud, reflected in turn in moon, symbolic of Incarnation | Ca65 |
| to manifest | manifestation of colors of sunrise, symbolic of redemption through Christ's death | Ca11 |

**to display / unfold:** unmixed expansions
  to display a book on a lectern [Led1:11-12]
  to display the pages [19] [SEE ALSO: B.3.3.1. to display:ue. to display marbled pages]
  [Ca65:14]
  to display marbled pages [Ca48:14-16;26:35-36;11:5-7]
  to hang a book from a chain [Vi3:96-97; Do:51-54]

**to open**
  abrir [Mon4:6; Ven:47,79,200,234,238,255; Vi3:39,276; Av2:1,2,7,8; Os:1; VgC5: 33; Cab10:3,5,9; ManA2:29,108,115; VgC8:7;13:6;17:12; LoA:12; Fue:56; Jau:26; VgC4:2; BaB:5; Ca9:31;62:59,62;12:6; Grc:24; Ca2:14; 41:25; 55:42; 36:26;44:12; Ag2:60,61; Ca10:13,16; Enc:3]
  desatar [Cab10:13]
  soltar [Cab10:3]

| Tenor | Referent | No. |
|---|---|---|
| to rupture the hymen | Virgin Birth | Mon4 |
| to comprehend | mystery of the Godhead | Ven |
| to make manifest | natural world as clear manifestation of God | Ven |
| to create; to make manifest | created heavens as clear manifestation of God | Ven |

---

[19] In his observations on distinctive characteristics of Spanish incunabula, Díez-Borque mentions exceptions to their relative lack of illustrations, including the *Viaje a Jerusalen* of Breidenbach (1489), which even contained "páginas desplegables" (70). Perhaps Calderón is thinking of such a book when he uses the motif of displaying or unfolding the pages in relation to the crucified and simultaneously glorious Christ.

| | | |
|---|---|---|
| to manifest or reveal | revelation of God's judgment of just and sinners | Vi3 |
| to manifest or reveal | revelation of secrets of conscience and of God's judgment | Vi3 |
| to manifest | manifestation of secrets of conscience | Av2 |
| to manifest | manifestation of those known to God as predestined for glory | Av2 |
| to manifest | Christ as manifestation of God's justice and truth; his manifestation as such on his ascension to heaven | Os |
| to be a constant part of | labor and pain as constant part of mortal life as result of original sin | VgC5 |
| to manifest, to demonstrate | Christ's manifesting in his person and by the mysteries of his life, his being fulfillment of Old Law | Cab10 |
| to make clear | Christ's making clear to the Apostles, by his words after resurrection and sending of Holy Spirit, that he is the fulfillment of Old Law | Cab10 |
| to present for consideration | Church's presentation of a particular Gospel text on Marian feasts | ManA2 |
| to have power over; to comprehend | inability of anyone but God to have any power over Mary or to comprehend the mysteries of her being | ManA2 |
| to wound | Christ in his Passion and crucifixion | VgC8 |
| to reveal | inability of those responsible for Christ's death to comprehend who he was unless he himself revealed it | VgC13 |
| to wound | wounding of Christ's face by blow from high priest's servant | VgC17 |

| Tenor | Referent | No. |
|---|---|---|
| to manifest | manifestation of hidden merits of saints in Last Judgment | LoA |
| to wound | stigmata of St. Francis | Fue |
| to comprehend | incomprehensible mystery of divinity of crucified and Eucharistic Christ | Jau |
| to open; to manifest | open petals of flower as manifesting God the Creator | VgC4 |
| to wound; to manifest | stigmata of St. Francis as manifesting Christ and his grace | BaB |
| to remember | remembrance of one's mortality | Ca9 |
| to make clear | Church as interpreter of law of grace, in accord with upright conscience | Ca62 |
| to make accessible | accessibility to all peoples of a place in sacred history, salvation through faith in Christ | Ca12 |
| to manifest in light of day | heavens as seen in light of day | Grc |
| to understand | St. John's understanding, through special divine revelation, of mysteries of Christ | Ca2 |
| to make accessible | accessibility of salvation to Jews and Gentiles alike through faith in Christ | Ca41 |
| to reveal | mysteries of God's providence | Ca55 |
| to reveal | revelation of mysteries of Christ | Ca36 |
| to reveal | revelation of mysteries of salvation | Ca44 |
| to be able to be affected by | Mary as completely free from power of sin, and completely informed by grace | Ag2 |
| to comprehend | incomprehensibility of mysteries of Christ's divinity | Ca10 |
| to reveal, to give understanding of | understanding of Christian mysteries through faith | Ca10 |
| to open the womb; to comprehend the mystery of | Mary's perpetual virginity; incomprehensibility of Marian mysteries to any but God | Enc |

**to unroll**
  extender [Ven:236-37,238,247; Grc:24-25]

| Tenor | Referent | No. |
|---|---|---|
| to make manifest | heavens as clear manifestation of God | Ven |
| to make manifest | heavens as God's creation and as manifesting him | Grc |

**to unroll:** unmixed expansions

  to unroll a skin / scroll [SEE ALSO: A.1.2.4.3. skin:ue. an unrolled skin] [Ven:236-37,238-39,247-48]


B.3.3.1.ue. *To Open the Text: Unmixed Expansions*

  to open a book [SEE ALSO: A.3.2.1:ue. an open book; B.3.3.1. to unroll:ue. to unroll a skin]
  [Vi3:39-40,276-77; Av2:1-3,8; Cab10:3,5-6,9; ManA2:25-28; LoA:12; Ca62: 48+ 59,62-63]
  to open a seal [Cab10:3-4; VgC13:6; Ca2:14-15;36:26]
  No one can open the book. [SEE ALSO: B.3.3.1.me. No one but the Lamb / Lion can open the book.]
  [Ven:78-79; ManA2:106-08,111-15]


B.3.3.1.me. *To Open the Text: Mixed Expansions*

  No one but the Lamb / Lion can open the book. [Ven:47-48; VgC13:2-6; Ca44:10-13;10:12-14; Enc:3-4]


B.3.3.2. *To Close the Text*

**to close**
  cerrar [Ven:249; To:1; Cam:65; VgC5:32; Rod2:4; ManA1:7; 2:106; Va19:1; VgC8:7; Fue:55; Ca12:5; Grc:23-24; Ca43:131]

| Tenor | Referent | No. |
|---|---|---|
| to make difficult to understand | natural world as clear manifestation of God | Ven |
| to be incomprehensible to human understanding | incomprehensible mystery of Christ in his divinity | To |

MOTIF INDEX 275

| Tenor | Referent | No. |
|---|---|---|
| to be incomprehensible to human understanding | incomprehensibility to mortals of mystery of God in himself | Cam |
| to be totally absent from | rest from labor and pain as totally absent from mortal life as result of original sin | VgC5 |
| to be incomprehensible to human understanding | incomprehensible mystery of Christ in his divinity | Rod2 |
| to not be known | Mary's destiny as not yet known at her birth | ManA1 |
| to allow no power over or comprehension of the mysteries of | inability of anyone but God to have any power over Mary or to comprehend the mysteries of her being | ManA2 |
| to preserve the virginity of | Mary's perpetual virginity | Va19 |
| to be hidden | divinity of newborn Christ as hidden to human vision | VgC8 |
| to allow no power over | Immaculate Conception | Fue |
| to end | end of time or sacred history | Ca12 |
| to be invisible | stars of heaven as invisible during light of day | Grc |
| to be incomprehensible or mysterious in significance | mystery of Christ's lineage as contained in the Scriptures | Ca43 |

**to roll up** [SEE ALSO: A.3.3.1. scroll]
arrollar [LoA:15]
plegar [Vi3:107,109,111]

| Tenor | Referent | No. |
|---|---|---|
| to come to an end; to be unnecessary | end of world, when sinners will be condemned and just will enjoy beatific vision | Vi3 |
| to hide | merits of saints as hidden in this life through humility | LoA |

**to roll up:** unmixed expansion
to roll up a scroll [SEE ALSO: A.3.3.1. scroll]
[Vi3:107-08,109-10]

**to seal**
cerrar [Jau:25]
echar el sello [Jau:18,36,54]
sellar [Mon4:6;3:7; To:4; Cam:65; Va13:7;15:2; Fue:55; Va1:3; Re:6; Grc:34]

| Tenor | Referent | No. |
|---|---|---|
| to preserve the virginity of | Virgin Birth | Mon4 |
| to be incomprehensible to human understanding | the Word, incomprehensible in his divinity, who is eternal life | Mon3 |
| to have secondary characteristics; to hide | Christ's divinity as hidden by the accidents of his humanity | To |
| to be incomprehensible to human understanding | incomprehensibility to mortals of mystery of God in himself | Cam |
| to hide | Christ's divinity as hidden by his humanity, and both as hidden in Eucharist | Va13 |
| to preserve the virginity of; to hide | Mary's perpetual virginity, even in pregnancy; the unborn John the Baptist's recognition of Christ hidden in Mary's womb | Va15 |
| to preserve from all sin | Immaculate Conception | Fue |
| to hide | Christ's humanity as hiding his divinity, specifically in crucifixion, and Eucharist as hiding both | Jau |
| to be incomprehensible | truth as incomprehensible to person oriented to worldly delights | Va1 |
| to keep track of | God's sure knowledge of all a person's sins | Re |
| to hide, to be incomprehensible | difficulty of understanding human intentions | Grc |

B.3.3.2.ue. *To Close the Text: Unmixed Expansions*

to close a book [SEE ALSO: A.3.2.1:ue. a closed book; B.3.3.2. to roll up:ue. to roll up a scroll]
[Ca12:5]

## B.3.4. TO READ THE TEXT

### B.3.4.1. *To Read the Text: Mental Activities*

**to interpret**
desenvolver [Ven:55]
leer [Ca49:43]

| Tenor | Referent | No. |
|---|---|---|
| to understand | understanding of mysteries of Godhead not meant for ordinary person | Ven |
| to understand | understanding of mystery of Eucharist through faith | Ca49 |

**to read**
deletrear / letrear [Cam:74; Va15:3]
leer / lectura [Mon10:3;2:6;1:8; Ven:7,40,42,45-46,57,60,62,64,68,70,80, 85,86,94,110,147,151,152,156,161,162,174,175,192,196,201,203,205,206, 216,233,250,254,257,270,273,278,280,291,293,311,363,365,372,374,376, 378,384,389,399; Cstj2:6; Vi3:7,44,50,51,53,56,75,76,77,79,94,99,108,110, 112,116,125,128,155,221,239,303;1:3,4,6,7;2:5,18; Av4:1,3,4; AD:10,17,19; Ter:31; Cor:4; Grn:18,19,47,53; Leo2:13; Grn:98,100; Gal:3; Cam:46,59,64, 74; Var:14,17; Sua:3,16,55,58; Rod1:5,8; Cab8:5; Mu2:12,32,36-37; ManA2: 108; Led18:3,8,11,14,18; Bo16:2; Que3:4; VgC15:8; LoA:6,16; Led4:3; Va3:7; Bo15:4,59; BaB:79; Hu:9; VgC6:5; Ca9:31;64:19;20:6; Car:2,9; Ca31:15,17, 36;18:14,16;62:42,64; Grc:31,39,45,46; Ca67:2; Do:29,33,73; Da:9,33,38,43, 46,51,52,57; Ca8:38,45,48;45:10;42:15,21;43:77,103,105,111,125,136,138;17: 27;49:21,25,47,63; Gue6:14,22,24; Ca65:2;55:12,44;68:30;61:9,14; Gue1:40, 102;2:3;4:5;3:5;15:5;14:4; Ag1:8;2:2,36,53,56,58,62,64,67; Bm:4; Gue12:5]
recorrer [Ca24:2]
registrar [Gue1:52,66,116;15:7]
repasar [Vi1:1; Va3:15]

| Tenor | Referent | No. |
|---|---|---|
| to contemplate | beatific vision of angels, in which they understand directly mystery of Eucharist | Mon10 |
| to scrutinize through the instrumentation of | vanity of certain widows | Mon2 |
| to contemplate in the flesh | contemplation of crucified Christ, divine King and omnipotent God | Mon1 |
| to recognize, to know | recognition or knowledge of God through creatures | Ven |

| Tenor | Referent | No. |
|---|---|---|
| to contemplate, to know | beatific vision or direct knowledge of God | Ven |
| to contemplate, to know | knowledge of God through the human Christ | Ven |
| to know | God's infinite self-knowledge | Ven |
| to comprehend | comprehension of Godhead as not meant for mortals | Ven |
| to understand | understanding of God and of his will for humankind through natural world | Ven |
| to reflect upon | understanding of God achieved by philosophers through applying natural reason to world | Ven |
| to reflect upon, to reason about | natural world as clear source of understanding of God | Ven |
| to contemplate, to understand | St. Anthony's understanding of God through contemplation of natural world | Ven |
| to understand | heavens as source of understanding of God clear to anyone | Ven |
| to contemplate | contemplation of ordered movements of heavens as providing clear evidence of Creator | Ven |
| to manifest | reflection upon ordered movements of heavens as clear evidence of Creator | Ven |
| to know | characteristics of matter as source of knowledge of Creator | Ven |
| to manifest | matter as manifesting God's stability | Ven |
| to know | knowledge of God's love for creatures through relationship between form and matter | Ven |
| to know | heavenly bodies as sources of spiritual knowledge | Ven |
| to be mindful of | heavens as reminders of spiritual lessons | Ven |
| to contemplate | knowledge of God through natural world as not diminishing importance of faith | Ven |

| Tenor | Referent | No. |
|---|---|---|
| to understand | faith as enhancing understanding of spiritual truths derived through reason | Ven |
| to reflect upon | reflection upon human body as source of moral knowledge | Ven |
| to know | one's own body as source of spiritual or moral knowledge | Ven |
| to understand | discontent with one's state in life as sign of not understanding moral significance of functioning of human body | Ven |
| to recognize | truth recognized in God's creation as source of spiritual understanding | Ven |
| to be the object of | danger of believing flattery | Cstj2 |
| to meditate on | spiritual benefit of meditating on certain topics | Vi3 |
| to contemplate | beatific vision | Vi3 |
| to know | God's eternal knowledge of the elect | Vi3 |
| to know directly | direct knowledge of God enjoyed in heaven and only very rarely on earth | Vi3 |
| to meditate on | meditation on natural world as source of knowledge of God accessible to all | Vi3 |
| to know through the instrumentation of | end of world | Vi3 |
| to recognize | failure to recognize God in beauty of natural world | Vi3 |
| to understand | understanding of God through natural world as taught by few pagan philosophers | Vi3 |
| to contemplate | contemplation of virtues of Christian life in person and life of Christ | Vi3 |
| to contemplate | contemplation of the divine Word by both angels and human beings | Vi3 |
| to know | beatific vision | Vi3 |
| to contemplate | Mary as model of all virtue | Vi1 |

| Tenor | Referent | No. |
|---|---|---|
| to recognize, to learn to know | Mary, mother of the Word, as the New Law, prefigured in Old Testament | Vi2 |
| to contemplate | superficial manner of contemplation of crucified Christ | Av4 |
| to contemplate | Mary's sorrow in contemplation of Christ's Passion | AD |
| to know | Mary's knowledge of her role in redemption | AD |
| to know | visions of Christ as source of understanding | Ter |
| to contemplate | contemplation of Christ | Cor |
| to contemplate | contemplation of natural world as source of knowledge of God for St. Anthony | Grn |
| to recognize | failure of human beings to recognize God's perfection and love in natural world | Grn |
| to see in bodily form | incarnation of the Word | Leo2 |
| to recognize | failure of some human beings to recognize God's grandeur and love in natural world, vs. recognition of same by others | Grn |
| — | wordless communication between mutually loving souls | Gal |
| to recognize and understand | recognition of God and understanding of his unity and sovereignty, through his creation | Cam |
| to contemplate directly | St. John the Evangelist's direct contemplation of divine mysteries, not permitted to most mortals | Cam |
| to contemplate | contemplation of spiritual truths | Var |
| to contemplate | natural world as manifesting God's grandeur | Sua |
| to recognize | beauty of natural world as evident manifestation of God | Sua |
| to contemplate | Mary as manifesting all virtue | Sua |

| Tenor | Referent | No. |
|---|---|---|
| to contemplate | Mary as mother of the Word | Sua |
| to see in human form, to know | incarnation of the Word | Rod1 |
| to contemplate | beatific vision | Cab8 |
| to reflect upon | reflection on meaning of name of Jesus in conjunction with his circumcision | Mu2 |
| to consider in faith | Jews' failure to understand correctly the Scriptures because of lack of faith in Christ | Mu2 |
| to comprehend | impossibility of mystery of Mary being understood during her mortal life | ManA2 |
| to meditate on | meditation on life and death of St. Lucy | Led18 |
| to recognize | unborn John the Baptist's recognition of Christ the Messiah in Mary's womb | Va15 |
| to understand | natural world as source of understanding of God | Bo16 |
| to regard | prayer in time of anguish | Que3 |
| to see | face of deceased priest as manifesting effects of God's presence in him during his life | VgC15 |
| to see | Moses as exemplar of the Law even before it was written | LoA |
| to know | hidden merits of the saints | LoA |
| to exemplify | Christ's life and person as exemplifying victory over sin | Led4 |
| to perceive | pursuit of worldly delights | Va3 |
| to anticipate | anticipation of enjoyment of worldly delights | Va3 |
| to regard; to grace | God's regarding Mary and thereby gracing her | Bo15 |
| to grace | God's gracing of Mary in Incarnation | Bo15 |
| to know | immortal fame of St. Francis and universality of Franciscan Order | BaB |
| to contemplate; to comprehend | contemplation of dying Christ and accompanying signs | Hu |

| Tenor | Referent | No. |
|---|---|---|
| | in heavens as resulting in spiritual illumination of St. Dionysius | |
| to contemplate through expressing | expression and contemplation of love | VgC6 |
| to reflect upon | consideration of one's mortality | Ca9 |
| to know, to experience | original sin as affecting entire human race | Ca64 |
| to study, to discover | heavens as source of knowledge of human destinies | Ca20 |
| to be reminded of | reminders of Lope and his writings in flora along Manzanares | Car |
| to consider | consideration of Christ's promise of hundredfold reward for almsgiving | Ca31 |
| to interpret | interpretation of human fortunes in stars | Ca31 |
| to interpret | interpretation of omens in flames | Ca18 |
| to reveal | revelation of the mysteries of nature | Ca18 |
| to know | Church as interpreter of law of grace | Ca62 |
| to consider | consideration of mysteries of New Dispensation | Ca62 |
| to interpret | difficulty of understanding human intentions | Grc |
| to appear | discrepancy between human appearances and human reality | Grc |
| to know | God's eternal self-knowledge, in which all things have their existence | Ca67 |
| to contemplate | St. Ignatius' contemplation of God's perfections in natural world | Do |
| to contemplate | contemplation of death as motivation to conversion of life | Do |
| to contemplate | contemplation of Christ's Passion | Da |
| to know | response in mind and heart to Christ's death sentence as reflected in faces of those present | Da |

| Tenor | Referent | No. |
|---|---|---|
| to contemplate | contemplation of Mary's sorrow in Christ's Passion | Da |
| to contemplate | grief of poet in contemplation of Mary's sorrow | Da |
| to interpret | fragmentary or imperfect nature of wisdom that depends on reason alone | Ca8 |
| to see | Christ's life and person as evidence to the Jews of his being Messiah | Ca45 |
| to commend to | commending of human needs and sufferings in faith and hope to divine love | Ca42 |
| to find included | Mary as not included among sinners, having been preserved from sin from first moment of conception | Ca43 |
| to prefigure | Job as prefiguration of Christ | Ca43 |
| to prophesy | Isaiah as prophet of Christ | Ca43 |
| to reflect upon, to study | consideration by Jews and Gentiles of prophecies regarding Messiah or Christ | Ca43 |
| to know, to experience | original sin as affecting entire human race | Ca17 |
| to contemplate | contemplation in faith of mysteries of Redemption signified and reenacted in Eucharist | Ca49 |
| to recognize | Gentiles' recognition of crucified Christ as divine King | Ca49 |
| to complete, to accomplish | Christ's resurrection as accomplishment or culmination of his redemptive acts, reenacted in Eucharist | Ca49 |
| to understand | sanctity of Sts. John of Matha and Felix of Valois as not understood by later generations or by sinners | Gue6 |
| to study, to interpret | study of stars as revealing human destiny | Ca65 |

| Tenor | Referent | No. |
|---|---|---|
| to interpret | Mosaic Law as revealing mysteries of New Dispensation of grace, but in a hidden way | Ca55 |
| to contemplate, to know directly | direct knowledge of God as manifesting that his justice is his mercy | Ca55 |
| to understand | understanding of mysteries of nature | Ca68 |
| to study, to reflect upon | fruitlessness of Gentiles' search for understanding of divine mysteries until enlightened by grace | Ca61 |
| to teach | Mary Magdalene as having much to teach Christians | Gue1 |
| to contemplate | contemplation of Mary Magdalene's life | Gue1 |
| to examine | Mary Magdalene's examination of conscience | Gue1 |
| to discern, to pay attention to | condemnation of Mary Magdalene by those who did not discern her change of heart | Gue1 |
| to do justice in preaching | Guerra y Ribera's declaration of his inability to speak adequately of Mary Magdalene's penitent love | Gue1 |
| to recognize | recognition of correspondence between heavenly bodies and characters of human beings | Gue2 |
| to recognize | recognition of the divine as more plainly manifest in burning bush than in Crucifixion | Gue4 |
| to learn | converted Mary Magdalene as exemplar for sinners | Gue3 |
| to understand | knowledge of Cardinal Cisnero's life as illumining the meaning of his death | Gue15 |
| to recapitulate | knowledge of Cardinal Cisnero's life as illumining the meaning of his death | Gue15 |

| Tenor | Referent | No. |
|---|---|---|
| to know | manifestation of secrets of conscience at Last Judgment? | Gue14 |
| to recognize | recognition of infant Christ as King and God by Wise Men from East | Ag1 |
| to meditate on | meditation on Mary | Ag2 |
| to contemplate | angels' contemplation of Mary's perfection | Ag2 |
| to prefigure, to prophesy | Old Testament patriarchs and John the Evangelist as prefiguring, or prophesying with regard to, Mary | Ag2 |
| to review | review of sins of humankind | Ca24 |
| to believe in | belief in Christ's divinity in Eucharist as possible only through faith | Brn |
| to recognize | recognition of Christian detachment or death to world and self as highest expression of living by truth rather than illusion | Gue12 |

**to relate the parts** [Ca12:10;8:45-48]
juntar las partes [Bo12:7]

| Tenor | Referent | No. |
|---|---|---|
| to comprehend | impossibility of comprehending mystery of the infinite God | Bo12 |
| to reveal the relationship | to explain the relationship between enmity among religions of world, dispersion of the Jews, and death of Christ | Ca12 |
| to interpret in relation to one another | to attempt to understand the meaning of the prophecies concerning redemption | Ca8 |

**to study**
apurar [Ca68:21]
estudiar / estudio [Grn:8,16-17,20-21,38; Mat:4,15; Sua:23; Led12:2; ManA2:6-7; Va4:10; Grc:5; Ca37:19; Grc:36,51-52; Ca13:14; ManL:2; Do:77; Ca8:30; 17:33;26:39; Gar:3; Ca44:22; Gue1:44]

| Tenor | Referent | No. |
|---|---|---|
| to ponder | natural world as source of knowledge of the divine for great philosophers | Grn |
| to contemplate | contemplation of natural world as source of knowledge of God for St. Anthony and King David | Grn |
| to reflect on | natural world as source of knowledge of God for all | Grn |
| to contemplate, to meditate on | contemplation of crucified Christ as source of all St. Bonaventure's wisdom | Mat |
| to contemplate | St. Anthony's contemplation of God's perfections in natural world | Sua |
| to contemplate | St. John the Evangelist's mystical vision while leaning on Christ's breast at Last Supper | Led12 |
| to contemplate | contemplation of Mary as source of wisdom in winning victory over sin | ManA2 |
| to repeat | orderly succession of days and nights as manifestation of God | Va4 |
| to contemplate | contemplation of divine perfections in natural world | Grc |
| practice of prudence | examples of good and ill from human history as teaching prudence | Ca37 |
| to reflect upon with discernment | need for constant and prudent discernment in order to understand human intentions | Grc |
| — | study of flight and song of birds as omens | Ca13 |
| meditation | meditation on one's relation to God | ManL |
| to meditate on | meditation on death as motivation to conversion of life | Do |
| to meditate on | study of stars; meditation on Cross, source of grace and redemption | Ca8 |

| Tenor | Referent | No. |
|---|---|---|
| contemplation of divine mysteries | tree of knowledge as giving foretaste of knowledge of divine mysteries enjoyed in heaven | Ca17 |
| to subsume | subsuming of the natural law and Mosaic law in New Dispensation of grace inaugurated by Christ | Ca26 |
| to exploit | Satan's use of natural world for evil purposes | Ca68 |
| to contemplate | natural world intended as source of contemplation of God | Gar |
| to know and will instantaneously and inalterably | fall of Lucifer | Ca44 |
| to practice | Mary Magdalene's acts of penitence | Gue1 |

**to study:** unmixed expansions
  to study an occult text [Ca13:14-15;68:21-23;61:9-13]

**to take note of**
  mirar (con los ojos) [Vi2:4,17-18; Va16:4]
  notar [Led18:4,8,11,14,18]

| Tenor | Referent | No. |
|---|---|---|
| to contemplate | Mary, mother of the Word, as the New Law, prefigured in Old Testament | Vi2 |
| to be particularly mindful of | meditation on significance of manner of St. Lucy's martyrdom | Led18 |
| to contemplate | contemplation of Christ's wounding on head and crowning with thorns | Va16 |

B.3.4.1.1. *To Learn*

**to learn** [SEE ALSO: A.3.7.2.lesson:ue. to derive a lesson]
  aprender [Vi3:53; VgC5:10; Bo16:8; Ca55:54;44:21]
  deprender [Va15:4]

| Tenor | Referent | No. |
|---|---|---|
| to experience | inexhaustible riches of Godhead enjoyed by blessed in heaven | Vi3 |
| to imitate | St. Isidore of Madrid's imitation of Christ | VgC5 |
| to comprehend | unborn John the Baptist's comprehension of unborn Christ as Messiah | Va15 |
| to understand the significance of | creatures as manifestation of God | Bo16 |
| to believe in | grace given to a Jew to understand the spiritual meaning of the Cross and believe in Christ | Ca55 |
| to know and will instantaneously and inalterably | fall of Lucifer | Ca44 |

**to memorize / learn by heart** [Var:14-15]
   decorar [Bo16:13;12:6;15:20]
   deletrear [Led21:11]
   repetir [Led16:22]
   saber bien [Grc:37]
   saber de dicho [Led21:10]

| Tenor | Referent | No. |
|---|---|---|
| to be ever mindful of | mindfulness of spiritual truths meditated upon | Var |
| to practice | practice of virtue as essential to knowledge of it | Led21 |
| to be informed by | to be informed by virtue through its practice | Led21 |
| to practice constantly | Christ's constant obedience to Father | Led16 |
| to recognize, to know | knowledge of God through reasoning from natural world, or effect, to God as cause | Bo16 |
| to comprehend | knowledge of God through reasoning about natural world, as necessarily incomplete | Bo12 |
| to comprehend | God alone as fully comprehending mysteries of Mary's person and life | Bo15 |

| Tenor | Referent | No. |
|---|---|---|
| to constantly practice | need for constant and prudent discernment in order to understand human intentions | Grc |

B.3.4.1.1.ue. *To Learn: Unmixed Expansions*

> to learn the Christus of the primer [SEE ALSO: A.3.8. Christus:ue. The Christus is the only lesson one needs to learn.]
> [VgC5:10; Led21:4-6;16:22-23; Va15:3; Ca42:28-30;55:54]
> to learn something new with each reading [Vi3:51-53]
> No one can learn the text completely. [SEE ALSO: A.3.2.1.ue. an inexhaustible book]
> [Bo12:6-8;15:19-20]

B.3.4.1.ue. *To Read the Text – Mental Activities: Unmixed Expansions*

> to understand the text [SEE ALSO: B.3.4.1.ue. to understand the smallest portion of a text; to be understood only when written and read; to be understood without being written or read; The text is easy to understand]
> [Vi3:127-31; Va4:16-17; So:3-5]
> to understand the smallest portion of a text [Ven:56-58,63-65]
> to not understand the text [SEE ALSO: B.3.4.1.ue. to not understand the smallest portion of a text; to not understand a character; The more one reads, the less one understands; The text is difficult to understand]
> [Rod2:4-5; Ca8:38+42,47-48]
> to not understand the smallest portion of a text [Grc:37-40]
> to not understand a character [SEE ALSO: A.3.19.5. character / lettering: ue. to delight in the beautiful letters without understanding their meaning; B.3.4.1.ue. to recognize a character but not understand its meaning]
> [Grn:98-99; Ca29:23-24]
> to recognize a character but not understand its meaning [Ca31:24-25;55:19-20]
> to neither recognize a character nor understand its meaning [Grc:49-51]
> to be understood only when written and read [Rod1:1-5]
> to be understood without being written or read [Av5:14-15; Gal:3-5]
> The more one reads, the less one understands. [Ca61:114]
> The text is easy to understand. [SEE ALSO: A.3.2.1.ue. The book is open to all; A.3.7.2. lesson:ue. a clear lesson]
> [Ven:199-204,231-34,243-45,253-59; Sua:15-16; Grc:28-29]
> The text is difficult to understand. [SEE ALSO: A.3.6. subject matter / discourse:ue. difficult subject matter; A.3.19.5. character / lettering:ue. an obscure character; B.3.3.1:ue. No one can open the book.]
> [Ven:152-55; Grc:30-35,45-47]

B.3.4.2. *To Read the Text – Physical Activities* [SEE ALSO: A.3.18.2:ue. to turn the page; to turn back to a preceding page]

**to leaf through**
  hojear [Led12:5; Va3:13; Ca43:15,72;26:66,68; Gue1:32]
  revolver [Do:71]

| Tenor | Referent | No. |
| --- | --- | --- |
| to experience mystic union with Christ | St. John the Evangelist's mystical experience while leaning on Christ's breast at Last Supper | Led12 |
| to think about worldly pleasures | anticipation of enjoyment of worldly delights | Va3 |
| to reflect upon | reflection upon the brevity of human life | Do |
| to affect the human race | sin as affecting whole human race with exception of Christ and Mary | Ca43 |
| to affect all of human history | grace won through Christ's death as affecting entire history of human race | Ca26 |
| to affect all of human history | sin as affecting entire history of human race | Ca26 |
| to review | Mary Magdalene's examination of conscience or review of her past life | Gue1 |

B.3.4.3. *To Sing / Chant the Text*

**to intone**
  entonar [Par2:5]

| Tenor | Referent | No. |
| --- | --- | --- |
| to pray, to call out | St. Stephen's prayer when he was being stoned to death | Par2 |

B.3.4.ue. TO READ THE TEXT: UNMIXED EXPANSIONS

  to learn to read [Vi3:88-89,302-04; Si:2-3; Pin:151-55,165-68; Led21:4-11; Bo16:1,8]
  to teach to read [Vi3:155; Bo16:1-8; VgC24:26-27]

*Readers of the Text*

Philosophers and wise men have read the book. [SEE ALSO: B.3.4.ue. Mercurius Trismegistus read the book.]
 [Ven:172-74; Grn:7-8; Grc:4-6,22-26; Ag1:1+8;2:2+62]
Mercurius Trismegistus read the book. [Cam:20-26; Sua:25-31]
Many saints have read the book. [SEE ALSO: B.3.4.ue. The psalmist King David read the book; Saint Anthony read the book; Saint John the Evangelist read the book.]
 [Cam:30-34; Ag2:53-67]
The psalmist King David read the book. [Grn:20-24; Cam:43-48]
Saint Anthony read the book. [Ven:204-06,216; Grn:15-16; Cam:10-18; Sua:18-25]
Saint John the Evangelist read the book. [Vi3:77-79; Cam:58-59; Ag2:66-67]
St. Paul read the book. [Vi3:76-77; Cam:45-49]
We should not try to read what is beyond our comprehension. [Ven:52-56,65-68,78-81]

*To Read a Certain Text*

to read the original [Ven:162-63; Ca64:18-19;17:26-27]
to read the title [Mon1:8-9; Mu2:32,36-37,40; Gue4:5]
to read the chapter titles to learn what the book is about [Var:17-18; Mu2:10-13; Gue1:52-53;15:5-8]

*To Read in a Certain Way*

to read according to one's capacity [Vi3:43-45]
to read from beginning to end [Ven:61-62; Vi3:50-51]
to read from the professorial chair [Led1:6-7;16:8-9; Bo15:70-71]
to read in a competitive examination [Led4:3; Ca62:41-42,62-65]
to read attentively [Ven:202-03; Vi1:1; Mu2:32-33; Ag2:2]
to read poorly [SEE ALSO: A.2.2. reader:ue. a poor reader; B.3.4.ue. to read superficially]
 [Ven:384,389]
to read superficially [SEE ALSO: A.3.19.5. character / lettering:ue. to delight in the beautiful letters without understanding their meaning]
 [Mon2:6; Av4:1-5]

*To Read a Certain Amount of Time / with a Certain Frequency*

to have a book always before one's eyes [Vi3:225-26; Var:5-7]
to read a text briefly [Vi3:76-77; Ca55:44]
to read a text frequently [SEE ALSO: B.3.4.ue. to have a book always before one's eyes]
 [Vi3:6-7]

*To Not Be Able to Read* [SEE ALSO: A.3.5. text / contents:ue. The text is illegible.]
[Vi3:106-08; Grn:96-98; LoA:13-16; Da:46,52; Gue6:21-24]


B.3.4.me. TO READ THE TEXT – MIXED EXPANSIONS

The angels read the text. [SEE ALSO: B.3.4.me. Only the angels / saints can read the book of life.]
[Mon10:1-3; Ag2:35-36]
Only the angels / saints can read the book of life. [SEE ALSO: B.3.4.me. Only the angels / saints can read the inside / original of the divine book.]
[Vi3:143-44,75-76]
Only the angels / saints can read the inside / original of the divine book. [SEE ALSO: B.3.4.me. Only the angels / saints can read the book of life.]
[Ven:39-41,59-61,65-67,79-81]
In this life we can read only the outside / copy of the divine book. [Ven:37-43,124-29; Cam:31-34]
In the book of Mary we read all the moral virtues. [Vi1:1-7; Sua:52-55]


B.3.5.ue. TO RESPOND / NOT RESPOND TO THE TEXT: UNMIXED EXPANSIONS

to make good use of a book [Cam:37]
to marvel at the binding [Ven:95-96]
to value a book highly [SEE ALSO: A.3.2.1:ue. a highly esteemed book]
[Bo15:6; Ag2:43-44]
to be moved by a text [Do:47-56; Da:9]
Believing what one reads can be harmful. [Cstj2:3-6]
The text is read throughout the world. [SEE ALSO: B.4.3. to disseminate:ue. to disseminate the text throughout the world]
[BaB:77-80]
The text is well received. [SEE ALSO: B.3.5.ue. The text is read throughout the world.]
[Mon2:11-12; Gue1:16,70]
The text is not well received. [Gue1:9-12]


B.4. *TO PRESERVE / NOT PRESERVE THE TEXT*

B.4.1. TO PRESERVE THE TEXT

**to preserve**
conservar [Vi3:240,244; Pin:28-29; Bo12:13; Ca30:43;53:15; 57:17]
depositar [Ca8:66]
esconder [Ca29:57]
guardar [Vi3:244; Snt2:8; Bo6:18; Ca2:22]

| Tenor | Referent | No. |
|---|---|---|
| — | Incarnation | Vi3 |
| to know eternally | God's eternal knowledge of the elect | Pin |
| — | memory's preserving learning and noble deeds of humankind | Snt2 |
| to keep in existence | God's eternal knowing of all his creatures as keeping them in existence | Bo12 |
| — | God's preserving Mary from original sin | Bo6 |
| to inhere in | mysterious designs of grace for redemption of humankind | Ca2 |
| to subsume | subsuming of natural law in law of grace | Ca30 |
| to bestow | King Solomon's God-given power and wisdom | Ca8 |
| to maintain in confidentiality | confidentiality maintained by confessors with regard to sins confessed | Ca53 |
| to remember | commemoration of a sacred festival | Ca57 |
| to conceal | mysterious designs of Providence | Ca29 |

### B.4.1.ue. TO PRESERVE THE TEXT: UNMIXED EXPANSIONS

to keep the text clean [SEE ALSO: B.4.1.ue. to not (ever) blot the text] [Vi3:297-98]

to not (ever) blot the text [Fue:39; Bo6:7-8,11-12,27-30, 39-40; Ca43:90-91]

to not bend / wrinkle a page [ManA2:103-05]

to not (ever) cross out of the text [Fue:15-16; BaB:51-52]

to not (ever) erase from the text [SEE ALSO: B.2.1.ue. to be written indelibly; B.4.1.ue. to not (ever) erase from the book; B.4.1:me. to not (ever) erase from memory]
[Vi3:295-96; Roc:7-8; Cab11:42-43; Va17:3; PrA:4-6; Lud:11-12; Ca44:23]

to not (ever) erase from the book [Vi3:63-64; ADJ:4]

to preserve one's ideas through writing [Vi3:240-45; Pin:28-30,65-66]

to preserve important / secret papers [Snt2:2-7; Led14:10; Va15:6-9]

to preserve in an archive [Snt2:6-9; BaB:39-40; Ca2:21-22;8:64-66;57:17;29: 56-57]

to preserve in a receptacle [Vi3:244-45]

to recover the leaves that have fallen out of a book [Ca8:38]

## B.4.1.me. TO PRESERVE THE TEXT: MIXED EXPANSIONS

to not (ever) erase from the book of life / glory [SEE: B.4.1:ue. to not (ever) erase from the book]
to not (ever) erase from memory [Re:3]


## B.4.2. TO NOT PRESERVE THE TEXT

### B.4.2.1. *To Deface / Damage the Text*

**to blot** [Bo6:24-25]
　borrar [ManA2:134; Gue1:67]
　manchar [Fue:39; Bo6:11,16; Ca43:17,20]

| *Tenor* | *Referent* | *No.* |
|---|---|---|
| to sin | saints as having sinned at times | ManA2 |
| to detract from the perfection of | Mary as free from even the tendency to sin | Fue |
| for sin to affect | Mary's freedom from original sin | Bo6 |
| for sin to affect | original sin as affecting whole human race | Bo6 |
| to sin | original sin | Bo6 |
| to negate | total negation of sin's power in case of Jesus | Ca43 |
| for sin to affect | Mary Magdalene's many sins | Gue1 |

**to blot:** unmixed expansions
　to blot a name [Bo6:24-25; Ca43:83-84]
　for an ink blot to fall on the text / writing material [Grn:64-65; Par3:6-9; Roj:3; Ca43:74-76,92; Gue1:30-31]

**to cross out**
　tachar [Fue:16]

| *Tenor* | *Referent* | *No.* |
|---|---|---|
| to affect negatively | Satan's powerlessness over Mary and St. Francis | Fue |

**to tear**
　rasgar [ManA2:95,102]

| Tenor | Referent | No. |
|---|---|---|
| to commit venial sin | saints as having sinned at times | ManA2 |

**to tear:** unmixed expansions [SEE: A.3.18.2:ue. Loose leaves are easily lost or torn.]

B.4.2.2. *To Get Rid of the Text* [SEE ALSO: B.2.3.2. to expurgate]

**to burn**
  echar en el fuego [Sua:43]

| Tenor | Referent | No. |
|---|---|---|
| to condemn to hell | condemnation of sinners | Sua |

**to burn:** unmixed expansions
  to burn a forbidden book [Sua:42-43]

**to cancel**
  cancelar [ManA3:23,33; Va2:13; Ca32:19]

| Tenor | Referent | No. |
|---|---|---|
| to put an end to | Christ's redemptive death as ending obligation to Old Law | ManA3 |
| to repeal | repealing of punishment due humankind for sin | ManA3 |
| to repeal | repealing of punishment due humankind for sin | Va2 |
| to annul | Baptism as annulling original sin | Ca32 |

**to cancel:** unmixed expansions
  to annul a law [ManA3:16+23]
  to cancel a debt [Av3:15-21; ManA3:71-72,96-97,110-11; Bo8:6,9,13-14; Va2:9+13]
  to cancel a stamp [Ca32:15-19]

**to erase / blot out**
  borrar [Cstj1:3; Vi3:64,68,71,284,295; Av3:18; ADJ:4; Pin:77,97; Vgs8:3;4:4; Roc:7; Cab11:42-43; Led10:12; ManA3:10,21,33,36,47,54,71,96,110; Cai7:4; Va17:3; Bo8:6,9,14; Va7:1;2:9,13,14,24; Hu:7; PrA:6; Ca9:78,84;22:49; 21:11; VgC24:3; Roj:8; Ca56:4,10,25;6:11; Grc:10; Ca7:19; Re:3; Ca8:32; 43:35;41:31; Mrt:3; Lud:11; Ca65:21;36:16;44:23; Gue1:57,80,88,102,105,109; Ag2:72; Ca24:15,17]
  dar un borrón [Lem:1]
  raer/raimiento [Vi3:65; Pin:84,93,94]

| Tenor | Referent | No. |
|---|---|---|
| to forget | forgetfulness of service rendered on part of unjust and inhumane king | Cstj1 |
| to change a soul's eternal destiny from salvation to condemnation | eternal predestination of the elect | Vi3 |
| to know as not saved | God's eternal knowledge of those who are not saved | Vi3 |
| to keep secret | revelation of secrets of conscience at Last Judgment | Vi3 |
| to undo | all a person's acts, even the most secret, as having everlasting effects that will some day be revealed | Vi3 |
| to repeal | repealing of punishment due humankind for sin | Av3 |
| to turn away from | conversion from sinful life | Lem |
| to condemn | eternal salvation of Asenet, figure of Mary and of soul | ADJ |
| to know as not in grace or saved | God's knowledge of those who are not in state of grace and thus not saved | Pin |
| to know as not in grace | willingness of Moses and St. Paul to be without God's grace for sake of salvation of others | Pin |
| to condemn | ignorance as to one's eternal destiny | Vgs8 |
| to condemn | fall of Lucifer and other rebellious angels | Vgs4 |
| to destroy | prayer for constancy in love of and obedience to God in all trials | Roc |
| to remove | Christ's bearing the effects of his now glorious wounds even in heaven | Cab11 |
| to forget | Christ's eternal love for souls, reason for his redemptive death | Cab11 |
| to preserve from | God's preservation of Mary from original sin | Led10 |
| to put an end to | Christ's redemptive death as ending obligation to Old Law | ManA3 |

| Tenor | Referent | No. |
|---|---|---|
| to repeal | repealing of punishment due humankind for sin | ManA3 |
| to prevent | prevention of punishment due for sin through participation in Christ's redemption | ManA3 |
| to abrogate | abrogation of humankind's debt of expiation for sin and its transferral to Christ | ManA3 |
| to abrogate | abrogation of King David's debt of expiation for sin and its transferral to Christ | ManA3 |
| to forgive | God's forgiveness of sins of repentant sinner | Cai7 |
| to forget | Christ's eternal love for souls, reason for his redemptive death | Va17 |
| to abrogate | abrogation of expiation owed by humankind for sin through Christ's redemptive death | Bo8 |
| to condemn | condemnation of unrepentant sinners | Va7 |
| to repeal | repealing of punishment due humankind for sin through Christ's redemptive death | Va2 |
| to obscure | storm-darkened sky at moment of Christ's death as sign of the mystery of his divinity | Hu |
| to destroy | powerlessness of a person's past sins to destroy God's love and grace in soul | PrA |
| to put an end to | annulment of Old Law with inauguration of New Dispensation of grace | Ca9 |
| to reject | rejection of false gods | Ca9 |
| to destroy | spiritual defeat caused by sin, from which Mary was free | Ca22 |
| to forget | forgetfulness of one's station in life | Ca21 |

| Tenor | Referent | No. |
|---|---|---|
| to surpass | sacrilegious treatment by Jews, of figure of St. Peter, as surpassing in infamy their ancestors' crucifixion of him | VgC24 |
| to obscure | obscuring of light of day in tumult of elements that accompanied death of Naboth, figure of Christ | Roj |
| to annul | annulment of original sin through Baptism | Ca56 |
| to forgive | prayer for God's mercy and forgiveness of one's sins | Ca6 |
| to be without substance or character | human beings who are not really persons | Grc |
| to undo the effect of | the sin of an instant as undoing the effects of long period of virtuous living | Ca7 |
| to forget | God's eternal mindfulness of each person or soul | Re |
| to forgive | forgiveness of sins through grace won by Christ's death | Ca8 |
| to annul | Christ's annulling effects of original sin through death on Cross | Ca43 |
| to condemn | God's eternal knowledge of those who are not saved | Ca41 |
| to destroy | destruction of loving relationship to God in grace | Mrt |
| to destroy | sin's inability to destroy St. Peter of Alcantara's unwavering obedience to God | Lud |
| to forgive | sinner who has been forgiven most, as loving most | Ca65 |
| to annul | annulment of original sin through Baptism | Ca36 |
| to change | inalterable nature of angelic knowledge and will | Ca44 |
| to repent of | Mary Magdalene's repentance for her sins | Gue1 |
| to annul | Christ's annulling the effects of sin | Gue1 |

# MOTIF INDEX

| Tenor | Referent | No. |
|---|---|---|
| to win forgiveness | Mary Magdalene's repentance for her sins as winning Christ's forgiveness | Gue1 |
| to forgive | prayer for Mary's intercession for divine forgiveness of one's sinful periods of life | Ag2 |
| to forgive | prayer for God's mercy and forgiveness of one's sins | Ca24 |

**to erase / blot out:** unmixed expansions
   to erase a brand [PrA:6; Ca56:3-4,6-7,25;36:16]
   to erase a section of the text [Gue1:57-58,80-81,104-05; Ag2:72-73]
   to erase one character with another [Ca56:9-10]
   to erase a defect [Led10:12; Cai7:4]
   to erase an error [Gue1:89-90,108-09]
   to erase from the book [SEE ALSO: B.4.2.2. to erase / blot out:me. to erase from the book of life / glory]
     [Cstj1:3; Vgs4:4; ManA3:54; Ca6:9-11;41:27-31;24:9-17]
   The more erasures, the fewer errors. [Ca65:21-22]

**to erase / blot out:** mixed expansions
   to blot out with blood [Av3:18-19; ManA3:10,21-22,33; Bo8:14; Va2:9-16]
   to erase from the book of life / glory [Vi3:65-66; Pin:77-80,96-97; Vgs8:3-4]
   to erase from memory [Va7:1; Ca21:9-11;43:33-35]

**to tear out**
   rasgar [Gue1:59,90,111]

| Tenor | Referent | No. |
|---|---|---|
| to abandon one's former sinful ways | Mary Magdalene's amendment of life | Gue1 |

**to tear out:** unmixed expansions
   to tear out pages [Gue1:59,90,110-11]

**to tear up**
   romper [ManA3:37; Par1:9; Ca9:51;45:17-19]

| Tenor | Referent | No. |
|---|---|---|
| to prevent | prevention of punishment due for sin through participation in Christ's redemption | ManA3 |

|   Tenor   |   Referent   |   No.   |
|---|---|---|
| to annul | Christ's annulling effects of sin through his redemptive death | Par1 |
| to distract from memory of | forgetfulness of death | Ca9 |
| to disobey, to pay no heed | Israel's disobedience in not heeding signs testifying to Christ as Messiah | Ca45 |

**to tear up:** unmixed expansions
   to tear up a document [SEE ALSO: B.4.2.2. to tear up:ue. to tear up and throw away a document]
   [ManA3:28-29+36-37; Par1:9; Ca45:17,19]
   to tear up and throw away a document [Ca9:51-52]

**to throw away**
   arrojar [Ca9:52]

|   Tenor   |   Referent   |   No.   |
|---|---|---|
| to cause to forget | forgetfulness of death | Ca9 |

**to throw away:** unmixed expansions [SEE: B.4.2.2. to tear up:ue. to tear up and throw away a document]


B.4.2.3. *To Lose the Text*

**to disappear**
   desvanecer [Da:57]

|   Tenor   |   Referent   |   No.   |
|---|---|---|
| to be indistinguishable | Mary's tears as rendered indistinguishable by torrent of weeping | Da |

**to disappear:** unmixed expansions
   The writing disappears as one reads. [Da:57]

**to lose** [Ca9:42-43]
   perder [Cab6:3; ManA2:96,101,183; Ca54:14,19]

|   Tenor   |   Referent   |   No.   |
|---|---|---|
| — | to know the principles of virtue even in the | Cab6 |

| Tenor | Referent | No. |
|---|---|---|
| | absence of written texts, through their embodiment in faithful Christians | |
| to sin mortally, to lose one's habit of virtue | saints as having sinned at times, or as being capable of mortal sin, in contrast to Mary | ManA2 |
| to forget | forgetfulness of death caused by concern for vanities of this world | Ca9 |
| to surrender | St. Augustine's willingness to surrender his need to understand divine mysteries and to accept gift of faith | Ca54 |

**to lose:** unmixed expansions
    to lose a leaf / page [SEE ALSO: A.3.18.2:ue. Loose leaves are easily lost or torn.]
        [ManA2:182-83]

**to scatter / disperse**
    arrojar esparcido [Ca8:12-13]
    esparcir [ManA2:89]

| Tenor | Referent | No. |
|---|---|---|
| to distribute | different virtues and graces given by God to different saints | ManA2 |
| to cause confusion and distress | spiritual confusion of Gentiles in midst of conflicting doctrines, before accepting faith in Christ | Ca8 |

**to scatter / disperse:** unmixed expansions
    to scatter / disperse the leaves / pages [ManA2:88-89; Ca8:11-13]


B.4.2.4.  *To Omit from the Text*

**to omit**
    no escribir [Vi3:69,70-71,73-74; Pin:120-21; Va7:4]
    no tener lugar [Va7:5-6]

| Tenor | Referent | No. |
|---|---|---|
| to know as not saved | God's eternal knowledge of those who are not saved | Vi3 |
| to know as not saved | God's eternal knowledge of those who are not saved | Pin |
| to condemn | condemnation of unrepentant sinners | Va7 |

B.4.2.4.ue. *To Omit from the Text: Unmixed Expansions*

to omit from a book [Vi3:70-74; Va7:4-6]

B.4.2.5. *The Text Deteriorates* [SEE ALSO: A.3.18.1:ue. a loose binding]

**to (cause to) come unbound**
descuadernar/se [Led1:12; Fue:29; Bo13:4;4:4; Per:15; Ca8:12; Ba:2-3; Mrn:2; Gue3:4]

| Tenor | Referent | No. |
|---|---|---|
| to be stretched to point of dislocation | crucified Christ | Led1 |
| to be stretched to point of dislocation | crucified Christ | Fue |
| to lose one's integrity | fasting as necessary to spiritual integrity of Christian | Bo13 |
| to cause to collapse | collapse of mountains in earthquake when Christ died | Bo4 |
| to collapse | collapse of mountain, allusion to Christ's death from perspective of evil that caused it | Per |
| to lack spiritual integrity | Gentiles as lacking spiritual integrity until finding it in Christ, divine Wisdom | Ca8 |
| to be destroyed | destruction of heavens at end of world | Ba |
| to cause to collapse | God's hypothetical destruction of heavens were St. Peter of Alcantara to pray for it | Mrn |
| to be unbound and loose | Mary Magdalene's unbound hair | Gue3 |

**to (cause to) come unbound:** unmixed expansions
for a book to come unbound [SEE ALSO: A.3.2.1:ue. a book with broken binding]
[Ba:2-3; Mrn:2]

**to (cause to) come unbound:** mixed expansions
The mountains come unbound. [Bo4:4; Per:12-15]

**to disintegrate**
deshacerse [LoU1:3]

| Tenor | Referent | No. |
|---|---|---|
| to die and turn to dust | mortality of body contrasted with immortality of soul | LoU1 |

**to fade** [SEE ALSO: A.3.18.1:ue. a faded binding]
relajarse el color [Do:93]

| Tenor | Referent | No. |
|---|---|---|
| to lose color and vigor | color of the skin of aged hermit | Do |

**to shrivel**
encogerse [VgC1:6-7]

| Tenor | Referent | No. |
|---|---|---|
| to die to self, to lose one's sense of self-importance | loss of egotism or self-attachment as one is more united with God | VgC1 |

B.4.2.ue. TO NOT PRESERVE THE TEXT: UNMIXED EXPANSIONS

(Part of) A text is missing. [SEE ALSO: A.3.7.2. signature:ue. to lack a signature; A.3.16. approbation:ue. without approbation; copyright:ue. without copyright; price limit:ue.without a price limit; A.3.19.4.2. seal:ue. to lack a seal; A.3.19.5. character / lettering:ue. to be missing a letter]
[Ca43:19;1:29-30]

B.4.3. TO TRANSMIT (THROUGH) THE TEXT

**to transmit**
comunicar [Vi3:168; ManA1:7-8]
transmitir [Vi3:164]

| Tenor | Referent | No. |
|---|---|---|
| to communicate | God's direct self-communication to angels | Vi3 |
| to manifest | natural world's manifestation of God to human beings | Vi3 |
| to give birth to | Mary's giving birth to the eternal Word | ManA1 |

**to dictate**
dictar [Sar:3; Do:43; Ca8:22; Gue1:42]

| Tenor | Referent | No. |
|---|---|---|
| to inspire | God's inspiration of St. Ignatius Loyola for his special mission in world | Sar |
| to govern | sun as creative agent of God | Do |
| to inspire | divine wisdom's inspiring Queen Saba or Gentiles | Ca8 |
| to teach through example | Mary Magdalene's sinful life as example that teaches negatively | Gue1 |

**to disseminate**
despachar [Gue1:14,61]
difundir [Mon2:11; Va4:21]
repartir [ManA2:99]

| Tenor | Referent | No. |
|---|---|---|
| to communicate | communication between John the Baptist and Christ in their mothers' wombs | Mon2 |
| to distribute | different virtues and graces given by God to different saints | ManA2 |
| to manifest to all | heavens' manifestation of God to all peoples | Va4 |
| to be received | heaven's approval of life of mortification | Gue1 |
| to make known | story of Mary Magdalene's great love and conversion as told wherever Gospel is preached | Gue1 |

**to disseminate:** unmixed expansions
   to disseminate the text throughout the world [Mu1:4-6; Va4:16-18; Gue1:113-15]

# MOTIF INDEX 305

B.4.3.1. *To Teach (through) the Text* [SEE ALSO: B.3.4:ue. to read from the professorial chair]

**to teach**
    aleccionar [Gue1:48]
    dictar [Bo15:71]
    enseñar / enseñanza [Ven:204; Vi3:155,214,240-41; Grn:14; VgC5:24; Led1:7; Cab8:13; Led16:3; Jau:29; Va4:10,11; Bo15:9; VgC24:27; Ca8: 39;55:26; Ag2:3]
    explicar [Bo15:17; Mrl:4]
    instruir [Vi3:158]
    leer [Cab8:9-10; Led16:2,8,18; ManL:5; SF2:3]

| *Tenor* | *Referent* | *No.* |
|---|---|---|
| — | natural world as clear manifestation of Creator, understandable to human reason | Ven |
| to enable to recognize God's presence | God's enabling Job to recognize, through natural world, mysteries of Providence, in contrast to lack of such enabling in pagan philosophers | Vi3 |
| to communicate | God's communicating himself and his will for humankind indirectly through natural world and Scripture | Vi3 |
| to communicate | God's self-communication in Christ | Vi3 |
| to enable to recognize | God's enabling Job to recognize and accept mysteries of Providence, through natural world | Grn |
| to manifest | St. Isidore of Madrid's contemplation of God's perfections in natural world | VgC5 |
| — | Christ's last words on Cross as teaching the whole of divine truth | Led1 |
| to communicate | God's direct self-communication to angels and saints | Cab8 |
| to communicate | God's self-communication to humankind in Christ | Cab8 |

| Tenor | Referent | No. |
|---|---|---|
| to exemplify | Christ as exemplar of all Christian virtues | Led16 |
| to manifest | Eucharist as manifesting Christ's redemptive acts in their entirety | Jau |
| to manifest | orderly succession of days and nights as manifesting Creator | Va4 |
| to manifest; to bring forth | Mary's manifesting extraordinary virtue and grace; Mary as mother of God | Bo15 |
| to reveal fully | God alone as able to explain fully the mysteries of Mary's person and life | Bo15 |
| to grace; to engender | God as source of Mary's unique graces, including her immaculate conception, and as engendering his Word in her virginal womb | Bo15 |
| to present as model | Christ the suffering Servant as model for Prince Baltasar Carlos | VgC24 |
| to demonstrate | St. Peter Martyr's witness, through his death, to truth of the faith which he affirmed in writing on ground with his blood | Mrl |
| to communicate | God's communication to soul in contemplative prayer | ManL |
| to make known | manifestation of prophecy of redemption and salvation | Ca8 |
| to manifest | miracles or special signs as unnecessary to faith of St. Ferdinand | Ca55 |
| to model | Mary Magdalene as example of penitent sinner | Gue1 |
| to manifest | Mary as manifesting incomprehensible divine mysteries | Ag2 |
| to communicate | Christ's communication to soul in prayerful solitude | SF2 |

B.4.3.1.ue. *To Teach (through) the Text: Unmixed Expansions*
    to teach concretely in one text what one has already taught in theoretical terms in another [Vi3:211-15; Led16:2-4]
    A brief text teaches more than immense volumes. [Jau:27-30]
    A text does not teach anything new. [Ca55:25-27]


B.4.3.ue. TO TRANSMIT (THROUGH) THE TEXT: UNMIXED EXPANSIONS

    to bequeath a book [VgC17:1,10]
    to carry letters back and forth [Cai16:2]
    to cite an earlier text [Bo6:15]
    to give someone a book [SEE ALSO: B.4.3.ue. to bequeath a book] [Vi3:83-84; Ter:19-20]
    to immortalize a text [Grc:12-16; GarE:6-9]
    to nail up a document [Av3:16-18; ManA3:10-13; Va2:9-10; Par1:10-11]
    to pay in books [Gue1:17-18]
    to publicize (through) a text [SEE ALSO: B.4.3.ue. to nail up a document] [Vi3:162-65; Car:17-19; Ca5:3-4]
    to sell a book [Var:8-9; Gue1:10-14]
    to send a letter [SEE ALSO: A.2.2. mail carrier; B.2.1:ue. to write a letter to a king]
    [AD:2-4; Mu1:5-6+17]


B.4.3.me. TO TRANSMIT (THROUGH) THE TEXT: MIXED EXPANSIONS

    a text transmitted from Adam [SEE ALSO: A.4.1. library:me. Adam's library]
    [AD:2-4; VgC5:31;17:1]

# WRITERS AND WORKS

Note: In the case of writers on whom information is abundant and easily accessible, I have in general selected data most directly pertinent to the passages included in this study.

ACTIO *quae inscribitur examen sacrum.* Before 1586? Represented in Colegio of Jesuits in Salamanca.

AGUILAR, Juan Bautista. Fl. second half 17th century. D. ca. 1714. Native of Valencia. Trinitarian; professed 1655. Master in Sacred Theology. Held important positions in his Order, including directorship of studies in convent in Valencia. *Varias, hermosas flores, del Parnaso,* published Valencia 1680, contains fifty-two of his poems, original or translated, including "A Christo Señor nuestro" and "A la Virgen Santissima." Translated various prose works from Latin and Italian.

AUCTO *de las donas.* 1520-50? From period between Gil Vicente and Lope de Vega. First published by González Pedroso.

AUCTO *de los desposorios.* Included in *Códice de Autos Viejos,* which contains plays written 1550-75. First published by González Pedroso.

ÁVILA, Juan de. B. 1499/1500. D. 1569. Native of Almodóvar del Campo. Of *converso* descent and wealthy parentage. Studied at Salamanca and Alcalá. Ordained priest 1526. Began preaching career 1529. Preached throughout Andalucía for nine years, then in all parts of Spain. Devoted to Jesuit Order, though not a member. The thirteenth of the *Sermones* was preached in 1543. In addition, Sermon 1 was preached in Zafra; Sermons 3, 78, and 79, to nuns. Forty-one sermons were published in 1596. *Colección de sermones inéditos* compiled between 1569 and 1576; with two exceptions, unpublished until 1947. Canonized 1970.

BALVAS BARONA, Antonio de. B. 1559. D. 1628. Native of Segovia. Unable to dedicate himself to literary career because of family's limited means, but continued to write poems on diverse subjects. "Romance a San Francisco" included in his *El poeta castellano,* published Valladolid 1627.

BALLESTER, Juan Bautista. D. 1672/73. Native of Valencia. "Catedratico [of Arts and Theology in Universities of Valencia and Seville], y Examinador el Dotor Iuan Bautista Ballester, Arcediano de Murviedro en la Santa Metropolitana Iglesia [i.e. cathedral] de Valencia, Calificador del Santo Oficio de la Inquisicion, y Iuez Ordinario en el mismo" (*Once sermones*). When Valencia divided into Thomists and anti-Thomists in 1655, 1658, 1662, he was chief among latter. Wrote poetry on sacred and secular subjects; contributed poems to all festival competitions in Valencia. *Aclamacion festiva* preached 1661/62, upon publication of papal brief of Alexander VII upholding doctrine of Mary's immaculate conception; sermon published 1664.

BERNAL, Juan. B. 1540/49. Died 1601. Native of Seville. Mercedarian for thirty-three years. Held important positions in his Order. Professor of Arts in Ecija and of Theology in Córdoba, Granada, Seville. Worked for redemption of captives in Morocco. Preacher to Philip II. Popularly considered a saint. *Sermon a las honras del Rey don Philipo II* preached 1598, published 1599.

BONILLA Y GARZÓN, Alonso de. B. ca. 1570. D. 1642. Native of Baeza. Married 1592. Member of Third Order of St. Francis. Very successful silversmith. With Alonso de Ledesma, considered one of originators of *conceptismo* in poetry. Proposed, with Ledesma and Quevedo, as poetic model by Baltasar Gracián in *Tratado de agudeza*. *Peregrinos Pensamientos* published 1614; *aprobación* dated September 5, 1612. *El nuevo jardin de flores divinas* and *Los Nombres y Atributos de la Virgen Maria* bear an *aprobación* by Lope de Vega, that for the former dated November 6, 1616. *Nuevo jardin* published 1617; *Nombres,* 1624. Of his poems, 1792 are known. Poetry primarily religious; favorite subjects Christ and Mary. His *villancicos* and *canzonetas sagradas* very popular in Córdoba, Seville, Granada, and Toledo, where they were regularly requested for religious festivals.

BRAONES [Brahones], Alonso Martín de. B. 1644. D. 1695. Native of Seville. First work published in 1665; *Epitome de los trivnfos de Jesvs,* in 1686. In 1689 published companion work *Epitome de las glorias de Maria.* Had published total of twelve works by that year. All his works are religious, most in verse.

BRAVO, Nicolás. D. 1648. Native of Valladolid. Member of Cistercians from 1594. Abbot in various monasteries. *Benedictina* published 1604. In the dedication, author says he wrote this work in "los primeros años de mi nueuo estado y profession" and refers to his "falta de experiencia, por auerla de edad y años."

CABRERA, Alonso de. B. ca. 1549. D. 1598. Native of Córdoba. Aristocratic family. Dominican. Completed studies at Salamanca. *Catedrático de prima* in Theology at University of Osuna. Very successful preaching career in Santo Domingo (before ordained priest), Córdoba, Osuna, Seville, Granada, Valencia, Toledo, and Madrid. Preacher to Philip II last four years of his life. Imitated Fray Luis de Granada. *Consideraciones sobre los Evangelios* first published 1601.

CAIRASCO DE FIGUEROA, Bartolomé. B. 1538. D. 1610. Native of La Gran Canaria. Of Italian descent. In 1553 acquired canonry in Las Palmas. Ordained 1559. In Castile 1560-69. Poet and musician. Translated Torcuato Tasso. His garden, consecrated to Apollo, was meeting place for group of writers from Las Palmas and elsewhere. Wrote some dramatic pieces on religious subjects. Major work *Templo de la Iglesia militante* or *Flos Sanctorum*, which contains the *Definiciones*. *Segunda parte* published 1603; *Cuarta parte*, 1615.

CALDERÓN DE LA BARCA, Pedro. B. 1600. D. 1681. Native of Madrid. Family of lesser nobility; father was Secretary of the Consejo de Hacienda. Studied under Jesuits at Colegio Imperial de Madrid, then at Alcalá and Salamanca. Began literary career ca. 1629. Member of Order of Santiago 1637. Ordained priest 1651. Named Chaplain of the Court by Philip IV in 1663.

CAMOS Y REQUESENS, Marco Antonio. B. 1542. D. 1606. Native of Barcelona. Of noble parentage. Studied humane letters. Married. Captain of cavalry. Governor of Sardinia ca. 1581. After death of wife and children, studied philosophy and theology. Entered Augustinians at age thirty-eight, professed 1583. Doctorate in Theology 1588 from University of Barcelona. Held important positions in his Order, including that of Provincial. Renowned as preacher. Wrote books on Christian life in prose and verse. *Microcosmia* published 1592; earliest *aprobación* dated April 21, 1592.

CARDOSO, Fernando. Would seem to be the Isaac Cardoso of whom Cejador speaks, who went by name of Fernando Cardoso. Native of Portugal. Doctor of medicine; practiced in Valladolid and Madrid ca. 1640. Returned secretly to Jewish faith and went to Venice. One of reformers of natural philosophy in Spain. Wrote several books on that subject and one on Jewish tradition. *Oracion funebre* in honor of Lope de Vega preached 1635.

CASTILLA, Antonio de. Fl. 1675-91. Native of Ubeda. Franciscan. *Auto* entitled *Al nacimiento del Hijo de Dios* published 1675. *Epistola a las monjas* dated September 26, 1691; published 1693.

CASTILLEJO, Cristóbal de. B. ca. 1494. D. 1550. Native of Ciudad-Rodrigo. Cistercian, with ties to Monastery of Nuestra Señora de

Valdeiglesias. Secretary to Ferdinand of Austria, brother of Charles V, king of Hungary and Bohemia. Died in Vienna. "Consiliatoria al Rey de Romanos Don Fernando" written January 1541, published in *Obras . . . corregidas*, 1573. "La invencion de la Cruz" and "Dialogo entre la Verdad, y la Lisonja" published 1614.

COELLO Y OCHOA, Antonio. B. 1611. D. 1652. Native of Madrid. Of middle class family, *hidalgos* but without much money. Recognized as poet by 1630. Wrote plays and collaborated with several dramatists, including Calderón de la Barca, Rojas Zorrilla, Solís, Vélez de Guevara. From 1638 primarily dedicated to military career, serving eighth duke of Albuquerque. Captain of Infantry. Knight of Santiago 1642. Gentleman-in-waiting to king. Named Minister of Real Junta de Aposentos 1652. Two of his three *autos* are extant: *El reyno en Cortes*, published 1655; *Auto famoso de la Virgen del Rosario*, published 1664.

CÓRDOBA SAZEDO, Sebastián de. Fl. ca. 1563-75. Native of Ubeda. *Obras de Boscán y Garcilaso trasladadas a materias cristianas y religosas* published 1575. Says it took him twelve years to complete. Apparently also wrote an *a lo divino* version of León Hebreo's *Diálogos de amor*.

DÁVILA, Juan Bautista [Ávila, Juan Bautista de]. B. 1597/98. D. 1664. Native of Madrid. Member of Jesuits since 1617. Held Chair in Hebrew, Chaldean, and Syriac in Colegio Imperial de Madrid for fourteen years. *Passion del Hombre-Dios* published 1661.

DICASTILLO, Miguel de [a.k.a. Miguel de Mencos]. B. ca. 1590. Native of Navarre. Descendant of titled nobility. In Tudela before entering Carthusians in Saragossa. *Avla de Dios, Cartvxa real de Zaragoza* augmented by another member of Order, Agustín Nagore. Preface by D. Joseph Pellicer de Ossavi y Tovar says, "Ambas [epístolas o partes] Me comunicó Manuscriptas el P. D. Miguel de Dicastillo, a los Fines del Año Mil Seiscientos i Treinta i Seis . . . . Imprimiólas el Año siguiente, Dandolos a la Estampa con Nombre de Don Miguel de Mencos."

DOMÍNGUEZ CAMARGO, Hernando [a.k.a. "el Doctor Camargo"]. B. beg. 17th century. D. 1659. Native of Santa Fe de Bogotá. Jesuit. Near end of his life was a "familiar del Santo Oficio y comisario del mismo" (Carilla 19). Poet, mainly of religious subjects. Imitated Góngora. Poem *S. Ignacio de Loyola* his most ambitious work, not quite complete upon his death. Completed by Jesuit Antonio Navarro Navarrete, who had it published in Europe, where he thought it would be better received.

ENCISO Y MONZÓN, Juan Francisco de. Fl. toward end of 17th cent. Native of Cádiz. At time of completion of *La Christiada*, published in 1694, had written several works, some in prose, including translation of five works of Tertullian, others in verse, in Latin and Castilian.

ENRÍQUEZ GÓMEZ, Antonio. B. 1600. D. 1663. Native of Cuenca/Segovia. Descendant of *conversos* on father's side, Old Christians on mother's side. Both religions exerted strong attraction for him, each appearing to predominate at different periods of his life. In 1618 married woman of Old Christian family. Established as merchant in Madrid by 1624. Self-exiled to France ca. 1636. Returned clandestinely to Spain ca. 1649 under alias Fernando de Zárate y Castronovo. Arrested by Inquisition in Seville 1661; died in prison, supposedly of natural causes, after having been reconciled to Church. Wrote verse, *comedias*, prose. *El Siglo Pitagórico y Vida de D. Gregorio Guadaña*, published 1644, in imitation of Lucian, considered his best work. The three "Epístolas de Job" were published in his *Academias morales de las musas*, 1642, in Bordeaux.

ESCOBAR Y MENDOZA, Antonio de. B. 1589. D. 1668. Native of Valladolid. Jesuit, priest; chaplain to Doña María de la Bastida, a member of Poor Clares in Valladolid. *Nveva Gervsalen Maria*, 4th printing, amended by author, published 1625; *privilegio* 1615. In "Al Lector" author says, "Tenia muchos años ha compuesto este librillo."

FERNÁNDEZ, Lucas. B. 1474. D. 1542. Native of Salamanca. Family thought to be *converso*. Father was carpenter and sculptor in wood. Maternal uncles connected with university, cathedral or *cabildo*. Degree in Arts from Salamanca. Ordained priest. Poet and musician. Dealt in real estate. Wrote *autos* for Corpus Christi, representados in Salamanca from 1501. Professor of music at Salamanca 1522-42. *Auto de la Pasión* written before 1503; published with rest of his dramatic production 1514.

FUENTE, Jerónimo [Gerónimo] de la. Fl. 1615-22. Resident of Granada? "Dezimas" written for competition in honor of Immaculate Conception, 1615; published 1616. One of poets in *Relacion de las Fiestas . . . en la Canonizacion de . . . San Isidro*, this last canonized March 1622.

GÁLVEZ DE MONTALVO, Luis. B. 1549? D. 1610? Native of Antequera/Guadalajara. Knight of San Juan de Jerusalén. "El llanto de San Pedro," based on Tansillo, published in *Primera parte del Tesoro de divina poesia*, 1587, compiled by Esteban de Villalobos.

GARAU, Francisco. B. 1640. D. 1701. Native of Catalonia. Jesuit. *Catedrático de Prima* in Theology at Barcelona. *Rector* of Colegio de Montesión in Majorca. *Calificador* for Inquisition. *El Olympo del Sabio instruído en la naturaleza y segunda parte de las máximas políticas y morales* published 1675.

GARCÍA DE ESCAÑUELA(S), Bartolomé. D. 1684. Franciscan. "Lector Iubilado, Padre, y Custodio de la Santa Provincia de Granada, Predicador de las Magestades Catolicas, y Calificador de la Suprema [i.e. Inquisition], y electo Obispo de Puerto Rico" (Huerta 418). Sermon in honor of St. Peter of Alcantara preached 1669, published 1670.

GODINEZ, Felipe. B. 1585. D. 1659. Native of Seville. Of Jewish descent. Cervantes mentions him in *Viaje al Parnaso* as young man beginning to write for stage. Studied theology in Seville. Renowned for knowledge of theology and Scripture, and as preacher. Embroiled in inquisitorial trial for *mosaísmo*. As result of auto de fe 1624, divested of property, rights and privileges of priesthood. Moved to Madrid, where associated with famous writers. Asked to preach sermons for various occasions. Wrote several *autos*. *Avto del nacimiento de Christo* and *Avto del nacimiento de Christo, y pastores de Belen* published by Juan Fernández in *Avtos sacramentales, y al nacimiento de Christo*, 1675.

GÓMEZ (Y) TEJADA DE LOS REYES, Cosme. Fl. 1634. "Licenciado. Capellán mayor de las Bernardas descalzas y patronazgo en S. Ildefonso de Talavera" (Simón Díaz. *Bibliografía* 10: 726-27). *Privilegio* for his *León prodigioso* dated 1634; published 1636. *Noche buena. Autos al nacimiento* published 1661.

GÓNGORA Y ARGOTE, Luis de. B. 1561. D. 1627. Native of Córdoba. Studied at Salamanca 1576-80. Received minor orders. *Racionero* of cathedral in Córdoba. Settled in Madrid 1617; named royal chaplain and ordained priest. "A la procesion que víspera del Corpus se hace al Sagrario" written 1609 for Corpus Christi festival in Córdoba.

GRACIÁN, Baltasar. B. 1601. D. 1658. Native of Calatayud (Aragón). Jesuit; professed 1619. *Rector* of Colegio of Tarazona. Part 1 *El Criticón* published 1651; Part 2, 1653; Part 3, 1657.

GRANADA, Luis de [a.k.a. Luis de Sarria]. B. 1504. D. 1588. Native of Granada. Of humble parentage. After father's death, became protege of Count of Tendilla. Entered Dominicans in Granada 1524; professed 1525. To Valladolid for advanced study 1529. Later Master of Theology. Renowned as preacher. Assignments in Córdoba and Badajoz; Provincial for Portugal 1556-60. Convent of Santo Domingo in Lisbon his home base until his death. Wrote in Castilian, Latin, Portuguese; works on spiritual life, biography, sermons, and sacred oratory. First original work, *Libro de la oración y meditación*, published 1554. First four volumes of *Introducción del símbolo* published 1582; fifth volume, 1585.

GUERRA Y RIBERA, Manuel. B. 1638. D. 1692. Trinitarian. Held Chair in Philosophy at Salamanca. Preacher to Charles II; preached also in Salamanca, Saragossa, Lisbon. *Sermones varios* published 1677-80. *Oracion de San Iuan de Mata, y San Felix de Valois* preached 1666. *Oracion en la Canonizacion de San Francisco de Borja* preached 1671. *Oracion en la beatificacion de onze Martyres, y San Francisco Solano* preached 1675. *Sermón de la conversion* published 1679. "Aprobación" for Rodríguez Monforte's *Sueños misteriosos de la Escritura* written 1686.

HURTADO DE MENDOZA Y LARREA [de la Rea], Antonio. B. 1586. D. 1644. Native of Castro Urdiales (Santander). Page (ca. 1608) and gentleman-in-waiting (ca. 1618) to Count of Saldaña. Favorite of Count-Duke of Olivares. *Secretario de cámara* to Philip IV (1621) and Secretary of Inquisition (1622/23). Knight of Calatrava (1623), *Comendador* of Zurita. Married 1623 and 1631. Credited with invention in January 1637 of *papel sellado*, government-stamped paper at different prices, necessary for all official documents. Secretary of Justice 1641. Lifelong friend of Lope de Vega. Greater part of *Vida de N. Señora* written by 1628, although poet was still working on it toward end of his life; unfinished when published 1666.

JAÚREGUI Y AGUILAR, Juan de. B. 1583. D. 1641. Native of Seville. Distinguished painter and poet. Resided some years in Rome; returned to Spain highly reputed as painter. Knight of Calatrava. He and wife resided in Madrid from 1619. Censor of books from 1621. Translated *El Aminta* of Torcuato Tasso. Collection of his *rimas* published 1618. Wrote *Apologia* on behalf of Paravicino, 1625.

LEDESMA BUITRAGO, Alonso de. B. 1562. D. 1633. Native of Segovia. Father was cloth merchant. Studied at Alcalá. Married. Held various municipal offices. Appears frequently in notarial documents. Maintained close ties with Jesuits throughout his life. Known as *divino* among contemporaries, for religious nature of most of his poetry. Did write secular verse also. *Aprobaciones* for several of his works written by such persons as Lope de Vega, José de Valdivielso, Paravicino. He wrote poems for works composed or compiled by others, including Lucas Rodríguez, Lope de Vega, Alonso de Salazar, Angel Manrique, Balvás [Balbás] Bar[ah]ona. Fray Juan de Arenas, prior of Monastery of San Agustín in Segovia, advises preachers in "Al lector," *Primera parte de Conceptos espirituales*, published 1600, to use the work as source of *conceptos* related to Scripture, in their sermons. This work extremely successful. "Epitetos a la Cruz de Christo nuestro Señor," which appeared in it, had been published previous year in Lucas Rodríguez (q.v.).

*Privilegio* for *Segunda parte* dated 1604; published 1606. A series of his *hieroglificos* (including IX, XVI, XXXIII) appeared in Alonso de Salazar's *Fiestas que hizo el insigne Colegio de la Compañia de Jesus de Salamanca a la Beatificacion del glorioso patriarca S. Ignacio de Loyola*, published Salamanca 1610. *Juegos de Nochebuena con cien enigmas hechas para honesta recreacion* published 1611. Was included in Zapata's *Indice Expurgatorio* of 1632; edition that circulated throughout Castile was that of 1613. *Juegos* are religious poems based on formulae in children's games and on traditional songs. *Privilegio* for *Tercera parte de Conceptos espirituales* dated November 12, 1611; published 1612. *Conceptos a las llagas de San Francisco* published 1621. His *décimas* "Ay, insaciable apetito" appeared in Angel Manrique's *Exequias* on death of Philip III, 1621. *Epigramas y jeroglificos a la vida de Cristo, festividades de Nuestra Señora, excelencias de santos y grandezas de Segovia* published 1625. See also: Bonilla y Garzón, Alonso de.

LEMOS, Jerónimo de. D. 1563. Native of Segovia. Hieronymite; professed 1537. *Torre de David* published 1567.

LEÓN, Luis de. B. 1527. D. 1591. Native of Belmonte (Cuenca). Licentiate in Theology from Salamanca 1551. Augustinian; professed 1544. *Maestría* from Alcalá 1558. *Catedrático* in Salamanca in Theology, Moral Philosophy, Scripture. Tried by Inquisition 1572-76 and 1582-84. *Nombres* published 1583. "Carta dedicatoria" dated September 15, 1587.

LÓPEZ DE ANDRADE, Diego. B. 1569. D. 1628/35. Native of Portugal. Augustinian. Preached in Pamplona, then in San Felipe el Real in Madrid. Archbishop of Otranto (Trent). *Aprobación* for *Tratados sobre los evangelios de la qvaresma* dated October 2, 1614; published 1616. Intends work to be useful to other preachers as source of material and model in composing sermons.

LÓPEZ DE UBEDA, Juan. D. ca. 1582-85. Native of Toledo. Founded Seminario de los Niños de la Doctrina Cristiana in Alcalá de Henares. *Cancionero general de Doctrina Cristiana* published 1579, *privilegio* 1578; second edition, unchanged, 1585. *Vergel de Flores Diuinas*, which contains "Dios puso en hombre su nombre" and "Tratado de la vida segura," published 1582, *privilegio* 1581; second edition, unchanged in content, 1588. Both works contain compositions by him and by others.

LUCAS DEL OLMO, Alfonso. Native of Jerez. Franciscan?

LUDEÑA, Juan de. Fl. 1650-71. Member of Order of St. Francis of Paola (Minim Friars). "Predicador de su Magestad, Calificador de la Suprema [i.e. Inquisition], Provincial de la Provincia de Castilla, y Vicario General de las de España" (Huerta 199). Also "Examinador sinodal del arzobispado de Toledo" (Simón Díaz. *Bibliografía* 13: 576-78). Sermon in honor of St. Peter of Alcantara preached 1669, published 1670.

MADRE DE DIOS, Lucas de la. Fl. 1669. Native of Tortuera. Discalced Carmelite. Prior of their Colegio in Toledo. "Lector de Sagrada Teologia, y Predicador mayor de su Conuento de Madrid" (Huerta 267). Sermon in honor of St. Peter of Alcantara preached 1669, published 1670.

MALÓN DE CHAIDE, Pedro. B. 1530. D. 1589. Native of Cascante (Navarre). Augustinian; professed 1557. Held chair at Universities of Huesca and Saragossa. Prior of convents in Saragossa 1575-77, and Barcelona 1586. *Tratado de la Conversión de la gloriosa María Madalena* probably written 1578-83; published 1588.

MANRIQUE, Angel [formerly Pedro de Medina y Manrique]. B. 1577. D. 1649. Native of Burgos. Old and noble family on mother's side. Father *regidor* of Burgos. Cistercian; occupied very important positions in Order. Held five different chairs at Salamanca, last being *Teología de prima*. Named one of king's preachers; renowned as preacher throughout Spain and Italy. Named bishop of Badajoz 1645. Several volumes in prose on religious subjects, including history of Cistercians. First collection of sermons published 1604-05. *Sanctoral y Dominical Cisterciense* first published 1610, *aprobaciones* dated March to May 1609; second edition, amended and augmented, published 1613. In prologue, author says it took him four years to write the *Sanctoral*. He adds, "Esto quiero que me agradezcan los predicadores, y en esto vna particularidad mas que a otros que escriuen: que ellos aguardan a sacar a luz sus obras, quando estan hartos ya de predicarlas; y consiguientemente quando las tienen hechas tan comunes, que apenas les pueden seruir a ellos, ni a otros: pero yo, los mas discursos que aqui escriuo passarán de mi pluma a agena boca, sin auerlos oydo nadie de la mia."

MANRIQUE, Luisa [Luisa Magdalena de Jesús]. B. 1604. D. 1660. Native of Naples. Of noble parentage. At very young age entered service of Queen Isabel, wife of Philip IV. Married Don Manuel Manrique de Lara, Count of Paredes; had two daughters. As widow, entered Discalced Carmelites in Malagón ca. 1648; served as prioress. *Romance* "¡Qué breves que son, Dios mio!" seems to have been first published in Serrano y Sanz' *Apuntes*.

MATA, Gabriel. B. first third 16th century. Native of Burgos. Franciscan. *Aprobación* for *El Cavallero del Asisio* dated 1586; published 1587, 1589. *Privilegio* for *Cantos morales* dated August 17, 1592.

MIRA DE AMESCUA, Antonio. B. 1574. D. 1644. Native of Guadix. Lawyer. Named *alcalde mayor* of Guadix in 1600. Named archdeacon in Guadix 1632. *Capellán de honor* to Philip IV. Wrote *comedias* and *autos sacramentales*. *Pedro Telonario* and *Las prvebas de Christo* published by Juan Fernández in *Avtos sacramentales, y al nacimiento de Christo*, 1675.

MONTESINO, Ambrosio. B. 1444-50. D. 1514. Native of Huete. Franciscan, Friars Minor. Confessor and preacher to Catholic Monarchs. Nominal bishop of Sarda (Albania), then bishop auxiliary to Cardinal Cisneros. Translated the first work printed in Alcalá, the *Vita Christi* by Ludolphus de Saxonia (1502). *Cancionero de diversas obras de nuevo trovadas* published 1508; dedication to King Ferdinand dated May 27, 1508.

MORALES, Jacinta María de. Fl. mid-17th cent. Wrote sonnet in praise of the *Poema tragico de Atalanta, y Hipómenes* of Juan de Moncayo y de Gurrea, Marqués de San Felices, published 1656 and dedicated to Philip IV.

MORCHÓN, Manuel [Dr.] Fl. 1669. "Canciones al assvmpto primero" [i.e., St. Peter of Alcantara's prayer that ended plague in *villa* of Albuquerque, Extremadura] written 1669, published 1670.

MORETO, Agustín. B. 1618. D. 1669. Native of Madrid. Parents Italian, prosperous. Studied at Alcalá. In 1642 was cleric with minor orders. Period of greatest literary activity 1642-56. In 1657 became chaplain to cardinal archbishop of Toledo and put in charge of Hermandad de San Pedro o del Refugio, for poor and abandoned. *La gran casa de Austria y divina Margarita*, his only known *auto*, first published in *Navidad y Corpus Christi festejados por los mejores ingenios de España*, 1664.

MURILLO, Diego. B. 1555. D. 1616. Native of Saragossa. Among his studies was jurisprudence. Entered Franciscans ca. 1576. Held important positions in his Order. Preached in Saragossa nearly thirty years; was its chronicler last two years of his life. Nine books published in his lifetime. His works were published "de todas las lenguas" ("Al Lector"). First *Discursos predicables* published 1601. *Divina, dvlce, y provechosa poesia*, his last work, published posthumously in 1616.

OROZCO [Horozco], Alonso de. B. 1500. D. 1591. Native of Oropesa (Toledo). Studied at Salamanca. Assumed habit of Augustinians 1522. Preacher to Charles V and Philip II; chaplain to Queen Isabel, Philip's wife. Reputed ascetic and mystic. Wrote more than fifty works. *Historia de la reyna Saba*, allegory for soul's journey to Christ, published 1565.

OSEGUERA, Diego de. Fl. ca. 1580. Native of Dueñas. "Contino de la casa de S. M." (Pérez Pastor 1: 215). *Estacionario de la Creacion y Redencion del Mundo* published 1593; dedicated to the "Señora Infante de Castilla Doña Isabel Clara Eugenia."

OVANDO, Gaspar de. Fl. 1615. Native of Málaga. Resident of Granada? Dramatist of post-Lopean period. Wrote *comedia* entitled *Atlanta poética*. "Dezimas" written for competition in honor of Immaculate Conception, 1615; published 1616.

PADILLA, Pedro de. B. 1549/50. D. after 1595. Resident of Linares at time of receiving gratis *Bachiller en Artes* 1564, University of Granada. Resident of Jaén when matriculated for course in Theology October 26, 1572, aged twenty-two. Knight of Santiago. Carmelite. *Iardin espiritual* published 1585. *Grandezas y Excelencias de la Virgen señora nuestra* published 1587.

PARAVICINO Y ARTEAGA, Hortensio Félix. B. 1580? D. 1633. Native of Madrid. Of Italian and Basque descent. Discalced Trinitarian. Professed 1600. Occupied Chair of Sacred Scripture in Madrid and, on occasion, Salamanca, Seville, and Barcelona, 1612-33. Highly celebrated as preacher in his lifetime. Preacher to Philip III and IV. He wrote "A San Esteuan" "siendo muchacho" (*Obras postvmas* 25). Dedication of *Iesv Cristo desagraviado* dated "dia de S. Bernabe" [June 11] 1633; he had preached the sermon before king.

PÉREZ DE MONTALBÁN [Montalván], Juan. B. 1601/02. D. 1638. Native of Madrid. Was priest by 1625. Admitted into Congregación de San Pedro de Sacerdotes Naturales de Madrid. Doctorate in Theology from Alcalá 1625-26. Works include *comedias* and *autos sacramentales*, biography of Lope de Vega. By 1633 was a notary of Inquisition. Toward end of life suffered severe mental ill health. *El Polifemo* apparently written for Madrid's Corpus Christi celebrations of 1628.

PINEDA, Juan de. B. ca. 1521. D. 1599. Probably native of Madrigal de las Altas Torres, in province of Avila. Parents Catholic, apparently not of nobility. Began studies at University of Salamanca 1537; undertook course in Theology 1540. Entered Franciscans 1544 at earliest. Preacher and professor of philosophy and theology. *Los treynta y cinco Diálogos familiares de la Agricultura Cristiana*, his masterwork, written 1578-80; approved March 7, 1581; published 1589. According to author, it is an imitation of the *Asclepius* of Hermes Trismegistus.

*POESÍAS varias*. Unpublished manuscript dated 1581. Includes "Alabanza a San Francisco."

PRADAS, Juan Valero. Fl. 1679. Franciscan. "Lector de Theologia, y Guardian del muy Religioso Conuento de San Gregorio, de la misma Ciudad [i.e. Orihuela], de Franciscos Descalzos" (*Once sermones*). *Sermon a Nuestra Señora de Monserrate* preached in cathedral of Orihuela, published 1679.

PRADO, Adrián de. Fl. ca. 1620. Hieronymite. Poet. His "Canción real a san Jerónimo en Siria" celebrated for realistic portrait of St. Jerome, apparently description of an unknown painting. "Al santísimo Sacramento" published as *pliego suelto* in Seville, 1629.

QUEVEDO VILLEGAS, Francisco de. B. 1580. D. 1645. Native of Madrid. Family of middle nobility in service of royalty. Studied under Jesuits at Colegio Imperial in Madrid, then at Alcalá. Knight of Santiago. Experienced some kind of moral conversion at age thirty-two. Dedication of *Lágrimas de Jeremías castellanas* dated May 8, 1613. *Las Tres Musas* published posthumously, 1670.

RAMILLETE *de divinas flores para el desengaño de la vida hvmana*. "Recopiladas con diligencia de los mejores y mas famosos Poetas de nuestros tiempos, por P. F. G. C. D"; published 1629. Includes "Glossa a la inmacvlada concepcion de Nvestra Señora."

REBOLLEDO, Bernardino. B. 1597. D. 1676. Native of León. Count. Began military career at age fourteen. Served in Italy and Flanders, where he held important military posts. Spanish minister to Denmark for Philip IV for twelve years, from end of 1647 or beginning of 1648. Member of Order of Santiago. His personal library consisted of some 225 works in Castilian, French, Italian, Portuguese, Latin, and German; one third each in the first two languages, one fourth in Italian. Inventory shows that among the works was an "Esposizion de los Salmos en berso castellano," which might have been that of José de Valdivielso. He recommended, in certain *tercetos*, Cairasco de Figueroa's "deuotos cantos" (Casado Lobato 234), i.e. *Templo militante*. Among works he himself wrote were three composed while in Denmark, translations of Psalms, Jeremiah, and Job. This last, *La constancia victoriosa*, published in Cologne 1655.

RIBERA, Luis de. B. 1555? D. 1620. Native of Seville. A sister was member of Order of the Conception. He was in Indies before publication of his poems, which constitute greater part of *Sagradas poesias*, in Seville by Clemente Hidalgo, 1612; *aprobación* 1611.

ROCABERTI, Hipólita [Hipólita de Jesús]. B. 1549. D. 1624. Native of Barcelona. Daughter of a Count. At age eleven entered Dominican Order; professed 1565. Said to have experienced extraordinary miracles and visions. Introduced as candidate for beatification and canonization. Epitome of her writings published posthumously. "¡Oh! llave piadosa" included in Volume I of *Obras* published in Valencia, 1683.

RODRÍGUEZ, Lucas. Fl. 1579-99. Resident of Alcalá de Henares. *Escritor* at University of Alcalá 1580-99. Anthologist or compiler. *Conceptos de divina poesia* published 1599, just before Ledesma's *Conceptos*.

RODRÍGUEZ CORONEL, Juan. B. 1618. D. 1700. Native of Madrid. Jesuit. Preacher. Sermon in honor of St. Peter of Alcantara preached 1669, published 1670.

ROJAS ZORRILLA, Francisco de. B. 1607. D. 1648. Native of Toledo. Probably studied at Salamanca. Ca. 1630 became active in literary circles in Madrid; began writing plays in collaboration with Vélez de Guevara, Coello, Calderón, and Peréz de Montalbán. Established as a court dramatist by 1635. Began writing sacramental plays in 1639. Married 1640. Admitted to Order of Santiago 1645.

SALAS BARBADILLO, Alonso Jerónimo de. B. 1581. D. 1635. Native of Madrid. Never married. Sonnet "A san Juan Bautista" included in *Flores de poetas ilustres* compiled by Pedro Espinosa; dedication dated September 20, 1603, published 1605.

SAN FELIX, Marcela de. B. 1605. Died 1688. Native of Toledo. Daughter of Lope de Vega and Micaela Luján. Entered Trinitarians in Madrid at age sixteen, professed 1622. Life devoted to prayer and to writing sacred poetry. "Coloquio espiritual" and "Loa a una profesión" from unpublished manuscript of seventeenth century.

SANTIAGO, Hernando de. B. 1557. D. 1639. Native of Seville. Of noble descent. Entered Mercedarians at age eighteen; professed 1576. At age twenty-two was winning name as preacher. Degree in Theology in 1587 from Valladolid; Master by 1593. Called affectionately "pico de oro" (Q. Pérez, 115, 142-43). *Licencia* for his *Cuaresma* dated May 4, 1597; published 1598.

SARRIERA, Elvira. Fl. 1622. "Oda a San Ignacio de Loyola" written for Gerona competition in celebration of saint's canonization in 1622.

SILVESTRE, Gregorio. B. 1520. D. 1569. Native of Lisbon. At fourteen entered service of Count of Feria in Zafra. Organist in cathedral of Granada from 1541. Married. Wrote poetry in traditional style until last several years of his life, when he cultivated Italian forms. "A una calavera" included in *Las obras del famoso poeta*, published 1582.

SOLÍS Y RIVADENEYRA, Antonio de. B. 1610. D. 1686. Native of Alcalá de Henares. Of noble parentage. Wrote *comedias*, first one at age seventeen; *Historia de la Conquista de la Nueva España* (second part incomplete); *Cartas familiares Politicas*. Member of Secretaría de Estado and secretary to Philip IV. *Coronista Mayor de las Indias* to Queen Mother. Ordained priest at age fifty-eight, whereupon he abandoned secular writing. "A la Conversion de San Francisco de Borja" (canonized 1671) included in *Varias poesias*, published posthumously 1692.

SUÁREZ DE GODOY, Juan. Fl. 16th century. Native of Badajoz. Mercedarian and priest. Renowned as preacher. *Thesoro de varias consideraciones sobre el psalmo de misericordias* published 1598.

TELLEZ, Gabriel [Tirso de Molina]. B. 1580? D. 1648. Native of Madrid. Entered Mercedarians 1600; professed 1601. Studied Arts at Salamanca; Theology at Toledo, Guadalajara, Alcalá de Henares. Began writing for stage ca. 1610. Moved to Madrid and began major period of literary activity 1620/21. Dramatic career virtually ended 1625 with edict of Committee for Reform of Council of Castile. *Deleitar aprovechando*, stories of saints' lives and *autos sacramentales*, written or compiled 1631-32, when he was in Toledo; published 1635. *No le arriendo la ganancia* probably written in early Toledan period, 1611-16; first represented in Madrid.

TERESA DE JESÚS, Santa [Cepeda y Ahumada, Teresa de]. B. 1515. D. 1582. Native of Avila. From age sixteen to eighteen was pupil of Augustinian nuns. Entered Carmelites 1535; received habit 1536; professed 1537. First mystical favor 1556. In 1559 Fernando de Valdés' *Index of Prohibited Books* deprived her of preferred books on mysticism. First foundation of Carmelite reform 1562. Canonized 1622. *El Libro de su Vida* completed 1565. Masterwork *El Castillo Interior* written 1577.

TIMONEDA, Joan. B. ca. 1520. D. 1583. Native of Valencia. Tanner, later bookseller. Married 1541. Wrote plays, poetry, prose fiction, and nonfiction. *Aucto de la fuente de los siete sacramentos* represented 1570 before Archbishop of Valencia, published 1575.

TORRES, Jaime. B. beginning 16th century. Fl. 1578-88. Native of Elche (Valencia). Of humble parentage. Degree in Arts in 1578 from University of Huesca; degree in Theology 1579. Mercedarian. Taught philosophy; Lupercio and Bartolomé Leonardo de Argensola were among his students. Translated various works from Italian. Wrote lyric poetry, *comedias* on religious subjects, *auto* entitled *Desafío moral del hombre contra los tres enemigos: Demonio, Mundo y Carne*, published in *Divina y varia poesia*, 1579.

VALDIVIELSO, José de. B. 1560/65. D. 1638. Native of Toledo? Chaplain to Cardinal of Toledo, Don Bernardo de Sandoval y Rojas, son of Philip III, from at least 1607. In Madrid by 1609. Censor of books. Highly esteemed as lyric and epic poet, and as writer of *autos sacramentales*. Admitted to Hermandad de los esclavos del Santísimo Sacramento after 1609. *Romancero espiritual en gracia de los esclavos del Santísimo Sacramento* published 1612. In "Al Lector" of *Exposicion parafrastica del Psalterio y de los Canticos del Breuiario*, he says the work, which is not intended as a "version" or "traducion," took him eight years. *Aprobación* dated June 9, 1620; published 1623. *Las ferias del alma* and *El hombre encantado* included in *Doze actos sacramentales, y dos comedias divinas*, published 1622. In "Al lector" Valdivielso says he chose these *autos* from the many he had written "por de pensamientos no trillados, y que han afectado imitar ingenios illustres, y algun buen bonete placeado porfiadamente por proprios."

VARONA DE VALDIVIELSO, Pedro. Fl. 1575-1606. Native of Villahermosa in Burgos mountains. Entered Franciscans in Toledo in 1575. Professor of Sacred Scripture and Moral Theology; preacher. Lived life of austerity, prayer and charity. Wrote religious works in Latin and Castilian; *Tractado sobre el Ave María* published 1596.

VÁZQUEZ, Dionisio. B. 1479. D. 1539. Native of Toledo. Augustinian; professed 1500. Preacher to Ferdinand the Catholic and Charles V. Named first professor of Sacred Scripture at Alcalá 1531. Awarded title of Doctor by Universities of Paris, Toledo, Alcalá. *Sermón de la Ascensión* preached 1538.

VEGA CARPIO, Lope Félix de. B. 1562. D. 1635. Native of Madrid. Father was *bordador*? Born close to home in which St. Isidore of Madrid labored. Admitted to "Hermandad de los esclavos del Santísimo Sacramento" 1610. Ordained 1614. Became censor of books. In old age he "habitually began every page of his writing with a cross" (Hayes 21). Began *El Isidro* in 1596; completed 1597? *Aprobación* by Pedro de Padilla dated January 22, 1599; published 1599. *De los cantares* probably written before 1599. *Pastores de Belén* completed by October 1611; published 1612. *Del pan y del palo* written ca. 1612. *Rimas sacras* published 1614. *El triunfo de la fe* written 1617, published 1618. *Filomela* (*Filomena*) published 1621. *Relacion de las fiestas . . . en la canonizacion de . . . san Isidro* written 1622. *Romancero espiritual* published 1625, though poems virtually same as in *Rimas sacras*. *Laurel de Apolo* written 1628-29, published 1630. *Rimas humanas y divinas del licenciado Tomé de Burguillos* published 1634; poems date from different periods. *Vega del Parnaso* published posthumously, 1637. "Sentimientos a los agravios de Cristo," included in Part 2 of latter, written when Prince Baltasar Carlos (1629-46) was child, probably 1630's.

VEGAS, Damián de. Resident of Toledo. "Del hábito de San Juan, en el convento de Santa María del Monte" (Cejador 3: 322). *Poesia cristiana, moral y divina* published 1590. *Comedia jacobina* included in this work.

VÉLEZ DE GUEVARA, Luis. B. 1579. D. 1644. Native of Ecija. Possibly of Jewish descent. Degree in Arts from Osuna 1596. Served in army in Italy and in Algiers. Returned to Spain (Valladolid) by 1603, began writing. Married four times. Served Count of Saldaña and Marquis of Peñafiel. Minor positions in household of Philip IV. Poet, playwright, author of prose work *El Diablo Cojuelo*. *Auto* entitled *La mesa redonda* first published by Isidro de Robles in *Navidad y Corpvs Christi*, 1664.

VENEGAS, Alejo. B. 1498/99. D. 1562. Native of Toledo. Family of noble blood but not distinguished or wealthy. Studied for priesthood but abandoned theological studies to marry. Professor at University of Toledo. Obtained title of Master 1531-37. Held Chair of Grammar of the Estudio de Madrid 1544-61. Censor of books with Inquisition of Toledo under Philip II and in Madrid. *Diferencia de libros que hay en el Universo* written 1538-39, published 1540.

VILLANUEVA, Tomás de. B. 1488. D. 1555. Native of Fuentellana or Fuenllana (Toledo); grew up in Villanueva de los Infantes. Family of noble lineage and well-to-do; maintained a mill for sole use of poor. Studied at Alcalá; professor of philosophy there at age twenty-six. Joined Augustinians in Salamanca in 1516, professed 1517. Ordained priest 1518, when he began preaching career. Preacher to Charles V. Archbishop of Valencia 1544/45 to end of his life. Canonized 1658.

VITORIA, Ignacio de. Fl. 1635. Native of Seville. Augustinian and priest. Held chair at University of Osuna. Chaplain to Doña Ana de Guzmán. *Oracion funeral panegyrica* in honor of Lope de Vega preached 1635.

# APPROXIMATELY CHRONOLOGICAL LIST OF TEXTS AND WRITERS

Note: Since the bibliography gives full citations, I list here only short titles of the original works, with the author's last name, and initials if necessary. Abbreviations: + = or after, a = *aprobación*, b = before, d = dedication, l = license, p = published, pr = preached, pv = *privilegio*, r = represented, w = written.

| Date | Writer | Text |
|---|---|---|
| p. 1508 | Montesino | *Cancionero* |
| w. b. 1503 p. 1514 | Fernández | *Auto de la pasión* |
| pr. 1538 | Vázquez | *Sermón de la Ascensión* |
| w. 1538-39 p. 1540 | Venegas | *Diferencias de libros* |
| w. 1514-50? p. 1614 | Castillejo | "Invencion de la Cruz" "La Verdad y la Lisonja" |
| w. 1541 p. 1573 | Castillejo | "Consiliatoria" |
| pr. 1518-55 ? | Villanueva | sermons on Virgin |
| pr. 1529-69 | Ávila | sermons |
| pr. 1543 | Ávila | *Sermón 13* |
| w. 1520-50? | — | *Aucto de las donas* |
| w. by 1565 p. 1588 | Teresa de Jesús | *Vida* |
| p. 1565 | Orozco | *Reyna Saba* |
| w. 1541-69 ? p. 1582 | Silvestre | *Obras* |
| w. by 1563 p. 1567 | Lemos | *Torre de David* |
| w. 1550-75 ? | — | *Aucto de los desposorios* |
| r. 1570 p. 1575 | Timoneda | *Aucto de la fuente* |

| Date | Writer | Text |
|---|---|---|
| w. ca. 1563-75 p. 1575 | Córdoba | "Soneto V" |
| p. 1579 | Torres | *Desafío moral* |
| w. 1578-80 p. 1589 | Pineda | *Diálogos familiares* |
| ms. 1581 | — | *Poesías varias*: "Alabanza a S. Francisco" |
| p. 1582 | Granada | *Introducción del símbolo* Vols. 1-4 |
| p. 1582 | López de Ubeda | "Dios puso en hombre" "Vida segura" |
| w. 1578-83 p. 1588 | Malón de Chaide | *Conversión de la Madalena* |
| p. 1583 | León | *Nombres* |
| p. 1585 | Granada | *Introducción del símbolo* Vol. 5 |
| p. 1585 | Padilla | *Jardín espiritual* (incl. "Niño sagrado y bendito") |
| w. b. 1586? | — | *Actio examen sacrum* |
| a. 1586 p. 1587 | Mata | *Caballero del Asisio* |
| p. 1587 | Gálvez de Montalvo | "Llanto de S. Pedro" |
| p. 1587 | Padilla | *Grandezas y Excelencias* |
| w. 1587 | León | "Carta dedicatoria" |
| p. 1590 | Vegas | *Poesia christiana* [Sancha] |
| a. 1592 p. 1592 | Camós | *Microcosmia* |
| p. 1593 | Oseguera | *Estacionario* |
| p. 1596 | Varona de Valdivielso | *Tractado sobre el Ave Maria* |
| l. 1597 p. 1598 | Santiago | *Quaresma* |
| w. 1596-97 p. 1599 | Vega Carpio | *Isidro* |
| p. 1598 | Suárez de Godoy | *Thesoro* |
| pr. 1598 p. 1599 | Bernal | *Sermon a las honras* |
| p. 1599 | Ledesma | "A la cruz de Christo" "A S. Sebastián" [in Rodríguez] |
| p. 1599 | Rodríguez | *Conceptos de divina poesía* |

| Date | Writer | Text |
|---|---|---|
| w. 1565-1624?<br>p. 1683 | Rocaberti | "¡Oh! llave piadosa" |
| pr. 1569-98?<br>p. 1601, 1609 | Cabrera | sermons |
| w. b. 1599 | Vega Carpio | *De los cantares* |
| w. 1594+<br>p. 1604 | Bravo | *Benedictina* |
| p. 1600 | Ledesma | *Conceptos espirituales I*:<br>(incl. "Dios y el hombre") |
| w. 1595-1600 ?<br>p. 1641 | Paravicino | "Quintillas a San Esteuan" |
| p. 1603 | Cairasco de<br>Figueroa | *Templo II*:<br>"A la Cruz bendita"<br>various poems from<br>*Definiciones* [Castro] |
| p. 1603 | Murillo | *Discursos en Adviento* |
| w. by 1603<br>p. 1605 | Salas Barbadillo | "A S. Juan Bautista" |
| ? | Lucas del Olmo | "Estaciones de la via sacra" |
| p. 1607 | Murillo | *Discursos en festividades* |
| w. ca. 1605-1609<br>a. 1609<br>p. 1610<br>2nd ed. p. 1613 | Manrique, A. | *Sanctoral* |
| w. 1609 | Góngora | "A la procesion [Mañana sá<br>Corpus Crista]" |
| p. 1610 | Ledesma | *hieroglificos* IX, XVI, XXXIII |
| w. by 1610<br>p. 1615 | Cairasco | *Templo IV*:<br>"San Dámaso, Papa"<br>various poems from<br>*Definiciones* [Castro] |
| p. 1611 | Ledesma | *Juegos de Noche Buena*:<br>"A la certidumbre"<br>"A la enseñanza"<br>"A la intencion"<br>"A santa Lucía"<br>"Al agradecimiento"<br>"Al nacimiento de Cristo" |
| pv. 1611<br>p. 1612 | Ledesma | *Conceptos espirituales III*:<br>"A la conversion"<br>"A la culpa de Adan" |

# APPROXIMATELY CHRONOLOGICAL LIST OF TEXTS AND WRITERS 327

| Date | Writer | Text |
|---|---|---|
| | | "Al juicio final" |
| | | "Discurso a la vida" |
| | | "Pintóse una hoja de oliva" |
| p. 1612 | Ribera | *Sagradas poesías* [Sancha] |
| w. 1609?-12 p. 1612 | Valdivielso | *Romancero espiritual* |
| w. 1611 p. 1612 | Vega Carpio | *Pastores de Belen* |
| a. 1612 p. 1614 | Bonilla | *Peregrinos pensamientos*: (incl. "De cómo se descubre" and "De la conciencia") |
| w. ca. 1612 | Vega Carpio | *Del pan y del palo* |
| d. 1613 | Quevedo | *Lágrimas de Jeremías* |
| p. 1614 | Vega Carpio | *Rimas sacras* |
| w. b. 1614 p. 1625 | Vega Carpio | *Romancero espiritual* |
| a. 1614 p. 1616 | López de Andrade | *Quaresma* |
| p. 1616 | Murillo | *Divina poesía* |
| w. 1615 p. 1616 | Fuente | "Dezimas" |
| w. 1615 p. 1616 | Ovando | "Dezimas" |
| a. 1616 p. 1617 | Bonilla | *Nuevo jardin*: "Cristo y san Pablo" "De la unidad" "De las excelencias" |
| w. 1611-16 ? | Téllez | *No le arriendo* |
| p. 1618 | Jáuregui | *Rimas* |
| w. 1617 p. 1618 | Vega Carpio | *Triunfo de la fe* |
| w. ca. 1613-20 a. 1620 p. 1623 | Valdivielso | *Exposicion parafrastica* |
| w. ca. 1615-20 ? | Escobar y Mendoza | *Nueva Gerusalen* |
| p. 1621 | Vega Carpio | *Filomena* |
| w. 1621 p. 1621 | Ledesma | "Ay, insaciable apetito" |
| p. 1622 | Valdivielso | *Doze actos* |
| w. b. 1622 ? | Valdivielso | *Peregrino del cielo* |
| w. 1622 | Sarriera | "Oda a San Ignacio" |
| w. 1622 | Vega Carpio | *Relacion de las fiestas* |

| Date | Writer | Text |
|---|---|---|
| p. 1624 | Bonilla | *Nombres y atributos* (incl. "Redondillas de la Virgen") |
| p. 1627 | Balvás Barona | "Romance a San Francisco" |
| w. by 1633 | Paravicino | "A la santa cruz" |
| w. by 1635 | Vega Carpio | *Cien jaculatorias* |
| w. 1628+ p. 1666 | Hurtado de Mendoza | *Vida de Nuestra Señora* |
| w. 1628 | Pérez de Montalbán | *Polifemo* |
| p. 1629 | — | *Ramillette*: "Glossa a la inmaculada" |
| p. 1629 | Prado | "Al santísimo Sacramento" |
| w. 1628-29 p. 1630 | Vega Carpio | *Laurel* |
| p. 1634 | Vega Carpio | *Rimas de Tomé de Burguillos* |
| w. b. 1634? b. 1630? | Calderón de la Barca | *El divino Jasón* |
| d. 1633 | Paravicino | *Iesucristo desagraviado* |
| r. 1634 | Calderón | *Cena de Baltasar* |
| r. 1634? | Calderón | *Veneno y triaca* |
| w. 1634 | Calderón | *Nuevo palacio* |
| w. by 1659 p. 1675 | Godínez | *Auto del nacimiento* *Auto del nacimiento y pastores* |
| w. b. 1640 r. 1634? | Calderón | *Hidalga del Valle* |
| w. 1633-35 ? | Calderón | *Gran teatro* |
| w. 1634-35 ? | Calderón | *Gran mercado* |
| w. b. 1635 p. 1637 | Vega Carpio | *Vega del Parnaso* |
| pr. 1635 p. 1635 | Cardoso | *Oracion funebre* |
| pr. 1635 p. 1635 | Vitoria | *Oracion funeral* |
| w. by 1636 p. 1637 | Dicastillo | *Aula de Dios* |
| w. 1637? | Calderón | *Devoción de la Misa* |
| w. 1639? | Calderón | *Gran duque de Gandía* |
| r. 1640 | Calderón | *Misterios de la Misa* |
| w. 1640 | Calderón | *Psiquis y Cupido* (Toledo) |
| w. 1640? b. 1657-58? | Calderón | *Lo que va* |
| w. 1603-44? p. 1664 | Vélez de Guevara | *Mesa redonda* |

| Date | Writer | Text |
|---|---|---|
| w. 1632-44?<br>p. 1675 | Mira de Amescua | *Pedro Telonario*<br>*Pruebas de Christo* |
| p. 1642 | Enríquez Gómez | *Epístolas de Job I* |
| r. 1644 | Calderón | *Humildad coronada* |
| r. 1644 | Calderón | *Socorro general* |
| w. by 1645<br>p. 1670 | Quevedo | *Las Tres Musas:*<br>"A don Alvaro de Luna"<br>"Con la voz del enojo" |
| w. 1639-48 | Rojas Zorrilla | *Viña de Nabot* |
| w. 1645-49? | Calderón | *Encantos de la culpa* |
| w. 1648-49? | Calderón | *Segunda esposa* |
| r. 1649 | Calderón | *Vacante general* |
| r. 1650 | Calderón | *Año Santo de Roma* |
| r. 1651 | Calderón | *Cubo de la Almudena* |
| p. 1651 | Gracián | *Criticón I* |
| w. by 1652<br>p. 1655 | Coello | *Reyno en cortes* |
| w. by 1652<br>p. 1664 | Coello | *Virgen del Rosario* |
| w. 1651-52? | Calderón | *Año Santo en Madrid* |
| w. 1653? | Calderón | *No hay más fortuna* |
| w. 1648-55<br>p. 1655 | Rebolledo | *Constancia* |
| w. b. 1655 | Calderón | *Siembra del Señor:* "Loa" |
| w. ca. 1655?<br>b. 1659 | Calderón | *Valle de la zarzuela* |
| w. 1656 | Calderón | *Protestación de la Fe* and "Loa" |
| 1650's ? | Morales | "A S. Pedro mártir" |
| p. 1657 | Gracián | *Criticón III* |
| w. 1657-58 | Calderón | *Cura y enfermedad* |
| w. 1635-73 | Calderón | *Vida es sueño* (1st) |
| w. b. 1659? | Calderón | *A tu prójimo* (1st) |
| r. 1659 | Calderón | *Sacro Parnaso* |
| w. 1648-60? | Manrique, L. | "¡Qué breves que son!" |
| w. 1659 | Calderón | *Maestrazgo del Toisón* |
| w. ca. 1659<br>p. 1666 | Domínguez Camargo | *S. Ignacio de Loyola* |
| w. 1660 | Calderón | *Lirio y azucena* |
| p. 1661 | Dávila | *Passion* |
| p. 1661 | Gómez Tejada de los Reyes | "Dime, pastor" |

| Date | Writer | Text |
|---|---|---|
| w. 1661 | Calderón | *Arbol del mejor fruto* |
| w. 1661 | Calderón | *Primer refugio* |
| pr. 1661-62 p. 1664 | Ballester | *Aclamacion festiva* |
| r. 1662 | Calderón | *Mística y real Babilonia* |
| w. 1662 | Calderón | *Ordenes militares* and "Loa" |
| w. b. 1663 | Calderón | *Divino Orfeo* (1st) |
| w. 1663? | Calderón | *Orden de Melchisedech* |
| p. 1664 | Moreto | *Gran casa de Austria* |
| w. 1664 | Calderón | *A María el corazón* |
| w. 1664 | Calderón | *Inmunidad* |
| w. 1665 | Calderón | *Psiquis y Cupido* (Madrid) and "Loa" |
| w. 1665 | Calderón | *Viático Cordero* |
| pr. 1666 | Guerra y Ribera | *Oracion de San Iuan de Mata* |
| w. 1669 p. 1670 | Morcho[n] | ["Cancion real"] to St. Peter of Alcantara |
| pr. 1669 p. 1670 | Ludeña | Sermon VI on St. Peter of Alcantara |
| pr. 1669 p. 1670 | Rodríguez Coronel | Sermon VII on St. Peter of Alcantara |
| pr. 1669 p. 1670 | Madre de Dios | Sermon IX on St. Peter of Alcantara |
| pr. 1669 p. 1670 | García de Escañuela | *Panegirico a San Pedro de Alcantara* |
| r. 1670 | Calderón | *Verdadero dios Pan* |
| w. 1670 | Calderón | *Sueños hay que verdad son* |
| pr. 1671 | Guerra y Ribera | *Oracion de San Francisco de Borja* |
| w. 1671 | Calderón | *Santo rey Fernando* (I) |
| w. 1671? p. 1692 | Solís y Ribadeneyra | "Conversion de S. Francisco de Borja" |
| w. ca. 1672 | Calderón | *Redención de cautivos* |
| r. 1673 p. 1676-77 | Calderón | *Vida es sueño* (2nd) |
| w. b. 1674 | Calderón | *Tu prójimo* (2nd) |
| r. 1674 | Calderón | *Nave del mercader* |
| r. 1674 | Calderón | *Viña del Señor* |
| p. 1675 | Castilla | *Al nacimiento* |
| p. 1675 | Garau | *Sabio instruído* |
| w. 1668-75 | Calderón | *Nuevo hospicio* |
| w. 1675 | Calderón | *Jardín de Falerina* and "Loa" |

| Date | Writer | Text |
|---|---|---|
| pr. 1675 | Guerra y Ribera | *Oracion de once Martyres y S. Francisco Solano* |
| w. b. 1676 b. 1659? | Calderón | *Primero y segundo Isaac* |
| w. b. 1676 r. 1672? | Calderón | *¿Quién hallará?* |
| r. 1676 | Calderón | *Serpiente de metal* |
| w. 1677? | Calderón | *Pastor Fido* |
| w. 1678 | Calderón | *El día mayor* |
| w. 1679 | Calderón | *Tesoro escondido* |
| p. 1679 | Guerra y Ribera | *Sermón de la conversión* |
| p. 1679 | Pradas | *Sermon a Nuestra Señora* |
| w. ca. 1666-80 p. 1677-80 | Guerra y Ribera | *Sermones varios*: "Declamacion dia de S. Catalina" "Oracion a la Vncion" "Oracion a S. Iorge" "Oracion a S. Tomás" "Oracion dia de S. Ana" "Oracion dia de S. Catalina" "Oracion dia de Quarenta Horas" |
| p. 1677+ | Guerra y Ribera | "Oración del Miércoles de Señales" "Sermón de la tempestad" "Sermón de las honras" "Sermón de S. Teresa" "Sermón del Santissimo Sacramento" |
| p. 1680 | Aguilar | "A Christo" "A la Virgen" |
| w. 1680 | Calderón | *Andrómeda y Perseo*: "Loa" |
| w. 1680 | Calderón | *Indulto general* |
| w. b. 1681 | Calderón | *Lepra de Constantino* |
| r. 1681 | Calderón | *Cordero de Isaías* and "Loa" |
| r. 1681 | Calderón | *Amar y ser amado* |
| p. 1686 | Braones | *Epitome de los triunfos* |
| w. 1686 | Guerra y Ribera | "Aprobación" for *Sueños* |
| w. 1622-88 | San Félix | poems [Serrano y Sanz] |
| p. 1694 | Enciso y Monzón | *Christiada* |

# ANTHOLOGY

Note: The basic order of texts is alphabetical by author or title. When individual pieces within a collection by the same author bear numbers, I have followed numerical order. When pieces by the same writer are taken from various sources, I have alphabetized first by the author or title of the source. The exception is Lope de Vega, whose texts are alphabetized by the title of each of his own complete works.

**Act** Excerpt from *Actio quae inscribitur examen sacrum.* González Pedroso 139.

Nequam:
  No tratar con religiosos
  Dice que es grave delito:
  Vestidos algo costosos
  Y el rostro nada marchito
  Firma que es de los viciosos.

**ActE** Excerpt from "Entremés." *Actio quae inscribitur examen sacrum.* González Pedroso 141.

Menguillo:
  Es muy recia condicion
  La de Theos Adonai:
  Vuestro Tetragrammaton . . . .

**Ag1** Aguilar, Juan Bautista. "A Christo Señor nuestro, considerandole misterioso Libro, por los misterios sagrados de su vida." Simón Díaz 169.

  Perfecto Libro, que a la Estampa ha
              [dado
  bien entendido Autor, eres confiesso [;]
  al Encarnarte, aduierto estás impresso,
  como al Nacer al mundo, a luz sacado.
    En la Circuncision fuiste cortado,
  y al adorarte Reyes miro expresso,
  Sabios, te leen Rey, Dios Hombre, y esso
  tu Autor, con una Estrella ha señalado.
    Haziendo huyas a Egipto, hizo cubrirte,
  para en Ierusalen, despues mostrarte
  tres dias a sus Doctos, y aplaudirte:
    a una Coluna, quiso rubricarte
  y si en la Cruz, el Titulo inscribirte,
  en el monte Tabor, illuminarte.

**Ag2** Aguilar, Juan Bautista. "A la Virgen Santissima, creyendola cabal perfectissimo Libro."[1] Simón Díaz 169-72.

  Celestial, sabia María,
  Libro, en que estudioso leo,
  a la enseñanza, cuydados,
  a la perfeccion, desvelos.
    Libro docto, libro raro;
  que en vos solamente es cierto,
  Libro soys en tiempo escrito,
  y enquadernado ab eterno.
    Dios es vuestro Autor, y puso
  tan cuydado al componeros,

---

[1] The term "perfectissimo" seems to mean, in the light of the poem itself, both "without error" and "complete."

que en gloria vuestra, ni un nombre
os sobra, ni os falta un Verbo.
    El Titulo os dio de Madre,
y esto Madre Reyna, a tiempo
que vos el titulo os diste
de esclava, pero sin yerros.
    Tres Personas os apruevan,
en docto aplauso escriviendo
azia vuestra Gracia glorias,
al lograros Privilegios.
    A un Rey estais dedicado,
Alto honor logrando en ello;
pues luego que impresso fuistes
a raras glorias impresso.
    En vuestra Concepcion pura,
blancas hojas miro, y veo
en abismos de candores,
sin Letras, muchos conceptos.
    Negras lineas, que me dizen
sacros discursos diversos,
son del Espiritu Santo
luzes, que sombra os hizieron.
    Admiraciones no os faltan,
que en voz no pocas adverto
pusieron Angeles, quando
toda esplendor os leyeron.
    Puntos, los que en vuestra vida
señaló veloz en tiempo
serán, mas ¡o con que gracia
teneys el punto primero!
    Solo Tassa no os señalan,
porque el que llega a quereros,
no pone en precio cuydados,
ponelos si en el aprecio.
    Erratas, no las teneis
y es que el Sabio Impressor vuestro
del Original os saca,
sin Erratas, todo aciertos.
    Siendo Libro, será en vos
Tabla, ser del bien Compendio;
Fin, vuestra Coronación
y Principio el Nacimiento.
    Libro pues, leeros quiso
Moyses . . .[2]
. . . .
    Noe os leyó . . .
. . . .
    Adan os leyó gozoso,

. . . .
jamás abierto a la culpa,
y a la gracia siempre abierto.
    Sabio os leyó Salomon,
. . . .
    Iacob os leyó . . .
. . . .
    El Evangelista, Libro
os leyó; y es claro esto
que con siete Sellos, Iuan,
de que soys Libro, echó el sello.
    Libro soys, tambien soy
Libro,
hazer borrando imperfetos
Capitulos: Libro ocupe
la Librería del Cielo.

**ASF** Excerpt from "Alabanza a San Francisco." *Poesias varias* 5: 225.

El mas bruñido papel
que en el mundo pudo hallar
Exceptando el virginal
papel donde fue estampado
el escriptor eterno
que mostro en este treslado
qual era el original.

**AD** Excerpt from *Aucto de las donas que envió Adán a nuestra Señora*. González Pedroso 24.

Lázaro:
    ¡Oh qué carta de cuidado
        Te daria,
    Que tu padre Adan te envia,
    Sellada con una cruz,
. . . .
Nuestra Señora:
    . . . .(Tómala de manos de san Lázaro.)
    ¿Quién ha de poder leella
        Sin llorar,
    Viendo esta cruz aquí estar
    Por firma de mi dolor,
. . . .
    Mas con lloro y sospirar
        Quiero ver

---

[2] Medieval writers like Hugh of St. Victor and Richard de Bury used as metaphors for books such images as "arca Noe" and "scala Jacob" (Carruthers 160). These images also occurred in litanies of the Virgin as types or figures of Mary. Perhaps an awareness of both uses suggested to Aguilar the structure of the second half of his poem. See also in this regard Enciso y Monzón.

El sobrescripto, y leer
A quién dice.
Lázaro: (Leyendo.)
"Para vos,
La Esposa y Madre de Dios."

**ADJ** Excerpts from *Aucto de los desposorios de Josef.* González Pedroso 59.

Angel:
En libro de los vivientes
Hoy tu nombre es asentado,
Y jamás será borrado;
. . . .
Hija, mi nombre está escripto
Con aquel dedo de Dios
En su registro infinito.
Es libro de maravillas;
Lo que hay en él, infalible;
Cosas que no es convenible
A veces hombre pedillas,
Ni decillas es posible.

**Av1** Avila, Juan de. Excerpt from *Sermón I. Dominica primera de Cuaresma. Coleccion* 40.

No tenemos pontífice que no se duela de nuestras flaquezas, compadesciéndose dellas, porque nos tiene en su corazón escriptos.

**Av2** Avila, Juan de. Excerpt from *Sermón 1. Domingo I de Adviento. Sermones* 41.

Sentarse ha el Juez a juzgar. *Abrirse han los libros,* que son las conciencias, *y abrirse ha otro libro, que es de la vida.* Cuando un señor tiene un mayordomo, demás de los libros del mayordomo, tiene el señor otro libro, en que escribe él la cuenta, porque no lo engañe el mayordomo. Abrirse han las conciencias y *abrirse ha allí el libro de la vida, y a quien no estuviere escripto en aquel libro, echarlo han en el infierno* para siempre. ¡Oh quién viere aquel libro para saber si estoy escripto en él!

**Av3** Avila, Juan de. Excerpts from *Sermón 3. En vísperas de Navidad. Sermones* 96, 97, 100.

¿Deseáis castidad y limpieza en vuestro corazón, de suerte que tengáis un nuevo corazón, como San Ignacio, que decía que tenía escripto en su corazón a Jesucristo, y que nadie se lo podía quitar de su corazón?

. . . . ¡Bendito sea tal niño como éste, pues echa sobre sus hombros todos cuantos pecados vos hecistes; . . . y cuidadoso de pagar esta deuda sale por fiador de ella, y hace luego recién nacido obligación firmada con la sangre de su circuncisión. Obligado se ha a pagar todo cuanto merecen vuestros pecados.

. . . . Y para eso envió a su Hijo . . . para pagar por nosotros. Y *la escriptura* que al demonio teníamos hecha, dice San Pablo que *la enclavó en la cruz* y la borró con su sangre, para que no nos tenga más que pedir el demonio.

**Av4** Avila, Juan de. Excerpt from *Sermón 13. Miércoles de la IV semana de Cuaresma. Sermones* 244.

Leemos al Crucificado y muerto en la cruz, y estamos nosotros vivos a las pasiones. Leo con corazón, y río de lo que leo. Leo palabras, no hay en mí obras ningunas.

**Av5** Ávila, Juan de. Excerpts from *Sermón 32. Martes de Pentecostés. Sermones* 464, 465.

Este es el día . . . en que se dió Ley mejor; que la otra Ley se dió en tablas, pero esta otra se dió en los corazones. *Dabo legem meam in visceribus eorum.* "Darles he –dice Dios por Jeremías– *una Ley en sus entrañas,* no escrita en papel ni piedra, sino en los corazones" . . . . Esta Ley que hoy se dió, es ley de evangelio. ¿De cuál? ¿De los evangelios que se escribieron? No, que ese evangelio no propiamente, sino segundariamente se llama evangelio. Ley evangélica y santa se dice lo que se escribió en los corazones, que, aunque no hubiera letras ni escritura, se puede bien entender y se puede cumplir; en dándosela les pegó amor de cumplirla. . . . *Vos estis Epistola mea.* No es menester carta para escrebir la Ley. "*Vosotros* –dice el apóstol San Pablo– *sois mi Epístola, vuestros corazones son carta;* y no penséis que tiene de ser escrita con tinta, sino con el dedo, que es el Espíritu Santo, que es el que escribió la Ley en vuestros corazones, predicándola yo; el Espíritu Santo la escrebía –dice San Pablo–; yo soy el ministro de lo que El escribe".

**Av6** Ávila, Juan de. Excerpt from *Sermón 33. Jueves Santo. Sermones* 481.

Este amor que ves . . . con éste te traía en su pecho escrito, como madre a su hijo en su vientre.

**Av7** Ávila, Juan de. Excerpt from *Sermón 78. San Francisco de Asís. Sermones* 1218-19.

¿Qué más habéis de negar? . . . . No ha de quedar nada; blanco, liso como un pergamino, que tiene despegada toda la carne para escrebir, has de quedar. Quita . . . todos esos males, si ha de escribir Dios en tu ánima su sabiduráa y los dones de su gracia. Limpia, lisa, relumbrando ha de estar; no ha de tener ni aun pelito ni aun rasguito; quitado has de estar de toda carne.

**Av8** Ávila, Juan de. Excerpt from *Sermón 79. Festividad de Todos los Santos. Sermones* 1234.

Esto es predestinación. Una escritura en el pecho de Dios de dar su gloria a fulano y a fulano.

**BaB** Balvás Barona, Antonio. "Romance a San Francisco." Simón Díaz 166-68.

Oy el Autor soberano
saca, diuino Francisco,
impresso en su misma imprenta
el cuerpo de vuestro libro.
 El Compendio, el libro abierto
de caxa, cuento, y recibo,
del mismo Dios celebrado
en las partidas del siglo.
 La Coronica admirable,
que en el discurso, y estilo,
lo que tiene de aspereza
es lo excelente, y lo rico.
 Mas aunque libro de un santo
al mismo Dios dirigido,
podreys seruir de cartilla,
pues comenzays por el Christus.
 La cruz, el título, y llagas,
que la hoja del principio (*sic*),
dice en quien es el autor
obra de Dios en vos mismo.
 La carta dedicatoria,
prólogo, y notas de auiso,
es la humildad, leuantada
sin puntos vanos de altiuo.
 Las materias que tratays
de un zelo piadoso, y limpio,
son de actos de penitencia,
para los contemplativos.
 La fe del libro, y volumen,
tan grande como infinito,
en fe de que error, o erratas,
podrá reprouar el vicio.
 Dios os aprueua, y imprime
por milagroso, y diuino,
pues libro que Dios aprueba
quáles serán los escritos.
 El priuilegio Real,
en honra de tantos hijos,
seruirá de executoria
en la Yglesia, y sus archiuos.
 La tassa, no si se aduierte,
es del priuilegio antiguo,
que en manos, y cuerpo impresso,
muestra valor excessiuo.
 Por escudo desta obra
impressa, blasón, y arrimo,
os haze assombras de amparo
un árbol del parayso.
 Las hojas son, que os coronan,
laureles de vuestro olimpo,
porque a un libro de memoria
no ofendan rayos de oluido.
 De Dios estays apuntado,
por espantoso prodigio,
mas qué mucho que os apunte
si soys blanco de sus tiros?
 Como a Géminis del Cielo
con brazos en Cruz de amigo,
se cifra en la estampa vuestra
por armas de su designio.
 En fe de amor se retrata,
porque como en libro quiso
estar en vos retratado,

de su pinzel peregrino.
   Buen tercero, y terzio os haze
pues tan acabado os hizo,
porque quedeys desta Orden
mejorado en tercio, y quinto.
   Y en la impressión milagrosa,
assumpto, y cuerpo de libro,[3]
forma, y letra colorada,
aprouación, y registro.
   A luz sales propiamente,
tan compendioso, y sucinto,
que soys un libro de Dios,
iluminado, y luzido.
   Desde el Christiano Español,
hasta los remotos Indios,
todos yrán con letura,
de como estays recíbido.
   Aunque en la enquadernación
y la estampa, el Letor pío,
dude en razón de admirado,
si soys Dios, o soys Francisco.
   El os bautiza, y da el nombre
de eterna alabanza digno,
que el nombre del libro santo
es gloria del Christianismo.
   Finalmente libro impresso,
cuyo discurso, y motiuo,
por Peregrino en la tierra
veneran los Cielos mismos.
   El libro soys con la tabla
del retrato de Dios viuo,
de quien la tierra y el cielo
podrán dezir lo que han visto.

**Ba**   Ballester, Juan Bautista. Excerpt from *Aclamacion festiva. Once sermones* 32.

En el fatal fenecimiento del Orbe, dará tal estallido su maquina, que se desquadernará el volumen de los cielos.

**Be**   Bernal, Juan. Excerpt from *Sermón a las honras del Rey don Philipo. II.* 9.

Si sales al campo, y por desechar tristezas
te passeas por las orillas de los rios, en
ellos y en sus aguas donde nada se escrive,
hallaras escripto aquel dicho tan discreto
de la muger de Thecua, todos morimos, y
como aguas vamos corriendo al mar de la
sepultura. *Omnes morimur, & quasi aquae dilabimur in terram.*

**Bo1**   Bonilla, Alonso de. "De excelencias de la Virgen." *Nombres y atribvtos* 67 [2nd series of foliation].

Para formar vn libro soberano,
   escriuió su concepto el Padre eterno
   en las dos hojas del mejor quaderno,
   el ser Diuino, con el ser Humano.
De la especie de Adan, mortal gusano,
   trazó vna Madre y Virgen abeterno,
   dos tablas que su Espiritu coeterno
   dio a la enquadernacion con sabia mano.
Mas para que el primor correspondiera
   al concepto del libro de María,
   su artifice argentó las tablas bellas.
Y ansi, en vez de florones por defuera,
   le dio la peregrina argenteria,
   de la Luna, del Sol, y las Estrellas.

**Bo2**   Bonilla, Alonso de. Excerpt from "Decima a los dos, S. Iusto y Pastor, Martires." *Nombres y atribvtos* 48 [2nd series of foliation].

Si en vuestra niñez florida
   el morir por Christo fue,
   el Christus del A.B.C.
   del principio de la vida....

**Bo3**   Bonilla, Alonso de. "Del inefable nombre de Iesvs." *Nombres y atribvtos* n. pág.

Como al Verbo engendró el Padre infinito
   Abeterno en su incognita clausura,
   Porque al Criador conozca la criatura

---

[3] Because of its context, the term *cuerpo* here conveys all the following significations: "En la Empressa y Emblema es la figura que se pinta, con que se expressa el contenido de ellas.... Se llaman tambien los tomos o volúmenes que componen una libreria, o en que se divide una obra grande.... Significa tambien el contenido y parte essencial de alguna obra escrita, libro o volumen de algun tratado y assunto" (*Diccionario de autoridades*).

Le dio en mortalidad su nombre es-
[crito.
El nombre se escriuio (caso exquisito)
En el valle del llanto y amargura,
Con roja tinta de la sangre pura
De la que al mundo dio fruto bendito.
La pluma fue su amor incontrastable
Y la carne el papel, cuya innocencia
Las presta luz a las volubles zonas:
El nombre fue, IESVS, Dios inefable,
Escrito por la mano de vna essencia,
Con los tres dedos de las tres personas.

**Bo4** Bonilla, Alonso de. Excerpt from "Discvrso de la soledad y angvstias de la siempre virgen; en el transito, y passion de Iesu Christo Señor y Dios nuestro." *Nombres y atribvtos* 189.

Ya...
En el hoyo trastornan el retrato
Del Padre inmenso, cuya fuerza eterna
Los montes con el golpe desquaderna.

**Bo5** Bonilla, Alonso de. Excerpts from "Nombres y atribvtos de la impecable siempre virgen María Señora nuestra." *Nombres y atribvtos* 66, 135, 163, 164, 169.

['Atribvto de cielo']
 Astro fue el sobreescrito que tuuiste
  En el papel del alma inmaculada....
['Atríbvto de palma']
 Hoja de palma fue el papel primero
  En quien letra escriuio el ingenio hu-
[mano,
 Y el Padre de la luz, Sol verdadero,
 En la palma estrenó su pluma y mano:
 Pues porque del Leon que es ya Cor-
[dero
  El nombre se escriuiera soberano,
  Plantó en su eternidad tu palma bella
  Y assi está su palabra escrita en ella.
['Del soberano y singular nombre de Inmaculada']
 Por antojo de amor el infinito
  Quiso ver en papel de carne humana
  Aquel consubstancial Concepto es-
[crito
  Que de su entendimiento eterno mana:

Y solo en ti halló (caso exquisito)
Blanco papel su tinta soberana,
Que del papel de la naturaleza
Son los demas la estraza y la bajeza.
....
Si el discipulo escriue con destreza
 Porque el maestro gouernó su mano,
 La gracia gouernó a Naturaleza
 Al formar tu sujeto soberano:
 Y assi las dos formaron tu belleza
 Que es la letra mejor del ser humano,
 Letra que quando fue del Criador vista
 Madre de Dios la hizo a letra vista.
....
Como alcanzó ambas leyes tu pureza,
 Fuyste de tablas libro enquadernado,
 Que la enquadernacion es la corteza
 De aquello que en el libro está ence-
[rrado.
 Y como tu eres libro en quien la al-
[teza
 Dios escribió de su concepto amado,
 Las tablas que a Moyses dio el infinito
 Son tu enquadernacion, y Dios lo es-
[crito.

**Bo6** Bonilla, Alonso de. "La Virgen fue aquel papel do quanto supo escriuio Dios, por cuya gracia no cayó mancha alguna en el. Glosa." *Nombres y atribvtos* 54 [2nd series of foliation].

 En papel tan excelente
que culpa no lo ha passado,
escriuió el Padre increado
la palabra omnipotente
de su concepto engendrado.
 Fue el papel carne mortal,
tan blanco que nunca en el
cayó mancha original;
y por auer de ser tal,
la Virgen fue aquel papel.
 No manchó el primer delito
el papel de vn alma bella
donde el mismo Dios fue escrito,
que pues Dios escriuio en ella,
a lo escrito me remito.
 Que aunque manchado quedó
el libro del ser humano,
sola esta hoja guardó
Dios en su ser soberano,
do quanto supo escriuio.

Dio el Maestro vniuersal
su ley por materia al hombre,
y el hombre escriuio tan mal,
que echó en el nuestro y su nombre
el borron original.
 Y al que preguntar pretende
si en la que a Dios concibio
cayó mancha o no cayó?
respondo que la defiende
Dios, por cuya gracia no.
 No fue este papel batido
con el golpe del pecado,
pero tan esclarecido
que con el sol fue dorado
y con la gracia bruñido.
 Que en el ser inmaculado
deste diuino papel
otro que Dios no ha tocado,
ni del borron del pecado
cayó mancha alguna en el.

**Bo7** Bonilla, Alonso de. "A la Sinagoga sobre los azotes de Christo." *Peregrinos pensamientos* 42.

Maestros de licion de hypocresias,
 Tan mala letra haze la inocencia,
 Que al que es la guia de la eterna ciencia,
 Dexays con los azotes en las guias?
 Si en vuestra escuela le contays los dias,
 Prouá a escreuir con el en competencia,
 Porque en papel de arena su potencia,
 Arrastrará vuestras escriuanias.
Bastardillo escreuis, que comprehende,
 Bastardos hijos de mortal veneno,
 Contra quien con su letra os dessafia:
Y el escriue de caxa, pues lo aprende
 De aquella sempiterna caxa y seno;
 Escuela de inmortal Sabiduria.

**Bo8** Bonilla, Alonso de. "De la sangre y agua del costado de Christo." *Peregrinos pensamientos* 46.

Hizo vna obligacion el tierno infante,
 De pagar por el hombre, y de presente
 Circuncidose. y dio sangre inocente
 Quanta para la firma fue bastante:
El plazo se cumplio, y pagó al instante,
 Do por borrar la obligacion patente
 Quedó el tintero seco del caliente
 Humor de tinta roxa y elegante:
Pero para borrarla por entero
 Por ser tan larga que ocupado auia
 Mil plumas de Profetas escriuanos:
Fue licito añadir agua al tintero,
 Y ansi la obligacion de los humanos
 Con sangre y agua se borró este dia.

**Bo9** Bonilla, Alonso de. "De la Santificacion del Baptista." *Peregrinos pensamientos 66.*

 Vn libro muy singular
a compuesto Zacharias,
por ser obra que en sus dias
a luz pretende sacar.
 Pues ylde a auisar
si es libro de tanta estima,
que primero que le imprima
le quiere Dios censurar.
 Por que causas y razones
tan bien censurado a de yr?
Por auerse de imprimir
en hojas de corazones.
 Si tanto fruto a de dar
el libro de Zacharias,
cercene sus demasias
quien las puede cercenar:
 Pues ylde a auisar,
si es libro de tanta estima,
que primero que le imprima
le quiere Dios censurar.
 En obra tan acabada,
que importara la censura?
Quitarle el censo que dura
de la ignorancia heredada:
 Pues si ay censo que quitar
de faltas y demasias
bien se yo que Zacharias
querra su libro apurar.
 Pues ylde a auisar
que este censo se redima,
pues primero que se imprima
le quiere Dios censurar.
 Mil conceptos nunca oydos
en su discurso a de auer.
Que conceptos pueden ser
siendo en culpa concebidos?
 Si ay culpas que desterrar
por culpas de Zacharias
destierrense pues ay dias
para poderlo apurar.
 No salga a bolar,
que será de poca estima,

si primero que se imprima
Dios no lo va a censurar.

**Bo10** Bonilla, Alonso de. Excerpt from "Romance de la Santa Cruz." *Peregrinos pensamientos* 52.

Soys el gran libro de caxa,
donde el rico fiador nuestro,
por henchir vuestras partidas
se desencajo los miembros.

**Bo11** Bonilla, Alonso de. Excerpts from "Cristo y san Pablo en su conversion." Sancha 232.

–Di: ¿por qué me has perseguido,
Pablo, y a los que incluido
Tienen mi cristiano sello?
. . . .
Mi colegio perseguido,
Donde yo me imprimo y sello.

**Bo12** Bonilla, Alonso de. Excerpts from "De la unidad y trinidad de Dios." Sancha 70, 71.

Es libro tan peregrino,
Que tiene mundos por letras,
Pues por las criaturas de ellos
El Criador se deletrea.
Pero aunque es deletreado,
Nadie a decorarlo acierta,
Pues no hay quien junte las partes
Del todo de su grandeza.
. . . .
Un Dios no hecho, es principio
De todas las cosas hechas
Que en su ser están escritas
Y en el mismo se conservan.

**Bo13** Bonilla, Alonso de. Excerpt from "De las excelencias del ayuno." Sancha 140.

Dirígete a la templanza;
Que sí tu cuerpo no templas,
Serás un cuerpo de libro
Descuadernado en la Iglesia.

**Bo14** Bonilla, Alonso de. "De la conciencia del hombre." Simón Díaz 165-66.

Dios imprimió su ley por su clemencia
en el papel del corazón humano;
porque no fuesse su apetito en vano,
ya que de Dios apeteció la ciencia.
  Es margen de este libro, la conciencia,
donde el inmenso con su nombre y mano
acota su precepto soberano,
por digno de obseruancia y reuerencia.
  Y porque si a tan alto beneficio
correspondiesse mal por darle nombre
a su diuina ley de ley injusta,
  estableció que en el final juyzio
sea la misma conciencia juez del hombre,
porque en ella acotó su ley por justa.

**Bo15** Bonilla, Alonso de. "Redondillas de la Virgen." Simón Díaz 162-64.

Vos soys, Reyna Virginal,
libro de sabiduría,
tal que el mismo Dios, María,
lee en vuestro Marial.
  El priuilegio es de Dios,
que como tanto os estima
no quiso que el mundo imprima
otro libro como vos.
  Las que vuestro libro enseña
letras mayúsculas son,
porque es Dios vuestra impressión
y en Dios no ay cosa pequeña.
  No quedó quaderno en Dios
de virtudes y excelencias,
que para espejo de ciencias
no lo enquadernasse en vos.
  Sólo Dios sabrá explicar
de vuestra ciencia el tesoro,
que entre los nueue no ay coro
que lo sepa decorar.
  Esse gran libro de Dios
jamás tuuo expurgatorio,
Virgen, porque el purgatorio
no se hizo para vos.
  No ay de alguna imperfección
género en el libro vuestro,
por ser del mayor Maestro
libro de generación.
  Libro de caja de Dios
soys, pues el Seno paterno
es caxa del Sempiterno
concepto que escriuió en vos.
  Las letras de vuestros dones
aprueuan por peregrinas

las tres personas diuinas,
ved qué tres aprouaciones.
    Como su antiguo sucesso
en vos no imprimió el pecado,
soys, por ser tan estimado,
libro nueuamente impresso.
    Porque quando en la impressión
naturaleza dio tinta,[4]
la gracia os hizo distinta
del mundo en la perfección.
    La materia que contiene
es fecunda y peregrina,
porque en razón de doctrina
más frutos que hojas tiene.
    No es materia essa lección
para ingenio material,
que es todo vuestro caudal
materia de saluación.
    No ay libro que por fauor
del borrón de Adan se libre,
pero vuestro libro es libre
por libro libertador.
    Es vuestro libro la muestra
de la ciencia eterna y pura
porque fue Dios con lectura
de ser la lectura vuestra.
    No ay en vos imperfección,
pero virtud insumable,
y ansí en libro tan loable
no ay tassa ni corrección.
    Pues no se puede admitir
que entre la gran librería
de Adán, tenga el de María
erratas que corregir.
    Es el libro Virginal
cátedra tan peregrina
que es quien dictó su dotrina
Teólogo original.
    Los renglones claramente
nos dan la virtud reglada,
y las hojas son de espada
contra la mortal serpiente.

**Bo16** Bonilla, Alonso de. "De cómo se descubre algo de Dios por las criaturas." Valdivielso. *Romancero espiritual* xxxiv, lx.

Para que un rudo Príncipe adquiriera
    Principios de leer, que an (sic) no sabía,
    De varios pajes le introduxo un día
    El ayo un ABC desta manera:
Dio nombre a cada qual que respondiera
    Con una de las letras que tenía
    El prolijo ABC, por cuya vía
    De curso de nombrarlos lo aprendiera.
Criaturas, Plantas, Cielo, Sol, y Estrellas,
    Son como pajes, letras, y figuras,
    Que redimen del hombre la rudeza;
Pues, qual por ABC, sube por ellas
    A decorar de Dios la suma Alteza,
    Que es libro universal de las criaturas.

**Brn** Braones, Alonso Martin. Excerpt from *Epitome de los trivnfos de Jesvs* 29.

    El ingenio inventó con sutileza,
Que en papel blanco letras se escriviessen,
Que ocultando a la vista su belleza
A la luz solamente se leyessen:
Mas de el Diuino Verbo la fineza
Quiso escrito en lo humano le atendiessen,
Y tanto en este Pan llegó a ocultarse,
Que solo a luz de Fe puede mirarse.

**Brv** Bravo, Nicolas. Excerpts from *Benedictina* 306, 418.

[Canto 11]
    Que como Dios el corazón penetra,
      Donde se escriue de lo que el se
                      [paga,
      Siempre atalaya y mira en esta letra....
[Canto 16]
    Y quan de veras de su mal se duela,
    Lo atestigua la vista, y frente roja,
    Que el pecho compassivo de los males,
    Sobre escriue en la frente las señales.

**Cab1** Cabrera, Alonso de. Excerpt

---

[4] The choice of "tinta" conveys the notion that in the *Catechism* of the Council of Trent is expressed with respect to the Incarnation: "Thus, in believing that the body of Christ was formed from the most pure blood of His Virgin Mother we acknowledge the operation of human nature, this being a law common to the formation of all human bodies, that they should be formed from the blood of the mother" (43).

from *La circuncisión de Jesucristo. Navidad y Año Nuevo* 97-98.

¿Queréis ver lo que tenemos en el nombre gloriosísimo de Jesús? ¿En cuánto estimaríais vos que el rey os diese una docena de firmas en blanco, cada una en medio pliego de papel, que dijese: *Yo el rey*, dejando a vuestra voluntad componer lo que quisieseis? En la una pondríais ... en otra ... y que en viendo esas cédulas reales, autorizadas con su firma, sin dilación se cumpliesen. Una sola firma de éstas se tendría en mucho.

Pues, mira, hombre desventurado, que te da Cristo una firma en blanco que vale por cuanto tú quisieres, ... y ésta es el Nombre dulcísimo de Jesús.

**Cab2** Cabrera, Alonso de. Excerpt from *La circuncisión del Señor. Navidad y Año Nuevo* 143.

¿Qué diré de San Ignacio, que como muchas veces nombrase a Jesús y los verdugos le preguntasen la causa, respondió: Porque la lengua habla lo que está escrito en el corazón? Sácanle el corazón después de muerto y por cualquiera parte que le cortaban parecía escrito con letras de oro, *Jesús*.

**Cab3** Cabrera, Alonso de. Excerpt "El dedo de Dios." *Navidad y Año Nuevo* lix.

Cosa llana es que el que con una caña hiciese mejor letra que otro con una pluma muy bien cortada, sería tenido por mejor escribano.... Pues este fué el ardid de Dios: ... usó de instrumentos ineptos para lo que pretendía, para que después de hecha la obra y conseguido el fin, no se atribuyese la gloria al instrumento, sino a Dios y todo el mundo conociese que *el dedo de Dios está aquí (Exod., 8)*... En la mano de Dios ... la caña es pluma....

**Cab4** Cabrera, Alonso de. Excerpt from *Del santísimo nombre de Jesús. Navidad y Año Nuevo* 166-67.

Mirad lo que dice el mismo Salvador: *Vincenti dabo ... calculum candidum, et in calculo nomen novum scriptum, quod nemo scit, nisi qui accipit*. Al soldado victorioso ... darle he una piedrecita blanca, una perla, y en ella sobrescrito un nombre nuevo, que ninguno sabe lo que es, sino quien lo recibe. Esta perla es Cristo nuestro bien....

Con esta piedra preciosa, con este diamante y carbunclo de infinito precio están ricos los que, por haberle, se deshicieron en esta vida de lo que poseían; y el sobrescrito que tiene, las armas esculpidas en el campo blanco de esta piedra, es este nombre, *Jesús*, que hoy le ponen; nombre nuevo cuanto al afecto y significado; escrito con su Sangre, que es el esmalte de tan rica joya.... Entre tanto que marchamos con las armas a cuestas ... este nombre es la voz de salud....

**Cab5** Cabrera, Alonso de. Excerpt from *Nacimiento de Jesucristo. Navidad y Año Nuevo* 47.

Celebra hoy la Iglesia católica la fiesta del invictísimo mártir San Esteban, el primer testigo que con su sangre firmó de su nombre la verdad del Evangelio, el primer pagador que procuró, en cuanto fué posible, salir de la deuda en que Cristo, con su pasión, puso a todo el linaje humano....

**Cab6** Cabrera, Alonso de. Excerpt from *Consideraciones del Miércoles después del Domingo Primero de Cuaresma. Sermones* 112.

Están estos tales tan aficionados y amadores de lo justo y bueno, que si las leyes de la virtud se perdiesen de los libros, las hallarían escritas en los corazones dellos, conforme a la promesa del Señor: *Dabo legem meam in visceribus eorum et in corde eorum scribam eam* (Jer., 31). Lo cual dice, no tanto porque la sepan de memoria, como porque el amor determinado de su corazón es aquello mismo que la ley dice de fuera, por estar ya su voluntad tan transformada en el amor del bien, ... hechos una viva ley y medida de las obras humanas, según atinaba Aristóteles.

**Cab7** Cabrera, Alonso de. Excerpt from *Consideraciones del Viernes después del Domingo primero de Cuaresma. Sermones* 124.

Dos excelencias de la ley nueva sobre la vieja se coligen deste lugar. La una, que aquella fué sombra y borrador; ésta, imagen acabada. El que quiere escribir una carta a un inferior suyo, no cura de muchos primores; toma la pluma con pelo, y no se le da nada que el papel se pase, ni que la tinta sea blanca, ni que los renglones no vayan derechos, ni las razones bien concertadas; pero quien ha de escribir a un rey, hace un borrador y dos, para después sacarle en limpio. No se contentó el Señor con hacer la ley evangélica y Sacramentos de nuestra redención así como quiera, sino como de cosa que pretendía sacar muy prima, hizo primero un borrador y otro. Las obras de la creación de la primera vez salieron; no hubo más que decir y hacer.... Eran obras ordinarias y andaderas, y como de menor cuantía. Pero acá para sacar un sacrificio de Cristo en la cruz, hizo un borrador en el sacrificio de Abraham y en la serpiente de metal levantada en el madero, ... y para sacar en blanco un sacrificio del altar hizo un borrador en Melchisedec, ... [y] puso primero el maná.... Por esto llama el Apóstol a lo antiguo borrones y sombras, y a lo nuevo, lo limpio y perfecto.

**Cab8** Cabrera, Alonso de. Excerpt from *Consideraciones del Martes después del Domingo cuarto de Cuaresma. Sermones* 294.

¡Qué gran beneficio que aquel Señor que tan docta escuela tiene en el cielo, no se desdeñó de venir a ser maestro de niños en la tierra, acomodándose a todo! .... [Allí] leyendo todos en aquel libro de la vida, que es su divina esencia, quedan resueltos y consumados en toda verdad, y graduados todos de doctores. Pero, ¿qué me aprovechara a mí, Señor, que tú leyeras esa doctrina tan alta, y por modo tan alto allá en el templo de tu gloria, si no tuvieras por bien de bajar al templo de tu iglesia a enseñar a estos pequeñuelos hombres, templando la doctrina con la corta capacidad de los oyentes? ¿O dándosela por modo que aunque en substancia es la misma, la pudiesen percebir?

**Cab9** Cabrera, Alonso de. Excerpt from *Consideraciones del Viernes después del Domingo cuarto de Cuaresma. Sermones* 317.

Si alguna vez en el año siquiera tuviéramos licencia de poder entrar en la consideración en ver aquellas cosas que dentro su beatísima alma pasan, ahí está... aquella alma por todas partes, en finísimo oro de gracia ... forrada de fuera y dentro, ... las tablas ambas de amor de Dios y del prójimo, escritas, no con la mano de Moisés, sino con el dedo del Espíritu Santo, en su voluntad ....

**Cab10** Cabrera, Alonso de. Excerpt from *Consideraciones del lunes después del Domingo de la Resurrección. Sermones* 499.

Pues esa cruz quebrantó a todos los enemigos; y por eso es cordero y león. Y este venció para abrir el libro y soltar sus sellos. Parece que no es buen orden. Acá primero se abren las manecillas y después el libro, ¿cómo allá lo dicen al revés ... ? Muy bien dice: porque Cristo nuestro bien, encarnando, muriendo, resucitando, subiendo a los cielos, abrió el libro, esto es, mostró con la obra ser en su persona cumplidos estos misterios que en la vieja ley estaban dél pronosticados. Verificólos en el hecho, y después desató los sellos, declarando de palabra a sus apóstoles las Escrituras y dándoles el Espíritu Santo para que las entendiesen.

**Cab11** Cabrera, Alonso de. Excerpt from *Consideraciones del Domingo en la octava de la Pascua de Resurrección. Sermones* 514-15.

Costumbre es entre dos que bien se quieren cuando se ofrece apartarse llevar consigo una sortija o un joyel en que suelen a veces escribir el nombre de su amada, para que esto les sea un perpetuo despertador o libro de memoria que no dé lugar al olvido. Cristo, nuestro bien, enamorado de su Iglesia y de cada una de nuestras almas, habiéndose de apartar della por la presencia visible y subirse al cielo, para mostrar que en él no puede caber olvido de quien bien quiere, lleva su nombre escrito, no en sortijas y joyeles, sino en sus sagrados pies y manos y en su amoroso pecho. Aquellas llagas preciosas que guardó en sus manos son las sortijas; aquella gran abertura del costado, es el joyel donde nos tiene escritos para nunca olvidarse de nosotros. Así lo dice por el profeta Isaías: . . . . *Ecce in manibus meis descripsi te* . . . . ¡Ah, que te tengo escrito en mis manos; no me puedo mirar a ellas sin acordarme de ti! ¿Qué hombre hay tan perdido por los amores de una mujer que consintiese escribir su nombre en su propia carne con un cauterio de fuego como suelen herrar a los esclavos? ¡Oh divino enamorado de nuestras almas, tan perdido . . . por sus amores, que quisiste escribir en tu carne virgínea los nombres dellas con plumas de hierro que son los clavos, y con la tinta, que es tu preciosa sangre, para nunca olvidarte de ellas! . . . . Lo que en la uña se escribe, está muy presente a los ojos y al corazón. Así Cristo tiene todos los nombres en la uña, en sus manos, pies y costado . . . . Escribiónos en las manos, para ayudarnos en nuestras necesidades; escribiónos en los pies, para nunca apartarse de nosotros . . . . En el corazón, para que nunca pierda nuestra memoria. . . . No quiso borrar la escritura de sus clavos, por no borrar el nombre de su esposa; antes la tiene por empresa y no por divisa, que trae por amor de su enamorada. Pues si Cristo te quiere tanto, alma cristiana, que te escribe en sus manos y corazón con plumas de hierro, ¿por qué no le escribirás tú con pluma de amor, estampando su nombre en tu corazón, imprimiéndole en tu pecho, para nunca olvidarte dél?

**Cai1** Cairasco de Figueroa, Bartolomé. Excerpt from "Afeccion cristiana." Castro 2: 481.

Y siempre está brotando documentos,
Palabras, pensamientos y obras buenas.

**Cai2** Cairasco de Figueroa, Bartolomé. Excerpts from "Apariencia santa." Castro 2: 473.

Es la bella Apariencia un sobrescrito
Que declara cuál es y lo que vale
La interna calidad que está encubierta.
. . . .
Aquesta es una carta encarecida
Que escribe de favor naturaleza
A los humanos ojos . . . .

**Cai3** Cairasco de Figueroa, Bartolomé. Excerpt from "Caridad. Otra difinicion." Castro 2: 493.

Dios Caridad se nombra, y el que en ella
Tuviere su alma bella esté seguro
Que a Dios tiene por muro y en él vive,
Y Dios en él se escribe y atesora.

**Cai4** Cairasco de Figueroa, Bartolomé. Excerpt from "Causa pia." Castro 2: 480.

Letrado es la conciencia,
. . . .
Verdad, el escribano,
. . . .
La tinta es dulce llanto,
Y la mano que escribe peticiones
Señala el obrar santo,
Y ellas son oraciones . . . .

**Cai5** Cairasco de Figueroa, Bartolomé. Excerpts from "Constancia virginal.–Viudez.–Voluntad resuelta." Castro 2: 494.

Constancia Virginal es un traslado,
A pocas en la tierra concedido,
Del angélico, firme y puro estado.
. . . .
Es en el bien la Voluntad Resuelta
Correo que despacha entendimiento,
Con cartas de importancia a rienda suelta.

**Cai6** Cairasco de Figueroa, Bartolomé. Excerpt from "Discrecion." Castro 2: 453.

Y están las hojas llenas
De lo que escribe el corazón augusto.

**Cai7**  Cairasco de Figueroa, Bartolomé. Excerpt from "Enmienda." Castro 2: 460.

Hará tal recompensa [el alma],
Representando enmiendas en su abono,
*Che trovará pietá, non che perdono;*
Y no solo en borrar faltas escritas,
....

**Cai8**  Cairasco de Figueroa, Bartolomé. Excerpt from "Gracia. Otra difinicion." Castro 2: 489.

Es un escrito con su firma y sello,
Donde sin obligarle, Dios se obliga
De darle a quien le da su eterna gloria,
....

**Cai9**  Cairasco de Figueroa, Bartolomé. Excerpt from "Honestidad. Otra difinicion." Castro 2: 476.

Y un sobrescrito y admirable sello
De lo que escribe Dios en la conciencia.

**Cai10**  Cairasco de Figueroa, Bartolomé. Excerpt from "Longanimidad." Castro 2: 466.

  Es prueba que la firma el tiempo y sella
De luengo amor y de ánimo constante,
Cual de Jacob con la serrana bella.

**Cai11**  Cairasco de Figueroa, Bartolomé. Excerpt from "Música." Castro 2: 469.

Y siendo *letra* el hombre, el ángel *punto*,
Y el mismo Dios la *clave*,
Ved si será la música suave.

**Cai12**  Cairasco de Figueroa, Bartolomé. Excerpts from "Oracion." Castro 2: 453.

... es un diálogo
Con Dios, por quien nos pone en su catá-
                                   [logo;
....
Y un elegante prólogo
Del libro de la vida ....

**Cai13**  Cairasco de Figueroa, Bartolomé. Excerpt from "Oracion. Otra difinicion." Castro 2: 453.

Es carta de favor, fiel mensajero,
....

**Cai14**  Cairasco de Figueroa, Bartolomé. Excerpt from "Perseverancia." Castro 2: 490.

Si escriben las virtudes una carta
En el papel del alma al Rey divino,
Esta virtud la sobrescribe y sella.

**Cai15**  Cairasco de Figueroa, Bartolomé. Excerpt from "Prision." Castro 2: 468.

  Esta prision es libertad hidalga,
Do al firme se promete ejecutoria,
....

**Cai16**  Cairasco de Figueroa, Bartolomé. Excerpt from "Soledad. Otra difinicion." Castro 2: 478.

Los buenos pensamientos son correos,
Que traen y llevan cartas con buen porte
Desta vida mortal a la suprema,
....

**Cai17**  Cairasco de Figueroa, Bartolomé. Excerpt from "Tranquilidad." Castro 2: 456.

Es una dulce carta,
Que escribe Dios al alma en gran secreto,
....

**Cai18**  Cairasco de Figueroa, Bartolomé. Excerpt from "Victoria." Castro 2: 462.

Es carta ejecutoria de nobleza,
....

**Cai19**  Cairasco de Figueroa, Bartolomé. Excerpt from "A la Cruz bendita." Sancha 310.

Por ti la gloria se nos firma y sella,
....

**Cai20** Cairasco de Figueroa, Bartolomé. Excerpts from "San Dámaso, Papa." Sancha 300.

La Madre virginal del Unigénito,
Visitando la prima, hizo, en viéndola,
Aquel divino canto, en voz clarífica,
De la sacra *Magnifica*,
Escrito en su alma santa con la péndola
Del soberano amor, que del ingénito
Y de su primogénito
Procede, dictador de esta poética;
. . . .
Salió la alta poesia en rico tálamo,
. . . .
Iba escribiendo con un aureo cálamo.
. . . .
Y en tanto que ejercita la aurea péndola,
Están siempre sirviéndola
Gramática, Retórica y Dialéctica,
Mensura, Esfera, Música, Aritmética.

**Ca1** Calderón de la Barca, Pedro. Excerpts from *A María el corazón*. Autos 1140, 1146, 1147, 1148.

Peregrino:
  En la santa
  imagen del crucifijo
  la Ley, pues la cruz la tabla
  es, donde el dedo de Dios
  escribió la ley de Gracia;
. . . .
Soberbia:
  Que templo vivo de Dios
  es el hombre, y más teniendo
  en él sacerdotal orden
  aquel carácter impreso,
  que al alma del alma obliga
  con más perfección a serlo.
. . . .
Peregrino:
  Porque tan grabado
  de María el nombre tengo
  en el corazón . . .
. . . .
Soberbia:
  Calla
  que vivo yo, que he de verlo,
  y como en entrañas, vida,
  alma y corazón impreso
  está el nombre de María.
. . . .

Ya el corazón arrancado
de sus entrañas, no veo
el nombre en él de María,
. . . .

**Ca2** Calderón de la Barca, Pedro. Excerpts from *A tu projimo como a ti* (Primera redacción). Autos 1891, 1906.

Culpa:
  A este fin diversos nombres
  me dan de que son testigos
  tantos sacros textos como
  contiene el cerrado libro
  de quien halla en la escritura
  si a algún águila examino
  Son [sic] Páginas los misterios,
  son los éxtasis registros
. . . .
  y siendo así que de todos
  estos oprovios me miro
  notada en aquel cuaderno
  que abrió a un quaderno los
    signos
. . . .
Sol:
  Que pues vienes a ser Ley
  de mi obedienzia y mi Grazia
  me descubras los secretos
  que en tus archivos se
    guardan
  para la cura del hombre
. . . .

**Ca3** Calderón de la Barca, Pedro. Excerpt from [A] *Tu prójimo como a ti* (Segunda redacción). Autos 1416.

Culpa:
  El Cielo diversos nombres
  me da, de que son testigos
  tantos sacros textos como
  contiene el cerrado libro
  de quien allá en la escritura
  si a alguna Aguila examino
  son páginas los arrobos,
  son los éxtasis registros.

**Ca4** Calderón de la Barca, Pedro. Excerpt from *Amar y ser amado y divina Filotea*. Autos 1787.

Príncipe:
   Quedaos, divinas escuadras,
   que me acompañáis, en esta
   nave que sobre las nubes
   el sol a rayos bosqueja,
   en láminas de zafiros,
   con caracteres de estrellas.

**Ca5** Calderón de la Barca, Pedro. "Loa." *Andrómeda y Perseo. Autos* 1690, 1694.

Dama:
   Silencio, silencio,
   al nuevo cartel
   que publican los vientos.
   ....
   Tú, ilustre Corregidor,
   cuyo acertado gobierno,
   con las plumas de la fama
   tiene que escribir el tiempo,
   ....

**Ca6** Calderón de la Barca, Pedro. Excerpts from *El Año Santo de Roma. Autos* 496, 510.

Amor:
   ... [A]quellos [preceptos]
      solamente
   del Decálogo, que impresos
   más en la Fe que en el mármol,
   siempre han de vivir eternos.
   ....
Hombre:
   [D]e tu piedad, del libro de
      los días
   borra, Señor, iniquidades mías.

**Ca7** Calderón de la Barca, Pedro. Excerpts from *El Año Santo en Madrid. Autos* 539, 547.

Pecado:
   ... [T]estigo,
   sea algún infausto tronco;
   que yerto esqueleto frío,
   entre siempre verdes copas
   es padrón vegetativo,
   en cuya corteza el tiempo
   tiene, a pesar de los siglos,
   con caracteres de arrugas,
   en quebrado idioma escrito:

   Aquí del Género Humano,
   yacen los villanos Hijos
   de Adán, infames pecheros
   ....
   ... Mira en qué instante
   perdió cuanto había adquirido
   en su peregrinación
   el Hombre; un punto indiviso
   bastó a borrarle, con solo
   un deseo consentido,
   méritos de tantos días:
   ....

**Ca8** Calderón de la Barca, Pedro. Excerpts from *El Arbol del mejor fruto. Autos* 989, 993, 994, 995, 996, 1001, 1002.

Salomón:
   ¿Quién soy yo para que vea
   rasgarse ese azul viril
   en iluminadas hojas
   de púrpura y de jazmín?
   ....
Mujer 2a:
   [P]arece que arrancar quiere del pecho
   el corazón.
   ....
Sale Saba, y saca un libro, y están las hojas descuadernadas, de modo que las arroja el aire esparcidas.
Saba:
         Espíritu divino,
   que sin duda en aquesa azul esfera,
   causa de causas, es causa primera,
   ....
   ya que escribir me dejan mis congojas
   en hojas de los árboles, que hojas
   son del papel del viento,
   lo que me dictas, cobrarme en mi alien-
                                    [to,
   para decir, sabed, sabed, mortales,
   que sé de la salud de vuestros males,
   esas líneas que lleva divididas
   el aire, en verde lámina esculpidas,
   misterios comprehenden
   que solo las estrellas los entienden;
   estudiad, pues, en ellas,
   que letras son del cielo las estrellas,
   borrados hallaréis vuestros delitos,
   si alcanzáis los caracteres que escritos
   van en ese cuaderno,

corónica inmortal de Dios Eterno.
. . . .

Idolatría:
[R]ecojamos las hojas y leamos
lo que su vaticinio nos enseña.
. . . .

Todos:
Nada hemos entendido.
. . . .

Idolatría:
    Leyendo todos juntos,
quizá no divididos los asuntos,
podremos de esos modos,
no entendiéndose uno, leerse todos.
. . . .

Saba:
[E]s pregonera la fama
llena de plumas y lenguas,

[Q]ue su mayor excelencia
es el precioso tesoro
de su imperio y de sus ciencias,
en quien dormido volumen
son a un tiempo para ella,
con caracteres de flores,
las pautas de las estrellas.
. . . .

Tú, que de la presencia
oráculo eres vivo,
libro con voz y archivo
en quien la Providencia
supo depositar Poder y Ciencia.
. . . .

[C]onvidada de la fama,
que como antes dije fue
verbal coronista al orbe
de tu ciencia y tu poder,
llega esta vez la no ociosa
curiosidad de mujer,
. . . .

**Ca9**  Calderón de la Barca, Pedro. Excerpts from *La cena del rey Baltasar*. Autos 166, 167, 168, 175, 176, 177.

Daniel:
[N]o quiero, no, que el
    decreto,
del libro que es en rigor
*de acuerdo*, aunque ya en los
    hombres
es *libro de olvido* hoy,

ejecutes . . .
. . . .

Muerte:
Aquí esta la obligación,
en un libro de memorias.
    (Saca un libro de
    memorias.)
. . . .

Baltasar:
"[Y] recibí ( ¡helado estoy!)
una vida, que a la Muerte
he de pagar (¡qué rigor!)
cada y cuando que la pida;
cuya escritura pasó,
ante Moisés, los testigos
siendo Adán, David y Job."
. . . .

Muerte:
[Y] para que se te acuerde
ser, Baltasar, mi deudor,
de la gran Sabiduría
este Memorial te doy.
    (Dale un papel y vase;
    ábrele Baltasar y lee.)

Baltasar:
Así habla en un proverbio
del espíritu la voz:
*polvo fuiste, y polvo eres,*
*y polvo has de ser.* . . .
. . . .

Idolatría:
¿Qué contendrá aquel papel,
que tanto le divirtió
de nosotras?
    (Quítale la Vanidad el
    memorial.)
. . . .

Pensamiento:
[L]a memoria de la Muerte
la Vanidad le quitó.
. . . .

Vanidad:
Hojas que inútiles son,
    (Rompe el papel y
    arrójale.)
el viento juegue con ellas.
. . . .

(Da un gran trueno, y con un cohete de pasacuerda sale una mano y viene a dar donde habrá un papel escrito con unas letras.)

Baltasar:
....
¿Quién vio, quién, rayo
          compuesto
de arterias? No sé, no sé
lo que escribe con el dedo;
porque en habiendo dejado
tres breves rasgos impresos,
otra vez sube la mano
....
Daniel:
Así la mano de Dios
tu sentencia con el dedo
escribió, ...
....
porque ningún mortal use
mal de los vasos del templo,
que son a la ley de gracia
reservado sacramento
cuando se borre la Escrita
de las láminas del tiempo.
....
Idolatría:
Yo, que fui la Idolatría,
que di adoración a necios
ídolos falsos, borrando
hoy el nombre de mí y de
          ellos,
seré Latría ....

**Ca10** Calderón de la Barca, Pedro. Excerpts from "Loa [del juicio de Paris]." *El Cordero de Isaías. Autos* 1744, 1745.

Hombre:
          De mi vida
este penoso Desierto
paréntesis es, y como
que haya de cerrarse espero,
cuando trocado el discurso
vuelva de mi Patria al centro
y paréntesis, es cuasi
síncopa Paris, ...
....
Fe:
[D]el Libro de Siete Sellos,
que ninguno [ha de] abrir, hasta
sacrificado Cordero,
te haré ver a ojos cerrados
los Capítulos abiertos:
y en uno, en sola una blanca

Hoja, el más Alto Misterio
....

**Ca11** Calderón de la Barca, Pedro. Excerpts from *El Cordero de Isaías. Autos* 1763, 1766, 1767.

Behomud:
[O] ver que en iluminados
bríos, esplendor alegre,
en Cordero, Sacrificio
y Paz el Día desplegue,
haciendo de este volumen
las hojas afable Oriente;
....
Pitonisa:
[Y]a que te opones rebelde
a la enseñanza de quien
no solo capaz mantiene
noticia de cuánto oculto
Misterio se encierra en ese
volumen, pero de cuantos,
con azul línea o con verde,
el Cielo señala a luces,
la Tierra a flores guarnece;
....
Behomud:
¿Y qué es Bautismo?
Philipo:
          Una breve
ablución, que aunque exterior
llega al cuerpo, la mantiene
el alma, como Carácter
Sacrosanto e indeleble
que la imprime; ...
....
Pitonisa:
Me dicen que has tocado
el último renglón de
          desdichado;
....

**Ca12** Calderón de la Barca, Pedro. Excerpts from *El cubo de la Almudena. Autos* 567, 568.

Secta [de Mahoma]:
Doblemos aquí la hoja,
mientras sus desdichas digo,
que yo la desdoblaré
antes que se cierre el libro,
que abierto a los dos es ya

volumen de cuatro siglos.
. . . .
Y así, al desdoblar la hoja,
vuelvo a enlazar el principio
. . . .

**Ca13**  Calderón de la Barca, Pedro. Excerpts from *La cura y la enfermedad*. Autos 752.

Sombra:
　　El más bello astro . . .
. . . .
　　saben todos que madrugue
　　mañana a ser otra vez,
　　sin que se le dificulte
　　el mejor párrafo de ese
　　encuadernado volumen.
. . . .
　　No hay parte en que no se
　　　　　　crucen
　　su canto y su vuelo a un
　　　　　　tiempo[;]
　　son[,] al que curioso estudie
　　sus secretos[,] caracteres
　　y vaticinios, si arguyes
　　que no acaso aquellas canten,
　　y no acaso estotras surquen.

**Ca14**  Calderón de la Barca, Pedro. Excerpt from *La devoción de la Misa*. Autos 267.

Conde:
　　Las plumas de aquestas flechas
　　que en vuestro pavés advierto,
　　¿no son con las que la fama
　　ha de escribir vuestros hechos
　　siendo la tinta esa sangre
　　en los anales del tiempo?

**Ca15**  Calderón de la Barca, Pedro. Excerpt from *El día mayor de los días*. Autos 1650.

Noche:
　　Tres enemigos el Trigo
　　tiene, sobre el de mis nieblas,
　　hasta ser Pan: El Primero
　　la langosta, ave tan fiera
　　que Ira de Dios trae en sus alas
　　iluminadas a letras.

**Ca16**  Calderón de la Barca, Pedro. Excerpt from *El divino Jasón*. Autos 64.

Idolatría:
　　[A]migos somos los dos,
　　mi mágica te he enseñado.
　　Sus caracteres oscuros
　　turbarán el Firmamento
. . . .

**Ca17**  Calderón de la Barca, Pedro. Excerpts from *El divino Orfeo* (Primera versión). Autos 1821-22, 1825, 1829.

San Orfeo:
　　Las letras que tú compones
　　de variedades distintas
　　son cielo y tierra; las dos
　　son soberana poesía;
　　verso, y poema, es el cielo,
　　con su acordada armonía;
　　poema y verso es la tierra:
. . . .

Aristeo:
　　Por triunfo tan soberano
. . . .
　　hareis que victoria igual
　　con la pluma de un puñal
　　en las cortezas escriva
　　de estos troncos, porque viva
　　quizá en alguno inmortal.
　　Lámina será tan rara,
　　el papel del tronco herido
　　que el carácter esculpido
　　en la que oy es tierna vara
　　con letra gótica, y clara
　　crezer al paso se vea
　　del árbol, hasta que sea
　　él gigante, ella inmortal,
　　una letra original,
　　que el género humano lea.
. . . .
　　　　(Escóndese en el árbol en
　　　　que está la sierpe.)
. . . .

Eurídize:
　　. . . [D]el estudio
　　del cielo, es rasgo breve,
　　que me dize, que en sí
　　altas ciencias contiene.

**Ca18**  Calderón de la Barca, Pedro. Excerpts from *Los encantos de la Culpa*. Autos 412, 415.

Entendimiento:
  Rasgo de luz, que has corrido
  por las campañas del viento,
  ....
Hombre:
  Fuese, dejándome impreso
  un renglón de tres colores
  en el papel de los Cielos.
  ....
Culpa:
  La grande Quiromancía
  verás, cuando en vivo fuego
  en los papeles del humo
  caracteres de luz leo.
  ....
  De las flores te leeré
  estos escritos cuadernos,
  donde la Naturaleza
  escribió raros misterios.

**Ca19**  Calderón de la Barca, Pedro. Excerpts from *El gran duque de Gandía*. Autos 107, 109, 110.

Hombre:
  Mas, ¡ay!, que enojada vives,
  y así con mi sangre escribes
  mi delito. . . .
Demonio:
  . . . Mis sellos
  haré que en su rostro esculpan.
  ....
  Mi sello pondré en tu frente.
  ....
Hombre:
  Iris que asoma entre
      eclipsados velos,
  carácter a dos líneas reducido,
  ....

**Ca20**  Calderón de la Barca, Pedro. Excerpts from *El gran mercado del mundo*. Autos 227, 229.

El Padre de Familias:
  Entre ellos los dos nacisteis,
  y yo, que a un tiempo me di
  a las ciencias, hacer quise
  una experiencia sutil

de vuestros hados, leyendo
en ese hermoso matiz
de quien la luz es pincel,
de quien la sombra es buril,
vuestros genios . . .
....
Culpa:
  ¿Qué tronco hay en todo el valle
  que en sus cortezas no escriba
  mi nombre, diciendo alguno
  más que otros en sus cifras?
  Vegetativo padrón
  soy, que en el confuso enigma
  de este carácter repito
  el tema; la Culpa viva.

**Ca21**  Calderón de la Barca, Pedro. Excerpts from *El gran teatro del mundo*. Autos 203, 220.

Autor:
  Es tu Autor Soberano.
  De mi voz un suspiro, de mi
      mano
  un rasgo es quien te informa
  y a su oscura materia le da forma.
  ....
Rey:
  ¿Tan presto de la memoria
  que fuiste vasallo mío,
  mísero mendigo, borras?

**Ca22**  Calderón de la Barca, Pedro. Excerpts from *La hidalga del valle*. Autos 115, 116, 117, 118, 119, 121.

Culpa:
  A vuestra naturaleza,
  mi esclava, traigo conmigo,
  herrada con esos duros
  hierros que en su rostro imprimo.
  ....
  Y así, cualquiera embrión,
  ....
  cuando se nombra mi esclavo,
  se confiese mi cautivo,
  ....
  señalado con mis hierros
  y marcado con mis signos,
  ....
Job:
  No te había conocido
  hasta que te vi los hierros

que traes en el rostro escritos,
humana Naturaleza.
Naturaleza:
   Son mis señas, no me admiro;
   . . . .
   ¡Ah del Gran Puebo escogido
   de Jehová, Israel, a quien
   en un terso mármol liso,
   buril el dedo de Dios,
   dejó el Decálogo escrito!
   . . . .
Culpa:
   [A]lgún tiempo, determino,
   que de sus habitadores,
   fiadora salgas, escrito
   dejando en este cuaderno,
   paguen, aunque sean mis hijos;
   . . . .
Gracia:
   [L]uego si ha de reservarse
   algo del incendio altivo,
   mal hará en firmar por todos;
   . . . .
   y así, por todos no tengo
   de obligarme en tus registros.
   . . . .
Culpa:
   ¿Qué importa? Que yo altiva,
         osada y fuerte,
   de esa que humilde está,
         presa y cautiva,
   los triunfos borraré; . . .
   . . . .
   presto en la Concepción haré
         que escriba
   en mi Libro esa Niña el vasallaje
   que debe, por nacer de su linaje.

**Ca23** Calderón de la Barca, Pedro. Excerpts from *La humildad coronada de las plantas*. *Autos* 390, 399, 400, 402.

Espiga:
   [A]quí pendiente una corona
         miro,
   que es en su vago asiento
   imperial jeroglífico del viento.
   . . . .
Moral:
   ¿A quién viene guiado
   este rasgo de luz iluminado?
   . . . .

Encina:
   Dice bien:
   y pues que venimos solo
   a dar nuestros memoriales,
   . . . .
Espino:
   Pues dad vuestros memoriales,
   que yo le daré el mío y todo.
   Sale el Olivo con un memorial
   . . . .
         (Da el memorial de
         rodillas. . . .)
   . . . .
Encina:
   [A]queste es mi memorial.
         (Dale el memorial. . . .)
Cedro:
   Con cuánto temor le tomo;
   pero es fuerza que lo admita,
   puesto que en él reconozco
   . . . .
   viene ya en papel sellado
   con el sello misterioso
   del carácter del Bautismo.
         (Toma el memorial.)
Laurel:
   Yo soy de reinos remotos,
   donde ese papel sellado
   no está admitido.
Cedro:
         Ya noto
   que eres la gentilidad,
   y aunque sin sello le tomo
   para hacer cuanto pudiere,
   gentilidad, en tu abono,
   . . . .
Espino:
   [A] escuchar van los decretos
   de sus memoriales todos
   . . . .
Moral:
   [L]a moral prudencia mía,
   rústicamente cortés,
   te pide en nombre de todos
   que a sus memoriales des
   respuesta . . . .

**Ca24** Calderón de la Barca, Pedro. Excerpts from *El indulto general*. *Autos* 1723, 1725, 1730, 1733.

Culpa:
   [Y] así, vamos recorriendo

las estancias para que
sea, cuando llegue el tiempo,
memoria de sus olvidos
el Libro de mis Acuerdos.
. . . .
David:
De tu Piedad, del Libro de los
           Días.
Música:
De tu Piedad, del Libro de los
           Días.
David:
Borra, Señor, iniquidades mías.
Música:
Borra, Señor, iniquidades mías.
. . . .
Ángel:
[L]a felicísima boda
a que a mi Ser se acomoda,
el tiempo en bronces escriba,
. . . .
Música:
En voz de pregón, que altiva,
el tiempo en bronces escriba,
. . . .
Culpa:
[P]arte tú en su seguimiento
y vuelva yo a mis registros.

**Ca25** Calderón de la Barca, Pedro. Excerpt from "Loa." *La inmunidad del sagrado. Autos* 1111.

Culpa:
[E]l boreal cartel del viento, ha
aplazado el desafío,
. . . .

**Ca26** Calderón de la Barca, Pedro. Excerpts from *La inmunidad del sagrado. Autos* 1116, 1117, 1120, 1121, 1124, 1125, 1126, 1128.

Mundo:
Ya que en cláusulas comunes
de tierra, mar, aire y fuego,
que quiso Dios que circunden
los términos de mi esfera,
quiere también me articulen.

Trae el Libro de la Vida,
en que la partida apunte
de la entrega de este preso.

            (Saca un libro la
             Malicia.)
Malicia:
Aquí está.
Mundo:
           ¡Oh blanco volumen,
en que cuantos nazcan consten,
hasta que su cargo ajusten,
y de la cárcel del mundo
salgan; . . .
. . . .
Culpa:
. . . [P]ues viste el error
del Hombre, su relator
un memorial ajustado
hagas dél.
Lucero:
         ¿Qué error mortal
hay, que en memoria no esté
mía? Poco, o nada haré
en hacer el memorial.
. . . .
Gracia: (Cantando.)
Las nubes, que en sí te
           recatan, despliega
en hojas de rosa, clavel y jazmín.
. . . .
Mercader:
. . . ¿[Q]ué estudiabas?
Gracia:
Las Leyes que he de alegar.
Mercader:
¿Y qué es lo que en ellas hallas?
Gracia:
Nada que no sea en el Hombre
romperlas y quebrantarlas,
pues la natural y escrita
ofendió.
Mercader:
         Esas Leyes pasa,
ve a la tercera, quizá
Texto habrá que satisfaga
la acusación de la Culpa.
Gracia:
Desde aquí las hojas blancas
del libro están todas.
Mercader:
                    Pues
muestra, que Yo he de llenarlas,
cumpliendo de ese Volumen
lo que a la Esperanza falta,
con la nueva Información,
que en Derecho en favor haga

del Hombre; ...
. . . .
Hablan los dos aparte hojeando el libro, y sale el Lucero, y Culpa, con otro libro, hojeándole.
Lucero:
   En fin, Culpa, que no hay
         Tabla
   de Primera y de Segunda
   Ley, que infinito no haga
   del Hombre el delito.
. . . .
Mercader:
   Con eso en la Sala
   alega esta Nueva Ley,
   que a escribir voy ...
. . . .
Culpa:
   [P]ues dijo, que a escribir ...
. . . .
   en el monte se queda,
   Nueva Ley, que la Gracia
         alegar pueda,
. . . .
   [Y]a una vez meditada
   la Ley que ha de escribir, no
         bien cortada
   caña la pluma infiero;
   el papel, la corteza de un
         madero;
   y la tinta, la sangre que derrama.
. . . .
Culpa:
         Aquí en blanco
   está lo demás del libro;
   ¿qué Ley es, que no la hallo?
Sale el Mercader, con una Cruz ...
Mercader:
   La que yo escribí con sangre
   en corteza deste árbol.

**Ca27**  Calderón de la Barca, Pedro. Excerpt from "Loa." *El jardín de Falerina. Autos* 1503.

Tierra:
   Lo humilde de los Vallados,
   de los Montes lo soberbio,
   lo culto de las Ciudades,
   lo inculto de los Desiertos,
   un pautado Libro
   son de Solfa . . . .

**Ca28**  Calderón de la Barca, Pedro. Excerpts from *El jardín de Falerina. Autos* 1511, 1512, 1518, 1520.

Hombre:
   [E]s cuando a la sombra de este
   Arbol defiende en la siesta
   las sañas del Sol; y más
   si advierto que su corteza
   en lo vegetable escribe
   de sus arrugadas quiebras
   algún gran Misterio, pues
   de tres especies compuestas,
. . . .
Gracia:
   Y no para aquí, si adviertes,
   que esas mal formadas letras,
   también en tres lenguas hablan,
   griega, latina y hebrea.
. . . .
Vista:
   En la fiera de sus fieras,
   que ya se sabe que es
   la Hidra, veo que triunfante
   viene una hermosa mujer,
   acompañada de otras.
Gusto:
   Sin duda, dar a entender,
   en metáfora de libro
   de caballería, que es
   alguna Mágica intenta.
. . . .
Culpa:
   [I]nnoble al pie del árbol
   le colocad; sea allí
   padrón vegetativo
   su tronco, en que escribir
   podréis el aquí yace
   quien murió sin morir.
. . . .
Lucero:
   Pues ¿cómo en tus coros entra
   (Culpa) sin que en tus registros
   a ti te conste quién sea?

**Ca29**  Calderón de la Barca, Pedro. Excerpts from *La lepra de Constantino. Autos* 1800, 1803, 1805, 1806, 1811.

Fe:
   ... [Y]a Elena su madre
   en Bretaña ha recibido

aquella indeleble marca
del carácter del bautismo;
. . . .

Aparece un Angel en un iris con la Cruz
en la mano . . . .
Constantino:
 [A]rdiente rasgo de nácar,
 que verde, roxo y pajizo,
 en mi deshecha fortuna
 ser iris de la paz quiso,
 desabrochando del seno
 purpúreas hojas de vidrio,
 iluminadas a líneas,
 . . . .
 Bien, que a despecho de
  tanto
 resplandor, como registro,
 formada cruz veo de fuego,
 . . . .
 ¿qué quiere decirme (¡oh raro
 carácter, que no he entendido!)
 de tu sacra astrología
 el soberano designio?
 . . . .
Ángel: (Cantando.)
 Por la Señal de la Cruz,
 que en líneas de fuego he
  visto,
 líbranos, Señor,
 . . . .
Constantino y Músicos:
 Por la Señal de la Cruz
 que en líneas de fuego vimos,
 líbranos, Señor,
 . . . .
[Preceding lines repeated several
  times]
Maxencio:
 Mas, ¡ay infeliz!, que no
 la causa de mi rugido
 es la ocasión de la fiebre,
 sino aquel astro que miro,
 que impreso en el aire forma
 la viva imagen de Cristo.
 . . . .
Gentilidad:
 [E]se vago carácter de la Cruz,
 que en el aire se vio,
 no ha de valerle . . .
 . . . .
Fe:
 Si el cielo, señor, por causas
 que allá en sus archivos tiene
 arcanamente escondidos,
 . . . .

**Ca30**  Calderón de la Barca, Pedro.
Excerpts from *El lirio y la azucena*.
*Autos* 920, 921, 922, 923, 935.

Discordia:
 [Q]ue teniendo una Ley antes
 y otra después, a ser vengo
 paréntesis de ambas, pues
 a la Natural, siguiendo
 la Escrita y luego a la
  Escrita
 la de Gracia, en sus extremos,
 fronteriza de ambas Leyes,
 estoy de las dos en medio;
 . . . .
 A este fin, yo buscaré
 imaginados pretextos
 . . . .
 . . . fingiendo
 que nos quieren alterar
 las exenciones y fueros
 de la Ley que recibimos
 en Sinaí, monte excelso,
 que es el Libro Verde en que
 se escriben mis Privilegios;
 . . . .
[Brazo] Seglar:
         Sí,
 pues por agua imprimo el sello,
 carácter de nuevo mundo,
 como chanciller supremo
 de las Indias de su Ophir.
 . . . .
Discordia:
 [Q]ue yo atenida a los fueros
 del gran Verde Libro mío
 ni otros admito ni acepto.
 . . . .
Fama:
 [Y] que la Discordia, puesto
 que es alusión de otra Ley,
 pues está en medio de entrambas,
 a entrambas sujeta esté,
 en dos Mandamientos, a uno
 y otro, hasta llegar a diez;
 . . . .
 Con que conservada en Fueros
 del Libro Verde, se ve

obligada a la obediencia
....⁵

**Ca31** Calderón de la Barca, Pedro. Excerpts from *Lo que va del hombre a Dios*. Autos 282, 283, 286, 287, 288, 290, 291, 296.

[S]aldrá a este tiempo [el Pobre] vestido de mendigo, con un plato, y en él, un papel....
Hombre:
 ¿De eso habrá fiador que yo
 le di y le he de recibir?
Pobre:
 Mateo, para pedir,
 esa facultad me dió.
  (Enséñale el papel.)
Hombre:
 Si es el del cambio, ya creo
 su abono.
Pobre:
  Lee, y lo verás.
  (Dásele.)
Hombre: (Lee.)
 "Ciento por uno tendrás
 si das limosna.–*Mateo*."
 ....
Pesar: (Aparte.)
  ¡Ay de ti,
 que ambicioso en esta parte
 prestas, habiendo entendido
 la letra, mas no el sentido!
 ....
Culpa:

 ¡Adüana del día,
 contra los contrabandos de
  la fría
 noche! ¡Lámina bella,
 en quien esculpe la dorada
  huella,
 ya del carro del sol, ya de la
  luna,
 caracteres que lee nuestra
  fortuna,
 siendo de sus iguales
 astros, padrón de bienes y
  de males!
 ....
Hombre:
 Placer, tú lo recibe;
 y tú, para que yo lo pague
  escribe.
  (Al Apetito)
 ....
 ¿Qué monta todo, en fin?
  (Hace que suma la
  cuenta.)
Apetito:
   Cinco talentos,
 mostrando que en poder del
  Apetito...
Músicos:
 Cada deleite cuesta un sentido.
Hombre: (Firma.)
 Firmaré la partida,
 ....
 Ya firmé.
 ....
Príncipe:

---

⁵ The ideas in this excerpt correspond markedly to those articulated in the *Catechism* of the Council of Trent in its discussion of the Decalogue:

> Who is not conscious that a law is inscribed on his heart by God, teaching him to distinguish good from evil, vice from virtue, justice from injustice? The force and import of this unwritten law do not conflict with that which is written. Who is there, then, who will dare to deny that God is the author of the written, as He is of the unwritten law?
> But, lest the people, aware of the abrogation of the Mosaic Law, may imagine that the precepts of the Decalogue are no longer obligatory, it should be taught that when God gave the Law to Moses, He did not so much establish a new code, as render more luminous that divine light which the depraved morals and long-continued perversity of man had at that time almost obscured. It is most certain that we are not bound to obey the Commandments because they were delivered by Moses, but because they are implanted in the hearts of all, and have been explained and confirmed by Christ our Lord. (358-59)

... [C]umpla
la deuda hasta lo que alcance,
pues se obligó en la escritura,
....
Naturaleza:
De mis naturales dotes,
obligada en la Escritura
a las deudas de mi esposo,
....
Culpa:
      Si queda
ya su esposo en prisión,
y ella obligada a la deuda,
¿cómo es posible ...
....
y siendo tan infinito
el alcance de la cuenta,
el que ella le satisfaga?

**Ca32** Calderón de la Barca, Pedro. Excerpts from *El maestrazgo del Toisón*. Autos 907, 908.

Duque [de Austria]:
Tú, Bautista, pues señala
el canciller los despachos
y es quien los firma y los
      marca
con el real sello que imprime
de mi carácter la estampa,
serás su gran canciller,
pues de tu Bautismo de Agua
ha de manar el Bautismo,
que es el carácter del alma.
....
[S]iendo el Bautista el que
      imprima
con el Bautismo la estampa,
que el proceso de la Culpa
Original la deshaga,
dando, como secretario,
de que queda cancelada
Juan el testimonio ....

**Ca33** Calderón de la Barca, Pedro. Excerpt from *Los misterios de la Misa*. Autos 304.

Sabiduría:
Ese libro soberano,
es el libro de Memoria
de Dios, donde su cuidado
tiene asentados y escritos
todos los predestinados;
....

**Ca34** Calderón de la Barca, Pedro. Excerpt from "Loa." *Mística y real Babilonia*. Autos 1044.

Voluntad:
Donde la hermosa azucena,
con divina candidez,
da a su Criador las gracias
en cinco hojas de papel.

**Ca35** Calderón de la Barca, Pedro. Excerpts from *Mística y real Babilonia*. Autos 1054, 1063, 1066.

Idolatría:
El interior oscura
cifra es ...
....
Daniel:
Vive en fe de la esperanza
del *Verbo*, que ha de venir
a redimirla y librarla[,]
de quien hoy es rasgo breve
el que a los tres acompaña,
....
Con que al místico sentido,
reducido en rasgos breves
lo historial, perdón merezca,
....

**Ca36** Calderón de la Barca, Pedro. Excerpts from *La nave del mercader*. Autos 1445, 1448, 1451, 1452, 1462, 1467, 1468.

Culpa:
Que si en sacras lecciones
las vagas ondas son tribulaciones,
no (para algún concepto) sin
      disculpa
marino monstruo, a tribular
      la Culpa
hoy sulca de la vida los
      pasajes.
....
Y es que cuando el hombre
      vuelva
al estado primitivo
de aquella primera Gracia,

candor y yugo sencillo
(borrándole el duro hierro,
que ya mi esclavo le hizo,
. . . .
A este efecto, viendo cuánto
su destrucción solicito,
diversos nombres me dan;
de que son fieles testigos
tantos sacros textos como
contiene el cerrado libro
de quien habiendo inmolado
cordero abierto los signos,
son páginas los arrobos,
son los éxtasis registros;
. . . .
Sale el Tiempo, con una cartera,
y pluma y papel.
Tiempo:
    ¿Qué me quieres?
Hombre:
    Que des fe de que recibo
aquestos cinco talentos,
y que con ellos me obligo...
    . . . .
Tiempo: (Escribe.)
    Así lo escribo,
y de la entrega doy fe,
    . . . .
Hombre:
    Con eso y con que al fin son
prestados bienes, lo afirmo.
            (Hácelo.)
    . . . .
Tiempo, ven, por si pidiere
otra escritura.
Tiempo:
          Es preciso
que si a la tierra te obligas
a volver lo recibido
de la tierra, que es el cuerpo,
hayas de volver lo mismo
al cielo, cuya es el alma.
    . . . .
Hombre:
    ¡Ah del celeste zafiro,
en quien del alma los dotes
tienen su sagrado archivo!
    . . . .
Tiempo:
         ¿Conoces
estas escrituras?
Hombre:
         Mías

son.
. . . .
Tiempo:
    ... Y pues ante mí
las escrituras pasadas
se hicieron, a espaldas de ellas,
para empezar a otorgarla,
pongo la cruz. Di tú ahora
a qué te obligas.
Mercader:
         Bien trazas
el que mi fianza entre
con la cruz a las espaldas.
       (Escribe el Tiempo.)
Pon que me obligo a pagar
las deudas del Hombre, cuantas,
se hallen en las escrituras,
    . . . .
Así lo firmo.–*Segundo Adán*.
           (Firmando.)
    . . . .
[Al Hombre] A mi nave te retira,
y que a ella te lleve aguarda
    [mandamientos de soltura
con su finiquito y carta
de pago.
    . . . .
Tiempo:
    Sabed que suelto y no libre
va debajo de fianza.
Todos:
    ¿Qué fianza?
Tiempo:
          La escritura
Lo dirá.

**Ca37** Calderón de la Barca, Pedro. Excerpts from *No hay más fortuna que Dios. Autos* 615, 624, 632, 633.

Demonio:
    Rásguese de ese tronco
la arrugada corteza,
que fue al Hombre padrón
         vegetativo
y en su cuaderno bronco
la Gran Naturaleza,
con aqueste puñal, verá que
         escribo:
    (Escribe en el tronco.)
*Muerto, aquí yace vivo
todo el Género Humano;*
    . . . .

Discreción:
[S]eas bien venido, donde
hallarás en mis desvelos
participada la varia
lección de que [yo] me aliento.
Entra, pues, en mis estudios,
daráte la Historia en ellos:
para el Bien, los ejemplares;
para el Mal, los escarmientos.
. . . .
Demonio:
¿Cómo capaz del Bien puede
nacer el Hombre, supuesto
que aquel Arbol de la Muerte,
donde escondido el Mal tengo,
tiene en su Padrón escrito
con la pluma de este acero
su Sentencia?
Todos:
    ¿Qué sentencia?
. . . .
Malicia:
*En este árbol yace todo
el Género Humano muerto.*
Discreción:
¿Qué importa, si el de la vida,
. . . .
contra ese Padrón, impreso
tiene en su corteza?
. . . .
Bien:
    Aquí
vive todo el Universo.

**Ca38** Calderón de la Barca, Pedro. Excerpt from *El nuevo hospicio de pobres. Autos* 1206.

Fortaleza:
[T]rayendo el *Ave-María,*
no solo en el alma impreso
por blasón, pero en grabadas
láminas de bronce al pecho,
tenga con su Patrocinio,
Fortaleza contra el tiempo;
. . . .

**Ca39** Calderón de la Barca, Pedro. Excerpt from "Loa." *El nuevo palacio del Retiro. Autos* 133.

Palacio:
    Pero

dime: ¿cómo salvarás
el que siendo esta merced
decreto de un memorial
de amor y pasión que baja
de la Triunfante Ciudad
despachado en toda forma
de la diestra natural
del Poderoso, no tenga
Palacio la principal
parte del sacro registro
de esta gracia?

**Ca40** Calderón de la Barca, Pedro. Excerpt from *El nuevo palacio del Retiro. Autos* 138.

Judaísmo:
[D]e Ley Natural pasé
a estado de Ley Escrita,
cuando en el duro papel
de una piedra Dios redujo
sus Mandamientos a diez
Preceptos, siendo su dedo
de su lámina el cincel.

**Ca41** Calderón de la Barca, Pedro. Excerpts from *El orden de Melchisedech. Autos* 1075, 1076, 1078.

Gentilidad:
    La extraña nueva
de no sé qué pregón, no sé
      qué edicto
en papel de aire con la voz
      escrito,
. . . .
Sinagoga:
¿[Q]ue soy yo la Esposa Osseas
no firma? . . .
. . . .
Emanuel:
[V]iendo en ti,
que hoy a ser infiel acudas,
cómo dudas,
que libre al Contrato quedo,
. . . .
[L]a repugnancia que ha hecho
el Edicto de la Fe,
ella fue
lo que en los dos te ofrecí;
. . . .
Fe:
. . . [Y]o el libro

para todos tengo abierto.
Judaísmo:
   ¿Qué libro es?
Fe:
   En el que escritos
   los predestinados tengo
   y a los prescritos borrados.

**Ca42**  Calderón de la Barca, Pedro. Excerpts from "Loa." *Las órdenes militares. Autos* 1013, 1014, 1015, 1016.

[V]an saliendo los más que puedan con memoriales, detrás la Caridad, en medio de la Fe y la Esperanza; y como los va recibiendo, los va remitiendo, uno a una, y otro a otra . . . .
Uno:
   Este humilde memorial,
   que decretes te suplico,
   . . . .
Caridad:
   . . . [Y] así en tanto
   que estos acuerdos registro,
   id a esperar allá fuera.
   . . . .
   . . . [L]eedme, os digo,
   los memoriales . . .
   . . . .
Fe:
   Este memorial, Señora,
   es el primero que vino.
            (Lee.)
   . . . .
Esperanza:
   Huérfanos de padre y madre,
   la Ronda encontró dos niños
   en la calle de Alcalá
   tan extremamente chicos,
   que apenas en la cartilla
   saben más letra que el
            Christus:
   Pastor y Justo se llaman,
   . . . .
Fe:
   Para aqueste memorial,
   Señora, atención te pido:
   . . . .
Caridad:
            Pues,
   siendo como es ejercicio,
   por estatuto en la Casa
   de mi segundo Francisco

(que por blasón a las puertas
tiene Caridad escrito)
enterrar ajusticiados;
¿cómo han tardado remisos
sus congregantes? . . . .

**Ca43**  Calderón de la Barca, Pedro. Excerpts from *Las órdenes militares. Autos* 1018, 1022, 1024, 1025, 1026, 1028, 1029, 1030, 1031, 1032, 1033.

Culpa:
   Yo, aquel padrón, que a la
            muerte
   de verdes hojas de un leño
   le encuaderno en este libro
   todos los humanos pechos
   del villanaje de Adán,
   para ir cobrando sus feudos.
   . . . .
   [P]ues de un joven nazareno,
   haber puesto en los padrones,
   que dije, de los pecheros
   villanos hijos de Adán,
   la partida, no me acuerdo.
(Hojea el libro, y como que va a escribir en él, con los cendales asidos a la pluma, mancha una hoja.)
   Y cuando para anotarla,
   buscándola, no la encuentro,
   solo saco haber manchado
   la turbación el cuaderno.
   . . . .
Segundo Adán:
   Si por mí no me conoces,
   conóceme por mis hechos.
   Estos los papeles son,
   y fes de Oficios del tiempo
   que milité en tus campañas.
(Van dando memoriales, como lo dicen los versos.)
   . . . .
   Con que yo a quien . . .
   de aquella ruina la memoria
            aflige,
   no solo he de borralla,
   mas tanto he de ilustralla,
   que exaltando el madero, hacer
            sospecho
   la infamia de la espalda honor
            del pecho.
   . . . .
Oyendo el pregón, sale la Gracia, por

una parte, y la Naturaleza por otra,
ambas con dos memoriales.
. . . .
Gracia:
   En este Origen presento.
Naturaleza:
   Traigo en este memorial.
. . . .
Gracia:
   Estos los lustres altivos
   son de su Divinidad.
(Da el memorial al Judaísmo.)
Naturaleza:
   Y estos por la Humanidad
   son los actos positivos
   de su limpieza y nobleza.
(Da el memorial al Judaísmo.)
[*Judaísmo* and *Gentilidad* read the *memoriales* throughout the rest of the scene.]
Culpa:
   . . . [N]adie ha nacido
   (sino él) que yo no le tenga
   asentado en este libro.
   Siendo así, ¿quién le habrá dado
   el ser, sin ser comprendido
   en el pechado tributo
   del padrón de mis registros?
. . . .
Culpa:
              (Hojea el libro.)
. . . .
   En la plana que juzgué
   que la había (¡ay de mí!) visto
   la tinta cayó, y no deja
   leerse; con que no distingo
   si es su nombre, o no es su
                  nombre
   el que está escrito, y no
                  escrito.
. . . .
   Un borrón no deja
   verse el nombre bien distinto.
Naturaleza:
   ¡Ay, que no es eso!
Culpa:
     ¿Pues qué es?
Naturaleza:
   Es que es por no haber caído
   en ella, Culpa, el borrón,
   cayó el borrón en el libro.
. . . .
Culpa:
   Y así, con un memorial

tengo de ver si consigo
el deslucirle en lo humano
pues no puedo en lo divino.
. . . .
[V]ense sentados Moisés y Josué, teniendo delante un bufete con recado de escríbir . . . .
([Josué] Dale [a Job] un memorial, léele para sí, y prosigue luego.)
Job: (Leyendo.)
. . . .
Moisés:
   Firmad, e id en paz.
              (Firma, y vase.)
. . . .
              (Lee [Isaías] para sí, y
              dice luego. . . . Firma y
              vase.)
. . . .
Culpa:
   Lo que yo puedo decir
   dirá aquese memorial.
              (Deja un memorial en el
              bufete, y vase.)
. . . .
Josué:
   Aunque con firma no viene,
   veamos lo que contiene
   el memorial que dejó.
Moisés: (Leyendo.)
. . . .
Josué:
   ¿Qué haremos en duda igual,
   los dos con aquestas nuevas?
Moisés:
   Llevar cerradas las pruebas,
              (Hace un pliego.)
   incluso este memorial,
. . . .
Judaísmo:
   . . . [M]ientras leamos,
   vuestros informes oigamos.
(Lee Judaísmo y Gentilidad para sí.)
. . . .
Inocencia:
   Que habiendo visto las pruebas,
   aunque la Gentilidad
   suspendió su voto en ellas,
   el Judaísmo le puso
   la Cruz; . . .
. . . .
Naturaleza:
   ¿Cómo a despacharle llegan,

puesto que la Antigua Ley
aun no ha pasado a la Nueva,
sin que esté en la información
la fe del Bautismo puesta?
. . . .
Gracia:
Cédula de Comunión,
que también llevar es fuerza,
¿quién se la dio?

**Ca44**  Calderón de la Barca, Pedro. Excerpts from *El pastor Fido. Autos* 1587, 1592, 1593.

Luzbel:
[Y] más si a dos Juanes veo,
. . . .
voz de los desiertos uno,
con el índice del dedo
decir: El Cordero es este,
que a quitar del universo
viene los pecados; y otro,
escritor de otros desiertos.
El Cordero, que inmolado
estaba en el ara puesto,
solo abrir pudo el cerrado
Libro de los Siete Sellos,
. . . .
¡Oh Humana Naturaleza,
. . . .
Un pobre Pastor, a quien
su patria arroja de sí,
. . . .
con genio tan querubín
que su aprender fue idear
y su estudiar esculpir,
tan a no borrar, que una
vez llegado a concebir
el concepto, fue carácter,
que al ábrego más sutil,
aunque le malogre el fruto,
no le arranque la raíz.

**Ca45**  Calderón de la Barca, Pedro. Excerpts from *El primer refugio del hombre y probática piscina. Autos* 977, 978, 980, 981.

Afecto 1 [vestido a lo judío]:
Pues siendo así, saber quiero
con qué pasaporte vienes,
peregrino y extranjero,
a estas provincias.

Peregrino:
    Aquí
estos testimonios tengo.
(Saca la cartera y de ella los testimonios, que va dando y los lee el Afecto 1.)
. . . .
Afecto 1 :
Pero yo me cobraré
para concluirte, haciendo
experiencias que me digan
si son o no verdaderos
los testimonios que rompo,
pues que no los obedezco.
(Vase rompiendo los testimonios.)
. . . .
Afecto 4 [vestido a lo romano]:
Pues hay más
. . . .
. . . que yo,
. . . .
. . . te ofrezco
con las letras y las armas
ejercitar los decretos
de tu soberbia y mi ira?
. . . .
(Hinca el peregrino la rodilla y escribe en la tierra.)
Demonio:
La rodilla inclina al suelo,
hecha lámina la tierra,
bien como buril el dedo
en ella escribe.

**Ca46**  Calderón de la Barca, Pedro. Excerpts from *Primero y segundo Isaac. Autos* 801, 814.

Duda:
Pues ese, que a escalar
    sube,
. . . .
de sus verdes pompas los
    campos azules,
teatro hoy del mayor, más grave
espectáculo que esculpe
en los cuadernos del tiempo,
del tiempo el veloz volumen,
. . . .
Rebeca:
[Y]o he llegado la postrera.
Teuca:
¿Qué importa, si en ti se rasga
la ley general de todas?

**Ca47** Calderón de la Barca, Pedro. Excerpt from "Loa. La fábrica del navío." *La protestación de la Fe. Autos* 727.

Cuidado:
    Aunque se lave las manos
    el que aqueste mote ha escrito,
    tan negra es su tinta, que
    no tendrá los dedos limpios.

**Ca48** Calderón de la Barca, Pedro. Excerpts from *La protestación de la Fe. Autos* 734, 737, 738, 742.

Sabiduría:
    Quizá Cristina, que el nombre
    hoy imperfecto conserva
    de Cristiano, mal viciado
    por la falta de una letra
    (siendo la A la que falta,
    que es la Alfa en frase griega
    significación de Dios,
    pues Dios es Alfa y Omega)
    podrá ser que se le añada
    algún día . . .
    . . . .
Cristina:
    [V]as desplegando a tu fin,
    entre rasgos de carmín,
    hojas de jazmín y rosa.
    . . . .
    . . . ¡Oh carta digna,
    que en corazones que son
    más que los bronces, se
            imprima!
    . . . .
Religión:
    Como ya Cristina
    (tú lo dijiste), a quien falta
    una letra para ser
    perfectamente Cristiana,
    siendo Alfa la letra, viene
    buscando a Dios, a buscarla,
    . . . .

**Ca49** Calderón de la Barca, Pedro. Excerpts from "Loa." *Psiquis y Cupido* (Madrid). *Autos* 362, 363, 364, 365, 366.

Sale Emanuel en cuerpo, con un Cáliz . . . y en el cáliz ha de estar preso un papel en forma de memorial . . . .
Música:
    En el altar, que es hoy paraíso,
    un memorial de un soldado diviso,
    que con tener escritos milagros,
    es memorial que le vemos en
            blanco.
Emanuel:
    Fe mía, ¿qué es lo que ves
    en aqueste altar, teatro
    del memorial misterioso
    de mi pasión?
Fe:
    . . . .
    [E]s memorial de vuestras finezas,
    [que con tener escritos milagros,
    es memorial que la Fe le ve
            en blanco.
    Leo que a campaña sales,
    soldado el más soberano;
    . . . .
(Llega al Cáliz, y toma el memorial, y hace que lee.)
    Este memorial me dice,
    te vista a mi modo . . .
    . . . .
            Yo pretendo
    vestir de pasión y gozo,
    de dolor y contento,
    a *Emanuel*, que es un soldado
    de quien en mis manos tengo
    este memorial que ves,
    y por él me pide aquesto.
    . . . .
Entendimiento:
    . . . [D]e aqueste memorial
    oigamos qué dice el dueño.
    . . . .
Fe:
    Atienda ahora el discreto
    y verá cómo se lee
    del memorial el misterio.
    . . . .
(Saca el Judaísmo el título de la fuente . . . y le lee la Gentilidad; ha de estar escrito con estas cuatro letras: I.N.R.I.)
Judaísmo:
    Pues has dado en que ha de serlo,
    de Rey el título grande
    a Emanuel darle pretendo:
    éste es el título.
Gentilidad:
            Y dice

así: Jesús Nazareno,
Rey de los judíos.
....

Entendimiento:
Este es el renglón postrero
de este memorial divino.
....

Pues leído está con esto,
todos a este material[6]
de adoración el decreto
demos postrados....

**Ca50**   Calderón de la Barca, Pedro. Excerpts from *Psiquis y Cupido* (Madrid). *Autos* 368, 383, 384.

Amor:
Como [ley] natural, dictamen
no hubo para su impresión
menester más que la tierna
lámina del corazón.
Odio:
La Escrita, como más dura,
más áspera, se imprimió.
Amor:
En mármoles de quien fue
buril el dedo de Dios.
....
Hebraísmo:
[L]e daré muerte cruenta
por tal escándalo.
Gentilidad:
    Y yo
te firmaré la sentencia.

**Ca51**   Calderón de la Barca, Pedro. Excerpts from *Psiquis y Cupido* (Toledo). *Autos* 348.

Apostasía:
... [E]s [la Fe] de quien yo
    enamorado,
viví un tiempo a sus leyes
    ajustado,
y aun hasta ahora la quiero,
que fue mi amor carácter al
    primero

paso que di...
....
Fe:
[T]odavía traes señales
de quién eres, y te veo
el carácter del Bautismo
indeleblemente impreso
en el alma.

**Ca52**   Calderón de la Barca, Pedro. Excerpt from *¿Quién hallará mujer fuerte? Autos* 675.

Sísara:
¡Ay de mí! No siento, no,
tanto el morir, como a manos
de una mujer, con baldón
tan vil, como que vea el mundo
clavo en mi frente, y que hoy
muera con señas de esclavo
el que ayer era señor.
....
Débora:
[C]omo profetisa, estoy
viendo en aquel misterioso
jeroglífico, un borrón,
un rasgo, un viso, una seña,
....

**Ca53**   Calderón de la Barca, Pedro. Excerpt from *La redención de cautivos. Autos* 1331.

Gracia:
Pues feliz mata, en fecundo
nuevo plantel de los cielos,
de azul, y rojo matiz
produjo una flor, que al pecho
víctima es del corazón,
en sus hojas escribiendo
orden especial de Dios,
dada, y dedicada a él mesmo.
....
[C]on sus limosnas acudan;
y principalmente aquellos,
que de las mandas forzosas,

---

[6] The final lines in this passage allude to the concept of matter in the sense in which it is used in sacramental theology. In the sacrament of the Eucharist the matter is twofold, the first element being wheaten bread, the second, wine pressed from the fruit of the vine (*Catechism* 150, 219, 221).

tienen a cargo el acuerdo
conservando en sus registros
testimonios verdaderos
de Ley Natural y Escrita.

**Ca54**  Calderón de la Barca, Pedro.
Excerpts from *El sacro Parnaso*. *Autos*
786, 787.

S. Agustín:
... [R]eclinarme quiero,
para hacer en este libro
de memoria apuntamientos.
    (Siéntase y saca un
    libro de memoria.)
....
    (Escribe.)
....
    (Cáesele el libro.)
....
Mas ¡ay! ¿Qué mucho, si el
    libro
de memoria perdí? Pero
¿qué me aflijo? ¿Qué me
    espanto?
....
[S]i quizá le he dado a logro,
pues en lugar de que pierdo
el libro de la memoria,
hallo el del entendimiento,
según me ilumina
hoy un rayo bello,
....[7]

**Ca55**  Calderón de la Barca, Pedro.
Excerpts from *El santo rey don Fernando (Primera parte)*. *Autos* 1273, 1274, 1278, 1280, 1281.

Sale el Hebraísmo alborotado, con un libro de Tablas....
Hebraísmo:
    [Y] rasgándose las fieras,
    empedernidas entrañas,
    hallé, que contenía dentro
    de madera aquestas tablas,
    hechas en forma de libro;[8]
....
Tres hojas tiene, que escritas
están en tres lenguas varias,
y no atreviéndome a leerlas,
aún no he hecho más que
    mirarlas.
    (Dale el libro.)
Rey:
Con los principios que yo
tengo de letras humanas,
los caracteres conozco,
y no más; esta es romana
forma, y su frase latina;
esta es griega; y esta
    hebraica.
....
Nada yo a este libro debo,
pues que no me enseña nada,
que yo no sepa: tan fijas
en mi corazón se estampan
sus Verdades...
....
[S]é, que más firme las graba
en mis entrañas la Fe,
que la peña en sus entrañas.
Toma allá, hebreo, tu libro,
de tus ojos me le aparta;
pues que tú le has menester,[9]
....

---

[7] Here the *libro de memoria*, especially because of the contrast with *libro de entendimiento*, seems to be closely associated with reason and logic, which must ultimately surrender to faith. Carruthers cites Augustine's *Confessions*: "How shall I reach God? he asks. 'I shall pass through ... even this power of mine which is called memory; I shall pass through it to reach Thee, sweet Light'" (199).

[8] The book discovered by *Hebraísmo* is reminiscent of the wax tablet referred to by Plato, which Carruthers describes as follows: "The tablet on which the wax is spread ... is the pair (though sets of as many as ten have been found) of wooden slabs fastened together, familiar to every ancient student" (22).

[9] This segment is reminiscent of the high value placed on memory in medieval culture, long after the increased use and availability of books, beginning in the eleventh century. The fifteenth-century Italian jurist Peter of Ravenna boasts of lecturing more accurately and completely from his memory than he could by depending on a book. "The primary factor in its conservation lies in the identification of memory with the formation of moral virtues" (Carruthers 109, 156).

¡Oh Señor, si a tu suma
                    Providencia
tal vez rastreara el Hombre
                    los motivos,
y abiertos de tu Seno los
                    Archivos,
leyera un punto el Libro de
                    tu Ciencia!
. . . .
Rústico:
                              Es,
que un anciano hebreo, que era
en su Ley Doti-Rabillo,
halló un Libro de Madera;
y como a los niños suelen
poner el Cristus en ella,
él en ella aprendió el Cristus.
. . . .
Hebraísmo:
                         Como
el Cielo para mí ordena,
que se abra un risco, que el
                    risco
dé un Libro, y que el Libro
                    venga
a manos de un Rey . . . .

**Ca56**   Calderón de la Barca, Pedro. Excerpts from *La segunda esposa y triunfar muriendo. Autos* 437, 438, 439.

Pecado:
            Pues ¿cómo
el hierro, que yo le imprimo,
podrá borrársele nadie?
. . . .
(Echale agua [al Hombre] y quítasele el hierro.)
¡ . . .
[C]on otro carácter veo
borrado el carácter mío!
. . . .
Hombre:
¿El Bautismo perdí?
Bautismo:
                         No,
que el carácter que te dimos,
fijo se queda en el alma.
. . . .
Hombre:
No quiero sino llorarlos [vicios],
. . . .
        por ver si segunda vez

con agua también te rindo;
porque si aquella primera
el hierro me borró esquivo,
. . . .
Pecado:
Yo también, porque segunda
vez no suceda lo mismo,
haré del hierro cadenas,
. . . .
una vez, porque le ato,
y otra vez, porque le imprimo[.]
[H]uye ahora.

**Ca57**   Calderón de la Barca, Pedro. Excerpts from *La serpiente de metal. Autos* 1530.

Moisés:
No os lo cuento, que os lo
                    acuerdo,
a efecto de que no ha habido
mejor arte de memoria,
de voluntad mejor libro
para el agradecimiento,
que acordar el beneficio,
. . . .
María:
Viendo, Moisés, cuánto aceptas
hoy el júbilo por digno,
. . . .
en celebración de ser
día de Dios tan benigno,
que su nombre la memoria
conservará en sus archivos,
. . . .

**Ca58**   Calderón de la Barca, Pedro. Excerpt from "Loa." *La siembra del Señor. Autos* 679.

Invierno:
. . . [V]iene
a ser Madre y quedar Virgen,
siempre Intacta y Pura sempre,
siendo el día de la O
jeroglífico que quiere
decir integridad, puesto
que en su Expectación la tiene,
y es la O letra que no dice
dónde acabe o dónde empiece.

**Ca59**   Calderón de la Barca, Pedro. Excerpt from *El socorro general. Autos* 319.

Bautismo:
  El Bautismo,
  primer Sacramento suyo,
  a cuyo cargo los libros
  de sus ejércitos vienen,
  pues yo sus gentes alisto.

**Ca60** Calderón de la Barca, Pedro. Excerpt from *Sueños hay que verdad son*. *Autos* 1214.

Copero:
  La buena presencia es
  el sobrescrito primero
  de las cartas de favor,
  que escribe piadoso el cielo,
  . . . .

**Ca61** Calderón de la Barca, Pedro. Excerpts from *El tesoro escondido*. *Autos* 1667, 1679.

Abrese un carro, y se ve en él pintada una librería, y en medio un bufete, y estará sentado el Gentilismo[.]
Gentilismo:
  . . . .
  De esta, pues, causa, habiendo mi cui-
                                              [dado
  las lejanas noticias de un traslado,
  no encuentro en su lectura
  ápice que no sea,
  o rasgo, o viso, símbolo, o figura
  de otra apartada idea
  de los dioses que adoro,
  pues cuanto más la leo más la ignoro.
  Y pues cuanto desea
  averiguar mi espíritu es en vano;
  volumen soberano,
  . . . .
  ¿Qué me quieres decir, voz no entendida?
  Paréntesis tu sueño es de mi vida.
  . . . .
  ¡Ah de la feliz Arabia
  Corte del indiano Imperio
  a quien en Oriente el Sol
  corona de sus primeros
  celajes, siendo sus montes
  al rayar el alba en ellos
  claros prólogos del día!

Calderón de la Barca, Pedro. Excerpt from *Tu prójimo como a ti* (Segunda redacción). SEE: [A] *Tu prójimo como a ti*.

**Ca62** Calderón de la Barca, Pedro. Excerpts from *La vacante general*. *Autos* 475, 477, 478, 482, 487.

Iglesia:
  Leyes Naturales, Leyes
  Sobrenaturales; pero
  no visiblemente escritas,
  ni dadas en aquel tiempo,
  sino impresas en el Alma,
  con los caracteres cuerdos
  de Gracia y Naturaleza.
  Mas . . .
  . . . dispuso el cielo
  que hubiese siempre visibles
  oráculos verdaderos
  a quien todos consultasen.
  . . . .
Diego:
                Juan,
  con la pluma de ese remo,
  en el papel de las ondas
  dejarás tu nombre impreso,
  si de la mareta vences
  con él los embates.
  . . . .
Judaísmo:
              Mucho lo temo
  oír metáforas de pluma,
  cuando de David me acuerdo;
  . . . .
Pablo:
  Decidme, humildes pobres
                     pescadores,
  . . . .
  ¿qué maravilla sea
  la de un público edicto,
  en papel de aire, con la voz
                          escrito,
  . . . ?
Aparece la Iglesia en un trono con un libro en la mano, corona y cetro[.]
  . . . .
Emanuel:
  Los puntos nos da
  a todos que hemos de leer
  nueva deidad de la Ciencia.
Iglesia:
  Ten tú este libro, Inocencia.
              (Dale el libro.)

Inocencia:
    ¿Qué libro es este?
Iglesia:
            El que ser
    mereció por su presencia
    de memoria, en que asentados
    están los predestinados.
Inocencia:
    De casos es de Conciencia.
Iglesia:
    Llegad, que porque malicia
    no se arguya al elegir,
    la Inocencia le ha de abrir
    y yo he de guardar justicia.
    . . . .
            Abre, Inocencia,
    ese libro de la Ciencia,
    y para leer y argüir
    da los puntos a los dos
    . . . .
Judaísmo [a Emanuel]:
            (Dale una cruz.)
    Toma, toma, que ésta es
    la cátedra que yo pierdo
    y tú ganas.
    . . . .
    ¿Quién sabrá si es Oriente o
            si es ocaso
    aquél, porque mezclándose a
            porfía
    en cifra el sol hoy nos ha escrito
            el día?
    Cobarde el mar, las verdinegras
            plumas
    que le rizan, fingiendo
            hermosos mayos,
    ansimismo abrevio, porque entre
            sumas
    angustias teme . . . .

**Ca63** Calderón de la Barca, Pedro. Excerpts from *El valle de la zarzuela. Autos* 702, 703.

Demonio:
    ¿ . . . [E]sa dorada copa,
    de sangre de áspides llena,
    es un emblema que dice
    lisonja a un tiempo y ofensa?
    . . . .
Culpa:
    Venid; que la sed
    satisface esta copa,
    . . . .
    pues de la mujer y el vino
    jeroglífico me veis.

**Ca64** Calderón de la Barca, Pedro. Excerpt from *El veneno y la triaca. Autos* 183-84.

Lucero:
    Si de este honor soberano
    logro el favor que apetezco,
    . . . .
    haréis que victoria igual,
    con la pluma de un puñal
    en las cortezas escriba
    de algún tronco, donde viva
    su carácter inmortal.
    Lámina será tan rara
    el papel del tronco herido,
    que ni trofeo esculpido
    en la que hoy es tierna vara,
    con letra gótica y clara,
    callar el paso se vea
    del árbol, hasta que sea
    él gigante, ella inmortal,
    un padrón original
    que el género humano lea.

**Ca65** Calderón de la Barca, Pedro. Excerpts from *El verdadero Dios Pan. Autos* 1241, 1246, 1251.

Pan:
    [L]eyendo en ese azul campo
            de yelo
    caracteres que en líneas
            desiguales
    dispensan ya el favor o ya el
            desvío,
    . . . .
Gentilidad:
    . . . [P]arece,
    si el deseo no me engaña,
    que boreal, diáfana nube,
    los azules velos rasga;
    y desplegando las hojas,
    . . . .
Luna:
    [Q]ue no desluce el borrón
    los primores, que antes
            llenos
    de mil aciertos verás,
    pues donde se borra más,
    es donde se yerra menos.

**Ca66** Calderón de la Barca, Pedro. Excerpt from *El viático cordero*. *Autos* 1176.

Finés:
   Esto digo, porque vean,
   quitando la *S*, a mis celos,
   y poniéndomela al rostro,
   que esclavo de noble dueño
   mis motivos sin la *S*,
   no son celos, sino celo
   de la honra de Dios ....

**Ca67** Calderón de la Barca, Pedro. Excerpt from *La vida es sueño* (Primera redacción). *Autos* 1864.

Verbo:
   [Y] leyendo mi conzepto,
   que son los mejores libros
   donde están todas las cosas
   asentadas por registro,
   ....

**Ca68** Calderón de la Barca, Pedro. Excerpts from *La vida es sueño* (Segunda redacción). *Autos* 1390-1391, 1398, 1399.

Sabiduría:
   Yo, que sé todas las
            Ciencias,
   de que son fieles testigos
   los astros, pues que no hay
   en todo ese azul zafiro,
   encuadernado volumen
   de quien el Sol es registro,
   ninguno que por su nombre
   no llame, adverso o propicio.
   ....
   Habiendo con mi presencia
   en ese dorado Libro
   de once hojas de cristal,
   previsto al Hombre, ...
   ....
Sombra:
   Soy, no tan solo en la Tierra
   agricultora, que estudia
   esmerar sus obras; pero
   tan sabia, que en ella apura,
   y en los demás elementos,
   las cualidades ocultas.
   Caracteres para mí

en valles, montes y grutas,
son sus plantas[;] las estrellas,
en su campana cerúlea,
mis Oráculos de Fuego
son: del Agua las espumas
mis libros; y porque lea
lo que sus vuelos anuncian,
siendo para mí del año
cualquiera estación fecunda,
los pájaros en el viento
forman Abriles de plumas.

**Ca69** Calderón de la Barca, Pedro. Excerpts from *La viña del Señor*. *Autos* 1481, 1482, 1487, 1488, 1492, 1499.

Padre [de Familias]:
   Planté, para mi recreo,
   esa viña, que en la tierra
   verde pedazo es de cielo.
   ....
   La elegí, no sin misterio,
   para cláusula primera
   de mi último testamento,
   ....
   ¿No te has resuelto?
Hebraísmo:
         Sí.
Padre:
         ¿En qué?
Hebraísmo:
         En firmar el contrato.
Padre:
   Y para su cumplimiento,
   ¿quién te ha de fiar?
Hebraísmo:
            Mi esposa,
   que es la Sinagoga, ofrezco
   que se obligue con su dote,
   ....
   [A Isaías] Tomarás la razón, para
   ajustar después la cuenta.
   ....
      ¡Ay, que es fuerza
   cumplir lo que contraté!
   ....
      ¡Oh justa pena
   del que ofrece o firma, antes
   de ver qué firme o qué
                  ofrezca!
   ....
Fe:

El tercer tesoro, que es
la ley escrita en el mármol,
toca a la Fe; y así, yo
la represento, pasando
los preceptos de la escrita
a la de Gracia....

**Cam** Camós, Marco Antonio de. Excerpt from *Microcosmia* 4-5 [Parte Tercera].

BENA[VENTE]. [S]olamente ay vna luz que no fue encendida jamas,... y este es Dios, por naturaleza vniuersal señor y Monarcha del Cielo y dela Tierra.... VALDI[GLESIA]. Y a ymitacion suya... ay vn Monarcha Espiritual solo en el mundo, vna ley, vna fe, vn baptismo... y por consiguiente vna manera de gouierno vniuersal y Monarchico. Esta verdad nos enseña, la misma naturaleza: siendo el Cielo, y el mundo, y las criaturas que en los Cielos y la Tierra se descubren, vn libro que no trata de otra cosa sino declararnos esta marauillosa vnidad, vnica y diuina Monarchia. Assi lo dixo sant Anthonio respondiendo a quien le pregentaua [sic] como podia viuir solo y sin companya en el desierto. BEN[AVENTE]. No hizo mucho en dezir esto vn sancto, que vn Philosopho lo dixo: toda esta machina del mundo (dixo el Trismegistra Mercurio) su diuersidad, su orden y su hermosura, nos da materia de contemplar a Dios y su gouierno: puesto que esto todo, y con ello la mesma naturaleza, es como vn libro lleno de diuinidad, y vn espejo de cosas diuinas, y de las marauillas que a la vnidad de vn Dios y su Monarchia se reduzen. VAL[DIGLESIA]. Demos agora de mano a los Philophos [sic], pues tenemos testimonios muchos de sanctos: entre los cuales es S. Basilio, que al mundo todo llamo libro escrito, que descubre las marauillas de vn solo Dios. Sant Ioan Damasceno dize estas palabras: la orden y concierto vniuersal que naturaleza creada guarda en si, es vn libro: del qual vsa bien el que conosce ser todas las cosas participantes del que es vno en ser, llamadas por el al ser que tienen y de que gozan. Sant Augustin dize que las criaturas, son vozes que dizen y testiguan vn solo Dios y su gloria: lo que aprendio enseñado de Dauid por boca del Spiritu Sancto, quando dixo, que en los cielos y en las obras que aca baxo se nos descubren, se lee la gloria que ellos manifiestan y dizen, de esse solo Dios: y del Apostol sant Pablo que dixo esto mesmo. No solamente, las criaturas solas hazen vn libro, que declara las marauillas de vn solo Dios: pero es esse Dios tan amigo de la vnidad ... que las criaturas y el mundo todo con el vno, hazen vn solo libro.... Segun comenzo por el su Euangelio el Euangelista sant Matheo, intitulando a esse Dios y sus obras y marauillas, libro de la generacion. Es verdad que este libro (segun testigua sant Ioan, que en espiritu leyo en el) esta escrito por dedentro, y por defuera.... Fue necessario, que este libro fuesse escrito por las cubiertas del, y por la enquadernacion: para que pues no podemos en esta vida leer en lo de dentro (por estar cerrado y sellado) hasta que, desatados deste mortal cuerpo, se quiten los impedimentos ... conoscamos por lo escrito en las cubiertas (como por las doraduras y lindezas de la enquadernacion la excellencia del libro) por las criaturas al criador: y por su orden, el que Dios señor y criador de ellas guarda: y por su gouierno de naturaleza, el que tiene de autor de essa naturaleza. Ora vamos letreando y leyendo en las cubiertas de este libro, y sacando por las cosas deste mundo la vnidad de Dios y de su Monarchia....

**Car** Cardoso, Fernando. Excerpt from *Oracion funebre*. Vega Carpio. *Coleccion de las obras sueltas* 489-90.

Manzanares, que ya suspenso, fue cuidadoso oyente de su lyra.... Lope se lee en los arboles, donde celebró lo ameno de su soto. Lope en las plantas, donde pintó lo agradable de sus flores. Lope en las arenas, donde estampó lo respetoso de sus pisadas. Toda la ribera se matiza de Epigramas y Epitaphios. En las hojas de algunas plantas se lee: Aquí cantó los amores de *Angelica*: aquí las ternuras de *Arcadia* .... En las violetas se estampan los dolores de las *Rimas humanas*, y en las azucenas los contentos de las *Divinas*. La corona de

rey encierra quantas historias de coronas
cantó con dulzura; y el cypres quantas
tragedias de heroes lloró con desengaño
.... Otras publican: Aqui disfrazado pulsó
las cuerdas de varios instrumentos en *Canciones* graves, y en *Eglogas* pastoriles.

**Cas** Castilla, Antonio de. Excerpts from *Al nacimiento del Hijo de Dios*. Fernández, J. 344, 347-48.

San Miguel:
    No huyais, y t[ú] fiera esfinge
    qu[é] intentas en este prado,
    donde ya los Serafines
    están inundando glorias;
    donde los Cielos escriuen
    agregaciones de Parques,
    multitudes de pensiles?
    ....
    No sabes que aqueste prado,
    con plumas de dos en dos
    escriue, aqui nace Dios
    para dar muerte al pecado?

**Cstj1** Castillejo, Cristóbal de. Excerpt from "Consiliatoria." Castro 1: 233.

Aunque haya sido privado,
Ya para siempre jamás
Queda del libro borrado.

**Cstj2** Castillejo, Cristóbal de. Excerpt from "Dialogo entre la Verdad y la Lisonja." Castro 1: 241.

Con dos puntas te pusieron,
....
Que pueden ambas herir
Como lanzas amoladas
A quien cree
Lo que en tu libro se lee....

**Cstj3** Castillejo, Cristóbal. Excerpt from "La invencion de la Cruz." Castro 1: 252.

Y la crueldad esquiva
De sus penas tan extrañas
En mi corazon se escriba,
Y quede con sangre viva
Imprimida en mis entrañas.

**Co1** Coello, Antonio. Excerpt from *El reyno en cortes, y rey en campaña. Avtos sacramentales* 3.

Reyno:
    La guerra nos han metido
    en el corazon del Reyno,
    essa Prouincia del alma,
    tan libre, que con sus fueros,
    a su mismo Rey no sabe
    sujetarse en no queriendo,
    el loco humano alvedrio,
    que rebelde, altiuo, y ciego,
    es mistica Cataluña,
    que tiene sus priuilegios
    en el libro verde escritos
    del Paraiso terreno.

**Co2** Coello, Antonio. Excerpt from *La Virgen del Rosario, la amiga mas verdadera*. Robles 345.

Clara:
    Dichoso el pueblo Christiano,
    donde aquesta deuocion [del
                            rosario]
    está siempre establecida.
Iacinta:
    En mi alma está imprimida,
    que es papel de corazon.

**Cor** Córdoba, Sebastián de. Excerpt from "Soneto V." *Garcilaso* 97.

Escrito está en mi alma vuestro
                            gesto
y quanto yo escrevir de vos desseo:
vos, Christo, lo escrevís, y yo lo leo.

**Da** Dávila, Juan. Excerpts from *Passion del Hombre-Dios* Bk. II: 4, 6; Bk. III: 80, 81; Bk. V: 19.

[Libro II. Estancia 1. Canto 1]
    (Porque vn Padron a tu furia
    No se estampe en tal paciencia)
    Suelta mano la violencia,
    ....
    Pero su golpe acrecienta
    Con la injuria que deshonra,
    Y, porque pueda la honra,
    Leella para sentilla,
    Con su sangre en la mexilla

Quiso imprimir la deshonra.
....
Al valor la bofetada
  Autoriza en su violencia,
  Que era grande su paciencia,
  Pero no andaba sellada:
Mas ya como confirmada
  puede entrar en el tormento,
  Que en vn alto Sacramento
  Cinco lineas carmesies
  Rubricaron de rubies
  Character al sufrimiento.
....
  Que, si a Moyses se declara
  Que la ley vieja estampara,
  En las dos Tablas sangrientas
  La ley de sufrir afrentas
  La escribió Dios en su cara.
[Libro III. Estancia 10. Canto 3]
Corre por los circunstantes
  Sin oirse la Sentencia,
  Pues quien, no oyó su violencia,
  La leía en los semblantes:
Eran tan desemejantes,
  Como sus facciones son,
  Y en cada qual su affeccion
  Tantas letras escribia,
  Que en su rostro se leía
  A todos el corazon.
....
  Y en la Madre. Ay Dios! andar
  Azia alli en vn llanto quedo
  Me parece (ah si leer puedo!)
  Que anda allí todo el pesar:
....
  Mas no puedo ya leer tanto,
  Que (como es mar) de su llanto
  Vajan nubes a mis ojos.
....
  La letra es clara, y constante,
  Mas que leeré en su semblante,
  Si no puedo leerla a ella?
....
  Allí a vnos ojos hacer
  Veo letras de crystal;
  Mas ay que con su raudal
  Me desuanece al leer!
....
Todo caracteres son
  De Cruz, y nos los declara
  Vna beldad, que está clara,
  Entre vn llanto, que es borron.
[Libro V. Estancia 2. Canto 2]

Calle la jara ya, calle,
  Que cinco llagas esten
  En su Flor, si en ella ven
  Que sus armas mi Rey halle:
Nazareno es, y al miralle
  A aquellas sienes diuinas
  Con declaraciones dignas
  Veo escritas en su cara
  Cinco llagas en la jara,
  Y un million en las espinas.

**Di** Dicastillo, Miguel de. Excerpt from *Avla de Dios* 47.

En vez aqui de Elogios, y Epitafios,
donde suelen cifrarse tantas glorias
de inutiles hazañas, y victorias,
produce flores misteriosamente
este comun Sepulcro,
haziendo vnas con otras laberintos,
de hermosos caracteres, que distintos,
en sus hojas nos pintan,
y en ellas, como Oraculos escriven,
que donde mueren ellos, ellas nacen,
y eternos viven, donde muertos jazen
con varios coloridos, y matizes
funebres Geroglificos les hazen
a aquellos que fomentan sus raizes,
y entre los bellos lazos que interponen,
este Epitafio lugubre componen.

**Do** Domínguez Camargo, Hernando. Excerpts from *S. Ignacio de Loyola* 27, 62, 89-90, 98, 329, 334, 364.

[Libro I. Canto 2]
Ventajosa Vizcaya a quanta cera
  Aró de Roma el castigado estilo,
  A quanto, carta, junco en la ribera
  Inuestigó solicita del Nilo,
  A quanta piel le desnudó a la fiera
  Del Pergamo sangriento agudo el filo,
  A quanta en telas tunica le pudo
  Dar a la antiguedad tronco desnudo.
De Ignacio doctrinó en la pluma arado,
  Que sulcasse al papel campos de nieue,
  Donde sembro sus letras el cuydado,
  Y colmo siempre le siguió no breue:
  O no de tardos bueyes arrastrado,
  De Aguilas si Reales yugo leue!
  Que tantas fecundaste en nuestros dias
  Troxes de Iesuitas librerias.
[Libro I. Canto 3]

Su esfera gira en su sangrienta espuma,
　La pluma tiñe en el rubi su gloria,
　Y la tinta le ofrece con la pluma
　Al volumen heroyco de su Historia:
　No tiempo avrá que su esplendor
　　　　　　　　　　　　　[consuma,
　Que a sus letras es tabla la memoria,
　Y por de Ignacio, que la dio constante,
　Es ya su sangre tinta de diamante.
[Libro II. Canto 1]
　Leo, Señor, en la menor Estrella,
　Que en cerulea piel escriues sabio,
　De tu poder vn tropo, vna sentencia
　Del Tulio de tu altissima eloquencia.
Clausulas en el mar vndosas leo,
　Que en punto, y punto paran de la arena,
　Parentesis las Islas suyos creo,
　Quando en corvas orillas las enfrenas.
　Perifrasis son tuyos el arreo,
　Que en cultas flores tu eloquencia ordena:
　Antonomasia el hombre a ser viviente,
　Y hyperbole de luz el Sol ardiente.
Metafora en las plantas translatiua,
　Cristal altera en esmeralda hojosa;
　Pluma de luz al Sol dictas, que escriua
　Retorica de Estrellas numerosa;
　Y en tu boca del mundo descriptiua,
　Vna voz cada Cielo es armoniosa;
　Aquesta (o marmol yo) no me mouia
　Oratoria de Dios, dulce energia?
Poca letra me intima execuciones,
　Quando el alma mas Aspid se me obstina;
　Quien cadenas le forja los renglones
　A la que al yugo leyes le declina?
　Quien las vezes le ha dado de eslabones
　Al libro que me alhaga, y me acrimina?
　Quien de dientes te armó pagina graue,
　Que mordiendo eficaz, ladras suaue?
Zozobrado el aliento en dulce calma,
　Las señas, que las letras imprimieron
　En los ojos caminos para el alma.
[Libro II. Canto 2]
Si excede esta beldad, Hijo la fia
　En sus brazos vn Niño tan amante,
　Que al cuello se eslabona de Maria;
　Hilado su cabello es vn diamante,
　Su cuerpo de las carnes es del dia,
　Quando aun en leche el Sol es luz
　　　　　　　　　　　　　[infante;

Deste volumen de hermosura, y gala,
Indice que la obtiene, y la señala.¹⁰
[Libro IV. Canto 6]
O, rebuelue la Historia de los dias
　En el volumen de vn sepulcro obscuro,
　Las letras lee, que en cenizas frias
　Este huesso, y aquel escriue impuro:
　En tantas de la muerte Librerias,
　Los cuerpos de essos huessos mal seguro
　Estudia Iulio, y en su letra aduierte,
　Que son Abecedarios de la muerte.
[Libro V. Canto 1]
Aquella mano Soberana, aquella,
　Que en el libro del Cielo la brillante
　Cerulea conscriuió pagina bella
　Con tinta de oro, y pluma de diamante,
　Y al caracter loquaz de tanta Estrella,
　En Zona, y Zona aró pauta radiante,
　La que en el Monte fue nubes vestido
　Estilo sobre el risco empedernido.
En un rasguño de su diestra mano,
　Al alma heroyca de Loyola fia
　Vn valiente designio, vn soberano
　Modelo de su ilustre Compañia.
[Libro V. Canto 4]
Relajado el color las pieles floxas,
　En el volumen de su cuerpo rudo
　Rebuelve el tiempo sinuosas hojas,
　En quien edades escriuiendo mudo
　Con las que bebe al pecho tintas rojas
　La dura pluma de su diente crudo
　Biblioteca le erige a las edades,
　En que prescriue el tiempo eternidades.

**Enc** Enciso y Monzón, Juan Francisco de. Excerpts from *La Christiada* 31, 47.

[First is a litany of biblical figures of Mary]
　Tu aquel Libro, que solo puede abrir
　el Leon generoso de Iudá
　　. . . .
　Diuino nombre, en cuyo fausto eterno
　tanta delicia, y suauidad se siente,
　quanta aquel libro da a quien le devora
　donde el nectar escrito se atesora.

---

¹⁰ "Indice" as used here denotes the index or table of contents but also, through the verb "señala," evokes the image of the pointing finger sometimes found in the margin of a book.

**Enr**  Enríquez Gómez, Antonio. Excerpt from *Epístolas de Job*. Castro 2: 386.

Obro de loco cuando en cuerdo escribo;
Ando con luz, y la virtud no veo,
Y alcánzame la cuenta en el recibo.

**Es**  Escobar y Mendoza, Antonio de. Excerpts from *Nveva Gervsalen Maria* 34, 41, 154.

[Fvndamento II. Canto 2. "El Nacimiento de Maria."]

    El escrito melon está firmando
Con letras de oro, que ya está oloroso.
. . . .
    Saluete aquel Señor, que te ha escogido
Por Madre dulce, por Esposa amada;
Y en tan poco papel ha epilogado
La belleza de todo lo criado.

[Fvndamento VIII. Canto 1. "Circuncision del Niño, y el dulcissimo nombre de IESVS."]

    Ya goza el mundo libertad segura,
Que el Redemptor diuino se ha obligado,
Y por seguridad haze escritura,
De no parar sin verle rescatado:
La escritura firmó con sangre pura,
Y para que el papel vaya sellado,
Tomando el sello Real, que Iesus era,
Le dexa impresso en colorada cera.

**Fe**  Fernández, Lucas. Excerpt from *Auto de la Pasión. Teatro español del siglo XVI* 40.

    ¡Lloren todas las naciones
. . . .
las muy ásperas pasiones
y afliciones
del gran Tetragrammatón!

**Fue**  Fuente, Gerónimo de la. "Dezimas." Ferriol y Caycedo 58-59.

Oy en la Yglesia se an visto
Con diuina aprouacion,
Vn libro de Concepcion,
Y otro de llagas de Christo,
Y aunque el fiscal ande listo,
Estos libros calumniando,
Ni en el vno tiene mando,
Ni al de Concepcion tocó
Iamas, porque se imprimio
Sin que el pudiesse ver, quando.
    Vn libro toca a Maria,
Y otro a Francisco le toca,
Este con llagas prouoca,
Y aquel con graue hidalguia;
Nunca inuidiosa porfia
Estos libros a tachado,
Que en el de Maria estampado
Dios viuo, por gracia está,
Y en el de Francisco ya
Christo, al viuo, trasladado.
    El de Concepcion diuina
Escrito en letras de plata,
Sin enmienda, y sin errata
Muestra gracia peregrina:
El otro con sangre fina,
En cinco letras escriue
Que Dios en su historia viue,
Pues con letras señalado,
Del que en Cruz desquadernado
Libro, la impression reciue.
    Desde que estuuo en la imprenta
El libro de concepcion,
Como hizo Dios la impression,
Siempre corrio por su cuenta:
No cupo letra de afrenta
En este libro excelente,
Que ni aun tinta se consiente,
Porque no manche el papel,
El en Dios, y Dios en el
Se incorporan juntamente.
    Si es Maria original
De Dios, Francisco es traslado,
Tan a la letra sacado,
Que parece a Dios ygual:
La misma marca, y señal,
Que en Christo impressa quedó,
En Francisco se imprimio,
Por modo tan eminente,
Que a Christo mira presente,
Quien assi a Francisco vio.
    Con la gracia enquadernado
Solo el libro de Maria,
Al tiempo, que se imprimia,
Se halló cerrado, y sellado:
Francisco abierto y rasgado:
Como le aprieta la imprenta,
Por dezir, quien es reuienta,
Y assi al mundo descubierto
Con cinco bocas abierto,
Su diuina historia cuenta.

**Gal** Gálvez de Montalvo, Luis. Excerpt from "El llanto de San Pedro." Sancha 254.

Y lo que puede asconderse
Dentro de un alma amorosa,
Sin escribirse o leerse,
Con la vista es fácil cosa
Escucharse y entenderse.

**Gar** Garau, Francisco. Excerpt from *El Sabio Instruído de la Naturaleza*. Qtd. in Soria Ortega 107.

Era este mundo un libro en cuyas páginas espaciosas con caracteres de varios colores ha querido dársenos a estudiar la Sabiduría Divina.

**GarE** García de Escañuela, Bartolomé. Excerpts from *Elogios de oradores. Panegirico vltimo . . . a la Canonizacion del Glorioso San Pedro de Alcantara*. Huerta 428, 431, 434.

Dirán que le vieron andar sobre las aguas, lo qual es Canonizarlo el Cielo, escriuiendo en hojas de zafir la bula con el portento. . . . De la tierra Mínimo elemento leuantó Dios a el Sol que puso por caracter significativo de sus prodigios. . . . Eterniza el buril de su ingenio en el bronze de sus aciertos, como en libro executorias que le coronen Principe de la eloquencia: y titulos en que se eternice la gratitud de nuestros corazones.

**Go1** Godínez, Felipe. Excerpt from *Avto del nacimiento de Christo*. Fernández, J. 109.

Baltasar:
   Vos Rey Melchor, aduertid,
   que aunque Negro, es gran
      ventura
   ser borron en la Escritura
   de los Salmos de Dauid.

**Go2** Godínez, Felipe. Excerpt from *Avto del nacimiento de Christo, y pastores de Belen*. Fernández, J. 94.

Ángel:
   Estaua el Verbo escondido
   en la mente de su Padre,
   palabra mental de Dios,
   de su concepto caracter.
   No se oía esta palabra,
   o no sabiades antes
   este concepto diuino,
   allá en Dios inescrutable.
   Agora se ha pronunciado;
   . . . .
   Venid, que aunque ya visible, y
   ya pronunciado os hable
   todo el concepto de Dios,
   vereis la palabra Infante.

**GoT** Gómez Tejada de los Reyes, Cosme. Excerpt from "Dime, pastor, así el cielo." Sancha 214.

–El Mesías prometido
De profetas, cuyas leyes,
Escritas con sangre propia,
Darán salud a las gentes.

**Gon** Góngora, Luis de. Excerpt from "A la procesion que víspera del Corpus se hace al Sagrario." Castro 1: 497.

Crara:
   Mas tinta sudamo Juana
   Que dos prumas de escribana.

**Grc** Gracián, Baltasar. Excerpts from *El Criticón*. Ed. Correa Calderón 1: 40, 46, 146; 2: 95-96, 98-99, 105-106, 108.

[Parte I. Cr. 3]
– . . . . Así que con razón definió un filósofo este universo espejo grande de Dios. Mi libro, le llamaba el sabio indocto, donde en cifras de criaturas estudió las divinas perfecciones.
[Parte I. Cr. 4]
– . . . . [N]o tienen más que el pellejo y todo lo demás borra, y así son hombres borrados.
[Parte I. Cr. 9]
Eternizaron con letras de oro los antiguos en las paredes de Delfos, y mucho más con caracteres de estimación en los ánimos de los sabios, aquel célebre sentimiento de Biante: *Conócete a ti mismo*.

. . . . Ellas [las manos] . . . encierran en sí la suerte de cada uno, no escrita en aquellas vulgares rayas, ejecutada sí en sus obras.
[Parte III. Cr. 4]
–Discurrió bien quien dijo que el mejor libro del mundo era el mismo mundo, cerrado cuando más abierto; pieles extendidas, esto es, pergaminos escritos llamó el mayor de los sabios a esos cielos, iluminados de luces, en vez de rasgos, y de estrellas por letras. Fáciles son de entender esos brillantes caracteres, por más que algunos los llamen dificultosos enigmas. La dificultad la hallo yo en leer y entender lo que está de las tejas abajo, porque como todo ande en cifra y los humanos corazones estén tan sellados e inescrutables, asegúroos que el mejor letor se pierde. Y otra cosa, que si no lleváis bien estudiada y bien sabida la contracifra de todo, os habréis de hallar perdidos, sin acertar a leer palabra ni conocer letra, ni un rasgo ni un tilde. . . .
–¿De modo que todas están en cifra?
–Dígote que sí, sin exceptuar un ápice . . . .
– . . . . Las más de las cosas no son las que se leen. . . . De modo que es menester ser uno muy buen letor para no leerlo todo al revés, llevando muy manual la contracifra . . . . La lástima es que ha malísimos letores, que entienden C por B, y fuera mejor D por C. No están al cabo de las cifras ni las entienden, no han estudiado la materia de intenciones, que es la más dificultosa de cuantas hay. . . .
– . . . . [T]odos estos sí que serán letras.
–De ningún modo, digo que no lo son.
–¿Pues qué?
–Añadiduras de letras, puntillos de íes y tildes de enes. . . . Al fin, ellos son abreviaturas de hombres y cifra de personillas. . . .
–Esas –replicó Critilo, . . . –me holgara yo saber en primer lugar; porque estas otras que nos han dicho, los niños las aprenden en la cartilla.

**Grn** Granada, Luis de. Excerpts from *Introduccion del simbolo*. *Obras* 183, 184, 186, 187, 192, 202, 214, 608.

[Parte I. Capítulo 1]
Por todo lo que este gran filósofo [Séneca] nos ha enseñado en todas estas palabras, vemos cómo por el conoscimiento de las criaturas nuestro entendimiento se levanta al conoscimiento del Criador . . . . Este era el libro en que los grandes filósofos estudiaban, y en el estudio y contemplacion destas cosas tan altas y divinas ponian la felicidad del hombre.
. . . . Y por estas cosas en que la sabiduría y omnipotencia divina resplandesce, se da a conoscer a aquel Sancto varon [Job], enseñándole a filosofar en este gran libro de las criaturas . . . .
En este libro dijo el gran Antonio que estudiaba. Porque preguntandole un filósofo, en qué libro leia, respondió el Sancto: El libro, oh filósofo, en que yo leo, es todo este mundo. En este mismo libro estudiaba tambien aquel divino cantor, el cual en muchos de sus Salmos recrea y apascienta su espíritu con la consideracion, así de las obras de naturaleza, como de gracia. Y así en aquel salmo que comienza: Los cielos predican la gloria de Dios, la mitad del salmo gasta en contemplar estas obras de naturaleza, y la otra en una de las principales obras de gracia, que es la pureza y hermosura de la ley de Dios. . . .
[Parte I. Capítulo 2]
Pues segun esto, ¿qué es todo este mundo visible, sino un grande y maravilloso libro que vos, Señor, escribistes y ofrecistes a los ojos de todas las naciones del mundo, así de griegos como de barbaros, así de sabios como de ignorantes, para que en él estudiasen todos, y conosciesen quien vos érades? ¿Qué serán luego todas las criaturas deste mundo tan hermosas y tan acabadas, sino unas como letras quebradas y iluminadas, que declaran bien el primor y la sabiduría de su autor? . . . .
Somos como los niños que cuando les ponen un libro delante con algunas letras iluminadas y doradas, huélganse de estar mirándolas, y jugando con ellas, y no leen lo que dicen, ni tienen cuenta con lo que significan. Así nosotros, muy mas aniñados que los niños, habiéndonos puesto vos delante este tan maravilloso libro de todo el universo, para que por las criaturas dél, como por unas letras vivas leyésemos y

conosciésemos la excelencia del Criador que tales cosas hizo, y el amor que nos tiene quien para nosotros las hizo; y nosotros como niños no hacemos mas que deleitarnos en la vista de cosas tan hermosas, sin querer advertir qué es lo que el Señor nos quiere significar por ellas. . . .
[Parte I. Capítulo 3]
¿Quién diria que un retablo muy grande, y de muchos y muy excelentes colores y figuras se hizo acaso, con un borron de tinta, que acertó a caer sobre una tabla? Pues ¿qué retablo mas grande, mas vistoso, y mas hermoso que este mundo? . . . .
[Parte I. Capítulo 8]
Este es pues el freno que él puso a este grande cuerpo de la mar, para que no cubra la tierra, y cuando corre impetuosamente contra el arena, teme llegar a los términos señalados, y viendo allí escripta la ley que le fué puesta, da la vuelta . . . .
[Parte I. Capítulo 13]
Para lo cual es de notar, que así como un grande escríbano, que quiere asentar en una ciudad escuela de escribir, hace muchas diferencias de letras, unas de tirado, otras de redondo, otras de letra escolástica, otras de hacienda, otras quebradas, otras iluminadas, para mostrar en esto la suficiencia que tiene: así aquel artífice soberano (aunque la comparacion sea muy baja) declaró las maravillas de su providencia no de una manera, ni en un solo género de animales, sino en todos ellos. . . .
[Parte V. Tratado 1. Capítulo 3]
Por donde el que tuviere ojos para saber mirar estas cosas, entenderá que todo este mundo es un grande libro escripto con el dedo de Dios, y que todas las criaturas son las letras dél; las cuales tienen sus propias significaciones con que predican la gloria de su hacedor. Mas los hombres dados a las ocupaciones y aficiones de las cosas temporales, no saben leer por este libro, ni entienden lo que estas letras significan. . . .
Mas por el contrario el que supiere leer por este libro, no podrá dejar de decir con el mismo profeta: ¡Cuán engrandecidas son, Señor, vuestras obras! . . . En este mismo libro hallará que no solo todo este mundo visible fue criado para servicio del hombre, sino tambien todas cuantas criaturas hay en él.

**Gue1** Guerra y Ribera, Manuel de. Excerpts from *Sermón de la Conversión*. Herrero García 175-79, 197.

En un libro que miraba Ezequiel, estaban escritas lamentaciones y versos: *Lamentationes, carmen, et vae*. . . . Volando le miró Zacarías: *Volumen volans*; y todo volar es subir. . . .

¿Pretendes acaso introducirte en el papel azul de esos cielos, donde aquel Supremo Escritor corrió las líneas de su Poder en tantos rasgos de luz? . . . . El [mundo] no gusta de libros de mortificación. Tienen tan mal despacho, que no se venden; y como estos libros no tienen salida en el mundo, porque no se compran, vuelan al cielo, donde se despachan, porque sólo en él se estiman.

Corren mucho en el cielo estos libros, porque a costa de tales hojas se compra el cielo . . . .

No extraño ya que vuele tan veloz el libro si están suspirando sus hojas. . . . [E]n el Libro universal de este mundo, cuyas trágicas hojas compone el desaliño de sus vivientes, representando la tragedia de esta fugitiva vida, tal vez recitamos un verso alegre, pero tropezando a los lados con endechas tristes . . . . No impropiamente consideraba yo a los hombres como animados libros de desengaños, en cuya alternación de accidentes meditase su providencia los errores de sus hojas. En el blanco papel de Magdalena cayó el borrón de la culpa. Hojeó el libro de su libro y hallóle lleno de versos y gozos profanos. Determina su dolor presentarle a Cristo, para que le corrija, y envolvió sus gustos entre lamentaciones y ayes; y como el libro de Ezequiel volaba al cielo, por tener sus versos entre suspiros, voló el de Magdalena por envolver sus gustos entre lamentos.

No extrañarán que tenga más que leer tan grande libro. . . . En este libro, que nos dicta Magdalena su culpa, nos escribe con mejor letra la penitencia . . . .

En las hojas de este libro estudió Magdalena sus ayes, pues supo discreta envolver sus profanidades entre ardientes suspiros.

. . . . Aliciona con este libro de penitencia a los delincuentes . . . .

Disimulen lo prolijo, que un libro tan grande encierra innumerables reparos.
.... Registremos en estos libros los capítulos de vida y penitencia, de errores y desengaños.

Todos saben lo que se necesita para que corra en el mundo un libro. Se imprime, se corrige, se borran las opiniones sospechosas, se notan las voces disonantes y tal vez se rasgan algunas hojas, si contienen escandalosos errores; ya expurgados, se aprueba, se imprime y se despacha.

Las docilidades de una trágica hermosura habían escrito en el libro de Magdalena varios capítulos de su profana historia.
.... Disgustada del hermoso título del libro, registró las hojas por de dentro, y al mirar el interior tan borrado, crecieron los borrones, las congojas y se cubrió el sol de nubes. Maldito está, Magdalena, mi libro.
... En el mundo ha corrido, por ser de buen gusto, pero ¿cómo podrá pasar en el cielo?

Tratemos, dice congojada su discreción, de enmendarle. Al autor le toca el corregirle, y siendo yo la autora, a mí me toca la enmienda. Para que salga a luz ya enmendado, necesito licencia y aprobación. Cristo sólo la puede dar; pero como tiene un divino entendimiento y bajó a encuadernarme los libros y borrar las hojas prohibidas que introdujo Adán en nuestros mortales cuerpos, es difícil que un libro tan escandaloso salga con su censura aprobado. Pero yo me arrojo a la censura por la enmienda. Aquí, Señor, dice Magdalena, ... os pongo el libro de mi vida a las plantas .... Bien conozco que está lleno de errores ... pero si el agua borra, ya mi llanto le limpia. ... Si es poco borrar los errores, también rasgaré sus hojas, porque ya arrojo las galas; y como a mí no me toca censurarle, sino corregirle, ya que yo pongo la enmienda, sed piadoso en la censura.

Admirados los circunstantes de tan escandaloso libro, no pudieron pasar el juicio sin censurarle. El fariseo le condena por escandaloso.... Los discípulos le notan de profano. Judas le censura por el desperdicio. Padecía tan terribles censuras porque miraban el libro por la exterioridad, sin leer lo borrado del interior.

Corra en paz, dice Cristo, libro tan hermoso. ... Era de bustos, pero ... se han borrado los gozos. Eran sus caracteres malditos porque se imprimían sus voces en el mundo, pero ahora son hermosos porque se imprimen en mis plantas. Tenía errores de la vista, pero se han borrado con tanta agua. Estaba lleno de profanas hojas, pero ha rasgado sus profanidades, y como ha quedado tan enmendado que parece libro nuevo, ha de correr con mi aprobación por el mundo por el más bello libro de desengaño....

Mal podré, Magdalena mía, registrar tu amante y discreto libro de penitencia....
.... Parecen tus arroyos deshecha fortuna y son apacible bonanza, porque como del llanto, que mira el sol, matiza el iris los colores de su serenidad, más matices le ofrece tu llanto que pueda escribir en el papel azul la Esfera.

**Gue2**  Guerra y Ribera, Manuel de. Excerpt from *Declamacion evangelica dia de Santa Catalina, Virgen, y Martyr. Sermones varios* 63.

Y si no me engaña mi especulacion; elevando la vista a la alternacion constante de essa esfera, leeremos en el papel azul dessos Cielos escrita esta verdad con caracteres de luz.

**Gue3**  Guerra y Ribera, Manuel de. Excerpt from *Oracion a la Vncion de la Madalena. Sermones varios* 393.

[S]alió de casa ansiosa buscando a su Maestro, y fio de los atrevimientos del viento la madeja hermosa, ... iba en culto desaliño desquadernado aquel bello libro de flamantes rayos, para que leyesse el mundo en sus rasgados caracteres mas desengaños, que bebió en sus compuestas ojas hechizos.

**Gue4**  Guerra y Ribera, Manuel de. Excerpts from *Oracion a San Iorge. Sermones varios* 189, 192.

Hablen en essas Campañas los azeros, y escriva la purpura derramada inmortales Caracteres de gloria, pues los nobles no an de tener mas boca, que la espada.

.... Mas patente se leía el Rotulo de Divino en las puntas de Horeb, que en el Calvario.

**Gue5** Guerra y Ribera, Manuel de. Excerpt from *Oracion a Santo Tomás Apostol. Sermones varios* 74-75.

El papel que me a cabido para leer la felizidad destos años, son las Llagas de Christo, renovadas por Tomas: No parece buen Libro, porque años llagados serán enfermos; pero mal temo, quando son unas heridas, que con el sobrescrito de pena, tienen verdades de gloria .... Y este Libro de immortales llagas, es el mas feliz registro de los años, que anelamos.

**Gue6** Guerra y Ribera, Manuel de. Excerpts from *Oracion de San Iuan de Mata, y San Felix de Valois. Sermones varios* 25, 26, 27.

Tanto dista lo material de lo espiritual, quanto el Cielo de la tierra. La distancia consiste, en ser lo material visible, y lo espiritual invisible ....

Y si elevamos la contemplacion al Cielo, veremos escrita esta verdad en aquellos rasgos de luz.

.... Dos colunas erigió Dios, estas son Iuan, y Felix. Subscrivió en ellas su nombre; porque las subscrivió con el nombre de la Trinidad. Dudavan la grandeza destas colunas, y era la causa, la que en las colunas de Seth; que si bien llenas de gloriosos caracteres, no se leían bien, a fuer de antiguos. Es verdad, que en estas colunas puso Dios su nombre, y como su nombre es su Gloria, alli estava su Gloria gravada; pero no se percibia, no porque no estuviesse bien escrita, sino, o por ser letra tan antigua, que no se percebia bien la letra, o por que como los hombres no leen, sino las letras que hazen, o conocen, como eran letras que las escrivió la Trinidad, no las acertavan a leer: y viendo Dios, que aun estando firmada de su nombre no reconocian su gloriosa letra, sale oy con la Bula a declararla.

**Gue7** Guerra y Ribera, Manuel de. Excerpt from *Oracion dia de Santa Ana. Sermones varios* 11.

La eleccion de Ana para Madre de la Madre de una Deidad, es la alta calificacion de su virtud; porque como Dios escrive los decretos con la tinta de los meritos, de puestos Gigantes, no pueden ser enanas las virtudes.

**Gue8** Guerra y Ribera, Manuel de. Excerpts from *Oracion dia de Santa Catalina. Sermones varios* 164, 175-76.

Hermosa prenda es la sabiduria. Es un rasgo, aunque en borron, de los limpios caracteres de la Deidad. ...

Los instrumentos dedicados para escrivir, aun siendo insensibles, por nacer destinados para la ciencia, nacieron infelices. El principal instrumento de la ciencia es la pluma; porque a pesar de lo caduco inmortaliza la ciencia: para que forme la pluma los caracteres, se necessita cortar, y cortarla es propriamente consumirla, y desazerla .... Entera formará borrones como gruessa, y cortada, escrivirá hermosas letras como delicada.

.... La pluma muere en las puntas que la cortan, porque cortandola, la acaban: y no espira Catalina en ellas.

**Gue9** Guerra y Ribera, Manuel de. Excerpts from *Oracion en dia de Quarenta Horas. Sermones varios* 212.

En las eminencias de las cumbres escriven colericos los elementos sus rigores ....

El viento que perdona la melancolica ociosidad del ciprés, desoja airado la purpura a la rosa. Es este breve rasgo de hermosura, relampago hermoso que enciende la vanidad del Abril ....

**Gue10** Guerra y Ribera, Manuel de. Excerpt from *Oracion en la beatificacion de onze Martyres. Sermones varios* 261.

Imprimió el amor en Francisco aquellas hermosas llagas, ... salió Francisco, o como una hechiza Deidad, o como una humanidad con gloriosos caracteres de Dios[;] mirando, los semblantes de las copias, no aciertan los ojos a distinguir entre el traslado, y el original, porque se equivoca con el original, como fue tan Divino el pincel.

**Gue11** Guerra y Ribera, Manuel de. *Oracion en la Canonizacion de San Francisco de Borja. Sermones varios* 469.

Es Ciudad de Letras, y . . . excede a la antigua en la grandeza de la libreria, pues aqui cae la voz de Lipsio, que llamó a los Sabios Bibliotecas animadas.

**Gue12** Guerra y Ribera, Manuel de. Excerpts from "Aprobación de los *Sueños misteriosos de la Escritura* [de Rodríguez Monforte]." Qtd. in Soria Ortega 348, 349, 352.

Yo reparaba el desengaño de este grande libro de la naturaleza, dar menos sueño a los peces . . . . [N]o son comparables los desengaños de palabra a los documentos de la obra. . . . Todos los prudentes leían en el libro vivo de este cristiano desprecio el más alto renglón del desengaño, nada se echaba menos para tan importante documento, pero faltaba que se juntase a lo hablo lo escrito, fuer primero el hacer . . . . Lo que se debe temer y sentir de este libro, es que tenga fin. Y si a la luz no la aprobó Moisés, sino Dios, porque solo un Dios que pudo hacerla podía aprobarla, en libro que todo es luz, llega a la censura con respetos de admiración.

**Gue13** Guerra y Ribera, Manuel de. Excerpt from *Oración del Miércoles de las Señales*. Qtd. in Soria Ortega 283-84.

Yo llamo al entendimiento libro universal, porque en su seno, como en embrión, se encierran las especies de todas las ciencias, aunque por faltas de salir a luz, confusas.

**Gue14** Guerra y Ribera, Manuel de. Excerpt from *Sermón de la tempestad*. Qtd. in Soria Ortega 341-42.

En el Juicio último, escribe Juan que se desviará el Cielo como un libro envuelto.

. . . . [L]o escrito con agrio de limón no se puede leer sino es al fuego . . . .

**Gue15** Guerra y Ribera, Manuel de. Excerpt from [*Sermón de las honras del Cardinal Cisneros*]. Qtd. in Soria y Ortega 261.

No es la vida y la muerte libro aparte. Es un libro con dos encuadernaciones. La vida le encuaderna con colores caducos. La muerte le descuaderna lo caduco para encuadernarle lo eterno. . . . Para leer en nuestro cardenal el grande libro de su muerte, registraré los insignes capítulos de su vida.

**Gue16** Guerra y Ribera, Manuel de. Excerpt from [*Sermón de Santa Teresa de Jesús*]. Qtd. in Soria y Ortega 242.

¿Qué culpas no pretenden sutilizar con tus discreciones en tus libros, para que nos parezcas capaz de borrones?

**Gue17** Guerra y Ribera, Manuel de. Excerpt from [*Sermón del Santissimo Sacramento*]. Qtd. in Soria y Ortega 170.

[Es el Sacramento] la pasión de Cristo en limpio.

Horozco, Antonio de. SEE: Orozco, Antonio de.

**Hu** [Hurtado de] Mendoza, Antonio de. Excerpts from *Vida de N. Señora*. [*Obras*] 145, 172, 177.

... [A]quella Arca,
No del viejo Testamento,
Sino de un Dios Hombre, siempre
Vivo Testamento Nuevo.
. . . .
   El Atheniense más sabio,
Por el borrado contexto
De obscuridades, las dudas
Leyó claras en el Cielo.
. . . .
   A los Discipulos santos
En toda ciencia, y perfecto

Saber, más que los gradua,
Los corona de Maestros.
   La Catedra de Dios Hombre
Maria substituyendo,
De la Ley fue Libro, y Alma
Impressa ya en doze Cuerpos.

**Jau**   Jáuregui, Juan de. "Al Santísimo Sacramento. Romance alegórico." *Rimas* 148-50.

   Mientras militaba Cristo,
sus hazañas se imprimieron
y grandezas en el mundo,
de quien hizo libro nuevo.
   Doce apostólicas hojas
tuvo su primer cuaderno,
y luego dél se tradujo
la dotrina a muchos cuerpos.
   Mas Dios, por dar a su historia
viva luz y nombre eterno,
en solas cuatro palabras
cifró sus heroicos hechos.
   Y con ellas, en el libro
y primer hoja de Pedro,
puso una hostia encarnada
para cerrar el proceso.
*Y en encarnada hostia, Dios eterno*
*a sus grandezas tiene echado el sello.*
   El sello fue de sus armas
forjado de nuestro hierro,
en fragua ardiente de amor,
y amor fue el raro maestro.
   El le formó de dos temples,
y abrióle en aquel más tierno;
pero lo que el sello cierra,
sólo Dios lo mira abierto;
   aunque hace tanta fee
el sobrescrito que vemos,
que enseña más la verdad
que volúmenes inmensos.
   Lenguaje de Dios al fin,
no del tosco estilo nuestro:
pan por pan, vino por vino,
mar de profundo misterio.
*Que en encarnada hostia, Dios eterno*
*a sus grandezas tiene echado el sello.*

   Dispuso que entre los hombres
vivo su valor y entero
viniese de lengua en lengua
hasta la fin de los tiempos.
   No le basta que sus obras
cuenten Marcos y Mateo,
que en sus corónicas dicen
verdad como el Evangelio.
   Y Juan, que con El trataba
y conoce bien su pecho,
nos deja toda su historia
escrita de verbo ad verbum.[11]
   Mas El, para quedar vivo
siempre en la boca del pueblo,
quiso cerrar la escritura
con otro milagro nuevo.
*Y en encarnada hostia, Dios eterno*
*a sus grandezas tiene echado el sello.*

**Led1**   Ledesma, Alonso de. Excerpts from "A la Cruz de Cristo." D'Ors 349-51.

Sois la pluma con que Dios,
mojando en su sangre mesma,
nos dio la carta de horro
de su mano y de su letra;
. . . .
sois la cátedra de prima
donde Cristo nos enseña
en solas siete leciones
todas las divinas sciencias;
. . . .
sois atril do el libro Cristo
descuadernado se muestra,
en quien cinco mil azotes
sirven de rasgos y letras;
. . . .
sois el banco do se libran
a letra vista mis deudas,
y cuando el cambio está alzado
mejor se pagan las letras;
. . . .

**Led2**   Ledesma, Alonso de. Excerpt from "A la culpa de Adán." D'Ors 158.

---

[11] This poem is in one sense a pun on the distinction explained by Carruthers, between *memoria ad verbum* and *memoria ad res* (73-74, 86-91, etc.). The Eucharist is *ad res*; the Gospels, John's in a special way, are *ad verbum*.

Por fiador le habéis salido
y, pues el plazo se viene
y la escritura contiene
que al fiador puedan pedir,
a Vos habrán de acudir,
pues el deudor no lo tiene.

**Led3** Ledesma, Alonso de. Excerpt from "Al glorioso San Sebastián." D'Ors 335.

Entre la riqueza summa
puede estar depositado
vuestro divino traslado,
por ser imagen de pluma.

**Led4** Ledesma, Alonso de. Excerpt from "Ay, insaciable apetito." D'Ors 330.

Fue su vida, ser y trato
una perpetua lección
do leyo de oposición
la materia "De Pecato".

**Led5** Ledesma, Alonso de. Excerpt from "Discurso a la vida de Christo." D'Ors 155.

En la cátedra de Hebreo
la resumió porque andaba
por dinero y no por sciencia
(que hay letras en oro y plata).

**Led6** Ledesma, Alonso de. Excerpt from "[Hieroglifico]. Pintóse una hoja de oliva." D'Ors 242.

Pintóse una hoja de oliva, y escrito en ella *Predestinatum*, y al otro lado una espada desnuda, y escrito en ella *Praecitum*.
  No tiene más de dos hojas
  el proceso de esta audiencia,
  y en la una, tu sentencia.

**Led7** Ledesma, Alonso de. Excerpt from "Hieroglifico IX." D'Ors 372.

Al mismo propósito, significando en la cara lo que tiene en el corazón. Píntase un papel cuyas letras se echan de ver por el envés, como escritas en papel que se pasa. . . .
  Aunque el papel tiene cuerpo,
  tanto la tinta penetra
  que se ve casi la letra.

**Led8** Ledesma, Alonso de. Excerpt from "Hieroglifico XVI." D'Ors 374.

Pintóse una letra de cambio y en ella escrito *Ihesus* y *Siete de setiembre de 1540, a letra vista.* . . .

**Led9** Ledesma, Alonso de. Excerpt from "Hieroglifico XXXIII." D'Ors 379.

Pintóse una moneda con las armas de Jesús y en el reverso el rostro del Beato Ignacio. . . .
  Si a Dios y a César se da
  lo que a cada cual se debe,
  bien será que Dios se lleve
  la moneda que aquí está.
  Sellada con *Ihesus* va . . . .[12]

**Led10** Ledesma, Alonso de. "A la natividad de nuestra Señora." [*Primera parte de*] *Conceptos* 97-98.

Oi se halló por mi ventura
  un blanco i limpio papel,
  para escrevir Dios en el,
  mi rescate i mi soltura.
Es papel de corazon,
  tan limpio que es maravilla,
  no papel de culebrilla,
  como los demas lo son.
Que aunque Adan por su locura
  echó esta marca al papel,
  para escrevir Dios en el,
  borrole tan ruin figura.
En este pliego tendras,
  la firma de Dios escrita,
  i aunque es la letra infinita,
  una palabra es no mas.
Toda cifralla procura,

---

[12] "Hugh [of St. Victor] likens the making of a memory image to a coin stamped by the coiner with a likeness which gives it value and currency" (Carruthers 39).

en este liso papel,
 i porque cupiese en el,
 está con abreviatura.

**Led11** Ledesma, Alonso de. "A S. Francisco." [*Primera parte de*] *Conceptos* 145-146.

De lo que Dios a lastado,
 ai hecha escritura Real,
 es Cristo el original
 i vos Francisco el traslado.
Perdio mi padre la gloria,
 de su eredada nobleza,
 i Cristo nuestra cabeza,
 ganonos la executoria.
El solo la a pleiteado,
 poniendo onor i caudal,
 i de aqueste original,
 sois vos Francisco el traslado.
Aunque el traslado firmó,
 el Rei con su sangre pura,
 la original escritura,
 es la que siempre valio.
Vos sois un simple traslado,
 que sirve de memorial;
 puesto que de mano Real,
 esteis assi rubricado.

**Led12** Ledesma, Alonso de. Excerpt from "A S. Ivan Evangelista recostado al pecho de Cristo." [*Primera parte de*] *Conceptos* 128.

Si en tal almohada dormis,
 i en tal libreria estudiais,
 dormid, que cuando durmais,
 liciones de prima ois.
Esse libro id hojeando,
 i dezid, lo que vais viendo,

pues que sabeis mas durmiendo
 que los mas dotos velando.[13]

**Led13** Ledesma, Alonso de. Excerpt from "Epitetos a la Cruz de Christo nuestro Señor." [*Primera parte de*] *Conceptos* 45-46. (Cf. Led1.)

Soys Retril do el libro Christo,
 desquadernado se muestra,
 en quien cinco mil azotes,
 sirven de rasgos i letras.

**Led14** Ledesma, Alonso de. Excerpt from "A la certidumbre de la muerte." Sancha 176-77.

Es la muerte un puerto seco,
Do, no solo registramos
Lo que llevamos allá,
Sino lo que acá dejamos.
. . . .
 En la aduana del mundo
Puesto que registran hartos,
Como no ven lo interior,
Mucho se les va por alto.
 Es secreto de escritorio
Este corazon humano,
Do pasa sin registrar
Nuestro pensamiento vario.
 Mas aqui tiene el registro
Quien le labró por sus manos,
. . . .
Y pues él tiene asentado
En su libro de memoria
Desde el recibo hasta el gasto,
 En papel de corazon
Escribid cargo y descargo,
Pues ni se escusa la cuenta
Ni se ignora vuestro trato.

---

[13] The Franciscan Francisco Tenorio writes in Chapter 16 of his *Passio duorum*, composed before 1519 and published in 1526, of the institution of the sacrament of the Eucharist and "del amortecimiento de San Juan sobre el pecho del Señor":

> En aquel arrobamiento vio San Juan muchos y grandes secretos de la eternidad del Verbo encarnado y de la unidad con el Padre y de la santa Encarnacion que a ninguno otro fueron tan abiertamente revelados . . . . Contempla, pues, a San Juan . . . arrimado al costado siniestro, sobre el corazón la cabeza acostada y rodeada y sostenida con los brazos que sostienen el mundo, haciendo el Señor de sus sacras manos almohada en que su amado discípulo reposase. (Sainz Rodríguez 2: 757, 765-66)

**Led15** Ledesma, Alonso de. Excerpt from "A la conversion de un pecador." Sancha 138.

Las paredes de Memoria
Sirvieron de papel blanco,
Donde el Ocio bosquejó
Mil gustos imaginados.

**Led16** Ledesma, Alonso de. Excerpts from "A la enseñanza de Cristo." Sancha 168.

La paciencia en los trabajos
Lee Dios en pública escuela,
Enseñándonos la práctica
Desta teórica excelsa.
. . . .
El culto en la religion,
Que es una grave materia,
Nos leyó aqueste maestro
En cátedra y fuera della.
. . . .
El libro de la justicia,
Por do todo lo govierna,
Y el de la misericordia,
Dios en su cuerpo encuaderna.
. . . .
La virtud de la humildad,
Desde que nace la muestra,
Leyéndola cada dia;
Que es una profunda ciencia.
. . . .
La obedencia hasta la muerte
La repite, por ser esta
El Christus de su cartilla,
. . . .

**Led17** Ledesma, Alonso de. Excerpt from "A la intencion." Sancha 155.

Aunque en una letra sola
Se juega para no errar,
Pues Dios es alfa y omega,
En cualquier letra jugad.

**Led18** Ledesma, Alonso de. Excerpt from "A santa Lucía." Sancha 175.

En la margen de tu vida
Pon, Lucía, esos dos ojos,
Porque leyendo esa plana
Noten lo que importa a todos.
Letor, de faltas ajenas,
Si ya de puro curioso
Tus ojos te escandalizan,
*Lee su vida y nota el ojo.*
Doncella desvanecida,
. . . .
*Lee su vida y nota el ojo.*
Viuda sola en el monjil,
. . . .
*Lee su vida y nota el ojo.*
Casada, que eres archivo
De la honra de tu esposo,
. . . .
*Lee su vida y nota el ojo.*

**Led19** Ledesma, Alonso de. Excerpt from "Al agradecimiento y a la ingratitud." Sancha 178.

Es en la corte del mundo
Agradecimiento un cambio,
Do paga el pobre sus letras,
Y cobra el rico a sus plazos.
. . . .
Las partidas de su libro
Obligaciones las llamo,
Pues da por reconocidas
Las firmas en cualquiero caso.
Las escrituras que otorga
Ante el Tiempo, su escribano,
Nunca alega prescribir,
Puesto que pasen diez años.

**Led20** Ledesma, Alonso de. Excerpt from "Al juicio final y particular del hombre." Sancha 138.

Todos ajusten sus libros;
*Que será la cuenta estrecha.*

**Led21** Ledesma, Alonso de. Excerpts from "Al nacimiento de Cristo." Sancha 162.

   Buen Respeto y Cortesía,
Hijos de Ingenio y Nobleza,
En casa de la Humildad
Aprenden virtud y letras.
. . . .
Empezaron por el *Christus,*
. . . .
El libro de la Virtud

Les dan por cartillas nuevas;
Que no se sabe de dicho
Cuando no se deletrea.
Pusiéronles a escribir,
Y ella les hizo materia
Para que imiten su forma;
Que esto es hacer buena letra.
En casa de la Humildad
Ninguno escribió sin reglas,
Ni da margen al papel
Hasta tener su licencia.

**Led22** Ledesma, Alonso de. Excerpt from "Dios y el hombre." Sancha 221.

Si a cobrar venis a mí,
Señor, mal podréis cobrar.
–No te pienso ejecutar;
Que yo pagaré por ti.
–Teneis, Señor, por escrito
Lo que debo de mi cuenta?
–Todo en mi libro se asienta,
Con que debes infinito.

**Lem** Lemos, Jerónimo de. Excerpt from *La torre de David*. Sainz Rodríguez 3: 226.

Por tanto desde hoy más doy un borrón a toda la vida pasada con sus liviandades y apetitos y comienzo a hacer un libro de nuevo tan iluminado como por la obra vera.

**Leo1** León, Luis de. Excerpt from "Carta dedicatoria." Sainz Rodríguez 3: 390.

Si no la vi mientras estuvo en la tierra, ahora la veo en sus libros y hijas; o, por decirle mejor, en Vuestras Reverencias solas las veo ahora, que son sus hijas, de las más parecidas a sus costumbres, y son retrato vivo de sus escrituras y libros.

**Leo2** León, Luis de. Excerpt from *De los nombres de Cristo* 162-63.

El nombre de Dios, de cuatro letras, que se encierra en este nombre, . . . no se pronuncia. . . . Mas aunque no se pronuncia en sí, . . . en el nombre de Jesús, por razón de dos letras que le añaden, tiene pronunciación clara y sonido formado y significación entendida, para que acontezca lo mismo que passó en Cristo; y para que sea . . . retrato el nombre del ser. Porque por la misma manera en la persona de Cristo se junta la divinidad con el alma y con la carne del hombre, y la palabra divina, que no se leía, junta con estas dos letras, se lee . . . .

**LoA** López de Andrade, Diego. Excerpts from *Tratado sobre el Euangelio del segundo [i.e. tercero] Martes. Tratados sobre . . . Qvaresma* 195, 203.

Porque auia de dar la ley, le abilitó mucho antes la diuina prouidencia, que le tenia destinado para este oficio, haziendole ley racional y biua: de suerte que todo lo que despues se auia de escriuir en tablas muertas, se podia primero leer en sus obras, como en escritura biua.

. . . . Assi entiende san Pedro Dam. en el cap. 7 de la Epist. 3 aquellas palabras del cap. 7 de Dan. Iudicium sedit, & libri aperti sunt. Sentose Dios a juzgar, abrieronse los libros, los quales (dice) no son otros, sino los Santos, cuyos merecimientos aora estan escondidos en la custodia de su humildad y arrollados como vna escritura, para que nadie la lea.

**LoU1** López de Ubeda, Juan [comp.]. "Dios puso en hombre su nombre." Sancha 336.

*Dios puso en hombre su nombre,*
*Y aunque el vaso quebradizo*
*En que estaba se deshizo,*
*Quedó su nombre en el hombre.*
   A las bestias parecemos
En esta parte inferior,
Mas en la otra superior
La imagen de Dios tenemos;
Si en esta se pone el nombre
De Jesus, no hay que dudar
De que se puede afirmar
Que está su nombre en el hombre.
   El alma segun su esencia
Es eterna, incorruptible;
Solo el cuerpo es corruptible,
Como muestra la experiencia.

Si estampa Jesus su nombre,
Luego se podrá decir
Que para mas le subir
Quedó su nombre en el hombre.
  Era Cristóbal pagano,
Como en su historia hemos visto,
Y púsole el mismo Cristo
Nombre dulce de cristiano;
Porque mas al mundo asombre,
Y alegre Cristóbal quede,
Así como hacello puede,
Puso su nombre en el hombre.

**LoU2** López de Ubeda, Juan [comp.]. Excerpt from "Tratado de la vida segura." Sancha 368.

En viento escribes y en agua,
Si por ti mismo te riges;
. . . .

**Luc** Lucas del Olmo, Alfonso. Excerpt from "Estaciones de la via sacra." Sancha 144.

En el corazón imprimo
Con carácteres del alma
Aqueste nuevo prodigio.

**Lud** Ludeña, Juan de. Excerpts from *Sermon VI*. Huerta 201.

Y assi las olas de el mar, quando llegan a los muros de arena, retroceden doblandose vnas sobre otras. Donde aduirtió San Basilio de Seleucia, que el retroceder las aguas del mar, es culto religioso, con que veneran a la arena, respetando la Ley, que miran alli impressa.
  . . . . Porque si en la arena imprimió Dios su Ley, aunque la impuso a las aguas; Pedro conseruó en su alma tan impressa la Ley de Dios, que jamás llegó a borrar sus caracteres la negra tinta de la culpa.

**Mad** Madre de Dios, Lucas de la. Excerpt from *Sermon IX*. Huerta 273.

En lo comun de la imitacion, al primer exemplar Christo Señor nuestro, hallo copiadas en S. Pedro de Alcantara las perfecciones mas heroicas. . . . La humildad, hasta huir los honores de Palacio, donde con sobrescrito de zelo pudiera aumentar creces al espiritu.

**Mal** Malón de Chaide, Pedro. Excerpt from "Salmo CIII." *Tratado de la Conversión. Escritores del siglo XVI* 295.

No pueden los humanos
Contar la diferencia
De peces que allí viven,
Porque solo se escriben
En tu eterna memoria y alta ciencia.

**ManA1** Manrique, Angel. Excerpt from *Discvrso I. De la . . . Reyna de los Angeles . . . en el dia de su purissima Concepcion*. Libro primero. *Sanctoral* 3.

. . . P]or ser la serenissima Reyna de los Angeles el libro, de quien habla S. Matheo: *Liber generationis Iesu Christi*: y celebrarse en esta fiesta el dia en que se hizo la primera impression del en las entrañas de Santa Ana. Salio a luz este libro, aunque cerrado, el dia feliz de su Natiuidad: comunicose la sabiduria que estaua escrita en el al mundo el dia que pario en Bethleen al Verbo eterno: rayaronle de dolores y tormentos, el dia que le crucificaron a su hijo: illuminaronle y retocaronle de gloria, el dia de su milagrosissima Assumpcion, en que la coronó Dios por Reyna de ella. Pero la primera impression que se hizo, del, no tiene duda, sino que fue el dia de su concepcion, que oy celebramos. Suelen mandar essos señores del Consejo, que en acabandose de imprimir vn libro buelua alla, juntamente con el original, para ver si corresponde el vno con el otro: y las faltas que huuiere auido en la impression, mandan que se saquen al fin del libro, juntamente con vna certificacion de como en todo lo demas concuerda con su original aquel impresso. Pues esto mismo es lo que haze nuestra Madre la Iglesia, en esta fiesta: que en acabandose de imprimir el libro de Maria en las entrañas de santa Ana, luego le presenta juntamente con el original, ante los Oydores de consejo de Dios, para que vean si ha sido bien impresso. *Liber generationis*, Veys ay el libro: *Iesu Christi*, veys ay el original de donde fue sacado: *Filii Dauid, filii Abraham, genuit Isaac, genuit Iacob*. Veys ay los oydores del

Consejo de Dios; todos essos Patriarcas, y Prophetas, con quien el comunicaua en aquel tiempo sus consejos. Y porque no dexe de auer fiscales en la causa, ni por falta de acusadores, salga menos calificada la sentencia, llama tambien a muchas pecadores a la vista: *Booz de Raab* . . . . Iuntanse todos al negocio, acusan los vnos, escusan los otros, sentencian los que mas saben de este caso, y dize quien no pudo errar en la sentencia, que concuerda con su original, sin faltar punto: *De qua natus est Iesus*: que le viene el original como nacido: y esso es lo que mandan poner al fin del libro. Esta es, en suma, la letra del santo Euangelio: y si della sacamos que no ay en la Virgen Maria ninguna errata, bien aproposito nos viene en este dia, en que la pretendemos sacar libre aun del yerro y culpa original, en que caen todos.

**ManA2** Manrique, Angel. Excerpt from *Discvrso II. De la . . . Reyna de los Angeles. . . en el dia de su dichoso Nacimiento*. Libro primero. *Sanctoral* 17-26.

Thema. *Liber generationis Iesu Christi*: Ex Euangelica lectione, Matth. cap. 1. Letra del Evangelio.

[Pensamiento primero. II] . . . . [No] solamente a la sabiduria es mejor que las armas; sino que los libros tambien, por estudiarse en ellos sirue de ellas; sus hojas de escudos, sus renglones de picas, o de estoques; sus partes, sus letras, sus apices, sus comas, de pelotas y valas, con que hazer guerra y vencer al enemigo, que sabe Dios jugar libros por armas, y con las hojas dellos, hazer temblar, como hojas de arboles, los hombres. . . . Pues aplicandolo aora todo a mi proposito; como esta Dios tan hecho a jugar libros por armas, como le va tan bien siempre con ellos, apenas se halla a vsar de otras en sus guerras: y assi vereys que para la mayor de todas, para conquistar al mundo, y desterrar de todo el a su tyrano, . . . las armas que escogio, fueron vn libro: y este es el que tenemos por Thema de todo este discurso, y es principio de nuestro Euangelio, que comienza. *Liber generationis Iesu Christi*. . . .

[Segundo pensamiento. III] Qvien sea este libro, no se le hara muy dificultoso a quien considerare los dias en que nuestra madre la Iglesia nos le abre, a quien viere que le saca a luz todos los dias que se celebra fiesta de la Virgen; clara señal de que deue de ser ella, y no otro alguno. *Sola enim Virgo María liber est generationis Iesu Christi*, dize Gregorio Nazianzeno, Oratione 2. Natiuitate Virginis, que sola la serenissima Reyna de los Angeles es este libro de que haze mencion nuestro Euangelio. . . . [L]ibro donde escriuio la generacion de Iesu christo el Padre Eterno. Su muerte escriuieronla los Iudios en las sangrientas tablas de la Cruz, Sus azotes en el bruñido papel de sus espaldas y con diuersas puas, en vez de plumas, señalaron su cuerpo de mil rasgos, con las espinas la frente, y el celebro: el costado con el yerro de la lanza: el rostro hermoso, con sus manos sacrilegas: y en las de Christo, y en sus pies diuinos hizieron con las puntas de los clauos puntos, en vez de letras, como Hebreos. Finalmente su vida escriuieronla los Euangelistas en sus libros, su Nacimiento, Dios en las comidas tablas de vn pesebre, su Circuncision, quien fue ministro della el propio cuchillo, con que se hizo su destierro en Egypto, su buelta en Iudea, su Baptismo en el Iordan, su Predicacion en las almas que le oian y sus milagros en los cuerpos que sanaua, pero su generacion, solamente fue escrita en las purissimas entrañas de la Virgen: que haziendo dellas papel, y de su sangre tinta, con la pluma del Espiritu Santo . . . con essa pluma pues, con essa tinta, y con esse papel, escriuio el Padre eterno en vna sola palabra quanto supo. Y si escriuio esse Verbo en las entrañas de Maria, ella es sin ninguna duda el libro de la generacion que aora tratamos. . . .

[IIII] . . . . [Y] como ni en los Angeles del Cielo, ni en todos los hombres de la tierra, auia de auer quien tuuiesse esta grandeza: quien llegasse a ser libro, en que escribiesse Dios su Verbo eterno . . . ; solamente echa mano de vna muger . . . [S]ola Maria sabia que auia de ser, *Liber, generationis Iesu Christi* . . . .

[Tercero pensamiento. V] Aqui comienzan las excellencias de la serenissima

Reyna de los Angeles, . . . todas las procuraré reduzir a estas tres palabras; *Liber generationis Iesu Christi:* Lo primero que es libro: Todos los demas santos son como hojas; esse es el titulo que les da Salomon por muy honrado. Prob. 11. *Iusti autem qua si virens folium,* los Iustos son como vnas hojas verdes. . . . Sola la Virgen es libro entero: y libro que solo el tiene mas hojas que todas quantas andan sueltas y esparzidas por el mundo. Doctrina recebida entre los Teologos, que en solo Maria depositó Dios mas gracia, que en todos los demas santos de la Iglesia. Desta excelencia sale otra no menor, en que se auentaja la Reyna de los Angeles a todos: que las hojas sueltas muy facil es el rasgarse y el perderse, pero en estado enquadernadas y hechas libro, luego parece que estan firmes y seguras. Mil hojas de oro de charidad y de virtudes estauan repartidas en los santos, pero como eran hojas sueltas, no podian dexar de estar sugetas a perderse vna vez y rasgarse otras. . . . Sola la Virgen es quien tiene enquadernadas estas hojas: y está tambien enquadernada en ellas, que ni aun doblarsele vna no es possible. Por eso prouey'o Dios que fuesse libro cerrado hasta la muerte; y que ni para escriuirle, ni para leerle no se abriesse: *Hortus conclusus, fons signatus*: aunque no con nombre de libro, pero ay estan las cerraduras claramente. Y para eso tambien le siruieron sus manos de manillas, no la dexando nunca vn punto dellas. Quien duda sino que todo el resto del infierno no fue bastante a abrirle, ni a quitarlas.

Padre en verdad que no teneys razon, en hazer a los Santos hojas sueltas. Quien duda que las de todas las virtudes, aunque se les perdiesse alguna, o alguna vez[,] ordinario las traerian en quadernadas en sus vidas, y ellos se enquadenarian en ellas, assi mismo. Especialmente, que es doctrina de los Theologos que todas las virtudes andan siempre encadenadas entre si y consiguientemente siempre juntas. En hora buena: yo digo que las ayan en quadernado todas en sus almas. No me negareys, que aunque mejor, y mas enquadernadas las ayan tenido, quando mucho fueren como vnos cartapacios (digamoslo assi) a diferencia de la Virgen, que fue libro.

Mirad, en los cartapacios vnas hojas estan en blanco, otras escritas: de las escriptas, vnas bien, y otras borradas. En vn libro no, sino que todo esta vniforme, y todo bien escrito. Desde la primera hoja hasta la vltima no hallareys vna plana si quiera que este ociosa, y hasta las margenes estan bien ocupadas con las cotas. Mas que en los cartapacios no todo lo que se escribe esta aprouado, que muchas cosas suele auer en ellos, que no fuera razon, que lo estuuieran: pero en los libros no puede auer nada, que no lleue su aprouacion, y su censura. Finalmente los cartapacios ni han menester priuilegio, ni le tienen: solos los libros son los que suelen siempre andar con priuilegio: y en el primer pliego, y aun en la primer plana del libro se dize, como se imprimio con priuilegio del Rey nuestro Señor, y aun le pueden poner alli muy a la larga. Pues estas son las diferencias y bentajas, que haze a los demas Santos nuestra Virgen. Que ellos, como no son libros, si no cartapacios, por mas enquadernados que traygan todas las hojas de su vida, y de sus obras, es fuerza hallar en blanco muchas dellas: y aunque en algunas tengan aprobacion, y en otras aprouacion y Priuilegio, en muchas es muy cierto que no llegaron a tener lo vno, ni lo otro. Quando Heirposeles paso a todos ellos, sin hazer cosa que fuesse de prouecho a muchos, la mocedad enteramente, a algunos aun la vejez, casi a todos la niñez, y a todos, sin auer casi ni excepcion (sino quando mucho vn Hieremias, o vn san Iuan Baptista, y essos por poco tiempo) lo que anduuieron en los vientres de sus madres: sin que en la primer hoja de la concepcion por lo menos pudiesse dezir ninguno, que se estampaua con gracia, y priuilegio. Y plege a Dios que muchas hojas de adelante no esten en muchos llenas de borrones, que sin aprouacion particular bien cierto es, que no seran pocas las que ay. Pero quando esten assi, no es marauilla; que assi suelen estar los cartapacios y ningun Santo ha llegado a ser mas que esso. Sola la Reyna de los Angeles es libro, *liber generationis Iesu Christi:* y assi es fuerza, que no tenga hoja perdida, ni que carezca de aprobacion, y priuilegio. Las de la niñez en el templo en exercicios santos, y deuotos, las de la adolescencia con los Angeles, cuyas visitas recibia muy de ordinario: las de la juuentud con su precioso Hijo, . . . las de la vejez con el Espiritu Santo, y los Apostoles. Todas en particular aprouacion del Cielo, aprouechada, llenas, y vniformes, libro en que no ay hoja ociosa, ni baldia, y en que aun las margenes siruen y aprouechan, y estan todas acotadas por Dios, y como cosa suya. Libro; en cuya primera plana, aunque sea la de la concepcion, esta la gracia; y el priuilegio (solo a ella concedido) de que fuesse concebida sin pecado: y cuya vltima plana) [sic] sin que aya entre las dos cosa, que desdiga, que la que cierra la obra, con la muerte, acaba (como suelen otros libros) con aquel LAVS DEO VIRGINI QVE MATRI, que le cantaron el dia de su gloriosa Assumpcion todos los Angeles. No veys? no veys que de ventajas les haze a todos los Santos, por ser libro. Pues todas ellas nos significa la Iglesia, con llamarla: *liber generationis Iesu Christi*.

Mas es libro la Virgen, y libro que compuso el Padre eterno. No se si me atreua a dezir, que vn tan buen libro bastara hazerle inmortal, quando el no lo fuera. No dize alla el Poeta, que los libros hazen a sus Autores inmortales? Pues si de otros libros se dize esto, del libro que contiene toda la sabiduria de Dios, que se puede dezir? No dixo Dios mejor palabra que la que escriuio en este libro; no la pudo dezir; no es el mejor. Mirad que mucho que diga yo, que pudiera por solo auerla escrito, hazerse eterno. Acabó vn Autor vn libro de mentiras, y fabulas prophanas; y apenas le huuo acabado, quando pareciendole que podia competir en la inmortalidad, de las estrellas, . . . dixo . . . .

Pues libro de verdades, y en quien esta la mesma verdad escrita: *Ego sum veritas* con quien podra competir? . . . . Preguntan los Theologos, supuesta la doctrina cierta, de que todos tenemos Angeles de guarda, desde quando enpiezan a hazer sobre nosotros centinela? . . . . Y resueluen casi todos . . . que desde que nace . . . y no antes, porque mientras está en el vientre de su madre, madre y hijo entrambos se reputan por vn mesmo supuesto. . . . Pues aora, si esta doctrina es cierta mirad a este libro mientras tiene dentro en sus hojas; la palabra en el espacio de los nueue meses, . . . que si ella y el se reputan por vn supuesto solo, esse supuesto tan bueno es como el de el Padre eterno. . . .

Ni aun son menester para esto Theologias, que solo el nombre del libro nos lo dize: sino dezidme, que se llama libro? Solo el papel? o el papel juntamente con lo que esta escrito en el? Padre esso es claro. El libro no le haze solo el papel sino el papel juntamente y la escriptura.

Y aun es la escriptura la que le constituye en razon de libro formalmente, que el papel solo, sea como materia. De suerte que lo que llamamos libro es el papel, con lo que tiene escripto. Pues miradme aora a la Reyna de los Angeles, con aquel Verbo solo, que escriuio en ella, como en blanquissimo y purissimo papel, el Padre eterno, hallareys que para ser tan buena como el, segun que le contiene, no es menester acudir a los supuestos. Libro es que assi nos lo dize el Euangelio: *liber generationis*, y libro que se constituye formalmente en razon de tal, por las palabras que estan en el escritas. Aprecialde como libro solamente que como libro hallareys, que no le debe al mismo Dios cosa ninguna, y que por lo que tiene de libro, es tan buena, como el, sin que el mismo nos pueda negar esto.

[VI] Passemos adelante. *Liber, generationis*: Y veremos como si por ser libro excede en tanto a todos los demas santos, y por ser libro en que escriuio su palabra el Padre Eterno, llega a competir y aun a ygualar con el en cierto modo, tambien por ser libro de generacion tiene particulares prerogatiuas y excellencias. Y que mayor, que ser libro que da vida, y sera lo que en el se escriue? cosa que en ninguno otro libro lo alcançamos. Oyreys vn sermon a vn predicador, y pareceos tan bien, que no juzgays palabra por perdida, ni que ay cosa que dejar en todas sus razones: Afficionado del y dellas, pedis el papel, leyes, y no os parece la mitad de bien que quando le oystes. En que va esto? en que el predicador daua vida a lo que dezia, con la voz, con las acciones, con el modillo de dezir, con los meneos: pero en el papel es impossible escriuirse nada de esto. No da mas vida lo que dize que lo que ello en si tiene. Pero si vuiesse vn libro tan precioso, que fuesse dando vida a lo que esta escrito en el: por ventura no seria de grande estima? vn libro que diesse alma a sus razones? no auria cosa como el en todo el mundo. Pus esso es la serenissima Reyna de los Angeles, vn libro que da ser, alma, y vida a quanto dize. Por que es libro de generacion: *liber generationis*: y la generacion en los viuientes consiste en comenzar a tener vida, en recebirla ellos de su parte, y de la del que los engendra en darsela. Escribase en todos los demas santos Dios por gracia, y escriuase tambien corporalmente en todos los fieles que comulgan: pero ninguno puede dezir que le da vida, antes por el contrario la reciben, del los vnos y los otros. Solo en la Virgen se escriuio el Veruo Eterno, de manera, que recibio de ella ser y vida: y si la recibio, sin duda que le debe de estar en grande obligacion. . . .

[Quarto Pensamiento. VII] . . . . Escriuile vna vez Dauid (o si acaso fue Asaph el autor della) vna carta a Dios, como regalandose con el, y dandole el parabien de sus grandezas . . . . Despues de auerle dicho otras razones, cierra la carta, y pone por sobrescrito estas palabras: *Terribili, et ei qui aufert spiritum Principum. terribili apud Reges Terrae*. . . . Que dezis Dauid? Mirad que deue de yr errado el sobrescrito. No escreuis a Dios manso, a Dios pacifico . . . ? ¿pues como le sobrescriuis al terrible . . . ? Muy bien sabe el Psalmista lo que haze que si en el sobrescrito se ha de poner el nombre de la persona, para quien es la carta, y esta se escriue a Dios, antes de su venida al mundo . . . esse era el nombre mas conocido que tenia.

. . . . Pues esto es ser la Virgen libro de la generacion de Iesu Christo: que no solamente es libro donde escribió su Verbo el Padre eterno, ni solo recibio della vida esse Verbo: sino que essa vida que le dio, fue de Iesu Christo: esto es de Saluador, blando y amoroso. . . . Pareceos que es poco bien de la naturaleza humana auer tenido a Maria, para que fuesse libro desta generacion y siglo de oro. *Liber generationis Iesu Christi.*

[VIII] . . . . Pues si sola Maria es el libro donde assentó el Padre eterno destas partidas, si de la resta dellas vuo bastante suma para la saluacion de tantos Angeles, quien duda sino que le estan muy obligados?

[IX] . . . . Gloriosa Virgen, Serenissima Maria, libro purissimo de santidad, . . . pues soys libro en quien escriuio quanto supo el Padre Eterno, libro que a lo que se escriue en vos days ser y vida; y vida tan en fauor de todos, como la de Iesus . . . . Pues soys la prima de las letras y las armas, acudid, acudid con todo a nuestro amparo: escriuidnos en el libro de vuestra memoria, jugad las armas contra nuestros enemigos, emplead las letras en abogar ante vuestro hijo por nosotros . . . .

**ManA3** Manrique, Angel. Excerpt from *Discvrso V. Del glorioso san Pedro de Castilnuouo.* Libro tercero. *Sanctoral* 199-202.

[Primer Pensamiento. I] De todos los beneficios y mercedes, que Christo nuestro bien, con su venida al mundo, hizo a los hombres sacando el Apostol san Pablo en vna suma todas las partidas en el ca. 2 de la Epistola que escriuio a los Colosenses, las zifró en quatro palabras con dezirnos: *Delens quod aduersus nos erat chiro graphum decreti, et affigens illud cruci,* que borró con su sangre la escriptura, que estaua decretada ya contra nosotros, y la clauó en el madero de la Cruz, palabras a que los expositores dan varios sentidos. Theophilato, santo Thomas . . . y otros muchos, sienten, que se habla aqui de la ley vieja, cuya obligacion . . . era tan pesada, ocasionó a san Pablo a que la llamasse con nombre de contraria. . . . Y como todo esto auia fenecido ya con la muerte de Christo . . . por esso dize san Pablo, que la borró a aquel tiempo con su sangre: y la clauó contra la Cruz y con sus clauos: para que cancelada de essa suerte, no pudiesse hazer fee en juyzio contra nadie. . . .

No es menos conforme al texto la segunda exposicion, que da la Glossa, que por chirographo, aqui entiende la sentencia que tenia Dios promulgada contra todos: assi por el pecado original de nuestro primero Padre ... como por los actuales de cada vno ..., esta dize: que borró Christo con su sangre, y canceló con los clauos de su Cruz. Porque desde el punto que la derramo, y le crucificaron, esta en nuestra mano el borrarla, y el romperla: y, quanto es de su parte, no le quedó obligacion ninguna en pie, de quantas hasta entonces tenia contra los hombres. Quadra esta exposicion bien con el texto, por las palabras que acabaua de dezir poco antes el Apostol. *Donans nobis omnia delicta*: que hizo vn perdon general Dios de todas nuestras culpas, y pecados. Y luego explicando, que modo de perdon fue este, añade .... Que los perdonó borrando el decreto y sentencia de muerte, en que estauamos todos contenidos ....

[II] Pero ... aun lo podriamos declarar de otra manera, y a mi parecer no menos rigurosa y propriamente, si dixessemos que el perdonarnos Dios nuestras culpas y pecados, fue borrandolas del libro, donde primero las tenia escriptas por nuestra cuenta, ... y assentandolas en las tablas de la Cruz, por la de Christo ... para que desde aquel punto quedassemos nosotros libres dellas, y comenzassen a correr todas por la suya. No se si se entendera esto mejor por vn exemplo. Deuenle a vn mercader vna gran suma de dinero, no tiene el deudor con que pagarla, y como es regla del derecho, que ... quien no tiene bienes pague con su persona; haze que se le prendan, hasta que busque con que satisfazerle por la deuda. Si en este tiempo saliesse alguna persona abonada que quisiesse cargarse della, y pagasse por el preso al punto le daria libre el mercader, pero esso seria borrandole toda la partida de la hoja donde se la tenia assentada por su cuenta: y assentandosela al que salio a pagarla en otra. Pues esto mismo dize san Pablo, que sucedio entre Dios, y entre los hombres. Toda la perdicion y ruyna nuestra, fue por deudas: porque deuiamos a Dios la satisfacion de la ofensa que le hizimos, y para tan gran cantidad, aunque todos nosotros nos vendiessemos, no veniamos a tener con que pagarle. Executaron nos en los dotes de la gracia: desposseyeron nos de la justicia original, y aunque nos quitaron todo quanto teniamos, ... no quedó por esso la duda [sic] pagada, antes tan entero el principal como si no nos vuieran quitado cosa alguna.... En estas deudas espirituales ... entregaron al hombre al brazo seglar, y quedó preso debaxo de la jurisdicion y dominio del demonio, hasta que hallasse quien tomasse a su cuenta la partida, y se encargasse de pagarla por entero. Vino Christo[,] fiole y encargose de pagar por el al Padre eterno.... Que se podia seguir de aqui: sino quedandonos a nosotros por libres, se borrasse la partida del cargo de nuestra oja ... y se assentasse en otra por cuenta de Christo.... Quereys saber qual fue essa: la hoja de la Cruz, ... ay es donde se passaron nuestras culpas, y ay donde se assentaron por cuenta y riesgo de Christo nuestras deudas....

[III] .... Pecó Dauid dos pecados tan grandes como sabidos .... Y apenas confesso su culpa, quando le dixo Natan, en nombre de Dios .... El Señor tambien ha trasladado, o traspassado tu pecado.... Pues donde la pudo traspassar.... Quereys saber adonde la passo: a la Cruz de Christo .... Borrosela a Dauid de su cuenta, mouido de su arrepentimiento y de sus lagrymas: ... pero porque la deuda no se quedasse por pagar, assentola en la Cruz por la de Christo....

[IIII] Pero mejor que todos ... es vn lugar del capitulo. 12. de san Iuan, que la Iglesia vsa cantar en vna festiuidad de la Cruz, en el dia de su Exaltacion, a catorze de Septiembre: *Nunc iudium est mundi* .... Ya esta para salir en fauor del mundo la sentencia.... Ya está para despacharse el auto de su libertad ... y sacarle de la jurisdicion y señorio del demonio.... Sacará el mundo executoria de rescate, ... porque yo, si me leuantare en el madero de la Cruz, lo tengo de atraer a mi todo.... [C]omo si dixera: En viendome en la Cruz, passaré a ella todas las ofensas y deudas de la naturaleza humana ... y cargando me a mi toda essa plana: ... pagaré las partidas della con mi muerte.... De suerte, que la escriptura de obligacion que Christo hizo por nuestras culpas y pecados, en cuya virtud fuymos nosotros dados por libres, fue la que el escriuio en las tablas de la Cruz con sangre propria: essa es la que nos essenta de la esclauitud y captiuerio del demonio, y la que cada y quando nos quisiessen obligar a el, . . . hemos de presentar en nuestro abono. . . . seguro, de que en presentando estos recados, no se le podra quitar persona alguna.

**ManL** Manrique, Luisa. Excerpt from "Romance. ¡Qué breves que son, Dios mio!" Serrano y Sanz 29.

¡Y qué de tiempo me falta
para el estudio, Señor,
de aquella profunda ciencia,
quién sois vos y quién soy yo!
   Y quando quereis leerme
tan importante lección,
¡qué de contrarios hallais
que impiden este favor!

**Mat** Mata, Gabriel de. Excerpt from *El Cavallero del Asisio* 119.

Mira por ver la Libreria rica
mas no la auiendo: no con poco espanto
a su deuoto familiar supplica
le enseñe el libro donde estudia tanto.
La vista luego, el de fidanza applica
a vn pintado Crucifixo sancto,
y dize con profunda reuerencia:
de este Original saco mi sciencia.
   Creedme fiel y verdadero amigo
que a los pies deste soberano espejo
hallo eloquencia, lo que escriuo, y digo,
y mucho mas por negligencia dexo.
Al mismo os pongo por leal testigo
que otro registro, libro, ni consejo
no lo tengo, ni estudio, excepto el curso
que en el seruicio de las Missas curso.

**Mi1** Mira de Amescua, Antonio. Excerpt from *Pedro Telonario*. González Ruiz 810.

Pedro:
   . . . [E]s loco
quien piensa que mucho vale,
siendo todos igualmente
rasgos de Dios . . . .

**Mi2** Mira de Amescua, Antonio. Excerpt from *Las prvuebas de Christo*. Fernández, J. 49.

Principe de Tinieblas:
   . . . [Y]o soy digno
de esse blason, pues coronan
diademas de luz mi frente,
y soy vn rasgo, vna copia
de la hermosura de Dios,
sin borrones, y sin sombras.

**Mon1** Montesino, Ambrosio. Excerpts from "Coplas de la cruz." Sancha 450, 451.

¡Quién te viera, cruz beata,
. . . .
Relumbrar muy mas que plata,
De un título que relata
El ser de tu fruto lleno!
. . . .
Oh cruz, y quién vivo fuera,
Para que entonces leyera
Tu virtud intitulada!
. . . .
Tanta memoria dejaron [los mártires],
Que sus nombres asentaron
En el libro de la vida.

**Mon2** Montesino, Ambrosio. Excerpts from "Coplas de san Juan Baptista." Sancha 408, 412, 413.

Su alma será su libro,
Sus estudios la conciencia,
. . . .
   Otras hay de torzalejos
Y de tocas azufradas,
Que por libros leen espejos,
. . . .
   Los gozos que el mundo espera
Para salir del peligro,
Uno a otro en su manera
Los difunde y reverbera,
Como libro.

**Mon3** Montesino, Ambrosio. Excerpts from "Coplas de san Juan evangelista." Sancha 443, 444.

El *Apocalipsi* fué
Tu ejercicio,
. . . .
Te demuestra
El Rey grande de los reyes
. . . .

La sellada vida nuestra,
Que es el centro,
....
   Y con fe la imploro tanto,
¡Oh reina mayor del siglo!
Que saque como de libro
Las virtudes deste santo,
Para reinar sin periglo.

**Mon4** Montesino, Ambrosio. Excerpt from "Coplas del santísimo parto." Sancha 440.

   Nunca fué parto tan fuera
De periglo,
....
La Virgen quedando entera,
Como libro
Muy sellado sin abrir.

**Mon5** Montesino, Ambrosio. Excerpt from "Coplas en gloria de nuestra Señora." Sancha 420.

   Si el mar Oceáno
Fuese la tinta,
Y el sol escribano,
Que el verano pinta,
No puede ni mano
De pluma distinta
Loarte, Señora.

**Mon6** Montesino, Ambrosio. Excerpt from "Coplas [del sudor de sangre en Getsemaní]." Sancha 422.

   Y de alli me sucediera
Serme impresa como libro
Tu pasion ....

**Mon7** Montesino, Ambrosio. Excerpt from "Del glorioso san Francisco." Sancha 435.

   La causa mas señalada
Que de todas estas tomo,
Es ver tan autorizada
Su regla y carne sagrada
Con tan adorable plomo.
   Que ha por sellos,
            pendientes
De cordones amarillos,
Las llagas de Dios recientes,
Que son, si paramos mientes,

Cinco anillos.
   No le debe ser molesto
Ninguno de los mortales,
Ni se le tenga mal gesto,
Pues que ha Dios en él puesto
Tan lucíferas señales;
   Tan lindas, tan rubricadas,
So hábito de pardillo,
Del muy alto fabricadas,
En fragua de amor labradas,
Sin martillo.

**Mon8** Montesino, Ambrosio. Excerpts from "Itinerario de la Cruz." Sancha 425, 429.

Te pido, oh Reina sin par,
Que tu claro original
Resplandezca en mi traslado.
....
   Golgotana, tierra buena
....
   No hay rosa ni clavellina
Que te sea comparada,
Pues tú sola fuiste dina
Ser de la sangre divina
Rubricada.
....
   Tanto quiso el Rey sagrado
Que entre nos cisma no haya,
Que nos lo dejó firmado
Con abrirnos su costado
....

**Mon9** Montesino, Ambrosio. Excerpt from "Romance del glorioso san Juan Evangelista." Sancha 458.

Sobre el corazon de Cristo
San Juan está reclinado,
De sus sentidos partido,
Y al centro, que es Dios, llegado,
....
Para ser de todo el cielo
En este mundo traslado,
O que original del credo
Por lo mas alto volado;
....

**Mon10** Montesino, Ambrosio. Excerpt from "Tractado del Santísimo Sacramento." Sancha 407.

Así que, como le ven [los ángeles]
En misterio mas secreto,
Determinan lo que leen,
Que es el gozo que poseen
Mas perfeto.

**Mrl** Morales, Jacinta María de. Excerpt from "A san Pedro mártir." Castro 2: 545.

La voz turbada ya, la mano yerta
Lámina hizo del hielo en que escribía,
Con excelente sangre que vertía,
Sacros misterios que a explicar acierta.

. . . .

Pues del sitio en que heroico padeciste
Tan eminente catedra fundaste.

**Mrn** Morchon, Manuel. Excerpt from "[Cancion real]." Huerta 55.

Pues si Pedro gustara,
su volumen azul desquadernara.

**Mrt** Moreto, Agustín. Excerpts from *La gran casa de Austria y divina Margarita.* González Pedroso 552, 563.

Demonio:
    Quítale la devocion,
    Borra de su frente el *Tao.*
. . . .

Margarita:
    Horror da sólo al pensarlo;
    Con ser cuanto se imagina
    Un borron, un punto, un rasgo.

**Mu1** Murillo, Diego. Excerpt from *En la festividad del glorioso apostol S. Andres. Discursos predicables . . . en. . . Adviento* 318.

Somos . . . como trapos viejos, rotos, inutiles, y podridos. Pues esso busco yo (dize Christo) para hazer vn papel blanquissimo, subtilissimo y terso: en quien escriuir la palabra eterna encarnada: y embiarla por el mundo a los Principes y Monarchas; para que los honren, y tengan en summa veneracion. Molerlos he con trabajos, que esso es necessario, para hazerse el papel: lauarlos he con el baño de mi gracia, hare vna pasta muy pura con la cola de la charidad: que cozida con el fuego de amor en los moldes de la diuina ley, quede hecha vn papel hermosissimo. Quereys ver, como los corazones, en que se escriue la doctrina Euangelica, se llaman papel, y essa doctrina escrita se llama carta en la Diuina escritura?

**Mu2** Murillo, Diego. Excerpt from *En la . . . Circvncision. Discvrsos predicables . . . en las festividades de Christo* 265.

Compara S. Vicente Ferrer el mysterio del nombre de Iesus, al titulo que se suele poner en el principio de los libros, escrito con letra colorada. Que si el titulo es a proposito, en el está virtualmente, todo lo que se contiene en el libro. Y no falta quien le compara a las rubricas de los capitulos del derecho, donde se haze vna suma, de todo lo que se contiene en el capitulo. Por lo qual es consejo entre los legistas y canonistas, que para entender el capitulo, se lea primero la rubrica que está escrita de letra vermeja en el principio del. *Lege rubrum* (suelen dezir) *si vis intelligere nigrum. In capite libri* (dize Dauid en persona de Christo) *scriptum est de me, vt facerem voluntatem tuam. Deus meus volui, & legem tuam in medio cordis mei.* Luego a la entrada del libro está escrito de mi, que me hize hombre para hazer vuestra santa voluntad. Y yo (Dios mio) assi lo quise, y puse vuestra ley en medio de mi corazon, para ponerla por obra. Esto han de presuponer los que entran a leer la sagrada Escritura, el fin della . . . es Christo. Y porque el fin que el author de vn libro, le suele poner en el titulo del, por esso dize Christo por Dauid, que en el principio del libro está escrito del. . . . Y el Padre eterno, quiso que al tiempo de ponerle este nombre a su hijo, se derramasse su sangre, porque el titulo se leyesse con mas atencion, viendole escrito de letra colorada, hecha no menos que con sangre de Dios. Y por esso los Hebreos no entienden la sagrada Escritura, porque no entran leyendo este titulo. Pero tú Christiano si quieres entendello, toma el consejo de los juriconsultos, *Lege rubrum, si vis intelligere nigrum.* Para en este titulo rubricado con sangre de Dios, que aqui hallarás cifrada toda la sagrada Escritura.

**Mu3** Murillo, Diego. Excerpt from *En la fiesta de las llagas. Discvrsos predicables . . . en las festividades de Christo* 448-50.

Responderé, que son cinco señales de recuerdo, para no poderse Christo oluidar del hombre, por quien las recibio. Suelen los amantes traer en las manos anillos de memoria con algunos symbolos, que les siruan de despertadores, para acordarse de las personas que aman. Y desto seruian al Sumo Sacerdote aquellas piedras, que traya en el superhumeral y en el racional, sobre los ombros y sobre el pecho, en las quales estauan escritos los nombres de los doze Tribus. . . . Christo nuestro Summo Sacerdote no se contento con esso, sino que quiso traer las señales de recuerdo, en las manos, en los pies, y en el costado, sobre su proprio corazon, para que el ver aquellos cinco hermosissimos Rubies, le representassen al hombre, por quien auia sido llagado. . . . Y si quieres ver los anillos de memoria, que traygo, para lleuarte siempre delante de mi, y no poder oluidarte. Abre tus ojos, y mira mis manos. *Ecce in manibus meis descripsi te.* Alli veras (o alma) que te lleuo escrita con puntas de agudos clauos. Y si miras mis pies, alli tambien te hallarás escrita. Y lo que mas es, que sobre mi corazon he querido escriuirte, con el buril de vn duro hierro de lança. De suerte, que en mirandome las manos, alli hallo escrito tu nombre: Y en mirandome los pies, alli hallo escrito tu nombre. Y quando quiera cerrar los ojos, y no ponerlos en pies, ni manos, la herida que traygo en el corazon, me representa tu nombre, y me sirue de señal de recuerdo. . . . Porque essas mismas llagas, que son las letras, con que te traygo escrita en manos, en pies, y en costado; son los muros, con que te defiendo de la indignacion de mi Padre. . . . Porque podemos dezir, que las llagas de Christo, son señales de recuerdo; son letras, con que nos escriuio en sus manos, en sus pies y en su corazon: y son muros, con que nos defiende de la ira de Dios. Y pues el trahe aquellas señales de recuerdo, con summa justicia nos puede pedir, lo que pidio a su Esposa en los Cantares. . . . Que le lleuemos a el por señal de recuerdo, escrito en lo interior del corazón; y por señal de memoria, en lo exterior del brazo: acordandonos del, en todos nuestros pensamientos, y obras.

**Mu4** Murillo, Diego. Excerpt from "En alabanza de San Francisco." *Divina, dvlce, y provechosa poesia* 159.

Y porque supiesse cuya
oueja soys, el Demonio,
os dio porque en veros huya,
los sellos del testimonio,
sellados con sangre suya.

Y aun quiso el Rey soberano,
por mas authentico hazello,
ser el mismo el escriuano,
autorizando su sello,
con la letra de su mano.

Porque le parecio a el,
viendo os tan enamorado,
que solo merecia el,
escriuir en el papel,
de vuestro cuerpo sagrado.

Y para mostrar la summa
del bien con que os satisfizo
su misericordia suma,
de su sangre tinta hizo,
y de su dedo hizo pluma.

Y escriuio Francisco en vos,
no la ley vieja terrible,
sino la letra apacible,
con que satisfizo a Dios,
por la culpa aborrecible.

Y para mayor corona,
de vuestra virtud sin par,
a nadie quiso embiar,
sino que el mismo en persona,
quiso a escriuirla baxar.

**Or** Orozco, Antonio de. Excerpt from *Historia de la reyna* 43.

Y pues queremos que nos hagan todos buen tratamiento, le hagamos a nuestros hermanos. Esta es la summa de la ley natural: que el rey celestial escriuio en lo alto de nuestra anima que es la razon.

**Os** Oseguera, Diego de. Excerpt from Libro segundo. *Estacionario* 171.

... de la justicia el libro abierto,
Y donde la verdad se muestra llana.

**Ov** Ovando, Gaspar de. Excerpt from "Dezimas." Ferriol y Caycedo 66.

Con elegante energia,
  Hasta en la tinta, y papel,
  (que es ceniza, y tierra es el)
  Se escriue nuestra hidalguia:
  Pues de la vuestra Maria,
  Diga esta enquadernacion,
  Qual es, pues las letras son,
  Sangre que Cristo desata,
  La imprenta incapaz de errata
  Y la tinta de borron.

**Pad1** Padilla, Pedro de. Excerpts from Canto II. *Grandezas* 21, 35.

Las lumbreras bellissimas del cielo,
Con vn mudo lenguaje, dan loores
....
Libro precioso; donde fue sacado
Lo mas fino de todos los primores,
Repartidos en todo lo criado
Como en menos perfetos borradores.

**Pad2** Padilla, Pedro de. Excerpt from "Cancion al sanctissimo nombre de Iesus." *Iardin espiritual* 34.

  Si el estendido transparente Cielo
blanco papel bruñido y limpio fuera,
y el mar que ciñe en torno el ancho suelo
para escriuir en tinta se boluiera,
y de su seca arena se hiziera
cada grano de aquellos una pluma,
no se pudiera referir en summa
la celestial riqueza
y diuina grandeza
deste ineffable nombre sacrosanto.

**Pad3** Padilla, Pedro de. Excerpt from "Niño sagrado y bendito." Sancha 211.

En el nombre descubris
Lo que pretendeis hacer,
Jesus dulce, ...
....
Y en solo este sobrescrito
Esperanza se nos da
....

**Par1** Paravicino y Arteaga, Hortensio Félix. Excerpt from "A la santa Cruz." Sancha 148.

Desmantelado hasta el globo
Impíreo, ¿qué maniatado
Ladron no le hará un gran robo?
Camina por ese atajo
Al hurto Dimas famoso,
Si es hurto escalar murallas
Por una pica un bisoño.
Llega a cobrar lo que es tuyo;
Que aquesos papeles rotos
La escritura son contraria
Que clava el fiador famoso.

**Par2** Paravicino y Arteaga, Hortensio Félix. Excerpt from "[A San Esteuan Protomartir]." *Obras postvmas* 26-27.

Piedras, y cantos atrozes
os obligan a hazer llanto,
y entre verdugos ferozes
sois con Dios, libro de canto,
que entonais diuinas vozes.

**Par3** Paravicino y Arteaga, Hortensio Félix. Excerpt from *Iesv Cristo desagraviado* 7.

Bueno es esto, cuando el estudio se presume tan largo de vista, que a descubierto en el Sol manchas como en la Luna. Pero cuando la embidia no vio mas, por hazer el credito de otro menos? Pues ni la Luna los tiene. Aviasele de caer a Dios al escrevir essos cielos, como David dijo, alguna gota de tinta en lo batido de essas ojas azules, papel de sus maravillas entre letras de plata i oro, que cuando allá passasse por rasgo, pudiesse acá parecer borron?

**Per** Pérez de Montalbán, Juan. Excerpts from *El Polifemo*. González Ruiz 815-16, 819, 829.

Polifemo:
    ... [T]raté de vengarme,
    ....
    en su estampa y en su idea,
    que es el hombre, que formó
    de su mano y de su letra,
    al sexto día del mundo,
    sobre el papel de la tierra.
    ....
        Abrácese cada cual
    con un árbol, y dé rienda
    a los pies, porque ya el
            monte,
    animado de mi espuela,
    se descuaderna y desquicia.
    ....
        Todo se lo tengo escrito
    y no ha de salir de aquí
    si no me paga.
    ....
Pastor:
    Y si la fiase yo,
    ¿no la darás libertad?
Polifemo:
    Sí; mas mientras tu
            piedad
    no firmare la escritura
    he de tenerla segura
    con mil grillos y cadenas,
    ....

**Pin** Pineda, Juan de. Excerpts from *Diálogos familiares de la Agricultura christiana* 1: 109-11; 2: 422, 443.

[Diálogo II. Capítulo IX. Libro de la vida]
Ferenico: De muchos libros habla la Escritura cuando trata en los negocios del juicio, y, por otra parte, predica todo el mundo que en Dios no hay más que un libro....
Filaletes: Digo, cuanto a lo primero, que donde San Juan trata de esos libros en su *Apocalipsi*, nos pinta un libro de Dios y muchos de las consciencias de los hombres. Porque Dios, como único juez, tiene un libro para juzgar, y los hombres, como muchos juzgados, cada cual tiene el suyo. Esta declaración es recebida comúnmente y la tiene Sant Gregorio, a la cual añade Ricardo, doctor autorado, que, ansí el libro de Dios como el de los hombres, se llama libro de vida, con tal que se guarde aquella diferencia entre ellos, que el libro de la vida en Dios sea el en que están escritos los predestinados, como dignos de galardón, y que los libros de los hombres sean en los que están escritos sus merecimientos, por los cuales deben ser premiados.

El nombre de libro se pone a Dios metafóricamente o por alguna semejanza, por cuanto como el libro sirve de conservar lo que en él se escribe, porque no se olvide y se entienda bien tal o tal negocio o cuenta, ansí la divina esencia se llama libro de la vida por la noticia que tiene de los que se han de salvar, y esta tal manera de escritura de los predestinados se llama libro de la vida. Alejandro y Sancto Tomás dicen que el libro de la vida se diferencia de la predestinación en que la predestinación significa los beneficios que Dios, antes con antes, determina hacer a los predestinados, mas que en el libro de la vida están escritos los merecimientos que los predestinados tienen para la vida eterna; de lo cual se arguye que en el libro de la vida está escrito el bien que los hombres hacen, y en el de la predestinación los bienes que Dios les hace.

Sube más Alejandro la consideración de este libro, diciendo que la esencia divina no se llama libro a semejanza de la cera o papel o pergamino, en que se dibujan las letras humanas, sino a semejanza del espejo, en que se figura lo que delante se le pone; mas que este espejo debe ser entendido el interior del alma, donde tenemos impresa la imagen de la inteligencia, y que, como el Padre Eterno es la fuente primera y original de las formas o ideas, ansí el Hijo es llamado espejo del mesmo Padre, en el cual resultan y se trasuntan aquellas formas ideales que primariamente emanan del Padre; y ansí se concluye que, pues el libro sirve de dar noticia, y el Hijo es la noticia del Padre, manifestadora de sí y del objecto, de que fué engendrada, que a él se apropia el nombre del libro, bien tal como el de conservador de las ideas.

Dice más y muy bueno Sancto Tomás: que en el libro de la vida ninguno se escribe sino respecto del fin para que se ordena, como en el de la guerra no se escriben los soldados para que se armen, sino para que peleen; y que como la gloria sea el fin sobrenatural del hombre, que no se escriben en aquel libro sino sólo los predestinados que llegan a gozar de Dios; porque si por estar en gracia hobiesen los hombres de ser escritos, muy borrado podríamos romanzar que estaría ya el libro, bien como muchos pierden la gracia y la gloria y no quedan más escritos.

Y como respecto de lo natural divino ni humano ni angélico no hay eleción, ansí ni libro de la tal vida natural. Y cuando alguno se dice ser raído del libro de la vida, no se entiende, como dice el Doctor Seráfico, que estaba escrito en él respecto de la divina predestinación, que le introduce en la vida eterna, sino según el estado de la gracia que tuvo por algún tiempo, y por ella derecho a la vida eterna; mas como perdió la gracia, que es la que se puede decir escrita, perdió el derecho para la gloria, y esto es haber sido raído este tal. Y si se deba entender deste raimiento por perdimiento de gracia por algún tiempo, sin entrevenir culpa, lo que Moisés y Sant Pablo pidieron ser borrados deste libro, determínelo la sancta Madre Iglesia, porque muchos muchas cosas dicen.

Policronio: Tan bien sabe Dios lo malo como lo bueno, y haber libro de lo bueno en Dios es saberlo Dios; luego, pues Dios sabe lo malo, también tiene libro dello.

Filaletes: En lo que presupuse de diferencia entre sciencia, presciencia, providencia y predestinacion, queda respondido a esa objeción; que Dios, con sciencia de simple inteligencia, sabe todas las cosas igualmente; mas el conocimiento predestinativo añade eleción por la sciencia práctica, por la cual aplica a lo bueno de gracia y gloria al tal predestinado, y esto toca al libro de la vida. Ansí los capitanes, en caso que conozcan a todos los de un reino, no asientan en su matrícula más de los que van por sus soldados, y no los soldados ajenos; porque allí se pone por fin la corona, la cual no gozará sino quien bien peleare, y los que no van a la guerra no serán coronados, pues no pelean, y ansí tampoco son escritos; como ni hay idea de cosa mala, sino que el mal, como privación del bien, sigue el género de la forma que priva, como la ceguedad sigue a la vista....

[Diálogo XII. Capítulo XXV.]

Filaletes: .... [M]as nuestras almas son en su criación como un libro en blanco en que nada está escrito, que es comparación de Platón y de Aristóteles, y como van viviendo y entendiendo, ansí van pintando sus entendimientos de diversas species inteligibles, y las que más cosas saben, más pintados los tienen; ... pues el conoscimiento de una cosa dispone y ayuda para entender otra, como vemos que el que ya sabe medianamente, deprende lo que ignora más facilmente que el principiante, que tiene rasa la tabla de su entendimiento.

Policronio: Muy gran libro han menester los muy sabios, para que no hagan borrones, topándose unas pinturas con otras.

Filaletes: Si fueran pinturas corporales, que ocuparan lugar, bien habíades dicho, mas como sean intenciones spirituales no se ordenan unas tras otras como renglones o como pinturas....

[Diálogo XIII. Capítulo VI.]

Filaletes: Todo este mundo es una cartilla en que está escrito el alfabeto de las criaturas, sirviendo cada criatura de una letra viva, por donde el alma comienza a deprender el conoscimiento de Dios, mediante la información de sus potencias exteriores, que se informan destos elementos de las criaturas, como de letras sueltas, que no hacen sentencia; y estas potencias exteriores enseñan a las interiores estos primeros principios y, por eso, llamados elementos, también como los cuatro naturales, de que se componen todas las cosas naturales deste mundo.

Cada letra es un elemento, y cada una por sí es objeto del ojo, mas el juntar las palabras significativas es de otra potencia más subida; y ansí sobre cada cosa deste mundo cae algún sentido que la conosce, y luego traspasa su conoscimiento al sentido común, que forma los conceptos particulares, y después sobreviene la operación del entendimiento, que compone los conceptos universales.

**PrJ** Pradas, Juan Valero. *Sermon... a Nuestra Señora de Monserrate. Once sermones 29.*

[He refers here to a previous sermon by a different preacher.]
En el Sabado, la luz de este Orador, nos descubrió a Maria de Monserrate, libro celestial de Medicina contra la peste, aprouado por el Supremo Medico, siendo el Impressor toda la Trinidad Santissima, libro Hierarchico con tres tratados de *Illuminare, purgare,* & *perficere*; siendo tan grande su luz, que al mismo Dios le abrió los ojos, obrando con tanto poder, que obró como persona Divina, y confessando Maria, que a ella con el titulo de Monserrate se le debe la preseruacion de la peste.

**PrA**  Prado, Adrián del. Excerpt from "Al santísimo Sacramento." Sancha 291.

Hoy por esclavo me escribo,
Dulce Pan, en tu prision,
. . . .
Ya no podrá, dulces clavos,
Todo mi pasado error
Borrarme aquellas señales
Que dicen que soy de Dios.

**Que1**  Quevedo y Villegas, Francisco de. Excerpt from "A don Alvaro de Luna. Romance." *Poesías* 334.

"¿Cuántas veces, Condestable,
  Entre burlas y entre veras,
  Te pedí de Dios firmada
  La cédula de firmeza?"

**Que2**  Quevedo y Villegas, Francisco de. Excerpt from "Con la voz del enojo de Dios suena. [Soneto]." *Poesías* 329.

Respóndanle lloviendo mis dos ojos,
Pues escrita en su luz mi noche miro.

**Que3**  Quevedo y Villegas, Francisco de. Excerpt from *Lágrimas de Jeremías. Poesías* 472.

Ya que no merezco de tu mano
Que tus ojos piadosos como justos
Vean mis desventuras,
Alcance que en mis entrañas lean
Las turbaciones mias.

**Ra**  "Glossa a la inmacvlada concepcion de Nvestra Señora: Sobre el verso de todo el mundo en general." *Ramillette de divinas flores* 206.

Libro singular soys vos
Donde el impressor perfeto
No imprimio qualquier conceto
Sino el Conceto de Dios:
Y en libro tan Celestial
No vuo errata conocida,
Porque fuystes concebida
Sin pecado original.

**Re**  Rebolledo, Bernardino de. Excerpts from *La constancia vitoriosa.* Castro 2: 397, 398.

Diom'espíritu entonces tu clemencia,
Consérvale despues tu providencia,
Y no de la memoria lo has borrado;
. . . .
Y tienes mis pecados,
Como en pliego, sellados,
. . . .

**Ri1**  Ribera, Luis de. Excerpt from "Contemplacion sobre la sentencia de los Cantares." Sancha 63.

Imprimiste en la frente el sacro nombre,
. . . .

**Ri2**  Ribera, Luis de. Excerpt from "De la entrada y triunfo de Cristo." Sancha 287.

Betis, que al canto de la sacra historia
La noble faz anciana enternecia,
Serenó mas la oreja y la memoria,
Y a la ninfa mas sabia le decia
Que en el oro en sus grutas encerrado
Con inmortales letras lo pondria.

**Ri3**  Ribera, Luis de. Excerpt from "Del nombre de Jesus." Sancha 58.

De ti, Rey, Sacerdote y Dios, se asombre
La escuadra que la luz y estrellas calza,
Y la que, de su amor propio descalza,
Vió escrito en fuego y zarza este renom-
                                                    [bre.

**Ri4**  Ribera, Luis de. Excerpt from "Del triunfo de Cristo en Jerusalen." Sancha 63.

Tal es, Jerusalen, tu gloria el dia
Que Salomon pacifico se muestra,
. . . .
Firmando con su muerte la concordia.

**Roc**  Rocaberti, Hipólita de Jesús, y. Excerpt from "¡Oh! llave piadosa." Serrano y Sanz 152.

¡Oh! llave de oro fino,
abre mi corazón a tu ley santa;
el espíritu ardiente
dél sea el escritor, y yo la tabla.
  Con su dedo divino
su amor tan firme grabe
que borrarle no puedan
ni penas, ni dolor, ni enfermedades.

**Rod1**  Rodríguez, Lucas [comp.]. Excerpt from "A la encarnacion." *Conceptos* 1.

Aquel concepto escondido
que Dios de si produco
nunca jamas fue entendido
hasta que en vos se escriuio
y assi pudo ser leydo.
Que para que se entendiesse
este concepto fiel,
y el hombre aca lo leyesse,
fue vuestra carne el papel
donde Dios escrito fuesse.

**Rod2**  Rodríguez, Lucas [comp.]. Excerpt from "A la gloriosa Magdalena." *Conceptos* 62.

[Mary Magdalene, kissing feet of Christ, offers her mouth as seal or stamp]
del pliego humano y diuino
tan cerrado, que no vino
por si ninguno a entendello.

**RodC**  Rodríguez Coronel, Juan. Excerpt from *Sermon VII.* Huerta 248.

El Hombre es vn compendio sucinto, vn conciso epitome de quantas perfecciones auia obrado la mano de Dios en el volumen dilatado de el Orbe.

**Roj**  Rojas Zorrilla, Francisco de. Excerpts from *La viña de Nabot.* González Ruiz 840, 859.

Trabajo:
  Soy del bien un torcedor
  borrón que cae sobre cuantos
  la buena dicha escribió;
. . . .
Nabot:
  Y ahora confúndase el orden
  natural, borre el dictamen
      (Hay terremoto.)
  de la luz el claro día;
. . . .

**Sal**  Salas Barbadillo, Alonso de. Excerpt from "A san Juan Bautista." Castro 2: 43.

Indice de aquel libro celebrado
  De la verdad que a la virtud inclina,
. . . .

**SF1**  San Félix, Marcela de. Excerpt from "Coloquio espiritual." Serrano y Sanz 257.

Oración:
  Y haz cuenta que todo es nada;
  es una coma, ni un rasgo
  de lo que gozan felices
  estos bienaventurados.

**SF2**  San Félix, Marcela de. Excerpt from "Loa a una Profesión." Serrano y Sanz 289.

Huid de todo y de todas
y mucho más de vos misma,
que es lección que Cristo lee
a sus esposas queridas.

**Snt1**  Santiago, Hernando de. Excerpt from [*Consideraciones para el*] *Jueves después de Ceniza. Consideraciones de Quaresma.* Qtd. in Pérez 132.

[Q]ue de los trapillos rotos no se pueda hacer un fino papel del peregrino, que siendo el papel peregrino, el peregrino sea papel.

**Snt2** Santiago, Hernando de. Excerpt from *De la conversión de San Pedro. Consideraciones de Quaresma.* Qtd. in Pérez 24-25.

¡Oh memoria, rico tesoro y guardajoyas del alma! . . . ¡Oh escritorio! ¡Oh hucha secreta y guarda de letrado y estudioso varón, donde guarda y atesora para el día que quiere hacer muestra de sí! . . . ¡Oh archivo de las escrituras importantes y títulos de nobleza y riqueza del hombre, y donde se guardan las verdades de las ciencias![14]

**Sar** Sarriera, Elvira. Excerpt from "Oda a San Ignacio de Loyola." Serrano y Sanz 392.

En silvo blando y en sutil marea
Se representa Dios a Ignacio santo,
Para dictarle leyes saludables
Escritas con su dedo inmenso, tanto
Que el orbe capacísimo rodea
Y pudiera ceñir innumerables
Leyes incomparables,
. . . .

**Si** Silvestre, Gregorio. Excerpt from "A una calavera." Sancha 331.

Mírate parte por parte,
Y aprende primero a ver
En el libro de humillarte,
Que, de no saber mirarte,
No te sabes conocer.

**So** Solís y Ribadeneyra, Antonio de. "A la Conversion de San Francisco de Borja." *Varias poesias* 133.

Letras ay, que declaran
El lenguage del Cielo;
Letras, que siempre duran,
Escritas en el polvo postrimero:
Y tu las entendiste,
Tan pronto a su concepto,
Que el mismo desengaño
Adquirió luzes en tu entendimiento.

**Sua** Suárez de Godoy, Juan. Excerpt from *Thesoro de varias consideraciones* 505-506.

No es otra cosa este mundo, sino vn hermoso y grande libro escrito por de dentro, y por de fuera, a do no se lee otra cosa, sino la grandeza de Dios todo poderoso. Las primeras letras son los elementos, fuego, ayre, agua, y tierra. Las silabas son los imperfectos mixtos. Las dictiones son los mixtos perfectos.[15] La oracion que tiene significacion, y perfecto sentido son los animales sensitiuos, o quan adornado esta este libro, de estrellas, de Sol, de Luna, de montes, de valles[,] de collados, de rios, de lagos, de bosques, de prados, de toda hermosura, que se puede

---

[14] Santiago's cluster of images corresponds to Carruthers' description of an important ancient metaphor for educated memory, the *thesaurus*, which meant "storage-room" and later "strongbox." It referred to both what was in the strongbox and the strongbox itself, i.e. to the contents of memory and its internal organization (33-35). A closely related metaphor was the *arca*, basically a wooden chest, box, or cupboard for transporting or storing valuables, including books (42-43).

[15] The sequence of textual elements in this segment accords with that in which a child learned to read in ancient and medieval schools. Carruthers cites Quintilian, who indicates that the pupil first learned his letters, "after which instruction proceded to syllables (ba-, be-, bo-, bi- bu-, etc.) and then to words" (111-12). Luis de Granada explains *mixtos perfectos* and *imperfectos* in the *Introducción del símbolo de la Fe*:

> En el segundo [grado] ponemos los mixtos imperfectos, como son nieves, pluvias, granizo, vientos, heladas y otras cosas semejantes que tienen alguna mas composicion [que los cuatro elementos, que son cuerpos simples, los cuales no tienen mas que dos cualidades]. En el tercero están los mixtos perfectos, como son piedras, perlas y metales; donde se halla perfecta composicion de los cuatro elementos. (188)

pensar, pues bien ignorante serias tu hombre sino acertasses a leer en este libro, mira aquestas figuras que todas ellas se muestran a Dios, y su grandeza: esta fue la respuesta de aquel beatissimo Heremita Antonio, el qual siendo preguntado como podia viuir en aquellos yermos sin libros, respondio que este mundo era su libro, en el qual estudiaua el orden de los cielos con sus estrellas, la mar con sus peces, la tierra llena de tan varias flores, assi lo llamo al mundo aquel famoso Mercurio Trismegistro en el primero libro de Prinando. *Liber tota mundi conspiratio, rerum pulcherrimus ordo contemplandi Deunda naturam sive gerit, est enim natura veluti liber vnus diuinitate plenus.* Toda esta machina deste mundo, y el hermosissimo orden de las cosas despierta la naturaleza a contemplar a Dios, no es otra cosa la naturaleza, sino como vn libro lleno de la diuinidad, y assi el mundo es libro, y el hombre es mundo, por que no sera por fuerza el hombre, y todos los hombres libretes pequeños; pero ay esta diferencia que vnos son libros aprouados, y otros reprouados y falsos, quales son los pecadores, que deshonrran a Dios. . . . Y assi en el libro prohibido, la echan en el fuego, assi al malo, solo el justo es libro dotado por la gracia, sellado con aquellas siete figuras de los siete dones del espiritu sancto, por de dentro, y por de fuera, porque alaba a Dios con el corazon alla dentro, y por de fuera con las obras: el hipocrita es libro por de fuera bueno, pero de dentro lleno de malos conceptos, y entre todos estos libros el que mas alaba a Dios es el libro de Maria, en este libro escriuio Dios aquel concepto eterno del verbo eterno, aqui se leen todas las virtudes morales, . . . luego con razon dize que engrandece su alma al Señor, pues le hizo mejor libro que ninguno del mundo . . . . Aqui se lee mejor que en otro libro, la sabiduria del Padre, porque. *Verbum caro factus est.* En medio deste libro en la carne de Maria se escriuio el verbo de Dios, la bondad del espiritu sancto, pues por obra suya, y no de varon fue escrita la potencia y grandeza de Dios, pues vn concepto, que no cabe en todo el mundo le zifro en mi tan angosto papel.

**Tel** Téllez, Gabriel [Tirso de Molina]. Excerpt from *No le arriendo la ganancia*. González Pedroso 269.

Escarmiento:
  Vuestro padre Entendimiento,
  A quien tengo por señor,
  Haciendo con él asiento
  En el libro del Temor,
  . . . .
  Pupilaje os dió en mi escuela,
  Donde hay letras y hay
    labranza;
  Que aquí, por más que
    presuma
  De sus libros el letrado,
  Muestra la experiencia, en
    suma,
  Que entre surcos del arado
  Caben surcos de la pluma.

**Ter** Teresa de Jesús. Excerpts from *Libro de la vida* 89, 171, 192.

[Capítulo 9]
Para las que van por aquí es bueno un libro para presto recogerse. Aprovechábame a mí también ver campo o agua, flores; en estas cosas hallaba yo memoria del Criador, digo que me despertaban y recogían y servían de libro . . . .
[Capítulo 23]
Es otro libro nuevo de aquí adelante, digo otra vida nueva. La de hasta aquí era mía; la que he vivido desde que comencé a declarar estas cosas de oración es que vivía Dios en mí . . . .
[Capítulo 26]
Cuando se quitaron muchos libros de romance, que no se leyesen, yo sentí mucho, porque algunos me daban recreación leerlos y yo no podía ya, por dejarlos en latín; me dijo el Señor. *No tengas pena, que Yo te daré libro vivo.* Yo no podía entender por qué se me había dicho esto, porque aún no tenía visiones; después . . . lo entendí muy bien, porque he tenido tanto en qué pensar y recogerme en lo que veía presente, y ha tenido tanto amor el Señor conmigo para enseñarme de muchas maneras, que muy poca o casi ninguna necesidad he tenido de libros; Su Majestad ha sido el libro verdadero adonde he visto las

verdades. ¡Bendito sea tal libro, que deja imprimido lo que se ha de leer y hacer, de manera que no se puede olvidar!

**Ti** Timoneda, Joan. Excerpt from *Aucto de la fuente de los siete sacramentos*. González Pedroso 98.

Y es de tan alto metal
El licor con que se enxalma
La cerviz, y frente y palma,
Que aquí os hacen la señal,
Y Dios la imprime en el alma.

**To** Torres, Jaime. Excerpt from *Desafío moral del hombre*. Dexeus de Moll 157.

Este es el libro cerrado
con dos tablas excellentes,
que es alma y cuerpo sagrado;
con siete sellos sellado,
que son varios accidentes.
Las hojas, ambas naturas,
que humana y diuina son;
los idiomas, escripturas;
las correas y ataduras,
la hypostática vnión.

**Va1** Valdivielso, José de. Excerpt from *El peregrino del cielo*. Autos 91.

Verdad:
 Soy piedra con muchos ojos,
 libro a los vuestros sellado,
  . . . .

**Va2** Valdivielso, José de. Excerpt from *Las ferias del alma*. Doze actos 91.

De rodillas la Yglesia con las escrituras en las manos.
  Señor vuestra Yglesia
   amada
  oy se postra en oracion,
  para pediros perdon
para aquesta alma humillada.
 . . . .
Borrad aquesta escritura,
que clauada a estos pies dexo[;]
aneguela el mar bermejo
dessa hermosa sangre pura.
Bien es se cancele y borre,
y bien se podra borrar
si alcanzare en ella a dar
la sangre que de vos corre.
 . . . .
 Visten de blanco al Alma.[16]
 . . . .
Demonio:
 Qual Leon herido bramo
 buelueme mis escrituras.
Iglesia:
 Ya mi esposo las borro.
Demonio:
 . . . .
 Pues y todos los pecados,
 que en sus processos auia?
  Muestra las escrituras
  en blanco.
Iglesia:
 Alza a verlos fiera Harpia,
 y podras verlos borrados.

**Va3** Valdivielso, José de. Excerpts from *El hombre encantado*. Doze actos 74, 77.

["Deleyte" is onstage dressed "de muger bizarra," with a book in one hand and a rod in the other.]
Hombre:
 Tan grande gusto recibo
 en las bellezas que veo,
 que lo que en tus ojos leo
 dentro el corazon lo escriuo.
 Tu adorada perfeccion,
 que es de la belleza suma
 mis desseos que son pluma
 trasladan al corazon.
 Aquesse libro ojeando,
 cuyos ojos son las hojas

---

[16] The white garment in which the Soul is clothed is, among other things, an allusion to one of the ceremonies of the sacrament of Baptism: "On the person baptized the priest then puts a white garment saying: 'Receive this white garment, which mayest though carry unstained before the judgment-seat of our Lord Jesus Christ; that thou mayest have eternal life'" (*Catechism* 196).

voy mis glorias repasando.
Ignorancia:
  Bien es que te satisfaga
  el libro que ves delante,
  que es libro de vn nigromante,
  y que le tiene vna Maga.
  . . . .
Aparece el Euangelio sentado, como Sol, en las manos vn libro con siete sellos, y sobre el libro vn cordero, a las quatro esquinas los quatro animales de los Euangelistas.
  Aquel libro que alli miras,
  por defuera, y por dedentro,
  escrito contra la magia,
  tiene poderosos versos.

**Va4** Valdivielso, José de. Excerpts from "Psalm. XVIII." *Exposicion parafrastica* 23.

1. Los cielos todos lenguas, con sonoras
vozes, la gloria del Señor ensalzan,
y el firmamento (libro cuyas letras
estrellas son) sus obras manifiestan,
y en ellas la excelencia de sus manos.
2. En orden militar marchan los dias,
del vno al otro passa la palabra,
deste al que viene, y del que viene a essotro,
vna noche es maestra de otra noche,
la vna estudia lo que la otra enseña,
copiada la que enseña en la enseñada,
con alternada sucession gozosas,
alabando las dos su autor eterno.
3. Con sus palabras y con su lenguaje,
sin hablar hablan, dando vozes mudas.
4. Por todo el orbe haziendo que se
  [entienda
por sus vltimos fines dilatada,
hablando en su lenguaje hasta el mas rudo,
dando vozes la eterna prouidencia,
por ellos altamente difundida.
. . . .
8. Deleytables son obras tan hermosas,
admirables son obras tan diuinas,
pero mas deleytosa y admirable
es la ley del Señor candida y pura.

**Va5** Valdivielso, José de. Excerpt from "Psalm. XXXVI." *Exposicion parafrastica* 50.

33. Porque en su corazon escrita tiene,
lamina de metal con letras de oro,
la ley de Dios que guarda, y que medita,
. . . .

**Va6** Valdivielso, José de. Excerpt from "Psalm. XXXIX." *Exposicion parafrastica* 55 [i.e. 54].

11. Y no sin causa, porque en el principio
del libro sin principio, done viuen
vuestros predestinados, el primero
lugar me distes, preferido a todos,
y en el principio de las escrituras
para que hiziesse la voluntad vuestra,
. . . .
y como la ley toda se endereza
a mi obediencia y muerte, y como enmedio
del corazón la tenga escrita . . . .

**Va7** Valdivielso, José de. Excerpt from "Psalm. LXVIII." *Exposicion parafrastica* 104.

33. Borrense sus memorias para siempre,
sin que dellos se acuerde hombre nacido,
como libros vedados se prohiban,
no los escriuan de los hombres justos
en el pio catalogo, ni tengan
lugar en los quadernos de la vida.

**Va8** Valdivielso, José de. Excerpt from "Psalm. LXXVI." *Exposicion parafrastica* 113.

9. Por ventura su enojo no aplacado
podrá oponerse a sus misericordias?
. . . .
10. No, no, y mas que empiezo libro nueuo,
y dixe agora empiezo nueuamente
. . . .

**Va9** Valdivielso, José de. Excerpt from "Psalm. CXXXVIII." *Exposicion parafrastica* 221.

15. Porque teneys escriptos exemplares
en las ideas vuestras libro eterno.

**Va10** Valdivielso, José de. Excerpt from "Ensaladilla buelta al Santíssimo Sacramento." *Romancero espiritual* 73.

Brasildo, Tyrsi y Damón,
Froniso, libres esclavos,
que traen las eses y clavos
de Dios en el corazón,
. . . .

**Va11**  Valdivielso, José de. Excerpt from "Letra al Santísimo Sacramento para las quatro vozes." *Romancero espiritual* 130.

Tiple:
  Pues mi voz sube del suelo
donde otra voz no penetra,
quiero cantar punto y letra
por aquel papel del cielo;
. . . .

**Va12**  Valdivielso, Jose dé. Excerpt from "Romance a la Circuncisión." *Romancero espiritual* 28-29.

Que la letra con sangre entra
dize el antiguo refrán,
y por ninguno se dixo,
mi Niño, con más verdad.
Es letra que a letra vista
en el cielo pagarán,
y más si con vuestra sangre
ven que rubricada va.
Es firma en blanco, Iesús,
que a vuestros amigos dais,
con que del cielo por ella
cobren a su voluntad.

**Va13**  Valdivielso, José de. "Romance al Santíssimo Sacramento, día de la Santíssima Trinidad." *Romancero espiritual* 55-56.

  A aquel libro de memoria
que en su blanco pergamino
dize mysterio de fe,
porque es de fe todo el libro;
el libro que vio San Iuan
por de dentro y fuera escrito,
sellado con siete sellos
y iluminados los cinco.
. . . .
  Libro de cifras de amor,
pues, siendo la pluma él mismo,
en aquella blanca hoja,
escrivió cifrado el *Christus*;
libro donde enquadernó
con soberano artificio
el ser de hombre y ser de Dios,
juntando humano y divino.
. . . .
  Libro que lo es de la vida,
tan sin fin y sin principio,
que tiene solas tres hojas,
el Padre, el Amor y el Hijo.
. . . .

**Va14**  Valdivielso, José de. Excerpt from "Romance al sudario de Nuestro Señor." *Romancero espiritual* 170.

En la imprenta de la muerte
en ti imprimió su trasunto,
estampando en tus dos hojas
todos sus dolores juntos.

**Va15**  Valdivielso, José de. Excerpt from 'Segundo mysterio [gozoso], de la Visitación de Nuestra Señora.' "Rosario de Nuestra Señora." *Romancero espiritual* 181.

Quando en el virginal libro,
sellado con siete sellos,
deletreó Iuan el *Christus*,
y le deprendió el primero.
. . . .
Quando en el rico escritorio
de nácar, marfil y cedro,
se gozó Iuan de mirar
de su redención el precio.

**Va16**  Valdivielso, José de. Excerpt from 'Tercero mysterio [doloroso], a la corona de espinas.' "Rosario de Nuestra Señora." *Romancero espiritual* 198.

Quando en la margen del libro
con estylo de hombre escriven
muchas notas coloradas
para que el letor las mire.

**Va17**  Valdivielso, José de. Excerpt from 'Primero mysterio glorioso, de la Resurrecion de Nuestro Señor.'

"Rosario de Nuestra Señora." *Romancero espiritual* 208.

Quando en pecho, pies y manos
escritos trae a los suyos,
para que no se le borren,
con plumas de hierros duros.

**Va18** Valdivielso, José de. Excerpt from 'Segundo mysterio glorioso, a la Ascensión de Nuestro Señor.' "Rosario de Nuestra Señora." *Romancero espiritual* 209.

Rosa en cuyas bellas hojas
con letras de oro escrivió
el deve y el ha de aver
de la humana redención.

**Va19** Valdivielso, José de. Excerpt from 'Quarto mysterio [glorioso], de la Assunción de Nuestra Señora.' "Rosario de Nuestra Señora." *Romancero espiritual* 217.

Quando esse libro cerrado
que vio el profeta bolar
a la librería del cielo
con su pergamino va.

**Var** Varona de Valdivielso, Pedro. Excerpt from *Tractado sobre el Ave*. Sainz Rodríguez 3: 679-80.[17]

**Basilio:** Es de tanto provecho el libro de Consideración, que sin él ninguno de los mortales pudo aprovechar en la vida espiritual. Y así los que no quieren volver atrás y pretenden ir adelante . . . deben traer siempre delante de los ojos de su entendimiento este libro de Consideración.
**Ruperto:** ¿En qué librería se vende ese libro tan provechoso, y que tanto vale?
**Basilio:** No se halla en las librerías famosas de París, ni Salamanca, sino en las del corazón humano, porque no es libro material sino espiritual, y con la voluntad le compra el entendimiento, y lo que lee en él lo encomienda a la memoria.
**Ruperto:** Pues tan a mano tenemos ese libro de Consideración, leed algunos capítulos, para que sepamos de qué trata.

**Vaz** Vázquez, Dionisio. Excerpt from *Sermón de la Ascensión*. *Sermones* 65-66.

Mirá quién . . . daba el testimonio, . . . y veréis . . . que fué una carta de crédito de Dios al mundo de su Hijo propio y natural.

**VgC1** Vega Carpio, Lope Félix de. Excerpts from "Cien jaculatorias a Cristo nuestro Señor." *Colección escogida* 182.

XXXIX. Ciencia infinita, con unos libros dijo un sabio que traía todos sus bienes; ¿qué dirá un alma que te tiene a ti?
XL. Fuego de mi alma, yo he pensado que quieres los pechos de pergamino, que mientras mas se acercan a ti, mas se encogen en sí. . . .
XLIII. A un hombre, Señor mio y Rey mio, que escribia tu nombre en una piedra, le dije que le escribiese en mi corazon, pues era lo mismo.

**VgC2** Vega Carpio, Lope Félix de. Excerpts from *De los cantares*. González Pedroso 185.

Cuidado:
    Esta, Señor, es la capa
    Que al ingrato mundo tapa
    Tu grandeza, donde el cielo,
    Que es aforro deste velo,

---

[17] This entire passage is reminiscent of the medieval book of memory discussed by Carruthers. Points of correspondence include the book of "Consideración" itself; the book as necessary for progress in the spiritual life; the book's being always before the eyes of one's understanding; the book's being accessible not in famous libraries, like those of Paris or Salamanca, but in the human heart; the involvement of the three faculties of will, understanding, and memory; and the act of reading the chapters, i.e. chapter titles, to see what the book is about.

Se cifra en tan corto mapa.
. . . .
Alegría:
  ¿Qué significa esta *E*?
Cuidado:
  De su *Esposa* el nombre tierno.

**VgC3** Vega Carpio, Lope Félix de. Excerpt from *Del pan y del palo*. González Pedroso 163.

Buen Año:
  ¿No ves que aquella oracion
  La escribió el Esposo mismo?
. . . .
Regocijo:
      Pues si es suya,
  Al mismo Dios se atribuya.
  ¿Y en qué la escribió?
      ¿En papel?
Buen Año:
  Y en los mismos corazones.

**VgC4** Vega Carpio, Lope Félix de. Excerpt from "A don Diego Felix Quijada y Riquelme [Epístola IV]." *La Filomena. Colección escogida* 420.

  ¿Quién mira de la flores la belleza,
Libro abierto en sus hojas? ¿Quién, sacan-
                              [do
El sol por el oriente la cabeza,
  Que no conozca que su autor, mostran-
                              [do
Su divino poder en las criaturas,
Es principio sin fin, sin cómo y cuándo?

**VgC5** Vega Carpio, Lope Félix de. Excerpts from *Isidro* 10, 15, 19, 22, 41, 48, 59, 150.

[Canto I]
  Y siendo el entendimiento,
Ojo del alma, este halló
En Dios lo que en el faltó,
Por vn infuso talento,
Como el que el libro comio.
  No supo letras, ni a quien
Preguntarselas tan bien,
Que vn abece que oyo,
Solo el Christus aprendio:
Pero este supole bien.
  Deste libro inescrutable,

Que abarca de Polo a Polo,
Fue una Sibila, vn Apolo,
Que es estudiante notable,
El que lo es de vn libro solo.
. . . .
  Los Lirios del campo via,
Y assi crecer pretendia,
Y con rustica atencion
La hormiga de Salomon,
Cuya prudencia aprendia.
  Que a donde libros, y ciencia,
No enseñauan sus primores
Con Retoricos colores,
Despertauan su inocencia
Los campos, aguas, y flores.
. . . .
  Quedole aquel viento manso
De la humildad para aliento,
Y de Adan el testamento,
Cerrado para el descanso,
Y abierto para el tormento.
. . . .
  Assi quien mas no sabia,
Porque no ay letras mejores
Entre rudos Labradores,
Libros divinos hazia
Los campos, aguas, y flores.
[Canto II]
  Y sufri que como en cera
Estamparse en el pudiera
La virtud . . .
. . . .
  Y atenta a ver que dezia,
Oyó que dixo, Cruz mia,
. . . .
  O Thao que a los varones
Vio en la frente Ezechiel,
. . . .
[Canto III]
  En efeto el cauallero,
. . . .
Venia a ver su distrito,
En vn Andaluz ouero,
De moscas negras escrito.
[Canto VI]
La verde pera en sazon,
Con el escrito melon,
. . . .
Te diera con manos francas.

**VgC6** Vega Carpio, Lope Félix de. Excerpt from "Silva IV." *Laurel de Apolo. Colección escogida* 200.

De amor es...
....
Pintar discursos, describir historias,
Que tiene amor sus guerras y victorias,
Y las quiere leer, aunque está ciego,
Porque son sus carácteres de fuego;
Y mas siendo el amor amor diuino,
Que amor que no es de Dios es desatino.

**VgC7**  Vega Carpio, Lope Félix de. Excerpt from "Egloga. Bato, Ergasto y el Rústico." *Pastores de Belen.* Sancha 270.

Bato:
  Adora en esa Madre y Hijo, a título
  De que él de Dios es firma, y ella es cé-
  [dula.

**VgC8**  Vega Carpio, Lope Félix de. Excerpt from "Egloga. Huid, lobos crueles." *Pastores de Belén. Colección escogida* 312.

Palmira:
  Causa en sus ecos las celestes aves
  Para cantar, que con humanos velos
  Está en la tierra el libro de los cielos.
Nectalvo:
  Está en la tierra el libro de los cielos,
  Cerrado ahora, y tan abierto un dia,
  Que llorarán, rompiéndose, los velos
  De cielo y tierra para gloria mia;
  ....

**VgC8.1**  Vega Carpio, Lope Félix de. Excerpt from *Relacion de las fiestas . . . en la canonizacion de . . . san Isidro. Colección escogida* 152.

Al santo Fray Pedro de Alcántara, cuya beatificacion celebran estos dias los padres franciscos descalzos, . . . correspondia este [jeroglífico]:
  Dos ángeles teniendo un libro, en que solo estaba escrito el nombre de Jesús, y en lo bajo, entre muchos libros cerrados, una mano y este rótulo: *Discere Jesum omni scibili salubrius.* Declarábase mas en español:
   Saber a Dios es saber,
   Ni de que sabe se alabe
   Quien este libro no sabe.

**VgC9**  Vega Carpio, Lope Félix de. Excerpt from 'Egloga primera.' "Al Nacimiento de Nuestro Señor." *Rimas de Tomé de Burguillos* 204.

Ya retozan en el prado
los corderos y cabritos;
los blancos y los escritos
piezas de ajedrez parecen.

**VgC10**  Vega Carpio, Lope Félix de. Excerpt from 'Egloga segunda.' "Al Nacimiento de Nuestro Señor." *Rimas de Tomé de Burguillos* 210.

  1. Agora sí, Niño santo,
que sois Libro y sois Cordero.

**VgC11**  Vega Carpio, Lope Félix de. Excerpt from "Espinelas al mismo [Santo] Niño." *Rimas de Tomé de Burguillos* 219.

Hablad, pues hablar podéis;
palabra sois, bien podéis,
tan sabia que cifra y sella
cuanto sabe Dios en ella.

**VgC12**  Vega Carpio, Lope Félix de. Excerpt from "Villancico al [Nacimiento de Nuestro Señor]." *Rimas de Tomé de Burguillos* 216.

  Dos corderillos, escritos
de amor y temor llevemos,
  ....

**VgC13**  Vega Carpio, Lope Félix de. Excerpt from "A la mudanza." *Rimas sacras. Colección escogida* 364.

Mudóse el leon airado
En cordero vendido;
No apólogo fingido,
Sino libro tan cierto, que llevado
Al sacrificio mudo,
Abrir sus sellos solamente pudo.

**VgC14**  Vega Carpio, Lope Félix de. Excerpt from "Cancion. Cantad, ruiseñores." *Rimas sacras.* Sancha 184.

  *Cantad, ruiseñores,*
*Al alborada,*

*Porque viene el Esposo*
*De ver al alma.*
. . . .
Poned en el libro
De sus hazañas
Los divinos ojos
Que han visto tantas;
. . . .

**VgC15**  Vega Carpio, Lope Félix de. Excerpt from "Elegía a la muerte del padre Gregorio de Valmaseda." *Rimas sacras. Colección escogida* 367-68.

Que el placer que tuviste a la partida
Dejaste impreso en tu difunta cara.
 Como el que va escribiendo influye vida
A las letras que animan sus concetos,
Y aunque se ausente, allí se ve esculpida,
 Así los gozos de tu bien perfetos,
Supuesto que te vas, quedan escritos,
Leyéndose en tu rostro los efetos.

**VgC16**  Vega Carpio, Lope Félix de. Excerpt from "Hombre mortal mis padres me engendraron." *Rimas sacras.* Sancha 52.

 La tierra y la miseria me abrazaron,
Paños, no piel o pluma, me envolvieron;
Por huésped de la vida me escribieron,
Y las horas y pasos me contaron.

**VgC17**  Vega Carpio, Lope Félix de. Excerpt from "A la prision." *Romancero espiritual.* Sancha 87.

Dejónos Adam un libro,
A quien del duelo llamaron
Sus míseros descendientes,
Que por él tuvieron tantos.
Con esas mortales iras
Dan los errores humanos
En vestir de honor al mundo
La venganza del agravio.
Mas ya, divino Señor,
Que el libro nos ha dejado
De tu soberano rostro
Abierto de aquella mano,
Perdonaremos injurias,
. . . .

**VgC18**  Vega Carpio, Lope Félix de. Excerpts from "A las llagas." *Romancero espiritual.* Sancha 121.

 Al tiempo que el alba llora
Sobre azucenas y lirios,
Y con letras de diamantes
Hojas escribe en jacintos;
. . . .
Francisco a Cristo pedia
. . . .
Le diese sus mismas penas,
Por ser su retrato vivo;
. . . .
Entonces con fuego ardiente
El serafin encendido,
Haciéndose todo un sello,
Con ser su ser infinito.
Imprimióle como estampa,
Viéndole papel tan limpio,
En el cuerpo a Cristo muerto,
Y en el alma a Cristo vivo.
Tal suele obediente cera
Mostrar el blason antiguo
Sobre la nema a su dueño,
En un instante esculpido.
Quedó Francisco sagrado
Como aquel lienzo divino,
Que si allí imprimió su sangre,
Aquí sus dolores mismos.

**VgC19**  Vega Carpio, Lope Félix de. Excerpt from "A san Ignacio de Loyola." *Romancero espiritual.* Sancha 124.

Mas dicen que fué alegria
De ver que quiere esculpir
Su santo nombre en los pechos
Del mas bárbaro gentil;
. . . .

**VgC20**  Vega Carpio, Lope Félix de. Excerpt from "Al Santísimo Sacramento. Los esclavos de la tierra." *Romancero espiritual.* Sancha 108.

Pan de vida, pues que sois
Sello del ser inmutable
De Dios, y en cerco pequeño
Su divina esencia cabe:
Selladnos de vuestras letras,

Para que ellas nos aparten
De los esclavos del mundo
....

**VgC21**   Vega Carpio, Lope Félix de. Excerpt from "Al seráfico padre san Francisco. Un mancebo mercader." *Romancero espiritual.* Sancha 121.

Hácense las escrituras,
Y escribe Dios de su letra
En sus pies, costado y manos
Lo que ha de haber de su hacienda.
¡Oh, qué rico mercader,
Pues Cristo mismo confiesa
Con cinco firmas de sangre
Que está pagada la deuda!

**VgC22**   Vega Carpio, Lope Félix de. Excerpts from *Triunfo de la fe.* Colección escogida 164, 169-70.

Fué forzoso dividirse estos padres, y el que por sus cartas me ha advertido destas relaciones, animado de aquel divino Pedro, gran defensor de la fe, que con su sangre misma escribió en la tierra el credo, se partió a Arima....

.... Finalmente, hallaron una nueva invencion con que sellar aquellas divinas cartas, para que fuesen conocidas por las armas del dueño adonde quiera que fuesen vistas, y fué imprimirles con un hierro ardiendo una cruz en la frente; cosa digna de ser ponderada por admirable, pues habiendo de ser las armas y el nombre del Emperador, como en algunas provincias es costumbre, sin saber lo que hacian, les pusieron las de su verdadero rey y señor, para que quedasen señalados con el *Tau* de Ecequiel, cuando aquel varon vestido de blanco los fué con este sello dividiendo de los que habian de morir en Jerusalen; y aquellos por quien dijo el ángel en el *Apocalipsi*... "Sellemos estos siervos suyos en las frentes con las señales de nuestro Dios."

**VgC23**   Vega Carpio, Lope Félix de. Excerpts from "El siglo de oro. Silva moral." *Vega del Parnaso* I. *Colección escogida* 370.

Matizando los prados de violetas,
De rosas y de cándidas mosquetas;
No de otra suerte que la alfombra pinta
El tracio con la seda de colores,
En cada rueda de labor distinta,
Arábicos carácteres y flores;
....
Pero felicidad tan soberana
Poco duró por la soberbia humana,
....
Bañó la ley la pluma
En pura sangre para tanta suma,
Que excede su papel todas las ciencias:
Tales son las humanas diferencias.
Pero, por ser los párrafos primeros,
....

**VgC24**   Vega Carpio, Lope Félix de. Excerpts from "Sentimientos a los agravios de Cristo." *Vega del Parnaso* II. *Colección escogida* 360, 363.

   Fué Pedro la figura de este dia,
....
   Como quien borra lo que tiene escrito,
Y entre renglones pone lo que inventa,
Añade afrenta a afrenta
Y delito a delito,
....
Purpúreos estampó duros matices
Sobre los muchos que en su cuerpo habia,
Porque secas tenia
Las rojas cicatrices.
....
Firme resplandeció Miguel triunfando,
La bandera divina tremolando.
   *¿Quién como Dios?* estaba en ella escrito,
Bordada de sus rayos orientales;
Las escuadras leales
Del rey incircunscrito
Al nuevo general en varias sumas
Postran hebras de sol y humillan plumas.
....
   Aquí, donde la fe tan verdadera
En nuestros corazones y almas vive,
Que en diamantes se escribe
....
   Esta cartilla, príncipe de Asturias,
En que os enseñen doctos sacerdotes,
Pues hay *Christus* y azotes,
Aunque de Dios injurias,
Vuestra santa licion primera sea;
Saldréis lector de cuanto Dios desea.

Que como Dios es un principio eterno
Sin principio ni fin, profundo abismo
De si mismo en si mismo,
Para tanto gobierno
Como os espera de uno y otro polo,
Dios ha de ser vuestro principio solo.

**Vgs1** Vegas, Damián de. Excerpt from "A los ángeles." Sancha 469.

Pues que traigo en mi frente
Vuestra memoria escrita, y en mi alma
Vuestro amor, ayudadme . . . .

**Vgs2** Vegas, Damián de. Excerpt from "A san Francisco. [Glosa tercera]." Sancha 535-36.

*Tal sello impreso traeis,*
*Francisco, en vos, que pregunto*
*Si sois Cristo o su trasunto,*
*Porque se le pareceis.*
  Francisco, tengo recelo,
Segun lo que he visto en vos,
Que o sois buleto de Dios
O algun despacho del cielo;
  Porque cual el sello veis
Con que Dios en carne tierna
Selló su Palabra eterna,
*Tal sello impreso traeis,*
  Francisco, y estos recados
Decidnos a fe si son
Cualque gracia o remision
De todos nuestros pecados.

**Vgs3** Vegas, Damián de. Excerpt from "Coloquio entre un alma y sus tres potencias." Sancha 533.

Memoria:
  . . . .
  ¿Hay cosa mas inhumana
Que gustes tú y que permitas
Que estén en mí siempre escritas
Las culpas de nuestra hermana?

**Vgs4** Vegas, Damián de. Excerpt from *Comedia llamada jacobina*. Sancha 510.

Isaac:
  A él [Lucifer] y a cuantos
    fueron de su emprenta
  Los borró de su libro . . . .

**Vgs5** Vegas, Damián de. Excerpt from "Endecha espiritual." Sancha 526.

Son leyes de aquel cuaderno
Que en la mundanesca guardan,
Aunque hay ley de Dios eterno
Que los que las guardan, ardan
Para siempre en el infierno.

**Vgs6** Vegas, Damián de. Excerpt from "Glosa al mememto homo." Sancha 550.

Medita frecuentemente
En aquel recuerdo extraño
Que tan cuidadosamente
Nos estampa cada año
La madre Iglesia en la frente:
*Memento homo quia pulvis es.*

**Vgs7** Vegas, Damián de. "Que no muere el justo." Sancha 353.

Esto en tu memoria escribe:
Que de aquel que bien viviere,
Aunque el cuerpo a tiempo muere,
El alma por siempre vive.

**Vgs8** Vegas, Damián de. Excerpt from "Razon para llorar." Sancha 481.

No tengo prenda notoria
De que soy predestinado,
Ni si escrito o si borrado
En el libro de la gloria.

**Vel** Vélez de Guevara, Luis. Excerpt from *La mesa redonda*. Robles 75.

Galalon [Judas]:
  Fue Cain en mi respecto
  traydor de papel de estraza.

**Ven** Venegas, Alejo. Excerpts from *Diferencias de libros* iii, v, vi, vii, viii, ix, x, xiii, xxx, xxxi, xxxii, xxxiii, xxxiiii, xxxvi, xxxvii, xxxix, xlii, xlvii, lxxxix, xcviii, xcix, cii, civ, cxii, cxiii, cxx, cxxxi, cxxxii, cxxxiii, cxli, cxlii, clxxi.

[Libro primero. Prologo]
Porque no aura quien con el no pueda deuotamente contemplar y hablar a su alma: para que vea quanta es la vanidad deste mundo[,] si las cosas que en el contempla no las refiere a dios cuyas son[,] para que en ellas lea la omnipotencia: sabiduria y bondad infinita de dios.
[Capitulo primero]
Libro es vna arca de deposito en que por noticia essencial[,] o por cosas o por figuras se depositan aquellas cosas que pertenescen a la informacion y claridad del entendimiento. . . . Dizese lo tercero por noticia essencial solamente por el libro diuino[,] que es la noticia y conoscimiento: que eternalmente tiene Dios de si mismo[,] por el qual conoscimiento conosce todas las cosas que fueron: son y seran: . . . y conosciendo su diuina essencia con este eterno conoscimiento: produze y engendra al verbo eterno: en el qual y por el qual cria todas las cosas. Deste libro Diuino dize sant Juan. Per quem omnia facta sunt. Que dios crio todas las cosas por el conoscimiento que tuuo y tiene de si mismo en este libro diuino. Añadese en la difinicion que tambien se depone algo por cosas: por todo aquello que fuera de si trae noticia de otra cosa: assi como son las . . . cosas señaladas en el libro de la razon.
[Capitulo ii]
Para lo qual es de notar que este nombre libro tomado assi generalmente en su primera diuision se diuide en libro Archetypo y en libro Metagrapho. El primero se dize exemplar o dechado. El segundo se dize trasunto o traslado. El primero es el libro Increado: en que leen los Angeles y los sanctos glorificados. Y en el segundo leen los hombres que biuen en este mundo. El primero avnque esta escripto de dentro y de fuera: que es la Diuinidad que de dentro se lee[,] y la Humanidad que avnque vnida al verbo Diuino se lee por defuera[,] no ay quien le abra . . . . Sino solo el Cordero[,] que murio por viuificar a los suyos: y hazerlos particioneros de aquella licion. La licion deste libro es la paga que dios tiene prometida al que trabajare en su viña. . . . Mas la gente comun que no tiene habilidad para juzgar de las tejas arriba[,] quien la entremete en presumir desemboluer la licion del libro diuino . . . . [E]l solo se basta a leer sin dexar hoja ni ringlon ni dicion ni syllaba ni letra ni tilde de todo este libro . . . . Digo mas que la mayor gloria que tienen los bienauenturados que leen en este libro: ya que ellos no le puedan acabar de leer (como dizen de pe a pa) es holgarse en extremo de todo plazer: que el mismo dios lea su libro y se entienda de todo punto . . . . Concluyamos pues que la licion deste libro diuino: pues es de dios y de los moradores del cielo: no nos anticipemos a querella leer: . . . y pues que gracias a dios tenemos tanta copia de libros en que leer: que son proprios nuestros[,] porque se escriuieron para nosotros: no perdamos el tiempo de nuestra licion . . . .
[Capitulo iii]
Assi diremos aqui que por la enquadernacion del libro diuino sacaremos . . . que tal deue ser el libro: que tal enquadernacion tiene de fuera. Porque avnque ni deuamos ni podamos abrir el libro para leer en el: porque es licion de los sanctos del cielo[,] no nos veda dios: que no veamos la enquadernacion por defuera: y por la hermosura y precio: de la qual podremos arguyr algo de lo mucho que ay dentro[,] . . . ni se veda al que sabe leer[,] que no lea el sobre escripto de la carta: que le viniere a las manos. Desta manera ya que con mucha razon dexemos el secreto del libro diuino a cuyo es: no seremos descomedidos si con la humildad y reuerencia deuida digamos con admiracion lo que dize el apostol. . . . Y con esta admiracion de humildad nos daran licencia que nos paremos: no para leer ni tantear la grandeza: sino para marauillarnos de la enquadernacion del libro diuino. La qual veremos muy guarnecida de la verdad. . . . Quiere dezir el euangelista que la luz diuina que resplandece en el ser de las criaturas es tan manifiesta: que con razon no se puede negar. . . . Sacaremos luego de la enquadernacion del libro diuino: que pues es verdad que dios es suma verdad: y por consiguiente es el sumo poder[,] saber y bondad que en quanto poderoso tiene poder para gouernar su mundo[,] y

en quanto sabio tiene orden para regirle: y en quanto bueno: quiere la perfeccion y bondad: que a sus criaturas conuiene. Esta theologia leeran los que confessaren ser dios la causa vniuersal de todas las causas: y confessaran a dios los que con atencion quisieren considerar este mundo.
[Capitulo v]
Hemos dicho de quanta excelencia es el libre aluedrio: que es como vn molde en que se imprimen las virtudes morales y theologales....
[Capitulo xvii]
Ia auemos dicho que la verdad es la enquadernacion del libro diuino.
[Capitulo xviii]
Sabido ya que la licion del libro archetypo que es el diuino: no pertenesce a los hombres que en esta vida caminan: ni del se puede saber otra cosa: fuera de lo que por la exterior enquadernacion (que es la verdad) por defuera paresce: o lo que en la escriptura sagrada esta reuelado. Queda de saber la segunda diferencia del libro que diximos que en griego se dize metagrapho: y en romance trasunto o traslado.... Digamos pues: que libro metagrapho: o trasunto es vna arca de deposito: en que por cosas o por figuras se deposita algo de lo que a la illustracion y claridad del entendimiento couiene. Este libro de traslado avnque es sacado del libro archetypo que es el diuino: no por esso se sigue que sea de tanto valor[,] o que contenga todo aquello que se contiene en el libro de donde se traslado: porque el traslador deste libro no saco mas de lo que el vido que conuenia a la licion de aquellos: para quien se escriuio. Que si todo lo que en la bienauenturanza ha de leer los sanctos: se lo diera dios escripto y deletreado en este traslado: aca tuuieran su gloria: y no se dieran mucho por yrle a leer en el cielo: pues a poca costa le pudieran leer en su tierra.... Avn en el libro deste traslado puso dios tantas dificultades que a penas se acabassen de entender en esta vida: porque leuantassemos el desseo de yrlas a leer a su reyno: y con todo esto quedos: que quedos haroneamos: contentandonos con esta licion imperfecta[,] que ni harta nuestra memoria ni entendimiento ni voluntad: que hiziera si leyeramos tan clara licion en este traslado: como la esperamos leer en el libro exemplar de donde este libro trasladado salio? De creer es que no boluieramos mas a nuestro exemplar....
[Capitulo xix]
Este traslado del libro exemplar que es el libro diuino: es en muchas diferencias: de las quales en esta primera parte diremos solamente de tres. La primera es natural. La segunda racional. La tercera es reuelada. La primera es el libro de la naturaleza de todas las cosas criadas: en que leyeron los philosophos guiados de sola la lumbre natural. Con la qual leyeron muchos secretos tocantes a la omnipotencia y sapiencia y bondad del hazedor de tal libro.... La segunda diferencia es el libro de la razon : que es todo el hombre compuesto: que no es otra cosa sino como vna cuenta de suma: en quien se suman todas las criaturas[,] y en este libro se halla la ymagen y semejanza del que le escriuio muy mas perfectamente que en el libro primero de la naturaleza. Mas porque avn este libro no era bastante a informarnos de la licion de su exemplar de donde por via de traslado salio: ... ordeno el trasladador destos de escreuirnos vn libro de su propria mano: y por conclusiones sacadas en limpio nos quiso informar de la licion: que claramente leeremos quando nos hallaremos con el en su reyno: y este es el libro reuelado de la escriptura sagrada.
[Libro segundo. Prologo]
De los libros que auemos de leer: porque se escriuieron para nosotros: el primero es el libro de la naturaleza: que es la vniuersidad de las criaturas: el qual esta tan abierto: que no tendra vso de razon: el hombre que en el no supiere leer. Porque es tan claro y legible: que si con atencion se leyere: se podra leer sin maestro exterior que le enseñe. En este libro leya sant Anton las marauillas y las virtudes del hazedor de las cosas en que leya. El qual siendo vna vez preguntado. Como podia biuir en el yermo sin conuersacion i sin libros: Respondio que el libro de la naturaleza era toda su libreria: en la qual tenia tantos volumines: quantas eran las cosas que contemplaua y tanto de mas

verdadera escriptura: quanto el libro escripto por las manos de dios: excede a los libros escriptos por las manos de hombres. En este libro leya sant Anton el gran poder de dios en la creacion: la sabiduria de dios en la gouernacion: la bondad de dios en la comunicacion. A cuyo exemplo en la licion deste libro nosotros podemos ser induzidos a temer a dios por razon de su immenso poder: a creerle por razon de su infinito saber[,] a amarle por su infinita bondad: porque no hagamos como los niños o como los locos: que viendo en el libro las letras muy galanas i muy luminadas[,] deleytanse en la pintura sin curar de lo que interiormente en la tal escriptura se representa.

[Capitulo primero. Que la vniuersidad de las criaturas es vn libro tan comun para todos[,] que no escusa a los que no le quisieren leer de la negligencia que tuuieren de tan clara y tan abierta licion.]

[Capitulo ii]
Esto es lo que dixo Dauid. Que dios estiende el cielo como pellejo. Quiere dezir: que le abre como se estiende el libro de pargamino: que era vna forma de libro arrollado comparado a manera de carta de marear que entoces se vsaua.

[Capitulo iii]
Concluyamos pues que no ay rudeza de ingenio: que impida la licion del libro de la naturaleza: cuyas principales hojas son los cielos: porque (como ya diximos) Dauid dize que dios estiende el cielo como pellejo: o como pargamino: porque no se escuse alguno que por estar cerrado el libro no le pudo leer.... El que mirando la orden y la constancia del mouimiento del cielo[,] pensare que se haze a caso: y no por prouidencia diuina[,] no es de creer sino que este tal leyendo en vn libro tan abierto y tan claro: que no tiene sentido de hombre. Pues niega lo que razon le pone delante tan leydo y deletreado: como tres y dos son cinco[,] que es vn a.b.c. tan manifiesto: que no le puede negar el sentido.

[Capitulo iiii]
En este libro segundo breuemente se tocaran en sus lugares las tres diferencias: que quedan de naturaleza. Porque son hojas del libro vulgar: que dios escriuio de su mano para todos los hombres.

[Capitulo vi]
Porque toda la philosophia: y el libro de la naturaleza esta armada sobre la materia.... Por las condiciones de la materia podremos leer algunas marauillas del criador.... Con todas aquestas tachas... de la materia[,] tiene tal propriedad que nos da muy leydo y deletreado: quan estabilissimo sea dios en su essencia.... Haga quanto pudieren los hombres y los angeles[,] que no son parte para anichilar la menor parte de la materia. De aqui subira el entendimiento a leer en su criador....

[Capitulo viii]
Leeremos en este passo el amor gratuyto con que dios ama a sus criaturas.... Pues vemos que la forma graciosamente appetece a la materia por solo hazelle bien sin esperar paga de su amor.

[Capitulo xi]
Sacaremos para nuestra licion....

[Capitulo xxxv]
Nosotros para nuestra licion sacaremos que....

[Capitulo xxxix]
Podemos aqui leer para nuestra licion.... Tambien leeremos.... [L]eeremos.... Leeremos.... En el cielo empyreo leeremos la vida celestial: y en nosotros la vida cotemplatiua: que es fiel traslado de aquella.... Nosotros sacaremos para nuestra licion....

[Capitulo xl]
Nosotros para nuestra licion sacaremos....

[Capitulo xlii]
Para que siendo induzidos por la licion de sus criaturas: creamos por la fe informada de charidad[,] y sustentada con la esperanza: los altos mysterios que sobrenaturalmente nos reuelo. Pues que avnque estrella criada en el ayre fue la guia de los reyes de oriente: no les menoscabo la fe: con que creyeron ser dios y hombre redemptor del mundo aquel que adoraron[,] assi nosotros leyendo en el libro de la naturaleza[,] no menoscabaremos el merito de la fe: cuya licion fundamentalmente se funda en otro fundamento tanto mas alto que la naturaleza: quanto mas alto es el criador que la criatura. Plega a la immensa misericordia de dios: que no permita que perdamos tan buena materia y

tan bien escripta: como es la licion de las criaturas: por la qual vengamos en el conocimiento que por ellas podemos tener de la omnipotencia y sabiduria y bondad inefable de dios: con que pudo y supo y quiso criarlas: para que de a.b.c. siruiessen al hombre.
[Libro tercero. Capitulo primero]
Que andando a buscar a dios por el rastro de las criaturas: no pudo bien atinar quien fuesse dios: hasta que se recogio en lo intimo de su alma: y alli le hallo en la ley de la razon: que (como dize el apostol) escriuio dios en los corazones de los hombres.... De modo que el menor grado de conoscer sera por las criaturas corporeas: el segundo que sube sobre este: es la ley de la razon escripta y sellada en los corazones de los hombres: y el supremo es la reuelacion de las cosas: que se contiene en la escriptura sagrada.
[Capitulo xiiii]
Porque este mundo es vna relucencia y traslado del original diuino[,] en el qual traslado conosce el entendimiento criado las perfectiones de vn dios....
[Capitulo xvi]
Que... fue cosa muy conueniente a la bondad liberalissima de dios: hazer vna criatura libre: en quien se summassen todas las criaturas que libremente crio. Esta criatura es el hombre summa de todas las criaturas....
[Capitulo xvii]
Esta magnificencia que las criaturas han de dezir de su criador[,] esta cargada y assentada a la cuenta del hombre: porque allende quel es la suma: en que se suman todas las criaturas: es claro que para su seruicio y prouecho se crio el mundo con todo lo que ay en el.
[Capitulo xviii]
La razon illustrada con la informacion de la fe: aproucha tanto: que ya se suelta a leer de letura: y saca algunas liciones por si: que avnque a ella le sean naturales con la illustracion de la fe las lee con mayor efficacia y prouecho notable....
[Capitulo xxiiii]
Desta composicion escriuio Marco Tulio .... Que pues cada vno tiene vn tan buen libro en su misma persona: como es la armonia y coposicion de su cuerpo:

razon es que se suelte a leer en el: si quiera (conforme al refran) como el ruyn lector: que sabe leer en el libro de su aldea. En este libro de la coposicion de su cuerpo leera que no esta en este mundo como bruto.... que algun fin tiene a que tira .... Leera lo segundo: que no deue querer para otro: lo que no quiere para si.
[Capitulo xxv]
Suelen dezir vn refran. Que quando la hormiga se ha de perder: alas le han de nascer. Este se dira por los hombres que por leer mal en su libro: se van de si mismos. Estos son los hombres que no estan contentos con la vocacion: para que fueron llamados: o con el estado en que biuen.... Estos tales... se van de si mismos[,] porque leyeron muy mal en la republica de su cuerpo.
[Libro quarto. Prologo]
[E]n los tres libros passados breuemente tocamos el conocimiento que el hombre puede alcanzar: assi por la enquadernacion del libro original: como por la licion de las criaturas y las leyes de la razon. Mas ... ha menester vna licion sobrenatural .. .. Porque ya que de la verdad que leyo en la enquadernacion del libro original: saco la libertad de su libre aluedrio: y de la luz que resplandesce en las tinieblas: conoscio la primera causa increada fuente de todas las causas. Y de las porciones de su alma superior y inferior hallo el desseo que tiene de la bienauenturanza: no pudo sacar de todas estas liciones: que cosa y que tal sea la substancia de la bienauenturanza....

**Vi1** Villanueva, Tomás de. Excerpt from *En la anunciación de la ... Virgen María. Sermón I. Obras* 246.

Repasad con asiduidad este libro de pureza, escrito por el dedo de Dios por dentro y por fuera: leed en él la santidad, leed el recato, la prudencia, la caridad, la mansedumbre, la humildad; en una palabra, leed la plenitud acabada de todas las virtudes. Leed por dentro la virtud, por fuera la modestia....

**Vi2** Villanueva, Tomás de. Excerpt from [*En la anunciación de la ... Virgen María.*] *Sermón V. Obras* 286-87.

Dice San Agustín: ¡Oh José!, hijo de David, el mismo Dios que escribió tales maravillas en su ley, realizó también maravillas en tu esposa. Mira con tus ojos en María, lo mismo que has leído en tus libros.... Ella misma es ciertamente la ley. Por consiguiente, quien esculpió sin punzón las palabras de la ley en las tablas, de un modo semejante, sin necesidad de punzón, valiéndose de su dedo, el Espíritu Santo esculpió al Verbo eterno en el seno de la Virgen sin el concurso de varón; y el que proporcionó pan en el desierto sin el arado, sin la menor corrupción dejó encinta a la Virgen; y el que hizo germinar a la vara seca, hizo que la Hija de David engendrara sin semilla. Mira, pues, con tus ojos en María lo mismo que has leído en tus libros.

**Vi3** Villanueva, Tomás de. *En la natividad de la Virgen María. Sermón I. Obras* 172-85.

1. De cinco diferentes libros tenemos noticia en la Sagrada Escritura, a saber: el libro de la vida, el libro de la naturaleza, el libro de la escritura, el libro del ejemplo y el pensamiento, el libro de la conciencia; quien tuviere éstos en su biblioteca y los leyere con frecuencia, será, sin duda, bienaventurado.[18] El primero es el libro de la vida, que, según San Agustín, es la presciencia o predestinación de los elegidos, por la cual son escogidos para la vida los nombres de aquellos que se hallan indeleblemente grabados en el conocimiento de Dios.... Por lo cual dice Casiodoro: El libro de la vida no es otra cosa que el conocimiento de los que son elegidos para la vida, y esto es la inscripción y elección que se llama libro de la vida: libro, porque están en la memoria de Dios; de la vida, porque contiene sólo a los que estan destinados a la vida, y, tomado así, sólo los elegidos se hallan en este libro. Y en este sentido habla el Apóstol cuando dice de algunos santos: *Cuyos nombres están es-* critos *en el libro de la vida*. También se entiende de otro modo más general, y entonces el libro de Dios o libro de la vida es la divina Sabiduría o el Verbo de Dios, en el cual se encuentran en grado eminente las razones ideales o ideas de todas las criaturas.... Y éste también recibe el nombre de libro de la vida: libro, porque en él se ven todas las cosas; de la vida, porque todas las cosas viven en él.... Y de este modo se interpreta el libro de la vida en el Salmo: *Todos están escritos en tu libro*, no sólo los buenos, sino también los malos; y también se entiende así en el Apocalipsis, cuando dice que se abrirá el libro *que es el de la vida*, y los muertos, tanto los buenos como los malos, serán juzgados según lo que en él estuviere escrito. Sólo los ángeles y los bienaventurados leen en este libro, y cada uno según la facultad de su entendimiento, por lo que los superiores iluminan a los inferiores. Dichosa escuela con tantos y tan aventajados estudiantes con un solo Maestro y un solo libro.

2. .... [T]odas leen desde el principio en este libro, leerán hasta el fin, y nunca se agotarán las enseñanzas del libro, siempre aprenderán allí cosas nuevas. Léanse en este libro los impenetrables consejos de la divina Sabiduría....

También aquí se leen los nombres de los predestinados.... Dichosos los que... tuvieron la suerte de ser escritos en este libro; porque la notación de destinados no proviene de nuestros méritos, sino puramente de un don gratuito de Dios....

[E]l que desde la eternidad está escrito en el libro de la vida, sin duda que jamás será borrado de él. Y aunque diga el Salmo: *Raídos sean del libro de los vivientes*, debe entenderse esto según la justicia actual de Dios o de una manera privativa; ... se dice que borra a los que no escribió; por lo cual se ha de entender como una exposición lo que sigue: *Y no queden escritos en el* (libro) *de los justos*;

---

[18] Cf. Carruthers in reference to Cassiodorus' *Institutiones* and to St. Jerome: "For memory is most like a library of texts, made accessible and useful through various consciously-applied hueristic schemes" (33).

que quiere decir, sean borrados por privación, no positivamente, es decir, no sean escritos. . . . Ningún mortal o muy raro, sino solos los ángeles pueden leer en este libro. En un éxtasis leyó muy breve espacio San Pablo . . . . Leía también en ese libro un poco el discípulo amado del Señor, y de aquella lectura brotó el admirable comienzo: *En el principio era el Verbo*, etc. El libro de esta primera clase es de solos los discípulos.

3. Pero la divina Providencia proporcionó a sus pequeñuelos otro libro que contiene los rudimentos y elementos primeros, es decir, este mundo sensible, que se llama libro de la naturaleza, para que en él pudieran aprender a juntar las letras y pronunciar las palabras, y llegar mediante el raciocinio, como los niños, del conocimiento de las cosas sensibles a la sabiduría de las inteligibles . . . . No llegan así al conocimiento las criaturas celestiales que leen en el libro de la vida. Por lo cual muy bien compara San Bernardo este mundo visible con el libro común que suele haber colgado de una cadena en los claustros de las iglesias, para que todos los que quisieren puedan leer en él. Así este mundo está puesto delante de todas las gentes, pueblos y naciones, para que conozcan por él la sabiduría, poder, bondad, grandeza, hermosura, eternidad y perfección del supremo Artífice, y así reconozcan y adoren al Señor cuanto durare esta escuela de niños . . . . Pues tiempo vendrá en que el cielo se plegará como un libro y nadie podrá leer ya en él; no porque se plieguen los cielos como un libro, sino porque nadie leerá en este libro. Se dice que se plegará, porque los condenados no tendrán ya lugar de leer, y los predestinados serán destinados a otro libro más levantado, el de la vida . . . .

Mientras tanto, ¡dichoso el que puede leer en este librito elemental! No le menospreciemos, puesto que es hermoso y esplende en él una gran sabiduría. ¡Qué admirable y hermoso! ¡Qué hermosos caracteres tiene! El sol, la luna, las estrellas, el cielo, la tierra, los mares y diversidad de animales, de aves, árboles y flores. Pero nosotros, como niños pasmados, admiramos la elegancia de los caracteres sin saber leer ni entender, cual les ocurre a los niños y rústicos con las hermosas máximas escritas en la iglesia. ¡Oh si entendiésemos, oh si leyésemos y penetráramos las criaturas como los justos y los santos, qué gusto y sabor encontraríamos dentro de la corteza! ¡Cómo penetraríamos la gran teología y filosofía que está oculta en todas estas cosas! Por lo que dice el Salmo: *Los cielos publican la gloria de Dios, y el firmamento anuncia las obras de sus manos*.

Por consiguiente, . . . este mundo se nos dió no sólo para nuestra utilidad y servicio, sino también para nuestra enseñanza y magisterio . . . .

4. Así es que en estas cosas se oculta una gran sabiduría y ciencia; pero ni la conocemos ni la entendemos, porque solamente, como los animales, buscamos y nos paramos en su utilidad, y no, como racionales, en las voces significativas de las cosas visibles. Por lo que es digno de admiración que, habiendo escrito tantos libros de filosofía Aristóteles, Platón, Teofrasto, Plinio, Disoscórides, Avicena y Galeno, sobre las propiedades de las cosas . . . , tan poco, sin embargo, se haya escrito de esta filosofía. Apenas hallamos quien al escribir haya cumplido su cometido de enseñarnos a leer este libro. En los últimos capítulos de Job, como queriendo abrirnos camino para filosofar sobre las cosas, instruye admirablemente Dios a Job en esta mística filosofía . . . .

Escuchemos ahora acerca de estos libros al Salmista, que entona solemnemente: *Los cielos publican la gloria de Dios, y el firmamento anuncia las obras de sus manos*. Cada día transmite con abundancia al siguiente estas voces, es decir, Dios al ángel: he aquí el primer libro y la primera escuela; *y la una noche*, es decir, la criatura sensible, *las comunica a la otra noche*, o sea, al hombre mortal: he aquí el segundo libro y la segunda escuela. Acerca de esta continúa: *No hay lenguaje ni idioma en los cuales no sean entendidas estas sus voces*. . . . ¡Con qué primor y elocuencia habló el Salmista acerca de esta escuela!

5. Veamos ahora el tercer libro y la tercera escuela. . . . Este libro es el de la Es-

critura, porque no le bastaba al hombre el conocimiento natural; érale necesaria la sabiduría revelada.... Dios, pues, por su piedad, viendo que no le bastaba aquel libro, añadió la revelación, para ejercer de maestro Él mismo, que había sido Creador; y se dignó mandar escribir para enseñanza del mundo, ampliando y explicando mediante la ley escrita aquella ciencia natural.... Pues lo que por la creación había impreso en la naturaleza, nos lo da más explícito con su enseñanza.... En Ezequiel se encuentra figurado este libro, en que *estaban escritas lamentaciones y canciones lúgubres y ayes*, y en el Apocalipsis, donde trata del libro escrito por dentro y por fuera, dulce en la boca, pero amargo en el vientre. El libro estaba cerrado y fué abierto....

El libro de que se habla es la Sagrada Escritura, libro escrito por dentro a causa del sentido místico, y por fuera, a causa del literal.... Muy dulce en la boca por el conocimiento de la bondad de Dios y de su misericordia, ... en cambio, es amargo en el vientre, porque *quien acrecienta el saber, también acrecienta el trabajo*.... Se hallan en este libro *escritas lamentaciones*, que es la penitencia; *canciones lúgubres*, el gozo de los bienaventurados; *ayes*, la condenación de los malos....

6. Bien conoció el Señor nuestra ... incapacidad para comprender sus palabras. ... Y por eso, movido de piedad, nos transcribió prácticamente en otro libro ejemplar, manifiesto e ideal, cuanto nos había enseñado teóricamente en el libro de la naturaleza y en el libro de la Escritura....

Este libro es el Verbo encarnado, en el cual nos ha sido representada toda la vida espiritual y cristiana que se nos ha dado en el Evangelio y en otros libros, para que leamos allí claramente la caridad, la penitencia, la humildad, la mansedumbre, la santidad, el desprecio del mundo y las demás virtudes. Este es el libro de los justos: a éste miran, tienen siempre este manual en las manos ante los ojos, manual del cual dice Job: ¡*Oh quién me diera uno que me oyese, y escribiese el proceso mismo que juzga!* Es decir, que el juez escriba en sí mismo la ciencia de la vida que ordena....

El amanuense de este libro es el mismo Dios; la pluma, el Espíritu Santo; el pergamino, el seno de la Virgen; la tinta, su purísima sangre. En su seno fué escrito, acomodado, y encuadernado este libro; de su sangre fué configurado el sacratísimo carácter del Verbo divino.... Y le plugo consignarlo escrito para los mortales, a fin de que el ángel y el hombre leyesen en un mismo libro. Así, para conservarlos y enseñárselos a otros, acostumbramos nosotros a grabar nuestros conceptos en caracteres, a estamparlos en la escritura y guardarlos, como para conservarlos en pequeñas vasijas.

7. Pero veamos cómo está escrito. *Mi lengua ha sido hecha pluma de amanuense que escribe muy ligero.*... Esta lengua se ha convertido en pluma dando forma y componiendo en el seno de la Virgen: *El Espíritu Santo descenderá sobre ti. Que escribe muy ligero.* Y ¡con qué velocidad escribe! En un instante fué formado el cuerpo.... ¡Oh ilustre escritura, oh excelentísima marca, en la cual se oculta tal Verbo eterno! ¡Oh escritura excelsa, que ahora se nos propone para lectura de todos los mortales.... Sobre la belleza y sublimidad de esta escritura continúa.... ¿En qué libro, en qué papiro se encuentra grabada esta escritura? En el purísimo pergamino virginal, sin marca infamante de pecado. Por lo que muy bien y justamente se puede decir del tema: *Genealogía de Jesucristo*. Excelentísima comparación.

Dos excelentes comparaciones encontramos acerca de la Virgen en la Escritura: una, en la que se la compara con el vellón.... Excelente comparación, aunque no le es inferior aquella en que se la compara con un purísimo pergamino, en el cual y del cual se formó el Verbo eterno....

8. Sólo nos queda ya el quinto, el de la conciencia, del cual se dice en el Apocalipsis: *Y abriéronse los libros, y abrióse también otro libro, que es el de la vida; y fueron juzgados los muertos por las cosas escritas en los libros*. Este es el libro de las cuentas; por tanto, serán juzgados por el libro del Señor y por éste. En este libro aparecerá consignado todo lo que hemos hecho: pensamientos, deseos, palabras y

obras. Están ahora como borrados, pero aparecerán entonces. Como en un papel escrito con el jugo de ciertos limones no aparecen los caracteres de las letras, pero arrimado al fuego se pone de manifiesto todo lo escrito, así con aquel fuego se iluminarán los secretos tenebrosos y se manifestarán los pensamientos del corazón que se habían dado al olvido. Y así, San Bernardo, hablando de la conciencia, dice: es una membrana sutil e impregnada de tinta; no puede borrarse lo que en ella se ha escrito, aunque al presente no se manifiesta la escritura. . . . Procuremos, por consiguiente, tener limpia la escritura de la conciencia, a fin de que, cuando aparezca el libro de la vida, seamos dignos de ser llevados de esta escuela de niños a la escuela de los ángeles, y con ellos aprendamos a leer la sabiduría de Dios en la gloria . . . .

**Vit** Vitoria, Ignacio de. Excerpt from *Oracion funeral*. Vega Carpio. *Coleccion de las obras sueltas* 438.

¿Hay duda, que al passo que es mas cendrada la criatura, mas se desenvuelven en ella las grandezas de su autor? . . . . No, pues sobre el ser criatura, ya señala, era nuevo sobrescrito de la mano de Dios ser excelente y lustrosa.

# WORKS CONSULTED

Primary Sources-Golden Age Authors or Texts

*Actio quae inscribitur examen sacrum.* González Pedroso 133-43.
Aguilar, Juan Bautista. "A Christo Señor nuestro." Simón Díaz. *El libro español* 169.
———. "A la Virgen Santissima." Simón Díaz. *El libro español* 169-72.
"Alabanza a San Francisco." *Poesías varias.* Ms. II-1581. Palacio Real, Madrid. 5: 225.
*Aucto de las donas que envió Adán a nuestra Señora.* González Pedroso 22-26.
*Aucto de los desposorios de Josef.* González Pedroso 54-61.
*Avtos sacramentales, con qvatro comedias nvevas, y svs loas, y entremesses.* Primera parte. Madrid: Maria de Quiñones, 1655.
Ávila, Juan de. *Sermón I. [Para la] Dominica primera de Cuaresma. Colección de sermones inéditos del Beato Juan de Ávila.* Ed. Ricardo G. Villoslada. Miscelánea Comillas 7. Comillas (Santander): Universidad Pontificia, 1947. 39-49.
———. *Sermón 1. [Para el] Domingo I de Adviento. Sermones. Pláticas espirituales.* Vol. 2 of *Obras completas del B. Mtro. Juan de Avila.* Ed. Luis Sala Balust. 2 vols. Madrid: Católica, 1952. 33-50.
———. *Sermón 3. En vísperas de Navidad. Sermones* 83-102.
———. *Sermón 13. [Para el] Miércoles de la IV semana de Cuaresma. Sermones* 231-45.
———. *Sermón 32. [Para el] Martes de Pentecostés. Sermones* 455-78.
———. *Sermón 33. [Para el] Jueves Santo. Sermones* 479-88.
———. *Sermón 78. [Para la fiesta de] San Francisco de Asís. Sermones* 1210-31.
———. *Sermón 79. [Para la] Festividad de Todos los Santos. Sermones* 1232-42.
Balvás Barona, Antonio. "Romance a San Francisco." Simón Díaz. *El libro español* 166-68.
Ballester, Juan Bautista. *Aclamacion festiva, del antiqvissimo ivramento de la concepcion.* Valencia: Gerónimo Vilagrasa, 1664. Rpt. in *Once sermones* no. 2.
Bernal, Juan. *Sermon a las honras que la Ciudad de Sevilla hizo a la Magestad del Rey don Philipo. II. nuestro Señor.* Sevilla: Francisco Perez, 1599.
Bonilla, Alonso de. "A la Sinagoga sobre los azotes de Christo." *Peregrinos pensamientos, de misterios divinos, en varios versos, y glosas dificultosas.* Baeza: Pedro de la Cuesta, 1614. 42.
———. "Cristo y san Pablo en su conversion." Sancha 232.
———. "De cómo se descubre algo de Dios por las criaturas." Qtd. in Valdivielso *Romancero espiritual* xxxiv, lx.
———. "De excelencias de la Virgen." *Nombres y atribvtos de la impecable siempre virgen Maria Señora Nuestra. En Octauas. Con otras rimas a diversos assumptos, y glosas dificiles.* Baeza: Pedro de la Cuesta, 1624. 67 [2nd series of foliation].

Bonilla, Alonso de. "De la conciencia del hombre." Simón Díaz. *El libro español* 165-66.
———. "De la sangre y agua del costado de Christo." *Peregrinos pensamientos* 46.
———. "De la Santificacion del Baptista." *Peregrinos pensamientos* 66.
———. "De la unidad y trinidad de Dios." Sancha 70-73.
———. "De las excelencias del ayuno." Sancha 139-41.
———. "Decima a los dos, S. Iusto y Pastor, Martires." *Nombres y atribvtos* 48 [2nd series of foliation].
———. "Del inefable nombre de Iesvs." *Nombres y atribvtos* n. pag.
———. "Discvrso de la soledad y angvstias de la siempre virgen; en el transito, y passion de Iesu Christo Señor y Dios nuestro." *Nombres y atribvtos* 182-203.
———. "Nombres y atribvtos de la impecable siempre virgen Maria Señora nuestra." *Nombres y atribvtos* 3-182.
———. "Redondillas de la Virgen." Simón Díaz. *El libro español* 162-64.
———. "Romance de la Santa Cruz." *Peregrinos pensamientos* 51-52.
———. "La Virgen fue aquel papel do quanto supo escriuio Dios, por cuya gracia no cayó mancha alguna en el. Glosa." *Nombres y atribvtos* 54 [2nd series of foliation].
Braones, Alonso Martín. *Epitome de los trivnfos de Jesvs, y finezas de su amor en la redempcion del hombre.* Sevilla: Lvcas Martin de Hermosilla, 1686.
Bravo, Nicolás. *Benedictina. En qve trata la milagrosa vida del glorioso S. Benito, con vna breue recapitulacion de las Religiones, que le reconocen por Padre, assi monasticas como militares.* Salamanca: Artvs Taberniel, 1604.
Cabrera, Alonso de. *La circuncisión de Jesucristo. Navidad y Año Nuevo. Nacimiento y niñez de Jesús.* Ed. Luis G. Alonso-Getino. Madrid: V. Fierro, 1920.
———. *La circuncisión del Señor. Navidad y Año Nuevo.*
———. *Consideraciones del Domingo en la octava de la Pascua de Resurrección. Sermones del P. Fr. Alonso de Cabrera.* Nueva Biblioteca de Autores Españoles 3. Madrid: Bailly/Bailliere, 1906. 461-71.
———. *Consideraciones del Lunes después del Domingo de la Resurrección. Sermones* 452-60.
———. *Consideraciones del Martes después del Domingo cuarto de Cuaresma. Sermones* 265-73.
———. *Consideraciones del Miércoles después del Domingo Primero de Cuaresma Sermones* 94-103.
———. *Consideraciones del Viernes después del Domingo cuarto de Cuaresma. Sermones* 288-97.
———. *Consideraciones del Viernes después del Domingo primero de Cuaresma. Sermones* 113-21.
———. "El dedo de Dios." Qtd. in *Navidad y Año Nuevo.* Ed. Luis G. Alonso-Getino. lix.
———. *Del santísimo nombre de Jesús. Navidad y Año Nuevo.*
———. *Nacimiento de Jesucristo. Navidad y Año Nuevo.*
Cairasco de Figueroa, Bartolomé. "A la Cruz bendita." Sancha 310.
———. "Afeccion cristiana." Castro 2: 481.
———. "Apariencia santa." Castro 2: 473.
———. "Caridad. Otra difinicion." Castro 2: 493.
———. "Causa pia." Castro 2: 479-80.
———. "Constancia virginal. – Viudez. – Voluntad resuelta." Castro 2: 494.
———. "Discrecion." Castro 2: 452-53.
———. "Enmienda." Castro 2: 460.
———. "Gracia. Otra difinicion." Castro 2: 489.
———. "Honestidad. Otra difinicion." Castro 2: 476.

Cairasco de Figueroa, Bartolomé. "Longanimidad." Castro 2: 466.
———. "Música." Castro 2: 469.
———. "Oracion." Castro 2: 453.
———. "Oracion. Otra difinicion." Castro 2: 453.
———. "Perseverancia." Castro 2: 490.
———. "Prision." Castro 2: 468.
———. "San Dámaso, Papa." Sancha 300.
———. "Soledad. Otra difinicion." Castro 2: 478.
———. "Tranquilidad." Castro 2: 456.
———. "Victoria." Castro 2: 462.
Calderón de la Barca, Pedro. *A María el corazón. Autos sacramentales.* Vol. 3 of *Obras completas.* Ed. A. Valbuena Briones. Nueva ed. 3 vols. Madrid: Aguilar, 1966-67. 1134-51.
———. *A tu prójimo como a ti* (Primera redacción). *Autos* 1889-1907.
———. *Amar y ser amado y divina Filotea. Autos* 1774-96.
———. *El Año Santo de Roma. Autos* 491-512.
———. *El Año Santo en Madrid. Autos* 539-58.
———. *El Arbol del mejor fruto. Autos* 986-1009.
———. *La cena del rey Baltasar. Autos* 155-77.
———. *El Cordero de Isaías. Autos* 1746-71.
———. *El cubo de la Almudena. Autos* 566-85.
———. *La cura y la enfermedad. Autos* 750-73.
———. *La devoción de la Misa. Autos* 246-69.
———. *El día mayor de los días. Autos* 1636-59.
———. *El divino Jasón. Autos* 61-72.
———. *El divino Orfeo* (Primera versión). *Autos* 1820-39.
———. *Los encantos.de la Culpa. Autos* 406-21.
———. *El gran duque de Gandía san Francisco de Borja. Autos* 97-110.
———. *El gran mercado del mundo. Autos* 225-42.
———. *El gran teatro del mundo. Autos* 203-22.
———. *La hidalga del valle. Autos* 115-29.
———. *La humildad coronada de las plantas. Autos* 389-404.
———. *El indulto general. Autos* 1722-40.
———. *La inmunidad del sagrado. Autos* 1115-31.
———. *El jardín de Falerina. Autos* 1506-25.
———. *La lepra de Constantino. Autos* 1798-1817.
———. *El lirio y la azucena. Autos* 916-39.
———. *Lo que va del hombre a Dios. Autos* 273-97.
———. "Loa [del juicio de Paris] para *El Cordero de Isaías.*" *Autos* 1742-46.
———. "Loa 'La fábrica del navío' para *La protestación de la Fe.*" *Autos* 1742-46.
———. "Loa para *Andrómeda y Perseo.*" *Autos* 1690-95.
———. "Loa para *La inmunidad del sagrado.*" *Autos* 1110-14.
———. "Loa para *El jardín de Falerina.*" *Autos* 1502-1506.
———. "Loa para *Mística y real Babilonia.*" *Autos* 1042-66.
———. "Loa para *El nuevo palacio del Retiro.*" *Autos* 132-36.
———. "Loa para *Las órdenes militares.*" *Autos* 1013-17.
———. "Loa para *Psiquis y Cupido*" (Madrid). *Autos* 362-66.
———. "Loa para *La siembra del Señor.*" *Autos* 677-81.
———. *El maestrazgo del Toisón. Autos* 894-913.
———. *Los misterios de la Misa. Autos* 300-14.
———. *Mística y real Babilonia. Autos* 1047-66.
———. *La nave del mercader. Autos* 1444-70.
———. *No hay más fortuna que Dios. Autos* 615-34.

Calderón de la Barca, Pedro. *El nuevo hospicio de pobres. Autos* 1185-1207.
——. *El nuevo palacio del Retiro. Autos* 137-52.
——. *El orden de Melchisedech. Autos* 1068-86.
——. *Las órdenes militares. Autos* 1017-39.
——. *El pastor Fido. Autos* 1585-1607.
——. *El primer refugio del hombre y probática piscina. Autos* 964-83.
——. *Primero y segundo Isaac. Autos* 801-20.
——. *La protestación de la Fe. Autos* 730-47.
——. *Psiquis y Cupido* (Madrid). *Autos* 367-86.
——. *Psiquis y Cupido* (Toledo). *Autos* 346-62.
——. *¿Quién hallará mujer fuerte? Autos* 656-76.
——. *La redención de cautivos. Autos* 1321-40.
——. *El sacro Parnaso. Autos* 776-97.
——. *El santo Rey don Fernando* (Primera parte). *Autos* 1269-88.
——. *La segunda esposa y triunfar muriendo. Autos* 428-47.
——. *La serpiente de metal. Autos* 1528-51.
——. *El socorro general. Autos* 317-35.
——. *Sueños hay que verdad son. Autos* 1212-34.
——. *El tesoro escondido. Autos* 1667-88.
——. *Tu prójimo como a ti* (Segunda redacción). *Autos* 1410-42.
——. *La vacante general. Autos* 473-88.
——. *El valle de la zarzuela. Autos* 700-21.
——. *El veneno y la triaca. Autos* 180-97.
——. *El verdadero Dios Pan. Autos* 1241-62.
——. *El viático cordero. Autos* 1158-78.
——. *La vida es sueño* (Primera redacción). *Autos* 1861-75.
——. *La vida es sueño* (Segunda redacción). *Autos* 1387-1407.
——. *La viña del Señor. Autos* 1473-99.
Camós, Marco Antonio de. *Microcosmia, y govierno vniversal del hombre christiano, para todos los estados y qvalquiera de ellos.* Barcelona: Monasterio de S. A., por Pablo Malo, 1592.
Cardoso, Fernando. *Oracion funebre en la muerte de Lope de Vega.* Vega Carpio. *Coleccion de las obras sueltas* 467-392 [i.e. 492].
Castilla, Antonio de. *Al nacimiento del Hijo de Dios.* Fernández, J. 339-53.
Castillejo, Cristóbal de. "Consiliatoria al Rey de Romanos don Fernando." Castro 1: 232-34.
——. "Dialogo entre la verdad y la lisonja." Castro 1: 236-45.
——. "La invencion de la Cruz." Castro 1: 248-52.
Coello, Antonio. *El reyno en cortes, y rey en campaña. Avtos sacramentales* 2-11.
——. *La Virgen del Rosario, la amiga mas verdadera.* Robles 366 [i.e. 339]-351 [2nd series of pagination].
Córdoba, Sebastián de. "Soneto V." *Garcilaso a lo divino.* Ed. Glen R. Gale. Madrid: Castalia, 1971. 97.
Dávila, Juan. *Passion del Hombre-Dios referida y ponderada en decimas españolas.* Leon de Francia: Horacio Boissat y Gorge Remevs, 1661.
Dicastillo, Miguel de. *Avla de Dios, Cartvxa real de Zaragoza.* Añadida y avmentada por otro monge de la misma Cartuxa. Zaragoza: Pasqual Bueno, 1679.
Domínguez Camargo, Hernando. *S. Ignacio de Loyola. Poema heroyco.* Dala a la estampa Antonio Navarro Navarrete. Madrid: Ioseph Fernandez de Buendía, 1666.
Enciso y Monzón, Juan Francisco de. *La Christiada: poema sacro, y vida de Jesv Christo Nuestro Señor.* Cádiz: n.p., 1694.
Enríquez Gomez, Antonio. *Epistolas de Job.* Castro 2: 385-88.

Escobar y Mendoza, Antonio de. *Nveva Gervsalen Maria. Poema heroyco.* IV. impression enmendada por su autor. Valladolid: Iuan Bautista Varesio, 1625.
Fernández, Juan, ed. *Avtos sacramentales, y al nacimiento de Christo, con svs loas, y entremeses.* Recogidos de los maiores ingenios de España. Madrid: Antonio Francisco de Zafra, 1675.
Fernández, Lucas. *Auto de la Pasión. Teatro español del siglo XVI.* Ed. Alfredo Hermenegildo. Madrid: Sociedad General Española de Librería, 1982. 11-47.
Ferriol y Caycedo, Alonso de, ed. *Libro de las fiestas que en honor de la immaculada Concepcion de la Virgen Maria, nuestra señora, celebró su deuota y antigua Hermandad. En san Francisco de Granada. Año de mil y seiscientos y quinze.* Granada: Martin Fernández. A costa de la Hermandad, 1616.
Fuente, Gerónimo de la. "Dezimas." Ferriol y Caycedo 58-59.
Gálvez de Montalvo, Luis. "El llanto de san Pedro." Sancha 253-56.
Garau, Francisco. *El Sabio Instruído de la Naturaleza.* Qtd. in Soria Ortega 107.
García de Escañuela, Bartolomé. *Elogios de oradores. Panegirico vltimo, qve en el sextodezimo dia, y Fiesta, que hizo la Coronada, e Imperial Villa de Madrid a la Canonizacion del Glorioso San Pedro de Alcantara, dixo* . . . . Huerta 418-34.
"Glossa a la inmacvlada concepcion de Nvestra Señora: Sobre el verso de todo el mundo en general." *Ramillette de divinas flores para el desengaño de la vida hvmana.* Recopiladas con diligencia de los mejores y mas famosos Poetas de nuestros tiempos, por P. F. G. C. D. Amberes: Cesar Ioachim Trognesius, 1629. 206.
Godínez, Felipe. *Avto del nacimiento de Christo.* Fernández, J. 100-11.
———. *Avto del nacimiento de Christo, y pastores de Belen.* Fernández, J. 89-99.
Gómez Tejada de los Reyes, Cosme. "Dime, pastor, así el cielo." Sancha 214.
Góngora, Luis de. "A la procesion que víspera del Corpus se hace al Sagrario." Castro 1: 497.
Gracián, Baltasar. *El Criticón.* Ed. Evaristo Correa Calderón. 3 vols. Madrid: Espasa-Calpe, 1971.
Granada, Luis de. *Introduccion del Simbolo de la Fe. Obras del V. P. M. Fray Luis de Granada.* Ed. José Joaquín de Mora. 2nd ed. Biblioteca de Autores Españoles 6. 3 vols. Madrid: Rivadeneyra, 1848-1910. 1: 181-733.
Guerra y Ribera, Manuel de. "Aprobación de los *Sueños Misteriosos de la Escritura* (1687) de P. Rodríguez Monforte." Soria Ortega 346-52.
———. *Declamacion evangelica, dia de Santa Catalina, Virgen y Martyr, en la possession de Rector, que tomó en la Vniversidad de Salamanca, Don Francisco de Adda, Conde de Sales, predicada en la Capilla Real de San Geronimo, con assistencia de los Graduados della. Sermones varios de santos.* Lisboa: Domingos Carneyro, 1683. 50-69.
———. *Oracion a San Iorge, patrono de los Reynos de Aragon, assistiendo el Supremo Consejo de Aragon, y Orden de Montesa. Sermones varios* 182-208.
———. *Oracion a su Magestad en la Real Capilla, en dia de Quarenta Horas. Sermones varios* 209-25.
———. *Oración del Miércoles de las Señales.* Qtd. in Soria Ortega 283-84.
———. *Oracion dia de Santa Catalina a la possession de Rector de la Vniversidad de Salamanca, que tomo el Señor Don Diego de Assanza. Sermones varios* 160-82.
———. *Oracion en la beatificacion de onze Martyres, y San Francisco Solano, predicada en su Convento de San Francisco. Sermones varios* 226-65.
———. *Oracion evangelica a la declaracion de NN. SS. PP. San Iuan de Mata, y San Felix de Valois, Patriarcas de la Santissima Trinidad, Redempcion de Cautivos. Sermones varios* 20-50.
———. *Oracion evangelica a la Vncion de la Madalena. Sermones varios* 392-419.
———. *Oracion evangelica a Santo Tomás Apostol, a sus Magestades. Sermones varios* 69-88.

Guerra y Ribera, Manuel de. *Oracion evangelica a sus Magestades, que predicó dia de Santa Ana en su Real Capilla. Sermones varios* 1-19.

———. *Oracion evangelica en la Canonizacion de San Francisco de Borja, predicada en su Colegio de la Compañia de Iesus de Salamanca. Sermones varios* 466-503.

———. *Sermón de la Conversión de la Magdalena.* Herrero Garcia 175-98.

———. *Sermón de la tempestad.* Qtd. in Soria Ortega 341-42.

———. [*Sermón de las honras del Cardinal Cisneros*]. Qtd. in Soria Ortega 260-61.

———. [*Sermón de Santa Teresa de Jesús*]. Qtd. in Soria Ortega 242.

———. [*Sermón del Santissimo Sacramento*]. Qtd. in Soria Ortega 170.

Huerta, Antonio de, ed. *Trivnfos gloriosos, epitalamios sacros, pomposos, y solemnes aparatos, aclamacion alegre, y ostentosas fiestas, qve se celebraron año de M. DC. LXIX. en ... Madrid, y en el Real Conuento de San Gil, Descalzos de la Serafica Orden. A la canonizacion de ... San Pedro de Alcantara.* Madrid: Bernardo de Villa-Diego, 1670.

Hurtado de Mendoza, Antonio de. *Vida de N. Señora.* [*Obras*]. Lisboa: Miguel Manescal, 1690. 141-80.

Jáuregui y Aguilar, Juan de. "Al Santísimo Sacramento. Romance alegórico." *Rimas.* Vol. 1 of *Obras.* Ed. Inmaculada Ferrer de Alba. Madrid: Espasa-Calpe, 1973. 148-50. 2 vols.

Ledesma, Alonso de. "A la certidumbre de la muerte y al gozo que halla el justo en ella." Sancha 176-77.

———. "A la conversion de un pecador." Sancha 138.

———. "A la Cruz de Cristo." D'Ors 348-52.

———. "A la culpa de Adán y encarnación del hijo de Dios. En metáfora de una esecución." D'Ors 157-59.

———. "A la enseñanza de Cristo nuestro Señor y a la imitacion de los fieles en sus virtudes." Sancha 167-68.

———. "A la intencion." Sancha 155-56.

———. "A la natividad de nuestra Señora." [*Primera parte de*] *Conceptos espirituales.* [Madrid, 1600]. 97-98.

———. "A S. Francisco." [*Primera parte de*] *Conceptos* 145-46.

———. "A S. Ivan Evangelista recostado al pecho de Cristo." [*Primera parte de*] *Conceptos* 128.

———. "A santa Lucía, virgen y mártir." Sancha 175.

———. "Al agradecimiento y a la ingratitud." Sancha 178.

———. "Al glorioso San Sebastián." D'Ors 334-35.

———. "Al juicio final y particular del hombre." Sancha 137-38.

———. "Al nacimiento de Cristo nuestro Señor, y milagros de su vida." Sancha 161-63.

———. "Ay, insaciable apetito." D'Ors 329-31.

———. "Dios y el Hombre." Sancha 221.

———. "Discurso a la vida de Cristo, desde su encarnación hasta que vuelva a juzgar a los hombres. En metáfora de un reformador de una universidad." D'Ors 154-57.

———. "Epitetos a la Cruz de Christo nuestro Señor." [*Primera parte de*] *Conceptos* 45-46.

———. "[Hieroglifico]. Pintóse una hoja de oliva." D'Ors 242.

———. "Hieroglifico IX." D'Ors 372.

———. "Hieroglifico XVI." D'Ors 374.

———. "Hieroglifico XXXIII." D'Ors 379.

Lemos, Jerónimo de. Diálogo IV. *La torre de David moralizada.* Sainz Rodríguez 3: 210-26.

León, Luis de. "Carta dedicatoria a las Madres Priora Ana de Jesús y religiosas carmelitas descalzas del monasterio de Madrid." Sainz Rodríguez 3: 385-97.

León, Luis de. *De los nombres de Cristo*. Ed. Federico de Onís. 3rd ed. 3 vols. Madrid: Espasa-Calpe, 1948. Vol. 3.
López de Andrade, Diego. *Tratado sobre el Euangelio del segundo [i.e. tercero] Martes. Tratados sobre los Evangelios de la Qvaresma*. Lisboa: Iorge Rodriguez, 1616.
López de Ubeda, Juan, comp. *Cancionero general de la Doctrina Cristiana hecho por Juan López de Ubeda (1579, 1585, 1586)*. Intro. Antonio Rodríguez Moñino. 2 vols. Madrid: Sociedad de Bibliófilos Españoles, 1962-64.
———. "Dios puso en hombre su nombre." Sancha 336.
———. "Tratado de la vida segura." Sancha 365-68.
Lucas del Olmo, Alfonso. "Estaciones de la via sacra." Sancha 144-46.
Ludeña, Juan de. *Sermon VI. Qve en la fiesta qve celebró el Excelentissimo Señor Duque de Villahermosa, predicó*.... Huerta 199-219.
Madre de Dios, Lucas de la. *Sermon IX. Qve en la fiesta, qve hizo la Excelentissima Señora Doña Antonia de la Cerda, Marquesa del Carpio, predicó*.... Huerta 267-99.
Malón de Chaide, Pedro. *La conversión de la Magdalena*. Ed. Félix García. Vol. 1. Madrid: "La Lectura," 1930. 3 vols. 1930-47.
———. *Tratado de la Conversión. Escritores del siglo XVI*. 2 vols. Madrid: M. Rivadeneyra, 1853-55. 1: 275-417.
Manrique, Angel. *Discvrso I. De la serenissima Reyna de los Angeles: Predicable en el dia de su purissima Concepcion. Libro primero de las excelencias de la serenissima Reyna de los Angeles, vnica abogada y Patrona de nuestra Orden. Sanctoral y Dominical Cisterciense, hecho de varios discvrsos, predicables en todas las fiestas de nuestra Señora, y otros Sanctos*. 2nd ed. Valladolid: Francisco F. de Cordoua, 1613. 3-16.
———. *Discvrso II. De la serenissima Reyna de los Angeles: Predicable en el dia de su dichoso Nacimiento. Libro primero. Sanctoral* 17-26.
———. *Discvrso V. Del Glorioso san Pedro de Castilnuovo Martyr, y primer Inquisidor de quantos ha auido en la Iglesia contra hereges. Libro tercero de algvnos apostoles y martires, entresacados de los mas ilustres de nuestro Orden. Sanctoral* 198-215.
Manrique, Luisa. "Romance. ¡Qué breves que son, Dios mio!" Serrano y Sanz 29.
Mata, Gabriel de. *Primera, segunda y tercera parte del Cavallero Assissio, en el nacimiento, vida y muerte del seraphico Padre Sanct Francisco. En octaua Rima*. 3 vols. Bilbao: Mathias Mares, 1587. Vol. 2.
Mira de Amescua, Antonio. *Pedro Telonario*. González Ruiz 797-814.
———. *Las prvebas de Christo*. Fernández, J. 37-56.
Montesino, Ambrosio. "Coplas de la cruz." Sancha 449-52.
———. "Coplas . . . de san Juan Baptista y del misterio de la santa visitacion que la Reina del cielo hizo a santa Isabel." Sancha 407-15.
———. "Coplas de san Juan evangelista." Sancha 441-44.
———. "Coplas . . . del santísimo parto de la Virgen nuestra Señora." Sancha 438-40.
———. "Coplas [del sudor de sangre en Getsemaní]." Sancha 421-23.
———. "Coplas . . . en gloria de nuestra Señora." Sancha 420-21.
———. "Del glorioso san Francisco." Sancha 430-35.
———. "Itinerario de la Cruz." Sancha 424-29.
———. "Romance del glorioso san Juan Evangelista." Sancha 458-59.
———. "Tractado del santísimo sacramento de la Hostia consagrada." Sancha 402-407.
Morales, Jacinta María de. "A san Pedro mártir." Castro 2: 545.
Morchon, Manuel. "[Cancion real a San Pedro de Alcantara]." Huerta 55.

Moreto, Agustín. *La gran casa de Austria y divina Margarita*. González Pedroso 551-63.

Murillo, Diego. "En alabanza de nuestro Serafico Padre San Francisco." *Divina, dvlce, y provechosa poesia*. Dispuesta, y sacada a luz por Iuan Calderon. Zaragoza: Pedro Cabarte, 1616. 158-67.

———. *En la festividad del glorioso apostol S. Andres. Discursos predicables sobre los Evangelios . . . en los quatro Domingos del Adviento, y fiestas principales que occurren en este tiempo hasta la Septuagessima*. Zaragoza: Angelo Tauanno, 1603.

———. *En la fiesta de la Circuncision de Christo, y del sanctissimo nombre de Iesus. Discursos predicables sobre todos los evangelios, qve canta la Iglesia, en las festividades de Christo Nvestro Redemptor*. Lisboa: Antonio Aluarez, 1608, 240-78.

———. *En la fiesta de las llagas de Christo Redemptor nvestro. Discvrsos predicables . . . en las festividades de Christo*. 412-53.

Navarra, Pedro de. Diálogo I. *Diálogos muy subtiles y notables*. Sainz Rodríguez 3: 155-66.

[*Once sermones a honra de la Virgen, y de su concepcion inmaculada*.] V. p., 1651-1731. [Ticknor Collection of Spanish and Portuguese Books. Boston Public Library. D.270b.63]

Orozco, Antonio de. *Historia de la reyna Saba, quando disputo con el rey Salomon en Hierusalem*. Salamanca: Andrea de Portonariis, 1568.

Oseguera, Diego de. *Estacionario de la Creacion y Redencion del Mundo*. Madrid: Pedro Madrigal, 1593.

Ovando, Gaspar de. "Dezimas." Ferriol y Caycedo 65-66.

Padilla, Pedro de. "Cancion al sanctissimo nombre de Iesus." *Iardin espiritval*. Madrid: Querino Gerardo Flamenco, 1585.

———. *Grandezas y Excelencias de la Virgen señora nuestra*. Madrid: Pedro Madrigal, 1587.

———. "Niño sagrado y bendito." Sancha 211.

Paravicino y Arteaga, Hortensio Félix. "A la santa Cruz, despues de haber descendido de ella nuestro Redentor Jesucristo." Sancha 148-49.

———. "[A San Esteuan Protomartir]." *Obras postvmas, divinas, y hvmanas, de Don Felix de Arteaga*. Alcalá: Maria Fernandez, 1650. 25-27.

———. *Iesv Cristo desagraviado: o oracion evangelica: de los vltrages de Iesvcristo Señor i Redentor nuestro, nueva i sacrilegamente repetidos por unos Hebreos*. Madrid: Francisco Martinez, 1633.

Pérez de Montalbán, Juan. *El Polifemo*. González Ruiz 815-36.

Pineda, Juan de. *Diálogos familiares de la Agricultura christiana*. Ed. Juan Meseguer Fernández. 5 vols. Biblioteca de Autores Españoles 161-63, 169-70. Madrid: Atlas, 1963-64.

Pradas, Juan Valero. *Sermon, qve se predico dia vltimo de la celebre Octaua, que en la Santa Iglesia Cathedral de la Ciudad de Origuela, se consagró a Nuestra Señora de Monserrate, en accion de gracias de auer cessado la peste*. Murcia: Miguel Lorente, 1679. Rpt. in *Once sermones* no. 10.

Prado, Adrián de. "Al santísimo Sacramento." Sancha 291.

Quevedo y Villegas, Francisco de. "A don Alvaro de Luna. Romance." *Poesías*. Vol. 3 of *Obras de don Francisco de Quevedo Villegas*. Ed. Florencio Janer. Biblioteca de Autores Españoles 69. 3 vols. Madrid: Atlas, 1946-53. 334.

———. "Con la voz del enojo de Dios suena [Soneto]." *Poesías* 329.

———. *Lágrimas de Jeremías castellanas, ordenando y declarando la letra hebraica, con paraphrasis y comentarios en prosa y verso*. *Poesías* 465-73.

Rebolledo, Bernardino de. "La constancia vitoriosa, égloga sacra." Castro 2: 394-407.

Ribera, Luis de. "Contemplacion sobre la sentencia de los cantares: *Osculetur me, osculo oris sui.*" Sancha 63.
———. "De la entrada y triunfo de Cristo en el cielo el dia de su gloriosa Ascension." Sancha 287-88.
———. "Del nombre de Jesus o Salvador." Sancha 58.
———. "Del triunfo de Cristo en Jerusalen." Sancha 63.
Robles, Isidro de, ed. *Navidad y Corpvs Christi, festejados por los mejores ingenios de España, en diez y seis avtos a lo divino, diez y seis Loas, y diez y seis entremeses.* Madrid: Ioseph Fernandez de Buendía, 1664.
Rocaberti, Hipólita de Jesús, y. "¡Oh! llave piadosa." Serrano y Sanz 151-52.
Rodríguez, Lucas, comp. "A la encarnacion." *Conceptos de divina poesia.* Alcala de Henares: Iuan Iñiguez de Lequerica, 1599. 1.
———. "A la gloriosa Magdalena." *Conceptos* 62.
Rodríguez Coronel, Juan. *Sermon VII. Qve en la fiesta, qve hizo el Excelentissimo Señor Conde de Oropesa, Presidente del Consejo de Italia, Predicó* . . . . Huerta 219-49.
Rojas Zorrilla, Francisco de. *La viña de Nabot.* González Ruiz 837-64.
Salas Barbadillo, Alonso de. "A san Juan Bautista.-Al *Ecce Agnus Dei.*" Castro 2: 43.
San Félix, Marcela de. "Coloquio espiritual entre el Alma, la Tibieza, la Oración, el Amor Divino." Serrano y Sanz 252-60.
———. "Loa a una Profesión." Serrano y Sanz 289-90.
Santiago, Hernando de. [*Consideración para el] jueves después de Ceniza. Consideraciones de Quaresma.* Qtd. in Pérez 132.
———. *De la conversión de San Pedro. Consideraciones de Quaresma.* Qtd. in Pérez 24-25.
Sarriera, Elvira. "Oda a San Ignacio de Loyola." Serrano y Sanz 392.
Silvestre, Gregorio. "A una calavera." Sancha 331.
Solís y Ribadeneyra, Antonio de. "A la Conversion de San Francisco de Borja, a vista del Cadauer de la Señora Emperatriz." *Varias poesias, sagradas, y profanas.* Recogidas, y dadas a lvz por Jvan de Goyeneche. Madrid: Antonio Roman, 1692. 133.
Suárez de Godoy, Juan. *Thesoro de varias consideraciones sobre el psalmo de misericordias "domini in eternum cantabo".* Barcelona: Sebastian de Cormellas al Call, 1598.
Téllez, Gabriel. *No le arriendo la ganancia.* González Pedroso 269-82.
Teresa de Jesús. *Libro de la vida.* Ed. Guido Mancini. Madrid: Taurus, 1982.
Terrones del Caño, Francisco. *Instrucción de predicadores.* Ed. Félix G. Olmedo. 1617, Madrid: Espasa-Calpe, 1960.
Timoneda, Joan. *Aucto de la fuente de los siete sacramentos.* González Pedroso 95-100.
Torres, Jaime. *Desafío moral del hombre contra los tres enemigos: "Demonio, Mundo y Carne". En la fiesta del Sanctissimo Sacramento.* Dexeus de Moll 143-58.
Valdivielso, José de. "Ensaladilla buelta al Santíssimo Sacramento." *Romancero espiritual.* Ed. J. M. Aguirre. Madrid: Espasa-Calpe, 1984. 73-77.
———. *Las ferias del alma. Doze actos sacramentales, y dos comedias divinas.* Toledo: Iuan Ruyz [por] Martin Vazquez de la Cruz, 1622. 81-91.
———. *El hombre encantado. Doze actos* 70-80.
———. "Letra al Santísimo Sacramento, para las quatro vozes." *Romancero espiritual* 130-31.
———. *El peregrino del cielo. Autos sacramentales eucarísticos.* Ed. Alejandro Sanvisens. Barcelona: Cervantes, 1952. 79-99.

Valdivielso, José de. 'Primero mysterio glorioso, de la Resurreción de Nuestro Señor.' "Rosario de Nuestra Señora." *Romancero espiritual* 206-209.

———. "Psalm. XVIII." *Exposicion parafrastica del Psalterio y de los canticos del Breuiario.* Madrid: Biuda de Alonso Martin, 1623. 23.

———. "Psalm. XXXVI." *Exposicion* 50.

———. "Psalm. XXXIX." *Exposicion* 55 [i.e. 54].

———. "Psalm. LXVIII." *Exposicion* 104.

———. "Psalm. LXXVI." *Exposicion* 113.

———. "Psalm. CXXXVIII." *Exposicion* 221.

———. 'Quarto mysterio [glorioso], de la Assunción de Nuestra Señora.' "Rosario de Nuestra Señora." *Romancero espiritual* 214-17.

———. "Romance a la Circuncisión y Nombre de Iesús." *Romancero espiritual* 26-30.

———. "Romance al Santíssimo Sacramento, día de la Santíssima Trinidad." *Romancero espiritual* 55-56.

———. "Romance al sudario de Nuestro Señor." *Romancero espiritual* 168-70.

———. 'Segundo mysterio glorioso, a la Ascensión de Nuestro Señor.' "Rosario de Nuestra Señora." *Romancero espiritual* 209-211.

———. 'Segundo mysterio [gozoso], de la Visitación de Nuestra Señora.' "Rosario de Nuestra Señora." *Romancero espiritual* 180-82.

———. 'Tercero mysterio [doloroso], a la corona de espinas.' "Rosario de Nuestra Señora." *Romancero espiritual* 196-99.

Varona de Valdivielso, Pedro. Capítulo 11. *Tractado sobre el Ave María.* Sainz Rodríguez 3: 679-93.

Vázquez, Dionisio. *Sermón de la Ascensión. Sermones.* Ed. Félix G. Olmedo. Madrid: Espasa-Calpe 1956. 45-72.

Vega Carpio, Lope Félix de. "A don Diego Félix Quijada y Riquelme. [Epístola IV]." *La Filomena. Colección escogida de obras no dramáticas.* Comp. Cayetano Rosell. Biblioteca de Autores Españoles 38. Madrid: Atlas, 1950. 419-20.

———. "A la mudanza." *Rimas sacras. Colección escogida* 363-64.

———. "A la prision." *Romancero espiritual.* Sancha 87.

———. "A las llagas." *Romancero espiritual.* Sancha 121-22.

———. "A san Ignacio de Loyola, cuando colgó la espada en Monserrate." *Romancero espiritual.* Sancha 124.

———. "Al mismo asunto [del santísimo Sacramento]. Los esclavos de la tierra." *Romancero espiritual.* Sancha 108.

———. "Al mismo asunto [del seráfico padre san Francisco]. Un mancebo mercader." *Romancero espiritual.* Sancha 121.

———. "Cancion. Cantad, ruiseñores." *Rimas sacras.* Sancha 184.

———. "Cien jaculatorias a Cristo nuestro Señor." *Colección escogida* 181-83.

———. *Coleccion de las obras sueltas, assi en prosa, como en verso, de D. Frey Lope Felix de Vega Carpio, del habito de San Juan.* 21 vols. Madrid: Don Antonio de Sancha, 1776-79. Vol. 19.

———. *De los cantares.* González Pedroso 181-91.

———. *Del pan y del palo.* González Pedroso 161-71.

———. "Egloga. Bato, Ergasto y el Rústico." *Pastores de Belen.* Sancha 270-71.

———. "Egloga. Huid, lobos crueles, que ha venido." *Pastores de Belén. Colección escogida* 312.

———. 'Egloga primera.' "Al Nacimiento de Nuestro Señor." *Rimas de Tomé de Burguillos.* Ed. José Manuel Blecua. Barcelona: Planeta, 1976. 201-206.

———. 'Egloga segunda.' "Al Nacimiento de Nuestro Señor." *Rimas de Tomé de Burguillos* 207-14.

Vega Carpio, Lope Félix de. "Elegía a la muerte del padre Gregorio de Valmaseda." *Rimas sacras. Colección escogida* 367-68.

———. "Espinelas al mismo [Santo] Niño [de la Cruz] cuando le trujeron del Monasterio de Santa Juana de la Cruz al de la Santísima Trinidad de Descalzas." *Rimas de Tomé de Burguillos* 218-19.

———. "Hombre mortal mis padres me engendraron." *Rimas sacras*. Sancha 52.

———. *Isidro. Poema castellano*. Madrid: Luis Sanchez, 1599. San Sebastian: Impresion Manul, 1935.

———. *Relación de las fiestas que la insigne villa de Madrid hizo en la canonización de su bienaventurado hijo y patrón san Isidro. Colección escogida* 148-58.

———. "Sentimientos a los agravios de Cristo nuestro bien por la nacion hebrea." *Vega del Parnaso. Colección escogida* 359-63.

———. "El siglo de oro. Silva moral." *Vega del Parnaso. Colección escogida* 369-71.

———. "Silva IV." *Laurel de Apolo. Colección escogida* 200-203.

———. *Triunfo de la fe en los reinos del Japón, por los años de 1614 y 1615. Colección escogida* 159-80.

———. "Villancico al [Nacimiento de Nuestro Señor]." *Rimas de Tomé de Burguillos*, 214-17.

Vegas, Damián de. "A los ángeles." Sancha 469.

———. "A san Francisco [Glosa tercera]." Sancha 535-36.

———. "Coloquio entre un alma y sus tres potencias, donde se introduce irse dellas, amotinada por el mal servicio que le hacen." Sancha 530-34.

———. *Comedia llamada jacobina, o bendicion de Isaac*. Sancha 509-24.

———. "Endecha espiritual sobre los vicios que comunmente hoy reinan en el mundo, ponderando la vanidad y ceguedad de los que los siguen." Sancha 525-26.

———. "Glosa al memento homo, etc." Sancha 550.

———. "Que no muere el justo." Sancha 353.

———. "Razon para llorar." Sancha 480-93.

Vélez de Guevara, Luis. *La mesa redonda [y el Diuino Carlo Magno]*. Robles 65-82.

Venegas, Alejo. *Primera parte de las diferencias de libros q ay en el universo*. Toledo: Juan de Ayala, 1546. Barcelona: Puvill, 1983.

Villanueva, Tomás de. *En la anunciación de la bienaventurada Virgen María. Sermón I. Obras de Santo Tomás de Villanueva. Sermones de la Virgen y obras castellanas*. Ed. Santos Santamarta. Biblioteca de Autores Cristianos 96. Madrid: Católica, 1952. 234-46.

———. *[En la anunciación de la bienaventurada Virgen María]. Sermón V. Obras* 281-98.

———. *En la natividad de la bienaventurada Virgen María. Sermón I. Obras* 172-85.

Vitoria, Ignacio de. *Oracion funeral panegyrica . . . a las celebres amables memorias de Lope Felix de Vega Carpio*. Vega Carpio. *Coleccion de las obras sueltas* 401-66.

Primary Sources – Twentieth Century Authors or Texts

Aldecoa, Josefina R. *La enredadera*. Barcelona: Seix Barral, 1984.

Atwood, Margaret. *Cat's Eye*. New York: Bantam, 1989.

Bishop, Elizabeth. *The Collected Prose*. Ed. Robert Giroux. New York: Farrar, Straus and Giroux, 1984.

Byatt, A. S. *Possession: A Romance*. New York: Vintage, 1990.

Cherryh, C. J. *The Faded Sun: Kutath*. New York: Daw, 1979.

Cisneros, Sandra. *Woman Hollering Creek and Other Stories*. New York: Random House, 1991.

Clarke, Arthur C. *The Songs of Distant Earth.* New York: Ballantine, 1986.
Cohen, Matt. *The Spanish Doctor. A Novel.* New York: Beaufort, 1984.
Crowther, Hal. "View from a high place." *Independent* [Durham, NC] 30 May-5 June, 1990.
Dallas, Ian. *The Book of Strangers.* Albany, NY: SUNY P, 1988.
"Decoding the Book of Life." *NOVA.* WGBH-TV, Boston. 31 Oct. 1989.
Dillard, Annie. *An American Childhood.* New York: Harper & Row, 1987.
Freire, Paulo, and Donaldo Macedo. *Literacy: Reading the Word and the World.* South Haley, MA: Bergin & Garvey, 1987.
Frost, Robert. "A Patch of Old Snow." *The Poetry of Robert Frost.* Ed. Edward Connery Lathem. New York: Holt, Rinehart and Winston, 1969.
George, Elizabeth. *A Great Deliverance.* New York: Bantam, 1988.
Gilster, Paul A. "An Unlikely Novel About an Unlikely Thinker." Rev. of *The World as I Found It,* by Bruce Duffy. *The News and Observer* [Raleigh, NC] 11 Oct. 1987: 6D.
Grimes, Martha. *The Anodyne Necklace.* New York: Dell, 1983.
———. *The Deer Leap.* New York: Dell, 1985.
———. *The End of the Pier.* New York: Knopf, 1992.
———. *The Five Bells and Bladebone.* New York: Dell, 1987.
———. *Help the Poor Struggler.* New York: Dell, 1985.
———. *Jerusalem Inn.* New York: Dell, 1984.
———. *The Man with a Load of Mischief.* New York: Dell, 1981.
———. *The Old Contemptibles.* New York: Ballantine, 1991.
———. *The Old Fox Deceiv'd.* New York: Dell, 1982.
———. *The Old Silent.* New York: Dell, 1989.
Guibert, Rita. "Miguel Angel Asturias." *Seven Voices: Seven Latin American Writers Talk to Rita Guibert.* Trans. Frances Partridge. New York: Knopf, 1973, 119-79.
Hambly, Barbara. *The Witches of Wenshar.* New York: Ballantine, 1987.
Hunt, Diana, and Pam Hait. *The Tao of Time.* New York: Simon & Schuster, 1990.
James, P. D. *The Black Tower.* New York: Warner, 1975.
———. *Death of an Expert Witness.* New York: Warner, 1977.
Janés, Clara. *Los caballos del sueño.* Barcelona: Anagrama, 1989.
Lambert, Darwin. "Playing the Earth-Man Game." *Park Guide. Shenandoah National Park.* Shenandoah Newspaper Corp., 1982.
Langton, Jane. *The Dante Game.* New York: Viking, 1991.
———. *The Transcendental Murder.* New York: Penguin, 1964.
———. *Murder at the Gardner.* New York: Penguin, 1988.
Leopold, Aldo. *A Sand County Almanac: With Other Essays on Conservation from "Round River."* New York: Oxford UP, 1966.
LeSueur, Meridel. "The Ancient People and the Newly Come." *Growing Up in Minnesota: Ten Writers Remember Their Childhoods.* Ed. Chester G. Anderson. Minneapolis: U of Minnesota P, 1976. 17-46.
MacDonald, John D. *Dress Her in Indigo.* New York: Fawcett Gold Medal, 1969.
Marsh, Ngaio, with H. Jellett. *The Nursing Home Murder.* New York: Jove, 1963.
———. *Grave Mistake.* Boston: G. K. Hall, 1979.
———. *Photo Finish.* Boston: Little, Brown, 1980.
Matousek, Mark. "The Crucible of Homelessness." *Common Boundary: Between Spirituality and Psychotherapy* 9 (Sept.-Oct. 1991): 12-17.
Michaud, Ellen, Alice Feinstein, and the Editors of Prevention Magazine. *Fighting Disease: The Complete Guide to Natural Immune Power.* Emmaus, PA: Rodale, 1989.
Middleton, Harry. "Treasure in the Sand." *Southern Living* 23 (August 1988): 28-31.
Moyes, Patricia. *Dead Men Don't Ski.* New York: Holt, 1959.

Peters, Ellis. *The Confession of Brother Haluin: The Chronicles of Brother Cadfael.* New York: Mysterious, 1988.
———. *The Knocker on Death's Door.* New York: Warner, 1970.
———. *A Morbid Taste for Bones: The First Chronicle of Brother Cadfael.* New York: Fawcett Crest, 1977.
———. *One Corpse Too Many: The Second Chronicle of Brother Cadfael.* New York: Fawcett Crest, 1979.
———. *The Raven in the Foregate: The Twelfth Chronicle of Brother Cadfael.* New York: Morrow, 1986.
———. *The Rose Rent: The Thirteenth Chronicle of Brother Cadfael.* New York: Fawcett Crest, 1986.
Preuss, Paul. *Hide and Seek.* Vol. 3 of *Arthur C. Clarke's Venus Prime.* 6 vols. New York: Avon, 1987-91.
Rendell, Ruth. *The Tree of Hands.* New York: Ballantine, 1984.
Robinson, Marilynne. *Housekeeping.* New York: Bantam, 1980.
Shulman, Lee S. "Toward a Pedagogy of Substance." *Network News & Views* [The Educational Excellence Network] 8 (July 1989): 15-21.
Siegel, Bernie S. *Love, Medicine & Miracles: Lessons Learned about Self-Healing from a Surgeon's Experience with Exceptional Patients.* New York: Harper & Row, 1986.
Tepper, Sheri S. *Grass.* New York: Bantam, 1989.
Tyler, Anne. *Breathing Lessons.* New York: Berkley, 1988.
Welty, Eudora. *Losing Battles.* New York: Random House, 1970.

SECONDARY SOURCES

Aguirre, J. M. *José de Valdivielso y la poesía religiosa tradicional.* Toledo: Diputación Provincial, 1965.
Alarcos García, Emilio. "Los sermones de Paravicino." *Selección antológica de sus escritos.* Vol. 1 of *Homenaje al Excmo. Sr. Dr. D. Emilio Alarcos García.* 2 vols. Valladolid: U de Valladolid. Facultad de Filosofía y Letras, 1965. 217-99.
Alborg, Juan Luis. *Historia de la literatura española.* 2nd ed. Vol. 2. *Epoca barroca.* Madrid: Gredos, 1970. 4 vols. 1970-81.
Amezúa y Mayo, Agustín G. de. "Cómo se hacía un libro en nuestro Siglo de Oro." *Opúsculos histórico-literarios.* 3 vols. Madrid: Consejo Superior de Investigaciones Científicas, 1951-53. 1: 331-73.
Arco, Ricardo del. "El poeta Fray Jaime Torres, maestro de los Argensolas." *Boletín de la Real Academia Española* 30 (Sep.-Dic. 1950): 369-88.
Arias, Ricardo. *The Spanish Sacramental Plays.* Boston: Twayne, 1980.
Arribas Arranz, Filemón. "Un documento de 1454 en forma de rollo." *Colaboración.* Vol 2 of *Homenaje al Excmo. Sr. Dr. D. Emilio Alarcos García.* 2 vols. Valladolid: Sever-Cuesta, 1965. 571-78 + 2 plates.
Barrera, Cayetano Alberto de la. *Nueva biografía de Lope de Vega.* 2 vols. Biblioteca de Autores Españoles 262-63. Madrid: Atlas, 1973-74.
Bayley, Peter. *French Pulpit Oratory 1598-1650.* Cambridge: Cambridge UP. 1980.
Berchorius, Petrus. *Dictionarium, vulgo Repertorium morale.* Tomus operum in ordine IV. Qui est *Dictionarii moralis* pars secvnda. Coloniae Agrippinae: Joannis Wilhelmi Huisch, 1731.
Biblia sacra juxta Vulgatam Clementinam. Rome: Desclée, 1938.
Blecua, Alberto. *Manual de crítica textual.* Madrid: Castalia, 1983.
Bohigas, Pedro. *El libro español (Ensayo histórico).* Barcelona: Gustavo Gili, 1962.

Bonaventure, Saint. *The Mind's Road to God.* Trans. George Boas. New York: Liberal Arts, 1953.
Briesemeister, Dietrich. "Die Buchmetaphorik in den Autos sacramentales." *Iberoromania* 4 (1981): 98-115.
Caballero Venzala, Manuel. *Diccionario bio-bibliográfico del Santo Reino.* 2 vols. Jaén: Instituto de Estudios Giennenses, 1979-86.
Carilla, Emilio. *Hernando Domínguez Camargo.* Buenos Aires: R. Medina, 1948.
Carruthers, Mary J. *The Book of Memory: A Study of Memory in Medieval Culture.* Cambridge Studies in Medieval Literature 10. Cambridge: Cambridge UP, 1990.
Casado Lobato, María Concepción. "La biblioteca de un escritor de siglo XVII: Bernardino de Rebolledo." *Revista de Filología Española* 56 (1973): 229-328.
Castañeda, James A. *Agustín Moreto.* New York: Twayne, 1974.
Castro, Adolfo de, ed. *Poetas líricos de los siglos XVI y XVII.* 2 vols. Biblioteca de Autores Españoles 32, 42. Madrid: Rivadeneyra, 1854-1857.
*Catechism of the Council of Trent for Parish Priests.* Trans. John A. McHugh and Charles J. Callan. New York: Joseph F. Wagner, 1934.
Cejador y Frauca, Julio. *Historia de la lengua y literatura castellana.* 14 vols. in 7. Madrid: Gredos, 1972-74.
Cerdan, Francis. "Historia de la historia de la Oratoria Sagrada española en el Siglo de Oro: Introducción crítica y bibliográfica." *Criticón* 32 (1985): 55-107.
Chevalier, Maxime. *Lectura y lectores en la España de los siglos XVI y XVII.* Madrid: Turner, 1976.
Cotarelo y Mori, Emilio. "Dramáticos españoles del siglo XVII: Don Antonio Coello y Ochoa." *Boletín de la Real Academia Española* 5 (Dic. 1918): 550-600.
———. *Ensayo sobre la vida y obras de D. Pedro Calderón de la Barca.* Madrid: Tip. de la "Revista de Archivos, Bibliotecas y Museos," 1924.
Cruickshank, D. W. "Some Aspects of Spanish Book-Production in the Golden Age." *Library* 31 (1976): 1-19.
Curtius, Ernst Robert. *European Literature and the Latin Middle Ages.* Trans. Willard R. Trask. London: Routledge & Kegan Paul, 1953.
Daly, Peter M. *Literature in the Light of the Emblem: Structural Parallels between the Emblem and Literature in the Sixteenth and Seventeenth Centuries.* Toronto: U of Toronto Press, 1979.
Davies, Gareth A. *A Poet at Court: Antonio Hurtado de Mendoza (1586-1644).* Oxford: Dolphin, 1971.
Defourneaux, Marcelin. *Daily Life in Spain in the Golden Age.* Trans. Newton Branch. Stanford, CA: Standford UP, 1970.
DeVinne, Theo. L. *The Invention of Printing.* 1876. Detroit: Gale Research, 1969.
Dexeus de Moll, Mercedes. "Cinco piezas teatrales de Jaime Torres (1579)." *Revista de Archivos, Bibliotecas y Museos* (Madrid) 74 (1967): 105-79.
Díaz-Migoyo, Gonzalo. "¿Qué debe la novela a la imprenta?" MLA Convention. New York, December 1986.
*Diccionario enciclopédico U.T.E.H.A.* 10 vols. México: Unión Tipográfica Editorial Hispano Americana, 1964.
*Diccionario Oxford de literatura española e hispanoamericana.* Ed. Philip Ward. Trans. and adapt. Gabriela Zayas. Barcelona: Crítica, 1984.
*Dictionnaire de Theologie Catholique.* Ed. A. Vacant and others. 15 vols. Paris: Letouzey et Ane, 1903-50.
Díez-Borque, José María. *El libro: De la tradición oral a la cultura impresa.* Barcelona: Montesinos, 1985.
Dille, Glen F. *Antonio Enríquez Gómez.* Boston: Twayne, 1988.

Domínguez Ortiz, Antonio. *Instituciones y sociedad en la España de los Austrias.* Barcelona: Ariel, 1985.
D'Ors, Miguel. *Vida y poesía de Alonso de Ledesma: Contribución al estudio del conceptismo español.* Pamplona: U de Navarra, 1974.
Fernández Álvarez, Manuel. *La sociedad española en el Siglo de Oro.* 2nd ed. 2 vols. Madrid: Gredos, 1989.
Fischer, Bonifatius, comp. *Novae concordantiae Bibliorum Sacrorum iuxta vulgatam versionem critice editam.* 5 vols. Stuttgart-Bad Canstatt: Frommann-Holzboog, 1977.
Frye, Northrop. *The Double Vision: Language and Meaning in Religion.* Toronto: U of Toronto P, 1991.
Gallardo, Bartolomé José. *Ensayo de una biblioteca española de libros raros y curiosos.* 4 vols. 1863-89. Madrid: Gredos, 1968.
Garrote Pérez, Francisco. *Pensamiento y Naturaleza en España durante los siglos XVI y XVII.* U de Salamanca, 1981.
Gellrich, Jesse M. *The Idea of the Book in the Middle Ages: Language Theory, Mythology, and Fiction.* Ithaca, NY: Cornell U P, 1985.
Gómez Uriel, Miguel. *Bibliotecas antigua y nueva de escritores aragoneses de Latassa. Aumentadas y refundidas en forma de diccionario bibliográfico-biográfico.* 3 vols. Zaragoza: Calista Ariño, 1884-86.
González Pedroso, Eduardo, ed. *Autos sacramentales desde su origen hasta fines del siglo XVII.* Biblioteca de Autores Españoles 58. Madrid: Rivadeneyra, 1865.
González Rivas, Trinidad. *Escritores malagüeños. Estudio bibliográfico.* Málaga: Diputación Provincial de Málaga. Instituto de Cultura, 1971.
González Ruiz, Nicolás, ed. *Autos sacramentales.* Vol 1 of *Piezas maestras del teatro teológico español.* 3rd ed. 2 vols. Madrid: Católica, 1968.
Goodrich-Dunn, Barbara. "Walking the Critical Path. Interview with Morris Berman." *Common Boundary* 9 (July / Aug. 1991): 12-21.
Green, Otis H. *Spain and the Western Tradition: The Castilian Mind in Literature from El Cid to Calderon.* 4 vols. Madison: U of Wisconsin P, 1963-66.
Hatzfeld, Helmut A. *Santa Teresa de Avila.* New York: Twayne, 1969.
Hauer, Mary G. *Luis Vélez de Guevara: A Critical Bibliography.* University of North Carolina Studies in the Romance Languages and Literatures: Texts, Textual Studies and Translations 5. Chapel Hill, 1975.
Hausman, Carl R. *Metaphor and Art: Interactionism and Reference in the Verbal and Nonverbal Arts.* Cambridge: Cambridge UP, 1989.
Hayes, Francis C. *Lope de Vega.* New York: Twayne, 1967.
Herrero García, Miguel, ed. *Sermonario clásico. Con un ensayo sobre la oratoria sagrada.* Madrid: Escelicer, 1942.
Herrero Salgado, Félix. *Aportación bibliográfica a la oratoria sagrada española.* Madrid: Consejo Superior de Investigaciones Científicas, 1971.
Iribarren, Manuel. *Escritores navarros de ayer y de hoy.* Pamplona: Gómez, 1970.
Jacopone da Todi. *The Lauds.* Trans. Serge and Elizabeth Hughes. New York: Paulist, 1982.
Jammes, Robert. *La obra poética de Don Luis de Góngora y Argote.* Madrid: Castalia, 1987.
Kurtz, Barbara E. "The *Agricultura cristiana* de Juan de Pineda in the Context of Renaissance Mythography and Encyclopedism." *Inti: Revista de Literatura Hispánica* 24-25 (1986-87): 191-202.
Lichtenstadtler, Ilse. *Introduction to Classical Arabic Literature.* New York: Twayne, 1974.
Lida de Malkiel, María Rosa. "La tradición clásica en España." *Revista de Filología Hispánica* 1 (1959) 20-63.

Lida de Malkiel, María Rosa. *La tradición clásica en España*. Barcelona: Ariel, 1975.
López Estrada, Francisco. *Introducción a la literatura medieval española*. 3rd ed. Madrid: Gredos, 1974.
MacCurdy, Raymond R. *Francisco de Rojas Zorrilla*. New York: Twayne, 1968.
Maravall, José Antonio. *La cultura del Barroco: Análisis de una estructura histórica*. Barcelona: Ariel, 1975.
⸻. "La literatura del emblema." *Teatro y literatura en la sociedad barroca*. Madrid: Seminarios y Ediciones, 1972.
Marín Ocete, Antonio. *Gregorio Silvestre: Estudio biográfico y crítico*. Granada: Publicaciones de la Facultad de Letras, 1939.
Martí Grajales, Francisco. *Ensayo de un diccionario biográfico y bibliográfico de los poetas que florecieron en el reino de Valencia hasta el año 1700*. Madrid: Tip. de la "Revista de Archivos, Bibliotecas y Museos," 1927.
Martínez Añibarro y Rives, Manuel. *Intento de un diccionario biográfico y bibliográfico de autores de la provincia de Burgos*. Madrid: Manuel Tello, 1889.
McMurtrie, Douglas C. *The Book: The Story of Printing & Bookmaking*. 3rd rev. ed. New York: Oxford UP, 1943.
Méndez Bejarano, Mario. *Diccionario de escritores, maestros y oradores naturales de Sevilla y su actual provincia*. 3 vols. Sevilla: Girones, 1922-25.
Menéndez Pidal, Juan. "Datos para la biografía de Cristóbal de Castillejo." *Boletín de la Real Academia Española* 2 (Feb. 1915): 3-20.
Menocal, María Rosa. *The Arabic Role in Medieval Literary History: A Forgotten Heritage*. Philadelphia: U of Pennsylvania P, 1987.
Meo Zilio, G. *Estudio sobre Hernando Domínguez Camargo y su "San Ignacio de Loyola, Poema heroyco."* Messina-Florencia: D'Anna, 1967.
Millares Carlo, Agustín, and Manuel Hernández Suárez. *Biobibliografía de Escritores Canarios (Siglos XVI, XVII y XVIII)*. 5 vols. Las Palmas: Museo Canario, 1975-87.
Millás Vallicrosa, José María. *La poesía sagrada hebraicoespañola*. Madrid: Consejo Superior de Investigaciones Científicas, 1940.
Moll, Jaime. "Problemas bibliográficos del libro del Siglo de Oro." *Boletín de la Real Academia Española* 59 (1979): 49-107.
Monroe, James T. *Hispano-Arabic Poetry: A Student Anthology*. Berkeley: U of California P, 1974.
Moore, John A. *Fray Luis de Granada*. Boston: Twayne, 1977.
Morrow, Carolyn Roberts. *Popular Lyric Tradition in the "autos" of Lope de Vega*. Diss. Tulane U, 1969. Ann Arbor: UMI, 1970. 6920493.
Moseley, William W., Glenroy Emmons, and Marilyn C. Emmons, comps. *Spanish Literature, 1500-1700. A Bibliography of Golden Age Studies in Spanish and English, 1925-1980*. Westport, Conn.: Greenwood, 1984.
*New Catholic Encyclopedia*. Ed. Catholic University of America. 15 vols. New York: McGraw Hill, 1967.
Palau y Dulcet, Antonio. *Manual del librero hispanoamericano. Bibliografía general española e hispanoamericana desde la invención de la imprenta hasta nuestros tiempos con el valor comercial de los impresos descritos*. 2nd ed. 28 vols. Barcelona: Lib. Anticuaria de A. Palau, 1948-77.
Parker, Jack Horace. *Juan Pérez de Montalván*. Boston: Twayne, 1975.
Pastor Fuster, Justo. *Biblioteca valenciana de los escritores que florecieron hasta nuestros días. Con adiciones y enmiendas a la de D. Vicente Ximeno*. 2 vols. Valencia: José Ximeno, 1827-30. Vol. 1.
Peale, C. George, ed. *Antigüedad y actualidad de Luis Vélez de Guevara: Estudios críticos*. Purdue University Monographs in Romance Languages 10. Amsterdam: John Benjamins, 1983.

Pérès, Henri. *Esplendor de Al-Andalus. La poesía andaluza en árabe clásico en el siglo XI. Sus aspectos generales, sus principales temas y su valor documental.* Trans. Mercedes García-Arenal. 2nd ed. Madrid: Hiperión, 1983.
Pérez, Quintín. *Fr. Hernando de Santiago, predicador del Siglo de Oro (1575-1639). Revista de Filología Española.* Anejo 43. Madrid: Consejo Superior de Investigaciones Científicas, 1949.
Pérez Pastor, Cristóbal. *Bibliografía madrileña o Descripción de las obras impresas en Madrid.* 3 vols. Madrid: Tip. de los Huérfanos, 1891-1907.
Peyton, Myron A. *Alonso Jerónimo de Salas Barbadillo.* New York: Twayne, 1973.
Pfandl, Ludwig. *Cultura y costumbres del pueblo español de los siglos XVI y XVII.* Barcelona: Araluce, 1929.
Real Academia Española. *Diccionario de autoridades.* 6 vols. in 3. 1726-39. Madrid: Gredos, 1964.
Reynolds, John J. *Juan Timoneda.* Boston: Twayne, 1975.
Richards, I. A. *The Philosophy of Rhetoric.* New York: Oxford UP, 1936.
Rodríguez, Lucas. *Romancero historiado (Alcalá, 1582).* Ed. Antonio Rodríguez-Moñino. Madrid: Castalia, 1967.
Rodríguez Moñino, Antonio R. *Juan López de Ubeda, poeta del siglo XVI: Estudio bibliográfico.* Madrid: Maestre, 1962.
———. *Los poetas extremeños del siglo XVI. Estudios bibliográficos.* Badajoz: Diputación Provincial de Badajoz, 1935. Badajoz-Cáceres, 1980.
Rodríguez Puertolas, Julio. *Cancionero de Fray Ambrosio Montesino.* Cuenca: Diputación Provincial, 1987.
Ruiz, Licinio, and Julián García Sainz de Baranda. *Escritores burgaleses. Continuación al "Intento de un Diccionario bio-bibliográfico de autores de la provincia de Burgos", de Martínez Añibarro y Rives.* Alcalá de Henares: Escuela de Reforma, 1930.
Sainz de Robles, Federico Carlos. *Escritores españoles e hispanoamericanos.* Vol. 2 of *Ensayo de un diccionario de la literatura.* 2 vols. Madrid: Aguilar 1964.
———. *La imprenta y el libro en la España del siglo XV.* Madrid: Vasallo de Mumbert, 1973.
Sainz Rodríguez, Pedro, comp. *Antología de la literatura espiritual española.* 4 vols. Madrid: U Pontificia de Salamanca. Fundación Universitaria Española, 1980-85.
Salstad, M. Louise. "Illustration and Decoration in Early Spanish Printed Books." Unpublished paper, 1983.
———. "Nature as Sign and Symbol of the Divine in Religious Verse of Sixteenth-century Spain." Diss. U of Wisconsin, 1976.
Sancha, Justo de, ed. *Romancero y cancionero sagrados. Colección de poesías cristianas, morales y divinas, sacadas de las obras de los mejores ingenios españoles.* Biblioteca de Autores Españoles 35. Madrid: Rivadeneyra, 1855.
Santiago Vela, Gregorio de. "Camós y Requesens (Fray Marco Antonio de)." *Ensayo de una biblioteca ibero-americana de la Orden de San Agustín. Obra basada en el Catálogo bio-bibliográfico agustiniano del P. Bonifacio Moral.* Madrid: Asilo de Huérfanos del S. C. de Jesus, 1913-31. 1: 551-56.
Scholz, B. F. "Jacob Cat's Silenus Akibiadis in 1618 and in 1862: changes in word-image relations from the seventeenth to the nineteenth century." *Word & Image* 4 (Jan.-Mar. 1988): 67-80.
Segre, Cesare, and Tomaso Kemeny. *Introduction to the Analysis of the Literary Text.* Trans. John Meddemmen. Bloomington: Indiana UP, 1988.
Serrano y Sanz, Manuel. *Apuntes para una biblioteca de escritoras españolas desde el año 1401 al 1833.* Vol. 3. II (Primera parte). Biblioteca de Autores Españoles 270. 1903. Madrid: Atlas, 1975. 2 vols. in 4.

Simón Díaz, José. *Bibliografía de la literatura hispánica.* 2nd ed. rev. and enl. 14 vols. Madrid: Consejo Superior de Investigaciones Científicas, 1960-84.

———. *Cien escritores madrileños del Siglo de Oro (Notas bibliográficas).* Monografías bibliográficas 7. Madrid: Instituto de Estudios Madrileños, 1975.

———. *El libro español antiguo: Análisis de su estructura.* Kassell: Reichenberger, 1983.

Smith, Hilary Dansey. *Preaching in the Spanish Golden Age: A Study of Some Preachers of the Reign of Philip III.* Oxford UP, 1978.

Soria Ortega, Andrés. *El Maestro Fray Manuel de Guerra y Ribera y la oratoria sagrada de su tiempo.* U de Granada, 1950.

Thurston, Herbert, and Donald Attwater, eds. *Butler's Lives of the Saints: Complete Edition.* 4 vols. New York: P. J. Kenedy & Sons, 1956-63.

Tillyard, E. M. W. *The Elizabethan World Picture.* London: Chatto & Windus, 1950.

Vergara y Martín, Gabriel María. *Ensayo de una colección bibliográfico-biográfica de noticias referentes a la provincia de Segovia.* Guadalajara: Colegio de Huérfanos de la Guerra, 1904.

Vernet Ginés, Juan. *Literatura árabe.* Barcelona: Labor, 1966.

Wardropper, Bruce W. *Introducción al teatro religioso del Siglo de Oro: Evolución del Auto Sacramental antes de Calderón.* Salamanca: Anaya, 1967.

Whitaker, Elaine. E. Rev. of *The Book of Memory: A Study of Memory in Medieval Culture,* by Mary J. Carruthers. *South Atlantic Review* 57 (May 1992): 95-97.

Wilson, Margaret. *Tirso de Molina.* Boston: Twayne, 1977.

Yamey, Basil S. *Art & Accounting.* New Haven: Yale UP, 1989.

Zamora Lucas, Florentino. *Lope de Vega, censor de libros. Colección de aprobaciones, censuras, elogios y prólogos del Fénix, que se hallan en los preliminares de algunos libros de su tiempo, con notas bibliográficas de sus autores.* Larache: Artes Gráficas Boscá, 1941.

# ALPHABETICAL KEY WORD INDEX OF ENGLISH MOTIFS

This index has two main purposes. The first is to enable the reader to more readily locate specific topical motifs in the Motif Index. The second is to bring together, for the reader interested in tracing them, all motifs in which particular semantic elements occur.

Key words include those nouns, verbs, adjectives, adverbs and pronouns derived from the motifs, under which I thought a reader might search, either as a discrete term or as part of a phrase. Key words do not include numbered subdivision headings. Items are alphabetized in the following order of priority: (1) key word alone, (2) if a word or words precede the key word and none follows it, by the first preceding word, (3) if the key word is followed by another word or words, by the first such word. Initial articles and the infinitive "to (be)" have been omitted. Numbers appear at the head of the list as Arabic numerals.

(have / need only) *1* book B.3.2.ue
*1* page alone is free of blots A.3.18.2.ue
(have / need only) *1* text B.3.2.ue
*2* boards A.3.18.1. binding / boards:ue
*2* leaves A.3.18.2.ue
*2* letters A.3.19.5. character / lettering:ue
*2* strokes A.3.19.5. stroke / flourish:ue
*3* approbations A.3.16. approbation:ue
*3* languages A.3.12.ue
(written in) *3* languages A.3.12.ue
*3* leaves A.3.18.2.ue
*3* strokes A.3.19.5. stroke / flourish:ue
*3* treatises A.3.15. treatise:ue
(book of) *3* treatises A.3.15. treatise:ue
*3* versions A.3.11.ue
*4* letters A.3.19.5. character / lettering:ue
*4* words A.3.9. word:ue
*5* books A.3.2.1.ue
*5* leaves A.3.18.2.ue
*5* letters A.3.19.5. character / lettering:ue
*5* seals A.3.19.4.2. seal:ue
*5* signatures A.3.7.2. signature:ue

*5* signet rings A.1.2.1. seal / signet ring / stamp:ue
*5* strokes A.3.19.5. stroke / flourish:ue
*7* lessons A.3.7.2. lesson:ue
*7* seals A.3.19.4.2. seal:ue
(book with) *7* seals A.3.2.1.me
*11* leaves A.3.18.2.ue
*12* copies A.3.11.ue
*12* leaves A.3.18.2.ue
(quire of) *12* leaves A.3.18.2. quire:ue

"*A*" A.3.19.5.
*abbreviate* B.2.1.1.
*abbreviate* a word so it will fit on the paper B.2.1.1. abbreviate:ue
*abbreviation* A.3.9.
*accommodate* for binding B.2.6.
(add an) *account* A.3.7.2. account / account entry:ue
(document of closing of an) *account* A.3.4.2.3.1.
(settle an) *account* A.3.7.2. account / account entry:ue

*account* / account entry A.3.7.2.
(write in an) *account* book B.2.1.ue
*account* book / ledger A.3.4.1.
*account* shows an excessive debt A.3.7.2. account / account entry:ue
*account* shows debits and credits A.3.7.2. account / account entry:ue
*accuracies* A.3.6.
(blot of) *Adam* A.3.20.2. blot:me
(text transmitted from) *Adam* B.4.3.me
*Adam's* library A.4.1. library:me
*adapt* a text according to the intended reader / listener B.2.1.1. copy / adapt / translate:ue
(copy /) *adapt* / translate B.2.1.1.
(copy /) *adaptation* / translation A.3.11.
(copy /) *adaptation* / translation is not as complete as the original A.3.11.ue
(copy /) *adaptation* / translation is not as valuable as the original A.3.11.ue
(copyist /) *adaptor* / translator A.2.1.
*add* a letter A.3.19.5. character / lettering:ue
*add* an account A.3.7.2. account / account entry:ue
*address* B.2.1.1.
*address* a letter B.2.1.1. address:ue
*adorn* the binding B.2.6.
(stroke / flourish or) *adornment* on initial A.3.19.5.
*adornments* A.3.18.1.
(more) *advanced* book A.3.2.1.ue
(school of) *advanced* students A.4.1. school:ue
(write on) *air* B.2.1.me
(write) *all* one knows B.2.1.ue
(God as) *Alpha* and Omega A.3.19.5. alphabet:me
*alphabet* A.3.19.5.
*ancient* lettering A.3.19.5. character / lettering:ue
(school of the) *angels* A.4.1. school:me
*angels* read the text B.3.4.me
(only the) *angels* / saints can read the book of life B.3.4.me
(only the) *angels* / saints can read the inside / original of the divine book B.3.4.me
(written) *animal* B.2.1.me
(chronicle) / *annals* A.3.4.1.
*annul* a law B.4.2.2. cancel:ue
*appetite* writes B.2.1.me
*apply* the press A.1.2.4. printing press:ue

*approbation* A.3.16.
(without an) *approbation* A.3.16. approbation:ue
(three) *approbations* A.3.16. approbation:ue
*approve* B.2.3.2.
*Arabic* characters A.3.19.5. character / lettering:ue
*archive* A.4.2.
(preserve in an) *archive* B.4.1.ue
(open) *archives* A.4.2. archive:ue
(write on the) *arm* B.2.1.me
(name as [part of] a coat of) *arms* A.3.7.2. name:ue
*arms* and letters A.3.6. science / branch of learning / letters:ue
*art* of memory A.3.4.1.
*artist's* brush A.1.2.1.
(write in dust /) *ashes* B.2.1.ue
*asterisk* A.3.19.8.2.
*assume* costs B.2.5.
*author* A.2.1.
(text immortalizes its) *author* A.2.1. author:ue
(wise) *author* A.2.1. author:ue
*authorize* B.2.3.1.
(correcting the text is the) *author's* responsibility B.2.1.1. correct:ue
*autobiography* A.3.4.1.

*baptismal* certificate A.3.4.2.6.2.
*baptismal* character A.3.19.5. character / lettering:me
*bear* an identical mark A.3.19.9.ue
*bear* an identical seal A.3.19.4.2. seal:ue
*bear* God's brand A.3.19.9.2. brand:me
*beautiful* book A.3.2.1.ue
*beautiful* letters A.3.19.5. character / lettering:ue
(delight in the) *beautiful* letters without understanding their meaning A.3.19.5. character / lettering:ue
*beautiful* page A.3.18.2.ue
*beautiful* script A.3.19.6.ue
*beautiful* title page A.3.16. title page:ue
*begin* a new book A.3.2.1.ue
*beginning* A.3.15.
(without a) *beginning* A.3.15. beginning:ue
*beginning* of a book A.3.15. beginning:ue
(from) *beginning* to end A.3.15. beginning: ue
(read from) *beginning* to end B.3.4.ue

## ALPHABETICAL KEY WORD INDEX OF ENGLISH MOTIFS 439

*believing* what one reads can be harmful B.3.5.ue
(name of the) *beloved* A.3.7.2. name:ue
*bequeath* a book B.4.3.ue
*best* book A.3.2.1.ue
*better* handwriting A.3.19.6. handwriting:ue
*bill* of exchange A.3.4.2.3.2.
*bind* B.2.6.
*bind* skillfully B.2.6.ue
*bind* together in a book B.2.6.ue
*binder* A.2.1.
(accommodate for) *binding* B.2.6.
(adorn the) *binding* B.2.6.
(book with broken) *binding* A.3.2.1.ue
(change the) *binding* B.2.6.ue
(faded) *binding* A.3.18.1.ue
(loose) *binding* A.3.18.1.ue
(marvel at the) *binding* B.3.5.ue
(precious) *binding* A.3.18.1.ue.
(remove the) *binding* B.2.6.
(trim the) *binding* B.2.6.
*binding* / boards A.3.18.1.
*binding* corresponds to the content A.3.18.1.ue
*black* ink A.1.2.2. ink:ue
*black* lines A.3.9. line of writing:ue
*blank* book A.3.2.1.ue
*blank* document A.3.1. document / piece of writing:ue
*blank* leaves and written leaves are juxtaposed A.3.18.2.ue
*blank* page A.3.18.2.ue
*blank* petition A.3.4.2.6.2. petition:ue
*blank* tablet A.3.3.3. tablet:ue
(paper) *bleeds* A.1.2.3.2. paper:ue
(blot out with) *blood* B.4.2.2. erase / blot out:me
(certificate of purity of) *blood* A.3.4.2.5.
(sign with) *blood* B.2.1.1. sign:me
(write with) *blood* B.2.1.me
*blot* B.4.2.1.
(without) *blot* A.3.20.2. blot:ue
*blot* a name B.4.2.1. blot:ue
*blot* / drop of ink A.3.20.2.
*blot* of Adam A.3.20.2. blot:me
(not [ever]) *blot* the text B.4.1.ue
(for an ink) *blot* to fall on the text / writing material B.4.2.1.
*blot out* with blood B.4.2.2. erase / blot out:me
(erase /) *blot out* B.4.2.2.
(full of) *blots* A.3.20.2. blot:ue

(one page alone is free of) *blots* A.3.18.2.ue
*blue* book A.3.2.1.ue
*blue* page A.3.18.2.ue
*blue* paper A.1.2.3.2. paper:ue
*blue* skin A.1.2.3.3. skin:ue
*blurring* / overlapping A.3.20.2.
(binding /) *boards* A.3.18.1.
(two) *boards* A.3.18.1. binding / boards:ue
*body* A.3.15.
(write on the) *body* / in the flesh B.2.1.me
*book* A.3.2.1.
(beautiful) *book* A.3.2.1.ue
(begin a new) *book* A.3.2.1.ue
(beginning of a) *book* A.3.15. beginning:ue
(bequeath a) *book* B.4.3.ue
(best) *book* A.3.2.1.ue
(bind together in a) *book* B.2.6.ue
(blank) *book* A.3.2.1.ue
(blue) *book* A.3.2.1.ue
(bound) *book* A.3.2.1.ue
(burn a forbidden) *book* B.4.2.2. burn:ue
(buy a) *book* B.3.1.ue
(census) *book* A.3.4.1.
(chant) *book* A.3.4.1.
(close a) *book* B.3.3.2.ue
(closed) *book* A.3.2.1.ue
(common) *book* A.3.2.1.ue
(complete) *book* A.3.2.1.ue
(complete a) *book* A.3.2.1.ue
(crude) *book* A.3.2.1.ue
(customs) *book* A.3.4.1.
(dedicate a) *book* B.2.1.1. dedicate:ue
(emblem) *book* A.3.4.1.
(ending of a) *book* A.3.15. ending:ue
(erase from the) *book* B.4.2.2. erase / blot out:ue
(false) *book* A.3.2.1.ue
(famous) *book* A.3.2.1.ue
(forbidden) *book* A.3.2.1.ue
(fruitful) *book* A.3.2.1.ue
(give someone a) *book* B.4.3.ue
(God's) *book* A.3.2.1.me
(golden) *book* A.3.2.1.ue
(good / excellent) *book* A.3.2.1.ue
(great) *book* A.3.2.1.ue
(green) *book* A.3.2.1.ue
(have / need only one) *book* B.3.2.ue
(highly esteemed) *book* A.3.2.1.ue
(illuminated) *book* A.3.2.1.ue
(in this life we can read only the outside / copy of the divine) *book* B.3.4.me

(inexhaustible) *book* A.3.2.1.ue
(large / vast) *book* A.3.2.1.ue
(law) *book* A.3.4.1.
(learned) *book* A.3.2.1.ue
(little) *book* A.3.2.1.ue
(living) *book* A.3.2.1.me
(make good use of a) *book* B.3.5.ue
(many saints have read the) *book* B.3.4.ue
(memorandum) *book* A.3.4.1.
(Mercurius Trismegistus read the) *book* B.3.4.ue
(more advanced) *book* A.3.2.1.ue
(music) *book* A.3.4.1.
(new) *book* A.3.2.1.ue
(no one but the Lamb / Lion can open the) *book* B.3.3.1.me
(no one can open the) *book* B.3.3.1.ue
(not [ever] erase from the) *book* B.4.1.ue
(only the angels / saints can read the inside / original of the divine) *book* B.3.4.me
(open) *book* A.3.2.1.ue
(open a) *book* B.3.3.1.ue
(perfect) *book* A.3.2.1.ue
(philosophers and wise men have read the) *book* B.3.4.ue
(printed) *book* A.3.2.1.ue
(psalmist King David read the) *book* B.3.4.ue
(rare) *book* A.3.2.1.ue
(recover the leaves that have fallen out of a) *book* B.4.1.ue
(Saint Anthony read the) *book* B.3.4.ue
(Saint John the Evangelist read the) *book* B.3.4.ue
(Saint Paul read the) *book* B.3.4.ue
(scandalous) *book* A.3.2.1.ue
(sell a) *book* B.4.3.ue
(single) *book* A.3.2.1.ue
(so emended as to seem a new) *book* B.2.1.1. correct:ue
(supreme) *book* A.3.2.1.ue
(true / trustworthy) *book* A.3.2.1.ue
(outstanding student of a single) *book* A.2.2. student:ue
(white) *book* A.3.2.1.ue
(wisdom) *book* A.3.4.1.
(write in a memorandum) *book* B.2.1.ue
(write in an account) *book* B.2.1.ue
(have a) *book* always before one's eyes B.3.4.ue
*book* as weapon A.3.2.1.ue
(marvelous) *book* / book of marvels A.3.2.1.ue

(judge a) *book* by the outside B.2.3.2.ue
*book* does not suffice by itself A.3.2.1.ue
(write a) *book* for everyone B.2.1.ue
(hang a) *book* from a chain B.3.3.1. display:ue
(value a) *book* highly B.3.5.ue
(have a) *book* in one's library B.3.2.ue
(read the chapter titles to learn what the) *book* is about B.3.4.ue
*book* is open to all A.3.2.1.ue
*book* is written in every language A.3.12.ue
(account) *book* / ledger A.3.4.1.
*book* of heaven A.3.2.1.me
*book* of heroic exploits A.3.4.1.
*book* of justice A.3.2.1.me
(only the angels / saints can read the) *book* of life B.3.4.me
*book* of life / glory A.3.2.1.me
(erase from the) *book* of life / glory B.4.2.2. erase / blot out:me
(not [ever] erase from the) *book* of life / glory B.4.1.me
(write [a name] in the) *book* of life / glory B.2.1.me
*book* of magic A.3.4.1.
(in the) *book* of Mary we read all the moral virtues B.3.4.me
*book* of medicine A.3.4.1.
*book* of moral theology / canon law A.3.4.1.
*book* of philosophy A.3.4.1.
*book* of the just A.3.2.1.me
*book* of theology A.3.4.1.
*book* of three treatises A.3.15. treatise:ue
*book* of truth A.3.2.1.me
(display a) *book* on a lectern B.3.3.1. display:ue
(censor a ) *book* / submit a book to the censors B.2.3.2.ue
*book* that flies to heaven A.3.2.1.me
*book* that was consumed A.3.2.1.me
(for a) *book* to come unbound B.4.2.5. (cause to) come unbound:ue
(dedicate a) *book* to the king B.2.1.1. dedicate:ue
*book* with broken binding A.3.2.1.ue
*book* with seven seals A.3.2.1.me
bookmark A.4.2.
(5) *books* A.3.2.1.ue
(have many) *books* B.3.2.ue
(pay in) *books* B.4.3.ue
bookstore A.4.1.

*bound* book A.3.2.1.ue
(science /) *branch* of learning / letters A.3.6.
*brand* A.3.19.9.2. B.2.1.2.
(bear God's) *brand* A.3.19.9.2. brand:me
(erase a) *brand* B.4.2.2. erase / blot out:ue
(slave) *brand* A.3.19.9.2. brand:ue
(without a) *brand* A.3.19.9.2. brand:ue
*brand* a slave B.2.1.2. brand:ue
*branding* iron A.1.2.1.
(write a name on the heart /) *breast* B.2.1.me
(write on the) *breast* B.2.1.me
(papal) *brief* A.3.4.2.2.
*brief* stroke A.3.9. stroke:ue
*brief* text teaches more than immense volumes B.4.3.1.ue
(read a text) *briefly* B.3.4.ue
*broadsheet* / *broadside* A.3.3.2.
(book with) *broken* binding A.3.2.1.ue
*bronze* A.1.2.3.4.
(engrave on) *bronze* B.2.1.2. cut / engrave:ue
(artist's) *brush* A.1.2.1.
(papal) *bull* of canonization A.3.4.2.2.
(engrave with a) *burin* B.2.1.2. cut / engrave:ue
*burn* B.4.2.2.
*burn* a forbidden book B.4.2.2. burn:ue
*burnished* paper A.1.2.3.2. paper:ue
*buy* a book B.3.1.ue

*calligrapher* A.2.1.
(skillful) *calligrapher* A.2.1. calligrapher:ue
(school of) *calligraphy* A.4.1. school:ue
*cancel* B.4.2.2.
*cancel* a debt B.4.2.2. cancel:ue
*cancel* a stamp B.4.2.2. cancel:ue
(book of moral theology /) *canon* law A.3.4.1.
(compose with great) *care* B.2.1.1. compose:ue
*carry* letters back and forth B.4.3.ue
*carte* blanche A.3.4.2.3.2.
*cast* type B.2.4.1.
*censor* A.2.1. B.2.3.2.
*censor* a book / submit a book to the censors B.2.3.2.ue
*census* book A.3.4.1.
*census* list A.3.4.2.4.
(entry on a) *census* list A.3.7.2.
(baptismal) *certificate* A.3.4.2.6.2.

*certificate* of having received the Eucharist A.3.4.2.5.
*certificate* of military service A.3.4.2.5.
*certificate* of purity of blood A.3.4.2.5.
*certificate* of ransom A.3.4.2.5.
*certification* of fidelity to the original A.3.16.
*chain* A.4.2.
(hang a book from a) *chain* B.3.3.1. display:ue
(professorial) *chair* A.4.1.
(read from the professorial) *chair* B.3.4.ue
*chancellor* A.2.1.
*change* the binding B.2.6.ue
*chant* book A.3.4.1.
*chapter* A.3.15.
(read the) *chapter* titles to learn what the book is about B.3.4.ue
*chapters* of a life A.3.15. chapter:me
(baptismal) *character* A.3.19.5. character / lettering:me
(imprint a) *character* B.2.1.2. impress / imprint:ue
(indelible) *character* A.3.19.5. character / lettering:ue
(not understand a) *character* B.3.4.1.ue
(obscure) *character* A.3.19.5. character / lettering:ue
(rare) *character* A.3.19.5. character / lettering:ue
(sacramental) *character* A.3.19.5. character / lettering:me
(recognize a) *character* but not understand its meaning B.3.4.1.ue
*character* composed of five strokes A.3.19.5. character / lettering:ue
*character* composed of two strokes A.3.19.5. character / lettering:ue
*character* from (a language of) the New World A.3.19.5. character / lettering:ue
*character* / lettering A.3.19.5.
(neither recognize a) *character* nor understand its meaning B.3.4.1.ue
(imprint a) *character* on the soul B.2.1.2. impress / imprint:me
(erase one) *character* with another B.4.2.2. erase / blot out:ue
(Arabic) *characters* A.3.19.5. character / lettering:ue
(God's) *characters* A.3.19.5. character / lettering:me
(ill-formed) *characters* A.3.19.5. character / lettering:ue

(immortal) *characters* A.3.19.5. character / lettering:ue
*chief* pages A.3.18.2.ue
*children's* school A.4.1. school:ue
(novel of) *chivalry* A.3.4.1.
*Christus* A.3.8.
*Christus* as the first lesson of the primer A.3.8. Christus:ue
*Christus* is the only lesson one needs to learn A.3.8. Christus:ue
(learn the) *Christus* of the primer B.3.4.1.1.ue
*chronicle* / annals A.3.4.1.
*chronicler* A.2.1.
*cite* an earlier text B.4.3.ue
*clause* A.3.15.
(first) *clause* in a will A.3.15. clause:ue
*clay* A.1.2.3.4.
(impress in) *clay* B.2.1.2. impress / imprint:ue
(keep the text) *clean* B.4.1.ue
*clean* paper A.1.2.3.2. paper:ue
*clean* parchment A.1.2.3.3. parchment:ue
(text is both) *clear* and unclear A.3.5. text / contents:ue
*clear* Gothic lettering A.3.19.5. character / lettering:ue
*clear* handwriting A.3.19.6. handwriting:ue
*clear* lesson A.3.7.2. lesson:ue
*clear* lettering A.3.19.5. character / lettering:ue
*clear* prologue A.3.16. prologue:ue
*clear* script A.3.19.6.ue
(king as notary/) *clerk* A.2.1. notary / clerk:ue
(notary /) *clerk* A.2.1.
(time as notary/) *clerk* A.2.1. notary / clerk:ue
*close* B.3.3.2.
*close* a book B.3.3.2.ue
*close* a parenthesis A.3.19.7 parenthesis:ue
*closed* book A.3.2.1.ue
*closed* document A.3.1. document / piece of writing:ue
*closed* will A.3.4.2.5. will:ue
(document of) *closing* of an account A.3.4.2.3.1.
*coat of arms* A.3.19.4.2.
(cross as part of a) *coat of arms* A.3.19.9.3. cross:ue
(name as [part of] a) *coat of arms* A.3.7.2. name:ue

*code* A.3.19.5.1.
(written in) *code* A.3.19.5.1.ue
*code* breaker A.3.19.5.1.
(need a) *code* breaker in order to read the text A.3.19.5.1.ue
*coin* A.3.3.3.
(stamp on a) *coin* B.2.1.2. impress / imprint:ue
*column* A.3.3.3. A.3.19.2.
([cause to]) *come unbound* B.4.2.5.
(for a book to) *come unbound* B.4.2.5. (cause to) come unbound:ue
(mountains) *come unbound* B.4.2.5. (cause to) come unbound:me
*comma* A.3.19.7.
*common* book A.3.2.1.ue
*compare* the first impression with the original A.3.11.ue
*compendium* A.3.3.1.
*compendium* of the Law A.3.3.1. compendium:ue
(human being as) *compendium* of nature A.3.3.1. compendium:me
*complete* a book A.3.2.1.ue
(copy / adaptation / translation is not as) *complete* as the original A.3.11.ue
*complete* book A.3.2.1.ue
(no one can learn the text) *completely* B.3.4.1.1.ue
*compose* B.2.1.1.
*compose* with great care B.2.1.1. compose:ue
(character) *composed* of five strokes A.3.19.5. character / lettering:ue
(character) *composed* of two strokes A.3.19.5. character / lettering:ue
(we should not try to read what is beyond our) *comprehension* B.3.4.ue
(God writes his Word /) *Concept* in Mary B.2.1.me
(forbid /) *condemn* B.2.3.2.
(write on the) *conscience* B.2.1.me
(writing materials are) *consumed* A.1.ue
(binding corresponds to the) *content* A.3.18.1.ue
(lofty) *content* A.3.6.ue
(superscription corresponds to the) *content* A.3.7.1. superscription:ue
(superscription does not correspond to the) *content* A.3.7.1. superscription:ue
(table of) *contents* A.3.16.
(text /) *contents* A.3.5.
*context* A.3.5.

# ALPHABETICAL KEY WORD INDEX OF ENGLISH MOTIFS 443

*contract* A.3.4.2.5.
(guarantor of a) *contract* A.2.1.
(witness to a) *contract* A.2.1.
(make many) *copies* B.2.1.1. copy / adapt / translate:ue
(twelve) *copies* A.3.11.ue
*copy* A.3.1.
(faithful) *copy* A.3.11.ue
(final) *copy* A.3.10.
(living) *copy* A.3.11.me
(virgin) *copy* A.3.17.
*copy* / adapt / translate B.2.1.1.
*copy* / adaptation / translation A.3.11.
*copy* / adaptation / translation is not as complete as the original A.3.11.ue
*copy* / adaptation / translation is not as valuable as the original A.3.11.ue
*copy* from the original B.2.1.1. copy / adapt / translate:ue
*copy* is indistinguishable from the original A.3.11.ue
*copy* material A.3.7.2.
(in this life we can read only the outside /) *copy* of the divine book B.3.4.me
*copy* serves as a reminder of the original A.3.11.ue
*copyist* / adaptor / translator A.2.1.
*copyright* A.3.16.
(old) *copyright* A.3.16. copyright:ue
(royal) *copyright* A.3.16. copyright:ue
(unique) *copyright* A.3.16. copyright:ue
(without a) *copyright* A.3.16. copyright:ue
*correct* B.2.1.1.
*correcting* the text is the author's responsibility B.2.1.1. correct:ue
*correction* A.3.20.3.
(without) *correction* A.3.20.3.ue
(superscription does not) *correspond* to the content A.3.7.1. superscription:ue
(outside does not) *correspond* to the inside A.3.14.ue
(binding) *corresponds* to the content A.3.18.1.ue
(superscription) *corresponds* to the content A.3.7.1. superscription:ue
(outside) *corresponds* to the inside A.3.14.ue
(first impression) *corresponds* to the original A.3.11.ue
(assume) *costs* B.2.5.
*counter text* A.3.5. text / contents:ue
(letter of) *credential* A.3.4.2.4.

(account shows debits and) *credits* A.3.7.2. account / account entry:ue
*Creed* A.3.8.
*crooked* lines A.3.9. line of writing:ue
*cross* A.3.19.9.3.
(mark with a) *cross* A.3.19.9.3. cross:ue
(sign of the) *cross* A.3.19.9.me
*cross* as part of a coat of arms A.3.19.9.3. cross:ue
*cross* as signature A.3.7.2. signature:ue
*cross out* B.4.2.1.
(not [ever]) *cross out* of the text B.4.1.ue
*crude* book A.3.2.1.ue
*customs* book A.3.4.1.
*cut* / engrave B.2.1.2.
*cut* in stone / marble B.2.1.2. cut / engrave:ue
*cut* on a tree B.2.1.2. cut / engrave:ue
*cut* the pages B.3.3.1.
*cut* the pen A.1.2.1. pen:ue

*decree* A.3.7.2.
(account shows) *debits* and credits A.3.7.2. account / account entry:ue
(account shows an excessive) *debt* A.3.7.2. account / account entry:ue
(cancel a) *debt* B.4.2.2. cancel:ue
(receipt of discharge of a) *debt* A.3.4.2.3.1.
*dedicate* B.2.1.1.
*dedicate* a book B.2.1.1. dedicate:ue
*dedicate* a book to the king B.2.1.1. dedicate:ue
*dedication* A.3.16.
(erase a) *defect* B.4.2.2. erase / blot out:ue
(without) *defect* A.3.20.ue
*delight* in the beautiful letters without understanding their meaning A.3.19.5. character / lettering:ue
*derive* a lesson A.3.7.2. lesson:ue
*design* A.3.19.4.2.
*desk* A.4.2.
*diamond* pen A.1.2.1. pen:ue
*dictate* B.4.3.
(write what God) *dictates* B.2.1.me
*dictator* A.2.2.
*difficult* subject matter A.3.6. subject matter / discourse:ue
(text is) *difficult* to understand B.3.4.1.ue
*dip* the pen in ink A.1.2.1. pen:ue
*dirge* A.3.7.2.
*disappear* B.4.2.3.
(writing) *disappears* as one reads B.4.2.3. disappear:ue

(subject matter /) *discourse* A.3.6.
*disintegrate* B.4.2.5.
*dispatch* A.3.4.2.1.
*dispatch* / issue B.2.3.1.
(scatter /) *disperse* B.4.2.3.
(scatter /) *disperse* the leaves / pages B.4.2.3. scatter / disperse:ue
*display* a book on a lectern B.3.3.1. display:ue
*display* marbled pages B.3.3.1. display:ue
*display* the pages B.3.3.1. display:ue
*display* / unfold B.3.3.1.
*disseminate* B.4.3.
*disseminate* the text throughout the world B.4.3. disseminate:ue
*doctrine* A.3.6.
(lofty) *doctrine* A.3.6. doctrine:ue
(blank) *document* A.3.1. document / piece of writing:ue
(closed) *document* A.3.1. document / piece of writing:ue
(important) *document* A.3.1. document / piece of writing:ue
(living) *document* A.3.1. document / piece of writing:me
(nail up a) *document* B.4.3.ue
(open) *document* A.3.1. document / piece of writing:ue
(royal) *document* A.3.1. document / piece of writing:ue
(signed and sealed) *document* A.3.1. document / piece of writing:ue
(tear up a) *document* B.4.2.2. tear up:ue
(tear up and throw away a) *document* B.4.2.2. tear up:ue
*document* of closing of an account A.3.4.2.3.1.
*document* / piece of writing A.3.1.
*documentation* A.3.4.2.6.1.
(rough) *draft* A.3.10.
(blot /) *drop* of ink A.3.20.2.
(write in) *dust* / ashes B.2.1.ue

"E" A.3.19.5.
(cite an) *earlier* text B.4.3.ue
(text is) *easy* to understand B.3.4.1.ue
(gild the) *edges* of pages B.2.6.
*elegant* prologue A.3.16. prologue:ue
*emblem* A.3.19.4.2.
(obscure) *emblem* A.3.19.4.2. emblem:ue
*emblem* book A.3.4.1.
(title /) *emblematic* motto A.3.7.2.
(so) *emended* as to seem a new book B.2.1.1. correct:ue

*encyclopedia* / miscellany A.3.4.1.
(from beginning to) *end* A.3.15. beginning:ue
(read from beginning to) *end* B.3.4.ue
*ending* A.3.15
(without an) *ending* A.3.15. ending:ue
*ending* of a book A.3.15 ending:ue
(cut /) *engrave* B.2.1.2.
*engrave* a name on a jewel / precious stone B.2.1.2. cut / engrave:ue
*engrave* on a jewel / precious stone B.2.1.2. cut / engrave:ue
*engrave* on a metal plate B.2.1.2. cut / engrave:ue
*engrave* on bronze B.2.1.2. cut / engrave:ue
*engrave* with a burin B.2.1.2. cut / engrave:ue
*engraving* tool A.1.2.1.
*entitle* B.2.1.1.
(account / account) *entry* A.3.7.2.
*entry* on a census list A.3.7.2.
*entry* on a roster of prisoners A.3.7.2.
*envelope* / folded sheet A.3.3.2.
*epigram* A.3.7.2.
*episcopal* letter A.3.4.2.2.
*epitaph* A.3.7.2.
(print without the usual) *equipment* B.2.4.me
(write without the usual) *equipment* B.2.1.me
(writing) *equipment* A.1.1.
*erase* a brand B.4.2.2. erase / blot out:ue
*erase* a defect B.4.2.2. erase / blot out:ue
*erase* a section of the text B.4.2.2. erase / blot out:ue
*erase* an error B.4.2.2. erase / blot out:ue
*erase* / blot out B.4.2.2.
*erase* from memory B.4.2.2. erase / blot out:me
(not [ever]) *erase* from memory B.4.1.me
*erase* from the book B.4.2.2. erase / blot out:ue
(not [ever]) *erase* from the book B.4.1.ue
*erase* from the book of life / glory B.4.2.2. erase / blot out:me
(not [ever]) *erase* from the book of life / glory B.4.1.me
(not [ever]) *erase* from the text B.4.1.ue
*erase* one character with another B.4.2.2. erase / blot out:ue
(more) *erasures*, the fewer errors B.4.2.2. erase / blot out:ue
*errata* sheet A.3.16.

*error* A.3.20.1.2.
(erase an) *error* B.4.2.2. erase / blot out:ue
(full of) *errors* A.3.20.1.2. error:ue
(more erasures, the fewer) *errors* B.4.2.2. erase / blot out:ue
(highly) *esteemed* book A.3.2.1.ue
(book is written in) *every* language A.3.12.ue
(write a book for) *everyone* B.2.1.ue
*excess* A.3.20.1.2.
*exclamation* mark A.3.19.7.
*expurgate* B.2.3.2.
(without) *expurgation* B.2.3.2. expurgate:ue
*eyes* A.3.19.8.2.
(have a book always before one's) *eyes* B.3.4.ue

*fable* A.3.7.2.
(write on the) *face* B.2.1.me
*fade* B.4.2.5.
*faded* binding A.3.18.1.ue
*faithful* copy A.3.11.ue
(for an ink blot to) *fall* on the text / writing material B.4.2.1.
(recover the leaves that have) *fallen* out of a book B.4.1.ue
(text) *falls* into one's hands B.3.1.ue
*false* book A.3.2.1.ue
*fame* writes B.2.1.me
*famous* book A.3.2.1.ue
*fastenings* / ligatures A.3.18.1.
(write a name on the hands /) *feet* B.2.1.me
(write on the hands /) *feet* B.2.1.me
(certification of) *fidelity* to the original A.3.16.
(illuminated) *figure* A.3.19.4.1.
(rhetorical) *figures* A.3.13.
*fill* a page with writing A.3.18.2.ue
*final* copy A.3.10.
*find* a (replacement for a) lost text B.3.1.ue
*fine* paper A.1.2.3.2. paper:ue
(make) *fine* paper A.1.2.3.2. paper:ue
(make) *fine* paper from old rags A.1.2.3.2. paper:ue
(pointing) *finger* A.3.19.8.2.
(written with the) *finger* of God B.2.1.me
(ink stains one's) *fingers* A.1.2.2. ink:ue
(write with) *fire* B.2.1.me
*first* clause in a will A.3.15. clause:ue
*first* impression A.3.11.

*first* impression corresponds to the original A.3.11.ue
(compare the) *first* impression with the original A.3.11.ue
(Christus as the) *first* lesson of the primer A.3.8. Christus:ue
*first* page A.3.18.2.ue
(from the) *first* to the last page A.3.18.2.ue
(palm leaf was the) *first* paper A.1.2.3.2. palm leaf:ue
*first* paragraphs A.3.9. paragraph:ue
*first* part of a text A.3.15.ue
*first* quire A.3.18.2. quire:ue
*flaw* A.3.20.1.1.
(without) *flaw* A.3.20.1.1. flaw:ue
(write on the body / in the) *flesh* B.2.1.me
(stroke /) *flourish* or adornment on initial A.3.19.5.
*forbid* B.2.3.2.
*forbidden* book A.3.2.1.ue
(burn a) *forbidden* book B.4.2.2. burn:ue
*forbidden* page A.3.18.2.ue
(insert a) *forbidden* page A.3.18.2.ue
(taw written on the) *forehead* A.3.19.5. taw:me
(write on the) *forehead* B.2.1.me
*forge* a stamp A.1.2.1. seal / signet ring / stamp:ue
*form* A.1.2.4.
(one page alone is) *free* of blots A.3.18.2.ue
*fruitful* book A.3.2.1.ue
*full* of blots A.3.20.2. blot:ue
*full* of errors A.3.20.1.2. error:ue

*genealogy* A.3.4.1.
*gild* the edges of pages B.2.6.
*give* someone a book B.4.3.ue
*gloss* B.2.1.1.
(note /) *gloss* A.3.7.2.
(written with the finger of) *God*
*God* as Alpha and Omega A.3.19.5. alphabet:me
(write what) *God* dictates B.2.1.me
(language of) *God* / heaven A.3.12.me
*God* signs a promissory note B.2.1.1. sign:me
*God* writes his Word / Concept in Mary
*God's* book A.3.2.1.me
(bear) *God's* brand A.3.19.9.2. brand:me
*God's* characters A.3.19.5. character / lettering:me
*God's* signature A.3.7.2. signature:me

(pages of) *gold* A.3.18.2.ue
*gold* ink A.1.2.2. ink:ue
*gold* lettering A.3.19.5. character / lettering:ue
*golden* book A.3.2.1.ue
*golden* pen A.1.2.1. pen:ue
*good* / excellent book A.3.2.1.ue
*good* reader A.2.2. reader:ue
(in) *good* taste A.3.13.
*Gothic* lettering A.3.19.5. character / lettering:ue
(clear) *Gothic* lettering A.3.19.5. character / lettering:ue
*great* book A.3.2.1.ue
*great* library A.4.1. library:ue
*green* book A.3.2.1.ue
*green* metal plate A.3.3.3. metal plate:ue
*green* page A.3.18.2.ue
(sign as) *guarantor* B.2.1.1. sign:ue
*guarantor* of a contract A.2.1.
(pupil writes skillfully because the teacher) *guides* his hand B.2.1.ue

*half-sheet* A.3.3.2.
(pupil writes skillfully because the teacher guides his) *hand* B.2.1.ue
(write by) *hand* B.2.1.ue
(write in one's own) *hand* B.2.1.ue
(write with the right) *hand* B.2.1.ue
(text falls into one's) *hands* B.3.1.ue
(write a name on the) *hands* / feet B.2.1.me
(write on the) *hands* / feet B.2.1.me
*handwriting* A.3.19.6.
(better) *handwriting* A.3.19.6. handwriting:ue
(clear) *handwriting* A.3.19.6. handwriting:ue
(not recognize the) *handwriting* A.3.19.6. handwriting:ue
*hang* a book from a chain B.3.3.1. display:ue
*have* a book always before one's eyes B.3.4.ue
*have* a book in one's library B.3.2.ue
*have* many books B.3.2.ue
*have* / need only one book B.3.2.ue
*have* / need only one text B.3.2.ue
(memorize / learn by) *heart* B.3.4.1.1.
(write on the) *heart* B.2.1.me
(write a name on the) *heart* / breast B.2.1.me
(law written on the) *heart* / soul A.3.7.2. law:me

(book of) *heaven* A.3.2.1.me
(book that flies to) *heaven* A.3.2.1.me
(language of God /) *heaven* A.3.12.me
*Hebrew* script A.3.19.6.ue
(extremely) *high* price limit A.3.16. price limit:ue
(value a book) *highly* B.3.5.ue
*highly* esteemed book A.3.2.1.ue
*Holy* Rule A.3.4.1.
*human* being as compendium of nature A.3.3.1. compendium:me

*idea* A.3.6.
(put an) *idea* in writing B.2.1.ue
(preserve one's) *ideas* through writing B.4.1.ue
(bear an) *identical* mark A.3.19.9.ue
(bear an) *identical* seal A.3.19.4.2. seal:ue
*ill-cut* pen A.1.2.1. pen:ue
(text is) *illegible* A.3.5. text / contents:ue
*ill-formed* characters A.3.19.5. character / lettering:ue
*illuminate* B.2.2.
*illuminate* a book B.2.2.ue
*illuminated* book A.3.2.1.ue
*illuminated* figure A.3.19.4.1.
*illuminated* letters A.3.19.5. character / lettering:ue
*illuminated* lines A.3.9. line of writing:ue
*illuminated* pages A.3.18.2.ue
*illuminated* strokes A.3.19.5. stroke / flourish:ue
(brief text teaches more than) *immense* volumes B.4.3.1.ue
*immortal* characters A.3.19.5. character / lettering:ue
*immortalize* a text B.4.3.ue
(text) *immortalizes* its author A.2.1. author:ue
*important* document A.3.1. document / piece of writing:ue
*important* lesson A.3.7.2. lesson:ue
*important* letter A.3.4.2.6.3. letters:ue
(preserve) *important* / secret papers B.4.1.ue
*impress* / impression A.3.19.1.
*impress* / imprint B.2.1.2.
*impress* in clay B.2.1.2. impress / imprint:ue
*impress* in wax B.2.1.2. impress / imprint:ue
(first) *impression* A.3.11.
(impress /) *impression* A.3.19.1.

ALPHABETICAL KEY WORD INDEX OF ENGLISH MOTIFS    447

(first) *impression* corresponds to the original A.3.11.ue
(compare the first) *impression* with the original A.3.11.ue
(impress /) *imprint* B.2.1.2.
*imprint* a character B.2.1.2. impress / imprint:ue
*imprint* a character on the soul B.2.1.2. impress / imprint:me
*imprint* a seal B.2.1.2. impress / imprint:ue
(tools are) *inadequate* to the subject A.1.ue
*indelible* character A.3.19.5. character / lettering:ue
(written) *indelibly* B.2.1.ue
*index* A.3.16.
(copy is) *indistinguishable* from the original A.3.11.ue
*inept* writing instrument A.1.2.1.ue
*inexhaustible* book A.3.2.1.ue
*inferior* paper A.1.2.3.2. paper:ue
*initial* A.3.19.5.
(stroke / flourish or adornment on) *initial* A.3.19.5.
*ink* A.1.2.2.
(black) *ink* A.1.2.2. ink:ue
(blot / drop of) *ink* A.3.20.2.
(dip the pen in) *ink* A.1.2.1. pen:ue
(gold) *ink* A.1.2.2. ink:ue
(invisible) *ink* A.1.2.2. ink:ue
(note in red) *ink* A.3.7.2. note / gloss:ue
(pale) *ink* A.1.2.2. ink:ue
(parchment saturated with) *ink* A.1.2.3.3. parchment:ue
(red) *ink* A.1.2.2. ink:ue
(water the) *ink* A.1.2.2. ink:ue
(letters written in invisible) *ink* appear when held before the fire / to the light A.1.2.2. ink:ue
(for an) *ink* blot to fall on the text / writing material B.4.2.1.
*ink* stains one's fingers A.1.2.2. ink:ue
*inkwell* A.1.2.2.
*inkwell* runs dry A.1.2.2. inkwell:ue
*inscribe* B.2.1.1.
*insert* a forbidden page A.3.18.2.ue
*inside* A.3.14.
(outside corresponds to the) *inside* A.3.14.ue
(outside does not correspond to the) *inside* A.3.14.ue
(written on the) *inside* and the outside B.2.1.ue

(only the angels / saints can read the) *inside* / original of the divine book B.3.4.me
(inept writing) *instrument* A.1.2.1.ue
(write well with a poor) *instrument* B.2.1.ue
*interpret* B.3.4.1.
*intone* B.3.4.3.
*invisible* ink A.1.2.2. ink:ue
(letters written in) *invisible* ink appear when held before the fire / to the light A.1.2.2. ink:ue
(branding) *iron* A.1.2.1.
*iron* pen A.1.2.1. pen:ue
(dispatch /) *issue* B.2.3.1.

*Jesus* A.3.8.
(name) *Jesus* A.3.7.2. name:ue
*jewel* A.3.3.3.
(engrave a name on a) *jewel* / precious stone B.2.1.2. cut / engrave:ue
(engrave on a) *jewel* / precious stone B.2.1.2. cut / engrave:ue
*jot* A.3.9.
*judge* a book by the outside B.2.3.2.ue
*judicial* report A.3.4.2.5.
(book of the) *just* A.3.2.1.me
(book of) *justice* A.3.2.1.me
(blank leaves and written leaves are) *juxtaposed* A.3.18.2.ue

*keep* the text clean B.4.1.ue
(dedicate a book to the) *king* B.2.1.1. dedicate:ue
(signed by the) *king* B.2.1.1. sign:ue
(write a letter to a) *king* B.2.1.ue
*king* as notary / clerk A.2.1. notary / clerk:ue
(psalmist) *king* David read the book B.3.4.ue
*king's* signature A.3.7.2. signature:ue
(write all one) *knows* B.2.1.ue

*lack* A.3.20.1.2.
*lack* a seal A.3.19.4.2. seal:ue
*lack* a signature A.3.7.2. signature:ue
(no one but the) *Lamb* / Lion can open the book B.3.3.1.me
*language* A.3.12.
(book is written in every) *language* A.3.12.ue
(mute) *language* A.3.12.ue
*language* of God / heaven A.3.12.me

(character from [a] *language* of] the New World A.3.19.5. character / lettering:ue
(three) *languages* A.3.12.ue
(written in three) *languages* A.3.12.ue
*large* / vast book A.3.2.1.ue
*last* line A.3.9. line of writing:ue
*last* page A.3.18.2.ue
(from the first to the) *last* page A.3.18.2.ue
*last* part of a text A.3.15.ue
*law* A.3.7.2.
(annul a) *law* B.4.2.2. cancel:ue
(book of moral theology / canon) *law* A.3.4.1.
(compendium of the) *Law* A.3.3.1. compendium:ue
(living) *law* A.3.7.2. law:me
(new) *law* A.3.7.2. law:ue
(tablets of the) *Law* A.3.3.3. tablet:ue
*law* book A.3.4.1.
(write a) *law* in the sand B.2.1.me
(statute-)*law* rights and privileges A.3.7.2.
(Old) *Law* vis-a-vis the New Law A.3.7.2. law:ue
*law* written on the heart / soul A.3.7.2. law:me
*leaf* A.3.18.2.
(loose) *leaf* A.3.18.2.ue
(palm) *leaf* A.1.2.3.2.
(lose a) *leaf* / page B.4.2.3. lose:ue
(palm) *leaf* was the first paper A.1.2.3.2. palm leaf:ue
*leaf through* B.3.4.1.
*learn* B.3.4.1.1.
(Christus is the only lesson one needs to) *learn* A.3.8. Christus:ue
(memorize /) *learn* by heart B.3.4.1.1.
*learn* something new with each reading B.3.4.1.1.ue
*learn* the Christus of the primer B.3.4.1.1.ue
(no one can) *learn* the text completely B.3.4.1.1.ue
*learn* to read B.3.4.ue
*learn* to write B.2.1.ue
(read the chapter titles to) *learn* what the book is about B.3.4.ue
*learned* book A.3.2.1.ue
(eleven) *leaves* A.3.18.2.ue
(five) *leaves* A.3.18.2.ue
(quire of twelve) *leaves* A.3.18.2. quire:ue
(three) *leaves* A.3.18.2.ue
(twelve) *leaves* A.3.18.2.ue
(two) *leaves* A.3.18.2.ue

(blank) *leaves* and written leaves are juxtaposed A.3.18.2.ue
(loose) *leaves* are easily lost or torn A.3.18.2.ue
(scatter / disperse the) *leaves* / pages B.4.2.3. scatter / disperse:ue
(recover the) *leaves* that have fallen out of a book B.4.1.ue
(display a book on a) *lectern* B.3.3.1. display:ue
*lectern* / shelf A.4.2.
(account book /) *ledger* A.3.4.1.
*lesson* A.3.7.2.
(clear) *lesson* A.3.7.2. lesson:ue
(derive a) *lesson* A.3.7.2. lesson:ue
(important) *lesson* A.3.7.2. lesson:ue
(morning ["prime time"]) *lesson* A.3.7.2. lesson:ue
(Christus as the first) *lesson* of the primer A.3.8. Christus:ue
(Christus is the only) *lesson* one needs to learn A.3.8. Christus:ue
(seven) *lessons* A.3.7.2. lesson:ue
*letter* A.3.4.2.4. A.3.4.2.6.3. A.3.9.
(add a) *letter* A.3.19.5. character / lettering:ue
(address a) *letter* B.2.1.1. address:ue
(episcopal) *letter* A.3.4.2.2.
(important) *letter* A.3.4.2.6.3. letters:ue
(make different styles of) *letter* A.3.19.5. character / lettering:ue
(missing a) *letter* A.3.19.5. character / lettering:ue
(remove a) *letter* A.3.19.5. character / lettering:ue
(seal a) *letter* B.2.1.2. seal:ue
(send a) *letter* B.4.3.ue
(single) *letter* A.3.9. letter:ue
(spirit gives life to the) *letter* A.3.19.5. character / lettering:ue
(superscription on a) *letter* A.3.7.1. superscription:ue
*letter* of credential A.3.4.2.4.
*letter* of manumission A.3.4.2.5.
*letter* of recommendation A.3.4.2.6.3.
(write a) *letter* to a king B.2.1.ue
(ancient) *lettering* A.3.19.5. character / lettering:ue
(character /) *lettering* A.3.19.5.
(clear) *lettering* A.3.19.5. character / lettering:ue
(clear Gothic) *lettering* A.3.19.5. character / lettering:ue

(gold) *lettering* A.3.19.5. character / lettering:ue
(Gothic) *lettering* A.3.19.5. character / lettering:ue
(red) *lettering* A.3.19.5. character / lettering:ue
(silver) *lettering* A.3.19.5. character / lettering:ue
(arms and) *letters* A.3.6. science / branch of learning / letters:ue
(beautiful) *letters* A.3.19.5. character / lettering:ue
(five) *letters* A.3.19.5. character / lettering:ue
(four) *letters* A.3.19.5. character / lettering:ue
(illuminated) *letters* A.3.19.5. character / lettering:ue
(living) *letters* A.3.19.5. character / lettering:me
(science / branch of learning /) *letters* A.3.6.
(straight writing / printed) *letters* A.3.19.6.1.
(two) *letters* A.3.19.5. character / lettering:ue
(without) *letters* A.3.19.5. character / lettering:ue
(carry) *letters* back and forth B.4.3.ue
*letters* patent A.3.4.2.2.
(royal) *letters* patent A.3.4.2.2. letters patent:ue
*letters* patent of nobility A.3.4.2.6.2.
(delight in the beautiful) *letters* without understanding their meaning A.3.19.5. character / lettering:ue
*letters* written in invisible ink appear when held before the fire / to the light A.1.2.2. ink:ue
*letters* written on a mantle A.3.19.5. character / lettering:ue
*library* A.4.1.
(Adam's) *library* A.4.1. library:me
(great) *library* A.4.1. library:ue
(have a book in one's) *library* B.3.2.ue
(living) *library* A.4.1. library:me
*license* A.3.16.
(chapters of a) *life* A.3.15. chapter:me
(only the angels / saints can read the book of) *life* B.3.4.me
(parenthesis in) *life* A.3.19.7 parenthesis:me
(saint's) *life* A.3.4.1.

(book of) *life* / glory A.3.2.1.me
(erase from the book of) *life* / glory B.4.2.2. erase / blot out:me
(not [ever] erase from the book of) *life* / glory B.4.1.ue
(write [a name] in the book of) *life* / glory B.2.1.me
(spirit gives) *life* to the letter A.3.19.5. character / lettering:ue
(fastenings /) *ligatures* A.3.18.1.
(last) *line* A.3.9. line of writing:ue
*line* of writing A.3.9.
(black) *lines* A.3.9. line of writing:ue
(crooked) *lines* A.3.9. line of writing:ue
(illuminated) *lines* A.3.9. line of writing:ue
(ruled) *lines* A.3.19.2.
(census) *list* A.3.4.2.4.
(entry on a census) *list* A.3.7.2.
*list* of signatures A.3.16.
*little* book A.3.2.1.ue
*living* book A.3.2.1.me
*living* copy A.3.11.me
*living* document A.3.1. document / piece of writing:me
*living* law A.3.7.2. law:me
*living* letters A.3.19.5. character / lettering:me
*living* library A.4.1. library:me
*living* New Testament A.3.4.1. New Testament:me
*living* prophecy A.3.7.2. prophecy:me
*lofty* doctrine A.3.6. doctrine:ue
*lofty* / profound science A.3.6. science / branch of learning / letters:ue
*loose* binding A.3.18.1.ue
*loose* leaf A.3.18.2.ue
*loose* leaves are easily lost or torn A.3.18.2.ue
*lose* B.4.2.3.
*lose* a leaf / page B.4.2.3. lose:ue
(loose leaves are easily) *lost* or torn A.3.18.2.ue
(find a [replacement for a]) *lost* text B.3.1.ue
*love* story A.3.7.2. story:ue
*lyrics* A.3.7.2.

(book of) *magic* A.3.4.1.
*mail* carrier A.2.2.
*make* different styles of letter A.3.19.5. character / lettering:ue
*make* fine paper A.1.2.3.2. paper:ue

*make* fine paper from old rags A.1.2.3.2. paper:ue
*make* good use of a book B.3.5.ue
*make* many copies B.2.1.1. copy / adapt / translate:ue
(letters written on a) *mantle* A.3.19.5. character / lettering:ue
*manual* A.3.4.1.
(letter of) *manumission* A.3.4.2.5.
(have) *many* books B.3.2.ue
(make) *many* copies B.2.1.1. copy / adapt / translate:ue
*map* A.3.4.2.7.
(navigational) *map* A.3.4.2.7.
*marble* A.1.2.3.4.
(cut in stone /) *marble* B.2.1.2. cut / engrave:ue
*marbled* page A.3.18.2.ue
(display) *marbled* pages B.3.3.1. display:ue
*margin* A.3.19.2.
(write in the) *margin* B.2.1.ue
*marginal* note A.3.7.2. note / gloss:ue
*Mariology* A.3.4.1.
*mark* B.2.1.1.
(bear an identical) *mark* A.3.19.9.ue
(exclamation) *mark* A.3.19.7.
(mysterious) *mark* A.3.19.9.ue
(printers) *mark* A.3.19.4.2.
*mark* / sign A.3.19.9.1.
*mark* with a cross A.3.19.9.3. cross:ue
*marvel* at the binding B.3.5.ue
*marvelous* book / book of marvels A.3.2.1.ue
(God writes his Word / Concept in) *Mary* B.2.1.me
(in the book of) *Mary* we read all the moral virtues B.3.4.me
(copy) *material* A.3.7.2.
(for an ink blot to fall on the text / writing) *material* B.4.2.1.
(smooth writing) *material* A.1.2.3.ue
(writing) *materials* are consumed A.1.ue
*maxim* A.3.7.2.
(delight in the beautiful letters without understanding their) *meaning* A.3.19.5. character / lettering:ue
(neither recognize a character nor understand its) *meaning* B.3.4.1.ue
(recognize a character but not understand its) *meaning* B.3.4.1.ue
(book of) *medicine* A.3.4.1.
(written) *melon* B.2.1.me
*memorandum* A.3.4.2.3.1.

*memorandum* book A.3.4.1.
(write in a) *memorandum* book B.2.1.ue
*memorial* A.3.4.3.
*memorize* / learn by heart B.3.4.1.1.
(art of) *memory* A.3.4.1.
(erase from) *memory* B.4.2.2. erase / blot out:me
(not [ever] erase from) *memory* B.4.1.ue
(write on the) *memory* B.2.1.me
*Mercurius Trismegistus* read the book B.3.4.ue
*metal* plate A.3.3.3.
(engrave on a) *metal* plate B.2.1.2. cut / engrave:ue
(green) *metal* plate A.3.3.3. metal plate:ue
(certificate of) *military* service A.3.4.2.5.
(encyclopedia /) *miscellany* A.3.4.1.
*misprint* A.3.20.2.
(without) *misprint* A.3.20.2. misprint:ue
([part of] a text is) *missing* B.4.2.ue
*missing* a letter A.3.19.5. character / lettering:ue
*more* erasures, the fewer errors B.4.2.2. erase / blot out:ue
*more* one reads, the less one understands B.3.4.1.ue
(title / emblematic) *motto* A.3.7.2.
*mountains* come unbound B.4.2.5. (cause to) come unbound:me
*moved* by a text B.3.5.ue
(sheet of) *music* A.3.4.2.7.
*music* book A.3.4.1.
*mute* language A.3.12.ue
*mysterious* mark A.3.19.9.ue
*mysterious* seal A.3.19.4.2. seal:ue

*nail up* a document B.4.3.ue
*name* A.3.7.2.
(blot a) *name* B.4.2.1.
(new) *name* A.3.7.2. name:ue
(superscribe a) *name* B.2.1.1. superscribe:ue
*name* as (part of) a coat of arms A.3.7.2. name:ue
*name* as superscription A.3.7.1. superscription:ue
(write [a] *name*] in the book of life / glory B.2.1.me
*name* Jesus A.3.7.2. name:ue
*name* of the beloved A.3.7.2. name:ue
(engrave a) *name* on a jewel / precious stone B.2.1.2. cut / engrave:ue
(write a) *name* on rock / stone B.2.1.ue

(write a) *name* on the hands / feet B.2.1.me
(write a) *name* on the heart / breast B.2.1.me
(write a) *name* on the soul B.2.1.me
(human being as compendium of) *nature* A.3.3.1. compendium:me
*navigational* map A.3.4.2.7.
(have /) *need* only one book B.3.2.ue
(have /) *need* only one text B.3.2.ue
(text does not teach anything) *new* B.4.3.1.ue
*new* book A.3.2.1.ue
(begin a) *new* book A.3.2.1.ue
(so emended as to seem a) *new* book B.2.1.1. correct:ue
*new* law A.3.7.2. law:ue
(Old Law vis-a-vis the) *New* Law A.3.7.2. law:ue
*new* name A.3.7.2. name:ue
*new* primer A.3.4.1. primer:ue
*New* Testament A.3.4.1.
(living) *New* Testament A.3.4.1. New Testament:me
(learn something) *new* with each reading B.3.4.1.1.ue
(letters patent of) *nobility* A.3.4.2.6.2.
*no one* but the Lamb / Lion can open the book B.3.3.1.me
*no one* can learn the text completely B.3.4.1.1.ue
*no one* can open the book B.3.3.1.ue
*not* be able to read B.3.4.
*not* bend / wrinkle a page B.4.1.ue
*not* (ever) blot the text B.4.1.ue
*not* (ever) cross out of the text B.4.1.ue
*not* (ever) erase from memory B.4.1.me
*not* (ever) erase from the book B.4.1.ue
*not* (ever) erase from the book of life / glory B.4.1.me
*not* (ever) erase from the text B.4.1.ue
*not* recognize the handwriting A.3.19.6. handwriting:ue
(text does) *not* teach anything new B.4.3.1.ue
(we should) *not* try to read what is beyond our comprehension B.3.4.ue
*not* understand a character B.3.4.1.ue
(recognize a character but) *not* understand its meaning B.3.4.1.ue
*not* understand the smallest portion of a text B.3.4.1.ue
*not* understand the text B.3.4.1.ue

(text is) *not* well received B.3.5.ue
(pen of a) *notary* A.1.2.1. pen:ue
*notary* / clerk A.2.1.
(king as) *notary* / clerk A.2.1. notary / clerk:ue
(time as) *notary* / clerk A.2.1. notary / clerk:ue
(God signs a promissory) *note* B.2.1.1. sign:me
(marginal) *note* A.3.7.2. note / gloss:ue
(promissory) *note* A.3.4.2.3.1.
(sign a promissory) *note* B.2.1.1. sign:ue
(signature on a promissory) *note* A.3.7.2. signature:ue
(signed and sealed promissory) *note* A.3.4.2.3.1. promissory note:ue
*note* / gloss A.3.7.2.
*note* in red ink A.3.7.2. note / gloss:ue
(take) *note* of B.3.4.1.
*notebook* A.3.2.2.
*note down* B.2.1.1.
*novel* of chivalry A.3.4.1.
"*O*" A.3.19.5.
*obscure* character A.3.19.5. character / lettering:ue
*obscure* emblem A.3.19.4.2. emblem:ue
(study an) *occult* text B.3.4.1. study:ue
*old* copyright A.3.16. copyright:ue
*Old* Law vis-a-vis the New Law A.3.7.2. law:ue
(God as Alpha and) *Omega* A.3.19.5. alphabet:me
*omit* B.4.2.4.
*omit* from a book B.4.2.4.ue
(Christus is the) *only* lesson one needs to learn A.3.8. Christus:ue
(have / need) *only* one book B.3.2.ue
(have / need) *only* one text B.3.2.ue
*only* the angels / saints can read the book of life B.3.4.me
*only* the angels / saints can read the inside / original of the divine book B.3.4.me
(in this life we can read) *only* the outside / copy of the divine book B.3.4.me
(understood) *only* when written and read B.3.4.1.ue
*open* B.3.3.1.
*open* a book B.3.3.1.ue
*open* a seal B.3.3.1.ue
*open* archives A.4.2. archive:ue
*open* book A.3.2.1.ue

*open* document A.3.1. document / piece of writing:ue
(no one but the Lamb / Lion can) *open* the book B.3.3.1.ue
(no one can) *open* the book B.3.3.1.ue
(book is) *open* to all A.3.2.1.ue
*open* will A.3.4.2.5. will:ue
*original* A.3.11.
(certification of fidelity to the) *original* A.3.16.
(compare the first impression with the) *original* A.3.11.ue
(copy / adaptation / translation is not as complete as the) *original* A.3.11.ue
(copy / adaptation / translation is not as valuable as the) *original* A.3.11.ue
(copy from the) *original* B.2.1.1. copy / adapt / translate:ue
(copy is indistinguishable from the) *original* A.3.11.ue
(copy serves as a reminder of the) *original* A.3.11.ue
(first impression corresponds to the) *original* A.3.11.ue
(print from the) *original* B.2.4.ue
(read the) *original* B.3.4.ue
(only the angels / saints can read the inside /) *original* of the divine book B.3.4.me
*outside* A.3.14.
(judge a book by the) *outside* B.2.3.2.ue
(written on the inside and the) *outside* B.2.1.ue
(in this life we can read only the) *outside* / copy of the divine book B.3.4.me
*outside* corresponds to the inside A.3.14.ue
*outside* does not correspond to the inside A.3.14.ue
*outstanding* student of a single book A.2.2. student:ue
(blurring /) *overlapping* A.3.20.2.

*page* A.3.18.2.
(beautiful) *page* A.3.18.2.ue
(beautiful title) *page* A.3.16. title page:ue
(blank) *page* A.3.18.2.ue
(blue) *page* A.3.18.2.ue
(first) *page* A.3.18.2.ue
(forbidden) *page* A.3.18.2.ue
(from the first to the last) *page* A.3.18.2.ue
(green) *page* A.3.18.2.ue
(last) *page* A.3.18.2.ue
(lose a leaf /) *page* B.4.2.3. lose:ue
(marbled) *page* A.3.18.2.ue
(not bend / wrinkle a) *page* B.4.1.ue
(purple) *page* A.3.18.2.ue
(rule the) *page* B.1.
(single) *page* A.3.18.2.ue
(spacious) *page* A.3.18.2.ue
(title) *page* A.3.16.
(turn back to a preceding) *page* A.3.18.2.ue
(turn the) *page* A.3.18.2.ue
(white) *page* A.3.18.2.ue
(worthless) *page* A.3.18.2.ue
(wrinkled) *page* A.3.18.2.ue
(one) *page* alone is free of blots A.3.18.2.ue
(insert a forbidden) *page* into a book A.3.18.2.ue
(fill a) *page* with writing A.3.18.2.ue
(chief) *pages* A.3.18.2.ue
(cut the) *pages* B.3.3.1.
(display marbled) *pages* B.3.3.1. display:ue
(display the) *pages* B.3.3.1. display:ue
(gild the edges of) *pages* B.2.6.
(illuminated) *pages* A.3.18.2.ue
(scatter / disperse the leaves /) *pages* B.4.2.3. scatter / disperse:ue
(tear out) *pages* B.4.2.2. tear out:ue
(well-ordered) *pages* A.3.18.2.ue
*pages* of gold A.3.18.2.ue
*pale* ink A.1.2.2. ink:ue
*palm* leaf A.1.2.3.2.
*palm* leaf was the first paper A.1.2.3.2. palm leaf:ue
*papal* brief A.3.4.2.2.
*papal* bull of canonization A.3.4.2.2.
*paper* A.1.2.3.2. A.3.2.3.
(abbreviate a word so it will fit on the) *paper* B.2.1.1. abbreviate:ue
(blue) *paper* A.1.2.3.2. paper:ue
(burnished) *paper* A.1.2.3.2. paper:ue
(clean) *paper* A.1.2.3.2. paper:ue
(fine) *paper* A.1.2.3.2. paper:ue
(inferior) *paper* A.1.2.3.2. paper:ue
(make fine) *paper* A.1.2.3.2. paper:ue
(smooth) *paper* A.1.2.3.2. paper:ue
(synthesize on a small amount of) *paper* B.2.1.1. synthesize:ue
(torn) *paper* A.3.2.3.ue
(white) *paper* A.1.2.3.2. paper:ue
(palm leaf was the first) *paper* A.1.2.3.2. palm leaf:ue
*paper* bleeds A.1.2.3.2. paper:ue

ALPHABETICAL KEY WORD INDEX OF ENGLISH MOTIFS 453

(make fine) *paper* from old rags A.1.2.3.2. paper:ue
(preserve important / secret) *papers* B.4.1.ue
*papyrus* A.1.2.3.2.
*paragraph* A.3.9.
(first) *paragraphs* A.3.9. paragraph:ue
*parchment* A.1.2.3.3.
(clean) *parchment* A.1.2.3.3. parchment:ue
(smooth) *parchment* A.1.2.3.3. parchment:ue
(white) *parchment* A.1.2.3.3. parchment:ue
(prepare a) *parchment* for writing A.1.2.3.3. parchment:ue
*parchment* saturated with ink A.1.2.3.3. parchment:ue
*parchment* shrivels near fire A.1.2.3.3. parchment:ue
*parenthesis* A.3.19.7.
(close a) *parenthesis* A.3.19.7. parenthesis:ue
*parenthesis* in life A.3.19.7. parenthesis:me
(first) *part* of a text A.3.15.ue
(last) *part* of a text A.3.15.ue
*part* of a text is missing B.4.2.ue
(relate the) *parts* B.3.4.1.
*passage* A.3.9.
*passport* A.3.4.2.6.2.
*pay* in books B.4.3.ue
*peace* treaty A.3.4.2.4.
(sign a) *peace* treaty B.2.1.1. sign:ue
*pen* A.1.2.1.
(cut the) *pen* A.1.2.1. pen:ue
(diamond) *pen* A.1.2.1. pen:ue
(golden) *pen* A.1.2.1. pen:ue
(ill-cut) *pen* A.1.2.1. pen:ue
(iron) *pen* A.1.2.1. pen:ue
(well-cut) *pen* A.1.2.1. pen:ue
(dip the) *pen* in ink A.1.2.1. pen:ue
*pen* of a notary A.1.2.1. pen:ue
*pen* of a skillful scribe A.1.2.1. pen:ue
*penitential* A.3.4.1.
*perfect* book A.3.2.1.ue
*period* A.3.19.7.
*petition* A.3.4.2.6.2.
(blank) *petition* A.3.4.2.6.2. petition:ue
*philosophers* and wise men have read the book B.3.4.ue
(book of) *philosophy* A.3.4.1.
(document /) *piece* of writing A.3.1.
*plate* A.3.19.3.
(engrave on a metal) *plate* B.2.1.2. cut / engrave:ue
(green metal) *plate* A.3.3.3. metal plate:ue
(metal) *plate* A.3.3.3.
*plowing* as writing / writing as plowing B.2.1.me
*poetry* A.3.7.2.
*point* of discussion A.3.7.2.
*pointing* finger A.3.19.8.2.
*polish* a work A.3.1. work:ue
*polished* style A.3.13.ue
*polished* work A.3.1. work:ue
(write well with a) *poor* instrument B.2.1.ue
*poor* reader A.2.2. reader:ue
(read) *poorly* B.3.4.ue
(write) *poorly* B.2.1.ue
*portfolio* A.4.2.
(not understand the smallest) *portion* of a text B.3.4.1.ue
(understand the smallest) *portion* of a text B.3.4.1.ue
*portrait* A.3.19.3.
*portray* B.2.1.1.
*poster* A.3.4.2.8.
*precious* binding A.3.18.1.ue
*precious* stone A.1.2.3.4.
(engrave a name on a jewel /) *precious* stone B.2.1.2. cut / engrave:ue
(engrave on a jewel /) *precious* stone B.2.1.2. cut / engrave:ue
*prepare* a parchment for writing A.1.2.3.3. parchment:ue
*preserve* B.4.1.
*preserve* important / secret papers B.4.1.ue
*preserve* in a receptacle B.4.1.ue
*preserve* in an archive B.4.1.ue
*preserve* one's ideas through writing B.4.1.ue
(to apply the) *press* A.1.2.4. printing press:ue
(printing) *press* A.1.2.4.
*price* limit A.3.16.
(extremely high) *price* limit A.3.16. price limit:ue
(without a) *price* limit A.3.16. price limit:ue
*primer* A.3.4.1.
(Christus as the first lesson of the) *primer* A.3.8. Christus:ue
(learn the Christus of the) *primer* B.3.4.1.1.ue
(new) *primer* A.3.4.1. primer:ue

*print* B.2.4.
*print* from the original B.2.4.ue
*print* without the usual equipment B.2.4.me
*printed* book A.3.2.1.ue
(straight writing /) *printed* letters A.3.19.6.1.
*printer* A.2.1.
(skillful) *printer* A.2.1. printer:ue
*printers* mark A.3.19.4.2.
*printer's assistant* A.2.1.
*printing* press A.1.2.4.
*professorial* chair A.4.1.
(read from the) *professorial* chair B.3.4.ue
*prologue* A.3.16.
(clear) *prologue* A.3.16. prologue:ue
(elegant) *prologue* A.3.16. prologue:ue
*promissory note* A.3.4.2.3.1.
(God signs a) *promissory note* B.2.1.1. sign:me
(sign a) *promissory note* B.2.1.1. sign:ue
(signature on a) *promissory note* A.3.7.2. signature:ue
(signed and sealed) *promissory note* A.3.4.2.3.1. promissory note:ue
*proofread* B.2.4.
*prophecy* A.3.7.2.
(living) *prophecy* A.3.7.2. prophecy:me
*psalmist* King David read the book B.3.4.ue
*publicize* (through) a text B.4.3.ue
*publish* B.2.5.
*punctuate* B.2.1.1.
*pupil* writes skillfully because the teacher guides his hand B.2.1.1.
*purple* lettering A.3.19.5. character / lettering:ue
*purple* page A.3.18.2.ue

*quire* A.3.18.2.
(first) *quire* A.3.18.2. quire:ue
*quire* of twelve leaves A.3.18.2. quire:ue

(certificate of) *ransom* A.3.4.2.5.
*rare* book A.3.2.1.ue.
*rare* character A.3.19.5. character / lettering:ue
*read* B.3.4.1.
(learn to) *read* B.3.4.ue
(not be able to) *read* B.3.4.ue
(teach to) *read* B.3.4.ue
(understood only when written and) *read* B.3.4.1.ue

(understood without being written or) *read* B.3.4.1.ue
*read* a text briefly B.3.4.ue
*read* a text frequently B.3.4.ue
*read* according to one's capacity B.3.4.ue
(in the book of Mary we) *read* all the moral virtues B.3.4.me
*read* attentively B.3.4.ue
*read* from beginning to end B.3.4.ue
*read* from the professorial chair B.3.4.ue
*read* in a competitive examination B.3.4.ue
(in this life we can) *read* only the outside / copy of the divine book B.3.4.me
*read* poorly B.3.4.ue
*read* superficially B.3.4.ue
(many saints have) *read* the book B.3.4.ue
(Mercurius Trismegistus) *read* the book B.3.4.ue
(philosophers and wise men have) *read* the book B.3.4.ue
(psalmist King David) *read* the book B.3.4.ue
(Saint Anthony) *read* the book B.3.4.ue
(Saint John the Evangelist) *read* the book B.3.4.ue
(Saint Paul) *read* the book B.3.4.ue
(only the angels / saints can) *read* the book of life B.3.4.me
*read* the chapter titles to learn what the book is about B.3.4.ue
(only the angels / saints can) *read* the inside / original of the divine book B.3.4.me
*read* the original B.3.4.ue
(angels) *read* the text B.3.4.me
(need a code breaker in order to) *read* the text A.3.19.5.1.ue
*read* the title B.3.4.ue
(text is) *read* throughout the world B.3.5.ue
(we should not try to) *read* what is beyond our comprehension B.3.4.ue
(formerly unreadable word becomes) *readable* A.3.7.1. word:ue
*reader* A.2.2.
(adapt a text according to the intended) *reader* / listener B.2.1.1. copy / adapt / translate:ue
(good) *reader* A.2.2. reader:ue
(poor) *reader* A.2.2. reader:ue
(learn something new with each) *reading* B.3.4.1.1.ue
(sign without) *reading* B.2.1.1. sign:ue

## ALPHABETICAL KEY WORD INDEX OF ENGLISH MOTIFS 455

(writing disappears as one) *reads* B.4.2.3. disappear:ue
(believing what one) *reads* can be harmful B.3.5.ue
(more one) *reads*, the less one understands B.3.4.1.ue
*receipt* given to one who has paid on behalf of another A.3.4.2.3.1.
*receipt* of discharge of a debt A.3.4.2.3.1.
(text is not well) *received* B.3.5.ue
(text is well) *received* B.3.5.ue
(preserve in a) *receptacle* B.4.1.ue
*recognize* a character but not understand its meaning B.3.4.1.ue
(neither) *recognize* a character nor understand its meaning B.3.4.1.ue
(not) *recognize* the handwriting A.3.19.6. handwriting:ue
(letter of) *recommendation* A.3.4.2.6.3.
*recover* the leaves that have fallen out of a book B.4.1.ue
*red* ink A.1.2.2. ink:ue
(note in) *red* ink A.3.7.2. note / gloss:ue
*red* lettering A.3.19.5. character / lettering:ue
*red* wax A.1.2.3.2. wax:ue
*reed* A.1.2.1.
*register* A.3.4.1. B.2.1.1.
(sacred) *register* A.3.4.1. register:ue
*relate* the parts B.3.4.1.
*remove* a letter A.3.19.5. character / lettering:ue
*remove* the binding B.2.6.
(find a) [*replacement*] for a] lost text B.3.1.ue
(judicial) *report* A.3.4.2.5.
*revise* B.2.1.1.
*rhetorical* figures A.3.13.
(write with the) *right* hand B.2.1.ue
(statute-law) *rights* and privileges A.3.7.2.
*roll up* B.3.3.2.
*roll up* a scroll B.3.3.2. roll up:ue
*roster* A.3.4.1.
(entry on a) *roster* of prisoners A.3.7.2.
*rough* draft A.3.10.
*royal* copyright A.3.16. copyright:ue
*royal* document A.3.1. document / piece of writing:ue
*royal* letters patent A.3.4.2.2. letters patent:ue
*royal* seal A.1.2.1. seal / signet ring / stamp:ue A.3.19.4.2. seal:ue
*rubricate* B.2.1.1.

(Holy) *Rule* A.3.4.1.
*rule* the page B.1.
*ruled* lines A.3.19.2.
*ruler* A.1.2.2.

"*S*" A.3.19.5.
*sacramental* character A.3.19.5. character / lettering:me
*sacred* register A.3.4.1. register:ue
*Saint Anthony* read the book B.3.4.ue
*Saint John* the Evangelist read the book B.3.4.ue
*Saint Paul* read the book B.3.4.ue
(only the angels /) *saints* can read the book of life B.3.4.me
(only the angels /) *saints* can read the inside / original of the divine book B.3.4.me
(many) *saints* have read the book B.3.4.ue
*saint's* life A.3.4.1.
(write a law in the) *sand* B.2.1.me
*scandalous* book A.3.2.1.ue
*scatter* / disperse B.4.2.3.
*scatter* / disperse the leaves / pages B.4.2.3. scatter / disperse:ue
*school* A.4.1.
(children's) *school* A.4.1. school:ue
*school* of advanced students A.4.1. school:ue
*school* of calligraphy A.4.1. school:ue
*school* of the angels A.4.1. school:me
(lofty / profound) *science* A.3.6. science / branch of learning / letters:ue
*science* / branch of learning / letters A.3.6.
(pen of a skillful) *scribe* A.1.2.1. pen:ue
*scrinium* A.4.2.
(beautiful) *script* A.3.19.6.ue
(clear) *script* A.3.19.6.ue
(Hebrew) *script* A.3.19.6.ue
*script* / writing A.3.19.6.
*scroll* A.3.3.1.
(roll up a) *scroll* B.3.3.2.
(unroll a skin /) *scroll* B.3.3.1.
*seal* A.3.19.4.2. B.2.1.2. B.3.3.2.
(bear an identical) *seal* A.3.19.4.2. seal:ue
(imprint a) *seal* B.2.1.2. impress / imprint:ue
(lack a) *seal* A.3.19.4.2. seal:ue
(mysterious) *seal* A.3.19.4.2. seal:ue
(open a) *seal* B.3.3.1.ue
(royal) *seal* A.1.2.1. seal / signet ring / stamp:ue A.3.19.4.2. seal:ue
(sign and) *seal* B.2.1.1. sign:ue

*seal* a letter B.2.1.2. seal:ue
*seal* / signet ring / stamp A.1.2.1.
(signed and) *sealed* document A.3.1. document / piece of writing:ue
(signed and) *sealed* promissory note A.3.4.2.3.1. promissory note:ue
(book with seven) *seals* A.3.2.1.me
(five) *seals* A.3.19.4.2. seal:ue
(seven) *seals* A.3.19.4.2. seal:ue
(preserve important /) *secret* papers B.4.1.ue
*secretary* A.2.1.
(erase a) *section* of the text B.4.2.2. erase / blot out:ue
*sell* a book B.4.3.ue
*send* a letter B.4.3.ue
*sentence* A.3.9.
(sign a death) *sentence* B.2.1.1. sign:ue
(verdict /) *sentence* A.3.7.2.
*separate* type B.2.4.1.
*sheet* A.3.3.2.
(envelope / folded) *sheet* A.3.3.2.
(errata) *sheet* A.3.16.
*sheet* of music A.3.4.2.7.
lectern / *shelf* A.4.2.
*shrivel* B.4.2.5.
(parchment) *shrivels* near fire A.1.2.3.3. parchment:ue
(write on the) *side* B.2.1.me
*sign* B.2.1.1.
(mark /) *sign* A.3.19.9.1.
*sign* a death sentence B.2.1.1. sign:ue
*sign* a peace treaty B.2.1.1. sign:ue
*sign* a promissory note B.2.1.1. sign:ue
*sign* and seal B.2.1.1. sign:ue
*sign* as guarantor B.2.1.1. sign:ue
*sign* as witness B.2.1.1. sign:ue
*sign* of the cross A.3.19.9.me
*sign* with blood B.2.1.1. sign:me
*sign* without reading B.2.1.1. sign:ue
*signature* A.3.7.2.
(cross as) *signature* A.3.7.2. signature:ue
(God's) *signature* A.3.7.2. signature:me
(king's) *signature* A.3.7.2. signature:ue
(lack a) *signature* A.3.7.2. signature:ue
*signature* on a promissory note A.3.7.2. signature:ue
(five) *signatures* A.3.7.2. signature:ue
(list of) *signatures* A.3.16.
*signed* and sealed document A.3.1. document / piece of writing:ue
*signed* and sealed promissory note A.3.4.2.3.1. promissory note:ue

*signed* by the king B.2.1.1. sign:ue
(seal /) *signet* ring / stamp A.1.2.1.
(5) *signet* rings A.1.2.1. seal / signet ring / stamp:ue
(God) *signs* a promissory note B.2.1.1. sign:me
*silver* lettering A.3.19.5. character / lettering:ue
*single* book A.3.2.1.ue
(outstanding student of a) *single* book A.2.2. student:ue
*single* letter A.3.9. letter:ue
*single* page A.3.18.2.ue
*single* word A.3.9. word:ue
(synthesize in a) *single* word B.2.1.1. synthesize:ue
*sketch* B.2.1.1.
*skillful* calligrapher A.2.1. calligrapher:ue
*skillful* printer A.2.1. printer:ue
(pen of a) *skillful* scribe A.1.2.1. pen:ue
(bind) *skillfully* B.2.6.ue
(pupil writes) *skillfully* because the teacher guides his hand B.2.1.ue
*skin* A.1.2.3.3.
(blue) *skin* A.1.2.3.3. skin:ue
(unrolled) *skin* A.1.2.3.3. skin:ue
(unroll a) *skin* / scroll B.3.3.1.
*slanted* writing A.3.19.6.1.
(brand a) *slave* B.2.1.2. brand:ue
*slave* brand A.3.19.9.2. brand:ue
(synthesize on a) *small* amount of paper B.2.1.1. synthesize:ue
(not understand the) *smallest* portion of a text B.3.4.1.ue
(understand the) *smallest* portion of a text B.3.4.1.ue
*smooth* paper A.1.2.3.2. paper:ue
*smooth* parchment A.1.2.3.3. parchment:ue
(imprint a character on the) *soul* B.2.1.2. impress / imprint:me
(law written on the heart /) *soul* A.3.7.2. law:me
(write a name on the) *soul* B.2.1.me
(write on the) *soul* B.2.1.me
*spacious* page A.3.18.2.ue
*spell* out B.2.1.1.
(ink) *stains* one's fingers A.1.2.2. ink:ue
*stamp* A.3.14.9.2.
(cancel a) *stamp* B.4.2.2. cancel:ue
(forge a) *stamp* A.1.2.1. seal / signet ring / stamp:ue
(seal / signet ring /) *stamp* A.1.2.1.

*stamp* on a coin B.2.1.2. impress / imprint:ue
*stone* A.1.2.3.4.
(engrave a name on a jewel / precious) *stone* B.2.1.2. cut / engrave:ue
(engrave on a jewel / precious) *stone* B.2.1.2. cut / engrave:ue
(precious) *stone* A.1.2.3.4.
(write a name on rock /) *stone* B.2.1.ue
(cut in) *stone* / marble B.2.1.2. cut / engrave:ue
*story* A.3.7.2.
(love) *story* A.3.7.2. story:ue
*straight* writing / printed letters A.3.19.6.1.
*strike-out* A.3.20.2.
*stroke* A.3.9.
(brief) *stroke* A.3.9. stroke:ue
*stroke* / flourish or adornment on initial A.3.19.5.
(character composed of five) *strokes* A.3.19.5. character / lettering:ue
(character composed of two) *strokes* A.3.19.5. character / lettering:ue
(five) *strokes* A.3.19.5. stroke / flourish:ue
(illuminated) *strokes* A.3.19.5. stroke / flourish:ue
(three) *strokes* A.3.19.5. stroke / flourish:ue
(two) *strokes* A.3.19.5. stroke / flourish:ue
*strokes* of light A.3.19.5. stroke / flourish:me
*student* A.2.2.
(outstanding) *student* of a single book A.2.2. student:ue
(school of advanced) *students* A.4.1. school:ue
*study* B.3.4.1.
*study* an occult text B.3.4.1. study:ue
*style* A.3.13.
(polished) *style* A.3.13.ue
(unpolished / low) *style* A.3.13.ue
(make different) *styles* of letter A.3.19.5. character / lettering:ue
(difficult) *subject* matter A.3.6. subject matter / discourse:ue
*subject* matter / discourse A.3.6.
(book does not) *suffice* by itself A.3.2.1.ue
*superscribe* B.2.1.1.
*superscribe* a name B.2.1.1. superscribe:ue
*superscript* A.3.19.8.1.
*superscription* A.3.7.1.
(name as) *superscription* A.3.7.1. superscription:ue

*superscription* corresponds to the content A.3.7.1. superscription:ue
*superscription* does not correspond to the content A.3.7.1. superscription:ue
*superscription* on a letter A.3.7.1. superscription:ue
*supreme* book A.3.2.1.ue
*syllable* A.3.9.
*synthesize* B.2.1.1.
*synthesize* in a single word B.2.1.1. synthesize:ue
*synthesize* on a small amount of paper B.2.1.1. synthesize:ue
*table* of contents A.3.16.
*tablet* A.3.3.3.
(blank) *tablet* A.3.3.3. tablet:ue
(worn) *tablet* A.3.3.3. tablet:ue
*tablets* of the Law A.3.3.3. tablet:ue
*take* note of B.3.4.1.
(in good) *taste* A.3.13.
*taw* A.3.19.5.
*taw* written on the forehead A.3.19.5. taw:me
*teach* B.4.3.1.
(text does not) *teach* anything new B.4.3.1.ue
*teach* concretely in one text what one has already taught in theoretical terms in another B.4.3.1.ue
*teach* to read B.3.4.ue
*teach* to write B.2.1.ue
*teacher* A.2.2.
(pupil writes skillfully because the) *teacher* guides his hand B.2.1.ue
(brief text) *teaches* more than immense volumes B.4.3.1.ue
*tear* B.4.2.1.
*tear* out B.4.2.2.
*tear* out pages B.4.2.2. tear out:ue
(write with) *tears* B.2.1.me
*tear* up B.4.2.2
*tear* up a document B.4.2.2. tear up:ue
*tear* up and throw away a document B.4.2.2. tear up:ue
(living New) *Testament* A.3.4.1. New Testament:me
(New) *Testament* A.3.4.1.
*Tetragrammaton* A.3.19.5.
(angels read the) *text* B.3.4.me
(cite an earlier) *text* B.4.3.ue
(clear) *text* A.3.5. text / contents:ue
(counter) *text* A.3.5. text / contents:ue

(erase a section of the) *text* B.4.2.2. erase / blot out:ue
(find a [replacement for a] lost) *text* B.3.1.ue
(first part of a) *text* A.3.15.ue
(have / need only one) *text* B.3.2.ue
(immortalize a) *text* B.4.3.ue
(last part of a) *text* A.3.15.ue
(living) *text* A.3.5. text / contents:me
(moved by a) *text* B.3.5.ue
(need a code breaker in order to read the) *text* A.3.19.5.1.ue
(not [ever] blot the) *text* B.4.1.ue
(not [ever] cross out of the) *text* B.4.1.ue
(not [ever] erase from the) *text* B.4.1.ue
(not understand the) *text* B.3.4.1.ue
(not understand the smallest portion of a) *text* B.3.4.1.ue
(publicize [through] a) *text* B.4.3.ue
(study an occult) *text* B.3.4.1. study:ue
(understand the) *text* B.3.4.1.ue
(understand the smallest portion of a) *text* B.3.4.1.ue
(adapt a) *text* according to the intended reader / listener B.2.1.1. copy / adapt / translate:ue
(read a) *text* briefly B.3.4.ue
(keep the) *text* clean B.4.1.ue
(no one can learn the) *text* completely B.3.4.1.1.ue
*text* / contents A.3.5.
*text* does not teach anything new B.4.3.1.ue
*text* falls into one's hands B.3.1.ue
(read a) *text* frequently B.3.4.ue
*text* immortalizes its author A.2.1. author:ue
*text* is both clear and unclear A.3.5. text / contents:ue
*text* is difficult to understand B.3.4.1.ue
*text* is easy to understand B.3.4.1.ue
*text* is illegible A.3.5. text / contents:ue
([part of] a) *text* is missing B.4.2.ue
*text* is not well received B.3.5.ue
*text* is read throughout the world B.3.5.ue
(correcting the) *text* is the author's responsibility B.2.1.1. correct:ue
*text* is well received B.3.5.ue
(brief) *text* teaches more than immense volumes B.4.3.1.ue
(disseminate the) *text* throughout the world B.4.3. disseminate:ue
*text* transmitted from Adam B.4.3.me

(teach concretely in one) *text* what one has already taught in theoretical terms in another B.4.3.1.ue
(for an ink blot to fall on the) *text* / writing material B.4.2.1.
(book of) *theology* A.3.4.1.
(book of moral) *theology* / canon law A.3.4.1.
*throw away* B.4.2.2.
(tear up and) *throw away* a document B.4.2.2. throw away:ue
*time* as notary / clerk A.2.1. notary / clerk:ue
*time* writes B.2.1.me
(read the) *title* B.3.4.ue
*title* / emblematic motto A.3.7.2.
*title* page A.3.16.
(beautiful) *title* page A.3.16. title page:ue
(read the chapter) *titles* to learn what the book is about B.3.4.ue
*tome* A.3.2.1.
(engraving) *tool* A.1.2.1.
*tools* are inadequate to the subject A.1.ue
(loose leaves are easily lost or) *torn* A.3.18.2.ue
*torn* paper A.3.2.3.ue
*tragedy* A.3.7.2.
(copy / adapt /) *translate* B.2.1.1.
(copy / adaptation /) *translation* A.3.11.
(copy / adaptation /) *translation* is not as complete as the original A.3.11.ue
(copy / adaptation /) *translation* is not as valuable as the original A.3.11.ue
(copyist / adaptor /) *translator* A.2.1.
*transmit* B.4.3.
(text) *transmitted* from Adam B.4.3.me
*treatise* A.3.15.
(book of three) *treatises* A.3.15. treatise:ue
(three) *treatises* A.3.15. treatise:ue
(peace) *treaty* A.3.4.2.4.
(sign a peace) *treaty* B.2.1.1. sign:ue
(cut on a) *tree* B.2.1.2. cut / engrave:ue
(write on a) *tree* B.2.1.ue
*tree* bark A.1.2.3.2.
*trim* the binding B.2.6.
*true* / trustworthy book A.3.2.1.ue.
(book of) *truth* A.3.2.1.me
*turn* back to a preceding page A.3.18.2.ue
*turn* the page A.3.18.2.ue
*type* A.1.2.4.
(cast) *type* B.2.4.1.
(separate) *type* B.2.4.1.
*typecase* A.1.2.4.

(text is both clear and) *unclear* A.3.5. text / contents:ue
(text is difficult to) *understand* B.3.4.1.ue
(text is easy to) *understand* B.3.4.1.ue
(not) *understand* a character B.3.4.1.ue
(neither recognize a character nor) *understand* its meaning B.3.4.1.ue
(recognize a character but not) *understand* its meaning B.3.4.1.ue
*understand* the smallest portion of a text B.3.4.1.ue
(not) *understand* the smallest portion of a text B.3.4.1.ue
*understand* the text B.3.4.1.ue
(not) *understand* the text B.3.4.1.ue
(delight in the beautiful letters without) *understanding* their meaning A.3.19.5. character / lettering:ue
(more one reads, the less one) *understands* B.3.4.1.ue
*understood* only when written and read B.3.4.1.ue
*understood* without being written or read B.3.4.1.ue
display / *unfold* B.3.3.1.
*unique* copyright A.3.16. copyright:ue
*unpolished* / low style A.3.13.ue
(formerly) *unreadable* word becomes readable A.3.7.1. word:ue
*unroll* B.3.3.1.
*unroll* a skin / scroll B.3.3.1. unroll:ue
*unrolled* skin A.1.2.3.3. skin:ue
(make good) *use* of a book B.3.5.ue

(copy / adaptation / translation is not as) *valuable* as the original A.3.11.ue
*value* a book highly B.3.5.ue
(large /) *vast* book A.3.2.1.ue
*verdict* / sentence A.3.7.2.
*versicle* A.3.7.2.
(three) *versions* A.3.11.ue
*virgin* copy A.3.17.
(write with the) *voice* B.2.1.me
(brief text teaches more than immense) *volumes* B.4.3.1.ue

*wall* A.3.3.3.
(write on a) *wall* B.2.1.ue
(write on) *water* B.2.1.me
*water* the ink A.1.2.2. ink:ue
*watermark* A.3.14.9.2.
*wax* A.1.2.3.2.

(impress in) *wax* B.2.1.2. impress / imprint:ue
(red) *wax* A.1.2.3.2. wax:ue
(write) *well* B.2.1.ue
(text is) *well* received B.3.5.ue
(text is not) *well* received B.3.5.ue
(write) *well* with a poor instrument B.2.1.ue
*well-cut* pen A.1.2.1. pen:ue
*well-ordered* pages A.3.18.2.ue
*white* book A.3.2.1.ue
*white* page A.3.18.2.ue
*white* paper A.1.2.3.2. paper:ue
*white* parchment A.1.2.3.3. parchment:ue
*will* A.3.4.2.5.
(closed) *will* A.3.4.2.5. will:ue
(first clause in a) *will* A.3.15. clause:ue
(open) *will* A.3.4.2.5. will:ue
(write on the) *will* B.2.1.me
(write on) *wind* B.2.1.me
*wisdom* book A.3.4.1.
*wise* author A.2.1. author:ue
(philosphers and) *wise* men have read the book B.3.4.ue
*without* a beginning A.3.15 beginning:ue
*without* a brand A.3.19.9.2. brand:ue
*without* a copyright A.3.16. copyright:ue
*without* a price limit A.3.16. price limit:ue
*without* an approbation A.3.16. approbation:ue
*without* an ending A.3.15. ending:ue
(understood) *without* being written or read B.3.4.1.ue
*without* blot A.3.20.2. blot:ue
*without* correction A.3.20.3.ue
*without* defect A.3.20.ue
*without* expurgation B.2.3.2. expurgate:ue
*without* flaw A.3.20.1.1. flaw:ue
*without* letters A.3.19.5. character / lettering:ue
*without* misprint A.3.20.2. misprint:ue
(sign) *without* reading B.2.1.1. sign:ue
(print) *without* the usual equipment B.2.4.me
(write) *without* the usual equipment B.2.1.me
(delight in the beautiful letters) *without* understanding their meaning A.3.19.5. character / lettering:ue
(sign as) *witness* B.2.1.1. sign:ue
*witness* to a contract A.2.1.
*word* A.3.7.1.
(single) *word* A.3.9. word:ue

(synthesize in a single) *word* B.2.1.1. synthesize:ue
(formerly unreadable) *word* becomes readable A.3.7.1. word:ue
(God writes his) *Word* / Concept in Mary B.2.1.me
*word* / phrase A.3.9.
(abbreviate a) *word* so it will fit on the paper B.2.1.1. abbreviate:ue
(four) *words* A.3.9. word:ue
*work* A.3.1.
(polish a) *work* A.3.1. work:ue
(polished) *work* A.3.1. work:ue
(disseminate the text throughout the) *world* B.4.3. disseminate:ue
(text is read throughout the) *world* B.3.5.ue
*worn* tablet A.3.3.3. tablet:ue
*worthless* page A.3.18.2.ue
(not bend /) *wrinkle* a page B.4.1.ue
*wrinkled* page A.3.18.2.ue
*write* B.2.1.1.
(learn to) *write* B.2.1.ue
(teach to) *write* B.2.1.ue
*write* a book for everyone B.2.1.ue
*write* a law in the sand B.2.1.me
*write* a letter to a king B.2.1.ue
*write* a name in the book of life / glory B.2.1.me
*write* a name on rock / stone B.2.1.ue
*write* a name on the hands / feet B.2.1.me
*write* a name on the heart / breast B.2.1.me
*write* a name on the soul B.2.1.me
*write* all one knows B.2.1.ue
*write* by hand B.2.1.ue
*write* in a memorandum book B.2.1.ue
*write* in an account book B.2.1.ue
*write* in dust / ashes B.2.1.ue
*write* in one's own hand B.2.1.ue
*write* in the margin B.2.1.ue
*write* on a tree B.2.1.ue
*write* on a wall B.2.1.ue
*write* on air B.2.1.me
*write* on the arm B.2.1.me
*write* on the body / in the flesh B.2.1.me
*write* on the breast B.2.1.me
*write* on the conscience B.2.1.me
*write* on the face B.2.1.me
*write* on the forehead B.2.1.me
*write* on the hands / feet B.2.1.me
*write* on the heart B.2.1.me
*write* on the memory B.2.1.me

*write* on the side B.2.1.me
*write* on the soul B.2.1.me
*write* on the will B.2.1.me
*write* on water B.2.1.me
*write* on wind B.2.1.me
*write* poorly B.2.1.ue
*write* well B.2.1.ue
*write* well with a poor instrument B.2.1.ue
*write* what God dictates B.2.1.me
*write* with blood B.2.1.me
*write* with fire B.2.1.me
*write* with tears B.2.1.me
*write* with the right hand B.2.1.ue
*write* with the voice B.2.1.me
*writer* A.2.1.
*writer* is present in his / her writing A.2.1. writer:ue
(appetite) *writes* B.2.1.me
(fame) *writes* B.2.1.me
(time) *writes* B.2.1.me
(God) *writes* his Word / Concept in Mary B.2.1.me
(pupil) *writes* skillfully because the teacher guides his hand B.2.1.ue
(document / piece of) *writing* A.3.1.
(fill a page with) *writing* A.3.18.2.ue
(line of) *writing* A.3.9.
(prepare a parchment for) *writing* A.1.2.3.3. parchment:ue
(preserve one's ideas through) *writing* B.4.1.ue
(put an idea in) *writing* B.2.1.ue
(script /) *writing* A.3.19.6.
(writer is present in his / her) *writing* A.2.1. writer:ue
(slanted) *writing* / cursive A.3.19.6.1.
*writing* disappears as one reads B.4.2.3. disappear:ue
*writing* equipment A.1.1.
(inept) *writing* instrument A.1.2.1.ue
*writing* material A.1.2.3.1.
(for an ink blot to fall on the text /) *writing* material B.4.2.1.
(smooth) *writing* material A.1.2.3.ue
*writing* materials are consumed A.1.ue
(straight) *writing* / printed letters A.3.19.6.1.
(plowing as) *writing* / writing as plowing B.2.1.me
(understood only when) *written* and read B.3.4.1.ue
*written* animal B.2.1.me

*written* in code A.3.19.5.1.ue
(book is) *written* in every language A.3.12.ue
(letters) *written* in invisible ink appear when held before the fire / to the light A.1.2.2. ink:ue
*written* in three languages A.3.12.ue
*written* indelibly B.2.1.ue
(blank leaves and) *written* leaves are juxtaposed A.3.18.2.ue
*written* melon B.2.1.me
(letters) *written* on a mantle A.3.19.5. character / lettering:ue
(taw) *written* on the forehead A.3.19.5. taw:me
(law) *written* on the heart / soul A.3.7.2. law:me
*written* on the inside and the outside B.2.1.ue
(understood without being) *written* or read B.3.4.1.ue
*written* with the finger of God B.2.1.me
*written* without the usual equipment B.2.1.me

# ALPHABETICAL KEY WORD INDEX OF SPANISH MOTIFEMES

Note: Words that occur more than once within a numbered subdivision are starred to alert the reader to check under all motifemes in that subdivision.

## A

A A.3.19.5.
A.B.C. A.3.4.1.
abecé A.3.4.1.
abecedario A.3.4.1.
abreviar B.2.1.1.
abreviatura A.3.9.
abrir B.3.3.1.
aciertos A.3.6.
acomodar B.2.6.
acotar B.2.1.1.
acto de libertad A.3.4.2.5.
acto de limpieza A.3.4.2.6.2.
acto de nobleza A.3.4.2.6.2.
admiración A.3.19.7.
adornar B.2.2.
afirmar B.2.1.1.
aleccionar B.4.3.1.
alfa A.3.19.5.
alfabeto A.3.19.5.
alistar B.2.1.1.
amanuense A.2.1.
anales A.3.4.1.
anillo A.1.2.1.
anillo de memoria A.3.3.3.
anotar B.2.1.1.
añadidura A.3.9.
ápice A.3.9.
aplaudir B.2.3.2.
apólogo A.3.7.2.
aprender B.3.4.1.1.
aprobación A.3.16.
aprobar B.2.3.2.

(hacer) apuntamientos B.2.1.1.
apuntar B.2.1.1.
apurar B.2.1.1. B.3.4.1.
arar pauta B.1.
archivo A.4.2.
argentar B.2.6.
argentería A.3.18.1.
armas A.3.19.4.2.
(libro) arquetipo A.3.11.
arrojar B.4.2.2.
arrojar esparcido B.4.2.3.
(libro) arrollado A.3.3.1.
arrollar B.3.3.2.
arte de memoria A.3.4.1.
artífice A.2.1.
asentar B.2.1.1.
astro A.3.19.8.2.
asunto A.3.6.
ataduras A.3.18.1.
atril A.4.2.
autor A.2.1.
autorizar B.2.3.1.
ayo A.2.2.
azote A.3.19.5.

## B

bastardillo A.3.19.6.1.
batidor A.2.1.
biblioteca A.4.1.
blasón A.3.19.4.2.
borrador A.3.10.
borrar B.4.2.1. B.4.2.2.

borrón A.3.20.2.*
(dar un) borrón B.4.2.2.
(en) borrón A.3.10.
bosquejar B.2.1.1. B.2.1.2.
bronce A.1.2.3.4.
bufete A.4.2.
bula A.3.4.2.2.
buleto A.3.4.2.2.
buril A.1.2.1.

## C

cadena A.4.2.
caja A.1.2.4.
(de) caja A.3.19.6.1.
(libro de) caja A.3.4.1.
cálamo A.1.2.1.
cancelar B.4.2.2.
canciller A.2.1.
canciller supremo A.2.1.
caña A.1.2.1.
capítulo A.3.15.
carácter A.3.19.5.
carbunclo A.1.2.3.4.
cargo A.3.7.2.
carta A.3.3.2. A.3.4.2.2. A.3.4.2.4. A.3.4.2.6.3.
carta de crédito A.3.4.2.4.
carta de favor A.3.4.2.6.3.
carta de horro A.3.4.2.5.
carta de marear A.3.4.2.7.
carta de pago A.3.4.2.3.1.
carta de pago y lasto A.3.4.2.3.1.
carta dedicatoria A.3.16.
carta ejecutoria A.3.4.2.6.2.
cartapacio A.3.2.2.
cartel A.3.4.2.8.
cartera A.4.2.
cartilla A.3.4.1.
catálogo A.3.4.1.
cátedra A.4.1.
cátedra de prima A.4.1. professorial chair: ue
cédula A.3.4.2.4. A.3.4.2.6.2.
cédula de Comunión A.3.4.2.6.2.
censura A.3.16. B.2.3.2.
censurar B.2.3.2.
cera A.1.2.3.2.
cercenar B.2.1.1.
(pliego) cerrado A.3.3.2.
cerraduras A.3.18.1.

cerrar B.3.3.2.*
certificación A.3.16.
Christus A.3.8.
ciencia A.3.6.
(libro de la) Ciencia A.3.4.1.
cifra A.3.9. A.3.19.4.2. A.3.19.5. A.3.19.5.1.
cifrar B.2.1.1.
(libro de) cifras A.3.4.1.
cincel A.1.2.1.
cláusula A.3.9. A.3.15.
columna A.3.3.3. A.3.19.2.
coma A.3.19.7.
compendio A.3.3.1.
componer B.2.1.1.
comunicar B.4.3.
concepto A.3.6.
concordia A.3.4.2.4.
condenar B.2.3.2.
configurar B.2.1.1.
conscribir B.2.1.1.
conservar B.4.1.
consignar B.2.1.1.
contexto A.3.5.
contracifra A.3.19.5.1.
contrato A.3.4.2.5.
copia A.3.1.
copiar B.2.1.1.
coronista A.2.1.
correas A.3.18.1.
corrección A.3.20.3.
corregir B.2.1.1.
correr las líneas B.1.
correr por la cuenta de uno B.2.5.
cortar B.2.6.
corteza A.1.2.3.2.
correo A.2.2.
cota A.3.7.2.
credo A.3.8.
crónica A.3.4.1.
cruz A.3.19.9.2. A.3.19.9.3.
cuaderno A.3.2.1. A.3.4.1.* A.3.18.2.
cubiertas A.3.18.1.
cubrir B.2.6.
cuenta A.3.7.2.
cuenta de suma A.3.7.2.
(correr por la) cuenta de uno B.2.5.
(libro de) cuentas A.3.4.1.
cuento A.3.7.2.
cuerpo A.3.2.1. A.3.15.
cultas flores A.3.13.
custodia A.4.2.

## D

dar a la encuadernación B.2.6.
dar a la estampa B.2.4.
dar forma B.2.1.1.
dar nombre B.2.1.1.
dar un borrón B.4.2.2.
de caja A.3.19.6.1.
de buen gusto A.3.13.
de dentro A.3.14.
debe A.3.7.2.
decorar B.3.4.1.1.
decreto A.3.7.2.
dechado A.3.11.
dedicar B.2.1.1.
(carta) dedicatoria A.3.16.
deletrear B.2.1.1. B.3.4.1. B.3.4.1.1.
demasía A.3.20.1.2.
dentro A.3.14
depositar B.4.1.
deprender B.3.4.1.1.
desatar B.3.3.1.
descargo A.3.7.2.
descuadernar/se B.2.6. B.4.2.5.
desencajar B.2.4.1.
desenvolver B.3.4.1.
deshacerse B.4.2.5.
designio A.3.19.4.2.
despachar B.2.3.1. B.4.3.
despacho A.3.4.2.1.
desplegar B.3.3.1.
desvanecer B.4.2.3.
diamante A.1.2.3.4.
dibujar B.2.1.1.
dicción A.3.9.
dictador A.2.2.
dictar B.4.3. B.4.3.1.
dicho A.3.7.2.
difundir B.4.3.
dirigir B.2.1.1.
discípulo A.2.2.
discurso A.3.6.
doctrina A.3.6.
documento A.3.1.
doraduras y lindezas A.3.18.1.

## E

E A.3.19.5.
echar el sello B.2.1.2. B.3.3.2.
echar en el fuego B.4.2.2.
edicto A.3.7.2.
ejecutoria A.3.4.2.6.2.
ejecutoria de rescate A.3.4.2.5.
(carta) ejecutoria A.3.4.2.6.2.
ejemplar A.3.11.
(libro) ejemplar A.3.11.
(primer) ejemplar A.3.11.
emblema A.3.19.4.2.
emendar B.2.1.1.
emienda B.2.1.1.
empresa A.3.19.4.2.
en limpio A.3.10.
encogerse B.4.2.5.
encuadernación A.3.18.1.
(dar a la) encuadernación B.2.6.
encuadernar B.2.6.
endecha A.3.7.2.
enigma A.3.19.4.2.
enmienda A.3.20.3.
(la) enseñada A.2.2.
enseñanza B.4.3.1.
enseñar B.4.3.1.
entonar B.3.4.3.
entrada A.3.15.
(libro) envuelto A.3.3.1.
epigrama A.3.7.2.
epilogar B.2.1.1.
epitafio A.3.7.2.
epítome A.3.3.1.
epístola A.3.4.2.2.
errata A.3.20.2.
(fe de) erratas A.3.16.
error A.3.20.1.2.
esconder B.4.1.
escribanía A.1.1.
escribano A.2.1.*
escribir B.2.1.1. B.2.1.2.*
escribir por huésped B.2.1.1.
(no) escribir B.4.2.4.
(recado de) escribir A.1.1.
escrito A.3.4.2.3.1. A.3.5.
(lo) escrito A.3.5. A.3.14. A.3.19.6.
escritorio A.4.2.*
escritura A.3.1. A.3.4.2.3.1.* A.3.5. A.3.19.6. B.2.1.1.
escritura de obligación A.3.4.2.3.1.
escudo A.3.19.4.2.
escuela A.4.1.
esculpir B.2.1.1. B.2.1.2.*
eslabones A.4.2.
(arrojar) esparcido B.4.2.3.
esparcir B.4.2.3.
estampa A.3.19.1. A.3.19.4.2.
(dar a la) estampa B.2.4.

estampar B.2.1.2. B.2.4.
estancia A.3.15.
estilo A.1.2.1. A.3.13.
estrella A.3.19.8.2.
estudiante A.2.2.
estudiar B.3.4.1.
estudio B.3.4.1.
estudios A.3.6.
explicar B.4.3.1.
expurgar B.2.3.2.
expurgatorio B.2.3.2.
extender B.3.3.1.
exterioridad A.3.14.

## F

fábula A.3.7.2.
falta A.3.20.1.1. A.3.20.1.2. A.3.20.2.
fe A.3.16.
fe de bautismo A.3.4.2.6.2.
fe de erratas A.3.16.
fe de oficio A.3.4.2.6.2.
fiador A.2.1.
figura A.3.19.4.1. A.3.19.4.2.*
(letras y) figuras A.3.19.5.
fin A.3.15.
finiquito A.3.4.2.3.1.
firma A.3.7.2.
firma en blanco A.3.4.2.3.2.
firmar B.2.1.1.
fiscal A.2.1.
(cultas) flores A.3.13.
florones A.3.18.1.
(de) fuera A.3.14.
fueros A.3.7.2.

## G

gasto A.3.7.2.
gota de tinta A.3.20.2.
gozos A.3.7.2.
grabar B.2.1.2.*
guardar B.4.1.
guarnecer B.2.6.
guía A.3.4.1.
guías A.3.19.2.
(de buen) gusto A.3.13.

## H

ha de haber A.3.7.2.
hacer apuntamientos B.2.1.1.
hacer una suma B.2.1.1.
herrar B.2.1.2.
hierro A.1.2.1. A.3.19.9.2.
historia A.3.7.2.
historia de corona A.3.4.1.
historia de los días A.3.4.1.
hoja A.3.18.2.
hoja de corazón A.1.2.3.2.
hoja de palma A.1.2.3.2.
hoja del principio A.3.16.
(primer) hoja A.3.16.
hojear B.3.4.2.

## I

idioma A.3.12.
iluminar B.2.2.
ilustrar B.2.2.
imperfección A.3.20.1.1.
imprenta A.1.2.4.
impresión A.3.19.1. B.2.1.2.* B.2.4.
(primera) impresión A.3.11.
impreso A.3.1.
(sacar) impreso B.2.4.
impresor A.2.1.
imprimir B.2.1.2.* B.2.4. B.2.4.1.
índice A.3.16. A.3.19.8.2.
información A.3.4.2.6.1.
inscribir B.2.1.1.
inscripción B.2.1.1.
instruir B.4.3.1.
instrumentos A.1.1.
interior A.3.14.
intitular B.2.1.1.

## J

jeroglífico A.3.19.4.2.
Jesús A.3.8.
joyel A.3.3.3.
juntar las partes B.3.4.1.

**L**

lámina A.3.3.3.
lección A.3.7.2.
(varia) lección A.3.4.1.
lector A.2.2.
lectura A.3.5. B.3.4.1.
leer B.3.4.1.* B.4.3.1.
lengua A.3.12.
lenguaje A.3.12.
letra A.3.5. A.3.7.2. A.3.9. A.3.19.5. A.3.19.6.
letra (de cambio) A.3.4.2.3.2.
letra mayúscula A.3.19.5.
letras A.3.6. A.3.19.9.2.
letras quebradas A.3.19.5. character:ue.
letras y figuras A.3.19.5.
(rasgos +) letras A.3.19.5.
letrear B.3.4.1.
ley A.3.7.2.
librería A.4.1.*
librete A.3.2.1.
librito A.3.2.1.
libro A.3.2.1.
libro arquetipo A.3.11.
libro arrollado A.3.3.1.
libro de caballería A.3.4.1.
libro de caja A.3.4.1.
libro de canto A.3.4.1.
libro de cifras A.3.4.1.
libro de cuentas A.3.4.1.
libro de ejércitos A.3.4.1.
libro de generación A.3.4.1.
libro de hazañas A.3.4.1.
libro de la Ciencia A.3.4.1.
libro de la vida A.3.4.1.
libro de los días A.3.4.1.
libro de medicina A.3.4.1.
libro de memoria A.3.4.1.
libro de mortificación A.3.4.1.
libro de nigromante A.3.4.1.
libro de penitencia A.3.4.1.
libro de sabiduría A.3.4.1.
libro de santo A.3.4.1.
libro de solfa A.3.4.1.
libro ejemplar A.3.11.
libro envuelto A.3.3.1.
libro metagrapho A.3.11.
libro original A.3.11.
libro trasladado A.3.11.
libro universal A.3.3.1.
libro verde A.3.4.1.
libro virginal A.3.17.
licencia A.3.16.
línea A.3.9. A.3.19.5.
(correr las) líneas B.1.
lo de dentro A.3.14.
lo escrito A.3.5. A.3.14. A.3.19.6.
lo interior A.3.14.
lucir B.2.6.

**M**

maestro A.2.2.
mancha A.3.20.2.
manchar B.4.2.1.
manecillas A.3.18.1.
manillas A.3.18.1.
manual A.3.4.1.
mapa A.3.4.2.7.
marca A.3.19.4.2. A.3.19.9.1.
marcar B.2.1.2.*
margen A.3.19.2.
marial A.3.4.1.
mármol A.1.2.3.4.
materia A.1.2.3.1. A.3.6. A.3.7.2.
material A.3.6.
matrícula A.3.4.1.
máxima A.3.7.2.
(letra) mayúscula A.3.19.5.
membrana A.1.2.3.3.
(arte de) memoria A.3.4.1.
(libro de) memoria A.3.4.1.
memorial A.3.4.2.3.1. A.3.4.2.6.2.
memorial ajustado A.3.4.2.5.
mirar B.3.4.1.
molde A.1.2.4.
moneda A.3.3.3.
mote A.3.7.2.

**N**

nema A.1.2.3.2.
no escribir B.4.2.4.
no tener lugar B.4.2.4.
nombre A.3.7.2.*
(dar) nombre B.2.1.1.
nota A.3.7.2.
notación B.2.1.1.
notar B.2.1.1. B.3.4.1.

# O

O A.3.19.5.
obligación A.3.4.2.3.1.
obra A.3.1.
oidor de Consejo A.2.1.
ojos A.3.19.8.2.
omega A.3.19.5.
oración A.3.9.
oráculo A.3.7.2.
orden A.3.7.2.
origen A.3.4.2.6.2.
original A.3.11.
(libro) original A.3.11.
oyente A.2.2.

# P

padrón A.3.4.2.4. A.3.4.3.
padrón de registros A.3.4.1.
página A.3.18.2.
paje A.3.19.5.
palabra A.3.7.1. A.3.9.
papel A.1.2.3.2. A.3.2.3.
papel de corazón A.1.2.3.2.
papel de culebrilla A.1.2.3.2.
papel de estraza A.1.2.3.2.
papel sellado A.1.2.3.2.
papiro A.1.2.3.2.
pared A.3.3.3.
paréntesis A.3.19.7.
párrafo A.3.9.
partida A.3.7.2.*
partidas A.3.4.1.
pasaje A.3.9.
pasaporte A.3.4.2.6.2.
pauta A.3.19.2.
(arar) pauta B.1.
pautar B.1.
pellejo A.1.2.3.3.
péndola A.1.2.1.
perder B.4.2.3.
pergamino A.1.2.3.3. A.3.18.1.
perla A.1.2.3.4.
petición A.3.4.2.6.2.
piedra A.1.2.3.4.
piedra preciosa A.1.2.3.4.
piedrecita A.1.2.3.4.
piel A.1.2.3.3. A.3.18.1.
pintar B.2.1.1.
pinzel A.1.2.1.
plana A.3.18.2.

plegar B.3.3.2.
pliego A.3.3.2.*
(medio) pliego A.3.3.2.
pliego cerrado A.3.3.2.
pluma A.1.2.1.
poema A.3.7.2.
poesía A.3.7.2.
poética A.3.7.2.
por de dentro A.3.14.
por defuera A.3.14.
por dentro A.3.14.
por fuera A.3.14.
precepto A.3.7.2.
pregón A.3.7.2.
primer ejemplar A.3.11.
primer hoja A.3.16.
primera impresión A.3.11.
principio A.3.15.
(hoja del) principio A.3.16.
privilegio A.3.16.
privilegios A.3.7.2.
proceso A.3.4.2.5.
prohibir B.2.3.2.
prólogo A.3.16.
prueba A.3.4.2.6.1.
puntillo A.3.9.
punto A.3.7.2. A.3.9. A.3.19.7.
punzón A.1.2.1.

# R

raer B.4.2.2.
raimiento B.4.2.2.
rasgar B.2.1.1. B.2.2. B.3.3.1. B.4.2.1. B.4.2.2.
rasgo A.3.9. A.3.19.5.*
rasgos + letras A.3.19.5.
rasguño A.3.19.5.
rayar B.2.6.
rayo/s A.3.18.1. A.3.19.5. A.3.20.2.
razón A.3.6.
recado de escribir A.1.1.
recados A.3.4.2.3.1.
recibo A.3.7.2.
recorrer B.3.4.1.
reducir B.2.1.1.
registrar B.2.1.1.* B.3.4.1.
registro A.3.2.1. A.3.4.1.* A.3.16.* A.4.2.
registro de los años A.3.4.1.
(padrón de) registros A.3.4.1.
regla A.1.2.2. A.3.4.1.
relajarse el color B.4.2.5.

renglón A.3.9.
repartir B.4.3.
repasar B.3.4.1.
repetir B.3.4.1.1.
reprobar B.2.3.2.
retóricos colores A.3.13.
retratar B.2.1.1.
retrato A.3.19.3.
retril A.4.2.
revolver B.3.4.2.
romper B.4.2.2.
rótulo A.3.7.2.
rúbrica A.3.7.2.
rubricar B.2.1.1.˙

**S**

S A.3.19.5.
saber bien B.3.4.1.1.
saber de dicho B.3.4.1.1.
sacar a luz B.2.5.
sacar impreso B.2.4.
salir a luz B.2.5.
salir a volar B.2.5.
secretario A.2.1.
(papel) sellado A.1.2.3.2.
sellar B.2.1.2.˙ B.3.3.2.
sello A.1.2.1. A.3.19.4.2. A.3.19.9.2.
(echar el) sello B.2.1.2. B.3.3.2.
sentencia A.3.7.2.˙ A.3.9.
sentencia de muerte A.3.7.2.
seña A.3.19.9.1. A.3.19.9.2.
señal A.3.19.4.2. A.3.19.5. A.3.19.9.1. A.3.19.9.2.
señalar B.2.1.1. B.2.1.2.
signo A.3.19.4.2. A.3.19.9.2.
sílaba A.3.9.
síncopa A.3.9.
sobrescribir B.2.1.1.˙
sobrescrito A.3.7.1. A.3.19.8.1.
soltar B.3.3.1.
sortija A.3.3.3.
suma A.3.3.1.
(cuenta de) suma A.3.7.2.
(hacer una) suma B.2.1.1.
surco A.3.9.
symbolo A.3.19.9.1.

**T**

tabla A.3.3.3. A.3.16. A.3.19.3.

tablas A.3.18.1.
tachar B.4.2.1.
Tao A.3.19.5.
tasa A.3.16.
Tau A.3.19.5.
teólogo A.2.2.
teórica A.3.6.
testamento A.3.4.2.5.
Testamento Nuevo A.3.4.1.
testigo A.2.1.
testimonio A.3.4.2.6.1.
Tetragrammatón A.3.19.5.
texto A.3.5.
Thao A.3.19.5.
tilde A.3.9.
tinta A.1.2.2.
(gota de) tinta A.3.20.2.
tintero A.1.2.2.
título A.3.4.2.6.2. A.3.7.2. A.3.16.
traducir B.2.1.1.
tragedia A.3.7.2.
transcribir B.2.1.1.
transmitir B.4.3.
(libro) trasladado A.3.11.
trasladar B.2.1.1.
traslado A.3.11.
trasladador A.2.1.
traslador A.2.1.
trasunto A.3.11.
tratado A.3.15.
tropo A.3.13.

**V**

varia lección A.3.4.1.
vasija A.4.2.
vaticinio A.3.7.2.
vedar B.2.3.2.
verbo A.3.7.1. A.3.9.
verso A.3.7.2.˙
vida A.3.4.1.
(libro de la) vida A.3.4.1.
virginal libro A.3.17.
volumen A.3.2.1.
voz A.3.7.1.

**Z**

zafiro A.1.2.3.4.

# NORTH CAROLINA STUDIES IN THE ROMANCE LANGUAGES AND LITERATURES

*I.S.B.N. Prefix 0-8078-*

## Recent Titles

METAPHORIC NARRATION: THE STRUCTURE AND FUNCTION OF METAPHORS IN "A LA RECHERCHE DU TEMPS PERDU", by Inge Karalus Crosman. 1978. (No. 204). *-9204-1.*

LE VAIN SIECLE GUERPIR. A Literary Approach to Sainthood through Old French Hagiography of the Twelfth Century, by Phyllis Johnson and Brigitte Cazelles. 1979. (No. 205). *-9205-X.*

THE POETRY OF CHANGE: A STUDY OF THE SURREALIST WORKS OF BENJAMIN PÉRET, by Julia Field Costich. 1979. (No. 206). *-9206-8.*

NARRATIVE PERSPECTIVE IN THE POST-CIVIL WAR NOVELS OF FRANCISCO AYALA "MUERTES DE PERRO" AND "EL FONDO DEL VASO", by Maryellen Bieder. 1979. (No. 207). *-9207-6.*

RABELAIS: HOMO LOGOS, by Alice Fiola Berry. 1979. (No. 208). *-9208-4.*

"DUEÑAS" AND DONCELLAS": A STUDY OF THE DOÑA RODRÍGUEZ EPISODE IN "DON QUIJOTE", by Conchita Herdman Marianella. 1979. (No. 209). *-9209-2.*

PIERRE BOAISTUAU'S "HISTOIRES TRAGIQUES": A STUDY OF NARRATIVE FORM AND TRAGIC VISION, by Richard A. Carr. 1979. (No. 210). *-9210-6.*

REALITY AND EXPRESSION IN THE POETRY OF CARLOS PELLICER, by George Melnykovich. 1979. (No. 211). *-9211-4.*

MEDIEVAL MAN, HIS UNDERSTANDING OF HIMSELF, HIS SOCIETY, AND THE WORLD, by Urban T. Holmes, Jr. 1980. (No. 212). *-9212-2.*

MÉMOIRES SUR LA LIBRAIRIE ET SUR LA LIBERTÉ DE LA PRESSE, introduction and notes by Graham E. Rodmell. 1979. (No. 213). *-9213-0.*

THE FICTIONS OF THE SELF. THE EARLY WORKS OF MAURICE BARRES, by Gordon Shenton. 1979. (No. 214). *-9214-9.*

CECCO ANGIOLIERI. A STUDY, by Gifford P. Orwen. 1979. (No. 215). *-9215-7.*

THE INSTRUCTIONS OF SAINT LOUIS: A CRITICAL TEXT, by David O'Connell. 1979. (No. 216). *-9216-5.*

ARTFUL ELOQUENCE, JEAN LEMAIRE DE BELGES AND THE RHETORICAL TRADITION, by Michael F. O. Jenkins. 1980. (No. 217). *-9217-3.*

A CONCORDANCE TO MARIVAUX'S COMEDIES IN PROSE, edited by Donald C. Spinelli. 1979. (No. 218). 4 volumes, *-9218-1* (set), *-9219-X* (v. 1), *-9220-3* (v. 2); *-9221-1* (v. 3); *-9222-X* (v. 4).

ABYSMAL GAMES IN THE NOVELS OF SAMUEL BECKETT, by Angela B. Moorjani. 1982. (No. 219). *-9223-8.*

GERMAIN NOUVEAU DIT HUMILIS: ÉTUDE BIOGRAPHIQUE, par Alexandre L. Amprimoz. 1983. (No. 220). *-9224-6.*

THE "VIE DE SAINT ALEXIS" IN THE TWELFTH AND THIRTEENTH CENTURIES: AN EDITION AND COMMENTARY, by Alison Goddard Elliot. 1983. (No. 221). *-9225-4.*

THE BROKEN ANGEL: MYTH AND METHOD IN VALÉRY, by Ursula Franklin. 1984. (No. 222). *-9226-2.*

READING VOLTAIRE'S CONTES: A SEMIOTICS OF PHILOSOPHICAL NARRATION, by Carol Sherman. 1985. (No. 223). *-9227-0.*

THE STATUS OF THE READING SUBJECT IN THE "LIBRO DE BUEN AMOR", by Marina Scordilis Brownlee. 1985. (No. 224). *-9228-9.*

MARTORELL'S TIRANT LO BLANCH: A PROGRAM FOR MILITARY AND SOCIAL REFORM IN FIFTEENTH-CENTURY CHRISTENDOM, by Edward T. Aylward. 1985. (No. 225). *-9229- 7.*

NOVEL LIVES: THE FICTIONAL AUTOBIOGRAPHIES OF GUILLERMO CABRERA INFANTE AND MARIO VARGAS LLOSA, by Rosemary Geisdorfer Feal. 1986. (No. 226). *-9230-0.*

When ordering please cite the *ISBN Prefix* plus the last four digits for each title.

Send orders to: University of North Carolina Press
P.O. Box 2288
CB# 6215
Chapel Hill, NC 27515-2288
U.S.A.

# NORTH CAROLINA STUDIES IN THE ROMANCE LANGUAGES AND LITERATURES

*I.S.B.N. Prefix 0-8078-*

## Recent Titles

SOCIAL REALISM IN THE ARGENTINE NARRATIVE, by David William Foster. 1986. (No. 227). -9231-9.

HALF-TOLD TALES: DILEMMAS OF MEANING IN THREE FRENCH NOVELS, by Philip Stewart. 1987. (No. 228). -9232-7.

POLITIQUES DE L'ECRITURE BATAILLE/DERRIDA: le sens du sacré dans la pensée française du surréalisme à nos jours, par Jean-Michel Heimonet. 1987. (No. 229). -9233-5.

GOD, THE QUEST, THE HERO: THEMATIC STRUCTURES IN BECKETT'S FICTION, by Laura Barge. 1988. (No. 230). -9235-1.

THE NAME GAME. WRITING/FADING WRITER IN "DE DONDE SON LOS CANTANTES", by Oscar Montero. 1988. (No. 231). -9236-X.

GIL VICENTE AND THE DEVELOPMENT OF THE COMEDIA, by René Pedro Garay. 1988. (No. 232). -9234-3.

HACIA UNA POÉTICA DEL RELATO DIDÁCTICO: OCHO ESTUDIOS SOBRE "EL CONDE LUCANOR", por Aníbal A. Biglieri. 1989. (No. 233). -9237-8.

A POETICS OF ART CRITICISM: THE CASE OF BAUDELAIRE, by Timothy Raser. 1989. (No. 234). -9238-6.

UMA CONCORDÂNCIA DO ROMANCE "GRANDE SERTÃO: VEREDAS" DE JOÃO GUIMARÃES ROSA, by Myriam Ramsey and Paul Dixon. 1989. (No. 235). Microfiche, -9239-4.

CYCLOPEAN SONG: MELANCHOLY AND AESTHETICISM IN GÓNGORA S "FÁBULA DE POLIFEMO Y GALATEA", by Kathleen Hunt Dolan. 1990. (No. 236). -9240-8.

THE "SYNTHESIS" NOVEL IN LATIN AMERICA. A STUDY ON JOÃO GUIMARÃES ROSA'S "GRANDE SERTÃO: VEREDAS", by Eduardo de Faria Coutinho. 1991. (No. 237). -9241-6.

IMPERMANENT STRUCTURES. SEMIOTIC READINGS OF NELSON RODRIGUES' "VESTIDO DE NOIVA", "ÁLBUM DE FAMÍLIA", AND "ANJO NEGRO", by Fred M. Clark. 1991. (No. 238). -9242-4.

"EL ÁNGEL DEL HOGAR". GALDÓS AND THE IDEOLOGY OF DOMESTICITY IN SPAIN, by Bridget A. Aldaraca. 1991. (No. 239). -9243-2.

IN THE PRESENCE OF MYSTERY: MODERNIST FICTION AND THE OCCULT, by Howard M. Fraser. 1992. (No. 240). -9244-0.

THE NOBLE MERCHANT: PROBLEMS OF GENRE AND LINEAGE IN "HERVIS DE MES", by Catherine M. Jones. 1993. (No. 241). -9245-9.

JORGE LUIS BORGES AND HIS PREDECESSORS OR NOTES TOWARDS A MATERIALIST HISTORY OF LINGUISTIC IDEALISM, by Malcolm K. Read. 1993. (No. 242). -9246-7.

DISCOVERING THE COMIC IN "DON QUIXOTE", by Laura J. Gorfkle. 1993. (No. 243). -9247-5.

THE ARCHITECTURE OF IMAGERY IN ALBERTO MORAVIA'S FICTION, by Janice M. Kozma. 1993. (No. 244). -9248-3.

THE "LIBRO DE ALEXANDRE". MEDIEVAL EPIC AND SILVER LATIN, by Charles F. Fraker. 1993. (No. 245). -9249-1.

THE ROMANTIC IMAGINATION IN THE WORKS OF GUSTAVO ADOLFO BÉCQUER, by B. Brant Bynum. 1993. (No. 246). -9250-5.

MYSTIFICATION ET CRÉATIVITÉ DANS L'OEUVRE ROMANESQUE DE MARGUERITE YOURCENAR, par Beatrice Ness. 1994. (No. 247). -9251-3.

TEXT AS TOPOS IN RELIGIOUS LITERATURE OF THE SPANISH GOLDEN AGE, by M. Louise Salstad. 1995. (No. 248). -9252-1.

CALISTO'S DREAM AND THE CELESTINESQUE TRADITION. A REREADING OF *CELESTINA*, by Ricardo Castells. 1995. (No. 249). -9253-X.

THE ALLEGORICAL IMPULSE IN THE WORKS OF JULIEN GRACQ: HISTORY AS RHETORICAL ENACTMENT IN *LE RIVAGE DES SYRTES* AND *UN BALCON EN FORÊT*, by Carol J. Murphy. 1995. (No. 250). -9254-8.

---

When ordering please cite the *ISBN Prefix* plus the last four digits for each title.

Send orders to:   University of North Carolina Press
P.O. Box 2288
CB# 6215
Chapel Hill, NC 27515-2288
U.S.A.

The Department of Romance Studies Digital Arts and Collaboration Lab at the University of North Carolina at Chapel Hill is proud to support the digitization of the North Carolina Studies in the Romance Languages and Literatures series.

www.ingramcontent.com/pod-product-compliance
Lightning Source LLC
Chambersburg PA
CBHW030600230426
43661CB00053B/1784